CAMPING AND CARAVANNING IN EUROPE

Editor: Mitzi Bales
Designer: Peter Gibbons
Art Editor: Glyn Barlow

Gazetteer: Compiled by the Publications Research Unit of the Automobile Association
Maps: Prepared by the Cartographic Services Department of the Automobile Association
Cover Picture: Lermoos, Tyrol, Austria (J Allen Cash Photolibrary)

Head of Advertisement Sales: Christopher Heard
Tel 0256 20123 (ext 22020)
Advertisement Production: Karen Weeks
Tel 0256 20123 (ext 23525)

Phototypeset by Tradespools, Frome, Somerset
Colour Supplement produced by J. B. Shears, Basingstoke
Printed and bound in Great Britain by A. Wheaton & Co Ltd, Exeter

Published by the Automobile Association, Fanum House, Basingstoke, Hampshire RG21 2EA

ISBN 0 86145 642 4

AA Reference 51017

Which of the 150 buildings is the most fascinating? This depends partly on your own taste, but for something different there's the turf-covered tent of the Lapps, or the studio of a well-known artist, or the house with one room which was the district court. Then there's the summerhouse of the famous naturalist Emanuel Swedenborg, painted with scenes from an epic Latin poem, or the savings bank arranged as it was in the 1840s. There's also the belfry in a separate tower, as they once used to be, or a glassworks with a spectator's stand from which you can watch the artisans at work. No-one should wish to miss Mora House, the first building to be re-erected at Skansen, and a fine example of log cabin construction.

If all that, and more, is not enough for you, Skansen also has a zoo and an aquarium.

MAIHAUGEN — NORWAY

In the heart of southern Norway, about 70 miles due north of Oslo, you will find one of the largest open-air museums in Europe. This is Maihaugen in the town of Lillehammer. Its extensive reconstruction of 120 buildings was the inspiration and lifework of a dentist called Anders Sandvig, who has been honoured by having a street named after him in the town.

The buildings are mainly from the Gudbrandsdalen region, to which Lillehammer is the gateway, but the workshops in the newer central building come from all over the country. There are 30,000 different articles on display, many of them from Sandvig's original private collections. These include old costumes, tapestries, silver and glass.

A visit to a large museum like Maihaugen can hardly be brief, but somehow it never seems too long.

HJERL HEDE — DENMARK

Jutland pays tribute to its rural past through the Hjerl Hede open-air museum, set in an untouched natural area. It was established in 1930 and contains 40 buildings, some from over 400 years ago. You can take the official route or choose your own.

Hjerl Hede offers a few buildings just that bit different. For example, the Vinkel farm is the oldest known Danish farmhouse in existence. It dates from 1530 and was built by a rich farmer of the region. The flimsy timber-frame peasant home of the 18th-century is a great contrast.

Then there is the dairy farm, which is still in full working order and which produces butter during the summer tourist season. The steam engine operating the machinery here was built in England in 1880. The grocer's house has a shop arranged as it would have looked at the beginning of this century.

DEN FYNSKE LANDSBY — DENMARK

Hans Christian Andersen created the fairy-tale world of Denmark, but his native city of Odense has preserved the real work-a-day world of its past in Den Fynske Landsby (The Funen Village). Andersen's world of imagination still has its place in this reconstructed village: one of his tales is performed at the theatre here every July and August.

Although the historical period of The Funen Village is the mid-19th century, parts of some of the 24 buildings date back to the 1600s and 1700s. The less usual buildings include an almshouse for eight families; an old brickworks that was in production until 1940; a one-cell district gaol and a toll house.

There may be inns at other such museums, but will they be as unique as Funen's? The Sortebro Inn, which was a post office from 1869 to 1925, operates as a sub-post office here in the summer so that you can get a special postmark from The Funen Village.

DEN GAMLE BY — DENMARK

One of the few open-air museums devoted entirely to town life in olden times is in Aarhus. Known as Den Gamle By (The Old Town), it comprises more than 60 buildings.

The mayor's residence is the heart of The Old Town. Dating from 1597, the house is furnished with outstanding pieces from prosperous homes of later periods. Some of the artisan's houses depict trades rarely found in the countryside: the xylographer, who produced book illustrations by an early form of woodblock printing, the photographer and the hatter, for example.

Also unmistakably non-rural are the Custom House and the Elsinore Theatre. The theatre dates from 1817 and is in use for performances at The Old Town. Of particular interest, too, is the reconstructed Pavilion from the National Exhibition of 1909. Among the oldest buildings are a saddler's shop and brewery, both dating from 1570 to 1580.

FRILANDSMUSEET — DENMARK

It may be in the city, but the Frilandsmuseet (Open-Air Museum) at Copenhagen is all about the country. There are 40 buildings here, broadly grouped by where they came from. We are told by the museum that we can expect to see about four buildings in an hour, and are advised to pick one from each of the groupings. This won't be an easy choice, but there are several unusual ones.

How about the lace school? This is a specially equipped room where the farmer's housewife taught lacemaking to young local girls. Then there's the twin farmstead, built for two neighbours who each lived in half of it. Or the open-air food storehouse from Faeroe. It is built of wooden slats with air spaces between them so that whale meat, caught in that region, could be preserved in the fresh air without salt.

There is folk dancing and other entertainment in the summer, and sometimes guided tours in English (information at the entrance).

UIDERZEE OPEN-AIR MUSEUM

NETHERLANDS

In preserving its past heritage, the Netherlands has looked to life on an inland sea for the Zuiderzee Open-Air Museum at Enkhuizen. The once busy fishing villages of the region are no more — but this reconstruction gives us an exact picture of what they were like.

You know you are in for a different sort of experience from the first, when you learn that the only way to reach the museum is by boat. This takes passengers and cars through the Krabbersgat channel alongside the city. Another difference is that the houses are furnished by what is known about the people who actually lived in them, not by what is typical of the time or region. Touches of disorder are arranged for realism: knitting left on a kitchen table, a message pinned to the notice board in a repair yard, glass bits on the floor of the glazier's. It works so well that the museum won the European Museum of the Year award in 1984, only one year after it opened.

The Zuiderzee Museum is one of Europe's largest with 131 buildings. These include a cottage, house and cheese warehouse which, unusually, were moved in one piece.

In the harbour are historic sailing ships, on one of which you can enjoy a free trip in the summer, as announced. There are demonstrations of trades connected with fishing, such as smoking fish, tanning fishnets and repairing sails, plus changing exhibitions, films and video shows. There is also a children's theatre and other events, a playgroup, and a special playground. Plenty to do, see, and admire.

EDERLANDS OPENLUCHTMUSEUM

NETHERLANDS

There is an interesting mix of city and country buildings, small industrial structures and commercial shops in the Nederlands Openluchtmuseum (Netherlands Open-Air Museum) near Arnhem. Here we can see what daily life was like in Holland as far back as 1600, with old crafts revived, mills turning, and even lively sounds from the local tavern.

The most famous part of the museum is the Zaanse area with its drawbridge in front, wooden huts, shops and the largest collection of regional costumes in the country. In another section is something not often seen: an eelmonger's shelter. It was used just for overnight stays in Amsterdam by eel sellers from Volendam. Other uncommon buildings among the 80 here are a dovecote, coach house, paper mill, and turf cabin of the meanest sort.

The museum, which was 75 years old in 1987, suggests three different-length routes to follow.

BOKRIJK — BELGIUM

How did people live in Belgium when it was ancient Flanders? Bokrijk in the northeastern part of the country will bring it alive for you. Like Skansen, the Swedish model for many European open-air museums, Bokrijk has a section known as Old Town. It exactly captures the age of Pieter Bruegel, when fine houses were built with beautiful ornamental gables, and its examples come from various cities.

Basically, however, Bokrijk is a reconstruction of a Kempen vilage with farms, stables and granges typical of rural Flemish architecture. There are more than 100 buildings here, making it one of the larger such museums. Some of these were brought from other provinces, although they are primarily from Limburg. Life seems to be going on about you as people in the dress of their ancestors are seen in and out of the buildings.

Bokrijk, tucked between the two villages of Hasselt and Genk some 70 miles south of Einhoven, is set in a large leisure park. This offers all sorts of recreation for nature lovers and a special children's playground with many games and varied equipment.

SWISS OPEN-AIR MUSEUM — SWITZERLAND

If you think of Switzerland as mountains, chalets and ski slopes, the Swiss Open-Air Museum at Ballengberg will give you another view: that of rural areas and ordinary country life as it once was. Ballenberg, which opened in 1978, comprises more than 50 buildings from 17 cantons. These are arranged by general geographical regions into 10 groups, all connected by footpaths. It takes about 3 hours to see everything.

There are a number of farmhouses, one a magnificent example from Villars-Bramard built around 1800. There are many other farm buildings, including a cheese dairy, cheese storehouse and grain mills. Interesting distillery equipment shows how distilling was done with charcoal and lime kilns and by the resin method.

The museum has people, too, here to demonstrate the old rural crafts such as spinning, weaving, carving, baking and basketweaving. Forestry and timber workers can be seen going about their jobs in this nature conservation area.

Each year one particular topic of rural life is the subject of a special exhibition, and the permanent exhibition of watches is a collection worth seeing. Ballenberg also gives space to the Swiss Museum for Bread and Pastry in one of the farmhouses.

Round about the museum you can take short or long scenic hikes.

CONTENTS

HOW OUR ANCESTORS LIVED:

OPEN-AIR MUSEUMS

If you think of museums as dull and fusty, you are in for a pleasant suprise in the lively open-air museums of Europe. Their subject is the daily life of people in times gone by, and the way they transplant a piece of the past makes it seem real to us today.

What is the magic of these places? First of all, the old buildings — some of them from hundreds of years ago — are brought to their new site brick by brick or board by board to keep them exactly as they were. Indeed, it has sometimes taken up to three years to re-erect a building. So we see exactly what sort of homes, workshops, stables and other structures people lived and worked in. Then, these are fitted out with furniture and furnishings of the right sort in the right arrangement in homes, and with the right tools and equipment in workplaces. They are generally exact to the tiniest detail. To all this, people dressed in regional costumes of old revive traditional handicrafts and local customs. So we feel like life is going on just as it did back then.

Although in different countries and of different periods, most of the museums described here have preserved many of the same sorts of buildings. These include farmhouses and farmsteads, cottages and manors, mills (including windmills), blacksmith's shops, schools and rectories. Most will also show many of the same trades: baker, saddler, tanner, printer and chemist, for example. So the individual descriptions that follow mainly mention things which are different in each museum.

Scandinavia, which seems particularly fond of open-air museums, often shows us skittle lanes (for the game of skittles) and ropewalks (long walkways along which the rope is twisted). They also reveal how people moonlighted long ago: a smallholder who was also a tailor or pottery maker, a teacher or vicar who also farmed.

Going to an open-air museum as a family is easy and pleasant because most of them offer children's playgrounds and entertainment, and sometimes other adult activities. All those in this article are in regions where there are plenty of camping and caravanning sites.

SKANSEN — SWEDEN

To begin at the beginning, as the saying goes, let's look at the oldest open-air museum in the world: Skansen in Stockholm. This reconstruction of a Swedish farming area and town quarter, which is also the world's largest museum of its kind, opened in 1891. The Swedes themselves love it, two million a year thronging to visit.

It's easy to see the attraction. Skansen gives us a broad picture of past life — sweeping across the centuries from 1500 to the 1920s, taking us into the humblest worker's hut and the wealthy landowner's manor, showing us both rural and town life of yore, letting us meet people in national costume as they work in the traditional way. It makes history fun.

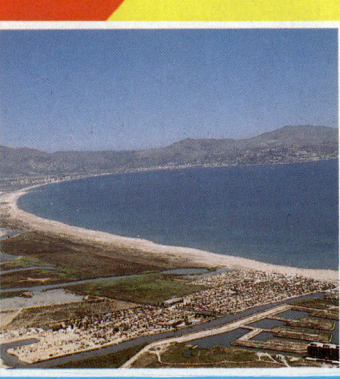

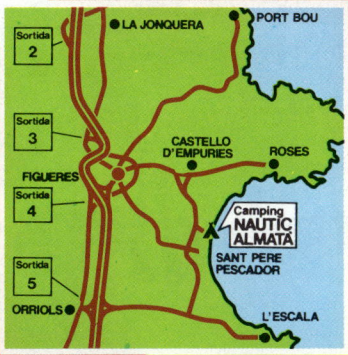

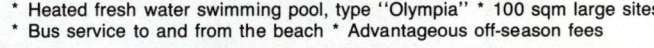

EL DELFIN VERDE

CARAVANING
CAMPING

TORROELLA DE MONTGRÍ, Costa Brava (España). Tel. (34-72) 75 84 50

1ª

e of the most beautiful camping and caravanning
›s of the Costa Brava, where you will always find an
ole pitch.

quiet, tranquile surroundings, by a magnificent, wide
mile-long sand beach, with the largest fresh-water
mming-pool of the Costa Brava and generously
asured pitches and sites. Many green areas and pine-
s groups.

nmercial centre. Gastronomy (3 bars, 2 snackbars, 2
aurants, 2 grills, 1 pizzeria).

ti-use sports area (handball, basket ball, volley,
mington, football), 5 tennis courts, minigolf (3000
n., 18 holes).

anization of fiestas, excursions, dancing, sports
npetition.

most modern ablution blocks. Hot water
rywhere.

ney exchange, safe, medical service, telephone,
s, bungalows, appartments for hire. - We speak
lish.

en: 20.5 - 20.9.

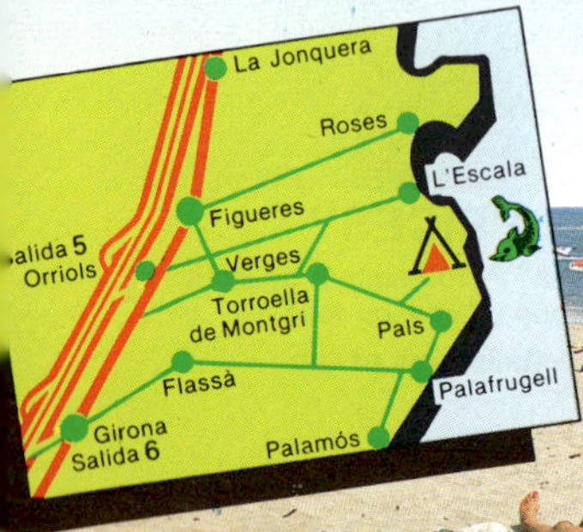

La Jonquera
Roses
L'Escala
Figueres
alida 5
Orriols
Verges
Torroella
de Montgrí
Pals
Flassà
Palafrugell
Girona
Salida 6
Palamós

Costa Brava
E-17470 Sant Pere Pescador
Tel. (34-72) 520302
Autopista A-17 salida 5

Discount on pitch fee:

70%	30.3./18.5.
40%	19.5./14.6. & 1.9./18.9.

- Beach frontage along the whole camp
- Windsurfing with complete service including repairs
- Restaurant, self-service restaurant, bars, supermarket, take-away meals . . .
- Quiet, friendly atmosphere, ideal also for children. Special installations for the handicapped
- Lead-free petrol 40 km
- English spoken

 SURF SHOP etc.

Camping
CALA
LLEVADÓ
First-Class
camping and caravanning
site. Fabulous situation
in the most beautiful
part of the COSTA BRAVA.
Isolated, quiet situation.
4 beaches. Swimming-pool.
Children's playground, bar,
restaurant, supermarket, medical
service, laundry service.
Numbered pitches.
Apartments for hire.
Tel. (010- -72) 34 12 77
Open 1.5. - 30.9.
Camping
CALA LLEVADO
TOSSA DE MAR (Costa Brava. España)
Sports and
Leisure:
Swimming-pool, tennis,
water-skiing, table tennis,
windsurfing, underwater-fishing,
diving, boat excursions.
For pitch reservations write to:
CAMPING CALA LLEVADO
Apartado 34, Tossa de Mar,
Costa Brava, Spain.
Tel. (010- -72) 34 03 14
APARTADO DE CORREOS 34 — Tel. (010- -72) 34 03 14
TOSSA DE MAR (COSTA BRAVA) — SPAIN

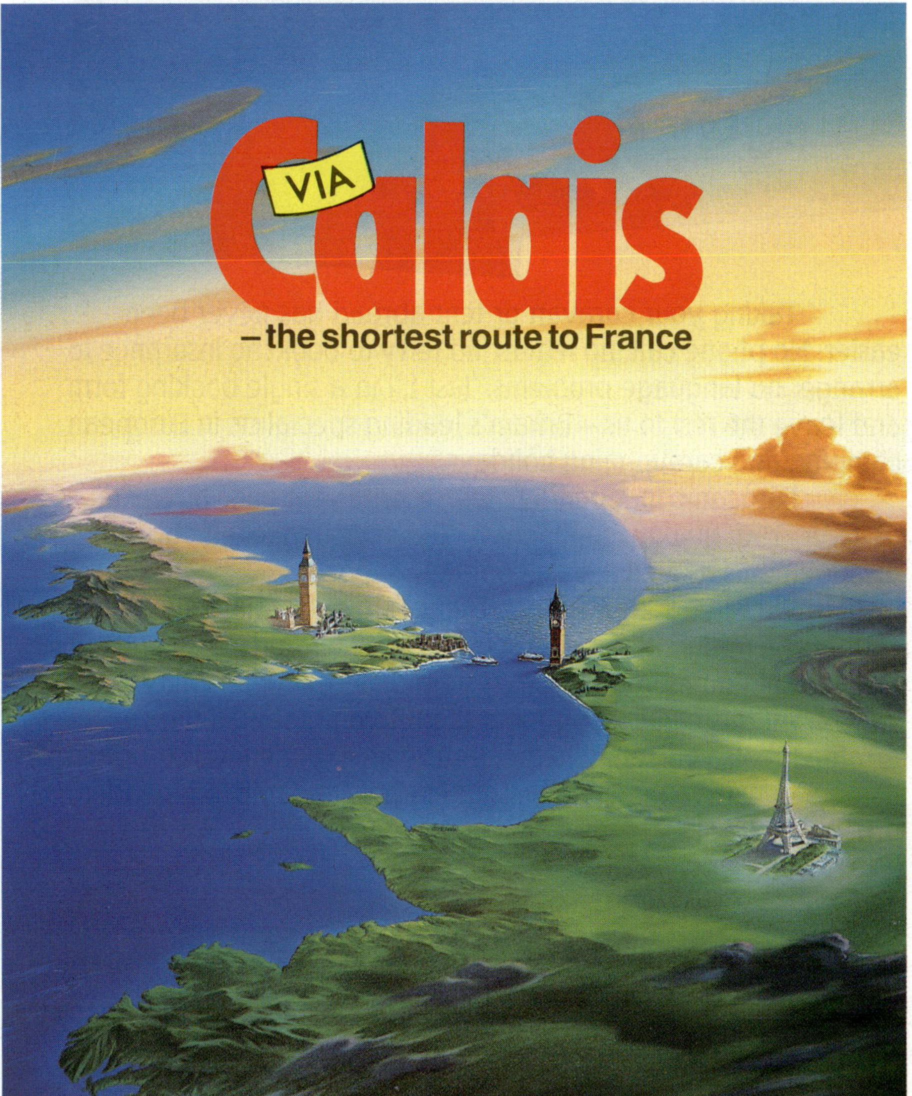
VIA
Calais
–the shortest route to France

BOOK
TOKEN
Book
Tokens
Book
Tokens

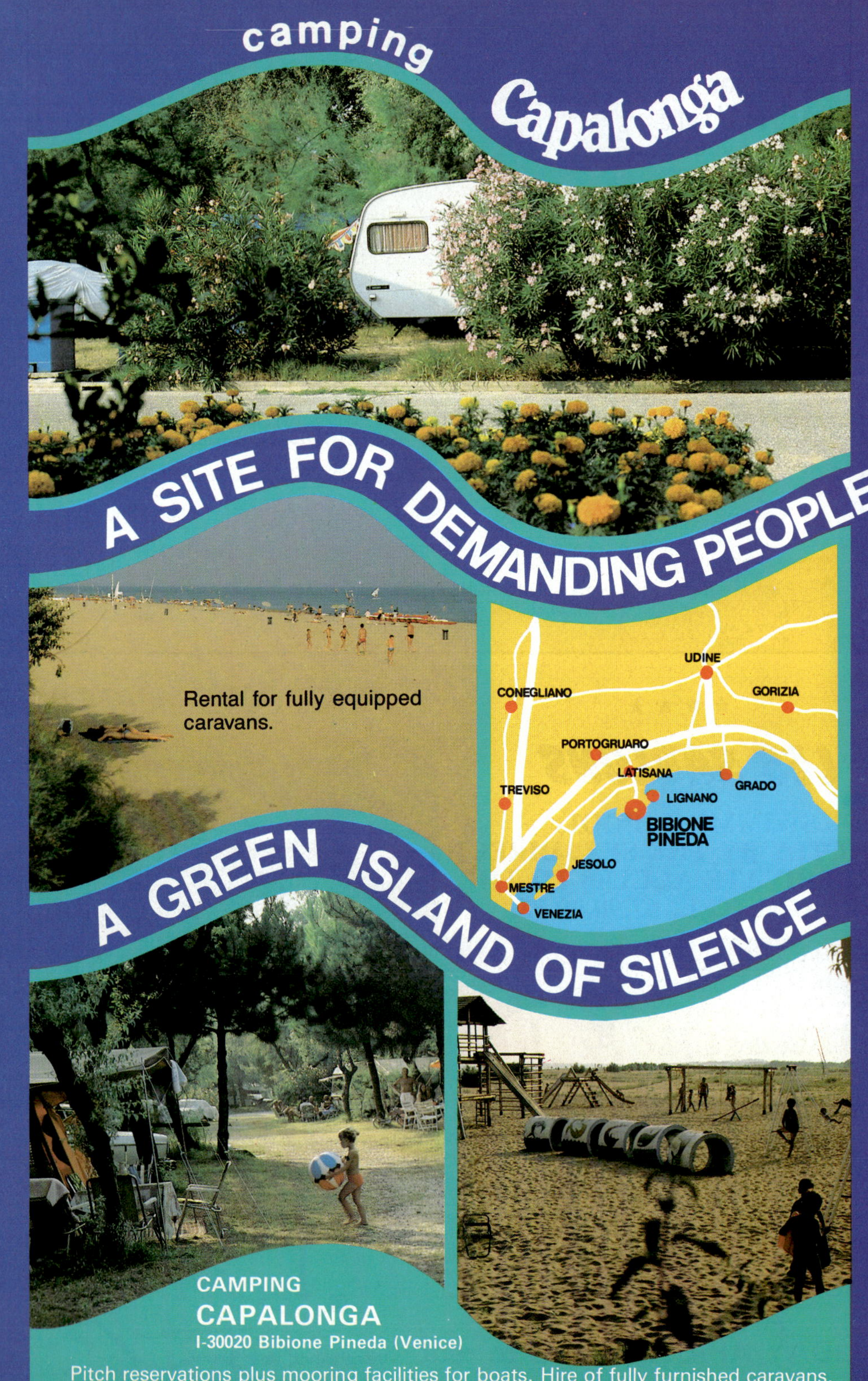

camping
Capalonga
A SITE FOR DEMANDING PEOPLE
Rental for fully equipped caravans.
UDINE
CONEGLIANO
GORIZIA
PORTOGRUARO
LATISANA
GRADO
TREVISO
LIGNANO
BIBIONE PINEDA
JESOLO
MESTRE
VENEZIA
A GREEN ISLAND OF SILENCE
CAMPING
CAPALONGA
I-30020 Bibione Pineda (Venice)
Pitch reservations plus mooring facilities for boats. Hire of fully furnished caravans.

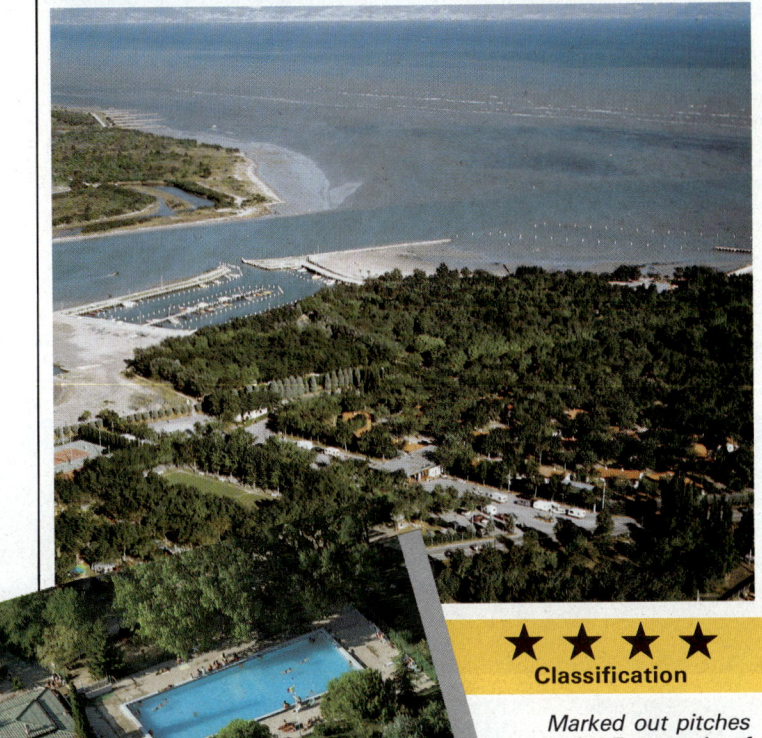

LEISURE PARK AND CAMPING

Duinrell Wassenaar: a unique combination of leisure park and camping. 110 hectares of forest and dunes. ANWB (dutch equivalent of the AA) classification: 3 stars and 5 flags. For your comfort: warm running water, showers, ironing and drying facilities, bar, restaurant, beauty parlour, supermarket etc. The leisure park contains not only attractions like bumper boats, the super slide, and the frog roller coaster but also the world famous tropical wavepool TIKI-BAD, with the longest covered waterslidescomplex in the world (almost 500 metres long!), sauna, whirlpool etc.

For detailed information call or write to: Duinrell B.V., Duinrell 5, 2242 JP Wassenaar/Holland, Tel: 010-31-175119314.

camping la siesta

Costa Brava / Catalunya (Spain)
Tel 30.00.16. and 30.02.58

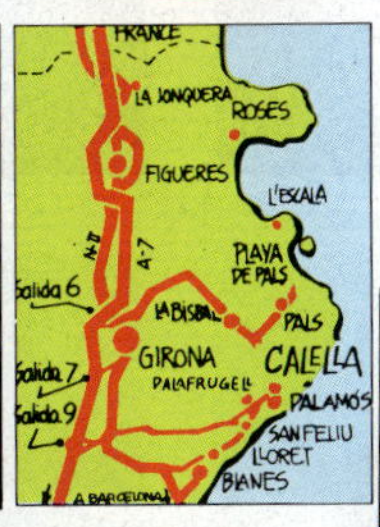

Situated in a big, shady pinewood, 200m from the beach, in the village.
3 Bars, 2 restaurants, 2 grills. Hairdresser, laundry, papershop, supermarket, souvenir shop, games room, dance.
Sports ground, tennis, volleyball, badminton. Two swimming pools. Change, Safe, doctor, apartments and bungalows.
Open: 1.5 — 30.9. Highway (autopista) A 17, exits nos. 6, 7 & 9.

In the picturesque, genuine Calella de Palafrugell, in the heart of the Costa Brava, with its beautiful bays.

Barcelona Costa Dorada

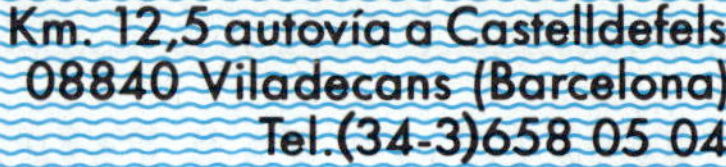

20% **Reduction** off-season

40% for stays over 10 days off-season

la ballena alegre

- Beach frontage along the whole camp
- Pine-tree wood throughout the campground
- All services of a modern holiday camp
- 12 km south of Barcelona. Friendly atmosphere and ideal also for children
- Money exchange
- Travel agency
- Very complete catering service
- Ideal also for water sports
- Lead-free petrol

This campsite has been distinguished by the Spanish Ministry of Tourism and the Autonomous Government of Catalonia

Recognised and inspected by the leading European motoring and camping organisations such as ADAC, DCC, AA, CARAVAN CLUB, ANWB, etc.

 etc.

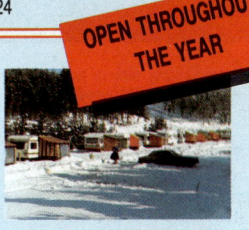

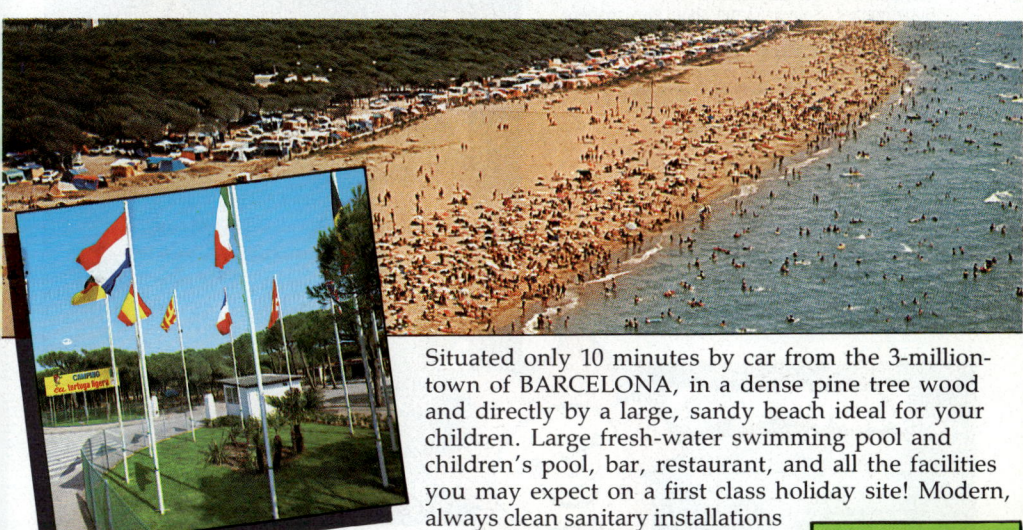

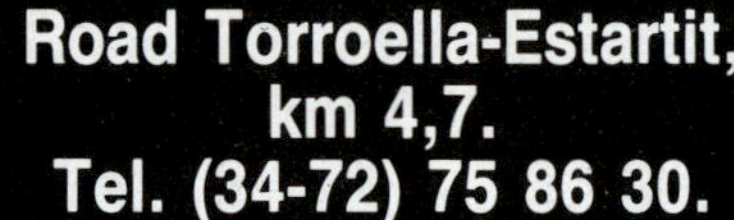

An exclusive holiday site in beautiful surroundings, in midst woods, with terraced sites on slope of mountain and on flat ground.

It's our guests who promote us.

We offer you, among other services:
- Panorama-swimming pool (70 × 40 metres, the largest in the Costa Brava).
- 2 Children's pools.
- Another 20 × 20m swimming pool.
- 2 bars. Pub. Sound-proof, underground disco with air-conditioning. Restaurant with air-conditioning. Piano-Bar with air-conditioning. 2 take-aways Barbecue.
- 2000 square metres of panorama terraces. 600 sq.m. free-covered terraces. 10,000 sq.m. of grass covered solarium.
- Folklore and shows daily.
- Minigolf, tennis, football, table tennis, trampoline. Children's castle. Children's playground. Free water slide.
- Supermarket. Souvenirs gift shop. Newspapers.
- Excursions. Money exchange. Car rental.
- Public Relations office.
- Daily doctor's visit.
- Car wash. Washing machines. Ironing room.
- Free hot water. Modern ablution blocks.
- 200,000 sq.m. tree covered square.
- Dogs only on lead.
- TV and Video Jumbo Screen. (4 × 3m)

Just come and see us. We are sure you will want to stay.

Open: 10.4 — 18.10
30% site fee reduction (except from 16.6-7.9) if you stay at least 5 days.

SPECIAL PRICE FOR PENSIONERS IN LOW SEASON.

***NEW:* ARTIFICIAL SWIMMING-LAKE WITH WATER-FALL**

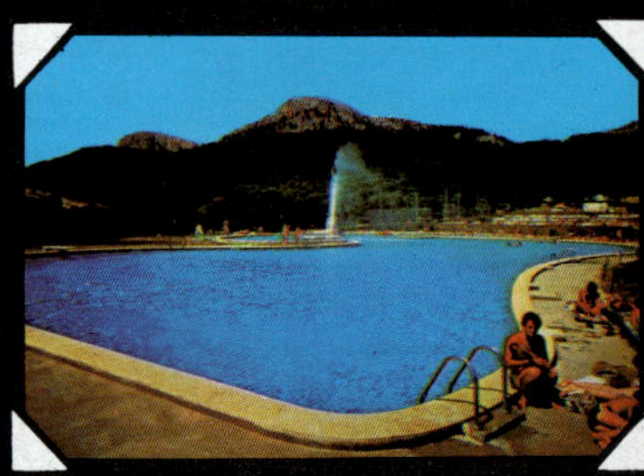

Special prices in low season.

Free bottle of Spanish champagne per family on showing this advertisement.

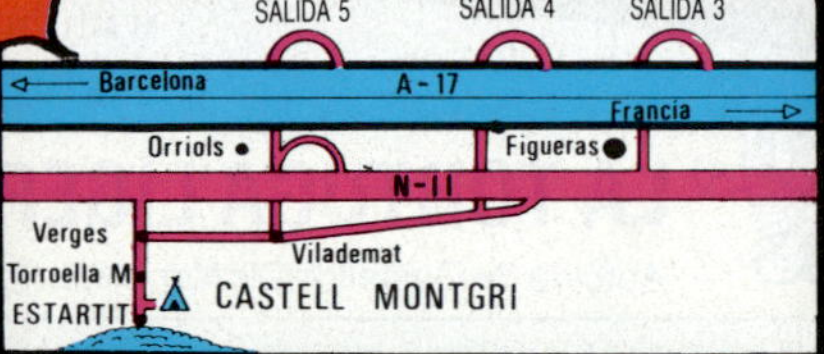

Camping-Caravanning

"TAMARIT"

Tel. (010-34-77) 650128
Tarragona/Costa Daurada

Exceptionally beautiful, quiet and isolated situation (1km from N-340 road and the railway), at the foot of the ruins of Tamarit Castle.

Over 250m beach frontage. Restaurant-bar directly on the beach. Supermarket.

Sports area with illuminated tennis court, football, basketball and volleyball ground. Table tennis, petanque. Open throughout the year.

Special off-main-season prices and reductions for old-age pensioners.

We speak English.

No resident campers.

Access: Autopista A-7 Barcelona-Tarragona, exit 32, then continue on N 340 in direction Tarragona.

Sign-posted turn towards the sea at km 259. Access road asphalted right down to the beach.

Camping-Caravanning

"GAVINA"

Creixell (Costa Daurada, Tarragona)
Tel. (010-34-77) 80 15 03

Directly at the long and wide sand beach of the COSTA DAURADA (only site in the area with 400 metres of own beach-front), ideal for all water sports (sailing, windsurfing school on camp, water-skiing). Beach also suitable for children — A good holiday site with modern sanitary installations, hot water showers, restaurant and bar with beach-terrace. Supermarket, medical service. Only touring campers, no residents. Sports area. Open 21.3—12.10. From 21.3 to 23.6 and from 8.9 until 12.10 special reduced prices, and reductions for old-age pensioners. We speak English. **Access:** autopista A-7 Barcelona-Tarragona, exit 31. Continue on N 340 in direction Tarragona until sign-posted turn towards the sea at km 268.

THINGS YOU NEED TO KNOW

Finding out at the last minute that a document you've never heard of before is vital to your travels. Getting in trouble with police because you don't know the traffic regulations of the country you are visiting. Being marooned through lack of thought in preparing your vehicle. Failure to ensure adequately against mishaps. These are some of the things which could spoil your holiday. Careful study of the following pages and of the Country Introductions will help you to avoid the snags of motoring abroad and ensure that you enjoy the freedom which a camping or caravanning holiday should offer.

DOCUMENTS REQUIRED

As well as a current passport (except for Republic of Ireland, see *Passports* page 38) a tourist temporarily importing a motor vehicle should always carry a full valid national driving licence, even when an International Driving Permit is held, the registration document of the car and evidence of insurance. The proper international distinguishing sign should be affixed to the rear of the vehicle and caravan or trailer if you are towing one. Other documentation comes in the form of a Customs *Carnet de Passage en Douane*, only required in certain circumstances, an *International Camping Carnet*, and special documentation required for vehicles equipped to carry 10 or more persons (including the driver). The appropriate papers must be carried at all times and secured against loss. Finally, the benefits of AA 5-Star Service are strongly recommended.

Boats

Tourists taking any type of boat by car to France,* Germany (Federal Republic of), Greece, Italy, Netherlands, Spain,* Switzerland or Yugoslavia are strongly advised to obtain boat registration documentation from the Royal Yachting Association, Queen Street, Gillingham, Dorset SP8 4PQ ☎(07476)4437. A Helmsman's (Overseas) Certificate of Competence is rarely needed, but is advisable for inland waters (except the French canals). The certificate can be obtained from the above address and is free to members of the RYA. Applications should be made well in advance. See also *Insurance* page 34, *Identification Plate* page 50 and *Customs regulations for European countries* page 57.

*Boat registration documentation is compulsory for all craft except very small craft under about 10ft. Check with the RYA if you are taking a boat to France.

Customs Documents

A Customs *Carnet de Passages en Douane* is necessary for some countries. See *Customs regulations for European countries* page 57.

Driving licence including International Driving Permit

You should carry your national driving licence with you when motoring abroad. If an International Driving Permit is necessary (see *IDP* below) it is recommended that you still carry your national driving licence. In most of the countries covered by this Guide a visitor can drive a temporarily imported car or motorcycle without formality for up to three months with a valid full licence (not provisional) issued in the United Kingdom or Republic of Ireland, subject to the minimum age requirements of the country concerned (see *Country sections*). If you should wish to drive a hired or borrowed car in the country you are visiting, make local enquiries.

If your licence is due to expire before your anticipated return, it should be renewed in good time prior to your departure. The Driver and Vehicle Licensing Centre (in Northern Ireland the licensing authority) will accept an application two months before the expiry of your old licence. In the Republic of Ireland licensing authorities will accept an application one month before the expiry of your old licence.

An International Driving Permit (IDP) is an internationally recognised document which enables the holder to drive for a limited period in countries where their national licences are not recognised (see *Country sections* under *Driving licence*). The permit, for which a statutory charge is made, is issued by the AA to an applicant who holds a valid full British driving licence and who is over 18 years old. It has a validity of 12 months, cannot be renewed and application forms are available from any AA Travel Agency or AA Centre. The permit cannot be issued to the holder of a foreign licence who must apply to the appropriate authority in the country where the driving licence was issued. *Note* Residents of the Republic of Ireland, Channel Islands and the Isle of Man should apply to their local AA Centre for the relevant application form or information as to where it may be obtained.

'E' card

This card may be displayed in the windscreen of your vehicle to assist the traffic flow across certain frontiers within the European Community. Full conditions of use are given on the card which may be obtained from AA Centres and AA Port Service Centres.

Insurance including caravan insurance

Motor insurance is compulsory by law in all the countries covered in this Guide and you are strongly advised to ensure that you are adequately covered for all countries in which you will travel. Temporary policies may be obtained at all frontiers except the Republic of Ireland, but this is a most expensive way of effecting cover. It is best to seek the advice of your insurer regarding the extent of cover and full terms of your existing policy. Some insurers may not be willing to offer cover in the countries that you intend to visit and it may be necessary to seek a new, special policy for the trip from another insurer. Should you have any difficulty, AA Insurance Services will be pleased to help you. *Note* Extra insurance is recommended when visiting Spain (see *Bail Bond* page 348). Third party insurance is compulsory for certain boats with engines in Italian waters and for craft used on the Swiss lakes (see also *Boats* page 33); it is recommended elsewhere for all boats used abroad. It is compulsory for trailers temporarily imported into Austria.

An international motor insurance certificate or Green Card is recognised in most countries as evidence that you are covered to the minimum extent demanded by law. Compulsory in Andorra, Greece* and Yugoslavia and strongly advised for Italy,* Portugal* and Spain* *the AA recommends its use elsewhere*. It will be issued by your own insurer upon payment of the additional premium for extension of your UK policy cover to apply in those countries you intend visiting. It will name all the countries for which it is valid. The document will not be accepted until you have signed it. Green Cards are internationally recognised by police and other authorities and may save a great deal of inconvenience in the event of an accident. If you are towing a caravan or trailer it will need separate insurance, and mention on your Green Card. Remember, the cover on a caravan or trailer associated with a Green Card is normally limited to third-party towing risks, so a separate policy (see *AA Caravan Plus* below) is available to cover accidental damage, fire or theft.

In accordance with a Common Market Directive, the production and inspection of Green Cards at the frontiers of Common Market countries is no longer a legal requirement and the principle has been accepted by other European countries who are not members of the EEC. However, the fact that Green Cards will not be inspected does not remove the necessity of having insurance cover as required by law in the countries concerned.

Motorists can obtain expert advice through AA Insurance Services for all types of insurance. Several special schemes have been arranged with leading insurers to enable motorists to obtain wide insurance cover at economic premiums. One of these schemes, *AA Caravan Plus*, includes damage cover for caravans, and their contents, including personal effects. While detached from the

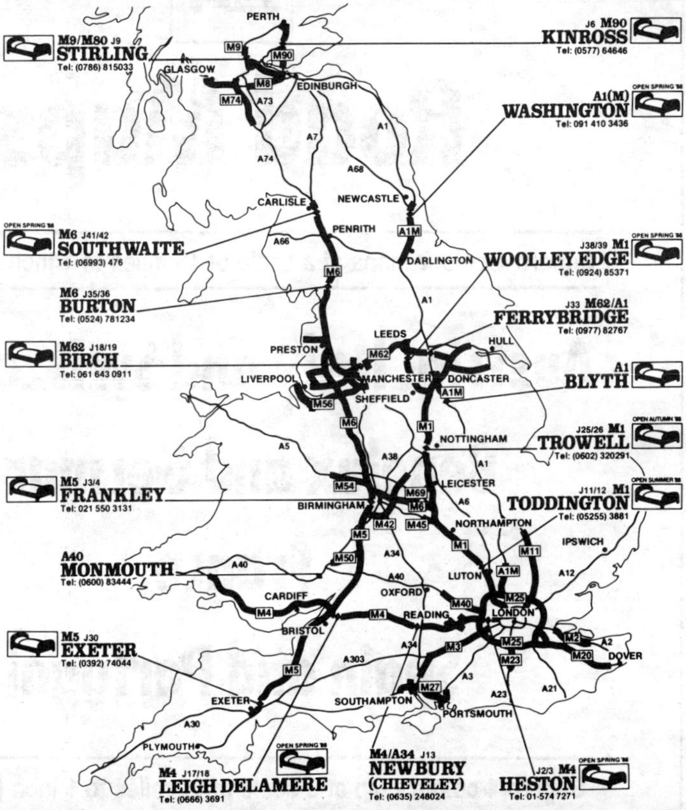

towing vehicle, protection against your legal liability to other persons arising out of the use of the caravan is also provided. Cover is extended to most European countries for up to 60 days without extra charge. *AA Caravan Plus* also provides cover for camping equipment. Full details of *AA Caravan Plus* may be obtained from any AA Centre or direct from AA Insurance Services Ltd, PO Box 2AA, Newcastle upon Tyne NE99 2AA.

Finally make sure you are covered against damage in transit (*eg* on ferry or motorail). Most comprehensive motor insurance policies provide adequate cover for transit between ports in the UK, but need to be extended to give this cover if travelling outside the UK. You are advised to check this aspect with your insurer before setting off on your journey.

*Although these countries are members of the EEC a Green Card is for the time being still a compulsory requirement or strongly advised as indicated.

International Camping Carnet

The **International Camping Carnet (ICC)**, available from organisations affiliated to the AIT, FIA or FICC for their own members, is recognised at most sites in Europe; in some cases it is essential and you will not be allowed to camp without it. At certain sites a reduction in the advertised charge may be allowed on presentation of the Carnet. No more than 12 persons may be covered by any one Camping Carnet.

On arrival at the site, report to the warden, who will tell you where you may pitch your tent or caravan. You may be asked to pay in advance, or alternatively to give into charge the Camping Carnet (which must bear the holder's photograph) for the length of your stay. Some wardens may also insist upon the retention of all passports.

The Camping Carnet bears an insurance stamp indicating that a premium has been paid in respect of third party liability to a total of £250,000 for accidents while camping abroad, provided that the accident was not caused directly or indirectly by a motor vehicle. The exclusions to the policy can be supplied upon application. The insurance cover is limited to 31 December of the year indicated by the stamp. The stamp can be renewed upon payment of a fee, and up to three stamps may be affixed to any one Camping Carnet.

Camping Carnets are issued subject to the following conditions:

- *i* that the holder is over 18 years of age and is a member of an organisation affiliated to one of the three major camping federations;
- *ii* that the holder has a permanent home address and enters this on the carnet;
- *iii* that the holder has never had a carnet withdrawn for an infringement of Camping regulations;
- *iv* that the holder will re-imburse the Automobile Association with any camping fees incurred even in th event of the loss of or fraudulent use of the Camping Carnet.

The applicant signs an undertaking that he/she will abide by the Principles of Good Camping as follows:

- *i* Camp only on permanent, authorised sites or on sites where permission is granted on special application.
- *ii* Leave the AIT Camping Carnet with the proprietor or guardian of the site during occupation of the site.
- *iii* Comply with the regulations of the camp and those of local authorities.
- *iv* Do not make a fire without permission or damage in any way the hedges and trees of the site. When permission for a fire has been given, first clear away any undergrowth – take extra care in woodlands and forests.
- *v* Leave the site as clean as you would wish to find it – leave no litter or rubbish on the site but dispose of it in accordance with the regulations of the camp.
- *vi* Respect the property and peace of others and do not offend them by word or bearing.
- *vii* Avoid making undue noise, particularly between 22.00 and 06.00 hrs.

Medical

Form E111 is required, see *Medical treatment* page 60.

Minibus (10 + seats)

A minibus constructed and equipped to carry 10 or more persons (including the driver*) and used outside the UK is subject to the regulations governing international bus and coach journeys. This will generally mean that the vehicle must be fitted with a tachograph and documentation in the form of a waybill, model control document and driver's certificate obtained. Apply to the Bus and Coach Council, Sardinia House, 52 Lincoln's Inn Fields, London WC2A 3LZ ☏01-831 7546 for waybill and model control document; for other information contact the appropriate authorities as follows:

i in respect of minibus registered in Great Britain (England, Scotland and Wales) contact the local Traffic Area Office of the Department of Transport;

ii in respect of minibus registered in Northern Ireland contact the Department of the Environment for Northern Ireland, Road Transport Department, Upper Galwally, Belfast BT8 4FY.
Residents of the Republic of Ireland should contact the Department of Labour, Mespil Road, Dublin 4 for details about tachographs and the Government Publications Sales Office, Molesworth Street, Dublic 2 for information about documentation.

When contacting any of the above authorities, do so well in advance of your departure.

*A minibus driver must be at least 21 years of age and hold a full driving licence valid for group 'A' or, if automatic transmission, group 'B'.

Passports and visas

Each person must hold, or be named on, an up-to-date *passport* valid for all the countries through which it is intended to travel. However, the UK together with the Republic of Ireland, Channel Islands and Isle of Man form a Common Travel Area. Persons born in the UK do not require a passport when travelling from the UK to the Republic of Ireland; similarly citizens of the Republic of Ireland may travel to the UK without holding a passport.

Passports should be carried at all times and, as an extra precaution, a separate note kept of the number, date and place of issue. There are various types of British passports including the standard or regular passport and the limited British Visitor's Passport. Standard UK passports are issued to British Nationals, *ie* British citizens, British Dependent Territories citizens, British Overseas citizens, British Subjects, and British Protected Persons. Normally issued for a period of 10 years, a standard UK passport is valid for travel to all countries in the world. A family passport may cover the holder, spouse and children under 16, but only the first person named on the passport may use it to travel alone. Children under 16 may be issued with a separate passport valid for 5 years and renewable for a further 5 years on application. Full information and application forms in respect of the standard UK passport may be obtained from a main Post Office or from one of the Passport Offices in Belfast, Douglas (Isle of Man), Glasgow, Liverpool, London, Newport (Gwent), Peterborough, St Helier (Jersey) and St Peter Port (Guernsey). Application for a standard passport should be made to the Passport Office appropriate for the area concerned allowing at least four weeks for passport formalities to be completed and should be accompanied by the requisite documents and fees.

British Visitor's Passports are issued to British citizens, British Dependent Territories citizens or British Overseas citizens over the age of 8 resident in the UK, Isle of Man or Channel Islands. Valid for one year only and acceptable for travel in Western Europe and West Berlin but not for Yugoslavia, they cannot be used for overland travel through the German Democratic Republic to West Berlin. A British Visitor's Passport issued to cover the holder, spouse and children under 16 may only be used by the first person named on the passport to travel alone. Children under 8 cannot have their own Visitor's Passport. Full information and application forms may be obtained from main Post Offices in Great Britain (England, Scotland and Wales) or Passport Offices in the Channel Islands, Isle of Man and Northern Ireland. However, Visitor's Passports or application forms for Visitor's Passports are NOT obtainable from Passport Offices in Great Britain. All applications for a Visitor's Passport must be submitted in person to a main Post Office or Passport Office as appropriate. Provided the documents are in order and the fee is paid, the passport is issued immediately.

Irish citizens resident in the Dublin

Metropolitan area or in Northern Ireland should apply to the Passport Office, Dublin; if resident elsewhere in the Irish Republic they should apply through the nearest Garda station. Irish citizens resident in Britain should apply to the Irish Embassy in London.

A *visa* is not normally required by United Kingdom and Republic of Ireland passport holders when visiting Western European countries for periods of three months or less (*Portugal* 60 days). However if you hold a passport of any other nationality, a UK passport not issued in this country or are in any doubt at all about your position you should check with the embassies or consulates of the countries you intend to visit.

Registration document

You must carry the original vehicle *registration document* with you. If the vehicle is not registered in your name, you should have a letter from the owner (for Yugoslavia this must be countersigned by a motoring organisation; for Portugal a special certificate is required, available *free* from the AA) authorising you to use it.

If you are using a UK registered hired or leased vehicle for touring overseas, the registration document will not be available and a *Hired/Leased Vehicle Certificate* (VE 103A), which may be purchased from the AA, should be used in its place.

If for any reason your registration document has to be sent to the licensing authorities you should bear in mind that, as processing can take some time, the document may not be available in time for your departure. Under these circumstances a certificate of registration (V379) will normally be issued and can be obtained free of charge from your nearest Vehicle Registration Office to cover the vehicle for international circulation purposes.

Vehicle excise licence

It is advisable for all vehicles temporarily exported from the UK for a period of 12 months or less to continue to be currently taxed in the UK. If your vehicle excise licence (tax disc) is due to expire whilst you are abroad, you may apply before you leave, by post to any main Post Office for a tax disc up to 42 days in advance of the expiry date of your present disc. You should explain why you want the tax disc in advance and ask for it to be posted to you before you leave, or to an address you will be staying at abroad. However, your application form must always be completed with your UK address.

VEHICLE AND EQUIPMENT MAINTENANCE HINTS

We know as well as anyone how expensive mechanical repairs and replacement parts can be abroad. Whilst not all breakdowns are avoidable, a vast number of those we deal with occur because the vehicle has not been prepared properly before the start of the journey. A holiday abroad involves many miles of hard driving over roads completely new to you, perhaps without the facilities you have come to take for granted in this country. The following hints we give here for preparing your car and caravan or tent may prevent problems arising during your holiday.

PREPARING YOUR CAR

We recommend that your car undergoes a major service by a franchised dealer shortly before your holiday or tour abroad. In addition, it is advisable to carry out your own general check for any audible or visible defects. If AA members would like a thorough check of their car made by one of the AA's experienced engineers, any AA Centre can arrange this at a few days' notice. Our engineer will then submit a written report complete with a list of the repairs required. There is a fee for this service. For more detailed information please ask for our leaflet Tech 8.

It is not practical to provide a complete list, but the following, used in conjunction with the manufacturer's handbook, should ensure that no obvious faults are missed. However, as a precaution, obtain a list of service agencies for your make of vehicle from your dealer and carry this with you on your journey. If it is necessary to take your vehicle to a garage for repairs always ask for an estimate before authorising the repair as some European garages make extremely high charges for repairing tourists' cars. **It cannot be emphasised too strongly that disputes with garages on the Continent must be settled on the spot**. It has been the AA's experience that subsequent negotiations can seldom be brought to a satisfactory conclusion.

Automatic Gearboxes

The fluid in an automatic gearbox does more work when it has to cope with the extra weight of a caravan. It becomes hotter and thinner, so there is more slip and more heat generated in the gearbox. Many manufacturers recommend the fitting of a gearbox oil cooler. Check with the manufacturer what is suitable for your car.

Automatic transmission fluid

Automatic transmission fluid is not always readily available especially in some of the more remote areas of Western Europe and tourists are advised to carry an emergency supply with them.

Brakes

Car brakes must always be in peak condition. Check both the level in the brake fluid reservoir and the thickness of the brake lining/pad material. The brake fluid should be completely changed in accordance with the manufacturer's instructions, or at intervals of not more than 18 months or 18,000 miles. However it is advisable to change the brake fluid, regardless of the foregoing, before departing on a Continental holiday, particularly if the journey includes travelling through a hilly or mountainous area.

Cold-weather touring

If you are planning a winter tour, make sure that you fit a high-temperature (winter) thermostat and make sure that the strength of your anti-freeze mixture is correct for the low temperatures likely to be encountered.

If you are likely to be passing through snow-bound regions, it is important to remember that for many resorts and passes the authorities insist on wheel chains or spiked or studded tyres. However, as wheel chains and spiked or studded tyres can damage the road surface if it is free of snow or ice, there are definite periods when these may be used and in certain countries the use of spiked or studded tyres is illegal. If wheel chains or spiked or studded tyres are compulsory this is usually signposted.

In fair weather, wheel chains or spiked or studded tyres are only necessary on the higher passes, but in severe weather you will probably need them (as a rough guide) at altitudes exceeding 2,000ft.

If you think you will need wheel chains, it is better to take them with you from home. They may be hired from the AA and further details are available from your nearest AA Centre.

Wheel chains fit over the wheels to enable them to grip on snow or icy surfaces. They are sometimes called *snow chains* or *anti-skid chains*. Full-length chains which fit right round a tyre are the most satisfactory, but they must be fitted correctly. Check that the chains do not foul your vehicle bodywork; if your vehicle has front-wheel-drive put the steering on full lock while checking. If your vehicle has radial tyres it is essential that you contact the manufacturers of your vehicle and tyres for their recommendations in order to avoid damage to your tyres. Chains should only be used when compulsory or necessary as prolonged use on hard surfaces will damage the tyres.

Spiked or *studded tyres* are sometimes called *snow tyres*. They are tyres with rugged treads on to which spikes or studs have been fitted. For the best grip they should be fitted to all wheels. The correct type of spiked or studded winter tyres will generally be more effective than chains.

Note The above comments do not apply where severe winter conditions prevail. It is doubtful whether the cost of preparing a car, normally used in the UK, would be justified for a short period. However, the AA's Technical Services Department will be pleased to advise on specific enquiries.

Direction Indicators

All direction indicators should be working at between 60–120 flashes per minute. Most standard car-flasher units will be overloaded by the extra lamps of a caravan or trailer and a special heavy duty unit or a relay device should be fitted.

Electrical

Check that all electrical connections are sound and that the wiring is in good condition. Should any problems arise with the charging system, it is essential to obtain the services of a qualified auto-electrician.

Engine and mechanical

If you suspect that there is anything wrong with the engine, however insignificant it may seem, it should be dealt with straight away. Even if everything seems in order, don't neglect such commonsense precautions as checking valve clearances, sparking plugs, and contact breaker points where fitted, and make sure that the distributor cap is sound. The fan belt should be checked for fraying and slackness. If any of the items mentioned previously are showing signs of wear you should replace them.

Any obvious mechanical defects should be attended to at once. Look particularly for play in steering connections and wheel bearings and, where applicable, ensure that they are adequately greased. A car that has covered a high mileage will have absorbed a certain amount of dirt into the fuel system and as breakdowns are often caused by dirt, it is essential that all filters (petrol and air) should be cleaned or renewed.

Owners should think twice about towing a caravan with a car that has already given appreciable service. Hard driving on motorways and in mountainous country puts an extra strain on ageing parts and repairs to items such as a burnt-out clutch can be very expensive.

The cooling system should be checked for leaks and the correct proportion of anti-freeze and any perished hoses or suspect parts replaced.

Consult your vehicle handbook for servicing intervals. Unless the engine oil has been changed recently, drain and refill with fresh oil and fit a new filter. Deal with any significant leaks by tightening up loose nuts and bolts and renewing faulty joints and seals.

Brands and grades of *engine oil* familiar to the British motorist are usually available in Western Europe but may be difficult to find in remote country areas. When available they will be much more expensive than in the UK and generally packed in 2-litre cans (3½ pints). Motorists can usually assess the normal consumption of their car and are strongly advised to carry what oil is likely to to be required for the trip.

Headlights

For driving abroad (except in the Republic of Ireland) headlights should be altered so that the dipped beam does not dazzle oncoming traffic. The alteration can be made by fitting headlamp converters (PVC mask sheets) or beam deflectors (clip-on lenses) which may be purchased from your nearest AA Centre. However, beam deflectors must not be used with halogen lamps. It is important to remember to remove the headlamp converters or beam deflectors as soon as you return to the UK. See also *Lights* page 50.

Note Remember to have the lamps set to compensate for the load being carried.

Mirrors

When towing a caravan it is essential to fit mirror accessories for better rear vision. The accessories available include: extensions that clip on existing wing mirrors; arms to extend wing mirrors; long-arm wing or door mirrors; and periscopes which are fitted on the car roof and reflect the rear view through the caravan window. A periscope and wing mirrors used together should eliminate all blind spots. The longer the mirror arm is, the more rigid its mounting has to be. Some mirrors have supporting legs or extra brackets to minimise vibration. A mirror mounted on the door pillar gives a wide field of vision because it is close to the driver. However, it has the disadvantage that it is at a greater angle to the forward line of sight. Convex mirrors give an even wider field of vision, but practice is needed before distances can be judged accurately due to the diminished image. Mirrors should be fitted to both sides of the towing vehicle.

Spares

The problem of what spares to carry is a difficult one; it depends on the vehicle and how long you are likely to be away. However, you should consider hiring an AA Spares Kit for your car; full information about this service is available from any AA Centre. AA Emergency Windscreens are also available for hire. In addition to the items contained in the spares kit, the following would also prove useful:

a pair of windscreen wiper blades
a length of electrical cable
an inner tube of the correct type
a roll of insulating or adhesive tape
a torch
a fire extinguisher
a tow rope

Remember that when ordering spare parts for dispatch abroad you must be able to identify them as clearly as possible and by the manufacturer's part numbers if known. When ordering spares, always quote the engine and chassis numbers of your car. See also *Lights* page 50.

Tyres

Inspect your tyres carefully; if you think they are likely to be more than three-quarters worn before you get back, it is better to replace them before you start out. If you notice uneven wear, scuffed treads, or damaged walls, expert advice should be sought on whether the tyres are suitable for further use. In some European countries, drivers can be fined if tyres are badly worn. The regulations in the UK governing tyres call for a minimum tread depth of 1mm over 75% of the width of the tyre all around the circumference, with the original tread pattern clearly visible on the remainder. European regulations are tougher: a minimum tread depth of 1mm or 1.6mm over the whole width of the tyre around the circumference.

If a caravan is to be towed, find out the recommended tyre pressures suitable for the extra load from the manufacturer. They will vary according to type, size and ply-rating of the tyres. If a lot of high speed driving is to be done, check that the ply-rating is adequate. The rear tyre pressures, for example, may have to be increased by 2–3lb per square inch. Pressures can only be checked accurately when the tyres are cold. Don't forget the spare tyre.

Warm climate touring

In hot weather and at high altitudes, excessive heat in the engine compartment can cause carburation problems. It is advisable, if you are towing a caravan, to consult the manufacturers about the limitations of the cooling system, and the operating temperature of the gearbox fluid if automatic transmission is fitted (see *Automatic gearboxes* page 40).

PREPARING YOUR CARAVAN

For the experienced, a pre-tour check of the caravan comes as a matter of routine; the newcomer may be unsure how to prepare. Therefore, assuming the caravan itself has been regularly serviced, here are a few tips which may prove useful.

Just before your trip give the caravan a good airing and if you have a water pump fitted, check the flow and flush with clean water to get rid of any staleness. Ensure that there are no leaks and replace any doubtful washers. Examine all potential leak spots especially around window rubbers and roof lights, applying sealing compound as necessary. Test all window, cupboard and locker catches to make sure that they shut firmly. Outside, clean rain gutters and make sure down-spouts and window channel drain-pipes are clear.

Brakes

Ensure that the caravan braking mechanism is adjusted to suit the car brakes. If a breakaway safety mechanism is used, the cable between the car and caravan must be firmly anchored so that the trailer brakes are pulled on immediately if the two part.

Level

The caravan should be level, or very slightly nose down when fully laden and linked to the car. A nose-up attitude can be corrected by a hitch height adjuster. These are available in various heights from the caravan manufacturer or dealer. An adaptor plate can be used to lower the tow-ball mounting, but it does put extra stresses on the bracket.

Lights

Make sure that all the lights are working: rear lights, stop lights, number-plate lights and flashers (check that the flasher rate is correct – 60–120 times a minute) and rear fog guard lamps, where fitted.

Nose weight

Ensure that the nose weight of the trailer complies with the car maker's recommendations but as a general guide the nose weight should be heavier than the rear by about 40–50kg (approx 90–110lb). Check the nose weight when the caravan is laden, using bathrooms scales and blocks of wood or a spring balance. A twin-axle trailer must be

THE ONLY DIRECT ROUTES TO HOLIDAY FRANCE & SPAIN

Our spacious, modern ships, with their abundant cabins and berths, are the most relaxing way to France, Spain and Portugal.
With our direct routes you'll easily avoid the congestion and wasted miles of Northern France.

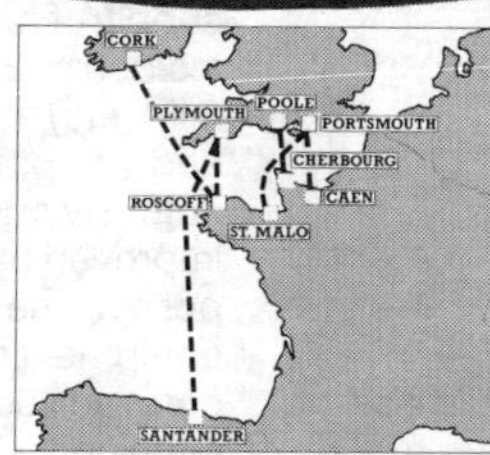

FLEET D'EXCELLENCE ON ALL ROUTES SOUTH

Our unique routes to Brittany, Normandy and Spain land you often hundreds of miles nearer your destination.
From there, our fast, clear picturesque roads make driving a sheer pleasure.

GREAT BARGAIN OFFERS FOR CARAVANNERS AND CAMPERS SAVE £££'s

We have some great offers for Caravanners and Campers:
we've Supersaver fares available on every sailing; superb bargain sites in Brittany, Normandy and Spain; and a FREE first night offer if you are taking one of our day sailings to France.

For your free 1988 Colour Brochures, ring our 24-hour brochure service on (0705) 751708 or (0752) 269926 or see your Motoring Organisation.

Brittany Ferries
The Holiday Fleet

Reservations: Portsmouth (0705) 827701. Plymouth (0752) 221321. Cork 277801.

weighed when the coupling is at the exact towing height. Too much weight can result in excessive pitching (see *Pitching* page 46), and too little can lead to instability.

Tyres

Both tyres on the caravan should be of the same size and type and it is advisable that they are the same type as those on the rear wheels of the car. Make sure that the tread depth is well above the legal minimum (see under *Preparing your car*) and that there is no uneven wear. Look also for cuts and for cracks that might have developed during the winter.

If the caravan tyres are not going to be used for a long period, they should be properly inflated and have the weight taken off them by jacking the axle on to wood blocks. Leave in an airy place where they will not be exposed to the sun, and cover if possible.

Weight and weight distribution

Caravan literature usually refers to weight as *ex-works* or *delivered* but this can be misleading due to the fact that it is normally based on a standard model and need not necessarily take into account any extras fitted. If the weight is referred to as above and the manufacturer cannot be contacted, it is recommended that the as-delivered weight be obtained by having it weighed at the nearest Public Weighbridge. This weight subtracted from the manufacturer's recommended maximum gross weight will give you the weight that can be utilised for personal effects and equipment. The kerbside weight of the towing car is defined as: the weight of the vehicle (inclusive of any towing bracket with which it is normally equipped) when it carries no person, a supply of fuel, a supply of other liquids incidental to its propulsion (*eg* water, oil, brake fluid, etc) and no load other than the loose tools and equipment with which the vehicle is normally equipped. Generally, stability will be improved by keeping as much weight as possible near the trailer axle. Heavier equipment should be stored on or near the caravan floor, to cut down the possibility of pitching (see *Pitching* page 46).

PREPARING YOUR CAMPING EQUIPMENT

Camp furniture, camp kitchens, utensils and other hardware generally take care of themselves much as do household items. However, stoves, airbeds, lanterns and sleeping-bags should always receive a check-over before departure.

The following camping equipment check list may prove to be a useful guide when planning your European camping holiday:

Air mattress and pump, or camp beds
All-purpose knife
Bucket
Camping clothes
Camp stove and fuel
Clothes-line and pegs
Cutlery, including cooking utensils
Dish-cloths, scouring pad, and tea towels
First-aid kit
Folding chairs or stools
Folding table
Food containers
Groundsheet
Icebox (portable)
Kettle
Mallet
Matches
Plastic bags or bags for litter
Plates, cups and saucers, or mugs
Rope
Saucepans, frying pan
Sleeping bags
Small brush (useful when camping on sand)
Teapot and teabags
Tent, poles, tent pegs (spares), sand pegs and discs
Tent-tidy (for scissors, string, needles, thread, etc)
Tin-opener, bottle opener, and corkscrew
Torch and batteries
Washing-up bowl and washing-up liquid
Water and milk containers
Water-purifying tablets
Windshield

PREPARING YOUR TENT

The tent, that basic item of the camping outfit, needs surprisingly little care considering the rugged service it is expected to give. Naturally, much depends on design, quality, and the amount of camping the owner pursues, but a good tent is very tough indeed. However, all this does not mean that you can ignore maintenance altogether.

Some weeks before your holiday, choosing a fine day, spread the tent on the lawn or some other open space so that a close inspection can be made of all potential stress points – that is, where guylines attach, where the groundsheet meets tent walls and where frame poles come into contact with fabric. The fabric of the tent can be damaged by branches or sharp objects. Additionally it can lose its proofing through long exposure to the weather or as a result of fat spattering on the fabric. If the tent is damaged in this way it is advisable to consult a good specialist camping supplier. Patch kits of a suitable colour and material are available, as are proofing preparations and sprays.

DRIVING AND TOWING HINTS

Before setting off check that:

1. the load is so arranged that the caravan is only slightly nose-heavy
2. roof lockers are free of equipment, if possible
3. heavy articles, tinned foods, etc are placed as near the axle as convenient
4. the brace for operating the four corner-steadies is in an accessible place
5. all doors and drawers are closed
6. there are no loose articles which could roll about
7. liquids are in containers which will not tip over
8. all windows, ventilators, and doors are firmly shut
9. any fires or flames are extinguished
10. the tap on the gas cylinder is turned off
11. the coupling is firmly in position
12. the over-run brake is working correctly
13. the two wing mirrors on your car show a good view down both sides of the caravan
14. the rear lights, brake lights and flashers on the caravan are working
15. the corner-steadies are fully wound up
16. the safety catch on the hitch is on
17. the fire extinguishers are operational and close at hand

Car and driver alike have a considerable weight of caravan or trailer to contend with. There will be increased strain on both. Much of the art of towing safely comes with experience – but by being aware of some of the problems before setting off, many dangers can be eliminated.

1. Know your car and how to drive it well – *before* attempting to tow.
2. Stop *before* you get tired.
3. Remember the three **Cs: Care, Courtesy** and **Consideration**.
4. Plan the journey in advance, checking that the roads are suitable for towing.
5. Have the right mirrors and use them. Remember *mirror, signal, manoeuvre*.
6. Keep well to the right of the road so that faster vehicles can overtake. If traffic builds up behind you, pull up in a safe place and let it pass.
7. Keep a safe stopping distance behind the vehicle in front.
8. *See and be seen* – switch on lights whenever visibility gets poor.
9. Keep to the speed limit and make good use of the gears, especially when descending hills.
10. Allow plenty of time when overtaking or pulling across a main road.
11. Never stop on narrow roads, bends, crests of hills, or anywhere that could be dangerous to yourself and other road users.
12. In case of breakdown or accident, use hazard flashers and advance warning triangles.

Overhang

Cars with more length at the rear, and therefore greater distance between the back axle and the towing ball, tend to be more difficult to handle than cars with less overhang. The design and weight distribution of the trailer would however, tend to have the greatest effect on overall performance.

Pitching

If the caravan starts to pitch, stability and control are reduced. If the nose weight (see *Nose weight* page 42) is right, and the heavier movable items are stored as near as practicable to the axle of the caravan (see *Weight distribution* page 44), pitching can be prevented by stiffening the towing car's rear suspension. To do this, a supplementary rubber or air spring unit can be fitted to the rear springs, or heavier duty shock absorbers can be used, although the latter are more expensive. Before any alterations are made, the car's front and rear shock absorbers must be in good condition.

Excessive pitching can lead to snaking, as the vertical movement starts to sway the caravan sideways.

Snaking

This can be caused by heavy pitching or bad weight distribution (see page 44). Snaking can be particularly dangerous as it is tempting for the driver to steer against the movement, making matters worse. It is best to steer straight and decelerate gently. Stabilisers are available, but it is better to cure the cause than to rely on preventative methods.

Soft ground

Avoid low sites liable to be waterlogged, sand that will not take the force of a driving wheel, and stone and shingle that may take the weight but not provide any grip.

If you have to drive over difficult ground, keep moving slowly with a very light throttle. If you stop, do not accelerate hard or the wheels will spin and dig in. Move gently backwards and forwards to get out of a dip. If the driving wheels do dig in, put brushwood or sacks in front of and behind the wheels. To move the trailer manually, pull sideways on the drawbar and work it forwards by chocking alternate wheels.

MOTORING REGULATIONS

Motoring laws in Europe are just as wide and complicated as those in the UK but they should cause little difficulty to the average British motorists, who are usually well trained. They should, however, take more care and extend greater courtesy than they would normally do at home, and bear in mind the essentials of good motoring – avoiding any behaviour likely to obstruct traffic, to endanger persons or cause damage to property. It is also important to remember that tourists are subject to the laws of the country in which they travel.

Road signs are mainly international and should be familiar to British motorists, but in every country there are a few exceptions. They should particularly watch for signs indicating crossings and speed limits. Probably the most unusual aspect of motoring abroad to the British motorist is the universal and firm rule giving priority to traffic coming from the right (**except in the Republic of Ireland**) and unless this rule is varied by signs, it must be strictly observed.

Accidents (See also Country sections)

The country sections give individual country information on summoning the fire, police and ambulance services. The international regulations are similar to those in the UK; the following recommendations are usually advisable.

If you are involved in an accident you *must* stop. A warning triangle should be placed on the road at a suitable distance to warn following traffic of the obstruction. The use of hazard warning lights in no way affects the regulations governing the use of warning triangles. Medical assistance should be obtained for persons injured in the accident. If the accident necessitates calling the police, leave the vehicle in the position in which it came to rest; should it seriously obstruct other traffic, mark the position of the vehicle on the road and get the details confirmed by independent witnesses before moving it.

The accident must be reported to the police: if it is required by law; if the accident has caused death or bodily injury; or if an unoccupied vehicle or property has been damaged and there is no one present to represent the interests of the party suffering damage. Notify your insurance company by letter if possible, within 24 hours of the

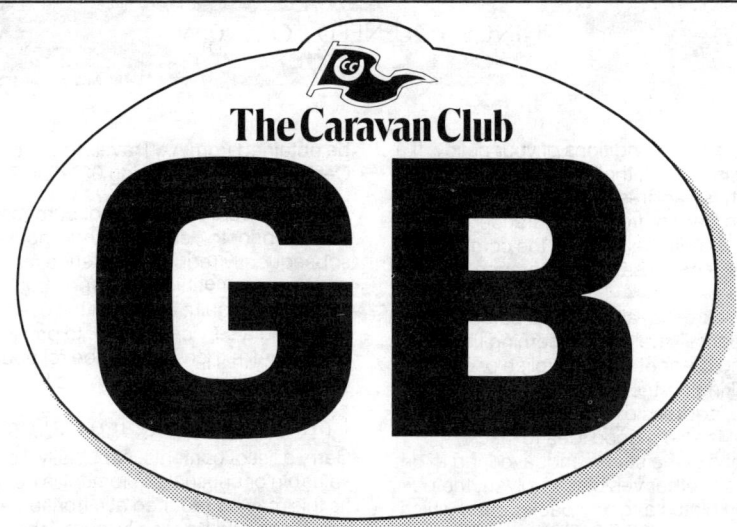

accident; see the conditions of your policy. If a third party is injured, the insurance company or bureau, whose address is given on the back of your Green Card or frontier insurance certificate, should be notified; the company or bureau will, if necessary, pay compensation to the injured party.

Make sure that all essential particulars are noted, especially details concerning third parties, and co-operate with police or other officials taking on-the-spot notes by supplying your name, address or other personal details as required. It is also a good idea to take photographs of the scene endeavouring to get good shots of other vehicles involved, their registration plates and any background which might help later enquiries. This record may be useful when completing the insurance company's accident form.

If you are not involved in the accident but feel your assistance as a witness or in any other useful capacity would be helpful then stop and park your car carefully well away from the scene. If all the help necessary is at the scene then do not stop out of curiosity nor park your car at the site.

Breakdowns

If your car breaks down, endeavour to move it to the side of the road or to a position where it will obstruct the traffic flow as little as possible. Place a warning triangle at the appropriate distance on the road behind the obstruction. Bear in mind road conditions and, if near or on a bend, the triangle should be placed where it is clearly visible to following traffic. If the car is fitted with hazard warning lights these may be switched on but they will only warn on the straight and will have no effect at bends or rises in the road. If the fault is electrical, the lights may not operate and it is for these reasons that they cannot take the place of a triangle. Having taken these first precautions, seek assistance if you cannot deal with the fault yourself.

Motorists are advised to take out AA 5-Star Service, the overseas motoring emergency service which includes breakdown and accident benefits, and personal travel insurance. It offers total security and peace of mind to all motorists travelling in Europe. Cover may be purchased by any motorist although a small additional premium must be paid by non-members. Further details and brochures may be obtained from AA Travel Agencies and AA Centres or by telephoning 021-550 7648.

Note Members who have not purchased 5-Star Service prior to departure and who subsequently require assistance may request spare parts or vehicle recovery, but in this case the AA will require a deposit to cover estimated costs and a service fee prior to providing the service. All expenses must be reimbursed to the AA in addition to the service fee.

Caravan and luggage trailers

Carry a list of contents, especially if any valuable or unusual equipment is being carried, as this may be required at a frontier. A towed vehicle should be readily identifiable by a plate in an accessible position showing the name of the maker of the vehicle and the production or serial number. If the vehicle does not have an *identification plate* see page 50. See also *Principal mountain passes* page 70.

Claims against Third Parties

The law and levels of damage in foreign countries are generally different to our own. It is important to remember this when considering making a claim against another motorist arising out of an accident abroad. Certain types of claims invariably present difficulties, the most common probably being that relating to the recovery of car hiring charges. Rarely are they recoverable in full and in some countries they may be drastically reduced or not recoverable at all. General damages for pain and suffering are not recoverable in certain countries but even in those countries where they are recoverable the levels are, in most cases, lower than our own.

The negotiation of claims against foreign insurers is extremely protracted and translation of all documents slows down the process. A delay of three months between sending a letter and receiving a reply is not uncommon!

If you have taken out the AA's 5-Star Service cover, this includes a discretionary service in respect of certain matters arising abroad requiring legal assistance including the pursuit of uninsured loss claims against third parties arising out of a road accident. In this event, members should seek guidance and/or assistance from the AA.

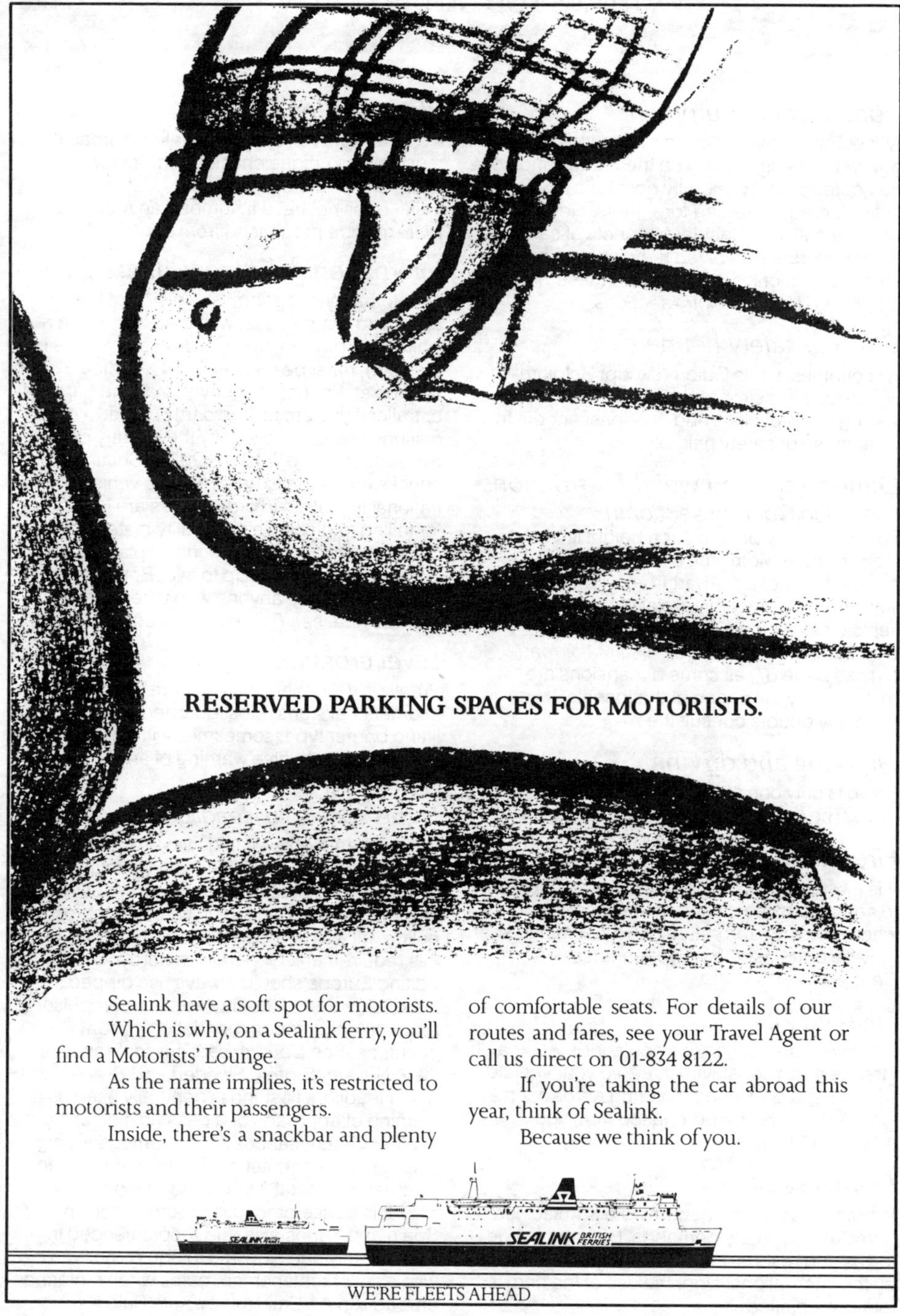
RESERVED PARKING SPACES FOR MOTORISTS.
Sealink have a soft spot for motorists.
Which is why, on a Sealink ferry, you'll find a Motorists' Lounge.
As the name implies, it's restricted to motorists and their passengers.
Inside, there's a snackbar and plenty of comfortable seats. For details of our routes and fares, see your Travel Agent or call us direct on 01-834 8122.
If you're taking the car abroad this year, think of Sealink.
Because we think of you.
SEALINK BRITISH FERRIES
WE'RE FLEETS AHEAD

Compulsory equipment

All countries have differing regulations as to how vehicles circulating on their roads should be equipped but generally domestic laws are not enforced on visiting foreigners. However, where a country considers aspects of safety or other factors are involved they will impose some regulations on visitors and these will be mentioned in the *Country sections*.

Crash or safety helmets

All countries in this Guide (except Belgium where they are strongly recommended) require visiting motorcyclists and their passengers to wear crash or safety helmets.

Dimensions and weight restrictions
(See also Country sections)

For an ordinary private car a height limit of 4 metres and a width limit of 2.50 metres is generally imposed. Apart from a laden weight limit imposed on commercial vehicles, every vehicle has an individual weight limit. See *Overloading* page 51. See also *Major road tunnels* page 67, as some dimensions are restricted by the shape of the tunnels. If you have any doubts consult the AA.

Drinking and driving

There is only one safe rule – if you drink, don't drive. The laws are strict and penalties severe.

Fire extinguisher

It is a wise precaution (compulsory in Greece) to equip your vehicle with a fire extinguisher when motoring abroad. An AA Fire Extinguisher may be purchased from your nearest AA Centre.

First-aid kit

It is a wise precaution (compulsory in Austria, Greece and Yugoslavia) to equip your vehicle with a first-aid kit when motoring abroad. An AA First-Aid Kit may be purchased from your nearest AA Centre.

Horn, use of

In built-up areas the general rule is not to use horns unless safety demands it; in many large towns and resorts, as well as in areas indicated by the international sign, the use of the horn is totally prohibited.

Identification plate

If a boat, caravan or trailer is taken abroad it must have a unique chassis number for identification purposes. If your boat, caravan or trailer does not have a number, an *identification plate* may be purchased from the AA.

International distinguishing sign

An international distinguishing sign of the approved pattern, oval with black letters on a white background, and size (GB at least 6.9in by 4.5in), must be displayed on a vertical surface at the rear of your vehicle (and caravan or trailer if you are towing one). These distinguishing signs signify the country of registration of the vehicle. On the Continent checks are made to ensure that a vehicle's nationality plate is in order. Fines are imposed for failing to display a nationality plate, or for not displaying the correct nationality plate, see *Police fines* page 51. Up to two (British or Irish) are issued free to anyone who takes out AA 5-Star Service, see *Breakdowns* page 48.

Level crossings

Practically all level crossings are indicated by international signs. Most guarded ones are the lifting barrier type, sometimes with bells or flashing lights to give warning of an approaching train.

Lights *(See also Headlights page 41)*

Dipped headlights should also be used in conditions of fog, snowfall, heavy rain and when passing through a tunnel, irrespective of its length and its lighting. In some countries police will wait at the end of a tunnel, checking this requirement. Generally motorcyclists visiting Europe should always use dipped headlights during the day as it is a compulsory requirement or recommendation in many countries. See *Country sections* for France, Italy, Norway, Spain, Sweden and Switzerland.

Headlight flashing is generally used as a warning of approach or a passing sign at night. In other circumstances it is accepted as a sign of annoyance or irritation and should be used with caution lest it be misunderstood.

It is a wise precaution (compulsory in Spain and Yugoslavia and recommended in France, Italy and Norway) to equip your vehicle with a set of replacement bulbs when motoring abroad. An AA Emergency Auto Bulb Kit suitable for most makes of car can be purchased from your nearest AA Centre.

Mirrors

When driving abroad on the right it is essential, as when driving on the left in the UK and Republic of Ireland, to have clear all-round vision. If your vehicle is not equipped with a rear view mirror on the left external side it is recommended that you fit one before travelling abroad. See also *Mirrors* page 41.

Overloading

This can create safety risks, and in most countries committing such an offence can involve *on-the-spot* fines (see *Police fines* page 51). It would also be a great inconvenience if your car were stopped because of overloading – you would not be allowed to proceed until the load had been reduced.

The maximum loaded weight, and its distribution between front and rear axles, is decided by the vehicle manufacturer and if your owner's handbook does not give these facts you should seek the advice of the manufacturer direct. There is a public weighbridge in all districts and when the car is fully loaded (not forgetting the passengers, of course) use this to check that the vehicle is within the limits.

When loading a vehicle, care should be taken that no lights, reflectors, or number plates are masked and that the driver's view is in no way impaired. All luggage loaded on a roof rack must be tightly secured and should not upset the stability of the vehicle. Any projections beyond the front, rear, or sides of a vehicle that might not be noticed by other drivers must be clearly marked.

Overtaking

When overtaking on roads with two lanes or more in each direction, always signal your intention in good time, and after the manoeuvre, signal and return to the inside lane. Do **not** remain in any other lane. Failure to comply with this regulation, particularly in France, will incur an *on-the-spot* fine (see *Police fines* page 51).

Always overtake on the left (on the right in the Republic of Ireland) and use your horn as a warning to the driver of the vehicle being overtaken (except in areas where the use of the horn is prohibited). Do not overtake whilst being overtaken or when a vehicle behind is preparing to overtake. Do not overtake at level crossings, at intersections, the crest of a hill or at pedestrian crossings. When being overtaken keep well to the right (left in the Republic of Ireland) and reduce speed if necessary – never increase speed.

Parking

Parking is a problem everywhere in Europe and the police are extremely strict with offenders. Heavy fines are inflicted as well as the towing away of unaccompanied offending cars. This can cause inconvenience and heavy charges are imposed for the recovery of impounded vehicles. In Athens number plates may be removed and confiscated from illegally parked vehicles. You should acquaint yourself with local parking regulations and endeavour to understand all relative signs. As a rule always park on the right hand side of the road (left-hand side in the Republic of Ireland) or at an authorised place. As far as possible park off the main carriageway but not on cycle tracks, pedestrian verges, railway lines or tram tracks.

Passengers

It is an offence in all countries to carry more passengers in a car than the vehicle is constructed to seat, but some have regulations as to how the passengers shall be seated. Where such regulations are applied to visiting foreigners it will be mentioned in the *Country sections*.

For passenger-carrying vehicles constructed and equipped to carry more than 10 passengers including the driver there are special regulations (see *Minibus* page 37).

Police fines

Some countries impose *on-the-spot* fines for minor traffic offences which vary in amount according to the offence committed and the country concerned. Other countries *eg* France, impose an immediate deposit and subsequently levy a fine which may be greater or lesser than this sum, but which usually matches it. Fines are either paid in cash to the police or at a local post office against a *ticket* issued by the police. They must usually be paid in the currency of the country concerned, and can vary in amount from £3–£690 (approximate amounts). The reason for the fines is to penalise and at the same time keep minor motoring offences out of the courts. Disputing the fine usually leads to a court appearance, delays and additional expense.

If the fine is not paid then legal proceedings will usually follow. Some countries immobilise vehicles until a fine is paid and may sell it to pay the penalty imposed.

Once paid a fine cannot be recovered, but a receipt should always be obtained as proof of payment. Should AA members require assistance in any motoring matter involving local police they should apply to the legal department of the relevant national motoring organisation.

Priority including roundabouts

The general rule is to give way to traffic entering a junction from the right (except in the Republic of Ireland), but this is sometimes varied at roundabouts (see below). This is one aspect of European driving which may cause British drivers the most confusion because their whole training and experience makes it unnatural. Road signs indicate priority or loss of priority and tourists are well advised to make sure that they understand such signs.

Great care should be taken at intersections and tourists should never rely on receiving the right of way, particularly in small towns and villages where local traffic, often slow moving, such as farm tractors, etc, will assume right of way regardless of oncoming traffic. Always give way to public services and military vehicles. Blind or disabled people, funerals and marching columns must always be allowed right of way. Vehicles such as buses and coaches carrying large numbers of passengers will expect and should be allowed priority.

Generally priority at roundabouts is given to vehicles entering the roundabout unless signposted to the contrary (see *France* page 125). This is a complete reversal of the United Kingdom and Republic of Ireland rule and particular care should be exercised when manoeuvring whilst circulating in an anti-clockwise direction on a roundabout. It is advisable to keep to the outside lane on a roundabout, if possible, to make your exit easier.

Road signs

Most road signs throughout Europe are internationally agreed and the majority would be familiar to the British motorist. Watch for road markings – do not cross a solid white or yellow line marked on the road centre. In *Belgium* there are two official languages and signs will be in Flemish or French, see *Roads* page 100 for further information. In the Basque and Catalonian areas of *Spain* local and national placenames appear on signposts, see *Roads* page 351 for further information.

Rule of the Road

In all the countries in this Guide except Ireland drive on the right and overtake on the left; in Ireland drive on the left and overtake on the right.

Seat belts

All countries in this Guide (except Italy where they are *strongly recommended*) require visitors to wear seat belts. If your car is fitted with belts then in the interest of safety, wear them; otherwise you may run the risk of a *police fine.*

Speed limits

It is important to observe speed limits at all times. Offenders may be fined and driving licences confiscated on the spot, thus causing great inconvenience and possible expense. The standard legal limits are given in the appropriate *Country sections* for private cars and for car/caravan/trailer combinations, but these may be varied by road signs and where these are displayed the lower limit should be accepted. At certain seasons limits may also be temporarily varied and information would be available at the frontier. It can be an offence to travel without good reason at so slow a speed as to obstruct traffic flow.

Traffic lights

In principal cities and towns traffic lights operate in a way similar to those in the United Kingdom and Republic of Ireland, although they are sometimes suspended overhead. The density of the light may be so poor that lights could be missed. There is usually only one set on the right-hand side of the road some distance before the road junction, and if you stop too close to the corner the lights will not be visible. Look out for 'filter' lights which will enable you to turn right at a junction against the

main lights. If you wish to go straight ahead do not enter a lane leading to 'filter' lights or you may obstruct traffic wishing to turn right.

Trams

Trams take priority over other vehicles. Always give way to passengers boarding and alighting. Never position a vehicle so that it impedes the free passage of a tram. Trams must be overtaken on the right except in one-way streets.

Warning triangles/Hazard warning lights (See also Country sections)

The use of a warning triangle is compulsory in most European countries and is a wise precaution in any case. It should be placed on the road behind a stopped vehicle to warn traffic approaching from the rear of an obstruction ahead. The triangle should be used when a vehicle has stopped for any reason – not only breakdowns. It should be placed in such a position as to be clearly visible up to 100m (109yds) by day and night, about 2ft from the edge of the road but not in such a position as to present a danger to on-coming traffic. It should be set up about 30m (33yds) behind the obstruction, but this distance should be increased to 100m (109yds) on motorways. A warning triangle is not required for two-wheeled vehicles.

An AA Warning Triangle, which complies with the latest international and European standards, can be hired from the AA or bought in AA Travel Agencies, AA Centres or by mail order.

Although four flashing indicators are allowed in the countries covered by this guide, they in no way affect the regulations governing the use of warning triangles. Generally hazard warning lights should not be used in place of a triangle although they may complement it in use, but see *France* page 126 and *Switzerland* page 394.

CAMPING FUELS

Gas in cylinders or bottles, as used in caravans, is mainly of two types: butane and propane. Both are kept in liquid under pressure and become a combustible gas once the pressure is released. They are available in Europe, but as they respond differently to weather conditions, propane is more widely distributed in countries where temperatures are likely to be very low in the winter. Propane has a higher pressure than butane. The branded gases and the manufacturers are listed on pages 55 and 56.

Carriage of gas by car ferries

Vehicles carrying unsealed cylinders of liquefied petrolem gas (LPG) must report at both United Kingdom and European ports for a leakage test 30 minutes before the published reporting time. A maximum of three Home Office approved cylinders, not exceeding 35lb net weight each, or up to 12 small expendable cartridges, sealed and packed in an outer container, are allowed for each caravan. Cylinders should be securely fixed in or on the caravan in the manner and position intended by the caravan manufacturer.

Virtually all campers and caravanners use LPG. New users particularly should follow safety instructions and experienced people sometimes need reminding of the safety rules which say in effect:

- change cylinders with care
- provide fresh air for safe combustion
- don't improvise or tamper with equipment
- carry out regular maintenance.

Gas safety rules

1. Always use the right type and length of hose for connecting a container to an appliance. If it is not supplied, or instructions are not given, ask the dealer's advice.
2. Replace any worn or faulty hose. Do not try to repair it.
3. When fitting the hose, where applicable use worm-drive clips and ensure they are tight.
4. Always use a spanner when fitting connections – finger tightness is not enough. Before fitting a regulator or other screwed connection to a butane cylinder, always ensure that the sealing washer is present and in good condition. When fitting to switch on or clip on type valves, refer to the manufacturer's/supplier's instructions.
5. Check for leaks by applying soapy water. Any leaks will be shown by bubbles.

6 **Never** check for leaks with a naked flame.
7 Always keep containers away from excessive heat or naked flames.
8 When starting up, open the container valve slowly.
9 If the container is not to be used for some time, close the valve, remove the pressure regulator and replace the valve cover if fitted.
10 When changing a cartridge or container, keep away from any naked light or flame, or any source of ignition. With cartridge appliances, check that the sealing washer, usually housed in the appliance inlet connection, is in position and in good condition. Make sure that the valve on the container, where fitted, and the tap on the regulator are fully closed.
Never try to change a pierceable cartridge (such as the Camping Gaz type) **until you are sure all the gas has been expended**. You can usually hear any gas remaining by gently shaking the equipment.
11 Once the pressure regulators are set they should not be tampered with. Any adjustments or repairs should be left to the dealer.
12 Containers must always stand upright, valves uppermost, whether in use or not. They should also be carried upright, but not by the valve.
13 Whether full or empty, never store the containers below ground or near drains, as all these gases are heavier than air and will collect at the lowest point in the event of a leak.
14 **Make sure there is good ventilation where gas burning appliances are used.** Unflued appliances must not be installed in sleeping accommodation. Only room sealed appliances should be installed in bath or shower rooms.
15 When moving, turn off all appliances and cylinder valves.
16 Do not sleep in a room where gas cylinders are used.
17 Permanent storage should always be out of doors.
18 When fitting cylinders, always check that the cylinder valve is fully closed in a clockwise direction before removing the valve-sealing cap or plug.

Branded gases

Shell Gas Butane This product is marketed in 15kg cylinders (approx 33lb) by Shell Gas in England, Scotland and Wales. The head office is at 7 Oxford Road, Manchester M60 7HH ☎061-277 2000. Lists of dealers are available from the LPG department. The distribution of *Butane* is confined to the United Kingdom (excluding Northern Ireland) and, because of differing official standards and regulations to which cylinders must conform, *Butane* cylinders cannot be exchanged for European ones. Neither can they be refilled abroad. Foreign cylinders must not be brought back to the United Kingdom, nor British cylinders left in Europe. For these reasons it is recommended that, if conditions permit, you take sufficient gas to last throughout the holiday.

A list of main agents from whom cylinders are available can be obtained from Shell Gas, 7 Oxford Road, Manchester M60 7HH ☎061-277 2000. The main agents will be able to supply you with the names and addresses of local sub-agents.

Butane is, however, marketed by Shell in France, the Netherlands, Switzerland, Belgium, Portugal and Luxembourg, usually in cylinders of 13kg capacity (approximately 29lb). British butane regulators will not connect directly with cylinders obtained in these countries because of differing connections. A regulator must be obtained on loan. Deposits on cylinders are payable at the time of purchase and it is essential that you get a receipt for this from the sub-agent so that you have no difficulty in getting the deposit refunded. If your burner is specifically designed for use with butane, it is inadvisable to use it with any other gas such as propane or a propane/butane mixture.

Shell Gas (propane): Marketed by Shell Gas in 4.7kg, 11kg, 18.5kg and 46kg cylinders in England, Scotland and Wales.

Calor Gas (butane): Marketed by Calor Gas Ltd, Appleton Park, Datchet, Slough, Berks SL3 9JG ☎40000. Although Calor Gas refills are not available abroad, it is possible to take sufficient with you to last for a short holiday. The following are suggested:

Camping: Single-burner picnic set or double-burner camping stove with 4.5kg cylinder;

Motor Caravan: Two-burner hotplate or two-burner hotplate grill with 4.5kg cylinder;

Trailer: Two-burner hotplate or small cooker, with 4.5kg cylinder with screw-on connection or 15kg cylinder which will accept the *switch-on* regulator.

If you follow the simple instructions on economical use, a 4.5kg cylinder will last a month on either the single or double-burner units. If you are travelling by car or motorcycle combination, one 4.5kg cylinder will be sufficient, especially if you are eating out occasionally.

If you cannot take enough Calor Gas cylinders in your outfit, you are advised to buy a Camping Gaz connecting tap before leaving this country. This enables a Calor Gas regulator or flow-control valve (or just the Calor Gas connecting nut in the case of appliances not using regulating equipment) to be connected to a Camping Gaz 904 or 907 cylinder (the exception to this is the quick-boiling ring or single burner, which fits directly to the 4.5kg cylinder shroud). The connecting tap is available from all Calor Gas sales and service centres, and other stockists.

Calor Gas (propane): Marketed by Calor Gas Ltd., in 3.9kg, 13kg and 47kg cylinders. This is suitable for those wishing to undertake all year round camping and caravanning.

Primus (propane): Primus cylinders are available in three sizes – 2000 (0.34kg), 2005 (0.82kg) and 2012 (1.98kg) – to complement the company's extensive range of leisure, DIY and industrial appliances. Cylinders are filled and distributed in this country by Calor Gas Ltd., and are available from most Calor Dealers or Calor-Primus stockists.

Primus (butane): Cartridges nos. 2201 (200g), 2202 (420g) and the new 2207 (220g) low profile, are widely available in this country and in Europe (with the exception of Spain and Eastern Europe).

Due to recent legislation in France and existing regulations in West Germany it is strongly advised to carry sufficient cartridges for passage through either of these countries.

Camping Gaz International (butane): Marketed in the United Kingdom by Camping Gaz (GB) Ltd, 9 Albert Street, Slough, Berks SL1 2BH ☏691707. This product is widely marketed throughout Europe (see below). A list of general agents can be obtained from the company. Cartridges and cylinders are available in the following sizes:

Cartridge 'GT' (3oz gas approx)
Cartridge 206 (7oz gas approx)
901 cylinder (0.51kg)
904 cylinder (1.86kg)
907 cylinder (2.78kg)

The cartridges are expendable but cylinders are fully interchangeable for use with cooking, lighting and heater units. A special connecting tap unit is available to fit Butagas or Calor Gas regulators to Camping Gaz 904 or 907 cylinders. Also, the Camping Gaz regulator with hexagon nut enables Calor Gas or Butagas cylinders to be connected to Camping Gaz low pressure stoves via the flexible hose supplied with these stoves.

Safety

— Always make sure you have the right size and type of gas cartridge for the appliance.
— Never put a cartridge in a cartridge holder unless the upper part of the appliance has been unscrewed and completely removed.
— A cartridge with gas in it must never be removed from an appliance nor must the upper part of the appliance be unscrewed.

The following shows the present availability in Europe: Andorra, Austria, Belgium, Denmark (not 901), Finland (not 901), France, West Germany, Greece, Italy, Liechtenstein, Luxembourg, Monaco, Netherlands, Norway (not 901; cartridge 206 and 904 refills limited; own cylinders can be filled at Progas depots; list of stockists available on request), Portugal, Spain including Majorca and Ibiza (cartridge 206 and 901 and 907 only), Sweden (not 901), through Optimus International, Switzerland, United Kingdom.

Paraffin

Paraffin (*pétrole* or *kerosene*) is not easily obtainable in country districts in Europe and you are advised to get supplies on arrival in large towns. Methylated spirit (*alcoöl à brûler*) is easier to get.

GENERAL INFORMATION

British Embassies/Consulates (See also Country sections)

In most countries there is usually more than one British Consulate and degrees of status vary. The functions and office hours of Vice-Consulates and Honorary Consuls are naturally more restricted. Generally Consulates (and consular sections of the Embassy) stand ready to help British travellers overseas, but there are limits to what they can do. A Consulate cannot pay your hotel, medical or any other bills, nor will they do the work of travel agents, information bureaux or police. Any loss or theft of property should be reported to the local police not the Consulate, and a statement obtained confirming the loss or theft. If you still need help, such as the issue of an emergency passport or guidance on how to transfer funds, contact the Consulate.

Credit/Charge Cards

Credit/Charge cards may be used abroad but their use is subject to 'conditions of use' set out by the issuing company who, on request, will provide full information.

Establishments display the symbols of cards they accept; it is not possible to produce any detailed lists.

Currency including banking hours (See also Country sections)

There is no limit to the amount of sterling notes you may take abroad. However, it is best to carry only enough currency for immediate expenses. As many countries have regulations controlling the import and export of currency, you are advised to consult your bank for full information before making final arrangements.

Customs regulations for European countries (other than the United Kingdom)

Bona fide visitors to the countries listed in this Guide may assume as a general rule they may *temporarily import personal articles* duty free, providing the following conditions are met:

a that the articles are for personal use and are not to be sold or otherwise disposed of

b that they may be considered as being in use and in keeping with the personal status of the importer

c that they are taken out when the importer leaves the country

d that the goods stay for no more than 6 months in any 12 months period, whichever is the earlier

All dutiable articles must be declared when you enter a country, otherwise you will be liable to penalties. Should you be taking a large number of personal effects with you, it would be a wise measure to prepare in advance an inventory to present to the Customs authorities on entry. Customs officers may withhold concession at any time and ask the traveller to deposit enough money to cover possible duty, especially on portable items of apparent high value such as television sets, radios, cassette recorders, pocket calculators, musical instruments, etc, all of which must be declared. Any deposit paid (for which a receipt must be obtained) is likely to be high; it is recoverable (but only at the entry point at which it was paid) on leaving the country and exporting the item. Alternatively the Customs may enter the item in the traveller's passport and in these circumstances it is important to remember to get the entry cancelled when the item is exported. Duty and tax free allowances may not apply (except for EEC countries) if travellers enter the country more than once a month, or if they are under 17 years of age (an alternative age may apply in some countries). However, residents of Channel Islands and Isle of Man do not benefit from EEC allowances due to their fiscal regimes.

A temporarily imported motor vehicle, caravan, boat or any other type of *trailer* is subject to strict control on entering a country, attracting Customs duty and a variety of taxes; much depends upon the circumstances and the period of the import and also upon the status of the importer. People entering a country in which they have no residence, with a private vehicle for holiday or recreational purposes and intending to export the vehicle within a short period, enjoy special privileges and the normal formalities are reduced to an absolute minimum in the interests of tourism. However, a *Customs Carnet de Passages en Douane* is required to temporarily import certain vehicles, boats and outboard engines into some countries (see *Country sections* for *Belgium, France*, and *Luxembourg*). The *Carnet*, for which a charge is made, is a valuable document issued by the AA to its members as part of the AA 5-Star Service – further information may be obtained from most AA Centres. If you are issued with a *Carnet* you must ensure that it is returned to the AA correctly discharged in order to avoid inconvenience and expense, possibly including payment of customs charges, at a later date. A temporarily imported vehicle, etc, should not:

a be left in the country after the importer has left;
b be put at the disposal of a resident of the country;
c be retained in the country longer than the permitted period;
d be lent, sold, hired, given away, exchanged or otherwise disposed of.

People entering a country with a motor vehicle for a period of generally more than six months (see also *Visa* information page 38) or to take up residence, employment, any commercial activity or with the intention of disposing of the vehicle should seek advice concerning their position well in advance of their departure. Most AA Centres will be pleased to help.

Customs regulations for the United Kingdom

If, when leaving Britain, you export any items of new appearance, such as watches, items of jewellery, cameras etc, particularly of foreign manufacture, which you bought in the UK, it is a good idea to carry the retailer's receipts with you if they are available. In the absence of such receipts you may be asked to make a written declaration of where the goods were obtained.

The exportation of certain goods *from the United Kingdom* is prohibited or restricted. These include controlled drugs; most animals, birds and some plants; firearms and ammunition; strategic and technological equipment (including computers); photographic material over 60 years old; and antiques and collectors' items more than 50 years old.

When you *enter the United Kingdom* you will pass through Customs. You must declare everything in excess of the duty and tax free allowances (see below) you have obtained outside the United Kingdom or on the journey and everything previously obtained free of duty or tax in the United Kingdom. You may not mix allowances between duty free and non-duty free sources within each heading except for alcohol which allows for example 1 litre of duty and tax free spirits in addition to 5 litres of duty and tax paid still wine. Currently as a concession only, travellers may use their alcoholic drinks not over 22% Vol entitlement to import table wine, in addition to the set table wine allowance. You must also declare any prohibited or restricted goods and goods for commercial purposes. Don't be tempted to hide anything or mislead the Customs. The penalties are severe and articles which are not properly declared may be forfeited. If articles are hidden in a vehicle, that too becomes liable to forfeiture. Customs officers are legally entitled to examine your luggage. Please co-operate with them if they ask to examine it. You are responsible for opening, unpacking and repacking your luggage.

The importation of certain goods into the United Kingdom is prohibited or restricted. These include controlled drugs such as opium, morphine, heroin, cocaine, cannabis, amphetamines, barbiturates and LSD (lysergide); counterfeit currency; firearms (including gas pistols, electric shock batons and similar weapons), ammunition, explosives (including fireworks) and flick knives, horror comics, indecent or obscene books, magazines, films, video tapes and other articles; animals and birds*, whether alive or dead (*eg* stuffed); certain articles derived from endangered species including furskins, ivory, reptile leather and goods made from them; meat and poultry and most of their products (whether or not cooked), including ham, bacon, sausage, pâté, eggs and milk; plants, parts thereof and plant produce, including trees and shrubs, potatoes and certain other vegetables, fruit, bulbs and seeds; wood with bark attached; certain fish and fish eggs, whether live or dead; bees; radio transmitters (*eg* citizen's band radios, walkie-talkies etc) not approved for use in the United Kingdom.

**Note* Cats, dogs and other mammals must not be landed unless a British import licence (rabies) has previously been issued.

Customs Notice No. 1 is available to all travellers at the point of entry or on the boat and contains useful information of which returning tourists should be aware. Motorists should obtain a copy of Customs Notice No. 15 on the ferry or ship, and display the appropriate red or green sticker that can be found in the notice on arrival. Advance copies of Customs Notices 1 and 15 can be obtained from HM Customs and Excise, Dorset House, Stamford Street, London SE1 9PS

Goods obtained duty and tax free in the EEC or duty and tax free on a ship or aircraft, or goods obtained outside the EEC	Duty and tax free allowances	Goods obtained duty and tax paid in the EEC
	Tobacco products	
200	Cigarettes	300
	or	
100	Cigarillos	150
	or	
50	Cigars	75
	or	
250g	Tobacco	400g
	Alcoholic drinks	
2 litres	Still table wine	5 litres
1 litre	Over 22% vol (eg spirits and strong liqueurs)	1½ litres
	or	
2 litres	Not over 22% vol (eg low strength liqueurs or fortified wines or sparkling wines)	3 litres
	or	
2 litres	Still table wine	3 litres
	Perfume	
50g		75g
	Toilet water	
250cc		375cc
	Other goods	
£32	but no more than: 50 litres of beer 25 mechanical lighters	£250

Note

I The tobacco allowances in the left-hand column are doubled for persons who live outside Europe.

II Persons under 17 are not entitled to tobacco and drinks allowances.

Electrical

The public electricity supply in Europe is predominantly 220 volts (50 cycles) AC (alternating current), but can be as low as 110 volts. In some isolated areas, low voltage DC (direct current) is provided. European circular two-pin plugs and screw type bulbs are usually the rule.

Electrical adaptors (not voltage transformers) which can be used in European shaver points and light bulb sockets are available in the United Kingdom, usually from the larger electrical retailers.

Emergency messages to tourists

In cases of emergency the AA will assist in the passing on of messages to tourists in Austria, Belgium, Denmark, France, Germany, Greece, Irish Republic, Italy, Luxembourg, Netherlands, Norway, Portugal, Spain, Sweden, Switzerland and Yugoslavia.

The AA can arrange for messages to be published in overseas editions of the *Daily Mail* and in extreme emergency (death or serious illness concerning next-of-kin) can arrange to have personal messages broadcast on overseas radio networks. Anyone wishing to use this service should contact their nearest AA Centre.

Before you leave home make sure your relatives understand the procedure to follow should an emergency occur.

If you have reason to expect a message from home you will be wise to contact the tourist office or the motoring club of the country you are staying in. They will be able to tell you to which frequency you should tune your radio and at what time such messages are normally broadcast.

No guarantee can be given, either by the AA or by the *Daily Mail*, to trace the person concerned, and no responsibility can be accepted for the authenticity of messages.

Ferry crossing

From Britain the shortest sea crossing from a southern port to the Continent would be obvious but it might not always be the best choice bearing in mind how it places you on landing for main roads to your destination. Your starting point is important because, if you have a long journey to a southern port, then a service from an eastern port might be more convenient.

Perhaps a Motorail service to the south might save time and possibly an overnight stop? In some circumstances the south-western ports may offer a convenient service and before making bookings it may be worth seeking advice so that the journey can be as economic and as comfortable as possible. Similarly, for crossings to Ireland, there are several departure points along the west coast and much depends on your starting location and ultimate destination for the most convenient ferry service. The AA provides a full information and booking service on all sea, motorail and hovercraft services and instant confirmation is available on many by ringing one of the numbers listed below (Monday to Friday, 09.00–17.00). Ask also if you want information and booking on Continental car-sleeper and ferry services.

The South-East
01-839 3555

The North
061-488 7290

The West and Wales
Bristol (0272) 24417

Scotland and Northern Ireland
041-812 2888

The Midlands
021-550 7648

Republic of Ireland
Dublin (0001)777004

Foodstuffs

What you take with you is largely a question of the space available and personal choice. Countries do have regulations governing the quantities of foodstuffs which may be imported, but generally they are not strictly applied. However visitors should be aware of the existence of these regulations and only take reasonable quantities of foodstuffs with them. Where specific regulations exist for a country, they are listed under the general section of the country heading.

Convenience foods offer great variety, are ideally suited to camping, and come in many forms; the three main types are tinned, dehydrated and, if you possess a cool box, frozen. Nevertheless resist the temptation to take too much as this only means a large number of tins making a long round trip.

It is far better to take only as much as you need until you can shop locally. Best value for money will be found in supermarkets or in the open markets in towns. However, the golden rule is to shop where you see locals shopping – a sure sign of good quality and the best prices.

Liquefied Petroleum Gas/LPG

The availability of this gas in Europe makes a carefully planned tour, with a converted vehicle, limited but feasible. The gas is retailed by several companies in Europe who will supply information as to where their product may be purchased. LPG is available in all the countries covered by this guide except Portugal and Spain. A motorist regularly purchasing the fuel in the UK could possibly obtain lists of European addresses from the retailer.

Hours of opening of filling stations vary from country to country but generally they operate during normal business hours, except for holidays and saints-days. At weekends LPG users are well advised to fill up on Saturdays and not rely on Sunday opening. It is recommended that a reducer nipple be carried as a precautionary measure. This accessory can normally be obtained from the importer/ manufacturer of the LPG unit at a minimal cost.

When booking a ferry crossing it is advisable to point out to the booking agent/ ferry company that the vehicle runs on a dual fuel system.

Medical treatment

Travellers who are in the habit of taking certain medicines should make sure that they have a sufficient supply to last for their trip since they may be very difficult to get abroad.

Those who suffer from certain diseases (diabetes or coronary artery diseases, for example) should get a letter from their doctor giving treatment details. Some Continental doctors will understand a letter written in English, but it is better to have it translated into the language of the country that it is intended to visit. The AA cannot make such a translation.

Travellers, who for legitimate health reasons carry drugs or appliances (hypodermic syringe etc) may have difficulty with Customs or other authorities. Others may have a diet problem which would be understood in hotels but for a language problem. The letter which such persons carry should therefore supply treatment details, a statement for customs, and diet requirements.

The National Health Service is available in the United Kingdom only and medical expenses incurred overseas cannot generally be reimbursed by the United Kingdom

Government. There are reciprocal health agreements with most of the countries covered by this Guide, but you should not rely exclusively on these arrangements as the cover provided under the respective national schemes is not always comprehensive *eg* the cost of bringing a person back to the UK in the event of illness or death is never covered nor is the cost of any medical care needed as a result of a road accident in the Republic of Ireland. The full costs of medical care must be paid in Andorra, Liechtenstein, Monaco, San Marino and Switzerland. Therefore, as facilities and financial cover can differ considerably between the various countries, you are strongly advised to take out comprehensive and adequate insurance cover before leaving the UK such as that offered by *Personal Security* under the *AA 5-Star Service*.

Urgently needed medical treatment in the event of an accident or unforeseen illness can be obtained for most visitors, free of charge or at reduced costs, from the health care schemes of those countries with whom the UK has health care arrangements. Details are in leaflet SA30 which is available from local social security offices of the Department of Health and Social Security or from its Leaflets Unit at PO Box 21, Stanmore, Middlesex HA7 1AY. In some of these countries visitors can obtain urgently needed treatment by showing their UK passport but in some a NHS medical card must be produced and in most European Community countries a certificate of entitlement (E111) is necessary. A form to obtain this certificate is included in the DHSS leaflet. Applicants should allow at least one month for the form to be processed although in an emergency the E111 can be obtained over the counter of the local DHSS office (residents of the Republic of Ireland must apply to their Regional Health Board for the E111). The DHSS will also supply on request a leaflet SA35 *Notice to Travellers – Health Protection* which gives advice on health precautions and guidance about the international vaccination requirements. This may be obtained by writing to the DHSS at the address given below or telephoning ext 6711.

Further information about health care arrangements overseas is obtainable from the Department of Health and Social Security, Alexander Fleming House, Elephant and Castle, London SE1 6BY, *Tel* 01-407 5522 ext 6641 (non-EEC countries), ext 6737 (EEC countries).

Motoring Clubs in Europe

Alliance Internationale de Tourisme (AIT) is the largest confederation of touring associations in the world and it is through this body that the AA is able to offer its members the widest possible touring information service. Its membership consists not of individuals, but of associations or groups of associations having an interest in touring. The Alliance was formed in 1919 – the AA was a founder member and is represented on its Administrative Council and Management Committee. The General Secretariat of the AIT is in Geneva.

Tourists visiting a country where there is an AIT club may avail themselves of its touring advisory services upon furnishing proof of membership of their home AIT club. AA members making overseas trips should, whenever possible, seek the advice of the AA before setting out and should only approach the overseas AIT club when necessary.

Off site camping

Apart from observing local regulations, you are strongly advised not to camp by the roadside and in isolated areas.

Petrol

In Western Europe, and indeed throughout the world, grades of petrol compare favourably with those in the UK. Internationally-known brands are usually available on main tourist and international routes, but in remote districts familiar brands may not be readily available. The minimum amount of petrol which may be purchased is usually five litres (just over one gallon). It is advisable to keep the petrol tank topped up, particularly in remote areas or if wishing to make an early start when garages may be closed, but when doing this use a lockable filler cap as a security measure. Some garages may close between 12.00 and 15.00hrs for lunch. Generally petrol is readily available and in most of the countries featured in this Guide you will find that petrol stations on motorways provide a 24hr service.

In the UK the motorist uses a fuel recommended by the vehicle manufacturer and this is related to a star method (2-Star 90 octane, 3-Star 93 octane and 4-Star 97 octane).

Overseas, petrol is graded as *Normal* or *Super* and the local definitions are generally recognisable. The motorist should be careful to use a grade in the recommended range as many modern engines designed to run on 4-Star petrol are critical on carburation and ignition settings.

Additionally, as unleaded petrol is also being sold in most of the countries in this Guide it is important to purchase the correct petrol. If a car designed to run on leaded petrol is filled with unleaded petrol it will do no immediate harm, provided it is the correct octane rating and the next fill is of leaded petrol. However, any queries regarding the performance of a vehicle on an unleaded or lower grade of fuel should be directed to the vehicle manufacturers or their agents. A leaflet containing further information on the subject of *Leaded and Unleaded Petrol in Europe* is available through AA Centres and AA Port Service Centres.

Petrol prices at filling stations on motorways will be higher than elsewhere whilst at self-service pumps it will be slightly cheaper. Although petrol prices are not quoted the current position can be checked with the AA. Petrol price concessions in the form of petrol coupons are available for Italy (see page 274) and Yugoslavia (see page 413) – check with the AA to ascertain the latest position.

The petrol contained in a vehicle tank may be imported duty-free. In some countries an additional quantity may be imported duty-free in cans, whilst others impose duty (Sweden and Yugoslavia) or forbid the carrying of petrol in cans in a vehicle (Greece, Italy and Spain). If you intend carrying a reserve supply of petrol in a can remember that on sea and air ferries and European car-sleeper trains operators insist that spare cans must be empty.

Note The extra weight of a caravan or roof-rack laden with luggage increases petrol consumption, which should be taken into consideration when calculating mileage per gallon.

Pollution

Tourists should be aware that pollution of the sea water at European coastal resorts, particularly on the shores of the Mediterranean, represents a severe health hazard. Not many popular resorts wish to admit to this, but many now realise the dangers and erect signs, albeit small ones, forbidding bathing. These signs would read as follows:

No bathing Bathing prohibited	**French** *Défense de se baigner* *Il est défendu de se baigner*
No bathing Bathing prohibited	**Italian** *Vietato bagnàrsi* *Èvietato bagnàrsi*
No bathing Bathing prohibited	**Spanish** *Prohibido bañarse* *Se prohibe bañarse*

Poste restante

If you are uncertain of having a precise address, you can be contacted through the local *poste restante*. Before leaving the United Kingdom, notify your friends of your approximate whereabouts abroad at given times. If you expect mail, call with your passport at the main post office of the town where you are staying. To ensure that the arrival of correspondence will coincide with your stay, your correspondent should check with the Post Office before posting, as delivery times differ throughout Europe, and appropriate allowance must be made. It is important that the recipient's name be written in full: *eg* Mr Lazarus Perkins, Poste Restante, Turnhout, Belgium. Do not use Esq.

Italy Correspondence can be addressed c/o post office by adding *Fermo in Posta* to the name of the locality. It will be handed over at the local central post office upon identification of the addressee by passport.

Spain Letters should be addressed as follows: name of addressee, *Lista de Correos*, name of town or village, name of province in brackets, if necessary. Letters can be collected from the main post office in the town concerned upon identification of the addressee by passport.

For all other countries letters should be addressed as in the above example.

Radio telephones/Citizen band radios and transmitters in tourist cars abroad

Many countries exercise controls on the temporary importation and subsequent use of radio transmitters and radio telephones.

Therefore if your vehicle contains such equipment, whether fitted or portable, you should approach the AA for guidance.

Tolls

Tolls are payable on many motorways in Europe. Charges on the French autoroutes are particularly expensive especially over long distances. For example, a single journey from Calais to Nice costs about £33 for a car and about £49 for a car with a caravan. Always have some currency of the country in which you are travelling ready to pay the tolls as travellers cheques etc., are **not** acceptable at toll booths. *Note* In Switzerland the authorities charge an annual motorway tax. See under Motorway tax page 394 for further information.

Tourist information

National Tourist Offices are especially equipped to deal with enquiries relating to their countries. They are particularly useful for information on current events, tourist attractions and information on specific activities such as skin diving and equipment hire, gliding, horse riding, etc. The offices in London (see *Country sections*) are most helpful but the local offices overseas merit a visit because they have information not available elsewhere. Tourists are advised to visit the office when they arrive at their destination if this is possible. When dealing with the offices in London, a letter will bring informative printed matter if a personal visit is not convenient. In either case approach them well in advance of your departure so that your application can be properly considered and the best use made of the services they offer.

Travellers cheques

We recommend you take Visa Travellers Cheques. You can use them like cash or change them for currency in just about any country in the world. If you should lose them a reverse charge telephone call will put you in touch with Visa's worldwide instant refund service. There are over 60,000 locations in 166 countries so help is never far away. Visa Travellers Cheques are available at any AA Travel Agency and are available on demand with cash payment.

Visitors' registration

All visitors to a country must register with local police which is a formality usually satisfied by the completion of a card or certificate when booking into a campsite. If staying with friends or relations it is usually the responsibility of the host to seek advice from the police within 24 hours of the arrival of guests.

For short holiday visits the formalities are very simple but most countries place a time limit on the period that tourists may stay after which a firmer type of registration is imposed. Therefore, if you intend staying in any one country for longer than three months (Portugal 60 days) you should make the appropriate enquiries before departure from the UK.

Weather information including winter conditions

Members of the public may telephone or call at the Met. Office Weather Centres listed below for information about local, national and continental weather forecasts. The centres **do not** provide information about road conditions:

Bristol
The Gaunts House,
Denmark Street
☎(0272)279298

Cardiff
Southgate House,
Wood Street
☎(0222)397020

Glasgow
33 Bothwell Street
☎041-248 3451

Leeds
Oak House,
Park Lane
☎(0532)451990

London
284–286 High
Holborn
☎01-836 4311

Manchester
Exchange Street,
Stockport
☎061-477 1060

Newcastle upon Tyne
7th Floor, Newgate
House, Newgate
Street
☎091-232 6453

Norwich
Rouen House, Rouen
Road
☎(0603)660779

Nottingham
Main Road, Watnall
☎(0602)384092

Southampton
160 High Street,
Below-Bar
☎(0703)228844

Met. Office Weather Centres are also being established in Aberdeen, Birmingham and Plymouth, but full details are not yet available.

If you require weather information as a guide when planning your holidays, you should contact the national tourist offices of the countries concerned (see *Country sections*). When you are abroad, you should contact the nearest office of the appropriate national motoring club. It is advisable to check on conditions ahead as you go along and campsites and garages are often helpful in this respect.

Winter conditions Motoring in Europe during the winter months is restricted because of the vast mountain ranges – the Alps sweeping in an arc from the French Riviera, through Switzerland, Northern Italy and Austria to the borders of Yugoslavia, the Pyrenees which divide France and Spain, as well as extensive areas of Spain, France and Germany which are at an altitude of well over 1,000ft. However matters have been eased with improved communications and modern snow clearing apparatus.

Reports on the accessibility of mountain passes in Austria, France, Italy and Switzerland are received by the AA from the European Road Information Centre in Geneva. Additionally, during the winter months and also under certain weather conditions, the AA Port Agents in Belgium and France collect information regarding the state of approach roads to the continental Channel ports. **To obtain information ring the AA Overseas Routes Unit at Basingstoke during office hours, ☏(0256) 20123, or the AA London Operations Centre (24-hr service) ☏01-954 7373 or enquire at the AA Port Service Centre before embarking.**

Details of road and rail tunnels which can be used to pass under the mountains are given on pages 67–69 and the periods when the most important mountain passes are usually closed are given on pages 70–79. If you want a conventional seaside holiday between October and March, you will probably have to travel at least as far south as Lisbon, Valencia, or Naples to be reasonably certain of fine weather. Further information on this subject is given in the leaflet entitled *Motoring in Winter and Continental Weather* which is available from the AA.

ROUTE PLANNING

EUROPEAN ROUTES SERVICE
Individually Prepared Routes to Your Own Requirements

The AA's Overseas Routes Unit has a comprehensive and unique database of road and route information built into the very latest computerised equipment. The database includes all relevant information needed for an enjoyable trouble-free route including distance in miles and kilometres for estimating journey times. The route also includes route numbers, road signs to follow, motorway services, landmarks, road and town descriptions, frontier opening times etc.

Overseas Routes can supply you with any route you may require: – scenic routes – direct routes – by-way routes – fast routes – coach routes – caravan routes – motorway routes – non-motorway routes – touring routes – special interest routes – etc.
You may believe you know the best route – we can confirm if you are correct or tell you if we believe you are wrong and we will probably save you time and money by doing so!

Can we help you further?

If we can please contact any AA Centre for a European Route Application form or either telephone Overseas Routes at Basingstoke (0256) 492182/492183 or complete the application form below and we will send you full details of the European Routes Service and the prices charged.

Send the form below to:
Overseas Routes, The Automobile Association, Fanum House, Basingstoke, RG21 2EA.

Application form for details of the European Route Service

Complete in BLOCK CAPITALS

Mr/Mrs/Ms/Miss/Title: Initials: Surname:

Address:

Postcode:

Membership number (or 5-Star number): Date of request:

(If you are not a Member of the AA an additional fee is payable unless you have paid the 5-Star non-member service fee.)

Countries/places to be visited:

Date of departure:

SYMBOLS USED FOR COUNTRY IDENTIFICATION (**See page 81**)

All location maps in this book use the following symbols to indicate adjoining countries.

AL	Albania	D	W. Germany	PL	Poland
AND	Andorra	DDR	Germany (DDR)	P	Portugal
A	Austria	GR	Greece	RO	Romania
B	Belgium	H	Hungary	E	Spain
BG	Bulgaria	IRL	Ireland (Rep of)	S	Sweden
CS	Czechoslovakia	I	Italy	CH	Switzerland
DK	Denmark	FL	Liechtenstein	TR	Turkey
SF	Finland	L	Luxembourg	SU	USSR
F	France	NL	Netherlands	YU	Yugoslavia
		N	Norway		

MAJOR ROAD TUNNELS

See *Lights* page 50. There are also minimum and maximum speed limits in operation in the tunnels. **All charges listed below should be used as a guide only.**

Bielsa France–Spain

The trans-Pyrenean tunnel is 3km (2 miles) long, and runs nearly 6,000ft above sea level between Aragnouet and Bielsa. The tunnel is usually closed from October to Easter.

Cadí (Spain)

A new road tunnel has been opened in Catalonia (road number C1411), between the villages of Bellver de Cerdanya and Bagá, and to the west of the Toses (Tosas) Pass.

The tunnel is 5km (3 miles) long and runs at about 4,000ft above sea level under the Sierra del Cadí mountain range. 18km (11 miles) of new access roads have also been completed.

Charges *(in Pesetas)*

cars	555
cars with caravans	1,215
motorcycles	450

Fréjus France–Italy

This tunnel (opened July 1980) is over 4,000ft above sea level; it runs between Modane and Bardonecchia. The tunnel is 12.8km (8 miles) long, 4.5m (14ft 9in) high, and the two-lane carriageway is 9m (29ft 6in) wide. Toll charges are as for the Mont Blanc Tunnel (see below).

Mont Blanc Chamonix (France)–Courmayeur (Italy)

The tunnel is over 4,000ft above sea level. It is 11.6km (7 miles) long. Customs and passport control are at the Italian end. The permitted maximum dimensions of vehicles are: height 4.15m (13ft 7in); length 18m (59ft); width 2.5m (8ft 2in). Total weight 35 metric tons (34 tons 9cwt); axle weight 13 metric tons (12 tons 16cwt). The minimum speed is 50kph (31 mph) and the maximum 80kph (49mph). Do not stop or overtake. There are breakdown bays with telephones. From November to March wheel chains may occasionally be required on the approaches to the tunnel.

Charges *(in French francs)*
The tolls are calculated according to the wheelbase.

cars	Wheelbase up to 2.30m (7ft 6½in)	65
	wheelbase from 2.30m to 2.63m (7ft 6½in to 8ft 7½in)	100
	wheelbase from 2.64m to 3.30m (8ft7½in to 10ft 10in) and cars with caravans	130
	wheelbase over 3.30m (10ft 10in)	330
vehicles	with three axles	495
	with four, or more axles	660

Grand St Bernard Switzerland–Italy

The tunnel is over 6,000ft above sea level; although there are covered approaches, wheel chains may be needed to reach it in winter. The Customs, passport control and toll offices are at the entrance. The tunnel is 5.9km (3½ miles) long. The permitted maximum dimensions of vehicles are: height 4m (13ft 1in), width 2.5m (8ft 2½in). The minimum speed is 40kph (24mph) and the maximum 80kph (49mph). Do not stop or overtake. There are breakdown bays with telephones on either side.

Charges *(in Swiss francs)*
The toll charges are calculated according to the wheelbase.

motorcycles		5
cars	wheelbase up to 2.08m (6ft 10in)	15
	wheelbase from 2.08m to 3.20m (6ft 10in to 10ft 6in)	22.50
	wheelbase over 3.20m (10ft 6in)	34
	with caravan	34
minibuses		34
vehicles	with three axles	67.50
	with four or more axles	112.50

St Gotthard Switzerland

The world's longest road tunnel opened in September 1980. The tunnel is about 3,800ft above sea level; it runs under the St Gotthard

Pass from Göschenen, on the northern side of the Alps, to Airolo in the Ticino. The tunnel is 16.3km (10 miles) long, 4.5m (14ft 9in) high, and the two-lane carriageway is 7.5m (25ft) wide. Forming part of the Swiss national motorway network, the tunnel is subject to the annual motorway tax, and the tax disc must be displayed (see page 934).

From December to February wheel chains may occasionally be required on the approaches to the tunnel, but they are *NOT* allowed to be used in the tunnel. (Lay-bys are available for the removal and refitting of wheel chains).

San Bernardino Switzerland

This tunnel is over 5,000ft above sea level. It is 6.6km (4 miles) long, 4.8m (15ft 9in) high, and the carriageway is 7m (23ft) wide. Do not stop or overtake in the tunnel. Keep 100m (109 yds) between vehicles. There are breakdown bays with telephones. From November to March wheel chains may occasionally be required on the approaches to the tunnel. Forming part of the Swiss national motorway network, the tunnel is subject to the annual motorway tax, and the tax disc must be displayed (see page 394).

Arlberg Austria

This tunnel is 14km (8¾ miles) long and runs at about 4,000ft above sea level, to the south of and parallel to the Arlberg Pass.

Charges
The toll charges for cars (with or without caravans) are 140 *Austrian schillings* for a single journey.

Bosruck Austria

This tunnel (opened October 1983) is 2,434ft above sea level. It is 5.5km (3½ miles) long and runs between Spital am Pyhrn and Selzthal, to the east of the Pyhrn Pass. With the Gleinalm Tunnel (see below) it forms an important part of the A9 Pyhrn Autobahn between Linz and Graz, now being built in stages.

Charges
The toll charges for cars (with or without caravans) are 60 *Austrian schillings* for a single journey.

Felbertauern Austria

This tunnel is over 5,000ft above sea level; it runs between Mittersill and Matrei, to the west of and parallel to the Grossglockner Pass. The tunnel is 5.3km (3¼ miles) long, 4.5m (14ft 9in) high, and the two-lane carriageway is 7m (23ft) wide. From November to April wheel chains may be needed on the approach to the tunnel.

Charges *(in Austrian schillings)*

		Single
cars	summer rate	180
	winter rate	100
caravans		free
motorcycles		100

Gleinalm Austria

This tunnel is 2,680ft above sea level; it is 8.3km (5 miles) long and runs between St Michael and Friesach, near Graz. The tunnel forms part of the A9 Pyhrn Autobahn which will, in due course, run from Linz via Graz to Yugoslavia.

Charges
The toll charges for cars (with or without caravan) are 120 *Austrian schillings* for a single journey.

Tauern Autobahn Austria

Two tunnels, the Katschberg and the Radstädter Tauern, form the key elements of this toll motorway between Salzburg and Carinthia.

The Katschberg tunnel is 3,642ft above sea level. It is 5.4km (3½ miles) long, 4.5m (14ft 9in) high, and the two-lane carriageway is 7.5m (25ft) wide.

The Radstädter Tauern tunnel is 4,396ft above sea level and runs to the east of and parallel to the Tauern railway tunnel. The tunnel is 6.4km (4 miles) long, 4.5m (14ft 9in) high and the two-lane carriageway is 7.5m (25ft) wide.

Charges *(in Austrian schillings)* for the whole toll section between Flachau and Rennweg:

		Single
cars/ motorcycles	summer rate	180
	winter rate	100
caravans		free

MAJOR RAIL TUNNELS

SWITZERLAND AND SWITZERLAND–ITALY

Vehicles are conveyed throughout the year through the **Simplon** Tunnel (Brig-Iselle) and the **Lötschberg** Tunnel (Kandersteg-Goppenstein). It is also possibe to travel all the way from Kandersteg to Iselle by rail via both the Lötschberg and Simplon Tunnels. Services are frequent and no advance booking is necessary and although the actual transit time is 15/20 minutes, some time may be taken by the loading and unloading formalities.

The operating company issues a full timetable and tariff list which is available from the AA (Overseas Routes, see page 65 for address), the Swiss National Tourist Office (see page 65 for address) or at most Swiss frontier crossings.

Albula Tunnel Switzerland

Thussis (2,372ft)–**Samedan** (5,650ft).
The railway tunnel is 5.9km (3½ miles) long. Motor vehicles can be conveyed through the tunnel, but you are recommended to give notice. Thusis ☏(081)811113 and Samedan ☏(082)65404.

Services
9 trains daily going south; 6 trains daily going north.

Charges
These are given in *Swiss francs* and are likely to increase.

cars (including driver)	67
additional passengers	8.80
car and caravan	125

Furka Tunnel Switzerland

Oberwald (4,482ft)–**Realp** (5,046ft).
The railway tunnel is 15.3km (9½ miles) long. Journey duration 20 minutes.

Services
Hourly from 06.50–21.00hrs.

Charges
Cars including passengers 18 *Swiss francs.* With caravan 36 *Swiss francs.*

Oberalp Railway

Andermatt (4,737ft)–**Sedrun** (3,728ft).
Journey duration 50 minutes.

Booking
Advance booking is necessary, Andermatt ☏(044)67220 and Sedrun ☏(086)91137.

Services
2–4 trains daily, winter only (Oct–Apr).

Charges
Cars including driver 51 *Swiss francs.* Additional passengers 8.40 *Swiss francs.* With caravan 102 *Swiss francs.*

Tauern Tunnel Austria

Böckstein (3,711ft) (near Badgastein)–**Mallnitz** 8.5km (5½ miles) long.
Maximum dimensions for caravans and trailers are height 8ft 10½in, width 8ft 2½in.

Booking
Advance booking is unnecessary (except for request trains), but motorists must report at least 30 minutes before the train is due to start. Drivers must drive their vehicles on and off the wagon.

Services
At summer weekends, trains run approximately every half-hour in both directions. 07.30–18.30hrs; and every hour during the night. During the rest of the year there is an hourly service from 06.30–22.30 hrs. *Duration 12 minutes.*

Charges
These are given in *Austrian schillings* and are for a single journey.

cars (including passengers)	160
motorcycles (with or without sidecar)	30
caravans	free

PRINCIPAL MOUNTAIN PASSES

It is best not to attempt to cross mountain passes at night, and daily schedules should make allowance for the comparatively slow speeds inevitable in mountainous areas.

Gravel surfaces (such as grit and stone chips) vary considerably; they are dusty when dry, slippery when wet. Where known to exist, this type of surface has been noted. Road repairs can be carried out only during the summer, and may interrupt traffic. Precipitous sides are rarely, if ever, totally unguarded; on the older roads stone pillars are placed at close intervals. Gradient figures take the mean on hairpin bends, and may be steeper on the insides of the curves, particularly on the older roads.

Before attempting late evening or early morning journeys across frontier passes, check the times of opening of the Customs offices. A number of offices close at night, *eg* the Timmelsjoch border crossing is closed between 20.00 and 07.00hrs.

Always engage a low gear before either ascending or descending steep gradients, keep well to the right side of the road and avoid cutting corners. Avoid excessive use of brakes. If the engine overheats, pull off the road, making sure you do not cause an obstruction, leave the engine idling, and put the heater controls, including the fan, into the maximum heat position. Under no circumstances remove the radiator cap until the engine has cooled down. Do not fill the coolant system of a hot engine with cold water.

Always engage a lower gear before taking a hairpin bend, give priority to vehicles ascending and remember that as your altitude increases so your engine power decreases. Priority must always be given to postal coaches travelling in either direction. Their route is usually signposted.

Caravans

Passes *suitable for caravans* are indicated in the table (pages 71–79). Those shown to be *negotiable by caravans* are best used only by experienced drivers in cars with ample power. The remainder are probably best avoided. A correct power-to-load ratio is always essential.

Conditions in winter

Winter conditions are given in italics in the last column. *UO* means usually open although a severe fall of snow may temporarily obstruct the road for 24–48 hours, and wheel chains are often necessary; *OC* means occasionally closed between the dates stated and *UC* usually closed between the dates stated. Dates for opening and closing the passes are approximate only. Warning notices are usually posted at the foot of a pass if it is closed, or if chains or snow tyres should or must be used.

Wheel chains may be needed early and late in the season, and between short spells (a few hours) of obstruction. At these times conditions are usually more difficult for caravans.

In fair weather, wheel chains or snow tyres are only necessary on the higher passes, but in severe weather you will probably need to use them (as a rough guide) at altitudes exceeding 2,000ft.

Conversion table gradients

All steep hill signs show the grade in percentage terms. The following conversion table may be used as a guide:

30%	1 in 3	14%	1 in 7
25%	1 in 4	12%	1 in 8
20%	1 in 5	11%	1 in 9
16%	1 in 6	10%	1 in 10

Pass and height	**From To**	**Distances from summit and max gradient**		**Min width of road**	**Conditions (See page 70 for key to abbreviations)**
***Albula** 7,595ft (2315m) Switzerland	Tiefencastel (2,821ft)	30km	1 in 10	12ft	*UC Nov–early Jun.* An inferior alternative to the Julier; tar and gravel; fine scenery. Alternative rail tunnel.
	La Punt (5,546ft	9km	1 in 10		
Allos 7,382ft (2250m) France	Barcelonnette (3,740ft)	20km	1 in 10	13ft	*UC early Nov–early Jun.* Very winding, narrow, mostly unguarded but not difficult otherwise; passing bays on southern slope, poor surface (maximum width vehicles 5ft 11in).
	Colmars (4,085ft)	24km	1 in 12		
Aprica 3,858ft (1176m) Italy	Tresenda (1,220ft)	14km	1 in 11	13ft	*UO.* Fine scenery; good surface, well graded; *suitable for caravans.*
	Edolo (2,264ft)	15km	1 in 16		
Aravis 4,915ft (1498m) France	La Clusaz (3,412ft)	8km	1 in 11	13ft	*OC Dec–Mar.* Outstanding scenery, and a fairly easy road.
	Flumet (3,008ft)	12km	1 in 11		
Arlberg 5,912ft (1802m) Austria	Bludenz (1,905ft)	35km	1 in 8	20ft	*OC Dec–Apr.* Modern road; short steep stretch from west easing towards the summit; heavy traffic; parallel toll road tunnel available. *Suitable for caravans*; using tunnel. Pass road closed to vehicles towing trailers.
	Landeck (2,677ft)	35km	1 in 7½		
Aubisque 5,610ft (1710m) France	Eaux Bonnes (2,461ft)	11km	1 in 10	11ft	*UC mid Oct–Jun.* A very winding road; continuous but easy ascent; the descent incorporates the Col de Soulor (4,757ft); 8km of very narrow, rough, unguarded road, with a steep drop.
	Argelès-Gazost (1,519ft)	32km	1 in 10		
Ballon d'Alsace 3,865ft (1178m) France	Giromagny (1,830ft)	17km	1 in 9	13ft	*OC Dec–Mar.* A fairly straightforward ascent and descent, but numerous bends; *negotiable by caravans.*
	St-Maurice-sur-Moselle (1,800ft)	9km	1 in 9		
Bayard 4,094ft (1248m) France	Chauffayer (2,988ft)	18km	1 in 12	20ft	*UO.* Part of the Route Napoléon. Fairly easy, steepest on the southern side; *negotiable by caravans* from north to south.
	Gap (2,382ft)	8km	1 in 7		
***Bernina** 7,644ft (2330m) Switzerland	Pontresina (5,915ft)	15.5km	1 in 10	16ft	*OC Dec–Mar.* A good road on both sides; *negotiable by caravans.*
	Poschiavo (3,317ft)	18km	1 in 8		

*Permitted maximum width of vehicles 7ft 6in

Pass and height	From To	Distances from summit and max gradient		Min width of road	Conditions (See page 70 for key to abbreviations)
Bonaigua 6,797ft (2072m) Spain	Viella (3,150ft)	23km	1 in 12	14ft	*UC Nov–Apr.* A sinuous and narrow road with many hairpin bends and some precipitous drops; the alternative route to Lleida (Lérida) through the Viella tunnel is open in winter.
	Esterri d'Aneu (3,140ft)	21km	1 in 12		
Bracco 2,011ft (613m) Italy	Riva Trigoso (141ft)	15km	1 in 7	16ft	*UO.* A two-lane road with continuous bends; passing usually difficult; *negotiable by caravans*; alternative toll motorway available.
	Borghetto di Vara (318ft)	18km	1 in 7		
Brenner 4,508ft (1374m) Austria–Italy	Innsbruck (1,883ft)	38km	1 in 12	20ft	*UO.* Parallel toll motorway open: heavy traffic may delay at Customs; *suitable for caravans using toll motorway.* Pass road closed to vehicles towing trailers.
	Vipiteno (3,110ft)	15km	1 in 7		
†Brünig 3,304ft (1007m) Switzerland	Brienzwiler Station (1,886ft)	6km	1 in 12	20ft	*UO.* An easy but winding road; heavy traffic at weekends; *suitable for caravans.*
	Giswil (1,601ft)	13km	1 in 12		
Bussang 2,365ft (721m) France	Thann (1,115ft)	22km	1 in 10	13ft	*UO.* A very easy road over the Vosges; beautiful scenery; *suitable for caravans.*
	St-Maurice-sur Moselle (1,800ft)	8km	1 in 14		
Cabre 3,871ft (1180m) France	Luc-en-Diois (1,870ft)	22km	1 in 11	18ft	*UO.* An easy pleasant road; *suitable for caravans.*
	Aspres-sur-Buëch (2,497ft)	17km	1 in 14		
Campolongo 6,152ft (1875m) Italy	Corvara in Badia (5,145ft)	6km	1 in 8	16ft	*OC Dec–Mar.* A winding but easy ascent; long level stretch on summit followed by easy descent; good surface; *suitable for caravans.*
	Arabba (5,253ft)	4km	1 in 8		
Cayolle 7,631ft (2326m) France	Barcelonette (3,740ft)	32km	1 in 10	13ft	*UC early Nov–early Jun.* Narrow and winding road with hairpin bends; poor surface and broken edges; steep drops. Long stretches of single-track road with passing places.
	Guillaumes (2,687ft)	33km	1 in 10		
Costalunga (Karer) 5,751ft (1753m) Italy	Cardano (925ft)	24km	1 in 8	16ft	*OC Dec–Apr.* A good, well-engineered road but mostly winding; *caravans prohibited*
	Pozza (4,232ft)	10km	1 in 7		
Croix 5,833ft (1778m) Switzerland	Villars-sur-Ollon (4,111ft)	8km	1 in 7½	11ft	*UC Nov–May.* A narrow and winding route but extremely picturesque.
	Les Diablerets (3,789ft)	9km	1 in 11		
Croix-Haute 3,858ft (1176m) France	Monestier-de Clermont (2,776ft)	36km	1 in 14	18ft	*UO.* Well-engineered; several hairpin bends on the north side; *suitable for caravans.*
	Aspres-sur-Buëch (2,497ft)	28km	1 in 14		
Envalira 7,897ft (2407m) Andorra	Pas de la Casa (6,851ft)	5km	1 in 10	20ft	*OC Nov–Apr.* A good road with wide bends on ascent and descent; fine views; *negotiable by caravans* (max height vehicles 11ft 6in on northern approach near L'Hospitalet).
	Andorra (3,375ft)	29km	1 in 8		

†Permitted maximum width of vehicles 8ft 2½in

Pass and height	From To	Distances from summit and max gradient		Min width of road	Conditions (See page 70 for key to abbreviations)
Falzárego 6,945ft (2117m) Italy	Cortina d'Ampezzo (3,983ft)	17km	1 in 12	16ft	*OC Dec–Apr.* Well-engineered bitumen surface; many hairpin bends on both sides; *negotiable by caravans.*
	Andraz (4,622ft)	9km	1 in 12		
Faucille 4,341ft (1323m) France	Gex (1,985ft)	11km	1 in 10	16ft	*UO.* Fairly wide, winding road across the Jura mountains; *negotiable by caravans* but it is probably better to follow La Cure–St.-Cerque–Nyon.
	Morez (2,247ft)	28km	1 in 12		
Fern 3,967ft (1209m) Austria	Nassereith (2,742ft)	9km	1 in 10	20ft	*UO.* An easy pass but slippery when wet; *suitable for caravans.*
	Lermoos (3,244ft)	10km	1 in 10		
Flexen 5,853ft (1784m) Austria	Lech (4,747ft)	6.5km	1 in 10	18ft	*UO.* The magnificent 'Flexenstrasse', a well-engineered mountain road with tunnels and galleries. The road from Lech to Warth, north of the pass, is usually closed between November and April due to danger of avalanches.
	Rauzalpe (near Arlberg Pass) (5,341ft)	3.5km	1 in 10		
Flüela 7,818ft (2383m) Switzerland	Davos-Dorf (5,174ft)	13km	1 in 10	16ft	*OC Nov–May* Easy ascent from Davos; some acute hairpin bends on the eastern side; bitumen surface; *negotiable by caravans.*
	Susch (4,659ft)	13km	1 in 8		
†Forclaz 5,010ft (1527m) Switzerland France	Martigny (1,562ft)	13km	1 in 12	16ft	*UO Forclaz; Montets OC Dec–early Apr.* A good road over the pass and to the frontier; in France narrow and rough over Col des Montets (4,793ft); *negotiable by caravans.*
	Argentière (4,111ft)	19km	1 in 12		
Foscagno 7,516ft (2291m) Italy	Bormio (4,019ft)	24km	1 in 8	11ft	*OC Nov–Apr.* Narrow and winding through lonely mountains, generally poor surface. Long winding ascent with many blind bends; not always well guarded. The descent includes winding rise and fall over the Passo d'Eira (7,218ft).
	Livigno (5,958ft)	14km	1 in 8		
Fugazze 3,802ft (1159m) Italy	Rovereto (660ft)	27km	1 in 7	10ft	*UO.* Very winding with some narrow sections, particularly on northern side. The many blind bends and several hairpin bends call for extra care.
	Valli del Pasubio (1,148ft)	12km	1 in 7		
***Furka** 7,976ft (2431m) Switzerland	Gletsch (5,777ft)	10km	1 in 10	13ft	*UC Oct–Jun.* A well-graded road, with narrow sections and several sharp hairpin bends on both ascent and descent. Fine views of the Rhône Glacier. Alternative rail tunnel.
	Realp (5,046ft)	13km	1 in 10		
Galibier 8,678ft (2645m) France	Lautaret Pass (6,752ft)	7 km	1 in 14	10ft	*UC Oct–Jun.* Mainly wide, well-surfaced but unguarded. Ten hairpin bends on descent then 5km narrow and rough. Rise over the Col du Télégraphe (5,249ft), then eleven more hairpin bends. (Tunnel under the Galibier summit is closed).
	St-Michel-de-Maurienne (2,336ft)	34km	1 in 8		
Gardena (Grödner-Joch) 6,959ft (2121m) Italy	Val Gardena (6,109ft)	6km	1 in 8	16ft	*OC Dec–Jun.* A well-engineered road, very winding on descent.
	Corvara in Badia (5,145ft)	10km	1 in 8		

*Permitted maximum width of vehicles 7ft 6in
†Permitted maximum width of vehicles 8ft 2½in

Pass and height	From To	Distances from summit and max gradient		Min width of road	Conditions (See page 70 for key to abbreviations)
Gavia 8,599ft (2621m) Italy	Bormio (4,019ft)	25km	1 in 5½	10ft	*UC Oct–Jul.* Steep and narrow but with frequent passing bays; many hairpin bends and a gravel surface; not for the faint-hearted; extra care necessary. (Maximum width vehicles 5ft 11in).
	Ponte di Legno (4,140ft)	16km	1 in 5½		
Gerlos 5,341ft (1628m) Austria	Zell am Ziller (1,886ft)	29km	1 in 12	14ft	*UO.* Hairpin ascent out of Zell to modern toll road; the old, steep narrow, and winding route with passing bays and 1-in-7 gradient is not recommended, but is negotiable with care; *caravans prohibited.*
	Wald (2,904ft)	15km	1 in 11		
†Grand St Bernard 8,114ft (2473m) Switzerland–Italy	Martigny (1,562ft)	44km	1 in 9	13ft	*UC Oct–Jun.* Modern road to entrance of road tunnel (usually open; see page 67) then narrow but bitumen surface over summit to frontier; also good in Italy; *suitable for caravans,* using tunnel. Pass road closed to vehicles towing trailers.
	Aosta (1913ft)	33km	1 in 9		
***Grimsel** 7,100ft (2164m) Switzerland	Innertkirchen (2,067ft)	25km	1 in 10	16ft	*UC mid Oct–late Jun.* A fairly easy, modern road, but heavy traffic at weekends. A long winding ascent, finally hairpin bends; then a terraced descent with six hairpins into the Rhône valley.
	Gletsch (5,777ft)	6km	1 in 10		
Gross-glockner 8,212ft (2503m) Austria	Bruck an der Glocknerstrasse (2,480ft)	33km	1 in 8	16ft	*UC late Oct–early May.* Numerous well-engineered hairpin bends; moderate but very long acent, toll road; very fine scenery; heavy tourist traffic; *negotiable preferably from south to north, by caravans.*
	Heiligenblut (4,268ft)	15km	1 in 8		
Hochtann-berg 5509ft (1679m) Austria	Schröcken (4,163ft)	5.5km	1 in 7	13ft	*OC Jan–Mar.* A reconstructed modern road.
	Warth (near Lech) (4,921ft)	4.5km	1 in 11		
Ibañeta (Ronces-valles) 3,468ft (1057m) France–Spain	St-Jean-Pied-de-Port (548ft)	26km	1 in 10	13ft	*UO.* A slow and winding, scenic route; *negotiable by caravans.*
	Pamplona (1,380ft)	52km	1 in 10		
Iseran 9,088ft (2770m) France	Bourg-St-Maurice (2,756ft)	49km	1 in 12	13ft	*UC mid Oct–late Jun.* The second highest pass in the Alps. Well graded with reasonable bends, average surface; several unlit tunnels on northern approach.
	Lanslebourg (4,587ft)	33km	1 in 9		
Izoard 7,743ft (2360m) France	Guillestre (3,248ft)	32km	1 in 8	16ft	*UC late Oct–mid Jun.* A winding and at times narrow road with many hairpin bends. Care required at several unlit tunnels near Guillestre.
	Briançon (4,396ft)	20km	1 in 10		
***Jaun** 4,951ft (1509m) Switzerland	Broc (2,378ft)	25km	1 in 10	13ft	*UO.* A modernised but generally narrow road; some poor sections on ascent, and several hairpin bends on descent; *negotiable by caravans.*
	Reidenbach (2,769ft)	8km	1 in 10		
†Julier 7,493ft (2284m) Switzerland	Tiefencastel (2,821ft)	36km	1 in 10	13ft	*UO.* Well-engineered road approached from Chur by Lenzerheide Pass (5,098ft). *suitable for caravans.*
	Silvaplana (5,958ft)	7km	1 in 7½		
Katschberg 5,384ft (1641m) Austria	Spittal (1,818ft)	35km	1 in 5	20ft	*UO.* Steep though not particularly difficult, parallel toll motorway, including tunnel available; *negotiable by light caravans,* using tunnel.
	St Michael (3,504ft)	6km	1 in 6		

*Permitted maximum width of vehicles 7ft 6in
†Permitted maximum width of vehicles 8ft 2½in.

Pass and height	From To	Distances from summit and max gradient		Min width of road	Conditions (See page 70 for key to abbreviations)
***Klausen** 6,391ft (1948m) Switzerland	Altdorf (1,512ft) Linthal (2,126ft)	25km 23km	1 in 11 1 in 11	16ft	*UC late Oct–early Jun.* Narrow and winding in places, but generally easy in spite of a number of sharp bends; *no through route for caravans as they are prohibited from using the road between Unterschachen and Linthal.*
Larche (della Maddalena) 6,542ft (1994m) France–Italy	Condamine (4,291ft) Vinadio (2,986ft)	19km 32km	1 in 12 1 in 12	10ft	*OC Dec–Mar.* An easy, well-graded road: narrow and rough on ascent, wider with better surface on descent; *suitable for caravans.*
Lautaret 6,752ft (2058m) France	Le Bourg-d'Oisans (2,359ft) Briançon (4,396ft)	38km 28km	1 in 8 1 in 10	14ft	*OC Dec–Mar.* Modern, evenly graded, but winding, and unguarded in places; very fine scenery; *suitable for caravans.*
Loibl (Ljubell) 3,500ft (1067m) Austria–Yugoslavia	Unterloibl (1,699ft) Kranj (1,263ft)	10km 29km	1 in 5½ 1 in 8	20ft	*UO.* Steep rise and fall over Little Loibl Pass to tunnel (1.6km long) under summit; from south to north *just negotiable by experienced drivers with light caravans.* The old road over the summit is closed to through traffic.
***Lukmanier (Lucomagno)** 6,286ft (1916m) Switzerland	Olivone (2,945ft) Disentis (3,772ft)	18km 22km	1 in 11 1 in 11	16ft	*UC early Nov–late May.* Rebuilt, modern road; *no throughroute for caravans as they are prohibited from using the road between the Lukmanier Pass and Olivone.*
†Maloja 5,955ft (1815m) Switzerland	Silvaplana (5,958ft) Chiavenna (1,083ft)	11km 32km	level 1 in 11	13ft	*UO.* Escarpment facing south; fairly easy but many hairpin bends on descent; *negotiable by caravans,* possibly difficult on ascent.
Mauria 4,285ft (1298m) Italy	Lozzo Cadore (2,470ft) Ampezzo (1,837ft)	14km 31km	1 in 14 1 in 14	16ft	*UO.* A well-designed road with easy, winding ascent and descent; *suitable for caravans.*
Mendola 4,472ft (1363m) Italy	Appiano (Eppan) (1,348ft) Sarnonico (3,208ft)	15km 8km	1 in 8 1 in 10	16ft	*UO.* A fairly straightforward, but winding road; well guarded; *suitable for caravans.*
Mont Cenis 6,834ft (2083m) France–Italy	Lanslebourg (4,587ft) Susa (1,624ft)	11km 28km	1 in 10 1 in 8	16ft	*UC Nov–May.* Approach by industrial valley. An easy broad highway but with poor surface in places; *suitable for caravans.* Alternative Fréjus road tunnel available (see page 67).
Monte Croce di Comélico (Kreuzberg) 5,368ft (1636m) Italy	San Candido (3,847ft) Santo Stefano di Cadore (2,978ft)	15km 21km	1 in 12 1 in 12	16ft	*UO.* A winding road with moderate gradients; beautiful scenery; *suitable for caravans.*
Montgenèvre 6,070ft (1850m) France–Italy	Briançon (4,396ft) Cesana Torinese (4,429ft)	12km 8km	1 in 14 1 in 11	16ft	*UO.* An easy, modern road; *suitable for caravans.*
Monte Giovo (Jaufen) 6,870ft (2094m) Italy	Merano (1,063ft) Vipiteno (3,115ft)	40km 19km	1 in 8 1 in 11	13ft	*UC Nov–May.* Many well-engineered hairpin bends; *caravans prohibited.*

*Permitted maximum width of vehicles 7ft 6in
†Permitted maximum width of vehicles 8ft 2½in

Pass and height	From To	Distances from summit and max gradient		Min width of road	Conditions (See page 70 for key to abbreviations)
Montets (see Forclaz)					
Morgins 4,491ft (1369m) France–Switzerland	Abondance (3,051ft) Monthey (1,391ft)	14km 15km	1 in 11 1 in 7	13ft	*UO.* A lesser used route through pleasant, forested countryside crossing the French/Swiss border.
***Mosses** 4,740ft (1445m) Switzerland	Aigle (1,378ft) Château-d'Oex (3,153ft)	18km 15km	1 in 12 1 in 12	13ft	*UO.* A modern road; *suitable for caravans*
Nassfeld (Pramollo) 5,020ft (1530m) Austria–Italy	Tröpolach (1,972ft) Pontebba (1,841ft)	10km 10km	1 in 5 1 in 10	13ft	*OC late Nov–Mar.* The winding descent in Italy has been improved.
Nufenen (Novena) 8,130ft (2478m) Switzerland	Ulrichen (4,416ft) Airolo (3,747ft)	13km 24km	1 in 10 1 in 10	13ft	*UC mid Oct–mid Jun.* The approach roads are narrow, with tight bends, but the road over the pass is good; *negotiable by light caravans* (limit 1.5 tons)
***Oberalp** 6,706ft (2044m) Switzerland	Andermatt (4,737ft) Disentis (3,772ft)	10km 22km	1 in 10 1 in 10	16ft	*UC Nov–late May.* A much improved and widened road with a modern surface; many hairpin bends but long level stretch on summit; *negotiable by caravans.* Alternative rail tunnel during the winter.
***Ofen (Fuorn)** 7,051ft (2149m) Switzerland	Zernez (4,836ft) Santa Maria im Münstertal (4,547ft)	22km 14km	1 in 10 1 in 8	12ft	*UO.* Good, fairly easy road through the Swiss National Park; *suitable for caravans.*
Petit St Bernard 7,178ft (2188m) France–Italy	Bourg-St-Maurice (2,756ft) Pré St-Didier (3,335ft)	31km 23km	1 in 16 1 in 12	16ft	*UC mid Oct–Jun.* Outstanding scenery; a fairly easy approach but poor surface and unguarded broken edges near the summit; good on the descent in Italy; *negotiable by light caravans.*
Peyresourde 5,128ft (1563m) France	Arreau (2,310ft) Luchon (2,067ft)	18km 14km	1 in 10 1 in 10	13ft	*UO.* Somewhat narrow with several hairpin bends, though not difficult.
***Pillon** 5,072ft (1546m) Switzerland	Le Sépey (3,212ft) Gsteig (2,911ft)	14km 7km	1 in 11 1 in 11	13ft	*OC Jan–Feb.* A comparatively easy modern road; *suitable for caravans.*
Plöcken (Monte Croce Carnico) 4,468ft (1362m) Austria–Italy	Kötschach (2,316ft) Paluzza (1,968ft)	14km 17km	1 in 7 1 in 14	16ft	*OC Dec–Apr.* A modern road with long reconstructed sections; heavy traffic at summer weekends; delay likely at the frontier; *negotiable by caravans.*
Pordoi 7,346ft (2239m) Italy	Arabba (5,253ft) Canazei (4,806ft)	9km 12km	1 in 10 1 in 10	16ft	*OC Dec–Apr.* An excellent modern road with numerous hairpin bends; *negotiable by caravans.*
Port 4,098ft (1249m) France	Tarascon (1,555ft) Massat (2,133ft)	18km 13km	1 in 10 1 in 10	14ft	*OC Nov–Mar.* A fairly easy road but narrow on some bends; *negotiable by caravans.*

*Permitted maximum width of vehicles 7ft 6in

Pass and height	From To	Distances from summit and max gradient		Min width of road	Conditions (See page 70 for key to abbreviations)
Portet-d'Aspet 3,507ft (1069m) France	Audressein (1,625ft)	18km	1 in 7	11ft	*UO.* Approached from the west by the easy Col des Ares (2,611ft) and Col de Buret (1,975ft); well-engineered road, but calls for particular care on hairpin bends; rather narrow.
	Fronsac (1,548ft)	29km	1 in 7		
Pötschen 3,221ft (982m) Austria	Bad Ischl (1,535ft)	19km	1 in 11	23ft	*UO.* A modern road; *suitable for caravans*
	Bad Aussee (2133ft)	10km	1 in 11		
Pourtalet 5,879ft (1792m) France–Spain	Eaux-Chaudes (2,152ft)	23km	1 in 10	11ft	*UC late Oct–early Jun.* A fairly easy, unguarded road, but narrow in places; poor but *being rebuilt on Spanish side.*
	Biescas (2,821ft)	34km	1 in 10		
Puymorens 6,283ft (1915m) France	Ax-les-Thermes (2,362ft)	28km	1 in 10	18ft	*OC Nov–Apr.* A generally easy modern tarmac road, but narrow, winding and with a poor surface in places; not suitable for night driving; *suitable for caravans* (max height vehicles 11ft 6in). Alternative rail service available between Ax-les-Thermes and Latour-de-Carol.
	Bourg-Madame (3,707ft)	27km	1 in 10		
Quillane 5,623ft (1714m) France	Quillan (955ft)	63km	1 in 12	16ft	*OC Nov–Mar.* An easy, straightforward ascent and descent; *suitable for caravans.*
	Mont-Louis (5,135ft)	5km	1 in 12		
Radstädter-Tauern 5,702ft (1739m) Austria	Radstadt (2,808ft)	21km	1 in 6	16ft	*OC Jan–Mar.* Northern ascent steep but not difficult otherwise; parallel toll motorway including tunnel available; *negotiable by light caravans, using tunnel.*
	Mauterndorf (3,681ft)	17km	1 in 7		
Résia (Reschen) 4,934ft (1504m) Italy–Austria	Spondigna (2,903ft)	29km	1 in 10	20ft	*UO.* A good straightforward alternative to the Brenner Pass; *suitable for caravans.*
	Pfunds (3,182ft)	20km	1 in 10		
Resterfond (La Bonette) 9,193ft (2802m) France	Jausiers (near Barcelonnette) (3,986ft)	23km	1 in 9	10ft	*UC Oct–Jun.* The highest pass in the Alps, completed in 1962. Narrow, rough, unguarded ascent with many blind bends, and nine hairpins. Descent easier, winding with twelve hairpin bends.
	St-Etienne-de-Tinée (3,766ft)	27km	1 in 9		
Rolle 6,463ft (1970m) Italy	Predazzo (3,337ft)	21km	1 in 11	16ft	*OC Dec–Mar.* Very beautiful scenery; bitumen surface; a well-engineered road; *negotiable by caravans.*
	Mezzano (2,098ft)	25km	1 in 14		
Rombo (see Timmelsjoch)					
Route des Crêtes 4,210ft (1283m) France	St-Dié (1,125ft)	—	1 in 8	13ft	*UC Nov–Apr.* A renowned scenic route crossing seven ridges, with the highest point at Hôtel du Grand Ballon.
	Cernay (902ft)	—	1 in 8		
†St Gotthard (San Gottardo) 6,916ft (2108m) Switzerland	Göschenen (3,629ft)	19km	1 in 10	20ft	*UC mid Oct–early Jun.* Modern, fairly easy two to three lane road. Heavy traffic; *negotiable by caravans* (max height vehicles 11ft 9in). Alternative road tunnel available (see page 67).
	Airolo (3,747ft)	15km	1 in 10		

†Permitted maximum width of vehicles 8ft 2½in

Pass and height	From To	Distances from summit and max gradient		Min width of road	Conditions (See page 70 for key to abbreviations)
***San Bernardino** 6,778ft (2066m) Switzerland	Mesocco (2,549ft)	22km	1 in 10	13ft	*UC Oct–late Jun.* Easy, modern roads on northern and southern approaches to tunnel (see page 68); narrow and winding over summit; via tunnel *suitable for caravans.*
	Hinterrhein (5,328ft)	9.5km	1 in 10		
Schlucht 3,737ft (1139m) France	Gérardmer (2,182ft)	15km	1 in 14	16ft	*UO.* An extremely picturesque route crossing the Vosges mountains, with easy, wide bends on the descent; *suitable for caravans.*
	Munster (1,250ft)	17km	1 in 14		
Seeberg (Jezersko) 3,996ft (1218m) Austria–Yugoslavia	Eisenkappel (1,821ft)	14km	1 in 8	16ft	*UO.* An alternative to the steeper Loibl and Wurzen passes; moderate climb with winding, hairpin ascent and descent.
	Kranj (1,263ft)	33km	1 in 10		
Sella 7,349ft (2240m) Italy	Plan (5,269ft)	9km	1 in 9	16ft	*OC Dec–Jun.* A finely engineered, winding road; exceptional views of the Dolomites.
	Canazei (4,806ft)	13km	1 in 9		
Semmering 3,232ft (985m) Austria	Mürzzschlag im Mürztal (2,205ft)	14km	1 in 16	20ft	*UO.* A fine, well-engineered highway; *suitable for caravans.*
	Gloggnitz (1,427ft)	17km	1 in 16		
Sestriere 6,670ft (2033m) Italy	Cesana Torinese (4,429ft)	12km	1 in 10	16ft	*UO.* Mostly bitumen surface; *negotiable by caravans.*
	Pinerolo (1,234ft)	55km	1 in 10		
Silvretta (Bielerhöhe) 6,666ft (2032m) Austria	Partenen (3,451ft)	16km	1 in 9	16ft	*UC late Oct–early Jun.* For the most part reconstructed; thirty-two easy hairpin bends on western ascent; eastern side more straightforward. Toll road; *caravans prohibited.*
	Galtür (5,195ft)	10km	1 in 9		
†Simplon 6,578ft (2005m) Switzerland–Italy	Brig (2,231ft)	22km	1 in 9	23ft	*OC Nov–Apr.* An easy reconstructed modern road, but 13 miles long, continuous ascent to summit; *suitable for caravans.* Alternative rail tunnel.
	Domodóssola (919ft)	41km	1 in 11		
Somport 5,354ft (1632m) France–Spain	Bedous (1,365ft)	31km	1 in 10	12ft	*UO.* A favoured, old established route; generally easy, but in parts narrow and unguarded; fairly good-surfaced road; *suitable for caravans.*
	Jaca (2,687ft)	30km	1 in 10		
***Splügen** 6,932ft (2113m) Switzerland–Italy	Splügen (4,780ft)	9km	1 in 9	10ft	*UC Nov–Jun.* Mostly narrow and winding, with many hairpin bends, and not well guarded; care also required at many tunnels and galleries (max height vehicles 9ft 2in).
	Chiavenna (1,083ft)	30km	1 in 7½		
††Stelvio 9,045ft (2757m) Italy	Bormio (4,019ft)	22km	1 in 8	13ft	*UC Oct–late Jun.* The third highest pass in the Alps; the number of acute hairpin bends; all well-engineered, is exceptional – from forty to fifty on either side; the surface is good, the traffic heavy. Hairpin bends are too acute for long vehicles.
	Spondigna (2,903ft)	28km	1 in 8		
†Susten 7,297ft (2224m) Switzerland	Innertkirchen (2,067m)	28km	1 in 11	20ft	*UC Nov–Jun.* A very scenic route and well guarded mountain road; easy gradients and turns; heavy traffic at weekends; *negotiable by caravans.*
	Wassen (3,005ft)	19km	1 in 11		

*Permitted maximum width of vehicles 7ft 6in †Permitted maximum width of vehicles 8ft 2½in ††Maximum length of vehicles 30ft

Pass and height	From To	Distances from summit and max gradient		Min width of road	Conditions (See page 70 for key to abbreviations)
Tenda (Tende) 4,334ft (1321m) Italy–France	Borgo S Dalmazzo (2,103ft) La Giandola (1,010ft)	24km 29km	1 in 11 1 in 11	18ft	*UO.* Well guarded, modern road with several hairpin bends; road tunnel at summit; *suitable for caravans; but prohibited during the winter.*
Thurn 4,180ft (1274m) Austria	Kitzbühel (2,500ft) Mittersill (2,588ft)	19km 10km	1 in 12 1 in 16	16ft	*UO.* A good road with narrow stretches; northern approach rebuilt; *suitable for caravans.*
Timmelsjoch (Rombo) 8,232ft (2509m) Austria–Italy	Obergurgl (6,322ft) Moso (3,304ft)	14km 21km	1 in 7 1 in 8	12ft	*UC mid Oct–late Jun.* Roadworks on Italian side still in progress. The pass is open to private cars (without trailers) only as some tunnels on the Italian side are too narrow for larger vehicles; toll road.
Tonale 6,178ft (1883m) Italy	Edolo (2,264ft) Dimaro (2,513ft)	30km 27km	1 in 14 1 in 8	16ft	*UO.* A relatively easy road; *suitable for caravans.*
Toses (Tosas) 5,905ft (1800m) Spain	Puigcerdá (3,708ft) Ribes de Freser (3,018ft)	25km 25km	1 in 10 1 in 10	16ft	*UO.* Now a fairly straightforward, but continuously winding two-lane road with many sharp bends; some unguarded edges; *negotiable by caravans.*
Tourmalet 6,936ft (2114m) France	Luz (2,333ft) Ste-Marie-de-Campan (2,811ft)	19km 17km	1 in 8 1 in 8	14ft	*UC Oct–mid Jun.* The highest of the French Pyrénées routes; the approaches are good though winding and exacting over summit; sufficiently guarded.
Tre Croci 5,935ft (1809m) Italy	Cortina d'Ampezzo (3,983ft) Auronzo di Cadore (2,835ft)	7km 26km	1 in 9 1 in 9	16ft	*OC Dec–Mar.* An easy pass; very fine scenery; *suitable for caravans.*
Turracher Höhe 5,784ft (1763m) Austria	Predlitz (3,024ft) Ebene-Reichenau (3,563ft)	20km 8km	1 in 5½ 1 in 4½	13ft	*UO.* Formerly one of the steepest mountain roads in Austria; now much improved; steep, fairly straightforward ascent, followed by a very steep descent; good surface and mainly two lane width; fine scenery.
***Umbrail** 8,205ft (2501m) Switzerland–Italy	Santa Maria im Münstertal (4,547ft) Bormio (4,019ft)	13km 19km	1 in 11 1 in 11	14ft	*UC early Nov–early Jun.* Highest of the Swiss passes; narrow; mostly gravel surfaced with thirty-four hairpin bends but not too difficult.
Vars 6,919ft (2109m) France	St-Paul-sur-Ubaye (4,823ft) Guillestre (3,248ft)	8 km 20km	1 in 10 1 in 10	16ft	*OC Dec–Mar.* Easy winding ascent with seven hairpin bends; gradual winding descent with another seven hairpin bends; good surface, *negotiable by caravans.*
Wurzen (Koren) 3,520ft (1073m) Austria–Yugoslavia	Riegersdorf (1,775ft) Kranjska Gora (2,657ft)	8km 5km	1 in 5½ 1 in 5½	13ft	*UO.* A steep two-lane road which otherwise is not particularly difficult; *caravans prohibited.*
Zirler Berg 3,310ft (1009m) Austria	Seefeld (3,870ft) Zirl (2,041ft)	7km 5km	1 in 7 1 in 6	20ft	*UO.* An escarpment facing south, part of the route from Garmisch to Innsbruck; a good modern road but heavy tourist traffic and a long steep descent, with one hairpin bend, into the Inn Valley. Steepest section from the hairpin bend down to Zirl; *caravans prohibited.*

*Permitted maximum width of vehicles 7ft 6in

ABOUT THE GAZETTEER

Booking

It is advisable to book in advance for peak holiday season travel although we find that some sites will not accept reservations. The AA cannot undertake to find accommodation or make reservations, but we suggest that you make use of the specimen booking letters on page 82. It should be noted that, although not common practice, some campsites may regard your deposit as a booking fee not deductible from the final account.

Campsites

You are advised to look over the site if possible before you decide to stay. Even if a site is shown with a high grade in one of the many other guidebooks available, the information for any publication must necessarily be obtained some time in advance and it may well be that ownership and standards have since changed. A site may be shown in the guide with a wide range of facilities but it may, nevertheless, be crowded when you call and the chances are that the next one you reach will afford more space.

When you are looking over a site consider the following points:

If you have found the general situation pleasant, check that the site is fenced and guarded. It should look both clean and tidy with a good supply of refuse bins.

The toilet block should have sufficient and clean lavatories and clean washing facilities with basins and showers. Check if there is hot water.

Individual pitches should not be cramped and there should be defined roads on the site, preferably lit at night

If you have a tent, the surface needs to be suitable for pegs; a caravan will need firmer ground.

In hot weather see that there is plenty of shade; in a damp spell the sites should appear well drained.

There should be safe drinking water. If you need any of the following, you should confirm their existence: electric points for razors, camping gaz, a well-stocked shop, laundry facilities, a restaurant serving reasonably priced food, ice for sale.

Additional lists of sites may be obtained free from most national tourist offices. In the country sections, details are given of local organisations which either publish a camping guide or provide more detailed information.

Although the large majority of sites have been selected for the high standards they maintain, we have included in addition, at the request of members, a number of sites along touring routes and others near the Channel ports which are suitable for overnight stops. These transit sites tend to become crowded at the height of the season but provide the necessary amenities

Complaints

Inform the site proprietor immediately if you have any complaints, so that the matter can be dealt with promptly. If a personal approach fails, please inform the AA as soon as possible on return to this country.

Gazetteer entry and example

Each country, with the exceptions of Andorra (following the Spanish section), Liechtenstein (following the Swiss section), and San Marino (following the Italian section), is listed alphabetically; likewise each placename and campsite.

Questionnaire cards are sent to all establishments each year to update the information. Where these have not been returned at the time of going to press, the *campsite name* will appear in italics.

The charges per night per adult, car, caravan and tent are given in the relevant currencies. Charges are not given in respect of children as these vary, but generally a 50% reduction is allowed for children (3–14 years).

To determine the cost of one night, add up each charge as it applies to the party, *ie* the cost for two adults, a car and a caravan for one night in the example would be *ASch*103.

However, campsites have different price structures, often depending on the country. The simplest is that where each member of the touring party is charged individually, as in the example – *ie* reach adult, car and caravan/tent. There can be different permutations of the four rates: some do not charge for the car, others do not charge for the person but for everything else. All variations will be reflected in the gazetteer.

There are exceptions and these are:

pp: Campsite charges per person. The charge for the vehicle and caravan/tent is included in each person's price. For a party of four people multiply the pp price by 4 for the total cost per night.

pitch: Campsite charges per person and for the pitch, immaterial of whether it is a caravan or tent. The word 'pitch' follows the 'A' with the price. For a party of four people multiply the 'A' charge by 4 and add the price of a pitch to the total; this will give the cost per night.

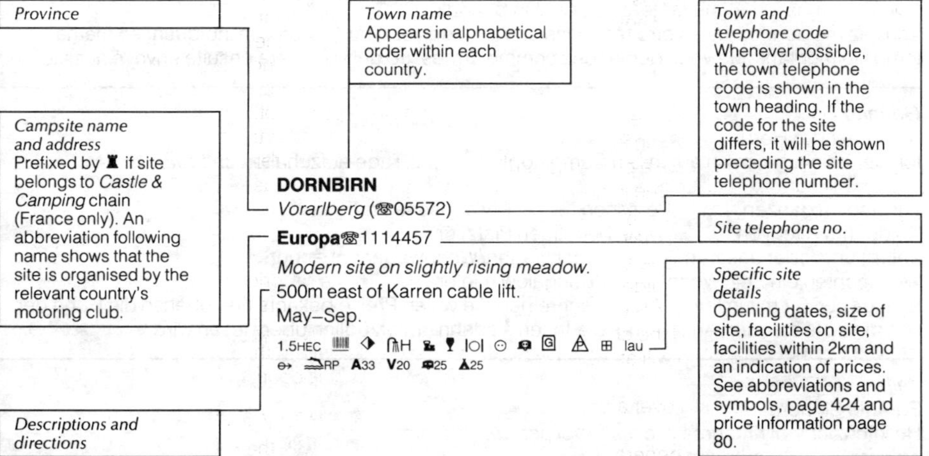

Province
Town name
Appears in alphabetical order within each country.
Town and telephone code
Whenever possible, the town telephone code is shown in the town heading. If the code for the site differs, it will be shown preceding the site telephone number.
Campsite name and address
Prefixed by ♜ if site belongs to Castle & Camping chain (France only). An abbreviation following name shows that the site is organised by the relevant country's motoring club.
DORNBIRN
Vorarlberg (☎05572)
Europa☎1114457
Modern site on slightly rising meadow.
500m east of Karren cable lift.
May–Sep.
1.5HEC lau
RP A33 V20 25 25
Site telephone no.
Specific site details
Opening dates, size of site, facilities on site, facilities within 2km and an indication of prices. See abbreviations and symbols, page 424 and price information page 80.
Descriptions and directions

Location maps

The location maps are at the beginning of each country section except those for Luxembourg, Portugal and Sweden which are incorporated in the Belgian, Spanish and Norwegian maps respectively. These maps are intended to assist the reader who wishes to stay in a certain area by showing only those places for which there is an entry in the gazetteer. Thus someone wishing to stay in the Innsbruck area will be able to select suitable places by looking at the map.

All location maps in this book use the symbols shown in the box on page 66 to indicate adjoining countries.

It must be emphasised that these maps are not intended to be used to find your way around the country and we recommend readers to buy the *AA Big Road Atlas of Europe*.

Opening times

Dates shown are inclusive opening dates. If the site is open all year, then 'All year' appears in the gazetteer entry. All information was correct at time of going to press, but we recommend you check with the site before arriving. Changes of date often occur because of demand and/or weather conditions. Sometimes restricted facilities only are available between October and April.

Specimen letters for booking sites

Please use block letters and enclose an *International reply coupon*, obtainable from the post office. Be sure to include your own name and address.

English

Dear Sir,
I intend to stay at your site for...........days
arriving on...........and departing on...........
We are a party of...........adults and...........children (aged...........)
and shall require a site for...........tent(s) and/or parking space for our car/caravan/caravan trailer.
We wish to hire a tent/caravan/bungalow.
Please quote full charges when replying and advise on the deposit required, which will be forwarded without delay.

French

Monsieur,
Je me propose de séjourner â votre terraine de camping pour...........jours
depuis le...........jusqu'au...........
Nous sommes...........personnes en tout, y compris...........adultes et...........
enfants (âgés de...........) et nous aurons besoin de'un emplacement pour...........tente(s) ainsi quel ou pour notre voiture/caravane/remorque.
Nous désirons louer une tente/caravane/un bungalow.
Veuillez me donner dans votre résponse une idée de votre tarif de prix, m'indiquant en même temps le montant que vous demandez comme arrhes, ce qui vous sera ensuite envoyé aussitôt.

German

Sehr geehrter Herr!
Ich beabsichtige, mich auf Ihrem Campingplatz...........Tage aufzuhalten und zwar vom-...........bis zum...........
Wir sind im ganzen...........Personen...........Erwachsene und...........
Kinder (im Alter von...........) und benötigen Platz für...........
Zelt(e) und/oder unseren Wagen/Wohnwagen/Wohnwagenanhänger.
Wir möchten ein Zelt/Wohnwagen/Bungalow mieten.
Bitte geben Sir mir in Ihrem Antwortschreiben die vollen Preise bekannt und ebenso die Höhe der von mir zu leistenden Anzahlung, die Ihnen alsdann unverzüglich überwiesen wird.

Italian

Egregio Signore,
Ho intenzione di rimanere presso di voi per...........giorni
arrivero il...........e partiro il...........
Siamo un gruppo di...........adultie...........bambini (de età...........e)
vorremmo un posto per...........tenda (e) e/o spazio per parcheggiare la nostra vettura/carovana/roulotte.
Desideriamo affittare una tenda/carovana/bungalow.
Vi preghiamo di quotare i prezzi completi quando ci risponderete ed darci informazioni sul deposito richiesto che vi sarà rimesso senza ritardo.

Spanish

Muy señor mio,
Desearia me reservara espacio por...........dias
a partir del...........hasta el...........
Nuestro grupo se compane de...........adultos y...........niños
(de...........años de edad).
Necesitarimos un espacio por...........tienda(s) y/o espacio para aparcar nuestro choche/caravana/remolque.
Deseariamos alquilar una tienda de campaña/caravana/bungalow.
Le ruego nos comunique los precios y nois informe sobre el depósito que debemos remitirle.

AUSTRIA

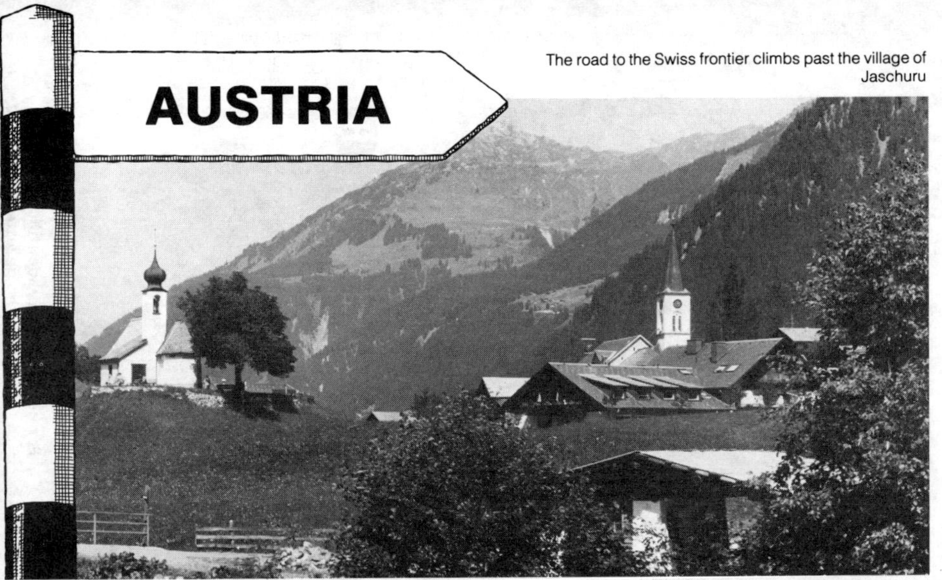

The road to the Swiss frontier climbs past the village of Jaschuru

Austria is a land of chalet villages and beautiful cities bordered by six countries: Czechoslovakia, Federal Republic of Germany, Hungary, Italy, Switzerland and Yugoslavia. The scenery is predominantly Alpine, an enchanting mix of mountains, lakes and pine forests. The splendour of the mountains is seen in the imposing Dachstein region of upper Austria and the massive Tyrolean peaks. The lakes of Burgenland and Salzkammergut, the river Danube, the forests and woods of Styria and the world-famous city of Wien (Vienna) are outstanding features of the landscape.

Most of the country enjoys a moderate climate during the summer, although eastern areas are sometimes very hot. The heaviest rainfall occurs in midsummer. The language of Austria is German, and English is not widely spoken.

HOW TO GET THERE

The usual approach from Calais, Oostende and Zeebrugge is via Belgium to Aachen to join the German *Autobahn* network, then onwards via Köln (Cologne) to Frankfurt. Here the routes branch southwards via Karlsruhe and Stuttgart for Innsbruck and the Tirol or eastwards via Nürnberg and München (Munich) to Salzburg for central Austria. The distance to Salzburg is about 700 miles and usually requires two night stops. Wien (Vienna) the capital is a further 200 miles east. Travelling via the Netherlands is a straightforward run joining the German *Autobahn* system near Arnhem. Alternatively, Austria can be reached via northern France to Strasbourg and Stuttgart or via Basel and northern Switzerland. This is also the route if travelling from Dieppe, Le Havre, Caen or Cherbourg.

GENERAL INFORMATION

(see also *Things you need to know*, pages 33–64

Boats

(see also page 33)

Motorboats are not allowed on most of Austria's lakes. It is advisable to check with the tourist office before taking a boat into Austria.

British Embassy/Consulates

(see also page 57)

The British Embassy together with its consular section is located at *1030 Wein* Reisnerstrasse 40 ☎(0222) 731575/9; consular section 756117/8. There are British Consulates with Honorary Consuls in Bregenz, Graz, Innsbruck and Salzburg.

Camping

Austria offers a variety of outdoor activities to suit everyone and there are numerous campsites throughout the country. Most are open from May to September, although a number remain open all year.

International camping carnet not compulsory but recommended. Some campsites will allow a reduction in the advertised charge to the holders of a camping carnet. See page 37 for

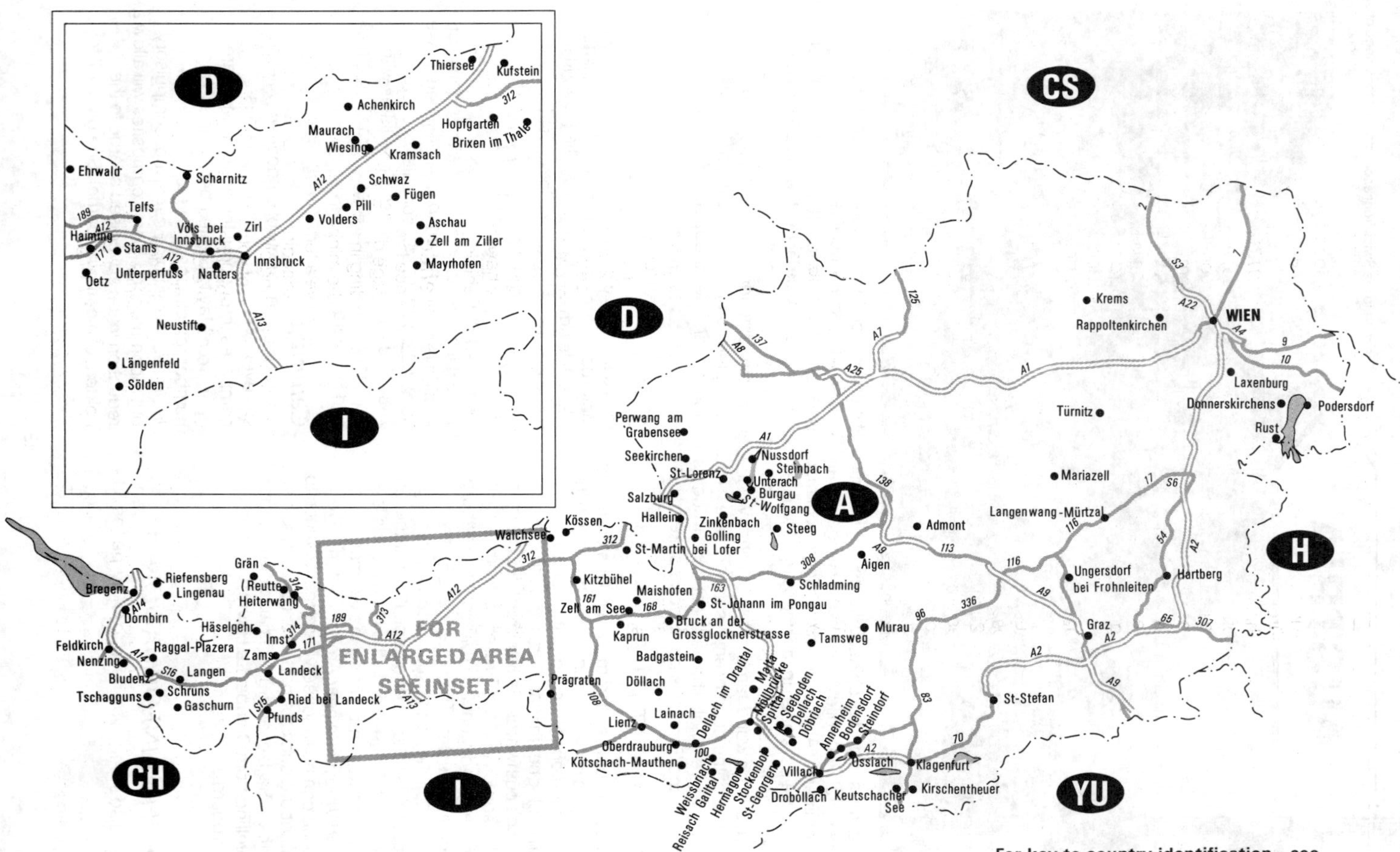

For key to country identification - see "About the gazetteer"

further information.
Off-site camping is possible in state forests with permission from the local Bürgermeister, but open fires are generally prohibited in woodland areas. Campers, not on an official site, staying in Austria for more than three days should report to the police as soon as possible, and also inform them of subsequent changes of location. Within Wien (Vienna) any form of off-site camping or caravanning is prohibited.

Currency including banking hours

(see also page 57)
The unit of currency is the Austrian Schilling (*ASch*) divided into 100 *Groschen*. At the time of going to press £ = *ASch* 20.40. Denominations of bank notes are *ASch* 20, 50, 100, 500, 1,000; standard coins are *Asch* 1, 5, 10, 20, 25, 50 and *Groschen* 2, 5, 10, 50. There are no restrictions on the amount of foreign or Austrian currency that a *bona fide* tourist may import into the country. No more than *ASch* 50,000 in local currency may be exported, but there is no restriction on the export of foreign currency.

Banks are open Monday to Friday from 08.00–12.30hrs and 13.30–15.00hrs extended to 17.30hrs on Thursday. The bank counter at the ÖAMTC head office is open during office hours; exchange offices at some main railway stations are open Saturdays, Sundays and public holidays.

Foodstuffs

(see also page 60)
Visitors may import tea, coffee and foodstuffs for their own personal use but meat and meat products from Italy, Spain, Portugal and Malta are prohibited.

Medical treatment

(see page 60)

Shopping hours

Generally shops are open from 08.00–18.00hrs Monday–Friday with a one or two hour break for lunch except in central Wien where shops do not close for lunch; on Saturday most shops close at midday throughout Austria.

Some shops operate a tax-free service whereby, on leaving the country, visitors are reimbursed for VAT paid. A special form (U34) must be obtained, completed and stamped, from the shop and presented to the Austrian Customs when crossing the border. Look for shops displaying the blue 'Tax-free Shopping' sign, or go to the local tourist information or ÖAMTC office for address lists.

Tourist information

(see also page 63)
The Austrian National Tourist Organisation maintains an information office in London at 30 St George Street, W1R 0AL ☎01-629 0461 and will be pleased to assist you with any information regarding tourism. In most towns in Austria there is a local or regional tourist office which will supply detailed local information.

Visitors' registration

(see page 63)

MOTORING

(see also *Things you need to know*, pages 33–64)

Accidents

(see also page 46)
Fire ☎122 police ☎133 ambulance ☎144

Breakdowns

(see page 48)

Dimensions and weight restrictions

Private **cars** and towed **trailers** or **caravans** are restricted to the following dimensions – height: 4 metres; width: 2.50 metres; length: 12 metres. The maximum permitted overall length of vehicle/trailer or caravan combination is 18 metres.

Trailers without brakes may weigh up to 750kg and may have a total weight of up to 50% of the towing vehicle.

Driving Licence

A valid UK licence is acceptable in Austria and although language difficulties may give rise to misunderstanding in a few isolated cases, it is legally valid. The minimum age at which a visitor may drive a temporarily imported car or motorcycle (exceeding 50 cc) is 18 years. The Austrian motoring club (ÖAMTC) will supply a free translation of your licence into German, but it is only available from their head office in Vienna and therefore will only be of use if touring in eastern Austria. However, an International Driving Permit is required by the holder of a licence issued in the Republic of Ireland. See under *Driving Licence and International Driving Permit* page 33 for further information.

First Aid Kit

(see also page 50)
In Austria all vehicles (including motorcycles) must be equipped with a first aid kit by law and visitors are expected to comply. This item will not be checked at the frontier, but any motorist can be stopped at the scene of an accident and his first-aid kit demanded; if this is not forthcoming the police may take action.

Lights

(see page 50 also *Headlights* page 41)

Motoring club

(see also page 61)
The *Österreichischer Automobil-, Motorrad-und Touring Club* (ÖAMTC) which has its headquarters at *1010 Wein* Schubertring 1–3 ☏(0222)72990 has offices at the major frontier crossings and is represented in most towns either direct or through provincial motoring clubs. The offices are usually open between 08.30 and 18.00hrs weekdays, 09.00 to 12.00hrs on Saturdays and are closed on Sundays and public holidays.

Passengers

(see also page 51)
Children under 12 are not permitted to travel in a vehicle as front seat passengers unless they are using special seats or safety belts suitable for children.

Petrol

(see page 61)

Roads

The motorist crossing into Austria from any frontier enters a network of well-engineered roads. In July and August, several roads across the frontier become congested. The main points are on the Lindau-Bregenz road; at the Brenner Pass (possible alternative – the Resia Pass); at Kufstein; on the München (Munich)–Salzburg *Autobahn* and on the Villach–Tarvisio road. For details of mountain passes see page 70.

Seat belts

(see page 52)

Speed limits

Car

Built-up areas
50 kph (31 mph)
Other roads
100 kph (62 mph)
Motorways
130 kph (80 mph)

Car towing caravan not exceeding 750 kg*

Built up areas
50 kph (31 mph)
Other roads
100 kph (62 mph)
Motorways
100 kph (62 mph)

Car towing caravan exceeding 750 kg*

Built-up areas
50 kph (31 mph)
Other roads
80 kph (49 mph)
Motorways
100 kph (62 mph)

*If weight of the trailer exceeds that of the towing vehicle or if the total weight of the two vehicles exceeds 3,500 kg then the following speed limits apply:

Built-up areas
50 kph (31 mph)
Other roads
60 kph (37 mph)
Motorways
70 kph (43 mph)

Note when the total weight of the two vehicles exceeds 3,500 kg it is not permissible to tow with a motor-car driving licence.

Warning triangle

The use of a warning triangle is compulsory in the event of accident or breakdown. The triangle must be placed on the road an adequate distance behind the vehicle or obstacle and must be clearly visible from 200 metres (219 yds). See also *Warning triangles/ Hazard warning lights* page 54.

Prices are in Austrian Schillings.
Abbreviation:
str strasse

ACHENKIRCH
Tirol (05246)
Achensee 6239
On N shore of lake, on level grassland with gravel paths.
Opposite Hotel Scholastika. Turn off B181 in Achenkirch.
All year.
3HEC lau A40 V27 27 A27

ADMONT
Steiermark (03613)
At **HALL** (3 km N)
Hall 2839
In level meadow on banks of the River Enns, near a farm.
Jun–Oct.
1HEC lau

AIGEN
Steiermark (03682)
Hohenberg 3383
Lakeside site on terraced hillside with some fruit trees.
Turn right in Wiler Ketten after the Military airfield and right again after the ARAL petrol station and follow narrow road to site.
Apr–Oct.
1.5HEC lau A24 V5 25–30 A25

ALT See **OSSIACH**

ANIF See **SALZBURG**

ANNENHEIM
Kärnten (04249)
Bad Ossiacher See (04248)2757
An extensive level site with adjoining meadow.
Situated on B94 Villach–Wien road.
15 May–15 Sep.
5.4HEC lau A45 Vn/c 45 A45

ASCHAU
Tirol
Aufenfeld (05282)2916
Level meadowland on forest slope.
Signposted.
All year.
3HEC lau A45–55 V50–60 n/c An/c

BADGASTEIN
Salzburg (06434)
Azur Erlengrund 2790
On meadowland below the road leading to the Tauern railway tunnel.
From Hofgastein turn left off B167 and

Austria

descend for 100 m.
All year.
4HEC lau A48–53 pitch50–75

BLUNDENZ
Vorarlberg (05552)
At **BRAZ** (7 km SE)
Traube 8103
On sloping grassland
7 km SE of Bludenz via E17, S16 (Blundenz–Arlberg–Innsbruck). Signposted. Near railway.
All year.
2HEC lau A45–50 V15 35–40 A25–40
At **NÜZIDERS** (2.5 km NW)
Sonnenberg 64035
Clean site with modern facilities in gently sloping meadow amid splendid mountain scenery.
Access from Bludenz–Nüziders road, at first fork follow up hill.
15 May–Sep.
2HEC lau A45 V35 35 A35

BODENSDORF
Kärnten (04243)
Glaser 568
On shore of Lake Ossiach with private bathing area. Quiet at night despite lying beside railway line. Badly signposted access.
Turn off B94 at BP garage towards lake. Cross railway and continue for 200 m.
Closed Nov.
1.5HEC lau A40–45 pitch130–160

BRAZ See **BLUDENZ**

BREGENZ
Vorarlberg (05574)
See Bodangasse 7 31895
Quite site on level meadow beside lake.
From town centre (Bahnhofsplatz) follow signs towards 'See Bühne'.
15 May–15 Sep.
8HEC lau
Weiss 35771
On a farm, 300 m from lake.
Access via Rheinstr and Felchenstr.
15 May–Sep.
3.4HEC lau A25 V25 35–45 A25–35

BRIXEN IM THALE
Tirol (05334)
Brixen im Thale 8373
On partly sloping grassland with some terraces and a fine view over the valley. Good leisure facilities.
Access via Kufstein–Innsbruck motorway (exit Wörgl-Ost). Site lies to the S of town past the level crossing.
All year.
3HEC lau A35 V30 30 A25

BRUCK AN DER GROSSGLOCKNERSTRASSE
Salzburg (06545)
Woferlgut 303
Access via exit Bruck-Süd on S11.
All year.
2HEC lau A30 V25 35 A20–35

BURGAU
Salzburg (07663)
Burgau 266
Mainly level site surrounded by trees between the road and the Attersee at Weissenbach.
On B152 at Km 27.6 opposite Hotel Burgau.
Apr–Oct.
2HEC A35–38 V26–29 26–29 A26–29

DELLACH
Kärnten (04766)
Neubauer 2530
Access from B100, Lienz–Spittal road. The turn-off is well signposted in the village.
May–Sep.
2HEC

DELLACH IM DRAUTAL
Kärnten (04714)
Waldbad 288
On NE shore of Millstatter See on W outskirts of town.
May–Sep.
2HEC lau A34–43 pitch25–36

DÖBRIACH
Kärnten (04246)
Brunner am See Glanzerstr 108 7189
Tidily arranged with poplar trees. Private bathing area.
The access road is at the E end of Lake Millstatt.
All year.
2.5HEC lau pitch160–230 (incl 2 persons)
Burgstaller Seefeldstr 7774
At SE end of lake. From B98 continue towards Lake Millstatt for 1 km.
All year.

7HEC pitch60–100 A40–50

Ebner Seefeldstr 1 ☎7315

On either side of the Seefeldstr, beyond Camping Burgstaller, at E end of Lake Millstatt.
All year.
1HEC lau

Mossler Glanzerstr 24 ☎7735

On meadowland, completely divided into pitches.

At SE end of the lake on right of Döbriach–Feistritz road.
20 Dec–Oct
3HEC lau

Winkler Strandweg 26 ☎7187

On level ground, divided into sections.

Approx. 400 m E of the lake.
15 Apr.–Oct.
1.7HEC lau A45
pitch60–70

DÖLLACH
Kärnten (☎04825)

Zirknitzer ☎451

Beside the River Möu.

Between Km 8 and Km 9 on the Glocknerstr (B107).
Jun–Sep.
0.6HEC A23 V12 18–20 15

DONNERSKIRCHEN
Burgenland (☎02683)

Sonnenwaldbad ☎8670

Grassy site with wide terraces beside a wood. View of the lake.

May–Sep.
10HEC lau A33 V33 33 33

DORNBIRN
Vorarlberg (☎05572)

In der Enz ☎69119

A municipal site beside a public park, some 100 m beyond the Karren cable lift

May–Sep.
1HEC lau A37 V32 32 32

DROBOLLACH
Kärnten (☎04242)

Mittewald ☎27392

In a hollow on slightly rising ground surrounded by trees and divided into pitches. Large children's playground.

Off Villach–Faaker See road. Signposted 'Serai'.
May–Sep.

Austria

2.5HEC lau A43 V19 33 28

EHRWALD
Tirol (☎05673)

International Dr-Ing E Lauth ☎2666

On undulating grassland, surrounded by high conifers, below the Wetterstein mountain range.

To the right of the access road to the Zugspitz funicular.
All year.
1HEC lau

Tiroler Zugspitzbahn ☎2254

Several grassy terraces. Modern sanitary installations with bathrooms.

Near the Zugspitz funicular station.
All year.
4HEC lau A42 pitch40

FAAK AM SEE See **VILLACH**

FELDKIRCH
Vorarlberg (☎05522)

Waldcamping ☎24308

On level grassland, surrounded by tall trees.

All year.
3HEC lau A30–35
V20–25 20–25 20

FÜGEN
Tirol (☎05288)

Zillertal-Hell ☎2203

In a meadow surrounding a farm.

1 km N of Fügen on the B169.
All year.
1.5HEC lau A40 V25 25
25

GANTSCHIER See **SCHRUNS**

GASCHURN
Voralberg (☎05558)

Nova ☎8548

A site on two levels. The upper level only is shaded.

Off B188 towards the river.
May–15 Oct.
1HEC lau

GOLLING
Salzburg (☎06244)

Torrener Hof ☎380

On the outskirts of the village on the B159.
All year.
1HEC lau A20 Vn/c 60 40

GOTSCHUCHEN See **KIRSCHENTHEUER**

GRÄN
Tirol (☎05675)

Tannheimer Tal ☎6570
1 km N of the village centre on the Pfronten–Tannheimer Tal road.
All year.
3HEC lau

GRAZ
Steiermark (☎03122)

S C Central Martinhofstr 3 ☎(0316)281831

A site with many lawns separated by asphalt paths and partly divided into pitches.

Turn off the B70 in Strassgang S of Graz and continue for 300 m.
Apr–Oct.
4HEC lau A33–38
pitch60–80

At **MANTSCHA**

Wald Riederhof ☎284380

A peaceful, terraced site surrounded by woodlands.

From Graz take Reininghalisstr and Steinbergstr towards Mantscha signposted from railway station.
All year.
5HEC lau

At **ST-PETER** (4 km SE)

Ost Neue Welthöhe 71 ☎(0316)45169

On terraced sloping ground.

3 km from the town centre off Waltendorfer Hauptstr.
Apr–Sep.
0.6HEC A25 V20 25 25

HAIMING
Tirol (☎05266)

Center Oberland ☎294

On a sloping meadow behind the BP garage.

Off B171 at Km 485.
All year.
4.5HEC lau A30 V25 25
25

HALL See **ADMONT**

HALLEIN
Salzburg (☎06245)

Susi ☎39194

Situated in well tended grassland on a tributary of the Konigsee.

Access from Salzburg–Villach motorway exit Salzburg Süd or Hallein, then on B159/E14 to turn off by Brückenwirt in Anif Niederalm.
Apr–Sep.
0.8HEC A30 V16–25 16
16

HARTBERG
Steiermark (☎03332)

Hartberg ☎2250

In quiet situation surrounded by trees, hedges in meadowland next to open-air pool.

Turn off B54 towards swimming pool and continue 300 m.
May–Sep.

0.9HEC ◆ H ⊙ lau P A25 V18 22 15

HÄSELGEHR
Tirol (☎05634)

Rudi Luxnach 122 ☎6425

All year.

1HEC ◆ H ⊙ G R P ⊞ lau A36 V22 25 18–26

HEILIGEN GESTADE See **OSSIACH**

HEITERWANG
Tirol (☎05674)

Heiterwanger See ☎5116

In a quiet situation in a meadow beside lake.

By Hotel Fischer am See.
All year.

1HEC ◆ H ⊙ G R L ⊞ lau A54 pitch30–50

HERMAGOR
Kärnten (☎04282)

Pressegger See ☎2039

6 km E.
May–Sep.

1HEC H ⊙ G R ⊞ lau L A25–30 V14 14–20 14–20

Schluga Hermagor ☎2051

1.5 km E on road to Pressegger See.
All year.

3.5HEC ◆ ◆ H ⊙ G R P ⊞ lau A33–40 pitch36–50

Schluga-Seecamping ☎2760

Approx. 300 m N of lake in meadowland with some terraces and fine views.

5.5 km E.
20 May–15 Sep.

7HEC ◆ ◆ H ⊙ G R ⊞ lau L A33–40 pitch36–50

HOPFGARTEN
Tirol (☎05335)

See also **BRIXEN IM THALE**

Reiterhof Penningberg 90 ☎2490

All year.

2HEC ◆ H ⊙ G R R lau

Schlossberg-Itter ☎2181

In terraced meadowland below Schloss Itter on the Brixental Ache.

2 km W on B170.
All year.

4HEC ◆ H ⊙ G R RP ⊞ lau A48 V33 30 30

IMST
Tirol (☎05412)

Imst-West ☎3364

On open meadowland in the Langgasse area.

Off the bypass near the turn for the Pitztal.
All year.

1HEC ◆ H ⊙ G R ⊞ lau LP A35 V20 20 20

At **OBERSTADT**

Böss Engererweg 5 ☎2866

In meadow surrounded by fruit trees.

Access from B197.
May–Sep.

1HEC ◆ H ⊙ G R LP ⊞ lau A31 V20 20 20

INNSBRUCK
Tirol (☎05222)

ARAL Tirol ☎84180

On rising meadowland partly surrounded by woods.

4.5 km W of town centre near Innsbruck airport. Access via A12/E17 exit Kranebitten in direction of Kranebitten.
15 Dec–Oct.

3.5HEC ◆ H ⊙ G R ⊞ lau R A55 V50 60–80 60–80

KAPRUN
Salzburg (☎06547)

Mühle ☎82540

On long stretch of meadow by the Kapruner Ache. S end of village towards cable lift.

All year.

1.5HEC ◇ H ⊙ G R ⊞ lau P A36–48 V29 34 29

KEUTSCHACHER SEE
Kärnten (☎04273)

Brückler Nord ☎2384

On N shore of the lake behind the public bathing area.
Apr–Oct.

2HEC ◆ H ⊙ L ⊞ lau

KIRSCHENTHEUER
Kärnten (☎04227)

Shell-Camping ☎2279

On road to Loibl Pass behind SHELL garage and motel.
May–Oct.

1.5HEC ◆ H ⊙ R PL lau

At **GOTSCHUCHEN** (10 km E)

Rosental Roz ☎246

Site in meadowland and small wood with pond suitable for bathing. Quiet, secluded situation.

Approach from Klagenfurt on B91 to Kirschentheuer. Turn onto B85 travelling E to Gotschuchen then turn left and continue to site.
15 Apr–Sep.

5HEC ◆ H ⊙ G L ⊞ lau

KITZBÜHEL
Tirol (☎05356)

Schwarzsee ☎2806

In meadowland on the edge of a wood behind a large restaurant.

2 km from town on B170 towards Wörgl turn right, 400 m after Schwarzsee railway station.
All year.

5HEC ◆ H ⊙ G R ⊞ lau L A54 V30 35 35

KLAGENFURT
Kärnten (☎04222)

Strandbad ☎21169

Large site divided into sections by trees and bushes.

From town centre take B83 towards Velden. Turn left just outside town in direction of bathing area.
May–Sep.

4HEC ◆ H ⊙ G ⊞ lau L A40 V20

KLÖSTERLE See **LANGEN**

KÖSSEN
Tirol (☎05375)

Wilder Kaiser ☎6444

Situated in a lovely position below Unterberg, this level site is adjoined on three sides by woodland.

For access follow road to Unterberg Lift, then turn right and continue for 200 m.
All year.

3.5HEC ◇ H ⊙ G R P ⊞ lau A50 pitch65–80

KÖTSCHACH-MAUTHEN
Kärnten (☎04715)

Alpen ☎429

In meadowland beside River Gail.

Turn off B110 in the S part of the village on the road to the Plöcken Pass and drive 800 m towards Lesachtal.
May–Sep.

1.4HEC ◆ H ⊙ G ⊞ lau RP A26–32 pitch26–37

KRAMSACH
Tirol (☎05337)

Seen-Camping Stadlerhof ☎3371

Near the Krumm lake behind a farm and on generally level meadow planted with fruit trees. ➤

From the Inntal Motorway (Rattenberg/ Kramsach exit) follow signs 'Zu den Seen'.
All year.

2HEC H G R lau L A38–40 V20 20–40

Tonis Ferien Comfort Seeblick Toni ☎3544

Rural site near the Brantlhof above Lake Reintaler.

From Inntal Motorway (Rattenberg/ Kramsach exit) follow signs 'Zu den Seen' for about 3 km, then drive through Seehof site.
All year.

2HEC H G lau L A45–55 V30–38 30–38 30–38

KREMS

Niederösterreich (☎02732)

Donau (ÖAMTC) Wiedengasse 7 ☎4455

By river opposite SHELL filling station.
May–Sep.

1HEC H R R

KUFSTEIN

Tirol (☎05372)

Kufstein ☎3689

Site has sporting facilities.

1 km W of Kufstein between River Inn and B171.
May–Oct.

1HEC H G R lau L A28 V25 25 20

Tiroler Fliegerstuben ☎4390

Site situated on level meadowland.

All year.

0.5HEC H L

LADIS See **RIED BEI LANDECK**

LAINACH

Kärnten (☎04822)

Bambi ☎376

On the undulating wooded meadowland.

By Km45.6 on Möutalstr (B106) behind Gasthof Planegger.
May–Sep.

0.5HEC H G A25 pitch40

LANDECK

Tirol (☎05442)

Huber Mühlkanal 1 ☎4636

All year.

Austria

1.3HEC H (summer only) R lau G R A35 V15 45–60 30–45

Riffler ☎39405

Site on meadowland between residential housing and banks of Sanna.

100 m from Camping Landeck-West.
All year.

0.3HEC H G lau P A30 V15 45–60 35–45

LANGEN

Vorarlberg (☎05582)

At **KLÖSTERLE** (2 km W)

Alpencamping ☎269

Well signposted.
All year.

1.5HEC H G lau P A40 V16 30 12–20

LÄNGENFELD

Tirol (☎05253)

Ötztal ☎5348

In meadowland with some tall trees on the edge of woodland.

Turn right off E186 at fire station.
All year.

3HEC H G R lau P A35 V20 35 35

LANGENWANG-MÜRTZAL

Steiermark (☎03854)

Europa ☎2950

On level meadow with some trees, surrounded by hedges.

The B306 (E7) by-passes the town, so be careful not to miss the exit 6 km S of Mürzzuschlag.
All year.

2HEC R lau R

LAXENBURG

Niederösterreich (☎02236)

Schlosspark Laxenburg Münchendorfer Str ☎71333

On level meadowland with surfaced roads. The site lies in a recreation centre within the grounds of the historic Laxenburg Castle.

Access 600 m S on the road leading to the B16.

Apr–Sep.

5.9HEC H P G lau

LEUTASCH

Tirol (☎05214)

Holiday ☎6570

A modern site on level grassland screened by trees on the Leutascher Ache.

Turn off B313 (Mittenwald-Scharnitz) towards Leutasch.
Closed Nov.

2.8HEC H G P lau pitch140–250 (incl. 2 persons)

LIENZ

Tirol (☎04852)

Dolomitenrast ☎2447

On B107 at Km0.8, at the foot of the ascent to the Isleberg and the Glocknerstr.

3HEC H P lau

Glocknerhof Schillerstr 4 ☎2167

The site lies on the E side of Lienz on B1074 close to town centre.
May–Sep.

1.8HEC H A38 V20 20 20

LINGENAU

Vorarlberg (☎05513)

Feurstein ☎6114

All year.

1HEC H G R lau RP A30 V15 35 30–35

MAISHOFEN

Salzburg (☎06542)

Kammerlander ☎8755

On B168.
Apr–Oct.

1HEC H L

MALTA

Kärnten (☎04760)

Malta ☎(04733)234

On a gently rising alpine meadow.

In Gmünd turn off B99 and drive 5.5 km through Malta valley.
May–Oct.

3HEC H G P lau A45 pitch60

MANTSCHA See **GRAZ**

MARIAZELL

Steiermark (☎02727)

Erlaufsee ☎2148

Small, quiet site on the edge of a wood, away from lake.

4 km N of Mariazell, off the B20. Access through a big car park in front of the Herrenhaus Hotel.
May–Sep.

0.5HEC L

MAURACH
Tirol (☎05243)

Bärenkopf ☎5297

On wooded hillside 0.5 km from lake.

In town turn off road B181 and follow the Pertisau road towards the lake. At lake turn left and continue by track for 300 m.
All year.

1.3HEC H G L lau

MAYRHOFEN
Tirol (☎05285)

Laubichl ☎2580

On a gently sloping meadow near a farm at N entrance to village.

All year.

2HEC H G R lau P A35 V18 18 18

MÖLLBRÜCKE
Kärnten (☎04769)

Rheingold Molltalstr 65 ☎2338

Site on main road from Spittal to Mallnitz, next to swimming pool.
All year.

1HEC H G P lau

MURAU
Steiermark (☎03532)

Olachgut ☎2162

All year.

2.5HEC H G R P lau A25 V15 25 25

NATTERS
Tirol (☎05222)

Natterer See ☎23988

Austria

A terraced site beautifully situated amidst woodland and mountains on the shore of Nattersee.

Approach via Brenner Motorway, exit 'Innsbruck Sud', via Natters, onto B182 and follow signs.
Jan–Sep.

NENZING
Vorarlberg (☎05525)

Garfrenga ☎2491

Signposted from B190 from Nenzing–2 km towards Gurtis.
Closed for 1 month after Etr.

3HEC H G R P lau

NEUSTIFT
Tirol (☎05226)

Gasthof Weiss ☎8104

Apr–Nov.

1.7HEC H G lau A20 Vn/c 50 30

Hochstubal ☎2610

On slightly sloping meadowland.

Near the Geier Alm approximately 5 km S of town on the road towards the Gletscher bahn.
Jan–Nov.

3HEC H R lau

NUSSDORF
Oberösterreich (☎07666)

See Camping Gruber ☎80450

On fairly long meadow parallel to the promenade.

S of village, access is at Km 19.7. Turn off B151 towards the lake (Attersee).
May–Sep.

1.6HEC H G R L

lau A36–40 pitch42–48

Strandcamping Graus ☎8088

Site on long meadow with fruit trees, sloping towards lake and bathing area. Access is within the village.

Turn off main road B151 at Km 19.5 towards the lake (Attersee).
May–Oct.

2.5HEC H L lau A40 pitch44

NÜZIDERS See **BLUDENZ**

OBERDRAUBURG
Kärnten (☎04710)

Dolomitenbad ☎481

On gently sloping meadow.

For access turn off the B100 onto the B110 Gailberg–Sattel road.
May–Sep.

1HEC H R lau

OBERSTADT See **IMST**

OETZ
Tirol (☎05252)

Oetz ☎6485

In a park-like area with hedges and trees.

Etr–Sep.

1.5HEC H G R lau LP

OSSIACH
Kärnten (☎04243)

Parth ☎421

On hilly ground on S shore of the lake. Steep, but there are some terraces.

Off B94 on S bank of Lake Ossiach.
Mar–Sep.

1.5HEC H G R lau L

Terrassen Camping ☎436

Divided into pitches with generally well-situated terraces.

Off B94 on E bank of Kale Ossiacher opposite ARAL garage.
May–Sep. ➔

8HEC lau A52
pitch43–52

At **ALT** (2 km NE)

Ideal Camping Lampele ☎529

On a tract of land sloping gently from shore road down to lake. Divided into plots by trees and hedges.

May–Sep.

3HEC lau

At **HEILIGEN GESTADE** (5 km SW)

Seecamping Berghof ☎(04242)41133

Terraced meadowland in attractive setting. 800 m long promenade with bathing areas.

E shore of Lake Ossiacher.
Mar–Oct.

8HEC lau

PERWANG AM GRABENSEE
Oberösterreich (☎06217)

Perwang ☎8247

Site beside lake.

May–Sep.

1HEC lau A40 pitch60

PFUNDS
Tirol (☎05474)

Sonnen ☎5232

Site in meadowland with some fruit trees.

On road B315 between SHELL Garage and Gasthof of Sonne.
All year.

1HEC lau A20 V20 20 A10–30

PILL
Tirol (☎05242)

Plankenhof ☎4195

Site in meadow.

On B171 near Gasthof Plankenhof.
Apr–Oct.

0.6HEC lau A35 pitch40

PODERSDORF
Burgenland (☎02177)

See 11 ☎309

Site between shore of lake and a line of poplar trees. Busy on Bank Holidays because of bathers.

Just before entering town, take by-pass to roundabout by lake and continue forward through an avenue of poplar trees.
May–Sep.

9HEC lau

PRÄGRATEN
Tirol (☎04874)

Venediger ☎5213

On uneven meadow next to a Pension.

500 m from Matrei-Hinterbichl road.
All year.

Austria

0.9HEC lau A35 V16 33 A35

RAGGAL-PLAZERA
Vorarlberg (☎05553)

Grosswalsertal ☎209

Situated in a quiet location on gently sloping terrain, with pleasant views.

All year.

0.8HEC lau A35 V6 16 A14

RAPPOLTENKIRCHEN
Niederösterreich (☎02274)

Rappoltenkirchen ☎389

Turn off B1 at Sieghartskirchen and continue S for 3 km.
Closed Jan.

2.4HEC lau A24 V18 35–38 A20

REISACH GAILTAL
Kärnten (☎04284)

Ferienpark Alpen ☎301

Terraced site almost entirely divided into pitches with fine mountain view.

Turn off B111 in town at the war memorial and continue 1.7 km on asphalt road with gradients of up to 13%.
Jun–20 Sep.

3.5HEC lau A29 pitch60–85

REUTTE
Tirol (☎05672)

Sennalpe ☎8115

In a quiet situation on a grassy mountain slope above the lake.

On Reutte–Oberamergau road 200 m from the Hotel Forelle.
15 Dec.–15 Oct.

4HEC

Sintwag ☎2809

Well kept site on a meadow on the edge of a forest near the sports centre. Modern swimming pool in town.

Turn right towards Waldrast.
Jan–Apr & Jun–Dec.

2.2HEC lau A46 V23 23 A23

RIED BEI LANDECK
Tirol (☎05472)

Dreiländereck ☎6294

Level site in centre of village.

Signposted.
All year.

1.5HEC lau A25 V20 20 A20

At **LADIS** (3 km N)

Sonnenterrasse ☎6607

Situated on gently sloping meadowland between a school and swimming pool. Views of the upper Inn and Burg Laidegg.

In Ried turn off the B315 towards Ladis, and follow a winding road with slight gradients for 4 km.
Etr–Oct.

0.4HEC lau A29 V11 17 A16

RIEFENSBERG
Vorarlberg (☎05513)

Hochlitten ☎8312

Site on terraced meadow next to the Berghof Inn.

All year.

1HEC A25–28 V10 45 A35–45

RODAUN See **WIEN (VIENNA)**

RUST
Burgenland (☎02685)

Rust ☎595

Situated on level meadowland with young trees.

From Rust follow the lake road.
Apr–Oct.

3HEC lau

ST-GEORGEN
Kärnten

Gerli St-Georgenstr 140 ☎(04242)27402

Level, quiet, isolated site, with heated swimming pool annexed to it which is open to the public.

From Spittal/Drau turn off B100, turn right just before Villach and continue for 2 km.
All year.

2HEC lau A40 V15 25–30 A20–25

ST-JOHANN IM PONGAU
Salzburg (☎06412)

Wieshof Rainbach 4 ☎519

On gently sloping meadow behind pension and farmhouse. Modern facilities. Big spa house with sauna, massage facilities and health bars, adjacent to site.

Off B311 towards Zell am Zee.
All year.

2HEC A35 pitch35

ST-LORENZ
Oberösterreich (☎06224)

Alten Ischler Bahn ☎(06232)2902

Clean orderly site, easily accessible in the beautiful Mondsee Valley.

May–Sep.

1HEC

P A ⊞ lau L A28 Vn/c 45 A35–40

Austria-Camp ☎(06232)2927

Level site on grassland bordered by trees and hedges and divided into fields by internal roads. Separate field for young people.

4 km from Mondsee, beside the lake.
Mid Apr–Oct.

1.7HEC H G R L A ⊞ lau A23 V22 27 A23

ST-MARTIN BEI LOFER
Salzburg (☎06588)

Park Grubhof ☎237

Situated in meadowland on the banks of the River Saalach. Separate sections for dog owners, families, teenagers and groups.

1.5 km S of Lofer turn left off B311.
May–Sep.

10HEC H G R R A ⊞ lau P A34 V19 22–28 A17–21

ST-PETER See **GRAZ**

ST-STEFAN
Kärnten (☎04352)

Streit ☎2273

E off B70 and then 2.7 km to site.
May–Sep.

0.8HEC H A

ST-WOLFGANG
Oberösterreich (☎06138)

Appesbach Au 99 ☎2206

On sloping meadow facing lake with no shade at upper end.

Austria

0.8 km E of St-Wolfgang between lake and Strobl road.
Apr–Oct.

2HEC H G R L A ⊞ lau A40 V20 pitch45–60

Berau Schwarzenbach 16 ☎2543

Site lies between lake and road from Strobl, N of lake.

1.3 km E of entrance to St-Wolfgang.
Etr.–Oct.

2.5HEC H G R L A ⊞ lau A39 V16 45–70 A35–70

SALZBURG
Salzburg (☎0662)

Nord Sam Samstr 22A ☎660611

Site divided into pitches.

400 m from Salzburg Nord Autobahn Exit.
Apr–Oct.

2HEC H G R P A ⊞ lau A34–45 pitch45–55

Schloss Algen ☎22079

Site divided into pitches in partial clearing on mountain slope.

From Salzburg–Sud motorway exit through Anif and Glasenbach.
May–Sep.

25HEC H G R A ⊞ A26 V13 13 A13

Stadtblick Rauchenbichlerstr 21 ☎50652

Leave motorway at exit Salzburg–Nord and follow signs.
Apr–Oct.

6HEC H G R A A ⊞ lau A40 V10 10 A10

At **ANIF**

Rif Reischenbachstr 27 ☎(06245)2221

Quiet isolated site in orchard clearing.

Leave motorway at Salzburg–Süd junc.
May–Sep.

0.6HEC H G A ⊞ lau RP A28 V17 17 A12–16

SCHARNITZ
Tirol

Alm

On level, open grassland. Near B313.

Access from S outskirts.
Closed Nov.

0.6HEC H G R A ⊞ lau A45 pitch45

SCHLADMING
Steiermark (☎03687)

Zirngast Langegasse 633 ☎23195

Site in meadow on left bank of River Enns next to railway.

Turn off B308 towards town as far as the MOBIL filling station.
All year.

2.5HEC H G R R A ⊞ lau P A40 V17 35 A22–26

SCHRUNS
Vorarlberg (☎05556)
At **GANTSCHIER** (2 km NW)
Rhätikon ☎29402
Site in level meadowland.
Off the Bludenz–Schruns road (B188) near River Ill.
All year.
0.7HEC H G lau

SCHWAZ
Tirol (☎05224)
At **WEER** (6 km W)
Alpencamping Mark Maholmhof ☎8146
Situated on meadowland by a farm on the edge of a forest.
Off B171.
Apr–Oct.
2HEC H G P lau A39 pitch25–40

SEEBODEN
Kärnten (☎04762)
Ferlendorf Lieseregg ☎2723
On large level meadows; some terraces and asphalt drives.
B99 from Spittal north to B98, then left for 1.5 km.
15 Apr–15 Oct.
4.5HEC H G R P lau A38–50 pitch64–74

Seecamping Penker ☎81267
Site situated on meadowland and divided into fields on both sides of the lakeside promenade. There are some rows of poplars and the lower part of the site is terraced.
For access turn off opposite ADEG store and continue for 300 m.
Apr–Oct.
1.3HEC H G L lau A38–55 pitch46–56

Strandbad Winkler Seepromenade 39 ☎81927
Level meadowland, separated from the beach by a road and small park.
For access, turn off opposite the ADEG store and drive for 300 m.
May–Sep.
0.6HEC H PL lau

Strandcamping Haupt Hauptstr 180 ☎81963
The site divides into terraces on sloping ground between main road and lake.
From B98 follow road down to Lake Millstätter.
May–Sep.
1.1HEC H G L lau

Terrassen Lärchenfeld ☎81267
Gently sloping site with terraces.
Access from village, opposite ADEG store, near the church turn uphill, then 300 m to site.
May–Sep.
1.6HEC H G lau L A30–45 pitch36–50

SEEKIRCHEN
Salzburg (☎06212)
Strand ☎488
Beside the Wallersee in beautiful meadow.
May–Sep.
2HEC H G P lau L

Zell am Wallersee ☎480
Level meadowland separated from the lake by the Lido.
Access from A1 exit Wallersee then via Seekirchen to Zell.
May–Oct.
3HEC H lau L A20 pitch100

SÖLDEN
Tirol (☎05254)
Sölden ☎2627
Situated on meadowland on left bank of Ötztaler tributary. Beautiful views of the surrounding mountains.
By Grauer Bär Inn at Km28 on the B186.
Closed May.
0.5HEC H G lau P A35–45 V20 35–45 30–35

SPITTAL
Kärnten (☎04762)
Draufluss ☎2466
A long, narrow riverside site, partly surrounded by a hedge.
From town centre follow road to river towards Goldeckbahn.
Apr–Oct.
1HEC H G P lau A40 V30 30 30

STAMS
Tirol (☎05263)
Eichenwald ☎6159
Well managed terraced site in oak wood.
Turn off B171 at ESSO filling station in direction of abbey, onto a steep, narrow access road.
15 May–Sep.
2HEC H G lau A30 60

STEEG
Oberösterreich
Strand ☎(06135)8166
Beside the Wallersee in a beautiful meadow.
May–Sep.
2HEC H G L lau

STEINBACH
Oberösterreich (☎07663)
Seefeld ☎3430
On meadowland sloping gently towards lake, behind Gasthof Föttinger.
Near MOBIL garage on B152 at Km 13.6.
May–Oct.
1.2HEC H L lau

STEINDORF
Kärnten (☎04243)
Nagele ☎8314
In the village of Steindorf on the lake shore.
Off B94 at Km 31.8 and cross railway.
Jun–Sep.
1HEC H G L lau

STOCKENBOI
Kärnten (☎04761)
Ronacher ☎256
Situated on meadow between forest slopes, gently sloping to the shore of Lake Weissensee.
Approach for caravans via Weissensee.
May–Sep.
1.7HEC H G R lau L

TAMSWEG
Salzburg (☎06474)
Tamsweg ☎385
Site lies 700 m N off main road at north entrance of village.
All year.
1.5HEC H G lau A25 V18 25 25

TELFS
Tirol (☎05262)
Schwimmbad ☎2849
150 m off B171.
All year.
0.7HEC H lau RP A25 V20 20 20

THIERSEE
Tirol (☎05376)
Rueppenhof ☎5419
Site made up of several meadows surrounding a farm that lies on the banks of a lake.
Apr–Sep.
1HEC H L lau A40 pitch35–40

TSCHAGGUNS
Vorarlberg (☎05556)
Zelfen ☎2326
Partly uneven, grassy site beside River Ill. Some residential housing and electricity switching station nearby.
All year.

2HEC fH G R lau A40 pitch60

TÜRNITZ
Niederösterreich (02769)

Gravogl 201
All year.
0.7HEC fH G lau R A25 V30 30 A30

UNGERSDORF BEI FROHNLEITEN
Steiermark (03126)

Lanzmalerhof 2360
Signposted 2 km S of Frohnleiten on the Graz road.
Apr–15 Oct.
0.5HEC fH G lau A30 V23 23 A12–24

UNTERACH
Oberösterreich (07665)

Insel 8311
Quiet site on shore of Lake Attersee; divided into two sections by River Seeache. Family site.
Entrance below B152 towards Steinbach at Km 24.5; about 300 m from fork with B151.
15 May–15 Sep.
1.8HEC fH L lau A33 V20 20 A15–20

UNTERPERFUSS
Tirol (05227)

Farm (05232)2209
Modern site on gently sloping meadow.
W end of village near Amberg railway and main road.
All year.
3HEC fH G S lau A45 V30 30 A30

VIENNA See **WIEN**

VILLACH
Kärnten (04242)

At **FAAK AM SEE** (10 km SE)

Strandcamping Anderwald 2297

Austria

Situated in pine forest near private beach.
From Villach approach via Drobollach and Egg to the site of E shore of Faaker See.
15 May–Sep.
3HEC fH L lau

Strandcamping Florian (04254)2261
A partially shaded site between the lakeside and the road.
Access from road by Hotel Fürst.
May–25 Sep.
2HEC fH G L lau A50–55 V25–30 30 A30

VOLDERS
Tirol (05224)

Schloss 2333
Well detached grassland site with lovely trees.
Access from the B171 by ARAL filling station or from motorway exit Schwaz or Wattens.
Etr–15 Oct.
2HEC fH G R P lau

VÖLS BEI INNSBRUCK
Tirol (05222)

Völs 303533
May–Oct.
3HEC fH lau R A40 V30 30 A30

WALCHSEE
Tirol (05374)

Seespitz 5359
Site made up of several plots of land.
Between B172 and bank of lake.
All year.
2HEC fH G L lau A50 V50 50 A50

Terrassencamping Süd-See 5339
Extensively terraced site, the lowest are reserved for tourers.
500 m W on B172 turn into 'no through road' and continue for 1500 m.
All year.
11HEC fH G R L lau A45 pitch60

WEER See **SCHWAZ**

WEISSBRIACH
Kärnten (04286)

Alpendorf 346
Access from Hermagor–Ilkmen road B87 5 km S of lake; turn by bridge then site is 300 m.
May–Sep.
1.5HEC fH R

WIEN (VIENNA)
Niederösterreich (0222)

See also **LAXENBURG, RAPPOLTENKIRCHEN**

Wien-Süd Brietenfurter Str 269 869218
Park-like site with interior roads and tall trees.
7 km from town centre in district Wien 23, also access from the Klest Kir.
21 May–9 Sep.
3HEC fH G lau

Wien-West 11 Hüttelbergstr 80 942314
On slightly rising meadow with asphalt paths.
From end of A1/E5 (Leinz–Wien) to Bräuhausbrucke, then turn left and across road to Linz, continue for approx. 1.8 km.
All year.
2.7HEC fH G P lau

See advertisement on p 96

At **RODAUN** (4 km SW)

Schwimmbad-Camping-Rodaun An der Au 2 884154
Between An der Austr and Leising River dam. Access from Breitenfurter Str N492.
20 Mar–16 Nov.
1.5HEC fH G P lau A40 V12 47–50 A40–47

WIESING
Tirol (☎05244)

Inntal-Stadt ☎2693

Partially terraced site on sloping grassland.

Access via Wiesing–Zillertal–Achensee exit on A12 in direction of Achensee.
All year.

1.8HEC lau

ZAMS
Tirol (☎05442)

Zams Magdalenaweg 1 ☎3289

3 km NE of Landeck on B1.
15 Jun–Aug.

0.2HEC A27 V16 20–40 20–40

ZELL AM SEE
Salzburg (☎06542)

Prielau ☎2115

Site on open meadowland on N shore of Lake Zeller.

Austria

Access off B311 N of the town in the direction of Thumersbach.
15 Dec–15 Oct.

2.4HEC A36 V18 35–40 25–30

ZELL AM ZILLER
Tirol (☎05282)

Hofer Gerlospasstr ☎2248

On meadowland with some fruit trees.

Site lies to the end of Zillertal off the road leading to the Gerlos Pass,
All year.

1.5HEC lau

ZINKENBACH
Oberösterreich (☎06138)

Terrassencamping Schönblick ☎2471

A terraced site with birch trees. Beautifully situated with views of St Wolfgang and the lake.

Turn off B158 between Zinkenbach and Strobl in direction of landing stage.
May–Oct.

1.4HEC lau A30 V12 30 30

ZIRL
Tirol (☎05228)

Alpenfrieden ☎27204

Near the B171.
15 Apr–15 Oct.

1HEC

BELGIUM

Namur is dramatically set at the foot of a steep hill

Belgium is a small, densely populated country bordered by France, Federal Republic of Germany, Luxembourg and the Netherlands. Despite the fact that it is heavily industrialised, it possesses some beautiful scenery, notably the great forest of the Ardennes. The resorts in the Oostende area offer a selection of wide, safe, sandy beaches and cover about forty miles of coastline.

The climate is temperate and similar to that of Britain. The variation between summer and winter is lessened by the effects of the Gulf Stream. French is spoken in the south, Flemish in the north and a German dialect in the eastern part of the province of Liège.

HOW TO GET THERE

Many cross-Channel ferries operate direct from Dover to Oostende or from Dover, Felixstowe and Hull to Zeebrugge. Alternatively, it is possible to use the shorter Channel crossings from Dover to France and drive along the coastal road to Belgium. Fast hovercraft services operate from Dover to Calais and Boulogne.

GENERAL INFORMATION

(see also *Things you need to know*. pages 33–64)

Boats

(see page 33 and *Customs regulations* page 57)

British Embassy/Consulates

(see also page 57)
The British Embassy is located at *1040 Bruxelles* Britannia House, 28 rue Joseph II ☎(02)2179000; consular section 32 rue Joseph II ☎(02)2179000. There are British Consulates with Honorary Consuls in Antwerpen and Liège.

Camping

Belgium is a varied charming country in which to spend a camping holiday, the rivers and gorges of the Ardennes contrasting sharply with the rolling plains which make up the rest of the countryside. There are now over 500 campsites officially authorised by local authorities. They are normally open from April to October, but some are open throughout the year. Coastal sites tend to be very crowded at the height of the season.

International camping carnet not compulsory but recommended. Some campsites will allow a reduction in the advertised charge to the holders of a camping carnet. See page 37 for further information.

Off-site camping is prohibited beside public roads for more than 24 consecutive hours, on seashores, within a 100-metre radius of a main water point, or on a site classified for the conservation of monuments. Elsewhere, camping is permitted free of charge, as long as the stay does not exceed 24 hours and the camper has obtained authorisation from the landowner.

Currency including banking hours

(see also page 57)
The unit of currency is the Belgian Franc (*BFr*) divided into 100 *Centimes*. At the time of going to press £ = *BFr* 60.55. Denominations of bank notes are *BFr* 50, 100, 500, 1,000, 5,000; standard coins are *BFr* 1, 5, 20 and *Centimes* 50. There are no restrictions on the amount of Belgian or foreign currency which may be taken in or out of Belgium.

Banks are open Monday to Friday from 09.00–15.30hrs; some close during the lunch hour and others remain open until 16.00hrs on Friday. Outside banking hours, currency may be changed in Bruxelles at special offices at the Gare du Nord and the Gare du Midi, open 07.00–22.00hrs daily and at Zaventem Airport, open 07.30–22.00hrs daily.

Customs regulations

A *Customs Carnet de Passages en Douane* is required for all pleasure craft temporarily imported by road, except craft without motors not exceeding 18ft (5.5 metres) in length, and for trailers not accompanied by the towing vehicle. See also *Customs regulations for European countries* page 57 for further information.

Foodstuffs

(see also page 60)
Visitors from EEC countries may import duty-free 1,000 g of coffee or 400 g of coffee extract and 200 g of tea or 80 g of tea extract bought duty and tax paid; a reduced allowance applies if bought duty-free. Visitors under 15 years of age do not qualify for the duty-free concessions on coffee.

Medical treatment

(see page 60)

Shopping hours

All shops are usually open from 09.00–18.00, 19.00 or 20.00hrs from Monday to Saturday however, food shops may close 1hr later.

Tourist information

(see also page 63)
The Belgian Tourist Organisation is at 38 Dover St. London W1X 3RB. Their telephone number is 01-499 5379 and they will be pleased to supply information on all aspects of tourism. In Belgium the national Tourist organisation is supplemented by the Provisional Tourist Federation, whilst in most towns there are local tourist offices. These organisations will help tourists with information and accommodation.

Visitors' registration

(see page 63)

MOTORING

(see also *Things you need to know*, pages 33–64)

Accidents

(see also page 46)
Fire and **ambulance** ☎900; **police** ☎901 (and also 906 in Antwerpen, Bruxelles, Brugge, Charleroi, Gent, Liège and Mechelen).

Breakdowns

(see page 48)

Dimensions and weight restrictions

Private **cars** and towed **trailers** or **caravans** are restricted to the following dimensions – height: 4 metres; width: 2.50 metres; length (including any coupling device) up to 2,500kg 8 metres, over 2,500kg 10 metres. The maximum permitted overall length of vehicle/trailer or caravan combination is 18 metres.

Trailers without brakes may have a total weight of up to 50% of the weight of the towing vehicle (unladen) with a maximum of 750kg.

Driving Licence

(see also page 33)
A valid UK or Republic of Ireland licence is acceptable in Belgium. The minimum age at which a visitor may drive a temporarily imported car or motorcycle is 18 years.

Lights

(see page 50 also *Headlights* page 41)

Motoring club

(see also page 61)
The *Touring Club Royal de Belgique* (TCB) has its head office at *1040 Bruxelles* 44 rue de la Loi ☎(02)2332211 and branch offices in most towns. The Bruxelles head office is open weekly 09.00–18.00hrs; Saturday 09.00–12.00hrs. Regional offices are open weekdays 09.00–12.30hrs (Monday from 09.30hrs) and 14.00–18.00hrs; Saturday 09.00–12.00hrs. All offices are closed Saturday afternoons and Sundays.

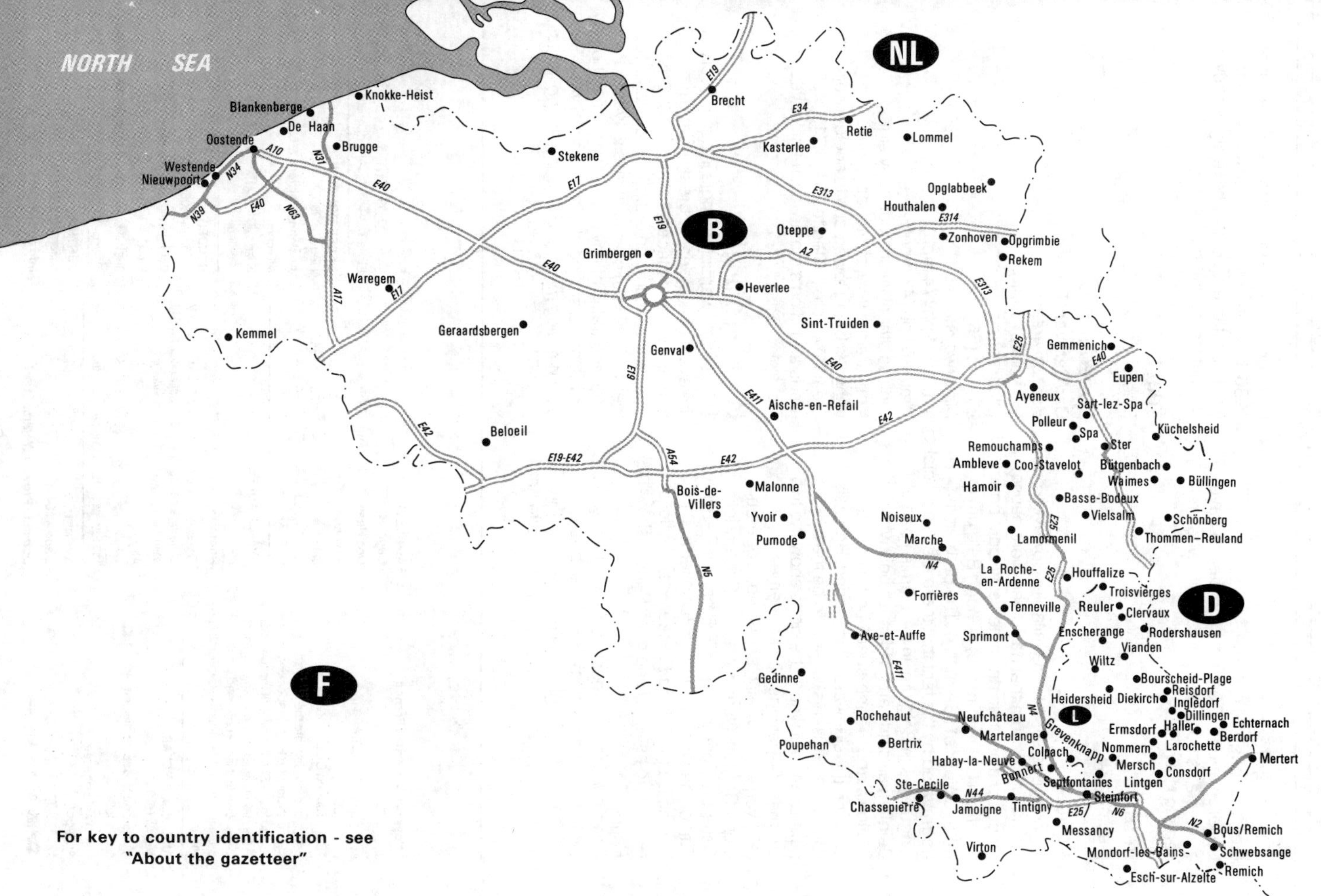

For key to country identification - see "About the gazetteer"

Passengers

(see also page 51)
Children under 12 are not permitted to travel in a vehicle as front seat passengers when rear seating is available.

Petrol

(see page 61)

Roads

A good road system is available. However, one international route that has given more cause for complaints than any other is, without doubt, that from Calais (France) through Belgium to Köln (Cologne) (Germany). The problem is aggravated by the fact that there are two official languages in Belgium; in the Flemish part of Belgium all signs are in Flemish only while in Wallonia, the French-speaking half of the country, the signs are all in French. Brussels (Bruxelles-Brussels) seems to be the only neutral ground where the signs show the two alternative spellings of placenames (Antwerpen-Anvers; Gent-Gand; Liège-Luik; Mons-Bergen; Namur-Namen; Oostende-Ostende; Tournai-Doornik. From the Flemish part of the country, Dunkirk (Dunkerque) in France is signposted *Duinkerke* and Lille is referred to as *Rijsel* and even Paris is shown as *Parijs.*

Road number changes A new numbering system, retaining the prefix N, has been introduced for Belgian main roads, with the exception of N1-N5 which retain their original numbers. The changeover took place during 1986, but some irregularities may still occur when the same road may have signs showing two different numbers.

Seat belts

(see page 52)

Speed limits

Car/Caravan/Trailer
Built-up areas
*60 kph (37 mph)
Other roads
90 kpm (56 mph)
Motorways
max 120 kph (74 mph)
**min 70 kph (43 mph)
*unless otherwise indicated by signs.
**on straight level stretches.
Vehicles being towed due to accident or breakdown are limited to 25 kph (15 mph) on all roads and, if on a motorway, must leave at the first exit.

Warning triangle

The use of a warning triangle is compulsory in the event of accident or breakdown. The triangle must be placed 30 metres (33 yds) behind the vehicle on ordinary roads and 100 metres (109 yds) on motorways to warn following traffic of any obstruction; it must be visible at a distance of 50 metres (55 yds). See also *Warning triangles/Hazard warning lights* page 54.

Prices are in Belgian Francs

Abbreviations:

av	avenue	rte	route
r	rue	str	straat
TCB	Touring Club de Belgique		

Belgium is divided into the Flemish region in the north and the French-speaking Walloon region in the South. Some of the town names in the gazetteer show both languages, and that shown first is the one used locally. Brussels (Bruxelles/Brussel) is officially bi-lingual.

AISCHE-EN-REFAIL
Namur (☎081)
Manoir de là Bas rte de Gembloux 180 ☎655353
5 km W of Eghezée.
Apr–Oct.
24HEC ▥ ◑ ⋒H ⚐ ▼ |O| ⊙ ⚑ ⩯P ⚠ ⊞ A40 V28 ⚑48 ▲48

AMBLÈVE
Liège (☎080)
Oos Heem Deidenberg 124 ☎349692
All year.
3HEC ▥ ◑ ⋒H ⚐ ▼ |O| ⊙ ⚑ Ⓖ Ⓡ ⊞ ⩯P ⚠ ⊞ lau A75 Vn/c ⚑75 ▲50–75

AVE-ET-AUFFE
Namur (☎084)
Roptai Roptai 32 ☎388319
The site is located in a hilly situation in pretty clearings amidst a large forest about 1 km along a dusty track from the village.
All year.
10HEC ▥ ◑ ⋒H ⚐ ▼ |O| ⊙ ⚑ Ⓖ Ⓡ ⌂ ⊞ ⩯P ⚠ ⊞ lau

AYENEUX
Liège (☎041)
Domaine Prov de Wegimont ☎771020
Feb–Dec.
3HEC ▥ ◑ ⋒H ▼ |O| ⊙ Ⓖ ⚠ ⊞ lau ⊖→ ⚐ ⩯P pitch200–275

BASSE-BODEUX
Liège (☎080)
Ancienne Barrière ☎684538
All year.
4HEC ▥ ◑ ⋒H ⚐ ▼ |O| ⊙ ⚑ ⚠ lau

BELOEIL
Hainaut (☎069)
Orangerie r du Major ☎689190
Etr–Oct.
3HEC ◑ ⋒H ⚐ ▼ |O| ⊙ ⚑ ⚠ ⊞ lau pitch245 (incl 4 persons)

BERTRIX
Luxembourg (☎061)
Info r de Mortehan 12 ☎412281

A terraced site on the edge of woodland with pleasant views.

Turn W off the N184 and continue for 1.5 km.
Apr–14 Nov.

0.9HEC ◆ H P ⊞ lau

BLANKENBERGE
West-Vlaanderen (050)

Dallas 418157

Mar–Sep.

3HEC H S

BOIS-DE-VILLERS
Namur (081)

Haute Marlagne r L-Fernand 22 433533

1 km from village. 200 m from main road.
Apr–Sep.

1HEC H ⊞ lau
A57 V40 40 40

BONNERT
Luxembourg (063)

Officiel rte de Bastogne 304 226582

E of E9–N4.
May–Sep.

1.4HEC H P
⊞ A77 V10 18 12

BRECHT
Antwerpen (03)

Het Veen Eekhoorlaan 1 6630165

Sports complex and mini zoo.

Leave Autoroute E10 at exit St Job in't Goor.
Apr–Sep.

7HEC ◆ H
A55 pitch80

BREDENE See **OOSTENDE (OSTENDE)**

BRUGGE (BRUGES)
West-Vlaanderen (050)

St-Michiel Tillegemstr 55 380819

2 km N of Autoroute E5 on W side of road.
All year.

6HEC H
⊞ lau L A65 V80 80
80

See advertisement page 102

At **LOPPEM** (5 km S. S of E5)

Lac Loppem 822264

Beautifully situated on a small lake with swimming facilities (also available to visitors).

At Brugge exit on Autoroute E5. Procede from E5 about 500 m towards Tourhout Entrance to site on right of ESSO filling station.
All year.

Belgium

14HEC ◆ H
L ⊞ lau

BÜTGENBACH
Liège (080)

Worriken Worriken 1 446358

Situated on the shores of a lake.

All year.

◆ H R
L ⊞ pitch293 (incl 4 persons)

BÜLLINGEN (BULLANGE)
Liège (080)

Hétraie r en Forêt 264 647703

This site is situated on a sloping meadow near a fish pond and is surrounded by groups of beautiful beech trees and conifers.

Leave village in direction of Amel then left and continue for 2 km.
All year.

3HEC ◆ H
P ⊞

CHASSEPIERRE
Luxembourg (061)

Cabrettes r de la Semois 7 312994

1 Apr–30 Sep.

23HEC H
⊞ lau R A59 V47 47 47

COO-STAVELOT
Liège (080)

Cascade chemin Faravennes 5 684312

Apr–Sep.

1.2HEC ◆ ◇ H
R ⊞ A53 V53 53
53

DE Each name preceded by 'De' is listed under the name that follows it.

EUPEN
Liège (087)

Hertogenwald Destr 78 743222

All year.

4.5HEC H ⊞
R

Hill Huette 40 744617

All year.

0.9HEC H
⊞ lau

FORRIÈRES
Luxembourg (084)

Pré du Blason r de la Ramée 80 212867

This well-kept site lies on a meadow surrounded by wooded hills and is completely divided into pitches and crossed by rough gravel drives.

Off N49 Masbourg road.
Apr–Sep.

3HEC H R
R ⊞ A51 V28 39 39

GEDINNE
Namur (061)

Melezes rte Dinant-Bouillon 588560

Etr–Oct.

1.5HEC ◆ H
A37 V29 37 37

GEMMENICH
Liège (087)

Kon Tiki Terstraeten 46 785973

All year.

12HEC H
P lau pitch400 (incl 4 persons)

GENVAL
Brabant (02)

Paul Charles 6535098

7.5HEC H ⊞

GERAARDSBERGEN
Oost-Vlaanderen (054)

Gavers Wolvenhoek Onkerzelestr 280
416324

All year.

6.5HEC ◆ H
L ⊞ lau pitch225

GRIMBERGEN
Brabant (02)

Grimbergen Veldkantstr 64 2692597

Apr–Oct.

0.3HEC H ⊞
P A70 V50 100
100

HAAN (DE)
West-Vlaandęren (059)

Townsend Thoresen Bredeweg 115
234475

Level subdivided grassland site behind a bungalow village.

Off the N72 Blankenberge/Oostende road.
Etr–Aug.

8HEC H
P ⊞ lau A100 V60 120
120

Belgium

HABAY-LA-NEUVE
Luxembourg (☎063)

RACB r du Bon-Bois 3 ☎42 312

Parklike, terraced site on a hill surrounded by woodland.

Turn off N48 and follow signs.
All year.

4.5HEC ◆ lau pitch220

HAMOIR-SUR-OURTHE
Liège (☎086)

Dessous Hamoir r de Moulin 31 ☎388925

All year.

◇ lau A47 V35 52 49

HEVERLEE
Brabant (☎016)

Ter Munck Kampingweg ☎238668

Leave Autoroute E5 at Leuven exit, then follow signs 'Leuven West' for 200 m.
15 Jun–15 Sep.

2.5HEC A48 pitch70

HOUFFALIZE
Luxembourg (☎062)

Chasse et Peche rte de la Roche 2 ☎288314

All year.

1.8HEC ◆ lau A75 V50 55 50

Moulin de Rensiwez Rensiwez 1 ☎289027

All year.

5HEC pitch400 (incl 4 persons)

Viaduc rte de la Roche ☎289067

All year.

4HEC pitch400 (incl 4 persons)

HOUTHALEN
Limburg (☎011)

Hengelhoef ☎382500

1 Apr–30 Sep.

15HEC ◆ lau pitch215–400

JAMOIGNE
Luxembourg (☎061)

Faing ☎311687

A municipal camp on a meadow situated behind a sports ground which separates the site from the road.

400 m W on N44.
15 Mar–Nov

5HEC A40 V40 20 20

KASTERLEE
Antwerpen (☎014)

Houtum Houtum 51 ☎556255

All year.

6HEC lau A62 V35 65 65

KEMMEL
West-Vlaanderen (☎057)

YPRA Pingelaarstr 2 ☎444631

Apr–Sep.

3HEC ◆

KNOKKE-HEIST
West-Vlaanderen (☎050)

Vuurtoren Heistlaan 168 ☎511782

On level meadow with tarred roads.

Turn S off Knokke-Oostende road 4 km from Knokke and follow signposts.
15 Mar–15 Oct.

6HEC ◇ lau pitch300 (incl 4 persons)

Zilvermeeuw Heistlaan 166 ☎512726

Mar–15 Nov.

7.5HEC ◇ lau A75 V25 50 50

At **WESTKAPELLE** (3 km S)

Holiday Natienlaan 70–72 ☎601203

Apr–Sep.

0.8HEC

KÜCHELSCHEID
Liège (☎080)

Küchelscheid Rickshelderweg 6 ☎446057

Situated in a wooded valley on a long, gently-sloping meadow with some terraces.

0.5 km SW of the frontier post Kalterherberg/ Küchelscheid.
15 May–Oct.

2HEC ◆ A40 V30 60 50

LA Each name preceded by 'La' is listed under the name that follows it.

LAMORMENIL
Luxembourg (☎086)

Euro Lamormenil ☎455350

All year.

3HEC ◆

LOMMEL
Limburg (☎011)

Luna Strand Luikersteenweg 313A ☎643708

On Leopoldsburg road (N446).
Apr–Sep

52HEC ◆ A68 V24 149 149

LOPPEM See **BRUGGE**

MALONNE
Namur (☎081)

Trieux r des Trieux 99 ☎445583

Apr–Oct.

1.8HEC ◇ lau A51 V34 34 34

MARCHE-EN-FAMENNE
Luxembourg (☎084)

Euro Camping Paola r du Panorama 10 ☎311704

A long site on a hill with a beautiful view. The only noise comes from a railway line, which passes right by the site.

Take road towards Hotton, turn right after cemetery and continue 1 km.
All year.

13HEC A59 V41 41 41

MARTELANGE
Luxembourg (☎063)

Vive Eau ☎600353

Leave N46 at the church, continue NW for 300m.
15 Mar–2 Nov.

4HEC A68 V47 65 65

MESSANCY
Luxembourg (☎063)

Lac r d'Arlon 52 ☎377129

All year.

13.5HEC lau

NEUFCHÂTEAU
Luxembourg (☎061)

Lac rte de Florenville ☎277615

All year.

◇ H ⊙ Ⓖ Ⓡ ⊞ lau ⊖ ♀ |O| L A40 V20 40 Å40

NIEUWPOORT
West-Vlaanderen (☎058)

Info Brugsesteenweg 49 ☎236037

A family site. Facilities for watersports.

On N67 between St Joris and Nieuwpoort.
3 Apr–15 Nov.

23HEC ◆ H ♀ |O| ⊙ P ⊞ lau pitch520 (incl 4 persons)

NOISEUX
Namur (☎086)

Noiseux r Chasseurs Ardennais ☎322586

All year.

2.1HEC ◆ H ♀ |O| ⊙ Ⓡ P ⊞ A52 V47 47 Å47

OOSTENDE (OSTENDE)
West-Vlaanderen (☎059)

At **BREDENE** (5 km NE)

Duinenpolder Duinenstr 198 bis ☎324202

All year.

3HEC H ♀ ⊙ ⊞ S A85 V21 84 Å84

KACB Camping Kon Astridlaan 53 ☎322475

Only Camping Carnet holders admitted.

Level grassland site on outskirts of village between other sites.

Off the N72 Oostende/Blankenberge road. Signposted in Bredene, 5 km NE of Oostende.
All year.

6.4HEC ◆ H ⊙ S ⊞ pitch210

OPGLABBEEK
Limburg (☎011)

Jeugdparadijs Speeltuinstr 4 ☎854587

Apr–Sep.

8HEC ◆ ◆ H ♀ |O| ⊙ P ⊞ lau A55 V35 55 Å55

OPGRIMBIE
Limburg (☎011)

Kikmolen ☎764619

2 km NW.
Mar–Oct.

30HEC ◆ H ♀ |O| ⊙ L ⊞ A45 V25 35 Å35

OTEPPE
Liège (☎085)

Hirondelle Château d'Oteppe ☎711131

Apr–Sep.

48HEC ◆ H ♀ |O| ⊙ Ⓖ Ⓡ P ⊞ lau A40 V30 60 Å60

POLLEUR
Namur (☎087)

Polleur r de Congrès 90 ☎541033

Apr–1 Nov.

3HEC ◇ H ♀ |O| ⊙ Ⓖ P lau A80 V80 80 Å80

POUPEHAN
Luxembourg (☎061)

Houlifontaine r des Sneviots ☎467315

Etr–Oct.

10HEC ◆ H ♀ |O| ⊙ R ⊞ A40 V26 26 Å26

PURNODE
Namur (☎082)

Bocq av de la Vallée 1 ☎612269

Apr–Sep.

2HEC ◆ ◆ H ♀ |O| ⊙ R ⊞ A55 V50 50 Å50

REKEM
Limburg (☎011)

Sonnevijer Heidestr 101 ☎713048

4 km S of Autoroute E39, exit 'Lanaken'.

All year.

30HEC ◆ H ♀ |O| ⊙ LP ⊞ lau A100 V100 100 Å100

REMOUCHAMPS
Liège (☎041)

Eden rte de Trois Ponts 92 ☎846313

Apr–15 Nov

3.2HEC ◆ H ⊙ ⊞ A58 V58 78 Å78

Idéal av de la Porallée ☎844419

On SW outskirts between river, railway and road behind SHELL petrol station.
Apr–Oct.

1.5HEC ◆ H ⊙ ⊞ A48 V48 78 Å78

RETIE
Antwerpen (☎014)

Berkenstrand Brand 78 ☎377590

3 km NE on road to Postel.
Apr–Sep.

10HEC ◆ H |O| ⊙ ⊞ ⊖ L A48 V41 48 Å48

ROCHE-EN-ARDENNE (LA)
Luxembourg (☎084)

Benelux r de Harze 14 ☎411559

Etr–Sep.

7HEC ◆ H ⊙ Ⓖ Ⓡ r ⊖ ♀ |O| P A53 V45 71 Å71

Florial rte de Houffalize 18 ☎411207

15 Mar–Sep.

8.5HEC ◆ H ♀ |O| ⊙ ⊞ lau ⊖ R A41 V28 41 Å41

Grillon r de Harzé 30 ☎412062

Apr–Oct.

3HEC ◆ H ♀ |O| ⊙ R A44 V38 44 Å44

Lohan rte d'Houffalize 20A ☎411545

In a park, on N bank of the River Ourthe.
Mar–Oct.

6HEC ◆ H ♀ |O| ⊙ L ⊞ A41 V31 39 Å39

Belgium

Ourthe ☎41159

Well-kept site, beside the River Ourthe.

On SW bank of the Ourthe below the N34.
15 Mar–10 Oct.

2.5HEC H R A43 V35 42 42

ROCHEHAUT
Luxembourg (☎061)

Laviot r Laviot 7 ☎466314

Apr–Oct.

6HEC H R lau A36 V25 25 25

SINT-TRUIDEN (ST-TROND)
Limburg (☎011)

Egel Bautershovenstr 97 ☎687637

Apr–Oct.

1.1HEC H A40 V35 40 35

STE-CECILE
Luxembourg (☎061)

Semois rte de Chassépierre 5 ☎312187

Apr–15 Oct.

3HEC H R A55 V48 48 48

SART-LEZ-SPA
Liège (☎087)

Touring Club (TCB) r Stockay 7 ☎474400

Signposted. The site lies to the E of Spa.
All year.

6HEC H

SCHÖNBERG
Liège (☎080)

Echo des Bois r en Forêt ☎548222

Spread over two valleys in wooded surroundings.

Turn W off N26 at Km 11.1 and continue for 0.5 km.
Apr–15 Nov.

3HEC H P lau

SPA
Liège (☎087)

Parc des Sources av de la Sauvenière 141 ☎772311

S of town centre on N32.
20 Mar–Jan.

2.7HEC H A69 V58 69 69

SPRIMONT
Liège (☎041)

Tultay r Fond Leval 22 ☎821621

Apr–Sep.

4HEC H A60 pitch45

STEKENE
Oost-Vlaanderen (☎03)

Eurocamping Baudeloo Heirweg 159 ☎7796663

All year.

3HEC H P A40 V25 30 25

Reinaert Lunterbergstr 4 ☎7798525

All year.

5HEC H lau A42 V32 32 32

STER
Liège (☎087)

Francopole ☎275099

In a secluded position beside the Eau Ronge River.

Off N32 in Francorchamps to Ster and Verviers, then turn right.
All year.

10HEC H lau

TENNEVILLE
Luxembourg (☎084)

Pont de Berguème r Berguème 9 ☎455443

Turn off E40/N4 towards Wyompont then turn right.
All year.

3HEC H G R RP A45 V45 45 45

THOMMEN-REULAND
Liège (☎080)

Hohenbusch Luxemburgstr 44 ☎227523

All year.

5HEC H G P lau A70 V70 70 70

TINTIGNY
Luxembourg (☎063)

Chenefleur chemin Ansart-Han ☎444078

15 Mar–15 Oct.

5HEC H P lau R A48 V42 42 42

VIELSALM
Luxembourg (☎080)

Casseroles ☎418808

All year.

0.4HEC H G R P A50 V100 150 100

VIRTON
Luxembourg (☎063)

Info r du Bonlieu ☎5701

Apr–14 Nov.

8HEC H P L

WAIMES
Liège (☎080)

Anderegg r Bruyères 4 ☎679393

Slightly sloping grassland site.

Entrance on outskirts of Bruyères at Km 11.4 km on N27.
All year.

2HEC H G A52 V45 45 45

WAREGEM
West-Vlaanderen (☎056)

Gemeentelijk Sportstadion Westerlaan ☎686289

Apr–Sep.

1HEC H P

WESTENDE
West-Vlaanderen (☎058)

Evergreen Lombardsijdelaan 171 ☎234804

200 m from the Lombardsijde centre.
Apr–Sep.

1.3HEC H R S pitch300 (incl 4 persons)

KACB Duinendorp Bassevillestr 81 ☎237343

Situated between Westende and Lombardsijde towards the sea.

All year.

6.6HEC H sP lau A89 V53 63 63

TCB (TCB) Lombardsijdelaan 153 ☎233797

All year.

6HEC H G S

WESTKAPELLE See **KNOKKE-HEIST**

YVOIR
Namur (☎082)

Repos r du Baty Bauche ☎611861

Beautiful site on bank of River Bocq.

4 km E on right bank of River Bocq.
Apr–Sep.

0.8HEC H G

ZONHOVEN
Limburg (☎011)

Berkenhof Teutseweg 33 ☎814439

Etr–15 Oct.

3.5HEC H A38 V24 38 38

Holsteenbron Hengelhoefseweg 7 ☎813727

All year.

6HEC H P lau

DENMARK

The banks of the River Gudenå in Jutland seem to invite campers

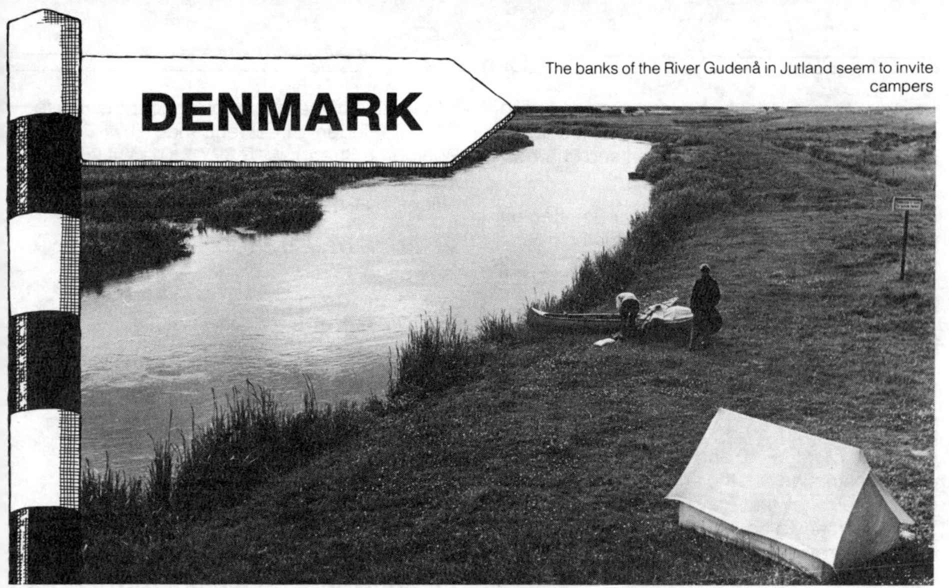

Denmark, the smallest of the Scandinavian countries, consists of the peninsula of Jutland and over 500 islands of various sizes, some inhabited and linked to the mainland by ferry or bridge. It is a low-lying country, its fertile lands broken by beech woods, small lakes and numerous fjords.

The climate is mild and equable similar to that of southern Scotland, although a little more extreme. Danish is the national language, but English is widely spoken as a second language. German and French will often be understood, but less frequently spoken, particularly in country areas.

HOW TO GET THERE

The two main ways of reaching Denmark are either by using the direct ferry service from Newcastle or Harwich to Esbjerg in western Jutland, Harwich to Hirtshals in northern Jutland, or by using one of the short Channel crossings to France or Belgium and driving through the Netherlands and northern Germany to Denmark. The distance from the Channel ports to København (Copenhagen) is roughly 660 miles and the journey would require one or two night stops.

Another possibility is to use the ferry operating between Harwich and Hamburg and drive the short distance to southern Denmark.

Inter-island travel is made easy by either bridge links or frequent vehicle ferries.

GENERAL INFORMATION

(see also *Things you need to know*. pages 33–64)

British Embassy/Consulates

(see also page 57)

The British Embassy together with its consular section is located at *DK-2100 København* Kastelsvej 36–40 ☎(01)264000. There are British Consulates with Honorary Consuls in Åbenrå, Ålborg, Århus, Esbjerg, Frederica and Odense.

Camping

Denmark has over 600 campsites approved and classified by the National Camping Committee, which have the approval of the health authorities. They are visited regularly by campsite inspectors to ensure that the required standards are maintained. Approved sites display a green wigwam symbol and the words *godkendt lejrplads*. The sites owned by the Danish motoring organisation (FDM) can only be used by members of the FDM and of motoring organisations affiliated to the Alliance Internationale de Tourisme (AIT). At most sites no noise is allowed between 22.00 and 07.00hrs. These sites close at 22.00hrs and early arrival is therefore advisable. Sites are usually open from May to September.

International camping carnet is compulsory on non-FDM campsites. When camping on FDM sites the carnet is advisable as it provides proof of AA membership. Generally campsites do not allow any reductions in the advertised charge. See page 37 for further information.

Off-site camping overnight is only permitted on private ground and only with permission from the owner.

Currency including banking hours

(see also page 57)
The unit of currency is the Danish Krone (*Dkk*) divided into 100 *Øre*. At the time of going to press £ = *Dkk* 11.10. Denominations of bank notes are *Dkk* 20, 50, 100, 500, 1,000; standard coins are *Dkk* 1, 5, 10 and *Øre* 5, 10, 25. There are no restrictions on the amount of foreign or Danish currency that may be imported. Visitors may export any amount of foreign or Danish currency provided:
a the foreign currency exported was declared on entry;
b the Danish currency exported was imported or obtained by conversion of imported foreign securities.

In København banking hours are 09.30–16.00hrs Monday, Tuesday, Wednesday and Friday and Thursday 09.30–18.00hrs. At the Central Railway Station and the Air Terminal banks are open until 22.00hrs. Outside København banking hours are generally 09.30–12.00hrs and 14.00–16.00hrs. All banks are closed on Saturdays, except Exchange offices on the Danish/German border which close between 13.00 and 15.00hrs. These offices may also open on Sunday during the summer.

Foodstuffs

(see also page 60)
Visitors over 15 years of age entering from an EEC country may import duty-free 1,000g of coffee or 400g of coffee extract and 200g of tea or 80g of tea extract; a reduced allowance applies in respect of visitors entering from a non EEC country.

Medical treatment

(see page 60)

Shopping hours

Shops are usually open between 09.00 and 17.30hrs (19.00hrs or 20.00hrs on Fridays). Most shops close on Saturday afternoons.

Tourist information

(see also page 63)
The Danish Tourist Board maintains an information office in London at Sceptre House, 169/173 Regent Street (entrance New Burlington Street), W1R 8PY ☎01-734 2637/8. In Denmark the Danish Tourist Board has offices in all main towns.

Visitors' registration

(see page 63)

MOTORING

(see also *Things you need to know*, pages 33–64)

Accidents

(see also page 46)
Fire, police, ambulance ☎000

Breakdowns

(see page 48)

Dimensions and weight restrictions

Private **cars** and towed **trailers** or **caravans** are restricted to the following dimensions – height: 4 metres; width: 2.50 metres; length: 12 metres. The maximum permitted overall length of vehicle/trailer or caravan combination is 18 metres.

Trailers without brakes may have a total weight of up to 50% of the weight of the towing vehicle; trailers with brakes may have a total weight up to 90% of the weight of the towing vehicle.

Driving Licence

(see also page 33)
A valid UK or Republic of Ireland licence is acceptable in Denmark. The minimum age at which a visitor may drive a temporarily imported car or motorcycle is 17 years.

Lights

(see page 50 also *Headlights* page 41)

Motoring club

(see also page 61)
The *Forenede Danske Motorejere* (FDM) has its headquarters at *2100 København Ø* 124 Blegdamsvej ☎(01) 382112 and branch offices are maintained in major towns throughout the country. The offices are usually open between 09.00 and 17.00hrs from Monday to Friday. During the summer the headquarters and many branch offices are open on Saturday to personal callers between 09.00–12.00hrs.

Petrol

(see page 61)

For key to country identification - see "About the gazetteer"

Roads

The roads in Denmark are generally of a very high standard and well signposted. They are classified into three categories, showing E-roads (green and white signs with prefix 'E'), primary roads (one or two digit black numbers on yellow boards) and secondary roads (three digit black numbers on white boards).

Seat belts

(see page 52)

Speed limits

Car
Built-up areas
50 kph (31 mph)
Other roads
80 kpm (49 mph)
Motorways
100 kph (62 mph)

Car/caravan/trailer
Built-up areas
50 kph (31 mph)
Other roads
70 kph (43 mph)
Motorways
70 kph (43 mph)
On-the-spot fines for exceeding the limits are very expensive.

Warning triangle

The use of a warning triangle is compulsory in the event of accident or breakdown. The triangle must be placed at least 50 metres (55 yds) behind the vehicle on ordinary roads and 100 metres (109 yds) on motorways to warn following traffic of any obstruction. See also *Warning triangles/Hazard warning lights* page 54.

Prices are in Danish Kroner
Abbreviations:
DCU Danske Camping Union
FDM Forenede Danske Motorejere

ÅBENRÅ
Jylland (☎04)

Åbenrå Vandererhjemmet Sønderskovvej 100 ☎622699

The site belongs to the local tourist association and lies in a semi-circle around a hill. It is partly terraced and divided by hedges.

For access turn off the E3 at the Åbenrå Fjord, near the CHEVRON petrol station, and drive inland. There is a youth hostel next to the site entrance.
All year.

2.4HEC H lau s **pp**29

ABILDØRE See **VIG**

AGERNÆS STRAND
Fyn (☎09)

Flyvesandet (DCU) ☎871320

The site lies on dunes interspersed with small pine trees.

From Odense turn N via Otterup and Krogsbølle. Turn off on Agerna road then take Flyvesandet road and continue for 3 km.
Etr–27 Sep.

7.7HEC H sR **pp**29

ÅLBÆK
Jylland (☎08)

Albæk Strand (FDM) Jerupvej 2 ☎488261

Site composed of large single pitches in a sand-dune area alongside an extensive sandy beach.

Access is S of road no. 40 near BP petrol station at Km 19.8.
May–1 Oct.

11HEC H lau s **pp**26

Bunken ☎487180

Very well-kept site in woods belonging to the Danish Forestry Commission. It is completely divided into pitches.

6 km N of town, off road no. 40 towards Skagen.
15 May–15 Sep.

14HEC H lau s **A**29

Limfjords Strandrej 5 ☎(07)560250

Grassland site subdivided by hedges and shrubs. Separated from the beach by a narrow stretch of grass and the promenade.

All year.

12.5HEC H sP lau **A**23–29

Skiveren ☎932200

Etr–Sep.

18HEC H lau s **pp**22

ALLINGE
Bornholm (☎03)

Sandkås ☎980441

Situated on a meadow, sheltered from the wind. Rocky coast not suitable for swimming.

2 km S of town.
15 May–15 Sep.

4HEC H lau sP

ALS
Jylland (☎08)

Havbakker (FDM) ☎581099

3 Apr–10 Sep.

1.2HEC H s

ÅRHUS
Jylland (☎06)

Århus Nord Randersvej 400 Lisbjerg ☎231133

The site lies in two hollows which are well protected from noise and wind, with sections surrounded by tall pine hedges and divided into pitches. There are a few terraces on the slopes between the two hollows.

4 km N of town, off the E3.
All year.

7HEC H P lau **pp**25

K C Blommehavn Orneredevej 15 ☎270207

In Marselisborg Forest on Århus bay. On sloping ground with paths and steps down to the bay.

From Århus drive towards the harbour and continue along the coast to the site.
mid Apr–Aug.

8HEC H lau s **pp**27

ÅRØSUND
Jylland (☎04)

Årøsund ☎584297

A well-designed site, mostly on level ground, and divided into sections. There are modern sanitary installations.

All year.

4.5HEC H lau s **pp**28

Denmark

ASSENS
Fyn (☎09)

Willemoes Naesvej ☎711543

1 May–15 Sep.

3.7HEC ◆ ⌂H ⊙ G R ⊞ lau ⟶ s
pp30

BALKE STRAND
Bornholm (☎03)

Balke Strand (FDM) ☎988074

Site in two parts in a pine forest on the lovely Bornholm bathing beach.

Well signposted from Snogebæk and Balke.
25 Apr–7 Sep.

3HEC ◆ ⌂H ⊙ R
lau ⟶ s

BANDHOLM
Lolland (☎03)

FDM ☎888485

On coast, near station.
10 Apr–10 Sep.

s ⟶ |O| **pp**30

BJERGE STRAND
Sjælland (☎03)

Bjerge Strand (FDM) Osvejen 30 ☎497028

3 Apr–12 Sep.

2.7HEC ⌂H ⊙ R
s lau

Urhøjgard ☎497200

Partly sloping site, subdivided by shrubs and separated from the beach by a stretch of pine woodland.

Turn off the Slagelse–Kalundborg road Km 23.1 in direction of Bjerge Strand and then 1 km to site.
Etr–Oct.

9HEC ◆ ⌂H |O| ⊙ G

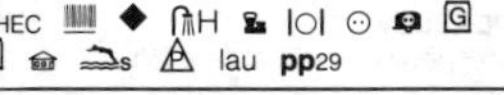

BLÅVAND
Jylland (☎05)

Hvidbjerg Strand ☎279040

On unshaded terrain set out around a former farm. Separate section for teenagers. Children's play area.

S of Osksby.
Apr–Oct

12HEC ⌂H |O| ⊙
G R ⊞ lau ⟶ s
pp29

BLOKHUS
Jylland (☎08)

Blokhus Ålborgvej 62 ☎249096

A large popular site sheltered by sand-dunes and a wood.

Turn off road no. 55 N of Pandrup onto road no. 559 and drive through Hune to Blokhus in 2 km.
Etr–15 Sep.

⊞ lau ⟶ |O| s **pp**29

BØJDEN
Fyn (☎09)

Bøjden ☎601284

The site lies on a field which is only partly sheltered from the wind and approx. 500 m from the Fynshav (Als) Ferry landing stage.

Etr–15 Sep.

4.5HEC ◆ ⌂H |O| ⊙
G R s ⊞ lau **pp**29

BORNHOLM (ISLAND OF) See **ALLINGE, BALKE STRAND, DUEODDE**

BORRE
Møns (☎03)

Møns Klint Klintevej 544 ☎812025

The site lies on several uneven meadows, surrounded by a forest. Separate section for young campers, fishing nearby.

Apr–Oct.

13HEC ◆ ⌂H ⊙ G R
P ⊞ ⟶ |O| **pp**32

BØTØ
Falster (☎03)

FDM Østersøparken ☎876786

Situated in a lovely, quiet position amidst woodland. Dunes separate the site from a wide beach.

Access from Nykøbing–Gedser road. Signed from Marrebæk.
Apr–14 Sep.

4.3HEC ◆ ⌂H ⊙ R
s ⊞ lau

BOULSTRUP
Jylland (☎06)

Hølken ☎556306

The site lies on meadowland which slopes gently down to the sea. It is divided into sections by rows of rose bushes. The long narrow beach is 100 m away.

From Odder and Sasald turn E to Hov and follow signposts.
Feb–Nov.

10HEC ◆ ⌂H ⊙ G R
⊞ lau ⟶ s **pp**26

BULBJERG
Jylland (☎07)

Skarrekilt Bulbjergvej ☎991128

N of Thisted–Ålborg road between Km 28 and Km 29.
15 Jun–15 Aug.

0.8HEC ◆ ⌂H |O| ⊙
lau **pp**21

COPENHAGEN See **KØBENHAVN**

DALBY
Fyn (☎09)

At **NORDSKOV** (8 km N)

Fyns Hoved ☎341014

On meadowland surrounded by close hedging and woodland. Very quiet. On NE point of Hindsholm peninsula.

Access is from Odense in NE direction via Munkebo and Dalby. From Nordskov continue N for 1.5 km.
Etr–15 Sep.

10HEC ⌂H ⊙ G
R ⊞ lau ⟶ |O| s

DRAGSTRUP
Jylland (☎07)

Dragstrup ☎744249

In natural pleasant terrain of pine woodland with some pitches on an open meadow.

Access is from the Nykøbing–Thisted road.
Etr–15 Sep.

3.8HEC ◆ ⌂H ⊙ G
R ⊞ lau ⟶ s **pp**28

DUEODDE
Bornholm (☎03)

Dueodde ☎988149

The site lies in the grounds of a youth hostel, near a beautiful beach in the S of the island amongst woodland and sand dunes. The site is very popular and crowded during the peak season. Adjoining the site is a car park for beach visitors. Each camper receives a key to sanitary blocks.

For access, take the southern coast road from Rønne to the Rønne–Nexø junction. Turn off SE towards Dueodde and follow signposts.
Jun–15 Sep.

4HEC ◆ ⌂H ⊙ G R
⊞ lau ⟶ |O| s **pp**30

ELSEGÅRDE
Jylland (☎06)

Blushoj ☎341238

This well-equipped site lies above the steep coast, on the side of the peninsula facing the Kattegat, on hilly land with sand dunes. There are pitches on and between the dunes and part of the site is pleasantly laid out with flowerbeds. The pebble beach is accessible via steps.

15 Apr–15 Sep.

9.5HEC ◆ ⌂H ⊙ G R
⊞ lau ⟶ s **pp**28

ESBJERG
Jylland (☎05)

Sjælborg ☎115432

On meadowland. Separate sections for residential vans and tourers.

At Ho Bay off the coast road towards Sjælborg.
15 Apr–15 Sep.

10HEC ◆ ⌂H ⊙ G R
⊞ lau ⟶ s

Strandskovens Gammel Vardevej 76 ☎125816

In the town next to a swimming pool and tennis court.

Parties of young people are not admitted without a responsible leader.
5 minutes from the ferry terminal.
15 May–15 Sep.

3.5HEC ◆ ⌂H ⊙ G R
⊞ lau ⟶ |O| P
pp28

FAKSE LADEPLADS
Sjælland (☎03)

Fed ☎825206

The site lies on a level meadow on a narrow strip of land leading to the Feddet peninsula, opposite a large bathing area. It is divided into many sections by hedges and bushes and almost completely surrounded by pine forests.

Approx. 5 km S of Fakse Ladeplads.
Apr–Oct.

9.6HEC ◆ H G R lau s

FÅREVEJLE
Sjælland (☎03)

KC Sandobberne Kalundborgvej 28 ☎453535

Between the sea and the Rudköbing road at Km 47.
Apr–15 Sep.

6HEC ◆ H G R s lau |O| **pp**27

FARSØ
Jylland (☎08)

Ertebølle ☎636375

On slightly rising grassland, next to the road, divided by hedges. Separate room for young campers. Pool open to the public. Well equipped children's play area.

On road S33, Viborg–Løgstør. Signposted
Apr–Sep.

3HEC ◆ H G R LRP lau |O| **pp**29

FJELSTRUP
Jylland (☎04)

At **KNUD**

Sandersvig ☎586225

A small site divided into pitches by hedges situated away from the beach, near a lonely farmstead in a quiet setting.

From Haderslev turn off E3 to Fjelstrup and continue for 5 km.
Apr–Sep.

8HEC ◆ H G R P lau s

FJERRITSLEV
Jylland (☎08)

Westpark Feriecenter ☎211800

This site is set amongst dunes and tall pines, adjoining the Kollerup plantation, near an hotel with a restaurant and discotheque.

Access 2 km NE of town towards the Svinkløv.
Mar–Dec.

4.5HEC ◆ H |O| P lau

FREDERICIA
Jylland (☎05)

Trelde Naes ☎957183

Well-kept site in a beautiful setting in a nature reserve. NE of Fredericia, above the steep coast and overlooking the Vejle Fjord. The beach is accessible via rather steep

Denmark

steps.

From Fredericia follow the coast road through Trelde for 4 km.
Apr–Oct.

10HEC ◆ H |O| G R lau s **pp**29

Trelde Sande (FDM) ☎957059

From Fredericia via Egeskov and Trelde villages.
12 Mar–9 Sep.

2HEC ◆ H G R s **pp**24

FREDERIKSHAVN
Jylland (☎08)

KC Nordstrand Apholmenvej 40 ☎429350

A local authority site situated on level, grassy ground close to a small wood on the outskirts of the town. Pitches are divided and facilities are modern.

Signposted from the E3 in Frederikshavn.
Apr–Sep.

9HEC ◆ H |O| G R lau s **pp**29

FREDERIKSSUND
Sjælland (☎03)

Frederikssund Omkørselsvejen ☎311423

900 m from Kronpins–Frederiks bridge; opposite Willsumen Museum.
Etr–15 Sep.

2.2HEC ◆ H G R lau |O| s

FURREBY
Jylland (☎08)

Løkken (FDM) Kirkevej 97 ☎991236

May–15 Sep.

2.6HEC ◇ H R s

FYNSHAV
Als (☎04)

Lillebælt ☎464332

The site covers a well-kept, partly sloping grass area divided into several sections bushy hedges.

If approaching from Sønderborg, take road no. 8 and drive to Fynshav. Take Mommark road and after approx. 300 m turn towards the beach.
20 Apr–Sep.

3HEC ◆ H G R lau |O| s **pp**28

GJERRILD
Jylland (☎06)

Gjerrild Nordstrand Langholmvej 26 ☎384200

A level, grassy site near the beach.

Signposted.
Etr–Sep.

10HEC ◆ H G R lau s

GRÆRUP
Jylland (☎05)

Grærup (FDM) ☎277049

Undulating terrain subdivided into sections by hedges and fencing which provide protection from the wind.

2 km W towards sea.
20 Apr–Aug.

2.5HEC H G R lau s

GRENÅ
Jylland (☎06)

KC Polderrev Fuglsangvej 58 ☎3217

A modern, pleasantly landscaped site level ground in a nature reserve, at the edge of a wood on the sand dunes. Separate section for tents and caravans each with its own sanitary block. Special washing cubicle for invalids. Spin driers and ironing facilities.

For access, drive towards the harbour past the Hotel du Nord, or coming from Århus, following signposts 2 km before Grenå.
Mar–25 Oct.

9HEC H |O| G R lau s **pp**30

At **STENSMARK**

Fornæs Stensmarkvej 36 ☎332330

The site lies on meadowland surrounded by fields sloping down to a quiet bay overlooking the sea.

Drive N from Grenå harbour, past Fornæs lighthouse and continue along the coast for 1 km.
Apr–Oct.

9.2HEC ◆ H G R s lau **pp**30

HADERSLEV
Jylland (☎04)

KC Haderslev Christiansfeldvej ☎527880

Meadowland surrounded by trees and shrubs.

N of town between E3 and Christiansfeldvej.
May–Aug.

1HEC ◆ H P lau **pp**25

Sønderballe Strand Djernaesveg 218 ☎698933

Etr–15 Sep.

3.7HEC ◆ H R lau Ls **pp**28

Vikær Strand Dundelum 29 ☎575464

Apr–Sep.

12HEC ◆ ◇ H G R s lau |O| **A**24 **V**n/c 10 10

HALS
Jylland (☎08)

Hals Strandvejen 14 ☎251425

NE on Fredrikshavn road.
Etr–15 Sep.

2.5HEC ◆ H R lau s **pp**28

HANSTHOLM
Jylland (07)

Hanstholm Hamborgvej 95 965198

Site is set in extensive meadowland and dunes with pines providing protection against the wind. View of the sea.

400 m from the beach.
Mar–Sep.

8HEC H P lau s **pp**29

HEGEDAL STRAND
Jylland (06)

Hegedal Strand (FDM) 317750

North of Hegedal; on beach.
May–Sep.

2.2HEC H G R s lau **pp**27

HEJLSMINDE
Jylland (05)

Hejlsminde Strand 574374

Site on slightly sloping meadowland with pleasant views 600 m from sea.

Turn off E3 about 4 km beyond Haderslev and continue via Fjelstrup to Hejlsminde.
Apr–15 Sep.

5HEC H |O|

HELNÆS
Fyn (09)

Strandbakkerls, Ebberup 771339

SW of Helnæs. 200 m from beach.
Apr–15 Oct.

2HEC H |O| G R lau s **pp**28

HELSINGØR
Sjælland (03)

Grønnehave Sundtolvej 9 215856

Sloping terrain between railway line and promenade within sight of sea. The site lies beyond several factory buildings. Out of season, the site is used by longstay campers.

For access from Kronberg harbour follow the Hornbæk road.
All year.

1.9HEC H G R lau |O|

HINDSGAVL
Jylland (09)

Hindsgavl (FDM) Søbadevej 10 415542

Site situated on level meadowland partially terraced with some fruit trees and surrounded by woodland on three sides.

From Kolding turn off the E66 near the SHELL filling station about 150 m beyond the old bridge over the Lille Bælt and continue for 200 m.
30 Mar–15 Sep.

2HEC H G R s

HINNERUP
Jylland (06)

Denmark

Hår Tåstrupvej 14 985847

On a terraced wooded hollow surrounded by a small wood above the Lilliå Stream. Good views across hills. Common room for children.

Turn off 6 km N of Århus on E3 in direction of Hinnerup–Hår.
Apr–Sep.

8HEC H G R P lau

HIRTSHALS
Jylland (08)

Hirtshals 942535

Situated on the Skagerrak below the lighthouse with a good view out to sea.

Approach from road no. 13 in direction of Fyr (lighthouse) to the site in 0.8 km.
15 Apr–15 Sep.

3HEC H G R lau s **pp**23–29

At **TORNBY** (6 km S)

Tornby Strand 977007

Spacious site in area of sand dunes and a nature reserve, protected from the wind by hedging and fences.

Take road no. 13 (Hjørring–Hirtshals) and turn left by the SHELL petrol station.
All year.

11HEC H |O| G R lau s

HJALLELSE See **ODENSE**

HJARBÆK
Jylland (06)

Hjarbæk 642309

By the Hjarbæk fjord on slightly sloping grassland.

NW of Viborg about 1.5 km via rough road.
Etr–15 Sep.

10HEC H |O| G R P lau

HJØLLUND
Jylland (06)

Hærvejens Ro Hovej 13 869011

All year.

0.1HEC H |O| G R lau **pp**17

HOBRO
Jylland (08)

Gattenborg 523288

This Tourist Office site has well-tended terraces offering lovely views of the town and its surrounds. There are four circular hollows for individual campers.

From the village follow Skive signs up the hill and past a dairy for the site.
Apr–Sep.

3HEC H |O| G

R P lau P **pp**23–29

HOLSTEBRO
Jylland (07)

Mejdal (DCU) 422068

Situated by the Storå River dam on a large well-kept and sloping meadow which is divided into several sections by rows of bushes and trees.

Access is from the bypass (which links the road no's. 11, 16 and 18) in the direction of Ringkøbing.
All year.

6HEC H G R P lau |O| **pp**29

HORBELEV
Sjælland (03)

Bregninge Bøgevang 10 845219

Peaceful location in rural and wooded country.

15 Apr–1 Sep.

3.3HEC H G R lau **pp**28

HOV
Langeland (09)

Hov Nordstrand (FDM) Vesterled 2 551880

N of Hov on beach.
30 Mar–15 Sep.

4.4HEC H G R lau s

HVALPSUND
Jylland (08)

Hvalpsund Overgaden 24 638123

A level grassy site divided into pitches by straw matting and separated from the beach by a strip of conifers.

Next to pine woodland. Well signposted.
15 May–15 Sep.

6HEC H P lau **pp**29

Stistrup 636176

In meadowland divided by hedges into separate fields, with numbered pitches. A belt of trees along the roadside provides protection against the wind. Swimming pool is open to the public.

Access from Viborg–Løgstør road at km 39.5
Etr–Sep.

6.5HEC H |O| G R P lau s **pp**29

HVIDE SANDE
Jylland (07)

Holmsland Klit Tingodden 141 (FDM) 311309

A modest site in pleasant dune country.

Access is S of Hvide Sande at Km27.8 of the Ringkøbing coast road.
20 Apr–Aug.

5HEC H G R s

Nordsø Tingodden 3 ☎311722

On level meadowland amidst dunes, this site is divided by a small fence and hedges.

6 km S of town.
Etr–Sep.

6HEC ◇ H ⊙ G R sP ⊞ lau **pp**30

ISHØJ

Sjælland (☎02)

Tangloppen ☎540767

May–8 Sep.

◇ H ⊙ G R s ⊞

JELLING

Jylland (☎05)

Friluftsbadets ☎871653

Located on meadowland next to a modern heated swimming pool.

Access from Vejle drive north on road no. 18 to Jelling and on outskirts turn into the Mølvangsvej.
15 Apr–15 Sep.

6.7HEC ◆ H |O| ⊙ G R P ⊞ lau **pp**23–29

JUELSMINDE

Jylland (☎05)

Juelsminde (FDM) ☎693210

Not far from the harbour. Protected from the wind and subdivided by groups of trees and hedges.

SE on beach.
Apr–20 Sep.

3.5HEC ◆ H ⊙ R G s ⊞ lau **pp**28

KARREBÆKSMINDE

Sjælland (☎03)

Hvide Svaner ☎742415

Caravan pitches are protected by hedges; sanitary blocks lie next to the tent area and the rates include hot showers and swimming pool. Well organised with dances and first class restaurant.

7 km SW of Næstved.
All year.

12HEC ◆ H |O| ⊙ G R P ⊞ lau **pp**29

KELDBY See **STEGE**

KELSTRUP STRAND

Jylland (☎084)

Kelstrup Strand ☎582246

Gently sloping site in meadowland divided by hedges.

Access is 8 km S of Haderslev, turning off road no. 170 in Hoptrup.
15 Apr–15 Sep.

2HEC ◇ H R ⊞ lau

KLIM STRAND

Jylland (☎08)

Klim Strand Havvejen 167 ☎225340

The site lies on a meadow between the coast road and a sandy beach. It is divided into large sections by hedges and fences which also provide shelter from the wind.

In Klim turn off onto the beach road and continue for 4.5 km.
Apr–15 Sep.

24HEC ◆ H |O| ⊙ G R ⊞ lau **pp**25

KLITMØLLER

Jylland (☎07)

Nordsø Vangsavej 25 ☎975071

Extensive well kept site among sand dunes with deep hollows providing shelter from wind. Fine beach. Bathing facilities for invalids.

At second crossroads in town take Vangså road and continue 150 m.
15 May–15 Sep.

1HEC ◆ H ⊙ R s ⊞ lau **pp**29

KNUD See **FJELSTRUP**

KØBENHAVN (COPENHAGEN)
(☎01)

Absalon (DCU) Kordalsvej Rødovre ☎410600

Divided into large pitches by low hedges.

The best approach is from the main railway station/tourist information office. Follow the Vesterbrogade and Roskildevej (signed Kosør) to the Korsdalsvej crossroads, situated by tower blocks and MOBIL filling station. The entrance lies 100 m away near BP filling station. Access from other directions is made difficult by bad signposting on ring road.
All year.

13HEC ◆ H ⊙ G R ⊞ lau |O| P

At **NÆRUM** (11 km NW)

Nærum (DCU) Ravnebakken ☎(02)801957

On Helsingør road.
11 Apr–13 Sep.

5.5HEC ◆ H ⊙ G R ⊞ lau **pp**29

KØGE

Sjælland (☎03)

Vallø Strandvej 102 ☎652851

The site lies in a wood of tall pine and oak trees, out of which many individual pitches of various sizes have been cut.

1.5 km S. 1 km from E4.
Apr–15 Sep.

10HEC ◆ H ⊙ G R ⊞ lau |O| s **pp**29

KOLDING

Jylland (☎05)

Vonsild Vonsildvej 19 ☎531853

Site lies in meadow broken by high trees and conifers. Adjoins bowling-alley.

Located 2 km S then E off E3.
All year.

2.5HEC ◆ H |O| ⊙ ⊞ lau **pp**30

KOLLUND

Jylland (☎04)

Kollund (FDM) Fjordvejen 29 ☎678515

Grassland site, partially sloping, divided by the coastal road.

From frontier follow E3, turn onto road no. 8 and drive several hundred metres towards Sønderborg, turn right and continue 4 km. Signposted from Km4.9 of the coastal road to Sønderborg.
3 Apr–24 Oct.

3.6HEC ◈ H ⊙ R lau R **pp**27

KORSØR

Sjælland (☎03)

Lystskov Skovvej 122 ☎570725

The site lies between Korsør Skov and road no. 150. Its well-kept field is divided into many sections by hedges.

15 Apr–15 Sep.

1.6HEC ◆ H ⊙ G R ⊞ lau |O| **pp**26

KRAKÆR

Jylland (☎06)

Krakær Gl-Kærvej 18 ☎362118

On several fields linked by asphalt road amid woods and heathland. Well protected from wind. There is a motel adjacent.

Access from Århus through Femmøller, turn off to Lyngsbæk and continue for 2 km.
All year.

8HEC ◆ H |O| ⊙ R G P ⊞ lau **pp**28

KRUSÅ

Jylland (☎04)

Frigård ☎678830

The large site, which is divided by low hedges, lies on undulating meadowland surrounded by trees. Playing fields, playgrounds and a miniature motorway.

Coast road 4 km E of Kruså.
All year.

15HEC ◆ ◈ H ⊙ G R ⊞ lau |O| s **pp**28

Grænse ☎671206

Grassland area subdivided by hedges.

All year.

10HEC ◆ H |O| ⊙ R P ⊞ lau

KULHUSE

Sjælland (☎03)

Kulhuse ☎330186

Situated near Islefjord in partly hilly grassland with some terraces and hedges.

From Frederikssund drive N for 17 km for site just before the Kulhuse–Sølager ferry.

Apr–20 Oct.
6HEC H lau

LAVEN See **SILKEBORG**

LEMVIG
Jylland (☎07)

K C Lemvig Vinkelhage ☎820042

Situated in meadowland and split into several sections. Well protected by 2 m high fence and a hedge.

Turn off Vestergade at the harbour and drive N for 2 km.
Apr–Sep.
3HEC H G R lau P pp29

LØKKEN
Jylland (☎08)

At **ULSTRUP** (4 km N)

Gl Kiltgård Lyngbyvei 331 ☎996566

24 Apr–7 Sep.
H G R lau S

LØNSTRUP
Jylland (☎08)

Egelunds Rubjergvej 19–21 ☎960135

The site consists of several level fields separated by wooden fences. It is adjacent to a hillside on which there are holiday cottages.

Well signposted from southern entrance of the village.
15 May–15 Sep.

LUNDBY
Sjælland (☎03)

Svinø Strand ☎769212

Divided into several fields by low fences and hedges reaching down to beach parking area.

9 km N of Vordingborg in the direction of Svinø Strand.
15 Apr.–15 Sep.

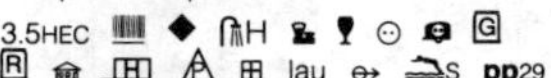

MARIAGER
Jylland (☎08)

Færgehagen ☎541342

Site in three parts on level meadowland surrounded by a wooden fence and wild rose bushes. Separated from the Mariager Fjord by a belt of reeds.

Signposted from bypass to the harbour.
Apr–Sep.

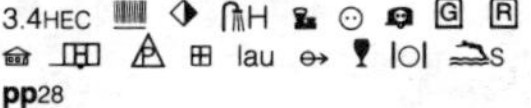

MARIBO
Lolland (☎03)

K C Maribo Bangshavevej 25 ☎880071

This municipal site lies next to the Søndersø.

From E4 at Maribo exit go to town centre and

Denmark

turn into Bangshavevej.
May–4 Nov.
6HEC H G R L pp29

MIDDELFART
Fyn (☎09)

Gals Klint ☎412059

Grassland site surrounded on three sides by woodland.

From Frederica turn right at bridge site 4 km.
10 Apr–Aug.
3HEC H S

At **RONÆS** (10 km SE)

Ronæs Strand Ronæsvej 10 ☎421763

Level meadowland with some trees. On the Gamborg Fjord.

Turn off Middelfart–Assens road in Udby and continue W to Ronaes for 2 km.
Apr–18 Sep.

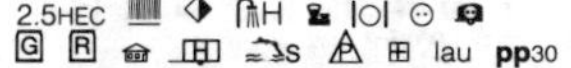

MØGELTØNDER See **TØNDER**

MOMMARK
Als (☎04)

Bellevue Fiskervej 17 ☎447208

Extensive, quiet site on meadowland with lovely view of Baltic Sea. High hedges divide the site into large pitches.

Etr–15 Sep.
5.3HEC H G R S lau
pp30

MØNSTED
Jylland (☎06)

Mønsted ☎645025

Level meadowland site subdivided by a number of hedges.

Access from Viborg direction is by road no. 16.
May–Oct.
1.8HEC H G R lau pp25

NÆRUM See **KØBENHAVN (COPENHAGEN)**

NEES
Jylland (☎07)

Nees Skalstrupvej 107 ☎884027

Site lies in a level field in secluded rural setting near the Nissumfjord.

For access take the Ringkøbing–Lemvig road.
May–15 Sep.
3.5HEC H G R P lau pp28

NIBE
Jylland (☎08)

Sølyst Logstørvej 2 ☎351062

The site lies on terraces which reach down to the road. Willow bushes offer some protection. Nearly all pitches are separated by low wooden barriers.

Situated 1 km W of town off the Løgstør road on the west bank of the Limfjordes.
All year.
3HEC H G R sP lau
pp29

NIVÅ
Sjælland (☎03)

Nivå Gl-Strandveg ☎245226

A meadowland site with close hedging and a small pond in the centre.

Apr–15 Sep.
2.6HEC H G R lau S

NORDBY ***Fanø***
(☎05)

Tempo Strandvej 34 ☎162251

Almost completely divided into squares, each one containing two pitches. There are separate sections for families and young people. Due to very good equipment and management, it is one of the best sites on the island. Opposite the site, there is a self-service shop and a gambling room, table tennis and billiard rooms. Excellent sanitary installations with dressing rooms.

W on Vesterhavsbadet road.
15 May–15 Sep.
5.5HEC H G R S lau P pp26

NORDBY ***Samsø***
(☎06)

Kiltgård ☎596169

On meadowland 10 m above sand and pebble beach.

1.5 km NE.
15.5HEC H lau S

NORDSKOV See **DALBY**

NØRRE SNEDE
Jylland (☎05)

Rørbæk Sø Rørbækveg 52 ☎736161

This holiday site is in the shape of a cloverleaf and is on the edge of a pine forest and a nature reserve.

Turn off road no. 13 in Nørre Snede and follow minor road for about 5 km towards Vesterlund
10 Apr–Sep.
5.5HEC H G lau pp27

NYKØBING ***Jylland***
(☎07)

Jesperhus Legindvej 30, Legindberge ☎723701

Modern holiday centre near the Jesperhus Blomsterpark in nature reserve. Large children's play areas. ➤

Approach from Nykøbing–Sallingsund in the direction of Blomsterpark.
28 Apr–4 Sep.
10HEC ▥ ◆ ⛰H ▪ ▾ |O| ⊙ ⊕ G R ⌂ ⩦P ⛺ ⊞ lau **pp**30

Morsø ☎721968
Beautifully situated site on level land. Divided into pitches; access to Limfjord. Camp is usually full in July, also weekends tend to be very busy.

From town centre follow signs to harbour then campsite signposts.
May–5 Sep.
1.6HEC ▥ ◆ ⛰H ▪ ⊙ ⊕ G R ⊞ ⛺ ⊞ lau ⊖→ ▾ |O| ⩦s **pp**26

NYKØBING *Sjælland*
(☎03)

Nykøbing Nordstrand (FDM)
Nordstrandvej 107 ☎411642
Site in woodland with clearings.

N on Nordstrand beach. Access from Nykøbing via Nordstrandvej.
27 Mar–14 Sep.
4.1HEC ▥ ◆ ⛰H ▪ ⊙ ⊕ R ⊞ ⩦s ⛺ ⊞ lau

NYSTED
Lolland (☎03)

Nysted ☎871411
1 km from town centre.
24 Apr–15 Sep.
2.1HEC ▥ ◆ ⛰H ▪ ▾ |O| ⊙ ⊕ G R Ⓟ ⊞ lau ⊖→ ⩦s **pp**30

ODENSE
Fyn (☎09)

At **HJALLELSE**

K C Odense Auto-Camping (DCU)
Odensevej 102 ☎114702
3.5 km S off road no. 9 towards Svendborg.
Apr–9 Sep.
4.5HEC ▥ ◆ ⛰H ▪ ⊙ ⊕ G R ⌂ ⛺ ⊞ lau **pp**29–31

OKSBØL
Jylland (☎05)

Oksbøl ☎271130
Etr–15 Sep.
2.5HEC ▥ ◆ ⛰H ▪ ⊙ ⊕ G R ⌂ ⛺ ⊞ lau ⊖→ ⩦P

ØSLØS
Jylland (☎07)

Bygholm Bygholmvej 27 ☎993139
Situated opposite motel and 300 m from northern shore of Lake Løgstør. Site is divided by several hedges and is sheltered from the wind.

Entrance is 100 m from MOBIL filling station.
15 Mar–Oct.
14HEC ▥ ◆ ⛰H ▪ ▾ |O| ⊙ ⊕ G R ⌂ ⊞ ⩦P ⛺ ⊞ lau ⊖→ ⩦s

ØSTER-HURUP
Jylland (☎08)

Toft ☎588032

Denmark

Site amongst dunes between coast road and beautiful beach. Separate sections for tents and caravans. Installations are excellent but some of the pitches are a considerable distance away. Children's play area.

At Km20.2 off coastal road.
Etr–15 Sep.
30HEC ▥ ◇ ⛰H ▪ ▾ |O| ⊙ ⊕ G R ⌂ ⊞ ⩦s ⛺ ⊞ lau **pp**29

RANDERS
Jylland (☎06)

Fladbro ☎429361
This grassland site which lies off the Fladbro road (6 km), is beautifully situated on a wooded hill and adjoins a golf course. It is divided into pitches by groups of pine trees.

Leave E3, drive through town and follow signposts to road no. 16.
Apr–15 Oct.
9.2HEC ▥ ◆ ⛰H ▪ ⊙ ⊕ G R ⌂ ⊞ ⛺ ⊞ lau **pp**25

RIBE
Jylland (☎05)

Ribe Farupvej ☎420887
Grassland site subdivided by shrubs.

Off road no. 11 N of the town about 1 km in direction of Farup.
Apr–15 Sep.
5HEC ⛰H ▪ ▾ |O| ⊙ ⊕ G R ⌂ ⊞ ⛺ ⊞ lau ⊖→ ⩦ **pp**26

RIIS
Jylland (☎05)

Fritidscenter ☎731433
Situated on grassland at edge of wooded area.

Access from town centre follow the Farre road.
May–7 Sep.
9HEC ▥ ◆ ⛰H ▪ ⊙ ⊕ G R ⌂ ⊞ ⛺ ⊞ lau ⊖→ ⩦P **pp**29

RINDBY
Fanø (☎05)

Feldberg Rindby Strand ☎163680
Site lies in a hollow surrounded by dunes near to beach. Divided by means of fences and bushes that also afford protection from the wind.

Etr–26 Oct.
2.7HEC ▥ ◆ ⛰H ▪ ⊙ G R ⌂ ⊞ ⛺ ⊞ lau ⊖→ ⩦s **pp**26

RINGKØBING
Jylland (☎07)

K C Ringkøbing Vellingvej 56 ☎320838
A well maintained municipal site subdivided into pitches by shrubs and situated between the coastal road and fjord.

For access drive from Ringkøbing towards Velling for 1 km.
Apr–Sep.
3.5HEC ▥ ◆ ⛰H ▪ ▾ |O| ⊙ ⊕ G R ⌂ ⊞ ⛺ ⊞ lau ⊖→ ⩦s **pp**28

RINGSTED
Sjælland (☎03)

Skovly Ortved ☎628261
7 km NE on the Roskilde road.
May–15 Sep.
3.5HEC ▥ ◆ ⛰H ▪ ⊙ ⊕ G R ⊞ ⛺ ⊞ lau **pp**27

RINKENÆS
Jylland (☎04)

Lærkelunden ☎650250
Site on well-tended grassland on two terraces partially subdivided on the gentle slope towards the bay.

Access from road no. 8, turn at Km 12 towards bay following signs. Site is near a large cafeteria.
Apr–1 Nov.
5HEC ▥ ◑ ⛰H ▪ |O| ⊙ ⊕ G R ⌂ ⊞ ⩦s ⛺ ⊞ lau ⊖→ ▾ **pp**29

RONÆS See **MIDDELFART**

ROSKILDE
København (☎03)

K C Roskilde – Vigen Strandpark
☎757996
This site lies on uneven, very hilly land overlooking the Roskilde Fjord.

N of town off A6 Hilerød road.
mid Apr–mid Sep.
27HEC ▥ ◆ ⛰H ▪ |O| ⊙ ⊕ G R ⌂ ⩦s ⛺ ⊞ lau **pp**28

RY
Jylland (☎06)

Birkhede Lyngvej 14 ☎891355
A well-kept site in a park-like setting on the slopes of a hill in the Knudsø.

Turn off road no. 15 at Mollerup and continue S, on unmade road.
May-15 Sep.
10HEC ▥ ◆ ⛰H ▪ ⊙ ⊕ G R ⌂ ⩦sP ⛺ ⊞ lau **A**20 **V**10 ⊕10 ⛺10

Holmens Klostervej 148 ☎891762
Well-kept site, laid out with flowerbeds.

On the Øm Kloster road S of town.
Apr–Sep.
5HEC ▥ ◆ ⛰H ▪ |O| ⊙ ⊕ G R ⌂ ⊞ ⩦s ⛺ ⊞ lau **pp**31

SÆBY
Jylland (☎08)

Hedebo Strand Frederikshavnsvej 108
☎461449
Meadowland divided by hedging with view of Baltic Sea. Traffic noise affects the quietness. Separate tent section.

2.4 km N of town on E3 Frederikshavn road.
All year.
10HEC ▥ ◆ ◑ ◇ ⛰H ▪ ▾ |O|

⊙ G R LP ⊞
lau pp29

Sæby Strand (FDM) Ndr Strandvej 69
☎463848

On meadowland sloping down to the beach.

2 km N of town on E3 Frederikshavn road.
Apr–15 Sep.

2.5HEC ◆ H ⊙ G R ⊞ S

SAKSKØBING

Lolland (☎03)

Sakskøbing Saxes Alle ☎894757

Grassy terrain divided into small fields by hedges.

Access from motorway Exit Sakskøbing continue along Nykøbingvej.
May–Aug.

1.5HEC ◆ H ⊙ G R ⊞ lau |O| P
pp28

SALTUM STRAND

Jylland (☎08)

Jambo Vesterhav Solvejen 48–60
☎881666

Holiday centre in quiet location on extensive meadowland which is divided into sections by hedges and wooden fences.

2km from beach. Separate section for tents and dog owners.
May–15 Sep.

13HEC ◆ H |O| ⊙
G R P ⊞ lau pp29

Saltum Strand Strandvej 141 ☎881159

Level open site on meadow, partly sheltered by pine forest.

May–1 Sep.

6HEC ◆ H |O| ⊙
G R ⊞ lau P pp29

SANDAGER

Fyn (☎09)

Sandager Næs Strandgårdsvej 12
☎791156

Site has own beach in Bay of Lille.

Apr–20 Sep.

2.5HEC ◆ H |O| ⊙
G R S ⊞ lau pp30

SEJERØ

Sejerø (☎03)

Sejerø Pedersberg ☎490138

NE of town near the beach.
All year.

2HEC ◆ H ⊙ G R
⊞ lau |O| S pp28

SEJS See **SILKEBORG**

SILKEBORG

Jylland (☎06)

K C Århus Bakken's Århusvej ☎822824

Level site on southern banks of Langsø, with numerous groups of trees.

Turn off road no. 15 in the direction of Silkeborg and continue for 2 km.
Etr–15 Sep.

Denmark

4HEC ◆ H ⊙ G R
L ⊞ lau |O| pp29

Jyllands–Ringen (FDM) Resenbro
☎853176

Extensive well tended site in wooded area above the Gudená valley. Partially on a hillock and garden-like in parts.

5 km E.
30 Mar–20 Oct.

10HEC ◆ H |O| ⊙ R
P lau

At **LAVEN** (12 km SE)

Askenoj ☎841282

Pleasant meadowland divided up on the edge of an extensive woodland area which protects the site from the west. Large sportsfield.

Turn off road no. 15 Århus–Silkeborg road in Linå–Bakke and continue S.
Apr–15 Sep.

3.5HEC ◇ H |O| ⊙
G R P Ⓟ ⊞ lau

At **SEJS** (6 km SE)

Sejs Bakker (FDM) Borgdalsvej 15
☎846383

A wooded site divided into sections by gravel paths and surrounded by hedges. 2 km to lakeside.

Access from Silkeborg; follow road towards Svejbæk. At the edge of Sejs at Km 13.2 turn left over the rarely used railway line, then 200 m to site.
27 Mar–18 Sep.

10HEC ◆ H ⊙ R
⊞ lau |O| pp27

SILKEBORG-VEST

Jylland (☎06)

Hesselhus (DCU) Funder ☎865066

Site divided into several sections by 1.5 m high dykes. Some pitches are in the shade and protected from the wind by the adjoining pine woodland.

From Silkeborg take road no. 15 towards Herning.
All year.

9.3HEC ◆ H ⊙ G R
⊞ lau |O| pp29

SKÆLSKØR

Sjælland (☎03)

Kildehus ☎594384

Site on level grassland between the Slagelsevej and Lake Noret, behind a small youth hostel.

Mar–Sep.

2.6HEC ◆ H |O| ⊙
⊞ pp27

SKAGEN

Jylland (☎08)

Grenen ☎442546

Partly wooded, divided by fences and hedges into numbered pitches.

N of town on road to Grenen.
May–Aug.

4.5HEC ◆ H ⊙ G R
S ⊞ lau |O| pp29

SØNDERHO

Fano (☎05)

Sønderhof Ny ☎164144

It is divided into pitches by shrubs and bushes.

2 km from the sea.
Etr–15 Oct.

5HEC ◆ H ⊙ G R
⊞ lau |O|

SPODSBJERG

Langeland (☎09)

Billevænge Spodsbjergvej 182 ☎501006

In a hollow with three terraces and partially surrounded by meadowland. Woodland adjoins one side of the site and there is a small ornamental lake in the centre.

1 km towards Rudkøbing.
May–20 Sep.

3.3HEC ◆ H ⊙ G R
⊞ lau |O| S pp28

Færgegårdens Spodsbjergvei 335
☎501136

On a field sheltered from the wind. The beach is narrow and stony, separated from the camp by a road to the ferry.

150 m from ferry terminus.
15 May–15 Aug.

3HEC ◆ H ⊙ G R
⊞ lau S pp 25

STAVNS See **TRANEBJERG**

STEGE

Møn (☎03)

At **KELDBY** (3 km NE)

Møns Familie ☎813456

In divided meadow surrounded by a hedge

100 m off Møns Klint road.
Etr–15 Sep.

4.8HEC ◆ H |O| ⊙
G R P ⊞ lau pp29

STENSMARK See **GRENÅ**

STRUER

Jylland (☎07)

Bredalsvig ☎861304

On level ground 100 m from beach.

N of town, 0.6 km beyond turning for Toftum Bjerge, turn right and follow signposts.
26 Apr–Aug.

20HEC ◆ H ⊙ G R
⊞ lau |O| S

K C Bremdal ☎851650

This well-kept and very popular site is divided into eighteen fields by wooden railings and completely enclosed by tall hedges. It lies next to a stadium and 50 m from a crowded beach. There is a good view of the town and harbour. ➤

From harbour take coast road N for 1.5 km.
May–15 Sep.

3HEC ◆ H lau s A28

STUBBEKØBING

Sjælland (03)

K C Stubbekøbing Gammel Landevej 841057

A well-kept municipal site in park-like setting. Separated from the sea-shore by a promenade.

May–Aug.

1.5HEC ◆ H lau s pp28

SVENDBORG

Fyn (09)

Carlsberg Sundbrovej 19 225384

Slightly sloping site divided by hedges.

From town centre follow road no. 9 over bridge to Tåsinge Island for Ny Nyby.
May–15 Sep.

6HEC ◆ H P lau s pp31

At **THURØ** (5 km SE)

Thurø (FDM) Smørmosevej 7 225384

On the edge of forestland and totally enclosed by hedges. Separated from the beach by a public play area.

The site is on the E side of the island of Thurø. From Svendborg follow signs 'Thurø'. Once on the island follow signs 'Grasten' and 'Camping'.
May–15 Sep.

5.5HEC ◆ H P lau s pp30

TANNISBY See **TVERSTED**

TARM

Jylland (05)

Lyne 250225

The site, on gently sloping land, is divided into many sections by young hedges and bordered on two sides by rows of pine trees.

For access take road no. 11, turn W near a farmhouse and continue for 1 km.

5HEC ◇ H P lau

TÅRUP-STRAND

Fyn

Mickleits 371199

Slightly hilly site divided into several sections by rows of low trees and hedges.

15 Apr–15 Sep.

6HEC ◆ H s lau pp28

THISTED

Jylland (07)

Thisted 921635

This clean and well-equipped site is divided into sections and lies on a very pleasant, completely enclosed meadow on the shores of the Limfjord.

Etr–Sep.

Denmark

3.2HEC ◆ H lau s pp29

THURØ See **SVENDBORG**

TJELE

Jylland (06)

Tjele Langsø 652312

This very popular site lies on gently sloping land on the south shore of Tjele Langsø. It borders a forest of pine and deciduous trees.

From Viborg continue on road no. 16 in easterly direction towards Randers. In 10km turn off for Hobro, then continue for 9 km via Tjele.
Etr–15 Sep.

4.4HEC ◆ H lau LP pp30

TØNDER

Jylland (04)

K C Tønder Holmevej 2A 721849

Municipal site in three sections next to swimming pool, tennis courts, stadium an indoor sports arena.

Access from road no. 11 at E end of town.
Etr–Sep.

1.6HEC ◆ H lau P pp26

At **MØGELTØNDER** (4 km W)

Møgeltønder 778460

A site with beautiful lawns surrounded by tall trees. Next to football ground.

Etr–Sep.

1.2HEC ◆ H lau

TORNBY See **HIRTSHALS**

TRANEBJERG

Samsø (06)

At **STAVNS**

Sælvigburgtens 590707

Situated on a meadow near the quiet Nordby road. Many of the pitches are screened by pine or willow trees.

Jun–30 Aug.

10HEC ◆ H lau s pp28

TRANEKÆR

Langeland (09)

Emmerbølle Strand 591226

Meadowland site divided into three large sections by rows of trees and surrounded by tall alder and poplar trees.

In Lejbølle at Km 16.8 turn off Rudkøbing Lohals road and continue 2 km to site.
29 Apr–15 Sep.

6HEC ◆ H

lau s pp29

TRUUST

Jylland (06)

Truust 871141

A quiet completely enclosed site in a small pine forest along the Gudenå.

Turn left off Århus road at Km37 in village and continue for 1.5 km.
All year.

5.5HEC ◆ H P lau pp29

TVERSTED

Jylland (08)

Aabo 931234

Situated on hilly grass and woodland on nature reserve which offers access to walkers.

Approach via Hirsthals–Skagen road. Turn towards beach in Tversted and in 500 m turn left to site.
May–Aug.

10HEC ◇ H lau sR

At **TANNISBY**

Tannisby 931250

The site lies off the road to the right behind a row of houses. It is divided into several sections by wooden fences. Modern sanitary installations with single wash places.

On road to beach, entrance is 1 km between houses.
15 Apr–15 Sep.

3.5HEC ◆ H lau A22 pitch20

ULBJERG

Jylland (06)

Ulbjerg Skrahedevej 6 697093

On hilly ground amidst beautiful heathland overlooking the Lorns Bredning in the Limfjord.

At Km23 turn off Viborg–Løgstør road towards site in 1.4 km (400 m is on unmade road).
Etr–15 Sep.

3.5HEC ◆ H P lau pp29

ULSLEV

Sjælland (03)

Gården 848350

This beautiful site lies in a nature reserve about 8 m above the sandy beach and is divided into several sections by hedges.

For access turn towards Horbelev on the southern outskirts of Nykøbing F, opposite SHELL petrol station. Turn again in Sdr. Vedbg, and drive towards Idestrupp, then to Sdr. Orslev and Ulslev.

6.4HEC ◇ H s lau

ULSTRUP See **LØKKEN**

VEDERSØ-KLIT
Jylland (☎07)

Campinggården ☎495160
Site lies in a meadow which is divided into several sections by hedges.
For access turn off road no. 6 in Ulfborg; in 9 km at Husby turn left for Vedersø-Klit.
All year.
2HEC 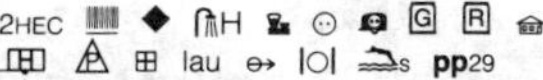 H lau pp29

Vedersø Klit ☎495202
Mainly open meadows, but partly wooded.
For access turn off road no. 16 in Ulfborg; in 9 km at Husby turn left for Vedersø-Klit, site entrance is opposite UNOX garage.
Apr–Oct.
5HEC H lau S

VEJBY
Sjælland (☎02)

Heatherhill Rågelejevej 37 (FDM) ☎306788
An extensive site on hilly meadowland which is divided into several fields and sheltered by bushes.
Access from København via Hillerød–Helsingør road to Vejby then on for 1 km.
27 Mar–19 Oct.
9.7HEC  H P lau

VEJEN
Jylland (☎05)

K C Vejen Vorupvænget 2 ☎362099
A completely enclosed municipal site sheltered from the wind and divided into pitches. Part of the site is pleasantly laid out with rose-beds and hedges. It lies on the SE outskirts of the village, near the E66 off Fugelsangsallee road.
Turn off the E66 between Km48.5 and BP filling station in direction of Haderslev and continue to site in 1.3 km.
Apr–28 Oct.
2.8HEC H lau P pp28

VEJERS STRAND
Jylland (☎05)

Schlüters ☎277036
Long strip of meadowland subdivided by wooden fences into three sections and sheltered on two sides by pine woods.
On outskirts of village behind ESSO garage.
Etr–23 Oct.
2.4HEC H lau pp30

Stjernelejrens ☎277054
Open level site divided into many sections by gravel paths and wire fences.
Near ESSO garage.
Apr–Sep.
6HEC H lau S pp27

VEJLE
Jylland (☎05)

K C Vejle Nørremarksvej 18 ☎823335
A well-kept site on hilly land at the edge of Nørreskov Forest. Protected from traffic noise by thick bushes.
N of town on E3.
15 Apr–15 Sep.
2.6HEC H lau pp29

VEMMETOFTE STRAND
Sjælland (☎03)

Vemmetofte ☎710226
The site lies in a nature reserve and is divided into many sections by young plants and surrounded by tall trees.
7 km E of Fakse and 1 km from Fakse Ladeplads road, near the beach.
All year.
5.6HEC H lau S pp29

VESTERVIG
Jylland (☎07)

Krik-Vig ☎941946
Partly in meadowland with wooded coppices.
Etr–15 Sep.
6.5HEC H lau S pp27

VIBORG
Jylland (☎06)

Viborg (DCU) Vinkelvej ☎611111
In a meadow on the Søndersø. Modern, well-maintained toilet facilities including bath for disabled.
Access is from road no. 16 in the direction of Randers, on E edge of town.
Apr–15 Sep.
4HEC H L lau pp29

VIG
Sjælland (☎03)

Vig ☎416227
Site uneven meadowland divided by shrubs.
Take local road to Høve for the sports and leisure centre.
Apr–Sep.
5HEC H lau SP pp30

At **ABILDØRE** (6 km SE)

Isefjordens ☎428710
All year.
3.25HEC H SR lau P pp30–32

VIPPERØD
Sjælland (☎03)

Paradisfjordens Kongvej 2, Ågerup ☎481060
All year.
4HEC H lau RP pp26

VORBASSE
Jylland (☎05)

Vorbasse (DCU) Drivvej 28 ☎333693
The site lies on level grassland at the edge of wooded country.
Turn S in the village for site.
All year.
3HEC H lau P pp29

VORDINGBORG
Sjælland (☎03)

Ore Strand Orevej 145 ☎770603
2 km SW.
All year
3HEC H S lau pp30

FRANCE

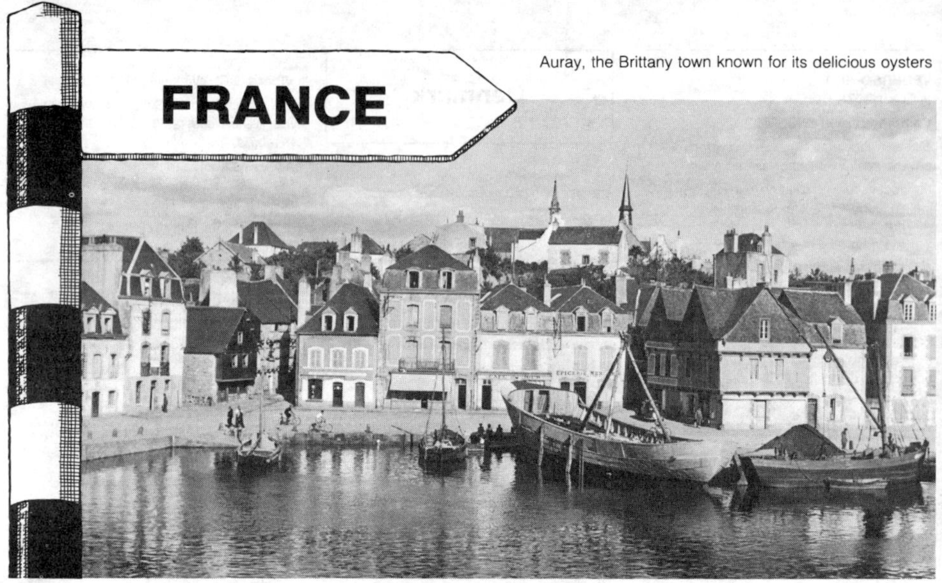

Auray, the Brittany town known for its delicious oysters

France, rich in history and natural beauty, is bordered by six countries: Belgium, Federal Republic of Germany, Italy, Luxembourg, Spain and Switzerland. The country offers a great variety of scenery from the mountain ranges of the Alps and the Pyrénées to the attractive river valleys of the Loire, Rhône and Dordogne. And with some 1,800 miles of coastline which includes the golden sands of the Côte d'Azur there is countryside appealing to everyone's taste.

The climate of France is temperate but varies considerably. The Mediterranean coast enjoys a sub-tropical climate with hot summers, whilst along the coast of Brittany the climate is very similar to that of Devon and Cornwall. The language is, of course, French and this is spoken throughout the country, although there are many local dialects and variations.

HOW TO GET THERE

Motorists can cross the Channel by ship or hovercraft services. Short sea crossings operate from Dover to Boulogne and Calais (1¼–1¾ hrs) and Folkestone to Boulogne (1¾ hrs). Longer Channel crossings operate from Ramsgate to Dunkerque (2½ hrs), Newhaven to Dieppe (4 hrs), Portsmouth to Le Havre (5½ hrs) or Caen (5½–6½ hrs) or Cherbourg (4–6½ hrs) or St Malo (9 hrs), Poole to Cherbourg (4½ hrs), Plymouth to Roscoff (6 hrs) and Weymouth to Cherbourg (4 hrs). Fast hovercraft services operate between Dover and Boulogne or Calais (30–35 mins).

GENERAL INFORMATION

(see also *Things you need to know*, pages 33–64)

Boats

(see page 33 and *Customs regulations* page 57)

British Embassy/Consulates

(see also page 57)

The British Embassy is located at *75008 Paris* 35 rue du Faubourg St-Honoré ☎42669142; consular section *75008 Paris* 16 rue d'Anjou ☎42669142. There are British Consulates in Bordeaux, Lille, Lyons and Marseilles; there are British Consulates with Honorary Consuls in Boulogne-sur-Mer, Calais, Cherbourg, Dunkerque, Le Havre, Nantes, Nice, Perpignan, St Malo-Dinard and Toulouse.

Camping

France has an enormous number of campsites, over 10,000 of them under the auspices of the French Federation of Camping and Caravanning. There are *castels et camping-caravanning* sites in the grounds of châteaux and many are included in this guide. A complete list of these sites can be obtained by AA members from Hotel and Information Services, Automobile Association, Basingstoke, Hants RG21 2EA. On sites in state forests *forêts domaniales* it is necessary to apply to the *garde forestier* for permission to camp and evidence of insurance must be produced (such as the *camping carnet*). Opening periods vary widely and some sites are open all year. Local information offices (see *Tourist information*) can supply detailed information about sites in their locality. During July and August there is over-demand around the French coasts, particularly on the Mediterranean.

All graded sites must display their official classification, site regulations, capacity and current charges at the site entrance. Some sites have inclusive charges per pitch, others show basic prices per person, vehicle and space, with extra facilities like showers, swimming pools and ironing incurring additional charges. In practice, most camp sites charge from midday to midday with each part day being counted as a full day. Reductions for children are usually allowed up to 7 years of age.

Camping information can also be obtained from 500 *Total* petrol service stations which have been equipped with information offices. The French radio station *France Inter* broadcasts special bulletins in English between 25 June and 25 August; transmitting on 1829 metres long wave the bulletins are after the news at 09.00hrs and 16.00hrs Monday to Saturday. Additionally the station maintains an advice line *Inter Service* in Paris between 09.00–18.00hrs which provides road and camping information in English ☎43061313.
International camping carnet not compulsory but recommended. However, a camping carnet is advisable when using *castels et camping-caravanning* sites and also the *forêts domaniales*. See page 37 for further information.
Off-site camping in the South of France is restricted because of the danger of fire; in other parts, camping is possible, provided that permission has been obtained, although camping is seldom allowed near the water's edge or at a large seaside resort. Casual camping is prohibited in state forests, national parks in the Landes and Gironde *départements* and in the Camarque. Camping in an unauthorised place renders offenders liable to prosecution or confiscation of equipment, or both, especially in the south. However, an overnight stop on parking areas of some motorways is tolerated, but make sure you do not contravene local regulations; overnight stops in a lay-by are not permitted. Camping is not permitted in *Monaco*. Caravans in transit are allowed but it is forbidden to park them.

Currency including banking hours

(see also page 57)
The unit of currency is the Franc (*Fr*) divided into 100 *Centimes*. At the time of going to press £ = *Fr* 9.70. Denominations of bank notes are *Fr* 10, 20, 50, 100, 200, 500; standard coins are *Fr* 1, 2, 10, 50, 100 and *Centimes* 5, 10, 20, 50. There is no restriction on the amount of foreign currency which may be taken into France. Travellers are, however, restricted to taking *Fr* 12,000 with them when leaving the country, unless they imported more currency on entry and completed the appropriate form at the time.

In most large towns banks are open from Monday to Friday 09.00–12.00hrs and 14.00–16.00hrs and closed on Saturday and Sunday; in the provinces they are open from Tuesday to Saturday as above and closed on Sunday and Monday. Banks close at midday on the day prior to a national holiday and all day on Monday if the holiday falls on a Tuesday.

The *Credit Lyonnais* has offices at the Invalides air terminal in Paris for cashing travellers' cheques, the *Société Générale* has 2 offices at Orly airport and at the Charles de Gaulle airport exchange facilities are available.

Customs regulations

A *Customs Carnet de Passages en Douane* is required for temporarily imported outboard engines, exceeding 92cc (5cv as applied to marine engines), imported without the boats with which they are to be used, and for cycles with auxiliary motors up to 50cc which are new or show no signs of use. See also *Customs regulations for European countries* page 57 for further information.

Foodstuffs

(see also page 60)
Visitors entering from an EEC country may import duty free 1,000g of coffee or 450g of coffee extract and 250g of tea or 80g of tea extract bought tax and duty paid; a reduced allowance applies if bought duty-free.

Medical treatment

(see page 60)

Shopping hours

Department stores are usually open from Monday to Saturday 09.00–18.30/19.00hrs. closing for lunch only in the provinces; *food shops* open at 07.00hrs and may also open Sunday morning.

Boulogr
ENGLISH
CHANNEL
Quend-Plage-
Noyell
Cayeaux-sur-
Le Trép
St-Aubin-sur-Mer
St-Valéry-en-Caux
Die
Campne
Sassetot-le-Mauco
Valmont
St-Léger-du-Bourg-Denis
N15
Le Havre
Jumièges
Bourg
Achard
Villerville
Pont-l'Evêque
Blangy-le-Château
Gros-Theil
Bernay
D834
Moyaux
Lisieux
Évre
St-Rémy-sur-
Maupertus-sur-Mer
Barfleur
Cherbourg
N13
Les
Pieux
St- Sauveur
-le-Vicomte
Barneville-Carteret
Carentan
La Haye -du-Puitts
Etréham
Arromanches-les-Bains
Bernières-sur-Mer
Lion-sur-Mer
Ouistreham-Riva-Bella
Cabourg
Bayeux
Martragny
Caen
Bénouville
Gonneville-en-Auge
Houlgate
Villers-sur-Mer
Deauville
1 St-Lunaire
2 Dinard
3 St-Malo
4 St-Coulomb
5 La Richardis
St-Germain- sur-Ay
Blainville-
sur-Mer
Coutainville
N175
Thury-Harcourt
Bréhal
St-Pair-
sur-Mer
D973
Villedieu-les-Poêles
Jullouville
Falaise
Avranches
Mont-St-Michel
Argentan
N138
Perros Guirec
Landrellec
Trébeurden
Locquirec
Trélévern
Plougasnou
Pleubian
Cléder
St-Michel-
en-Greve
Plouha
Carantec
St-Quay-Portrieux
Landéda
Plouezoch
Plestin-les-Greves
Etables-sur-Mer
Louargat
Binic
St-Cast
Cancale
Bougonvelin
Le
Fret
Pordic
Erquy
St-Briac
Plougastel-Daoulas
N165
Callac
Pléneuf-
val-André
Dol-de-Bretagne
St Marcan
Dinan
Epiniac
Camaret-
sur-Mer
Crozon
Morgat
Argruc-sur-Mer
Pentrez-Plage
Plomodiern
Plonévez-Porzay
Douarnenez
St-Domineuc
La Chapelle-aux-Filzméens
Bagnoles-de-l'Orne
Pre-en-Pail
Tinténiac
Fougères
Javron
Alençon
Caurel
Quimper
Landudec
St-Yvi
St-Evarzec
Tregunc
La Forêt-Fouesnant
Bannalec
Pont-l' Abbé
Névez
Querrie
Châtillon-en-Vendelais
Mayenne
Fresnay-sur-Sarthe
St-Guénolé
Sillé-le-Guillaume
A81
A11
Rennes
Beaumont-sur-Sarthe
Brou
Lesconil
Guilvinec
Bénodet
Mousterlin
Beg-Meil
Concarneau
Clohars-Carnoet
Ploërmel
St-Thurial
Sillé-le-Philippe
Raguenès-Plage
Port-Manech
Pont-Aven
Le Pouldu
Cloyes-sur-
Plouhinec
Plouharnel
La Trinité-sur-Mer
St-Philibert-sur-Mer
Erdeven
Carnac
Arradon
Noyal-Muzillac
Pouancé
Daon-de-Feins
Bessé-sur-Braye
La Chapelle-St-M
Pezou
St-Pierre-Quiberon
Muzillac
Guémené-Penfao
Marcon
Vendôme
Quiberon
Sarzeau
Billiers
La Flèche
Château-
du-Loir
Montoire-sur-
le-
Loir
Sauzon
La Roche-Bernard
Le Lion d'Angers
Le Palais
Ste-Reine-de-Bretagne
Le Lude
Château-Renault
Blois
St-Gildas-de-Rhuys
Pénestin-sur-Mer
Mesquer
Guérande
Héric
Angers
Les Rosiers
Piriac-sur-Mer
La Turballe
Le Croisic
Savenay
Sucé-sur-Erdre
La Membrolle-sur-
Choisille
Mesland
Les Mon
Batz-sur-Mer
La Baule
Pornichet
St-Nazaire
St-Brévin-les-Pins
St-Florent-le-Vieil
Les Ponts-de-Cé
Limeray
St-Brévin-
l' Océan
Nantes
Chalonnes-sur-Loire
Gennes
Luynes
Tours
Montlouis
-sur-Loire
Romora
-Lanthe
St-Brévin-Chef-Chef
St-Michel-Chef-Chef
Pomic
Les Moutiers-en-Retz
Saumur
Varennes-
sur-Loire
Azay-le-
Rideau
Bléré
St-Ai
sur-C
Bourgneuf-en-Retz
Montreuil-
Bellay
Montsoreau
Chinon
Ste-Catherine
-de-Fierbois
Barbâtre
Cholet
Loches
La Barre-de-Monts
Argenton-Château
Notre-Dame-de-Monts
St-Jean-de-Monts
St-Malô-du-Bois
Port-de-Piles
St-Hilaire-de-Riez
Apremont
Ingrandes
St-Gilles-Croix-de-Vie
St-Julien-des-Landes
Châteauroux
Bretignolles-sur-Mer
Olonne-sur-Mer
Les Sables-d'Olonne
Talmont-St-Hilaire
St-Cyr
Jard-sur-Mer
Avrille
Verruyes
La Tranche-sur-Mer
Longeville
Chauvigny
L'Aiguillon-sur-Mer
Coulon
La Faute-sur-Mer
Marans
L'Hommaize
La Trimouille
St-Clément-des-Baleines
St-Martin-
de-Ré
Lusignan
Montmorillon
Ars-en-Ré
L'Hommeau
Lagord
La Rochelle
La Courade-sur-Mer
Angoulins
Couhé-Verac
Le Bois-Plage-en-Ré
La Noue
Châtelaillon-Plage
St-Denis-d' Oléron
St-Georges-d' Oléron
Domino
Bessine-sur-Gartempe
La Cotinière
Boyardville
Gu
La Château-d'Oléron
La Palmyre
Vaux-sur-Mer
Saintes
Bonnac-la-Cote
Roy
Vas
Les Mathes
Saujon
Limoges
St-Palais-sur-Mer
Médis
Cognac
St-Léonar
de-Noblat
Royan
St-Georges-de-Didonne
Le Verdon-sur-Mer
Pons
Angoulême
Soulac-sur-Mer
Meschers-
sur-Gironde
Eymouthiers
Magnac-Bourg
N20
Nontron
Buge
Montalivet-les-Bains
Mareuil
M
BAY OF BISCAY
A10
Montendre
Hourtin Plage
Hourtin
Bombannes
Blaye
La Roche-
Chalais
Lacanau-Océan
Laruscade
Le Porge
Ambarès
Fronsac
Abzac
N89
Mussidan
Arès
Andernos-
les-Bains
Villenave
D'Ornon
Petit Palais
St-Emilion
Ste-Foy-la-Grande
Claouey
Lanton
Sadirac
St-Seurin-

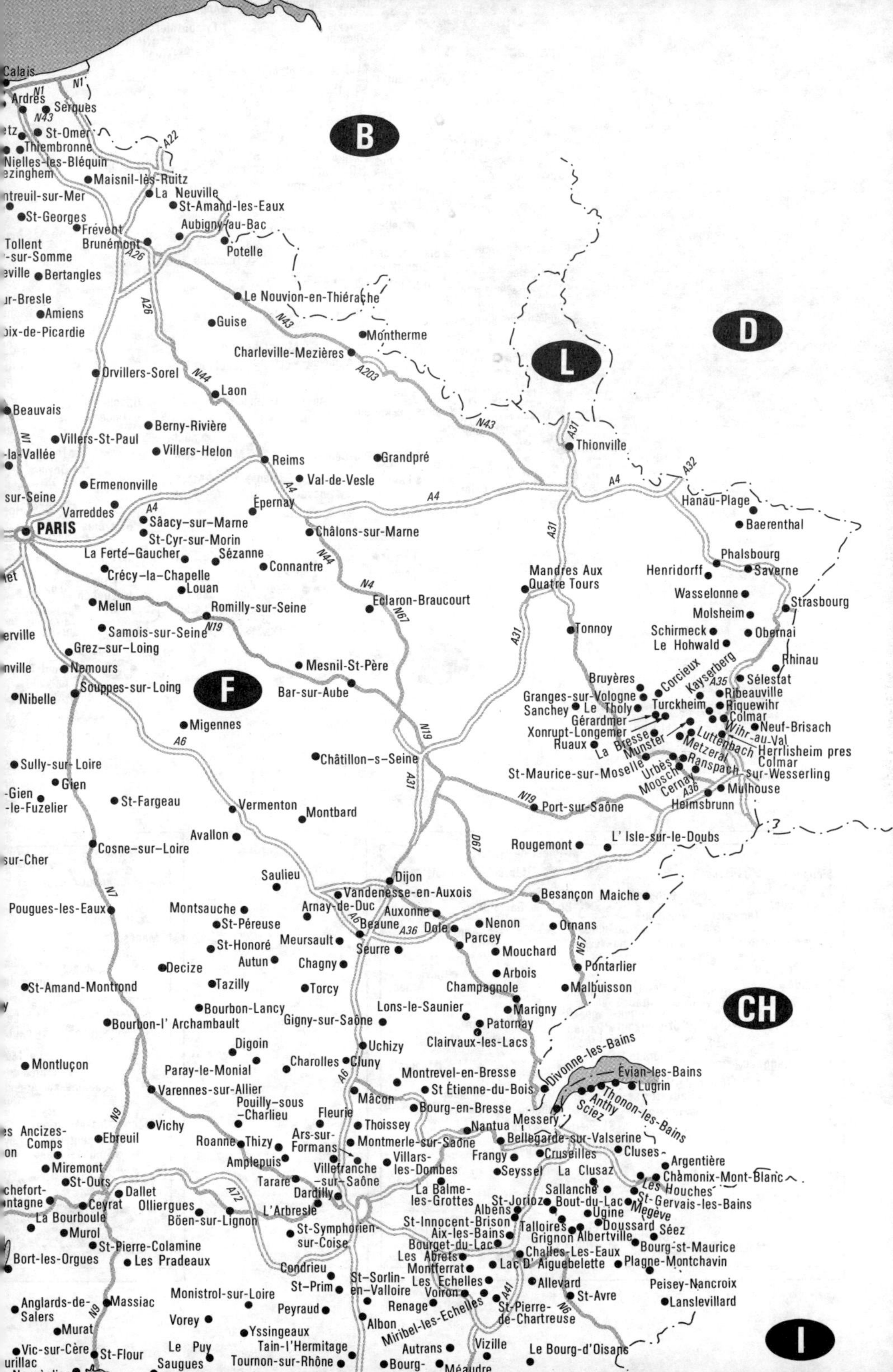

B
L
D
F
CH
I
Calais
N1
Ardres
Serques
N43
St-Omer
A22
Thiembronne
Nielles-les-Bléquin
Maisnil-lès-Ruitz
La Neuville
St-Amand-les-Eaux
St-Georges
Frévent
Aubigny-au-Bac
Tollent
Brunémont
A26
Potelle
Bertangles
Le Nouvion-en-Thiérache
Amiens
Guise
N43
Montherme
Charleville-Mezières
A203
Orvillers-Sorel
N44
Laon
Beauvais
Berny-Rivière
N43
Thionville
A31
Villers-St-Paul
Villers-Helon
Reims
Grandpré
A32
Val-de-Vesle
A4
Ermenonville
A4
Hanau-Plage
Épernay
Baerenthal
Varreddes
A4
PARIS
Sâacy-sur-Marne
Châlons-sur-Marne
St-Cyr-sur-Morin
La Ferté-Gaucher
Sézanne
N44
Connantre
Phalsbourg
Henridorff
Saverne
Crécy-la-Chapelle
Mandres Aux Quatre Tours
Louan
N4
Wasselonne
Melun
Romilly-sur-Seine
Eclaron-Braucourt
N67
Strasbourg
Molsheim
Samois-sur-Seine
N19
Tonnoy
Schirmeck
Obernai
Grez-sur-Loing
Le Hohwald
Nemours
Mesnil-St-Père
Rhinau
Nibelle
Souppes-sur-Loing
Bar-sur-Aube
Bruyères
Corcieux
Kayserberg
Sélestat
A35
Granges-sur-Vologne
Ribeauville
Sanchey
Le Tholy
Turckheim
Riquewihr
Migennes
Gérardmer
Colmar
N19
Neuf-Brisach
Xonrupt-Longemer
Wihr-au-Val
A6
La Bresse
Luttenbach
Herrlisheim pres Colmar
Ruaux
Munster
Metzeral
Sully-sur-Loire
Châtillon-s-Seine
Urbès
Ranspach-sur-Wesserling
A31
St-Maurice-sur-Moselle
Gien
Moosch
Cernay
Mulhouse
N19
A36
St-Fargeau
Port-sur-Saône
Heimsbrunn
Vermenton
Montbard
Avallon
D67
Rougemont
L' Isle-sur-le-Doubs
Cosne-sur-Loire
Saulieu
Dijon
Vandenesse-en-Auxois
Besançon
Maiche
Pougues-les-Eaux
Montsauche
Arnay-de-Duc
Auxonne
A6
Nenon
St-Péreuse
Beaune
A36
Dole
Ornans
N7
Meursault
Parcey
St-Honoré
Seurre
Mouchard
N57
Autun
Chagny
Decize
Pontarlier
Arbois
St-Amand-Montrond
Tazilly
Torcy
Champagnole
Malbuisson
Bourbon-Lancy
Lons-le-Saunier
Marigny
Bourbon-l' Archambault
Gigny-sur-Saône
Patornay
Digoin
Uchizy
Clairvaux-les-Lacs
Divonne-les-Bains
Montluçon
Charolles
Cluny
Évian-les-Bains
Paray-le-Monial
A6
Montrevel-en-Bresse
Lugrin
Varennes-sur-Allier
St Étienne-du-Bois
Thonon-les-Bains
Pouilly-sous-Charlieu
Mâcon
Anthy
N9
Bourg-en-Bresse
Messery
Sciez
Fleurie
Vichy
Thoissey
Nantua
Ebreuil
Roanne
Thizy
Ars-sur-Formans
Montmerle-sur-Saône
Bellegarde-sur-Valserine
Cluses
Frangy
Cruseilles
Argentière
Miremont
Amplepuis
Villefranche-sur-Saône
Villars-les-Dombes
Seyssel
La Clusaz
St-Ours
Tarare
Chamonix-Mont-Blanc
Dallet
A72
Dardilly
La Balme-les-Grottes
Les Houches
Sallanche
Ceyrat
Olliergues
St-Jorioz
Bout-du-Lac
St-Gervais-les-Bains
L'Arbresle
Albens
Megève
La Bourboule
Böen-sur-Lignon
St-Innocent-Brison
Ugine
Doussard
Séez
Murol
St-Symphorien-sur-Coise
Aix-les-Bains
Talloires
Grignon
Albertville
Bourg-st-Maurice
St-Pierre-Colamine
Bourget-du-Lac
Bort-les-Orgues
Les Pradeaux
Les Abrets
Challes-Les-Eaux
Lac D' Aiguebelette
Plagne-Montchavin
Condrieu
Montferrat
St-Sorlin-en-Valloire
Les Echelles
Allevard
Peisey-Nancroix
St-Prim
Voiron
A41
St-Avre
Monistrol-sur-Loire
Anglards-de-Salers
Massiac
N9
Renage
Peyraud
Miribel-les-Echelles
St-Pierre-de-Chartreuse
N6
Lanslevillard
Vorey
Murat
Albon
Yssingeaux
Vic-sur-Cère
Tain-l'Hermitage
Le Puy
Autrans
Vizille
St-Flour
Le Bourg-d'Oisans
Saugues
Tournon-sur-Rhône
Méaudre

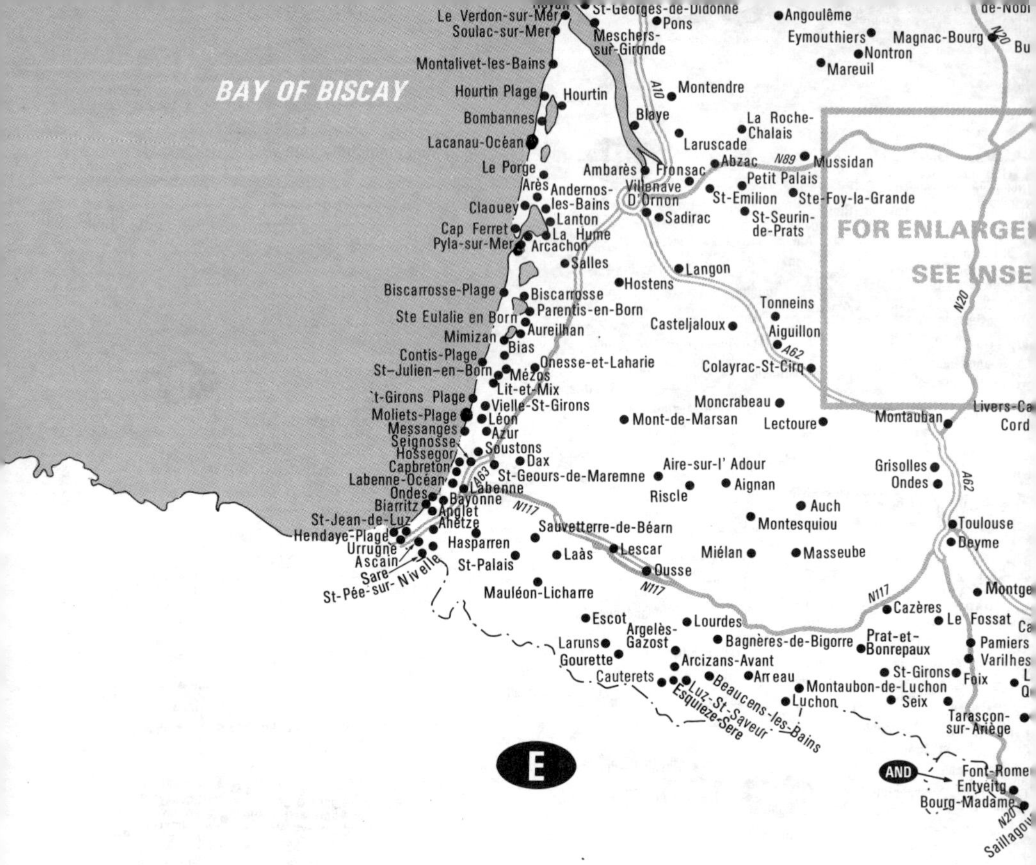

BAY OF BISCAY
Le Verdon-sur-Mer
Soulac-sur-Mer
St-Georges-de-Didonne
Meschers-sur-Gironde
Pons
Angoulême
Eymouthiers
Magnac-Bourg
Nontron
Mareuil
Montalivet-les-Bains
Hourtin Plage
Hourtin
A10
Montendre
Bombannes
Blaye
La Roche-Chalais
Lacanau-Océan
Laruscade
Le Porge
Ambarès
Fronsac
Abzac
N89
Mussidan
Arès
Andernos-les-Bains
Villenave D'Ornon
Petit Palais
St-Emilion
Ste-Foy-la-Grande
Claouey
Lanton
Sadirac
St-Seurin-de-Prats
Cap Ferret
La Hume
FOR ENLARGE
Pyla-sur-Mer
Arcachon
SEE INSE
Salles
Langon
Biscarrosse-Plage
Hostens
Biscarrosse
Parentis-en-Born
Tonneins
N20
Ste Eulalie en Born
Casteljaloux
Aiguillon
Mimizan
Aureilhan
Bias
A62
Contis-Plage
St-Julien-en-Born
Onesse-et-Laharie
Colayrac-St-Cirq
Mézos
Lit-et-Mix
St-Girons Plage
Vielle-St-Girons
Moncrabeau
Moliets-Plage
Léon
Mont-de-Marsan
Lectoure
Montauban
Livers-Ca
Cord
Messanges
Azur
Seignosse
Soustons
Hossegor
Dax
Capbreton
A63
Aire-sur-l' Adour
Grisolles
Labenne-Océan
St-Geours-de-Maremne
Aignan
Ondes
Labenne
Riscle
Ondes
A62
Biarritz
Bayonne
Auch
N117
St-Jean-de-Luz
Anglet
Montesquiou
Toulouse
Hendaye-Plage
Ahetze
Sauveterre-de-Béarn
Deyme
Urrugne
Hasparren
Lescar
Miélan
Masseube
Ascain
Laàs
St-Palais
Ousse
Sare
N117
Montge
St-Pée-sur-Nivelle
Mauléon-Licharre
N117
Cazères
Escot
Lourdes
Le Fossat
Ca
Argelès-Gazost
Prat-et-Bonrepaux
Laruns
Bagnères-de-Bigorre
Pamiers
Gourette
Varilhes
Arcizans-Avant
Cauterets
Arreau
St-Girons
Foix
Montaubon-de-Luchon
Beaucens-les-Bains
Luz-St-Saveur
Esquieze-Sere
Luchon
Seix
Tarascon-sur-Ariège
E
AND
Font-Rome
Entveitg
Bourg-Madame
N20
Saillago

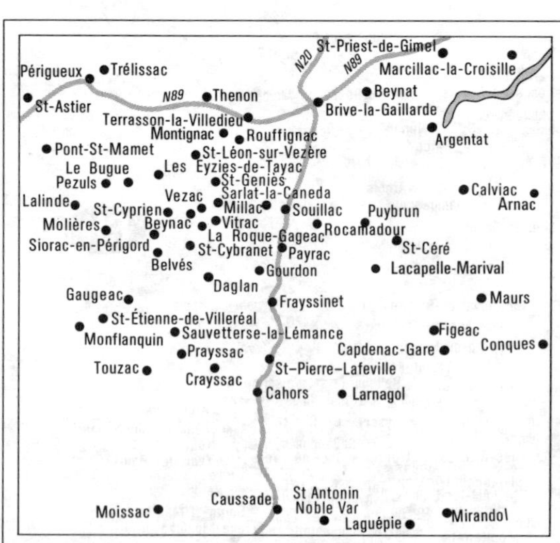

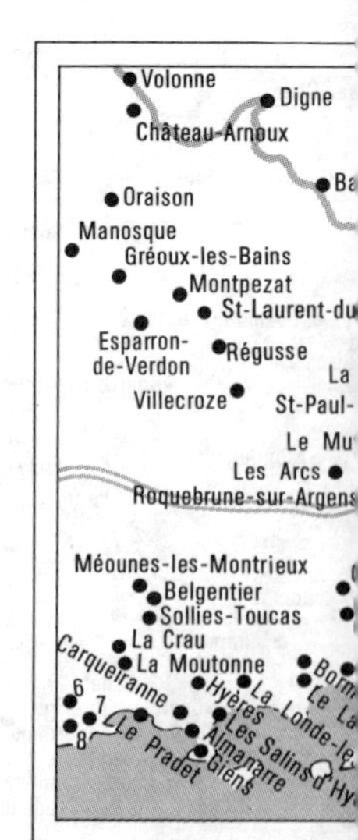

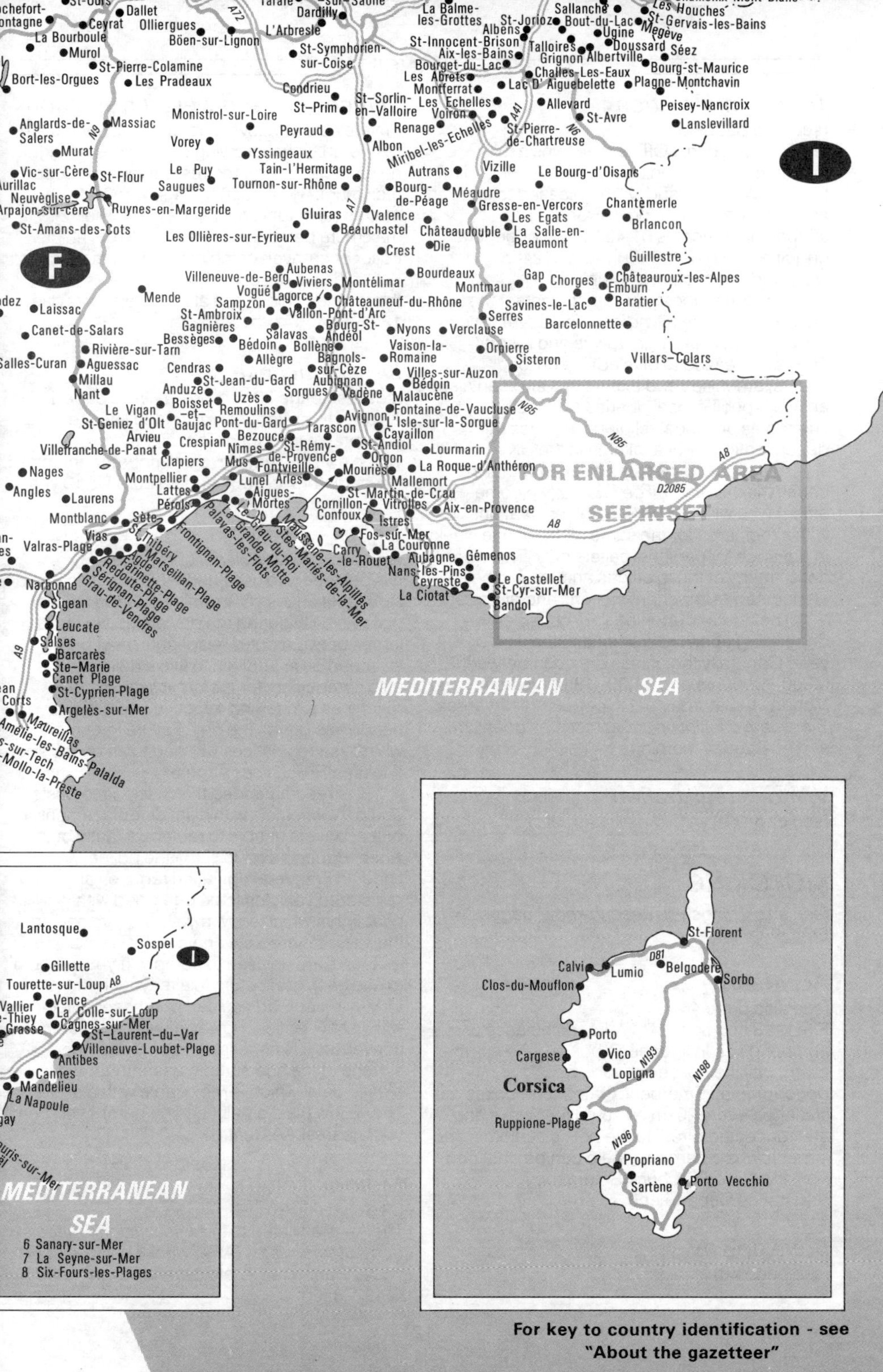

For key to country identification - see "About the gazetteer"

Tourist information

(see also page 63)

The French Tourist Office maintains a full information service in London at 178 Piccadilly, London W1V 0AL and will be pleased to answer any enquiries on touring in France. The telephone number is 01-491 7622 for general enquiries and 01-499 6911 for the 24hr recorded information service.

Once in France you should contact the local tourist office (*Syndicat d'Initiative*) which will be found in all larger towns and resorts. They are pleased to give advice on local events, amenities and excursions and can also answer specific local queries such as bus timetables and local religious services (all denominations) not available in the UK.

A further source of information within the country is the *Accueil de France* (welcome office) who will also book hotel reservations within their area for the same night, or one week in advance for **personal callers only**. There are not so many of these offices and mainly they are located at important stations and airports.

The hours of opening vary considerably depending upon the district and the time of year. Generally the offices are open between 09.00–12.00hrs and 14.00–18.00hrs from Monday to Saturday but in popular resort areas *Syndicats d'Initiative* are sometimes open later and on Sunday mornings.

Visitor's registration

(see page 63)

MOTORING

(see also *Things you need to know*, pages 33–64)

Accidents

(see also page 46)

Fire ☎18 and **police** ☎17. For **ambulance** use number given in telephone box or, if no number given, call the police (*brigade de gendarmerie*). Emergency telephone boxes are stationed every 20km on some roadways and are connected direct to the police station. In the larger towns emergency help can be obtained from the *Police Secours* (Emergency Assistance Department).

Breakdowns

(see page 48)

Dimensions and weight restrictions

Private **cars** and towed **trailers** or **caravans** are restricted to the following dimensions – height: no restriction, but 4 metres is a recommended maximum; width: 2.50 metres; length: 11 metres (excluding towing device). The maximum permitted overall length of vehicle/ trailer or caravan combination is 18 metres.

If the weight of the trailer exceeds that of the towing vehicle, see also *Speed limits* page 125.

Driving licence

(see also page 33 and *Speed limits* page 125)

A valid UK or Republic of Ireland licence is acceptable in France. The minimum age at which a visitor may drive a temporarily imported car or motorcycle (exceeding 80cc) is 18 years.

Lights

(see page 50 also *Headlights* page 41)

It is obligatory to use headlights as driving on sidelights only is not permitted. In fog, mist or poor visibility during the day either two fog lamps or two dipped headlights must be switched on in addition to two sidelights. It is also compulsory for *motorcyclists* riding machines exceeding 125cc to use dipped headlights during the day. Failure to comply with these regulations will lead to an on the spot fine (see *Police fines* page 51).

It is recommended that visiting motorists equip their vehicle with a set of replacement bulbs; drivers unable to replace a faulty bulb when requested to do so by the police may be fined. In France a regulation requires all locally registered vehicles to be equipped with headlights which show a yellow beam and, in the interests of safety and courtesy, visiting motorists are advised to comply. If you are able to use beam deflectors to alter your headlights for driving abroad you can purchase deflectors with yellow lenses. However, with headlamp converters it is necessary to coat the outer surface of the headlamp glass with a yellow plastic paint which is removable with a solvent. The yellow plastic paint can be purchased from your nearest AA Centre.

Motoring club

(see also page 61)

The AA is affiliated to the *Association Française des Automobilistes* (AFA) whose office is at *F-75017 Paris* 9 rue Anatole-de-la Forge ☎42278200.

Parking

(see also page 51)
In Paris cars towing caravans are prohibited from the *blue zone* between 14.00 and 20.30hrs. Cars towing trailers with an overall surface of 10 sq metres or more may neither circulate nor park in the central *green zone* between 14.00–20.30hrs, except on Sundays and public holidays. Vehicle combinations with an overall surface exceeding 16 sq metres may neither circulate nor park in the *green zone* between 08.00–20.30hrs. Those wishing to cross Paris during these hours with vehicle/trailer combinations, can use the boulevard Péripherique, although the route is heavily congested, except during public holiday periods. In some parts of the *green zones* parking is completely forbidden. It is prohibited to park caravans, even for a limited period, not only in the *green zone* but in almost all areas of Paris.

Passengers

(see also page 51)
Children under 10 are not permitted to travel in a vehicle as front seat passengers when rear seating is available.

Petrol

(see page 61)

Priority including Roundabouts

(see also page 52)
In built-up areas drivers must slow down and be prepared to stop at all road junctions. If there are no priority signs give way to traffic from the right, but you have priority on roads bearing the sign *Passage Protégé*. New signs are being introduced (inverted triangle with red border) some of which bear an additional panel with the word 'STOP' and distance in metres to the stop sign or the words *Cédez le passage.* A major road which has priority over side turnings will generally display signs to indicate this, usually a yellow square within white square with points vertical; a thick black band through the sign indicates end of priority. At roundabouts with signs bearing the words *Vous n'avez pas la priorité* traffic on the roundabout has priority; where no such sign exists traffic entering the roundabout has priority.

Roads

France has a very comprehensive network of roads, the surfaces of which are generally good; exceptions are usually signposted *Chaussée deformée.* The camber is often severe and the edges rough.

During July and August and especially at weekends traffic on main roads is likely to be very heavy. Special signs are erected to indicate alternative routes with the least traffic congestion and wherever they appear it is usually advantageous to follow them even though you cannot be absolutely sure of gaining time.

The alternative routes are quiet but they are not as wide as the main roads. They are **not** suitable for caravans.

A free road map showing the marked alternative routes, plus information centres and petrol stations open for 24 hours is available from service stations displaying the *Bison Futé* poster (a Red Indian chief in full war bonnet). These maps are also available from *Syndicat d'Initiatives* and information offices.

Seat belts

(see page 52)

Speed limits

Built-up areas
60 kph (37 mph)
Outside built-up areas on normal roads 90kph (56mph); on dual carriageways separated by a central reservation 110kph (68mph).
On Motorways 130kph (80mph) (*Note* The Minimum speed in fast lane on level stretch of motorway during good daytime visibility is 80kph (49mph) and drivers travelling below this speed are liable to be fined. The maximum speed on urban stretches of motorway is 110kph (68mph).

In wet weather speed limits outside built-up areas are reduced to 80kph (49mph), 100kph (62mph) and 110kph (68mph) on motorways.

These limits also apply to private cars towing a trailer or caravan, if the latter's weight does not exceed that of the car. However, if the weight of the trailer exceeds that of the car by less than 30% the speed limit is 65kph (39mph), if more than 30% the speed limit is 45kph (28mph). Additionally these combinations must:
i Display a disc at the rear of the caravan/trailer showing the maximum speed.
ii Not be driven in the fast lane of a 3-lane motorway.

Both French residents and visitors to France, who have held a driving licence for less than one year, must not exceed 90kph (56mph) or any lower signposted limit when driving in France.

Tolls

(see page 63)

Warning triangle/Hazard warning lights

The use of a warning triangle or hazard warning lights† is compulsory in the event of accident or breakdown. As hazard warning lights may be damaged or inoperative it is recommended that a warning triangle be carried. The triangle must be placed on the road 30 metres (33yds) behind the vehicle and clearly visible from 100 metres (109yds). For vehicles over 3,500kg warning must be given by at least a warning triangle. See also *Warning triangles/Hazard warning lights* page 54.

†If your vehicle is equipped with hazard warning lights it is also compulsory to use them if you are forced to drive temporarily at a greatly reduced speed. However, when slow moving traffic is established in an uninterrupted lane or lanes this only applies to the last vehicle in the lane(s).

Prices are in French Francs.

Abbreviations:

av	avenue
bd	boulevard
espl	esplanade
fbg	faubourg
Gl	Général
Ml	Maréchal
pl	place
Prés	President
r	rue
rte	route
Sgt	Sergent
sq	square

CM Camping Municipal (local authority site)

ABBEVILLE
Somme

At **PORT-LE-GRAND** (5 km NW)

Château des Tilleuls ☎22240775

On gently sloping meadow surrounding a farm.

1 km SE of Port-le-Grand on D940A.
Mar–Oct.
4HEC lau

ABJAT See **NONTRON**

ABRETS (LES)
Isère

Coin Tranquille ☎76321348

Completely divided into pitches with attractive flower beds in rural surroundings.

2 km E of village, 500 m off N6.
Apr–Oct.
3HEC lau **A**10 **V**7 pitch9

ABZAC
Gironde

Paradis ☎57490510

On meadowland near an artificial lake. Pedal boats and fishing nearby.

Drive W on N89 from the direction of Périgueux. After St-Médard-de Guizières turn onto D17E and follow signposts.
15 Apr–15 Oct.
5HEC lau **A**10 **V**9 10 10

AGAY
Var

Agay Soleil rte de Cannes ☎94820079

A small, sandy site beside a narrow beach. All kinds of watersports nearby.

Between N98 and the sea.
Apr–Oct
0.8HEC lau pitch88–95 (incl 4 persons)

Esterel rte de Valescure ☎94820328

10 Apr–Sep.
13HEC lau pitch79 (incl 2 persons)

Rives de l'Agay av du Gratadis ☎94820274

A level site below a country road.

Turn off N98 at Agay beach and continue for 0.5 km towards Valescure.
15 Feb–5 Nov.
1.25HEC lau **A**16 pitch20

Vallée du Paradis rte du Gratadis ☎94820146

On a large meadow and a narrow strip of land between the road and the river.

800 m inland from N98.
15 Mar–15 Oct.
3HEC lau

At **DRAMONT (LE)** (2 km SW)

International du Dramont ☎94820768

A hilly site, set among pine trees, beside a country house on the Cap du Dramont. Reserved for families only during August. Youths under 21 only admitted if accompanied by parents.

Entrance on the N98.
25 Mar–10 Oct.
7HEC lau

AGDE
Hérault

Agde Domaine des 7 Fonts ☎67941462

A park-like site amongst mature pine trees. 3 km from sea.

Turn off road between Agde and Sète by a furniture store and the ELF petrol station. Site in 400 m.
Jun–Sep

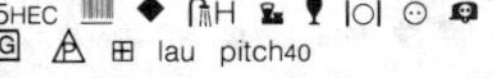

International de l'Hérault rte de la Tamarissière ☎67941283

A grassy site on W bank of the River Hérault.

Take the exit for 'Agde' off autoroute A9, then continue via D13 and D32E.
Etr–Sep.

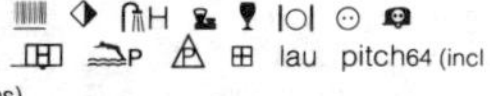

At **ROCHELONGUE-PLAGE** (4 km S)

Champs Blancs ☎67942342

Apr–1 Oct.

20HEC H G R sP lau pitch95 (incl 2 persons)

AGUESSAC
Aveyron

CM ☎65598467

A large level site beside the River Tarn.

10 Jun–Sep.

3HEC H G R lau A7 V7 7 7

AHETZE
Pyrénées-Atlantiques

Campagne ☎59235583

On an open field divided by hedges.

Off D655 Bidart-Ahetze road.
Etr–15 Sep.

5HEC H G lau

AIGNAN
Gers

Castex ☎62092513

800 m from D48.
15 Jun–15 Sep.

France

1.8HEC H P lau pitch52 (incl 2 persons)

AIGUEBELETTE (LAC D')
Savoie

At **LÉPIN-LE-LAC**

Peupliers ☎79360048

300 m S of Aiguebelette.
Apr–Oct

5HEC H G L lau A8 pitch10

AIGUES-MORTES
Gard

Petite Camargue ☎66538477

A grassy site lying amongst vineyards on the D62.3 km from the sea.

Access via autoroute exit Gallargues in direction of La Grande Motte.
Etr–Sep.

10HEC H G P lau

AIGUILLON
Lot-et-Garonne

CM du Vieux Moulin ☎53796143

Beside the River Lot.

500 m E of village off D666.
15 Jun–15 Sep.

0.8HEC H lau R

AIGUILLON-SUR-MER (L')
Vendée

Bel Air ☎51564405

A long, level stretch of meadowland in rural surroundings.

1.5 km NW on D44 then turn left.
15 May–15 Sep.

7HEC H G R P lau s pitch62 (incl 3 persons)

AIRE-SUR-L'ADOUR
Landes

Ombrages de l'Adour ☎58716470

A clean, tidy site next to a sports stadium beside the river. Clean sanitary installations.

May–Oct

4HEC H lau P A8 pitch8

AIX-EN-PROVENCE
Bouches-du-Rhône

Arc en Ciel ☎42261428

A pleasant terraced site on both sides of a stream.

Near motorway exit Aix-Est on N7 towards Toulon. 3 km SE near Pont des Trois Sautets.
All year.

3HEC H G P lau A17 pitch17

Chantecler av du Val ☎42261298

Widespread, uneven site on hill. Terraced pitches. Some separate showers for men and women. Cabins with wash basin and wc.

Access off motorway exit Aix-Est on A8. 2.5 km SE of town.
All year.

10HEC H G P lau

AIX-LES-BAINS
Savoie

Sierroz bd R-Barrier ☎79612143

A wooded site divided into 2 parts each with pitches, separated from the lake by 150 m strip of land and the Culoz road. Bathing area nearby on lake.

2.5 km NW
15 Mar–15 Nov.

5HEC H G R lau L A10 pitch20

At **VIVIERS-DU-LAC** (6 km S on N201)

Terre Nue ☎79634026

In rural surroundings on edge of lake.

1 km W on N201.

2HEC H G P lau

ALBENS
Savoie

Beauséjour ☎79547812 ➔

15 Jun–15 Sep.
2HEC ◆ H ⊙ G ⊞ lau A8 V5 5 5

ALBERTVILLE
Savoie

CM Adoubes av des Chasseurs-Alpins ☎79320662

Situated between N525 and River Arly on E side of town.
15 Jun–Sep.
2.5HEC ◆ H ⊙ G R ⊞ lau P A6 V2 4 4

ALBI
Tarn

Caussels 78 r E-Marty ☎63603706

The site is owned by the local automobile club. It lies on terraced land in a forest next to municipal swimming pools. International Camping Carnet required.

From village take N99 towards Millau, then turn left onto D100 and left again into site.
All year.
1.7HEC ◆ H ⊙ ⊞ lau |O| P

ALBON
Drôme

Château de Senaud ☎75031131

On an elevated meadow.

S of village between N7 and motorway.
Mar–Oct.
3HEC ◇ H ⊙ G P ⊞ lau A16 V8 12 12

ALENÇON
Orne

Guéramé r de Guéramé ☎33263495

Situated in open country near a stream, 500 m from town centre.

Access via the Boulevard Périphérique in the SW part of town.
Apr–Nov.
1.5HEC ◆ H ⊙ ⊞ lau |O| A6 V7 8 8

Jacques Fould ☎33292329

All year.
1HEC ◆ H ⊙ ⊞ lau |O| G A5 V3 3 3

ALLÈGRE
Gard

Château de Boisson Boisson ☎66248561

E of village on D37 towards Lussan.
May–Sep.
5HEC ◇ H |O| ⊙ G P ⊞ lau A18 pitch35

Domaine des Fumades ☎66857078

On sloping meadow near the river. Extensive leisure facilities. Liable to flooding at certain times.

Turn off D7 (Bourgot-les-Allègre) at TOTAL filling station and follow signs.

France

Apr–Sep.
13HEC ◇ H |O| ⊙ G P ⊞ lau A13 pitch41

ALLEVARD
Isère

Clair Matin ☎76975519

Gently sloping terraced area divided into pitches.

S of village, 300 m off D525.
15 May–Sep.
3HEC ◆ ◇ H ⊙ G R P ⊞ lau |O| pitch46 (incl 2 persons)

ALMANARRE (L')
Var

St-Pierre-des-Horts chemin de la Font des Horts ☎94576531

A site divided into many fields on meadowland surrounded by bushy hedges, next to a nursery.

Turn off the N559 at the northern edge of the town and follow a wide asphalt road westward for 0.5 km, then turn right.
All year.
1.8HEC ◇ H |O| ⊙ G R ⊞ lau S

AMBARÈS
Gironde

Clos Chauvet ☎56388108

Surrounded by vineyards.

100 m from A10 via D911.
May–15 Oct.
0.8HEC ◇ H ⊙ G ⊞ |O| A14 pitch10

AMÉLIE-LES-BAINS-PALALDA
Pyrénées-Orientales

Gaou av Beausoleil ☎68391919

All year.
7HEC ◇ H ⊙ ⊞ lau |O| RP

AMÉLIE-SUR-MER (L') See **SOULAC-SUR-MER**

AMIENS
Somme

CM l'Étang St-Pierre r Massey ☎22445421

Apr–Sep.
4HEC ◇ H ⊙ ⊞ lau |O| A4 V3 3 3

AMPHION-LES-BAINS See **EVIAN-LES-BAINS**

AMPLEPUIS
Rhône

Lac des Sapins ☎74895283

On a partially wooded meadow, sloping towards a lake.

Access via D10 and D504.
Etr–Sep.
4HEC ◇ H ⊙ G ⊞ lau |O| L

ANCIZES-COMPS (LES)
Puy-de-Dôme

CM Comp-les-Fades ☎73868164

2 km N on D62
Jun–15 Sep.
2HEC ◇ H ⊙ G ⊞ lau

ANDERNOS-LES-BAINS
Gironde

Fontaine-Vieille 4 bd du Cl-Wurtz ☎56820167

On level ground in sparse forest.

S of village centre.
15 May–15 Sep.
12.6HEC ◆ ◇ H |O| ⊙ G R sP ⊞ lau pitch66 (incl 2 persons)

Pleine Forêt ☎56821718

Situated in a quiet location among pines.

Off D106E or D106 Andernos-les-Bains-Bordeaux road.
All year.
6.5HEC ◇ H ⊙ G ⊞ lau A11 pitch21–25

ANDONVILLE
Loiret

Cheval Blanc ☎38395707

2.3 km S of rte de Richerelles.
All year.
14HEC ◆ ◇ H |O| ⊙ G P ⊞ lau A18 pitch18

Domaine de la Jouillière ☎38395846

1 km E on road to Richerelles.
All year.
15HEC ◇ H |O| ⊙ R P ⊞ lau

ANDUZE
Gard

Castel Rose rte de St-Jean-du-Gard ☎66618015

1 km NW on D907.
Etr–Sep.
8HEC ◇ H |O| ⊙ G R R ⊞

At **ATTUECH** (5 km SE on D907)

Fief ☎66618171

On level meadow, divided by flowerbeds and shrubs.

Turn off D982 E of Attuech and continue for 400 m on partially rough track.
Jun–Sep.
3.5HEC ◆ ◇ H |O| ⊙ G P ⊞ lau R pitch45 (incl 2 persons)

Pommeraie rte de Lasalle, Thoiras ☎66852052

May–Sep.

7HEC ◆ H G R RP ⊞ lau A12 pitch36

At **CORBÈS** (5 km NW on D907)

Cévennes Provence Mas-de-Pont ☎66617310

Near railway station.
Apr–15 Oct.

30HEC ◆ ◇ H G R R ⊞ lau A10 V3 9 A9

ANGERS

Maine-et-Loire

Lac de Maine ☎41730503

Access via A11 (Angers/Nantes) at Lac de Maine exit.
All year.

4HEC ◇ H (Jul–Aug) (summer only) G R lau L pitch40

Parc de la Haye ☎41693363

4.5 km NW on D122.
Jul–Aug.

3HEC ◆ H G lau P pitch28

ANGLARDS-DE-SALERS

Cantal

CM Fraux ☎71400002

Jul–Aug.

0.6HEC ◇ H ⊞ lau R A5 V2 2 A2

ANGLES

Tarn

Manoir ☎63709606

Site lies in the grounds of an old Manor House.

S of village, on rte de Lacabarède
Etr–Oct.

3HEC ◇ H P ⊞ lau pitch69 (incl 2 persons)

ANGLET

Pyrénées-Atlantiques

Barre de l'Adour 130 av de l'Adour ☎59631616

France

In a hollow between noisy road and jetty, adjacent to River Ardour.

6 Jun–20 Sep.

2.5HEC ◇ H G ⊞ lau S A9 V4 12 A12

Chambre d'Amour rte de Bouney ☎59037166

The site stretches over rising meadows with a few terraces near a water tower.

Turn off the coast road and follow signposts for 1 km.
Apr–Sep.

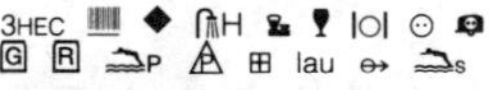

3HEC ◆ H G R P ⊞ lau S

Parme ☎59230300

A beautiful park-like terraced site near the airport, 3 km from sea.

Turn off the N10 at Km8 and follow the road for 500 m.
All year.

4.6HEC ◆ H G ⊞ lau A10 pitch19

ANGOULÊME

Charente

CM de Bourgines ☎45928322

On well-kept lawns, completely divided into pitches, next to swimming pool.

From Angoulême take road to Saintes (N141) and follow camp site signs after crossing bridge.
All year.

2.3HEC ◇ H lau

ANGOULINS-SUR-MER

Charente-Maritime

Chirats rte de la Platère ☎46569416 (Summer)

Modern site 150 m from a large, sandy beach. Booking advised.

Apr–15 Oct

H S

ANTHY

Haute-Savoie

Clos Pallin ☎50703209

Clean and tidy site with attractive flowerbeds on gentle slope.

Signposted from town via D33 and N5.
15 Apr–Sep.

1.7HEC ◇ H G ⊞ lau LP A6 V4 9 A5

ANTIBES

Alpes-Maritimes

Logis de la Brague ☎93335472

On a level meadow beside a small river.

On N7.
May–Sep.

1.7HEC ◇ H G ⊞ lau S pitch60 (incl 3 persons)

At **BIOT** (7 km N on N7 and A8)

Airotel Parc l'Eden chemin du Val de Pome ☎93656370

Site on level meadow, no tents allowed.

On D4.
15 May–15 Sep.

2HEC ◆ H G ⊞ lau S pitch89 (incl 2–4 persons)

Embruns ☎93333335

Small site with proper sanitary installations and divided into pitches.

Access via N7 and D4; 3 km from Antibes.
May–Sep.

0.9HEC ◇ H G ⊞ lau S pitch76

Prés quartier la Romaine ☎93656106

15 May–25 Sep.

1.25HEC ◆ ◇ H G ⊞ lau S pitch50 (incl 2 persons)

At **BRAGUE (LA)** (4 km N on N7)

Frênes ☎93333652

Opposite Biot railway station.
Jun–Sep.

2.5HEC ◆ G ⊞ lau S pitch70–80 (incl 2 persons)

Pylone ☎93335286

A grassland site, subdivided by hedging, with ample shade. Separate section for young people.

Access via N7 west from La Brague, onto D4 direction Biot and continue 200 m – follow signs.
All year.

2HEC ◆ H ⊙ G R ⊞ lau sR A24 V13 20 13

ANTIGES See **NEUVIC**

APREMONT
Vendée

Prairies ☎51557058

1.5 km NE on D40 rte de Maché.
May–Sep.

1.5HEC ◆ H ⊙ G ⊞ lau |O| LP A8 V3 7 7

ARBOIS
Jura

CM Vignes av Gl-Leclerc ☎84661412

Terraced site.

E on D107 Mesnay road at stadium.
Apr–Sep.

1.8HEC ◆ H |O| ⊙ G ⊞ lau P

ARBRESLE (L')
Rhône

CM ☎74011150

On N7.
Etr–Oct.

1.6HEC ◆ ◇ H ⊙ P ⊞ lau

ARCACHON
Gironde

CM des Abatilles allée de la Galaxie ☎56832415

1.5 km S.
Etr–15 Oct.

4.2HEC ◆ H ⊙ lau

ARCANGUES See **BIARRITZ**

ARCIZANS-AVANT
Hautes-Pyrénées

Lac ☎62970188

Set in Pyrenean landscape on outskirts of village, with very clean sanitary installations.

S on N21 take D101 through St-Savin.
Jun–Sep.

2.2HEC ◆ H ⊙ G ⊞ lau |O| P A11 Vn/c 11 11

ARCS (LES)
Var

Eau Vive quartier du Pont d'Argens ☎94474066

2 km S on N7.
All year.

2.5HEC ◆ H |O| ⊙ G RP ⊞ lau A12 V5 15

France

ARDRES
Pas-de-Calais

At **AUTINGUES** (2 km S)

St-Louis 197 r Leulene ☎21354683

Turn off N43 approx 1 km SE of Ardres onto D227 and follow signs.
Apr–Sep.

1.5HEC ◆ H ⊙ ⊞ lau |O| Ls A10 pitch11

ARÈS
Gironde

Abberts ☎56602680

Follow signs from D106.
15 May–Sep.

2HEC ◆ ◆ H (15 Jun–10 Sep) ⊙ ⊞ lau |O| s A14 V5 16 16

Canadienne rte du Cap Ferret ☎56602491

1 km N off D106.
Jun–6 Sep.

2HEC ◆ H (Jun–Aug) |O| ⊙ G P ⊞ lau pitch57 (incl 2 persons)

Cigale ☎56602259

Clean tidy site amongst pine trees. Grassy pitches.

0.5 km N on D106.
Apr–15 Oct.

2.5HEC ◆ ◆ H |O| ⊙ G ⊞ lau s pitch50 (incl 2 persons)

CM Goelands ☎56825564

Apr–Sep.

10HEC ◆ ◆ H ⊙ G ⊞ lau Ls A10 Vn/c 35 30

ARGELÈS-GAZOST
Hautes-Pyrénées

At **ARRAS-EN-LAVENDAN** (2 km SW on N618)

Relais de l'Aubisque rte du Col de l'Aubisque ☎62970211

Apr–Oct.

1HEC ◆ H ⊙ G ⊞ lau |O| A8 V4 4

ARGELÈS-SUR-MER
Pyrénées-Orientales

Bois Fleuri rte de Sorède ☎68810257

Etr–Sep.

13HEC ◆ H |O| ⊙ G R P ⊞ lau

Clos Joli chemin de C-Magnus ☎68810514

800 m E on N618.
Apr–Sep.

2HEC ◆ H |O| ⊙ G R Ⓟ ⊞ lau s

Criques de Porteils ☎68811273

Terraced site with beautiful view of sea.

4 km S on N114 turn left through railway underpass and continue for 0.3 km.
Mar–Oct.

5HEC ◆ H |O| ⊙ G s ⊞ lau A17 pitch23

Dauphin 6 rte de Taxo d'Avall ☎68811754

On a long stretch of grassland shaded by poplars, 1500 m from sea.

3 km N of town; at Taxo d'Avall turn right onto unclass road.
Apr–Sep.

5.5HEC ◆ H |O| ⊙ G P Ⓟ (pm) ⊞ lau pitch59 (incl 2 persons)

Haras Palau de Vidre ☎68221450

Off D11.

All year.

2.5HEC ◆ H |O| ⊙ G P ⊞ lau A14 pitch27

Massane ☎68810685

Well laid-out site in shady garden 1 km from sea.

Beside D618 near the municipal sports field.
15 Mar–15 Oct.

2.7HEC ◆ ◆ H |O| ⊙ G ⊞ lau sP A10 V5 31 31

Neptune plage Nord ☎68810298

Etr–Sep.

3.3HEC ◆ H |O| ⊙ G Ⓟ (from 22.00hrs) ⊞ lau s pitch58 (incl 2 persons)

Piscines 1 rte de Taxo d'Avall ☎68810638

Off N114, to the right of the Plage Nord/Route d'Avall road.
15 May–15 Sep.

3.8HEC ◆ H |O| ⊙ G P ⊞ lau pitch60–100

Romarin rte de Sorède ☎68810263

2.5 km SW on D2.
15 Jun–15 Sep.

2HEC ◆ H ⊙ Ⓟ

CM Roussillonnais ☎68811042

On a long stretch of sandy terrain adjoining a fine sandy beach.

In N part of town. Well signposted.
15 Apr–15 Oct.

10HEC ◆ H |O| ⊙ G s ⊞ lau A17 pitch20

Sardane ☎68811082

Enclosed pitches under tall trees.

3 km E of N114.
Etr–Sep.

4HEC ◆ H ⊙ G R ⊞ lau |O| s

Sirène rte de Taxo ☎68810461

Etr–Oct.

14HEC ◆ ◆ H |O| ⊙ G R P ⊞ lau pitch95 (incl 2 persons)

At **ARGELÈS-PLAGE** (2.5 km E by D618)

Beauséjour ☎68811063

On a long stretch of grassland on the landward side of D81.

15 Jun–15 Sep.

3HEC H lau s

Pins av du Tech ☎68811046

On a narrow stretch of grassland with some poplar trees.

Jun–15 Sep.

4HEC H lau s A15 pitch22

Soleil ☎68811448

Peaceful site in wide meadow surrounded by tall trees. Private beach, natural harbour. Best site in region, but pitches must be booked in advance.

Follow rte du Littoral N out of town then 1.5 km towards beach.
15 May–Sep.

15HEC H s lau A20 pitch35

ARGENTAN
Orne

At **MAUVAISVILLE** (2.8 km SE off N158)

Val de Baize ☎33672711

All year.

1HEC H lau A7 V4 4 4

ARGENTAT
Corrèze

Gibanel ☎55281011

Pleasant site situated in grounds of a château next to a lake.

Jun–15 Sep.

6HEC H (Jul–Aug) LP lau A13 V6 9 9

Saulou ☎55281233

6 km S on D116.
May–20 Sep.

7HEC H RP lau A12 Vn/c 13 13

At **MONCEAUX-SUR-DORDOGNE** (3 km SW)

Vaurette ☎55280967

On the banks of the River Dordogne.

May–Sep.

3.5HEC H R lau A10 pitch10

ARGENTIÈRE
Haute-Savoie

Glacier d'Argentière ☎50540392

Clean site on sloping meadowland in beautiful quiet situation at the foot of the Mont Blanc Massif.

Access is 1 km S of Argentière, turn off N506 towards Cableway Lognan et des Grandes Montets, then a further 200 m to site.
Jun–Sep.

1HEC H lau P A8 V4 6 5

ARGENTON-CHÂTEAU
Deux-Sèvres

CM Pont de Ciron ☎49659189

0.4 km S on D748.
Jun–Sep.

1HEC H lau L A5 pitch5

ARLES
Bouches-du-Rhône

City 67 rte de Crau ☎90930886

1.5 km SE off N453 towards Salon.
Apr–Sep. ➔

France

2.5HEC H P lau A11 V5 10 10

Crin Blanc ☎66874878

Apr–Sep.

4.5HEC H G R P P lau

ARLES-SUR-TECH

Pyrénées-Orientales

Riuferrer ☎68391106

Quiet holiday site on gently sloping ground in pleasant area. Clean sanitary installations. Separate area reserved for overnight stops.

Signposted from N115.
All year.

4HEC H G R R lau A10 pitch15

Rive ☎68391554

On N115, 200 m NE.
May–15 Oct.

2.5HEC H G R lau A13 pitch15

ARNAC

Cantal

Gineste ☎71629190

On Lake Enchanet.

3HEC H L

ARNAY-LE-DUC

Côte-d'Or

CM de Fouché ☎80900223

0.7 km E on D17C.
All year.

4HEC H G L lau A6 V3 4 4

ARPAJON-SUR-CÈRE

Cantal

See also **AURILLAC**

Sapinière Cros de Ronesque ☎71624786

S via D459.
All year.

1HEC H G R lau pp5

ARRADON

Morbihan

Penboch ☎97447129

May–15 Sep.

4HEC H G P lau S A13 pitch23

ARRAS-EN-LAVENDAN See ARGELÈS-GAZOST

ARREAU

Hautes-Pyrénées

Refuge International rte de Lannemezan ☎62986334

Enclosed terraced site.

2 km N on D929.
8 Jun–15 Sep.

4HEC H G lau

ARROMANCHES-LES-BAINS

Calvados

CM av de Verdun ☎31223678

1.5HEC H

ARS-EN-RÉ See RÉ (ÎLE DE)

ARS-SUR-FORMANS

Ain

Bois de la Dame ☎74007723

Access from A6, exit Villefranche. Continue E via D904.
Apr–Sep

1.1HEC H G lau pitch39 (incl 2 persons)

ARVIEU

Aveyron

Rêve du Pêcheur Notre-Dame d'Aures ☎65463111

Beside Lake Pareloop.

Jun–15 Sep

2HEC H G R L lau pitch68 (incl 2–3 persons)

ASCAIN

Pyrénées-Atlantiques

Nivelle rte de St-Pee-sur-Nivelle ☎59540194

2 km N of town on D918 to St-Jean-de-Luz.
15 Jun–15 Sep.

3HEC H G lau P

ATTEUCH See ANDUZE

AUBAGNE

Bouches-du-Rhône

Claire-Fontaine rte de la Tuilliere ☎42030228

3 km NW on D44.

4HEC H G lau

AUBENAS

Ardèche

CM Pins ☎75351815

Terraced site with special pitches for caravans.

2.7 km NW on D235 (rte de Lazuel).
Etr–Oct.

8HEC H G lau

AUBIGNAN

Vaucluse

Intercommunal du Brégoux chemin du Vas ☎90626250

A level site with good views of Mt. Ventoux.

On southern outskirts of town turn off D7 onto D55 and continue towards Caromb for 0.5 km
15 Mar–Oct.

4HEC H lau A10 pitch8

AUBIGNY-AU-BAC

Nord

Moderne 25 r L-Lagrange ☎27809139

Surrounded by hedges beside canal.
Signposted
Apr–Oct.

3HEC H R lau P

AUBUSSON

Creuse

CM ☎55661800

1.5 km S on D982, rte de Felletin.
Jun–Sep.

3HEC H G P lau P A5 V5 5 5

AUCH

Gers

CM ☎62050022

S on N21 (rte de Tarbes).
All year.

1.5HEC H lau P

AUMALE

Seine-Maritime

CM Grand Mail

Apr–15 Sep.

0.5HEC H lau P A5 V3 3 3

AUREILHAN

Landes

CM ☎58090339

Quiet site separated by a small road on the banks of the Étang d'Aureilhan

15 May–15 Oct.

6HEC H G lau A9 V3 15 7

Domaine de Vacances Eurolac ☎58090287

Well tended site under deciduous trees providing shade, partially on open meadow.

Turn right at Labouheyre off N10 on D626 to Aureilhan. Follow signs.
Jun–Sep.

13HEC H G lau L pitch60–70 (incl 2 persons)

AURILLAC

Cantal

See also **ARPAJON-SUR-CÈRE**

CM Ombrade ☎71482887

Well-kept site on meadow with clean sanitary installations.

On NE outskirts of town near river.
15 May–Sep.

6HEC H

AUTINGUES See ARDRES

AUTRANS

Isère

Caravaneige du Vercors ☎76953188

All year.

1.5HEC H G lau P A10 V6 9 A9

Joyeux Réveil 76953344

NE of town via rte de Montaud.
All year.

1.5HEC H G R P lau pitch42 (incl 2 persons)

AUTUN
Saône-et-Loire

CM fbg d'Arroux 85521082

Partly divided by hedges with an open meadow for tents.

On D980, 500 m N of Roman gateway into the town.

2HEC H G P

AUXONNE
Côte-d'Or

CM Arquebuse 80373436

Clean, well-equipped site on right bank of River Saône near bathing area.

From Auxonne travel W on N5 for 3 km. Then turn northwards on D24 towards Athée and Pontailler-sur-Saône.
14 May–15 Sep.

2HEC H G R lau RP

AVALLON
Yonne

CM Sous Roche 86341039

2 km SE by D944 and D427.
15 Mar–15 Oct.

2HEC H lau A6 V3 3 A3

AVIGNON
Vaucluse

Bagatelle 90863039

Pleasant site with tall trees on the Isle of Barthelasse. All pitches are numbered; on hard standing and divided by hedges. Separate section for young people.

Travel alongside the old town wall and the Rhône onto the Rhône bridge (Nîmes road). About halfway along turn right and follow signs.
All year.

4HEC H G lau P A10 V5 5 A5

CM Pont St-Bénézet l'ile de la Barthelasse 90826350

On island opposite bridge with fine views of town. Several tiled sanitary blocks with individual wash cabins. Individual pitches. Common room with TV, souvenir shop, car wash. Several playing fields for volleyball and basketball. Definite divisions for tents and caravans.

NW of the town on the right bank of the Rhône, 370 m upstream from bridge on right. (N100 leading to Nîmes).
Mar–Oct.

9HEC H G lau P A11 Vn/c 13 A11

France

AVRANCHES
Manche

Mares 10 r de Verdun 33580545

Etr–15 Sep.

1HEC H lau P

At **GENÊTS** (10 km W on D911)

Coques d'Or rte de la Plage 33708257

1 km from the sea.
Etr–Sep.

2HEC H lau S A10 V5 5 A5

AVRILLE
Cantal

Mancelières rte de Longeville-sur-Mer 51903597

15 Jun–15 Sep.

2.6HEC H G lau pitch41 (incl 2 persons)

AXAT
Aude

Crémade 68205064

All year.

3HEC H G lau A7 V5 pitch6

Station des Pyrénées 68205327

1 km N on D117.
Apr–15 Oct.

2HEC H G R lau pitch45 (incl 3 persons)

AYGUADE-CEINTURON See **HYÈRES**

AYTRÉ See **ROCHELLE (LA)**

AZAY-LE-RIDEAU
Indre-et-Loire

Parc du Sabot r du Stade 47454272

Site lies in large meadow on bank of River Indre.

Near Château in town centre.
Etr–Oct.

6HEC H lau P A6 5 A5

AZUR
Landes

Paillotte 58481212

Site on N shore of lake with strip of pitches over 200 m long between forest and lake. Quiet family site (special toilets and washbasins for children) with own private sandy bathing area.

1.5 km SW.
Jun–15 Sep.

7HEC H L lau pitch109 (incl 3 persons)

BAERENTHAL
Moselle

Ramstein Plage 87065073

Apr–Sep.

6HEC H G R lau L A8 pitch5

BAGNÈRES-DE-BIGORRE
Hautes-Pyrénées

Bigourdan rte de Tarbes 62951357

Etr–Sep.

0.6HEC H G lau P A12 pitch10

Fruitiers 91 rte de Toulouse 62952597

5 May–30 Oct.

1.6HEC H lau R A10 pitch9

Tilleuls av A-Brooke 62952604

May–Sep.

2.6HEC H G lau P A12 pitch10

At **CAMPAN** (5.5 km S on D935)

Layris 62953534

On level meadow; asphalt drives.

All year.

1HEC H G R lau

At **TRÉBONS** (4 km N on D935)

Parc des Oiseaux 62953026

Clean, well-kept site with large pitches.

All year.

2.8HEC H G R lau A13 V6 8 A8

BAGNOLES-DE-L'ORNE
Orne

Vée au du Prés-Coty 33378765

Spread over two terraces, partially divided by hedges. Lunchtime siesta 12.00–14.00 hrs.

S on D335. Signposted.
Apr–Sep.

4HEC H G lau P

BAGNOLS-SUR-CÈZE
Gard

Genêts d'Or rte de Carmignan 66895867

Hilly terrain on the banks of the Cèze.

Turn off in outskirts towards Pont St-Esprit. Turn right off N86 at TOTAL filling station and continue 1.5 km in the direction of Carmignan.
15 Mar–15 Oct.

3.5HEC H G RP lau pitch32 (incl 2 persons)

BAGUER-PICAN See **DOL-DE-BRETAGNE**

BALLAN-MIRÉ See **TOURS**

France

BALME-LES-GROTTES (LA)
Isère

Domaine Beauséjour ☎74946157

Beside the River Rhône
May–Sep.

1.5HEC ◆ H lau

BANDOL
Var

Vallongue ☎94294955

Terraced site, parts of which have lovely sea views.

3 km NW on N559.
Apr–Sep.

1.5HEC H lau pitch38–43

BANNALEC
Finistère

Genêts d'Or rte du Trevoux ☎98968067

1 km S off N165.
Mid Apr–Oct.

1HEC ◆ H lau

BARATIER
Hautes-Alpes

Verger ☎92431587

Terraced site in plantation of fruit trees with fine views of Alps. Divided into pitches. Rest room with TV.

From N94 drive 2.5 km S of Embrun, 1.5 km E on D40.
All year.

2.5HEC H lau LP pitch55 (incl 3 persons)

BARBÂTRE See **NOIRMOUTIER (ÎLE DE)**

BARCARÈS (LE)
Pyrénées-Orientales

Bousigues ☎68861619

Quiet site standing about 1 km from the sea.

Etr–15 Dec.

3HEC H (Jul & Aug) lau s pitch42 (incl 2 persons)

California rte de St-Laurent ☎68861608

May–Sep.

5HEC H (20 Jun–Aug) P lau pitch68 (incl 2 persons)

Europe ☎68861536

Via D90 2 km SW, 200 m from Agly.
All year.

6HEC ◇ H P Rs

Floride et Embouchure rte de St-Laurent de la Salanque ☎68861175

On N9 SW of village.
Apr–Sep.

11HEC ◆ H R lau s pitch62 (incl 2 persons)

Paris ☎68861550

Widespread level site, between road and river. Modern sanitary installations. Pitches 100 sq m.

1.5 km SW on N9.
Etr–Sep.

3HEC ◆ H P Ⓟ (from 23.00 hrs) lau s pitch110 (incl 2–3 persons)

Presqu'île ☎68861280

2 km on rte de Leucate, turn right.
May–Oct.

3HEC ◆ H lau s

Sables d'Or av du Lido ☎68861841

Off D627 between Le Barcarès and Port Barcarès.
All year.

4HEC ◆ H P lau s pitch65 (incl 2 persons)

BARCELONNETTE
Alpes-de-Haute-Provence

Plan ☎92810811

Well-managed site divided into pitches.

Turn off D900 in town and head towards Col de la Coyalle.
25 May–Sep.

0.5HEC H lau P

BARFLEUR
Manche

Tamaris 21 r de Réville ☎33540158

SE on D1.
Apr–15 Sep.

1.5HEC H lau s A8 pitch13

BARNEVILLE-CARTERET
Manche

At **BARNEVILLE-PLAGE**

Pré Normand ☎33534864

On slightly hilly meadow away from traffic noise but exposed to sea winds. Vehicles allowed on beach but beware of tide.

Off D166.
Etr–15 Sep.

1.4HEC H lau s A13 pitch13

At **CARTERET**

CM Bocage ☎33538691

Opposite town hall.
Etr–Sep.

3HEC H lau s A11 pitch13

BARRE-DE-MONTS (LA)
Vendée

Corsive ☎51685006

Situated in quiet setting on two large fields.

2 km on D38A rte de la Grande Côte.
Jun–15 Sep.

1.3HEC H s

Grande Côte ☎51685189

In pine forest behind dunes.

3 km from village beside Noirmoutier toll bridge.
Apr–Sep.

10HEC H

BARRÊME
Alpes-de-Haute-Provence

Napoléon ☎92342015

SE off rte de Castellane.
15 Jun–5 Sep.

2.5HEC ◇ H lau P Ⓟ

BAR-SUR-AUBE
Aube

Gravière r des Varennes ☎25271294

0.5 km E of D13.
Apr–15 Oct.

2.75HEC ◆ H lau P

BAR-SUR-LOUP (LE)
Alpes-Maritimes

Gorges du Loup chemin des Vergers ☎93424506

Terraced site divided into pitches, in an olive grove. Very steep entrance.

Access from Grasse on D2085 towards Le Pré du Lac (NE), then turn left on to D2210 in the direction of Vence.
Apr–Oct.

1.6HEC ◆ H P lau pitch39–99

BATZ-SUR-MER
Loire-Atlantique

Govelle rte de la Côte Sauvage ☎40239163

On D45 between Le Pouliguen and Batz.
Apr–Sep.

1HEC ◇ H s lau pitch52–88 (incl up to 3 persons)

BAULE (LA)
Loire-Atlantique

Ajoncs d'Or ☎40603329

Etr–Oct.

2.9HEC ◆ H lau s A17 pitch18

CM av P-Minot & av R-Flandin ☎40601740

Site consists of two sections, one for caravans, one for tents, each with separate entrance. Caravan site (off av R-Flandin) is level and has good sanitary installations. Tent site (off av P-Minot) is in hilly, sandy woodland with only simply installations.

27 Mar–Sep.

6HEC ◆ H lau s pitch34–49 (incl 2 persons)

Eden ☏40600323

May–Sep.

3HEC H lau P

Roserale 20 av J-Sohier, rte du Golf ☏40604666

Apr–Sep.

2.5HEC H sP lau A16 pitch46

BAYEUX
Calvados

CM Calvados bd d'Eindhoven ☏31920843

Very clean and tidy site with tarmac drive and hardstanding for caravans. Adjoins football field.

N side of town on Boulevard Circulaire.
Mar–Oct.

3.5HEC H lau P A10 pitch11

BAYONNE
Pyrénées-Atlantiques

Airotel la Chêneraie ☏59550131

On gently sloping field divided by hedges.

4 km NE off N117 Pau road.
Etr–30 Oct.

12HEC H P lau A13 pitch22–38

BEAUCENS-LES-BAINS
Hautes-Pyrénées

Viscos ☏62970545

1 km N on D13, rte de Lourdes.
25 May–25 Sep.

2HEC H (Jul–Aug) lau A9 pitch9

BEAUCHASTEL
Ardèche

CM Volliers ☏75622404

900 m S of N86.
All year.

1.5HEC H P lau R A8 V5 6 6

BEAUMONT-DE-VENTOUX See **MALAUCÈNE**

BEAUMONT-SUR-SARTHE
Sarthe

CM du Val de Sarthe ☏43970193

E on D26 then turn right.
May–Sep.

2HEC H lau P A5 V3 3 3

BEAUNE
Côte-d'Or

CM Cent Vignes 10 r A-Dubois ☏80220391

On outskirts of town. Site divided into pitches; clean, well-looked after sanitary installations. From 20 Jun–31 Aug it is advisable to arrive before 16.00 hrs.

On N74 on Savigny-les-Beaune road.
15 Mar–Oct.

2HEC H lau P A9 V5 8 8

BEAURAINVILLE
Pas-de-Calais

CM de la Source ☏21814071

All year.

1.5HEC H lau R A11 Vn/c 11 11

BEAUVAIS
Oise

CM chemin de Carmard ☏44020022

S off r Binet.
15 Jun–15 Sep.

2HEC H lau A6 V2 2 2

BÉDOIN
Vaucluse

Domaine de Belezy ☏90656018

Situated in a fine park with a 'Club House' in a 17th-century mansion. **Part of the site is reserved for naturists.**

H P

BEG-MEIL
Finistère

Roche Percée ☏98949415

Jun–15 Sep.

2.2HEC H R lau s

Vorlen Plage de Kerambigorn ☏98949736

In field, partly surrounded by hedges and divided into pitches near beach. Supervised beach with children's playground.

20 May–20 Sep.

10HEC H P lau s A13 V6 20 20

BELGENTIER
Var

Peiresc ☏94489755

Divided into pitches in an orchard.

W of D554 next to Le Gapeau River.
All year

2HEC H lau

BELGODÈRE See **CORSE (CORSICA)**

BELLEGARDE-SUR-VALSERINE
Ain

Crêt d'Eau 2 av de Lattre-de-Tassigny ☏50482370

3 km N of town, 200m from N84.
Jun–Aug.

4.5HEC lau P

BELLE-ILE-EN-MER
Morbihan

PALAIS (LE)

Rosbossère ☏97318386

Quiet holiday site behind farm, part lying in small orchard.

1 km from town. Signposted.
Apr–Sep.

2.5HEC H lau s A5 V4 4 4

SAUZON

CM Pen Prad ☏97318104

On meadow in valley.

Off D30 towards Le Palais.
mid Apr–Sep. ➔

1.5HEC H lau s

BELLERIVE See **VICHY**

BELVÈS
Dordogne

Moulin de la Pique ☎53290115

A quiet site. Surroundings include an old mill which has been converted into high class apartments.

500 m S on D710.
Etr–Sep.

3HEC H LP lau **A**18 **V**n/c 23 **Å**23

At **STE-FOY-DE-BELVÈS** (5 km SE by D710 and D54)

Hauts de Ratebout ☎53290210

An old Périgord farm, set in extensive grounds.

May–Sep.

10HEC H P lau **A**20 pitch30

BÉNODET
Finistère

Lanrivoal ☎98561078

15 May–20 Sep.

3HEC H lau s

Letty ☎98570469

Site divided into sectors. Good sanitary installations; ironing rooms and games room. Good beach for children.

By the sea 1 km SE.
22 Jun–6 Sep.

10HEC s lau **A**12 **V**6 19 **Å**19

Mer Blanche ☎98570075

3.5 km E on D44 (Fouesnant road).
All year.

7HEC H lau s

Pointe St-Gilles ☎98570537

Holiday site south of village, on fields by beach. Divided into several sectors; individual pitches. Well-equipped sanitary blocks.

May–Sep.

6HEC H sP lau **A**13 **V**6 21 **Å**21

Port de Plaisance Prat Poulou ☎98570238

15 Apr–Sep.

4HEC H P lau s **A**13 **V**6 19 **Å**19

BÉNOUVILLE
Calvados

Hautes Coutures rte de Ouistreham ☎31447308

All year.

3HEC H P lau **A**17 pitch17

BERNAY
Eure

CM ☎32433047

1 km S on N138.
Jun–Sep.

1HEC H lau P **A**8 **V**7 10 **Å**7

BERNIÈRES-SUR-MER
Calvados

Havre de Bernières ☎31966709

300 m to the village in the direction of Courseulles.
All year.

6HEC H (Jul–Aug) lau sP **A**13 pitch13

BERNIÈRES-SUR-SEINE
Eure

Château-Gaillard ☎32541820

All year.

25HEC H (wknds Jun–Aug) P lau R **A**22 pitch18–32

BERNY-RIVIÈRE
Aisne

Croix du Vieux Pont ☎2355002

North of N31; cross River Aisne, site is 500 m E of Vic-sur-Aisne on D91.
All year.

8HEC H P lau pitch65 (incl 2 persons)

BERTANGLES
Somme

Château ☎22936803

Site in old orchard of Château.

Signed off Amiens – Doullens road.
May–Aug.

1HEC lau **A**11 pitch11

BESANÇON
Doubs

At **ROCHE-LEZ-BEAUPRÉ** (NE on N83)

CM Plage ☎81880426

Mar–15 Dec.

2.5HEC H P lau

BESSÈGES
Gard

At **PEYREMALE** (3 km W)

Drouilhèdes ☎66250480

2 km W on D17 rte de Génolhac, and continue 1 km on D386.
15 Mar–Oct.

1.8HEC H R lau pitch52 (incl 2 persons)

BESSÉ-SUR-BRAYE
Sarthe

CM Val de Braye ☎43353113

Beside River Braye.

On D303.
15 Mar–15 Oct.

2HEC H P lau **A**5 **V**3 3 **Å**3

BESSINES-SUR-GARTEMPE
Haute-Vienne

At **MORTEROLLES-SUR-SEMME** (4.5 km N on N20)

CM ☎55760928

100 m from N20; in town centre.
All year.

10HEC H lau **A**5 pitch5

BEYNAC
Dordogne

Beynac-Plage ☎53295003

Jun–Sep.

3HEC H R lau **A**10 **V**n/c 10 **Å**10

BEYNAT
Corrèze

Étang de Miel ☎55855066

Beside lake.

4 km E on N121 Argentat road.
Etr–Sep.

16HEC H lau LP **A**8 pitch7

BEZINGHEM
Pas-de-Calais

Aulnes ☎21909388

Mar–Oct.

5HEC H lau **A**9 pitch18

BEZOUCE
Gard

Cyprés ☎66262430

Slightly sloping meadow; divided into pitches with fruit and poplar trees.

Off N86 N of town centre.
15 Mar–Sep.

0.6HEC H lau

BIARRITZ
Pyrénées-Atlantiques

Biarritz 28 r d'Harcet ☎59230012

Site lies 200 m from beach; 2 km from town centre on N10, follow signs 'Espagne'.
Apr–Oct.

3HEC H lau s **A**10 **V**4 19 **Å**12

Splendid 12 r d'Harcet ☎59230129

On gently sloping ground.

3 km S.
Apr–Sep.

1.6HEC lau s A10 V5 13 12

At **ARCANGUES** (4 km S on D254)
Aldabénia 59430730

4 km from beaches.

D254 leave N10, 2 km E of Biarritz at La Négresse.
Jun–Sep.

1HEC lau A9 pitch11

At **BIDART** (4 km SW)
Berrua rte d'Arbonne 59549666

Level meadowland with young plantation in rural surroundings. 800 m to sea.

May–Sep.

5HEC sP lau A12 pitch 9

Ferme Oyamburua 59549161

Level meadow site near farm. Views of the Pyrénées. Simple but pleasant site.

Turn off beyond the church in the direction of Arbonne, via N10, for approx 1 km.
15 May–Sep.

3HEC P lau **pp**11

Itsasoa-la-Mer 59265221

On meadowland, divided by a road.

Turn by ESSO filling station onto D655 Ahetze road.
Jun–Sep.

2.5HEC lau s

Jean Paris quartier M-Pierre 59265558

400 m from beaches.

S of town, cross railway line, site on S side of N10.
Jun–Sep.

1HEC lau s A10 pitch15

Pavilion Royal av Prince de Galles 59230054

Beautiful, well-kept site, divided into pitches, most of which have open view of sea. Beside rocky beach.

2 km N.
15 May–Sep.

5HEC sP lau pitch95 (incl 2 persons)

Résidence des Pins rte de Biarritz 59230029

Terraced site with numbered pitches, 800 m from sea.

2 km N on N106 Biarritz road.
Jun–Sep.

6HEC lau Ls pitch52 (incl 2 persons)

Ruisseau rte d'Arbonne 59235456

2 km E on D255.
23 May–Sep.

14HEC LP lau A15 V5 18 18

France

BIAS
Landes

CM Tatiou 58090476

Seasonal.

8HEC lau

BIDART See **BIARRITZ**

BILLIERS
Morbihan

Guerandière rte de Penlan Billiers 97416224

1 km from sea.

S of village on D5 Pointe de Pen-Lan road.
May–Sep.

2HEC lau s A7 V4 4 4

BINIC
Côtes-du-Nord

Fauvettes r des Fauvettes 96736083
1 km from Binic to coast.
15 Jun–15 Sep.

1HEC lau s

Korrigans No 2 96736234

100 m from the beach.

15 Mar–15 Oct.

1HEC lau Ps A14 V9 10 10

Panoramic 96736043

On a meadow divided into pitches, on a hill above the town.

On S outskirts of village.
20 Mar–Sep.

3HEC lau s A14 V6 10 10

Papliou r de l'Ic 96736156

15 May–Sep.

1HEC lau Ps A17 V8 7 7

BIOT See **ANTIBES**

BISCARROSSE
Landes

Mayote 58780000

Level well tended woodland meadow on Etang de Cazaux.

Turn off N652 on the road to Sanguinet about 5 km beyond Biscarrosse.
All year.

8HEC lau L

Rive 58781233

Level site in tall pine forest on E side of lake.

N of town off D652 Sanguinet road.
Apr–Sep.

10HEC lau L A13 V7 11 11

BISARROSSE-PLAGE
Landes

CM de la Plage 58782124

On S outskirts of village 1 km from beach in large pine forest.
All year

22HEC lau

BLAINVILLE-SUR-MER
Manche

Mélette 33471484

1 km W on D651.
15 Jun–15 Sep.

12HEC lau s

BLANGY-LE-CHÂTEAU
Calvados

Brévedent 31647288

3 km SE on D51 beside lake.
15 May–15 Sep.

3.5HEC P lau A22 pitch25

Domaine du Lac rte du Mesnil-sur Blangy 31646200

All year

6.5HEC P lau

BLANGY-SUR-BRESLE
Seine-Maritime

CM 14 r G-Chekroun 35935005

300 m on N28.
Apr–Sep.

0.4HEC

BLAYE
Gironde

At **MAZION** (5.5 km NE on RN937)
Tilleuls 57421813

All year

0.7HEC lau P

BLÉRÉ
Indre-et-Loire

CM 47579260

Well-kept site beside River Cher. Two entrances.

Mar–Sep.

4HEC P lau R

BLOIS
Loir-et-Cher

CM Boire rte de St-Dye 54742278

1.5 km E on D751
Mar–1 Dec.

1HEC lau A7 V4 10 10

BOCCA (LA) See **CANNES**

BOËN-SUR-LIGNON
Loire

Domaine de Giraud rte de Feurs 77240891

1 km SE on N89.
Apr–Nov.

2HEC H G lau R A5 V3 3 A3

BOIS-PLAGE-EN-RÉ (LE) See **RÉ (ÎLE DE)**

BOISSET-ET-GAUJAC
Gard

Domaine de Gaujac 66618065

4 km SE.
15 Apr–15 Sep.

11HEC H G lau RP pitch58 (incl 2 persons)

BOLLÈNE
Vaucluse

Barry 90301320

Well-kept site near ruins of Barry.

Signposted from Bollène via D26.
All year

3HEC H G P lau A15 pitch12

BOMBANNES
Gironde

Base de Bombannes 56033101

Quiet, extensive site in a large recreation ground. Separate sections for caravans and tents.

From Carcans W on D3E, and turn right after Maubuisson.
All year.

22HEC H (Jul & Aug) (Jun–Sep) P lau P

BONNAC-LA-CÔTE
Haute-Vienne

Château de Leychoisier 55399343

Well-managed site on ground sloping gently towards the woods. Divided into roomy pitches.

1 km S off N20.
Apr–Sep.

8HEC H G lau L

BONNAL See **ROUGEMONT**

BORMES-LES-MIMOSAS
Var

Manjastre 98 rte de Dom 95710328

All year

3.5HEC H G lau A11 pitch13

At **FAVIÈRE (LA)** (3 km S)
Domaine 94710312

In a very attractive setting with a long sandy beach and numbered pitches. Food supplies in peak season only. Fine views of sea. Sports facilities.

0.5 km E of Bormes Cap Bénat road.
Apr–Oct.

4HEC H G s lau A16 Vn/c 20–44 17–20

France

BORT-LES-ORGUES
Corrèze

CM Beausoleil rte de Ribeyrolles 55960031

1.5 km SW via D979.
Jun–15 Sep.

4HEC H G

BOSSONS (LES) See **CHAMONIX-MONT-BLANC**

BOULOGNE-SUR-MER
Pas-de Calais

At **PORTEL (LE)** (1 km SW)
Phare 21316920

Situated on the edge of the town beside the sea.
Apr–15 Sep.

7HEC H G R s lau pitch60 (incl 4 persons)

BOULOURIS-SUR-MER
Var

Ile d'Or 94955213

Apr–Oct.

6HEC H G lau s pitch62 (incl 2 persons)

Val Fleury 94952152

Terraced site with tarred drives.

Off N98 at Km 93.1
All year

1HEC H lau s

BOURBON-LANCY
Saône-et-Loire

CM de St-Prix 85891485

By the swimming pool off the D979a.
15 Apr–15 Oct.

2.5HEC H G P A8 V4 5 4

BOURBON-L'ARCHAMBAULT
Allier

CM Parc Bignon 70670883

1 km SW on N153, rte de Montluçon, turn right.
Mar–1 Dec.

3HEC H lau P A6 V3 3 3

BOURBOULE (LA)
Puy-de-Dôme

Clarines 73810230

Best site in district. Partly gravelled, part terraced with 100 m sq pitches. Good sanitary installations with individual washbasins in women's section.

1.5 km E.
Feb–15 Oct.

3.5HEC H G lau

BOURDEAUX
Drôme

At **POËT-CÉLARD (LE)** (3 km NW)
Couspeau 75533014

May–Sep.

3HEC H G P lau pitch40 (incl 2 persons)

BOURG-ACHARD
Eure

Clos Normand 129 rte de Pont Audemer 32563484

Apr–Sep.

1.4HEC H G lau A8 V4 7 7

BOURG-DE-PÉAGE
Drôme

CM du Parc des Sports 75701280

In football ground near swimming pool.

Well signposted from edge of town.
May–Sep.

1.5HEC H G P lau A12 V3 3 V3

BOURG-D'OISANS (LE)
Isère

Caravaneige le Vernis 76800268

Well-kept site with modern sanitary facilities. At foot of mountain in summer ski-ing area.

2.5 km on N91, rte de Briançon.
15 Jun–15 Sep.

1.5HEC H G R lau R

Cascade 76801011

Completely divided into pitches at the foot of a mountain with a waterfall and modern, very well-kept sanitary arrangements. Television lounge with library, open fireplace. Booking essential.

All year.

2HEC H G R lau P

Rencontre du Soleil rte de l'Alpe d'Huez 76800033

Charming site in a lovel setting in the Dauphiny Alps at the foot of a mountain. Fine rustic common room with open fireplace. TV, playroom for children.

At the foot of the hairpin road to L'Alpe-d'Huez, leave N91 (Grenoble–Briançon road) in the Le Bourg d'Oisans.
20 Mar–Apr & 20 May–10 Sep.

1.6HEC H G lau P pitch69 (incl 3 persons)

At **ROCHETAILLÉE** (6 km N)

Belledonne ☎76800718
15 Jun–5 Sep.
3.5HEC ▥ ◈ ⋔H ▪ ▼ |O| ⊙ ▪
Ⓖ ≈P ⛺ ⊞ lau
pitch57 (incl 3 persons)

At **VENOSC** (10 km SE on N91 and D530)

Champ du Moulin ☎76800738
15 Jun–15 Sep & 10 Nov–2 May.
1HEC ▥ ◈ ⋔H ▪ ▼ |O| ⊙ ▪
Ⓖ Ⓡ ⊞ ≈RP ⛺ ⊞ lau

BOURG-EN-BRESSE
Ain

CM de Challes av de Bad Kreuznach ☎74222779
In football ground near swimming pool.
Well signposted from outskirts of town.
All year.
2.7HEC ▥ ∴ ◈ ⋔H ▪ ⊙ ▪ Ⓖ
≈P ⛺ ⊞ lau ⇴ ▼ |O|

BOURGET-DU-LAC (LE)
Savoie

CM Ile aux Cygnes ☎79250176
May–Sep.
3.8HEC ▥ ◈ ⋔H ▪ ⊙ ▪ Ⓖ ≈L
⛺ ⊞ lau **A**11 **V**8 ▪17 **▲**17

BOURG-MADAME
Pyrénées-Orientales

Ségre rte d'Ax-les-Thermes ☎68045176
100 m N on N20
1HEC ▥ ◈ ⋔H ⊙ ▪ Ⓖ Ⓡ ⛺ ⊞
⇴ ▪ |O|

BOURGNEUF-EN-RETZ
Loire-Atlantique

CM du Collet ☎40214055
Flat, well-kept site. Sea unsuitable for swimming.
3 km SW on N758
Jun–15 Sep.
0.2HEC ▥ ∴ ⋔H ⊙ ▪ Ⓖ ⛺ ⊞
lau ⇴ ≈s

BOURG-ST-ANDÉOL
Ardèche

Lion ☎75545320
Large well-shaped park in wooded terrain, beside River Rhône.

France

Apr–Sep.
8HEC ▥ ◆ ⋔H ▪ ▼ |O| ⊙ ▪
Ⓖ ≈PR ⛺ ⊞ lau pitch51 (incl. 2 persons)

BOURG-ST-MAURICE
Savoie

Versoyen rte des Arcs ☎79070345
Two communal sanitary blocks – one heated. Ski-ing facilities. Many secluded pitches in a wood.
On S outskirts of town. Access via N90.
All year.
3HEC ▥ ◇ ⋔H ⊙ ▪ Ⓖ ⊞ ⛺
⊞ lau ⇴ ▪ ▼ |O| ≈P **A**14
pitch12

BOUT-DU-LAC
Haute-Savoie

CM ☎50443344
Extensive site divided into pitches in attractive surroundings.
150 m off N508 at S of Lac d'Annecy.
May–Sep.
7HEC ▥ ◈ ⋔H ▪ ▼ |O| ⊙ ▪
Ⓖ ≈L ⛺ ⊞ lau **A**8 pitch9

Lac Bleu rte d'Albertville ☎50443018
Modern, well-kept site. Overflow area with own sanitary blocks.
On the southern shores of Lake Annecy via the N508, opposite ANTAR Garage.
Apr–15 Oct.
3HEC ▥ ◆ ⋔H ▪ ▼ |O| ⊙ ▪
Ⓖ ⌂ ≈L ⛺ ⊞ lau pitch55 (incl. 3 persons)

BOYARDVILLE See **OLÉRON (ILE D')**

BRACIEUX
Loir-et-Cher

CM des Châteaux rte de Blois ☎54464184
N on left bank of River Beauvron.
20 Mar–Oct.
7HEC ▥ ◆ ⋔H ⊙ ▪ ⌂ ≈P ⛺
⊞ ⇴ ▪ ▼ |O| **A**7 **V**n/c ▪4 **▲**4

BRAGUE (LA) See **ANTIBES**

BRÉHAL
Manche

Vanlée ☎33616380
Site by sea on uneven, sandy meadow behind strip of dunes. Quiet situation. Magnificent beach. Good for children. Not crowded in peak season. Big common room, bar, games room, TV room. Golf and stables nearby.
5 km W at St-Martin.
May–15 Sep.
12HEC ∴ ◇ ⋔H ▪ ▼ ⊙ ▪ Ⓖ Ⓡ
≈s ⛺ ⊞ lau **A**10 pitch10

BRESSE (LA)
Vosges

Terrain des Écorces ☎29254129
In beautiful situation beside River Moselotte.
Off D34.
All year.
1.5HEC ▥ ∴ ◈ ⋔H ⊙ ▪ ⛺ ⊞
lau ⇴ ▪ ▼ |O| **A**7 **V**4 ▪6 **▲**5

BRETIGNOLLES-SUR-MER
Vendée

Dunes Plage des Dunes (3 km S) ☎51905532
2 km S turn right off D38 and proceed for 1 km across the dunes. 150 m from beach.
Etr–Oct.
12HEC ▥ ∴ ◈ ◇ ⋔H ▪ ▼ |O|
⊙ ▪ Ⓖ ⛺ ⊞ lau ⇴ ≈s **A**12
pitch67

Motine r des Morinières ☎51900442
Pleasant site situated 350 m from the town centre and 400 m from the beach.
May–Sep.
1.1HEC ▥ ◈ ⋔H ▼ |O| ⊙ ▪ Ⓖ
⊞ ⛺ ⊞ lau ⇴ ▪ ≈s pitch58–70 (incl. 3 persons)

Vagues 20 bd du Nord ☎51901948
Jun–Sep.
3HEC ▥ ◈ ⋔H ▼ ⊙ ▪ Ⓖ ⊞
⛺ ⊞ lau ⇴ ▪ ≈s pitch52–68 (incl 3 persons)

BRIANÇON
Hautes-Alpes

Cinq Vallées ☎92210627

Level site divided into pitches on natural wooded terrain next to River Durance.

2 km S on N94 towards St-Blaise.
Jun-15 Sep.

4HEC lau A15 pitch15

BRIVE-LA-GAILLARDE
Corrèze

CM des Iles bd Michelet ☎55243474

Beside River Corrèze.

All year.

2HEC lau P A8 pitch5

BRIVES-CHARENSAC See **PUY (LE)**

BROU
Eure-et-Loir

Base de Plein Air et de Loisirs ☎37470217

Apr–Oct.

4HEC P lau A7 pitch7

BRUNÉMONT
Nord

Parc de Pleine Air de la Sensée ☎27809128

S on D247.
Apr–Oct.

6HEC A11 pitch11

BRUYÈRES
Vosges

At **CHAPELLE-DEVANT-BRUYÈRES (LA)** (5 km SE by N423)

Pinasses ☎29585110

All year.

3HEC P lau A12 pitch17

BUGEAT
Corrèze

CM des Trois Ponts ☎55955003

1 km NW on D97, rte de Tarnac.
Apr–15 Oct.

11HEC R lau

BUGUE (LE)
Dordogne

CM du Port ☎53062460

On the Les Eyzies road (D703) 500 m from town.
15 Jun–15 Sep.

1.8HEC lau P

At **LIMEUIL** (5.5 km SW by D703 and D31)

Port de Limeuil ☎53220210

Adjacent to the confluence of the Rivers Dordogne and Vézère and facing Limeuil.

Jun–10 Sep.

6.4HEC R lau

France

CABELLOU (LE) See **CONCARNEAU**

CABOURG
Calvados

Vert Pré rte de Caen ☎31914168

2 km SW on D513.
Apr–Sep

6HEC lau S A11 pitch11

CAEN
Calvados

CM rte de Louvigny ☎31736092

S along left bank of the River Orne on the D212.
Jun–Sep.

2.2HEC lau P A6 V3 3 3

CAGNES-SUR-MER
Alpes-Maritimes

Country Club Cocagne Camp'otel ☎93209119

A small luxurious family site with numbered pitches divided by hedges. There is a tractor to help vehicles climb the entrance ramp, which is 300 m long with a 25% (1 in 4) gradient.

N of Cagnes-sur-Mer on D36.
All year.

0.5HEC P lau pitch76–135 (incl 2 persons)

Oasis rte de Grasse ☎93207567

Level terrain partially gravelled, 2 km from beach.

1 km W on D2085 towards Grasse.
Mar–Nov.

1.8HEC P lau SR

Rivière chemin des Salles ☎93206227

4 km N beside River Cagne.
All year.

1HEC P lau pitch40 (incl 2 persons)

At **CROS-DE-CAGNES** (2 km S)

Panoramer chemin des Gros-Buaux ☎93311615

Pleasant terraced site with sea view. Separate sections for tents and caravans.

2 km N of town.
Etr–20 Sep.

1.4HEC lau A12 V9 pitch70–90 (incl 3 persons)

CAHORS
Lot

CM St-Georges ☎65350464

All year.

0.7HEC lau RP A5 pitch5

At **ESCLAUZELS** (18 km SE)

Pompit ☎65315340

5 km NW of Esclauzels village.
15 Jun–15 Sep.

2.5HEC P lau A12 Vn/c 8 8

CALAIS
Pas-de-Calais

Peupliers 394 r du Beau Marais ☎21340356

Apr–Oct.

1.5HEC lau P pitch50

CALLAC
Côtes-du-Nord

CM Verte Vallée ☎96455850

15 Jun–15 Sep.

1.5HEC lau L A7 V3 4 4

CALVI See **CORSE (CORSICA)**

CALVIAC
Lot

Chênes Verts ☎53592107

May–Sep.

8.5HEC P lau A13 V10 15 15

Trois Sources ☎65330301

May–Oct.

9HEC R lau

CAMARET-SUR-MER
Finistère

Lambézan ☎98279141

3 km NE on rte de Roscanvel (D355).
May–15 Sep.

1.8HEC P lau S

CAMIERS
Pas-de-Calais

At **St-GABRIEL-PLAGE** (2.5 km W)

Dunes ☎21946177

Isolated site. Very bushy. Next to beach.

Etr–Sep.

4HEC S lau

At **STE-CÉCILE-PLAGE** (3 km NW)

Mer ☎21849225

Etr–Oct.

1HEC S lau

CAMPAN See **BAGNÈRES-DE-BIGORRE**

CAMPNEUSEVILLE
Seine-Maritime

Monchy-le-Preux ☎35937703

2 km N on D260.

CAUSSADE
Tarn-et-Garonne

Piboulette rte de Carjac ☎63930907

800 m NW from Caussade.
May–Oct.

1.5HEC ⊙ ⊞ lau |O| LRP

CAUTERETS
Hautes-Pyrénées

Mamelon-Vert av du Mamelon-Vert ☎62925156

Nov–Apr & 15 May–Sep.

3HEC ⊙ ⊞ lau |O| P **A**10 pitch10

CAVAILLON
Vaucluse

Durance ☎90711178

2 km S.
All year.

4HEC ⊙ ⊞ lau P

CAVALAIRE-SUR-MER
Var

Bonporteau ☎94640324

Site divided into pitches and partly terraced, 50 m above coast road.

Drive W on N559 on outskirts of town, turn N and continue 0.2 km.
25 Mar–15 Oct.

3HEC |O| ⊙ R ⊞ lau S pitch45–74

Canissons r des Canissons ☎94643181

SW via rte du Lavandou in a residential area.
Apr–Oct.

3HEC |O| ⊙ G ⊞ lau S

Cros de Mouton ☎94641087

Terraced site with individual pitches, separated for caravans and tents. Good view of sea, 1.5 km distance.

Turn off N559 in town centre and continue inland, 1.5 km.
Mar–Oct.

4.5HEC |O| ⊙ G ⊞ lau S **A**14 pitch16

Pinède rte du Lavandou ☎94641114

400m from sea.
Mar–Oct.

2HEC ⊙ G ⊞ lau |O| S **A**14 pitch14

CAVALIÈRE
Var

Mimosas rte du Lavandou ☎94058294

Very well-kept and divided into pitches. Specially designed for caravans.

NE of town off N559.
Feb–Oct.

5HEC |O| ⊙ ⊞ lau S **A**11 pitch29

Parc de Pramousquler ☎94058395

2.5 km E on N559, rte de Cavalière to Pramousquier.
15 May–Sep.

3HEC |O| ⊙ G ⊞ lau S **A**10 **V**n/c 14 14

CAYEAUX-SUR-MER
Somme

Brighton rte Littorale D225 ☎22257104

Situated 500 m from the sea.

Access from the rte Littorale D225.
All year.

4HEC ⊙ G ⊞ lau |O| S

Voyeul rte d'Eu ☎22266084

1.5 km S on D140.
All year.

1.4HEC ⊙ G ⊞ lau |O| S **A**6 **V**n/c 9 9

CAZÈRES
Haute-Garonne

At **PALAMINY**

Intercommunal le Plantaurel ☎61970371

Well-kept site, divided into pitches by hedges, on large open meadow. Open camp-fire clearng.

On S bank of the Garonne.
All year.

3.5HEC ⊙ P

CENDRAS
Gard

Croix Clementine ☎66865269

An extensive, partly terraced site.

Signposted W of town towards La Baume via D160.
Etr–Sep.

8HEC |O| ⊙ G R P ⊞ lau pitch60–77

CERNAY
Haut-Rhin

CM Acaclas r R-Guibert ☎89755697

Clean, quiet site on right bank of River Thur.

Off N83 between Colmar and Belfort.
May–Sep.

5HEC |O| ⊙ G ⊞ lau P **A**8 pitch9

CEYRAT
Puy-de-Dôme

CM av J-B Marrou ☎73613073

On undulating meadow on partly terraced hill. Large common room with games. Supplies only available peak season.

All year.

6HEC |O| ⊙ P ⊞ lau

CEYRESTE
Bouches-du-Rhône

Airotel de Ceyreste av E-Julien ☎42830768

Best-kept terraced site in the area, sutiated in a pine forest. Most sanitary arrangements are in individual cabins.

From La Ciotat turn left off D3 in town and continue uphill for 0.5km to entrance on left.
Etr–Oct.

3HEC ⊙ G ⊞ lau **A**12 pitch14

CHAGNY
Saône-et-Loire

CM Pâquler Fané ☎85872142

A clean site 600 m W of the church.

Follow the D974 from town centre.
2 May–Sep.

1.5HEC ⊙ G ⊞ lau P **A**9 pitch12

CHALLES-LES-EAUX
Savoie

Mont St-Michel chemin St-Vincent ☎79852073

Clean transit site on road to Chambéry and Grenoble.

15 May–Sep.

1.1HEC |O| ⊙ G ⊞ lau

CHALONNES-SUR-LOIRE
Maine-et-Loir

CM Candals ☎41780227

On the banks of the River Loire.

May–Oct.

2.5HEC ⊙ ⊞ lau |O| P **A**5 **V**4 4 4

CHÂLONS-SUR-MARNE
Marne

CM 51 rte de Sarry ☎26683800

On a park-like meadow broken up by hedges and flower beds.

At S end of town, signposted from town centre.
All year.

7HEC ⊙ G ⊞ lau |O| **A**10 **V**6 10 10

CHAMONIX-MONT BLANC
Haute-Savoie

Mer de Glace ☎50530863

2 km NE on N506 to Les Praz. On approach to village (from Chamonix) turn right under railway bridge.
Jun–Sep.

2HEC ⊙ G ⊞ lau |O| P **A**15 pitch15

Rosières ☎50531042

1 km NE on N506
All year. ➤

France

1.7HEC H G R lau P A13 pitch13

At **BOSSONS (LES)** (3 km W)

Cimes ☎50531900

In a wooded meadow at the foot of Mont Blanc Massif. Ideal for hiking and mountain tours.

15 Jun–15 Sep.

1HEC H G lau

Deux Glaciers ☎50531587

A glacial stream runs through the site. Pitches shaded by trees, very modern, well-kept sanitary installations. Rustic common room with open fires.

Leave N506 towards road underpass. 250 m to site.
15 Dec–15 Nov.

1.6HEC H G lau pitch45 (incl 3 persons)

Verneys

Well-kept terraced site on slightly sloping meadow. Views to Mont Blanc Massif.

Same access as Camping les Deux Glaciers.
Jun–Sep.

1HEC H G lau

CHAMPAGNOLE
Jura

CM Boyse rte de Voiteur ☎84520032

Clean and tidy site with asphalt drives and completely divided into pitches. In grounds of municipal swimming pool.

Turn onto D5 just before town and continue 1.3 km to site.
15 Jun–15 Sep.

0.7HEC H G P lau

CHAMPIGNY-SUR-MARNE See **PARIS**

CHANTEMERLE
Haute-Alpes

Serre-Chevalier ☎92240114

15 Jun–8 Sep.

3HEC H G R P lau

CHAPELLE-AUX-FILZMÉENS (LA)
Ille-et-Vilaine

Château ☎99452155

A quiet, pleasant site.

15 May–15 Sep.

5HEC H G R P lau

CHAPELLE-DEVANT-BRUYÈRES (LA) See **BRUYÈRES**

CHAPELLE-ST-MESMIN (LA)
Loiret

CM Château ☎38436046

500 m from N152.
Apr–Sep.

2.5HEC H lau P A9 pitch7

CHARLEVILLE-MEZIÈRES
Ardennes

CM Mont Olympe ☎24332360

Level meadowland near the town centre and 100 m from municipal indoor swimming pool.

Well signed from town centre.
Etr–15 Oct.

2HEC H lau P

CHAROLLES
Saône-et-Loire

CM ☎85240490

Mar–Oct

1.6HEC H G R P lau A6 V5 5 6

CHASTEUIL See **CASTELLANE**

CHÂTEAU ARNOUX
Alpes-de-Haute-Provence

CM Salettes ☎92640240

All year.

4HEC H G R RP lau A11 Vn/c 12 12

CHÂTEAU-D'OLÉRON (LA) See **OLÉRON (ÎLE D')**

CHÂTEAUDOUBLE
Drôme

Grand Lierne ☎75598314

Etr–15 Oct.

5HEC H G P lau pitch63 (incl 2 persons)

CHÂTEAU-DU-LOIR
Sarthe

CM Coëmont ☎43794463

2 km SE on N138.
May–15 Sep.

0.5HEC H lau A4 V2 2 2

CHÂTEAUDUN
Eure-et-Loire

CM Moulin-à-Tan r de Chôlet-St-Jean ☎37450534

15 Mar–15 Oct.

1.5HEC H lau A5 V3 5 5

CHÂTEAUNEUF-DU-RHÔNE
Drôme

CM ☎75908096

N end of village.
Jun–6 Sep.

0.6HEC H lau P

CHÂTEAU-RENAULT
Indre-et-Loire

CM Parc de Vauchevrier r P-L-Courier ☎47295443

Clean, well-kept site on a large field beside a swimming pool.

Singposted from N10.
Apr–Sep.

3.5HEC H P

CHÂTEAUROUX
Indre

CM Rochat ☎54342656

1 km N on Paris road.
All year.

3.5HEC H P A6 pitch5

CHÂTEAUROUX-LES-ALPES
Hautes-Alpes

Carlamas ☎92432263

On a meadow in an attractive mountain setting beside the River Durance.

1.5 km SE.
Jul–24 Aug.

10HEC H P lau A13 pitch17

CHÂTELAILLON-PLAGE
Charente-Maritime

Clos de Rivages av des Boucholeurs ☎46562609

Level, well-kept site.

15 Jun–10 Sep.

3HEC H G Ⓟ (after 22.00 hrs) lau sP

Deux Plages ☎46562753

19 Jun–15 Sep.

4.5HEC H G lau s

CHÂTILLON-EN-VENDELAIS
Ille-et-Vilaine

CM du Lac ☎99760622

0.5 km on D108.
Etr–Oct.

0.6HEC H G lau L A7 V3 4 4

CHÂTILLON-SUR-SEINE
Côte-d'Or

CM espl St-Vorles ☎80910305

SE of town off rte de Langres (D928).
Apr–Sep.

0.8HEC G P lau

CHÂTRES-SUR-CHER
Loir-et-Cher

CM des Saules ☎54980455

On N76 near bridge.
15 May–15 Sep.

1.8HEC H G lau A5 Vn/c 5 5

CHAUVIGNY
Vienne

CM Fontaine r de la Fontaine ☎49463194

NE of town in town park.

On N151 and follow signs.
All year.

1.5HEC lau P

CHAVAGNAC See **GAGNIÈRES**

CHÊNE-EN-SEMINE See **FRANGY**

CHERBOURG
Manche

Pins ☎33430078

5 km S of town off N13.
All year

5HEC lau **A**8 **V**n/c 10 10

CHINON
Indre-et-Loire

CM ☎47930835

On the banks of the river opposite the Château and off D951.

All year.

3HEC lau RP **A**6 **V**5 5 5

CHOISY-LE-ROI See **PARIS**

CHOLET
Maine-et-Loire

Lac de Ribou av du Lac ☎41624704

Well set-out site bordering a lake, with fishing, boating, tennis and volleyball.

France

3 km from town centre.
All year.

5HEC P lau

CHORGES
Hautes-Alpes

Prévalière ☎92506758

Clean site, on meadowland, partly terraced.

From village follow D3 southwards to Baie des Moulettes, then 500 m on.
15 Jun–Aug.

2HEC lau **A**9 pitch10

CIOTAT (LA)
Bouches-du-Rhône

Oliviers rte de Toulon ☎42831504

Terraced site between the N559 and the railway line from Nice.

Turn inland off the N559 at Km34, some 5 km E of the centre of the town and drive for 150 m.
Mar–Sep.

10HEC lau s **A**13 pitch17

St-Jean 30 av de St-Jean ☎42831301

Site on the right side of the coast road.

Between N559 and sea behind the motel in NE part of town.
Etr–Sep.

1HEC s lau pitch39–87 (incl 2–4 persons)

Soleil rte de Marseille (N559) ☎42835311

Divided into pitches.

Apr–Sep.

0.5HEC lau sP pitch58 (incl 4 persons)

CLAIRMARAIS See **ST-OMER**

CLAIRVAUX-LES-LACS
Jura

Grisière et Europe Vacances ☎84258048

Fenced in meadowland with some trees, sloping down to the Grand Lac. The site is guarded during July and August.

From village centre turn off N78, follow D118 towards Châtel-de-Joux for 800 m to the site.
May–Sep.

11HEC L lau **A**9 pitch7

CLAOUEY
Gironde

Airotel les Viviers rte du Cap Ferret ☎56607004

Beautiful, widespread site in a forest divided by seawater channels. ➤

On the D106, 1 km S of the town.
May–27 Sep.
33HEC H G P lau
pitch99–106 (incl 3 persons)

CM les Embruns ☎56607076

All year.

30HEC H lau G S

CLAPIERS
Hérault

Plein Air des Chênes ☎67591098

All year.

8HEC H P lau

CLÉDEN-POHER
Finistère

Moulin Vert ☎98938205

3.8 km SW off N787.
Jun–Aug.

3HEC H G R lau **A**9 **V**5 10 10

CLÉDER
Finistère

CM Roguennic ☎98696388

5 km N on coast.
15 Jun–15 Sep.

8.5HEC H lau

CLOHARS-CARNOËT
Finistère

Kergariou ☎98715465

Take rte du Porte de Doëlan on left in village centre.
All year

5HEC H G R R lau **A**10 **V**10 10 **V**10

CLOS-DU-MOUFLON See CORSE (CORSICA)

CLOYES-SUR-LE-LOIR
Eure-et-Loir

Parc des Loisirs ☎37985053

On the bank of the River Loire. Extensive leisure facilities. Separate section for teenagers. Lunchtime siesta 12.00–15.00 hrs.

Access from Châteaudun S on N10 towards Cloyes, then right onto Montigny-le-Gamelon road.
15 Jun–15 Sep & 15 Dec–Apr.

1HEC H R lau pitch60 (incl 3 persons)

CLUNY
Saône-et-Loire

CM St-Vital ☎85590834

G lau P **A**8 **V**5 5 5

CLUSAZ (LA)
Haute-Savoie

Plan du Fernuy ☎50024475

Airing rooms. 30 ski-lifts nearby. Several cable cars. Well-situated for skiing or walking.

At the road fork E of La Clusaz leave N50 the Col des Aravis road, and drive towards Les Confins from road fork 2 km to site.
15 Jun–15 Sep.

0.8HEC H R lau pitch98

CLUSES
Haute-Savoie

Corbaz ☎50984403

NW off D19 (rte de Marignier).
All year.

2HEC H G R lau **A**10 **V**5 12 12

COGNAC
Charente

CM rte de Ste-Sévère ☎45321332

2 km N on D24.
15 May–15 Oct.

1.5HEC H lau P

COGOLIN
Var

Argentière ☎94545786

Landscaped, partly terraced site.

1500 m NW along D48 rte de St Maur.
May–15 Oct.

8HEC H G R P lau **A**14 **V**n/c 14 14

COLAYRAC-ST-CIRQ
Lot-et-Garonne

CM 113 rte de Bordeaux ☎53875373

Bordering river.

200 m from N113.
Jun–Sep.

1.2HEC H G lau

COLLE-SUR-LOUP (LA)
Alpes-Maritimes

Pinèdes ☎93328612

Well-kept terraced site on steep slope with woodland providing shade.

Turn right off D6 towards Roquefort.
Mar–Oct.

3HEC H G lau pitch50–56 (incl 2 persons)

Vallon Rouge ☎93328612

Forest-like area, divided into pitches.

3 km W of town, 100 m to right of D6 towards Gréolières.
Mar–Oct.

3HEC H G R RP lau

COLMAR
Haut-Rhin

Intercommunal de l'Ill ☎89411594

On meadow beside the river. Liable to flooding at certain times. Separate section for campers in transit.

2 km E on N415.
Feb–Nov.

2.2HEC H G R lau **A**8 **V**5 5 5

CONCARNEAU
Finistère

Prés Verts ☎98970974

1.2 km NW.
Etr–15 Sep.

3HEC H lau S **A**12 **V**6 16 16

At **CABELLOU (LE)** (5 km S on N783)

Cabellou ☎98971040

21 May–20 Sep.

1HEC H S lau

CONCHES (LES) See LONGEVILLE

CONDRIEU
Rhône

Bell Rive ☎74595108

Bordering the Rhône.
Apr–Sep.

5HEC H G lau L

CONNANTRE
Marne

Château ☎26424876

In woodland with large marked pitches.

On left of N4 (Strasbourg-Paris) road.
All year.

1.5HEC H L

CONQUES
Averyron

Beau Rivage ☎65698223

On D601n.
Apr–Sep.

1HEC H G R lau **A**6
pitch7

CONTIS-PLAGE
Landes

Lous Seurrots ☎58428281

In pine forest on outskirts of village between road and stream. Beware of current if bathing in stream.

Etr–Sep.

15HEC H G R lau sR **A**14 **V**5 14 14

CONTRES
Loir-et-Cher

Charmoise ☎54795515

N956.
All year.

2HEC lau RP pp9

CORBÈS See **ANDUZE**

CORCIEUX
Vosges

Tour et Domain des Bains pl Notre Dame ☎29506742

On meadow-land divided into pitches.

E of village off D8.
Jun–15 Sep.

15HEC H lau P

CORDES
Tarn

Moulin de Julien ☎63560142

900 m E on D600 and D922.
Apr–Sep.

8HEC H G P lau pitch38 (incl 2 persons)

CORNILLON-CONFOUX
Bouches-du-Rhône

Pinède ☎90508464

800 m N on D70.
All year.

2HEC H G R P lau A11 V7 11 11

CORSE (CORSICA)
BELGODÈRE *Haute-Corse*

Belgodère ☎95602020

Jun–14 Sep.

2HEC H lau sR

CALVI *Haute-Corse*

Clé des Champs ☎95650086

1 km S on N197.
Apr–20 Oct.

0.4HEC H lau s

Dolce Vita Ponte Bambino ☎95650599

4 km SW of Calvi between N197 to l'Ile Rousse and the sea.
May–Sep.

6HEC H G lau s A16 V6 7 6

CARGESE *Corse-du-Sud*

Torraccia ☎95264239

4 km N on N199.
Jun–Sep.

4HEC H G lau A16 V5 8 5

CLOS-DU-MOUFLON *Haute-Corse*

Mouflon ☎95650353

Terraced site, divided into pitches. Very steep access via partly asphalted, winding road with gradient of 20%. **Tents and motorised caravans only**.

15 km from Calvi on D81 on the coastal road, in the direction of Porto.
13 Jun–24 Sep.

France

2.5HEC H G s lau A20 V11 12

LOPIGNA *Corse-du-Sud*

Truggia ☎95529021

Jun–Sep.

12HEC H G R lau

LUMIO *Haute-Corse*

Panoramic rte de Belgodère ☎95607313

Very clean and tidy site divided into pitches.

From Calvi, 12 km on N197, 200 m from main road.
15 Jun–15 Sep.

3HEC H G P lau A15 V5 10 10

PORTO *Haute-Corse*

At **SERRIERA** (6 km N)

Bussaglia ☎95261118

In sparse pasture with a few olive trees providing little shade. Lovely beach with sandy and rocky bays.

6 km N of Porto off D81.

4HEC H G lau s

PORTO VECCHIO *Corse-du-Sud*

Arutoli ☎95701273

1.5 km N of N198

4HEC H G lau

Golfo di Sogno ☎95700898

8 km NE on N198 turn right towards Ste-Trinité.
May–15 Oct.

45HEC H G sR lau A20 V8 10 8

PROPRIANO *Corse-du-Sud*

Corsica rte d'Ajaccio ☎95760057

Terraced site.

2.5 km NE by N196.
All year.

1.5HEC H G lau s

RUPPIONE-PLAGE *Corse-du-Sud*

Sud ☎95254051

Terraced site with sun shade roofs.

NE of D55 near Accelasca road.
May–Sep.

4HEC H G lau s

ST-FLORENT *Haute-Corse*

U Pezzo chemin de la Plage ☎95370165

Pleasant site; partly level, partly terraced under eucalyptus trees. Private access to large beach.

S of town on road to beach.
May–Sep.

2HEC H G R lau s A9 V4 7 6

SARTÈNE *Corse-du-Sud*

Olva les Eucalyptus ☎95771158

Apr–Sep.

8HEC H G P lau A18 V7 9 7

SORBO *Haute-Corse*

Marina-di-Sorbo ☎95365246

Level site.

S of Bastia in direction of Querciolo.
Jun–Sep.

3HEC H R s

VICO *Corse-du-Sud*

Sposata ☎95266155

On partly terraced, partly sloping ground.

1 km SW on N195.
All year.

2.5HEC H G lau A15 V4 12 8

COSNE-SUR-LOIRE
Nièvre

CM l'Ile de Cosne rte de Bourges ☎86282792

Site borders River Loire.

Follow D955 W towards Sancerre.
All year.

7.5HEC H (Jul–Aug) G R (Jul–Aug) lau P

COTINIÈRE (LA) See **OLÉRON (ÎLE D')**

COUARDE-SUR-MER (LA) See **RÉ (ÎLE DE)**

COUHÉ-VERAC
Vienne

Peupliers ☎49592116

N of village on N10 Poitiers road.
Etr–Sep.

8HEC H G RP lau A14 pitch18

COULON
Deux-Sèvres

Venise Vert ☎49359036

2 km SW on D123.
All year.

3HEC H G lau A5 V2 5 5

COURONNE (LA)
Bouches-du-Rhône

Arquet ☎42428100

Apr–Oct.

6HEC H lau s A12 V10 15 15

Cap ☎42807302

On road leading to the sea. Signposted from village.
All year. ➔

3HEC ◆ H lau A13 V8 13 A13

Mas Plage de Ste-Croix ☎42807034

On sparse, stony grassland on a plateau with a fine view of the bay, and access to a sandy beach.

Access from D49.
Apr–Sep.

6HEC ◆ H lau A14 V8 14 A14

COUNTAINVILLE
Manche

Mouettes r du Dr-Viaud le Passous ☎33470621

Apr–Sep.

1.25HEC H lau

COUX-ET-BIGAROQUE See **SIORAC-EN-PÉRIGORD**

CRAU (LA)
Var

Bois de Mont-Redon ☎94667334

15 Jun–15 Sep.

5HEC H lau pitch58 (incl 3 persons)

CRAYSSAC
Lot

Reflets du Quercy ☎65309148

1.8 km NW via D23 (rte de Catus), then turn left.
Apr–Oct.

7HEC ◆ H lau

CRÉCY-LA-CHAPELLE
Seine-et-Marne

Pré St-Jean rte de Serbonne ☎64367875

All year.

3.5HEC H

CRESPIAN
Gard

Mas de Reilhe ☎66778212

Individual pitches with hedges and trees dividing them. Recreational facilities.

On N110.
22 May–15 Sep.

3HEC ◆ H lau A16 Vn/c 37 A37

CREST
Drôme

CM Corinthe quai de Soubeyran ☎75750528

Follow D538 towards Montélimar, cross bridge over River Drôme and continue on embankment to stadium. Site is adjacent to stadium.
Apr–Sep.

2.5HEC H lau RP

CROISIC (LE)
Loire-Atlantique

Océan ☎40230769

Apr–Sep.

5HEC H lau A14 V9 13 A13

Stella Maris ☎40230371

May–15 Sep.

4HEC H lau

CROIX-VALMER (LA)
Var

Sélection ☎94796197

Site in scattered pinewood; protected from wind. Many terraces, divided into pitches.

Turn off N559 at roundabout at Km78.5 and continue W for 300 m along bd de Mer.
May–10 Oct.

5HEC ◆ H lau pitch95 (incl 1–3 persons)

CROS-DE-CAGNES See **CAGNES-SUR-MER**

CROZON
Finistère

Pen Ar Menez ☎98271236

On fringe of a pinewood. Water sport facilities 5 km away. Cycles for hire.

Jun–Sep

3HEC H lau A9 V4 9 A9

At **ST-FIACRE** (6 km NW)

Pieds dans l'Eau ☎98276243

Site on several meadows divided by trees. In quiet secluded situation reaching as far as a pebbly beach. Bathing is dependent on tides.

15 Jun–15 Sep.

2HEC H lau A10 V5 12 A12

Trez Rouz Prés de Camaret ☎98279396

Etr–Sep.

1HEC H lau A15 V5 pitch12

CRUSEILLES
Haute-Savoie

Parc des Dronières ☎50441395

Access from D15 several hundred metres NE of village.
Feb–Oct.

4.2HEC H LP lau

DAGLAN
Dordogne

Moulin de Paulhiac ☎53282088

Jun–Sep.

5HEC ◆ H RP lau

DALLET
Puy-de-Dôme

Ombrages rte de Pont du Château ☎73831097

Beside River Allier.

May–Sep.

2.5HEC H R lau pitch36 (incl 2 persons)

DAON-DE-FEINS
Mayenne

CM Ville de Château-Gontier ☎43073478

A well-kept site in a meadow on several levels, beside the River Mayenne.

From Château-Gontier take the D22 SE for 26 km.
Etr–Oct.

1HEC H R

DARDILLY
Rhône

Porte de Lyon ☎78356455

Generously arranged and equipped site divided into pitches. Ideal for overnight stays near motorway.

9 km N of Lyon La Garde exit off A6.
Mar–Oct.

6HEC H lau pitch41–74

DAX
Landes

Chênes Bois de Boulogne ☎58900553

W of town beside River Ardour.
Apr–Oct.

5HEC H lau P A13 pitch29

DEAUVILLE
Calvados

Clairfontaine r de Clairfontaine ☎31881406

Site on meadow with flower beds. Near racecourse.

W of town off D513 Villers road.
Etr–Sep.

5HEC H P lau S A18 V7 19 19

At **ST-ARNOULT** (3 km S)

Vallée rte de Beaumont ☎31885817

Etr–Oct.

3HEC H lau A16 pitch16

France

At **TOUQUES** (3 km SE)

Haras chemin du Calvaire ☎31884484

N on D62, to Honfleur.
All year.

4HEC H lau P A18 pitch16

DECIZE
Nièvre

CM Halles á la Promenade ☎86251405

Water sports on River Loire and tennis nearby.

NW of town centre.
May–Sep.

3.5HEC H RP lau

DESVRES
Pas-de-Calais

CM ☎21916374

In a sports ground near the forest.

Etr–Oct.

1HEC H lau P

DEYME
Haute-Garonne

Violettes ☎61817207

Adjacent to N113.
All year.

2.5HEC H lau

DIE
Drôme

Chamarges ☎75220677

Children's games.

Site lies 1.5 km W on D93 road to Crest adjacent to River Drôme. The site is the first on the right from Die.
Etr–15 Oct.

2HEC H P lau

Pinède quartier du Pont-Neuf ☎75221777

15 May–15 Sep.

5HEC H P lau A15 V7 7 7

CM Piscine

On slightly sloping meadow with young trees. Next to swimming pool and sports stadium.

Jun–15 Sep.

2HEC H lau P A8 V4 4 4

DIEPPE
Seine-Maritime

At **GRAINCOURT** (8.5 km NE by D925)

Bois Clieu Château de Derchigny ☎35836219

Very pleasant site in wooded countryside.

All year.

2.5HEC H lau

At **HAUTOT-SUR-MER** (6 km SW)

Source Petit-Appeville ☎35842704

15 Mar–15 Oct.

2.5HEC H lau A14 pitch14

DIGNE
Alpes-de-Haute-Provence

CM Bourg rte de la Javie ☎92310487

In a narrow valley with wooded slopes and a stream.

Turn off D900 1 km NE.
All year.

0.4HEC H P

DIGOIN
Saône-et-Loire

CM Chevrette r de la Chevrette ☎85531149

W of village on N79.
All year.

1.6HEC H lau P A8 V3 5 5

DIJON
Côte-d'Or➔

CM Lac 43 av Albert-1 er ☎80435472

1.5 km W on N5.
Apr–15 Nov.

3HEC H lau LR A5 V3 3 3

DINAN
Côtes-du-Nord

Châteaubriand 103 r Châteaubriand ☎96399611

1 km S of town centre towards Lehon and the hospital.
May–15 Oct.

1HEC H G lau s

At **TADEN** (3.5 km NE)

CM Hallerais ☎96391593

Beautiful clean site with level pitches on gentle slope near a country estate. Asphalt drives. Good sanitary installations.

SW of Taden off D12.
Mar–Oct.

10HEC H (in season) G lau A14 V3 17 17

DINARD
Ille-et-Vilaine

Mauny ☎99469473

Off St. Briac road (CD603).
Etr–Oct.

4HEC H G lau A12 V6 31 31

CM Port Blanc r du Sgt-Boulanger ☎99461074

Large site between horse riding field and coast. Numbered pitches. Busy, but sanitary installations very clean.

On western edge of town in quartier de St-Enogat near D786.
Apr–Sep.

7HEC H s lau A8 V5 8 8

Prieuré 20 av Vicomté ☎99462004

May–15 Sep.

1.2HEC H G R P lau s A13 pitch27

France

DIVONNE-LES-BAINS
Ain

CM ☎50200195

3 km N.
Apr–Sep.

7HEC H P

DOL-DE-BRETAGNE
Ille-et-Vilaine

See also **EPINIAC**

CM ☎99481468

On level meadow.

SW on rte de Dinan 400 m from town centre.
May–Sep.

1.7HEC H lau A8 V4 4 4

At **BAGUER-PICAN** (4 km E on N176)

Ferme-Camping du Vieux Chêne ☎99480955

Spacious site in pleasant lakeside situation. Farm produce available.

5 km E of Dol-de-Bretagne on N176.
Etr–Sep

4HEC H G P lau A15 pitch23

DOLE
Jura

Pasquier ☎84720261

Clean meadow site near River Doubs.

900 m SE of town centre.
15 Mar–Oct.

2HEC H G lau R A9 pitch13

DOMINO See **OLÉRON (ÎLE D')**

DOUARNENEZ
Finistère

Ferme de Kerleyou ☎98740352

Family site situated 1 km W on rue de Préfet-Collignon towards the sea.

May–Sep.

3HEC H G lau s A10 V5 10 10

Trézulien Tréboul ☎98741230

Etr–15 Sep.

3HEC H G lau s A9 V5 pitch10

At **POULLAN-SUR-MER** (5 km W on D765)

Pil Koad ☎98742639

Etr–Sep.

3.5HEC H G R P lau A15 V5 18 18

DOUSSARD
Haute-Savoie

Serraz ☎50443068

Modern site divided into pitches. Cosy bar in rustic style.

At E end of village 500 m from N508 on D181.
15 May–Sep.

3HEC H G lau LR pitch48 (incl 2 persons)

DRAMONT (LE) See **AGAY**

EBREUIL
Allier

Filature rte de Chauvigny ☎70907201

Beside River Sioule.

Etr–Sep

3HEC H G R lau pitch38 (incl 2 persons)

ECHELLES (LES)
Isère

At **ENTRE-DEUX-GUIERS** (1 km S)

Arc en Ciel ☎79660697

On D520 300 m from N6.
Mar–Oct.

1HEC H G R lau P A9 V5 8 8

ÉCLARON-BRAUCOURT
Haute-Marne

Presqu'Ile de Champaubert ☎25041320

Situated on lake peninsula.

Apr–15 Oct.

3.5HEC H G lau L A12 V8 11 11

EGATS (LES)
Isère

Belvédère de l'Obiou ☎76304080

Situated in beautiful scenery; modern sanitary installations.
May–Oct.

1HEC H G R lau A8 V6 5 5

EMBRUN
Hautes-Alpes

CM Clapière ☎92430183

Well managed site with shaded pitches on stony ground, on N shore of lake. Site shop open during summer only.

2.5 km SW on N94.
May–Sep.

6HEC H G lau LP pitch45 (incl 2 persons)

ENTRE-DEUX-GUIERS See **ECHELLES (LES)**

ENVEITG
Pyrénées-Orientales

Robinson ☎68048038

On gently sloping meadow surrounded by tall bushes.

All year.

4HEC H G lau

ÉPERNAY
Marne

CM ☎26553214

A site with poplar trees beside the River Marne within the Municipal Sports Park.

In NW suburbs of the town follow signs for Cumières and Damery.
Apr–Sep.

2HEC H lau A8 V2 8 8

EPINIAC
Ille-et-Vilaine

Château des Ormes ☎99481019

Site in grounds of château.

7 km S of Dol-de-Bretagne on D795 Rennes Road.
20 May–10 Sep.

4HEC H G P lau A19 pitch40

ÉQUEMAUVILLE See **VILLERVILLE**

ERDEVEN
Morbihan

Kerzerho ☎97556317

France

Level site divided and surrounded by bushes and trees. Each pitch has water and electricity.

1.5 km SE on the D781.
Etr–Sep.

9HEC H G P lau

Sept Saints ☎97555265

2 km NW via D781 rte de Plouhinec.
May–15 Sep.

5HEC H G R P lau A13 pitch32

ERMENONVILLE
Oise

Parc Jean-Jacques Rousseau ☎44540008

SW on D84.
All year.

8HEC H G R lau pitch35 (incl 2 persons)

ERQUY
Côtes-du-Nord

Pins rte du Guen ☎96723112

Situated in a pine forest.

1 km NE of village.
May–Sep.

8HEC H G P lau

Roches ☎96723290

15 May–15 Sep.

1.6HEC H G lau S A8 V4 7 7

St-Pabu ☎96722465

On big open meadow with several terraces in beautiful, isolated situation by sea. Divided into pitches.

W on D786 then follow signposts from La Coutre.
Etr–Sep.

3.6HEC H G S lau A10 V4 8 8

Vieux Moulin ☎96723423

Clean tidy site divided into pitches and surrounded by a pine forest. Suitable for children.

On D783.
Apr–Sep.

2.5HEC H G P lau S A13 V8 11 11

ESCLAUZELS See **CAHORS**

ESCOT
Pyrénées-Atlantiques

Centre de Loisirs le Mont Bleu ☎59344192

Quiet site in beautiful Pyrénéan landscape.

At railway bridge take D294 for approx 6 km.
25 Jun–5 Sep.

3.5HEC H G P lau A6 V4 16 16

ESPARRON-DE-VERDON
Alpes-de-Haute-Provence

Soleil ☎92780378

May–Sep

2HEC H G L lau A16 Vn/c 22–35 18

ESQUIÈZE-SÈRE
Hautes-Pyrénées

Airotel Pyrénées ☎62928918

Access directly off N927.
All year.

2.5HEC H G R lau P pitch70 (incl 3 persons)

ÉTABLES-SUR-MER
Côtes-du-Nord

Abri Côtier r de la Ville-es-Rouxel ☎96706157

1 km N of town centre on D786.
Apr–Sep.

2HEC H G R lau sP A12 V6 11 11

See advertisement page 152

ETRÉHAM
Calvados

Reine Mathilde ☎31217655

Jun–Sep.

3HEC H G lau A16 pitch16–18

EU
Seine-Maritime

CM r Mozart ☎35503017

About 7 km SE of town at Incheville, on the road to Beauchamps.
All year.

2HEC H G lau A7 V6 6 6

ÉVIAN-LES-BAINS
Haute-Savoie

At **AMPHION-LES-BAINS** (3.5 km W on N5)

Plage ☎50700046

NW of town on N5, 150m from lake.
All year.

1.5HEC H (Jul–Aug) lau L A12 pitch18

At **GRANDE-RIVE** (1.5 km E on N5)

Braconnay ☎50754219

Clean and tidy terraced site with main drives asphalt surfaced.

On N5.
May–Oct.

1HEC H lau L A8 Vn/c 13 13

At **MAXILLY** (2.5 km E on N5)

Clos Savoyard ☎50752584

Very clean and tidy site. ➤

Turn onto D21 in town 1200 m after Hotel de l'Etoile and continue uphill.
Apr–Sep.
1.5HEC ◇ H ⊙ G ⊞ lau |O| P pitch42 (incl 3 persons)

ÉVREUX
Eure
CM No 2 rte de Conches ☎32394359
W on D830.
Apr–Sep.
1.4HEC ◇ H ⊙ lau |O| P

EYMOUTHIERS
Charente
Gorges du Chambon ☎45707170
15 May–15 Sep.
7HEC ◇ H |O| ⊙ G P ⊞ lau A19 V9 30 A30

EYZIES-DE-TAYAC (LES)
Dordogne
At **SIREUIL** (7 km E off D47)
Mas ☎53296806
N of D47 (Sarlat-Les-Eyzies).
Jun–Sep.
3HEC ◇ H |O| ⊙ G R P ⊞ lau pitch42 (incl 2 persons)

FALAISE
Calvados
CM Château ☎31901655
W of town.
Etr–Sep.
1HEC ◇ H Ⓟ

FARINETTE-PLAGE
Hérault
Hélios ☎67940121
On level ground divided into pitches.
On D137 S of village signposted 'Farinette'.
Jun–Sep.
2.5HEC ◆ ◇ H ⊙ G R ⊞ lau S pitch52 (incl 2 persons)

FAUTE-SUR-MER (LA)
Vendée
Fautals ☎51564196
Situated in centre of village. Numbered pitches.
On D46.
28 Jun–Aug.
1HEC ◇ H ⊙ G ⊞ lau |O| LS pitch37 (incl 3 persons)

FAVIÈRE (LA) See **BORMES-LES-MIMOSAS**

FAYENCE
Var
Camping Club de St-Cassien ☎94761384
Booking recommended.
6 km from lake.
All year.
17HEC ◆ H |O| ⊙ G P ⊞ lau

Grillon ☎94760936
Large level meadow by hotel of same name.
SE of Fayence on N562 (Grasse-Draguignan) road.
All year.
2.7HEC ◆ H |O| ⊙ G P ⊞ lau

Lou Cantaire rte de Draguignan ☎94762377
Partly terraced. Pitches separated by low walls. Lunchtime siesta 12.15–16.30 hrs.
By the D562 about 6 km S. Signposted.
Mar–15 Oct.
4HEC ◆ H |O| ⊙ G P ⊞ lau A14 V5 10 A10

FERTÉ-GAUCHER (LA)
Seine-et-Marne
CM Joël Teinturier ☎64202040
All year.

4.5HEC ◇ H ⊙ P ⊞ lau |O| A10 Vn/c 10 A10

FIGEAC
Lot
Carmes av de Carmes ☎65340856
On well-kept meadow with flower beds and gravel drives.
From village centre follow N140 towards Brive, turn right at TOTAL garage.
All year.
0.7HEC ◇ H ⊙ G ⊞ lau |O| RP A10 pitch10

FLÈCHE (LA)
Sarthe
Route d'Or allée de la Providence ☎43945590
All year.
3HEC ◇ H ⊙ G ⊞ lau |O| P A8 V3 5 A4

FLEURIE
Rhône
CM la Grappe Fleurie ☎74041044
0.6 km SE on D119 E.
20 Mar–15 Oct.
1.6HEC ◇ H ⊙ ⊞ lau |O| G P A11 pitch12

FOIX
Ariège
CM Lac de Labarre rte de Pamiers ☎61651158
On well-kept meadow.
3 km N on N20.
Jun–Oct.
3.7HEC ◇ H ⊙ ⊞ lau |O| LR A6 V4 5 A5

FONTAINE-DE-VAUCLUSE
Vaucluse
CM Prés ☎90206954
SW on D24.
All year.
0.6HEC ◇ H ⊙ ⊞ lau |O| A9 V4 8 A8

FONT-ROMEU
Pyrénées-Orientales

CM Menhir rte de Mont Louis ☎68300932

N on N618.
15 June–Sep.

7HEC H lau pitch43 (incl 2 persons)

FONTVIELLE
Bouches-du-Rhône

CM Pins ☎90977869

1 km from village.
Apr–15 Oct.

3HEC H lau P A9 pitch17

FORÊT-FOUESNANT (LA)
Finistère

Kérantérec ☎98569811

Well-kept terraced site, divided into sections by hedges and extending to the sea.

3 km SE.
Etr–Sep.

3.5HEC H G S lau A6 V4 17 17

Manoir de Pen Ar Steir ☎98569775

NE off D44.
All year.

3HEC H G lau S

Plage Plage de Kerleven ☎98569625

2.5 km SE on D783.
May–Sep.

1HEC H S lau G A10 V4 15 15

Pontérec ☎98569833

0.5 km on D44 towards Bénodet.
Apr–Sep.

3HEC H G lau A6 V3 9 9

St-Laurent rte de Kerleven ☎98569765

On rocky coast. Divided into pitches.

3.5 km SE of village.
Jun–8 Sep.

5.25HEC H G S lau A12 pitch24

Stéréden-Vor Plage de Kerleven ☎98569643

2.5 km SE.
15 May–15 Sep.

1HEC H S lau

FORGES-LES-EAUX
Seine-Maritime

CM Minière bd N-Thiessé ☎35905391

800 m towards Lyon-la-Forêt.
Apr–Oct.

1.8HEC H G lau P A10 V3 3 3

FOSSAT (LE)
Ariège

Laillères ☎61685233

On D626.
Apr–Oct.

0.3HEC H G lau A3 V3 3 3

FOS-SUR-MER
Bouches-du-Rhône

Estagnon Plage St-Gervais ☎42050119

Level, rather dusty site. Public beach on other side of road.

Situated S of an industrial zone–quartier St-Gervais.
15 May–Sep.

2HEC H G lau S A15 pitch20

FOUGÈRES
Ille-et-Vilaine

CM Paron ☎99994081

All year.

2.5HEC H G R lau A7 V4 7 7

FRANGY
Haute-Savoie

At **CHÊNE-EN-SEMINE** (6 km NW)

Centre de Loisirs de la Semine ☎50779006

May–Sep.

2.9HEC H P lau A12 V2 10 10

FRAYSSINET
Lot

Tirelire ☎65310019

All year.

2HEC H G RP lau A6 pitch7

At **PONT-DE-RHODES** (1 km N on N20)

Plage du Relais ☎65310016

15 Jun–10 Sep.

2HEC H G P lau

FRÉJUS
Var

Acacias ☎94532122

On meadowland, divided into several sections. Quiet. Sea views.

NE on N7, then follow D37 towards Valescure.
All year.

1.8HEC H G lau P pitch32 (incl 2 persons)

Baume rte de Bagnols-en-Forêt ☎94959482

Partly residential site.

4.5 km N via D4.
Etr–Sep.

13HEC H G P lau pitch115 (incl 3 persons)

Bellevue rte de Bozon ☎94520052

2 km N.
All year.

2.3HEC H G lau A14 pitch19

Colombier ☎94515601

Widespread site on hill on some individual terraces under pine trees.

Turn N off N7 onto D4 towards Bagnols and continue for 500 m.
15 Mar–Sep.

10HEC H G R P lau A22 pitch22

Dattier rte de Bagnols-en-Forêt (CD4) ☎94534251

Laid out in terraces with a view of the Esterel mountains.

Access from A8 via RN7, then CD4.
Etr–15 Oct

3HEC H G R lau pitch80 (incl 2 persons)

Fréjus rte de Bagnols-en-Forêt ☎94521674

Access via N7 and D4.
Etr–Oct.

40HEC H G R P lau A15 pitch20

Holiday Green rte de Bagnols-en-Forêt ☎94522268

6 km N via D4.
Apr–Oct.

15HEC H G R P lau

Montourey rte de Bagnols-en-Forêt, St-Jean-les-Caïs ☎94522236

2 km N.
15 Jun–15 Sep.

4HEC H R P lau pitch61 (incl 2 persons)

See advertisement page 154.

Pierre Vert 4 rte de Bagnols-en-Forêt ☎94521748

Mar–15 Oct.

28HEC H G R P lau pitch55 (incl 2 persons)

Pins Parasols ☎94523187

4 km N via D4, rte de Bagnols-en-Forêt.
Etr–Sep.

4HEC H G P lau pitch77 (incl 3 persons)

See advertisement page 154.

At TOUR-DE-MARE (4 km NE)

Europa 7 rte Nationale ☎94402038

Dutch orientated site.

On N7.
15 Mar–Oct.

1HEC H G R lau S

Motel Camping le Kangourou rte de Valescure ☎94532169

2 km NE of N7.
All year.

1HEC [symbols] lau

FRESNAY-SUR-SARTHE

Sarthe

CM Sans Souci ☎43973287

1 km SE on D310.
Apr–Sep.

1.5HEC [symbols] lau [symbols] A6 V4 5 5

FRET (LE)

Finistère

Gwel-Kaër ☎98276106

On terraced meadow with fine views.

4 km W on D55.
15 Jun–Sep.

1.5HEC [symbols] lau [symbols]

FRÉTHUN

Pas-de-Calais

Village ☎21852542

1 km from village centre via D243
All year.

3HEC [symbols] lau [symbols] pitch37 (incl 2 persons)

France

FRÉVENT

Pas-de-Calais

CM ☎21037879

Apr–Oct.

5HEC [symbols] lau [symbols] A11 pitch8

FRONSAC

Gironde

CM Fronsadalis ☎56513133

Clean, well kept site beside River Dordogne.

From Libourne D670 then D128 in village.
7 May–6 Jun.

0.4HEC [symbols] lau [symbols]

FRONTIGNAN-PLAGE

Hérault

Miami ☎67481549

Modern, pleasantly landscaped site next to saltwater lagoon.

NE via D60.
Mar–Dec.

3HEC [symbols] lau

Soleil ☎67481443

Family site bordering the beach.

NE via D60.
18 Apr–Sep.

3HEC [symbols] lau pitch63 (incl 2 persons)

Tahiti 66 av d'Ingril ☎67481243

NE via D60.
18 May–15 Sep.

2.6HEC [symbols] lau [symbols]

Tamaris ☎67481691

From N108 take D129 for 6 km.
Jun–11 Sep.

4.5HEC [symbols] lau pitch74–89 (incl 2 persons)

GAGNIÈRES

Gard

At **CHAVAGNAC** (2 km N on D430)

Mines d'Or ☎66250667

Well-situated quiet site.

15 Jun–15 Sep.

1.8HEC [symbols] lau [symbols] pitch34 (incl 2 persons)

GAP

Hautes-Alpes

Provence rte de St-Jean ☎92511325

Very clean well-kept site, divided into pitches. On outskirts S of town.

On N85 (rte Napoléon).
15 Apr–15 Oct.

1.7HEC H G lau P A10 pitch12

GARDE-CASTELLANE See **CASTELLANE**

GASSIN
Var

Parc Montana rte du Bourrian ☎94561303

Park-like site on slopes of a hill. 2.5 km E of N559.

Access from main road at Km84.5 and 84.9 on D89.
Apr–Sep.

20HEC H G R P lau A13 V5 35 35

GASTES See **PARENTIS-EN-BORN**

GAUGEAC
Dordogne

Moulin de David ☎53226525

23 May–15 Sep.

14HEC H G R P lau pitch59 (incl 2 persons)

GÉMENOS
Bouches-du-Rhône

Clos rte de Toulon ☎42820629

On SE outskirts of town, N of N96, on rte de Toulon.
All year.

2HEC H P

GENÊTS See **AVRANCHES**

GENNES
Maine-et-Loir

Districal du Bord de l'Eau ☎41518177

Etr–Oct.

3HEC H lau P A5 pitch8

GÉRARDMER
Vosges

Ramberchamp ☎29630382

On S side of Lac de Gérardmer.
May–15 Sep.

3.5HEC H lau L

GIEN
Loiret

CM ☎38671250

Apr–15 Oct

7HEC H lau P A6 V4 6 6

GIENS
Var

Cigales pl de la Badine ☎94582106

A well-kept site with numbered pitches. Special places for caravans.

0.3 km E of D97.
11 Apr–15 Oct.

2HEC H G lau s A14 pitch17

Presqu'ile ☎94582286

Access from N559 via D97 to Giens peninsula. Site 500 m from D97.
Apr–Sep.

6HEC H G lau s pitch52 (incl 2 persons)

GIGNY-SUR-SAÔNE
Saône-et-Loire

Château de d'Epervière ☎85448323

1 km S at L'Epervière
Etr–15 Oct.

10HEC H G lau

GILETTE
Alpes-Maritimes

Moulin Noù Pont Ch-Albert ☎93089240

Apr–Sep.

2.5HEC H G R RP lau pitch56 (incl 2 persons)

GLUIRAS
Ardèche

Ardèchois ☎75666187

Meadow with trees, quiet and pleasantly situated by River Gluèyre.

From St-Sauveur via D102 in direction of Mezilhac and continue for 7 kms to site.
5 Jun–30 Sep.

37HEC H G R lau pitch59 (incl 2 persons)

GONNEVILLE-EN-AUGE
Calvados

Clos Tranquille ☎31242136

On D95A.
Apr–Sep.

1.3HEC H G R lau A12 pitch12

GONNEVILLE-SUR-MER
Calvados

Falaise ☎31910966

Has terraces and lawns. Steep access to beach by means of many steps. Section reserved for parties of young British campers.

On steep coast road to Deauville, 2.9 km NE from village.
Apr–Oct

8HEC H G P lau A14–16 pitch13–17

GOURDON
Lot

CM Écoute s'Il Pleut ☎65410619

1 km from town centre via D704.
15 Jun–15 Sep.

5HEC H P lau

At **GROLÉJAC** (15 km N on D704)

Granges ☎53281115

Beautifully situated terraces on a hill with big pitches. Site beside railway bridge. Facilities for sports and entertainment. ➤

Turn off D704 in village towards Domme.
May–Sep.
4HEC H P lau pitch81 (incl 3 persons)

At **ST-MARTIAL-DE-NABIRAT** (6 km W)

Carbonnier ☎53284253
Off the D46.
Jun–15 Sep.
9HEC H G R P lau A10 pitch15

GOURETTE
Pyrénées-Atlantiques

Ley ☎59051147
Terraced site with gravel and asphalt caravan pitches. TV, common room.
From Laruns drive E to Eaux-Bonnes and drive uphill to Gourette.
20 Dec–10 Apr & 15 Jun–15 Sep.
2HEC H R pitch30 (incl 2 persons)

GRAINCOURT See **DIEPPE**

GRAND MOTTE (LA)
Hérault

Cigales ☎67565085
Near crossroads for Palavas/Grand Travers and D62.
2HEC H G S

FFCCIATC ☎67565475
International Camping Carnet holders only are allowed.
W on D59.
15 Mar–Sep.
3.6HEC H

Garden ☎67565009
Completely divided into pitches separated by hedges and surrounded by a wall. 0.3 km from beach.
Access from D62. Site by crossroads towards Palavas/Grand Travers.
Mar–30 Oct.
3.5HEC H G R lau S pitch115 (incl 3 persons)

France

Lous Pibols ☎67565008
Well-organised. Divided into level pitches.
W on D59, 0.4 km from sea.
Apr–15 Oct.
3HEC H G R lau S pitch87–115 (incl 3 persons)

Or ☎67565210
Operated by family welfare organisation. Individual pitches separated by hedging each with water and electricity.
May–Sep.
5HEC H

GRANDE-RIVE See **EVIAN-LES-BAINS**

GRANDPRÉ
Ardennes

CM ☎24305218
150 m from village centre on D6.
Apr–Sep.
1.7HEC H R lau G A5 V3 3 3

GRANGES-SUR-VOLOGNE
Vosges

Gina-Park ☎29514195
1 km SE of town centre.
All year.
4.5HEC H G R lau A8 pitch13

Sténiole ☎29514375
1 km SE on D423, rte de Gérardmer, then 3 km on side road – signposted.
All year.
8HEC H G R lau A9 V5 5 5

GRASSE
Alpes-Maritimes

CM bd A-de-Rothschild ☎93362869
Terraced site on wooded slopes.
1.4 km N on D111.
All year.
0.5HEC H lau

At **OPIO** (8 km E by D2085 & D3)

Caravan Inn ☎93773200
Terraced rustic site for caravans only. Occupied largely by static caravans. Steep approach to site (15%) – free towage available.
1.5 km S of Opio on D3.
Closed Dec.
5HEC H G P lau pitch70–141 (incl 4 persons)

GRAU-DE-VENDRES
Hérault

Foulègues ☎67373365
Signposted.
Jun–Sep.
4HEC H G lau SR pitch60 (incl 2 persons)

GRAU-DU-ROI(LE)
Gard

Abri de Camargue rte du Phare de l'Espiguette, Port Camargue ☎66515483
2.5 km from town.
Apr–15 Oct.
4HEC H G P lau S pitch50–140 (incl 3 persons)

Bon Séjour rte de l'Espiguette ☎66514711
Clean, tidy, well-kept site.
3 km E of village off road to lighthouse.
Apr–Sep.
5HEC H G R L lau pitch51 (incl 3 persons)

Boucanet ☎66514148
Flat sandy site bordering beach.
3 km NW on D255.
May–Sep.
7.5HEC H G R S lau

Eden Port-Camargue ☎66514981

Quiet site on both sides of access road. 300 m from beach.

On D626 towards Espiguette.
Apr–6 Oct.

5HEC lau pitch102 (incl 3 persons)

Elysée Residence rte de L'Espiguette ☎66519888

Mar–Nov.

38HEC lau

CM l'Espiguette ☎66514392

42HEC lau

International de la Marine ☎66514622

3.5 km SW towards lighthouse.
25 Mar–Sep.

4.5HEC lau pitch90–115 (incl 4 persons)

Jardins de Tivoli ☎66518296

15 Mar–15 Oct.

7HEC

Mouettes rte de Port-Camargue ☎66514400

1.2 km SE.
Etr–Oct.

2.8HEC lau pitch 40 (incl 2 person)

Salonique rte de l'Espiguette ☎66515973

15 Mar–15 Oct

3HEC lau pitch35–66 (incl 2 persons)

GRÉOUX-LES-BAINS
Alpes-de-Hautes-Provence

Cygnes la Raludette ☎92780808

15 Mar–15 Oct.

40HEC lau

GRESSE-EN-VERCORS
Isère

4 Saisons ☎76343027

15 Jun–15 Sep. & Nov–3 May

2.2HEC lau pitch45 (incl 2 persons)

GREZ-SUR-LOING
Seine-et-Marne

CM Près ☎64457275

Apr–Dec.

3.8HEC

GRIGNON
Savoie

Belle Étoile ☎79324239

15 Jun–15 Sep.

2HEC lau

GRIMAUD
Var

At **PORT GRIMAUD** (4 km E)

Mûres ☎94561697

The site is divided into two parts by the N98. The land alongside the sea is level and mainly without shade. The other section of the site is on a slope and has some shade.

NE on N98.
Apr–Sep.

7.5HEC lau

Plage ☎94563115

Wide area of land near Km59.6 on N98 on both sides of road beside sea. Partly terraced and divided into pitches.

25 Mar.–Sep.

18HEC lau pitch57 (incl 2 persons)

Prairies de la Mer ☎94562529

Huge holiday centre on beach with all amenities. Nine sanitary blocks. Children's playground with trampoline.

Access N of Giscle Bridge near Km59.2 off N98.
15 Mar–Oct.

20HEC lau

At **ST-PONS-LES-MÛRES** (4 km E)

ACF ☎94563008

Site on hilly land with terraces divided into pitches and with many modern facilities.

Access via N98 and D244, then turn right and continue uphill.
Etr–Oct.

12HEC lau pitch116 (incl 4 persons)

GRISOLLES
Tarn-et-Garonne

Aquitaine rte de Montauban ☎63673322

1.5 km N off 'X' roads N20/N113.
All year.

3HEC lau A13 pitch11

GROIRE See **MUROL**

GROLÉJAC See **GOURDON**

GROS-THEIL (LE)
Eure

Salverte rte de Brionne ☎32355134

2.5 km SW on D26.
All year.

15HEC lau A19 V9 9 9

GUÉMENÉ-PENFAO
Loire-Atlantique

CM Hermitage av du Paradis ☎40792348

1.5 km E on rte de Châteaubriant.
All year.

2.5HEC

GUÉRANDE
Loire-Atlantique

CM Bréhadour ☎40249312

2 km NE on D51, rte de St-Lyphard.
All year.

5HEC lau A14 pitch14

Parc de Leveno ☏40247930

15 May–15 Sep.

6HEC H P lau pitch58–66

Pré du Château de Careil ☏40602299

Divided into pitches. Caravans only. Booking recommended for Jul & Aug.

2 km N of La Baule on D92.
Apr–Sep.

2.5HEC H P lau s pitch75 (incl 2 persons)

Tremondec ☏40600007

Subdivided terraced site with view of La Baule.

Approach road opposite Camping Pré du Château de Careil.
Etr–Sep.

0.6HEC H P (pm) lau s pitch41 (incl 3 persons)

GUÉRET

Creuse

CM r de Pommeil ☏55520702

On undulating terrain on a hillock above Guéret.

1.5 km SE via r de Pommeil.
All year.

1.5HEC H

GUILLESTRE

Hautes-Alpes

CM Rochette ☏92450215

On right bank of River Chagne.

W on D902A.
10 Jun–15 Sep.

2HEC H P lau

Villard ☏92450654

2 km W via D902A & N94, rte de Gap.
All year.

2HEC H P lau pitch46 (incl 2 persons)

GUILVINEC

Finistère

Karreg Skividen ☏98582278

Jun–15 Sep.

1HEC H lau s

Plage rte de Penmarc'h ☏98586190

On level meadow. Divided into pitches. Flat beach suitable for children.

2 km W of village on the Corniche towards Penmarc'h.
Etr–Sep.

7HEC H lau s A14 V6 19

GUINES

Pas-de-Calais

Bien Assise ☏21352077

France

A nice site in the country near to a large forest and a charming little town.

May–25 Sep.

5HEC H P lau A16 pitch23

GUISE

Aisne

Vallée de l'Oise r du Camping ☏23611486

1 km SE on D960.
Apr–Oct.

4.5HEC H R lau A8 V4 4 4

HANAU-PLAGE

Moselle

CM ☏87065155

Site lies beside Hanau lake. Busy at weekends and has many residential campers.

3 km NW of Philippsbourg on N62.
May–Sep.

7HEC H lau L A6 V4 6 6

HASPARREN

Pyrénées-Atlantiques

Chapital ☏59296294

15 June–Sep.

1HEC H lau P A9 V5

HAUTOT-SUR-MER

See **DIEPPE**

HAVRE (LE)

Seine-Maritime

CM Forêt de Montgeon ☏35465239

Quiet, well-kept site, with lawns, in forest. Cement stands for caravans.

Signposted from harbour and station.
15 Apr–Sep.

3.8HEC H lau A9 V3 8 6

HAYE-DU-PUITS (LA)

Manche

Etang des Haizes St-Symphorien-le-Valois ☏33460116

Bordering a lake.

15 Mar–1 Nov.

3HEC H L lau A9 pitch12

HEIMSBRUNN

Haut-Rhin

Chaumière ☏89819343

Signposted from village centre.
All year.

1HEC H lau A8 V5 5 5

HENDAYE-PLAGE

Pyrénées-Atlantiques

Acaclas ☏59207876

Apr–Sep.

5HEC H lau s A10 V6 12 12

Airotel Eskualduna rte de la Corniche ☏59200464

On gently sloping meadow.

2 km from village on N10c.
15 Jun–Sep.

8HEC H lau sP A12 V5 11 11

Airotel Sascoénéa bd du Gl-Leclerc ☏59200544

On hill, 1 km from sea.

From N10C turn into r d'Elissacilio then into r des Lilas.
Etr–Sep.

5HEC H lau s pitch40 (incl 2 persons)

Alturan r d'Elissacilio ☏59200455

Situated by the sea.

Jun–Sep.

4HEC H lau s A11 V5 13 13

Ametza rte de l'Empereur ☏59200705

Jun–Sep.

5HEC H P lau s A11 V4 15 15

Moulin ☏59207635

Partly terraced, very clean and well-kept site.

500 m E on N10C turn into rte de la Glacière.
15 Jun–15 Sep.

1.5HEC H sR

HENRIDORFF

Moselle

Plan Incliné ☏87253013

The site lies on a narrow strip of grassland below the railway, beside the canal.

3 km W of Lutzelbourg towards Dabo.
Apr–Sep.

3.5HEC H P lau A9 V4 4 4

HÉRIC

Loire-Atlantique

Pindière ☏40576541

1 km from town on D16.
All year.

0.8HEC H lau A10 V6 6 6

HERRLISHEIM

Haute-Rhin

Egulsheim ☏89231939

On sloping grassland, within a vineyard area. Lovely view of 3 castles.

Access via N83 turning west onto the D14. Follow signs though town to site.

Etr–30 Sept.
2HEC lau A8 pitch8

HOHWALD (LE)
Bas-Rhin
CM 88083090
All year.
2HEC lau A9 V5 7 7

HÔME (LE) See **HOULGATE**

HOMMAIZE (L')
Vienne
Vertoux 49427595
All year.
1HEC lau pitch28 (incl 2 persons)

HOSSEGOR
Landes
Rey 58435200
Off D652.
14 Jun–4 Sep.
10HEC lau Ls A11 Vn/c 14 14

HOSTENS
Gironde
Hostens 56885019
Off route to St-Symphorien.
May–Oct.
4HEC lau L

France

HOUCHES (LES)
Haute-Savoie
Airhôtel du Bourgeat 50544214
1.5 km NE.
15 Dec–Sep.
0.6HEC lau pitch62 (incl 3 persons)

Petit Pont 50544130
Terraced site with individual pitches in grounds of a renovated farmhouse dating from 1867.
2 km E on N506. 120 m above N506.
15 June–15 Sep.
1.2HEC

HOULGATE
Calvados
Vallée 88 rte de la Vallée 31244069
15 Apr–Sep.
8HEC lau s A15 pitch18

At **HÔME (LE)** (3 km W)
Pasteur av Gl-Leclerc 31912308
Apr–Sep.

4HEC lau s A10 pitch6

HOUMEAU (L')
Charente-Maritime
Trépied au Plomb 46509082
Jun–Sep.
2HEC lau s pitch33 (incl 2 persons)

HOURTIN
Gironde
Airotel Mauriflaude rte de Pauillac 56091197
Level meadowland, shaded by pines, in rural setting.
Turn onto D4 at the chemist and continue E towards Pauillac.
May–15 Sep.
9HEC P lau pitch79–84 (incl 4 persons)

Orée du Bois rte d'Aquitaine 56091588
1500 m from town centre beside the lake.
15 Jun–15 Sep.
1.5HEC lau pitch37 (incl 2 persons)

Ourmes 56091276
On well-kept field. Boating nearby.
Follow D4 towards lake. ➔

Apr–Oct.
6HEC H G R lau L
See advertisement page 159

HOURTIN-PLAGE
Gironde
Côte d'Argent ☎56091025
500 m from beach.
15 May–15 Sep.
20HEC H G R lau s A17 pitch 34–40

HUME (LA)
Gironde
At **TESTE (LA)** (3 km SW)
Domaine de la Forge rte des Lacs ☎56660772
Secluded site in very quiet woodland.
3 km S on D652.
All year.
12HEC H G R P lau pitch33

HYÈRES
Var
At **AYGUADE-CEINTURON** (4 km SE)
Ceinturon II ☎94663265
A popular site on level meadowland divided into pitches. Some individual washing cubicles.
4 km SE of Hyères on D42.
Jun–Aug.
5HEC H G lau s A13 pitch15
Ceinturon III ☎94663265
Well-kept and divided into numbered pitches. Individual washing cubicles.
4 km SE of Hyères on D42.
15 Mar–Sep.
3HEC H G lau s A14 pitch17
At **CAPTE (LA)** (7 km S)
CM de la Capte ☎94580020
Mar–Oct.
8HEC H G R lau s
At **HYÈRES-PLAGE** (4 km SE)
Pins Maritimes ☎94576388
Situated in a pine wood close to the beach.
Turn off D42 between Hyères-Plage and L'Ayguade by the water ski lift (Téléskinautique) and continue inland for 0.2 km.
Jun–15 Sep.
15HEC H G lau s

IBARRON See **ST-PÉE-SUR-NIVELLE**

ILLKIRCH-GRAFFENSTADEN See **STRASBOURG**

INGRANDES
Vienne

France

At **ST-USTRE** (2 km NE)
Petit Trianon de St-Ustre ☎49026147
In beautiful park surrounding small castle, part of which is open to the public.
Turn off N10 at signpost N of Ingrandes and continue for 1 km.
15 May–Sep.
4HEC H G P lau A18 V8 8 8

ISLE-SUR-LA-SORGUE (L')
Vaucluse
CM Sorguette rte d'Apt ☎90380571
Borders the N100 towards Apt.
15 Mar–Oct.
2.5HEC H G R lau A12 pitch11

ISLE-SUR-LE-DOUBS (L')
Doubs
CM Lumes ☎81927305
The site lies close to the town. Common room with TV.
Off N83. Entrance near bridge over the Doubs.
15 May–15 Sep.
1HEC H lau R A10 pitch12

ISTRES
Bouches-du-Rhône
At **ESTAGEL**
Vitou rte de St-Chamas ☎42565157
All year.
3HEC H P lau L pitch44–80 (incl 2–4 persons)

JARD-SUR-MER
Vendée
Coquille r de l'Océan ☎51334267
1 km SW on D19.
15 Jun–Aug.
0.4HEC H lau s pitch40 (incl 3 persons)
Écureuils r des Goffineaux ☎51334274
Quiet woodland terrain near to the sea.
Signposted.
Jun–15 Sep.
3HEC H G R P lau s

JAVRON
Mayenne
CM rte de Mayenne ☎43034067
200 m SW of town off N12. Signposted.
Etr & Jun–Sep.
1.5HEC H lau LR A4 V2 2 2

JULLOUVILLE
Manche
Chaussée av de la Libération ☎33618018
On large meadow, completely divided into pitches. Separated from beach and coast road by row of houses.
Apr–Sep.
4.7HEC H G lau s pitch44 (incl 2 persons)
Docteur Lemmonier ☎33514260
N on rte de Granville.
Etr–Sep.
1.5HEC H G lau s A9 pitch7
At **ST-MICHEL-DES-LOUPS** (4 km SE)
Chaumière ☎33488293
4 km SE on D21 via Bouillon.
15 Jun–15 Sep.
4HEC H G lau A9 V5 5 5

JUMIÈGES
Seine-Maritime
CM r Mainberte ☎35372415
Apr–15 Nov.
2HEC H lau A6 V3 3 3

KAYSERSBERG
Haut-Rhin
CM rte de Lapoutroie ☎89471447
Between a sports ground and the River Weiss. Subdivided by low hedges.
200 m from N415. Signposted.
Apr–Sep.
1.6HEC H lau P A10 V5 7 7

LA Each name preceded by 'La' is listed under the name that follows it.

LAÀS
Pyrénées-Atlantiques
Parc de Château ☎59389153
All year.
1HEC H lau A8 pitch10

LABENNE
Landes
Savane ☎59454113
On RN10.
All year.
6HEC H G lau s A9 pitch6

LABENNE-OCÉAN
Landes
Boudigau ☎59454207
Situated in pine forest.
Turn right into site after bridge.
Jun–Sep.
6HEC H G P lau s **pp**12

Côte d'Argent ☎59454202

Very well-managed modern site attached to holiday village.

3 km W on D126.
All year.

4HEC lau

Mer ☎59454209

On D126 (rte de la Plage).
Jun–Sep.

6HEC lau A11 pitch16

LACANAU-OCÉAN
Gironde

Airotel de l'Océan r du Repos ☎56032445

On rising ground in pine forest. 800 m from beach.

May–Sep.

9.5HEC lau pitch77 (incl 3 persons)

Grands Pins ☎56032077

On very hilly terrain in woodland. 400 m from the beach, access to which is through dunes.

All year.

11HEC lau pitch80–100 (incl 3 persons)

At **MOUTCHIC** (5 km E)

Ermitage ☎56202522

In village centre 150 m from lake.
Jul–Aug.

3HEC lau A15 V15 15 15

Lac ☎56030026

On D6 rte de Lacanau, 60 m from lake.
Apr–15 Oct.

2HEC lau A10 V5 20 20

Tedey ☎56030015

Quiet site in pine forest, on edge of Lake Lacanau. Private bathing area.

Turn off D6 and continue along narrow track through forest for 0.5 km.

30 Apr–25 Sep.

14HEC lau pitch37–55 (incl 1–3 persons)

LACAPELLE-MARIVAL
Lot

CM Bois de Sophie ☎65408259

May–Sep.

lau A5 pitch5

LAGORCE
Ardèche

Domaine de Chaussy ☎75396245

On D559 near Ruoms.
Etr–30 Sep.

4.5HEC lau pitch58–75 (incl 2 persons)

LAGORD
Charente-Maritime

CM Parc ☎46676154

20 May–Sep.

2HEC lau

LAGUÉPIE
Tarn-et-Garonne

Eaux Vives ☎63302458

On bank of Aveyron.

N on N658 and N122.

0.3HEC

LAISSAC
Aveyron

Moulinet ☎65696184

May–Sep.

0.6HEC lau

LALINDE
Dordogne

Moulin de la Guillou rte du Bugue ☎53610291

2 km E on D703.
Jun–Sep.

2HEC lau A8 V3 6 7

LANDÉDA
Finistère

Abers aux Dunes de Ste-Marguerite ☎98049335

Very quiet beautiful site among dunes. Ideal for children.

2.5 km NW on a peninsula between bays of Aber-Wrac'h and Aber Benoît.
June–15 Sep.

5HEC lau A9 V4 9 9

LANDRELLEC
Côtes-du-Nord

Port ☎96238779

Beautiful site by the sea with numbered pitches surrounded by hedges.

3 km from Trégastel turn towards Tréburden.
Etr–Sep.

2HEC lau pitch50 (incl 2 persons)

LANDUDEC
Finistère

Bel Air ☎98915027

Situated in an orchard.

18 km W from Quimper on D784.
June–15 Sep.

5HEC lau A11 V5 17 17

LANGON
Gironde

CM allées Marine 2 av de l'Hippodrome ☎56630756

In the centre of the town.
Jun–Sep.

0.8HEC lau

LANSLEVILLARD
Savoie

CM ☎79059052 ➔

From Lanslebourg E off D902.
13 Dec–15 May & 15 June–15 Sep.
3.1HEC ◇ H |O| ⊙ R ⊞ lau G

LANTON
Gironde

Roumingue ☎56829748

Level terrain under a few deciduous trees partially in open meadow on the Bassin d'Arcachon.

1 km NW of village towards sea.
4 Jun–17 Sep.
33HEC H |O| ⊙ G Ls ⊞ lau A18 pitch53

At **CASSY** (2 km N on D3)

Coq Hardi ☎56820180

A subdivided grassland site on the Bassin d'Arcachon. Limited swimming facilities.

15 May–15 Sep.
8.5HEC H ⊙

LANTOSQUE
Alpes-Maritime

Deux Rivers ☎93030544

Apr–Oct.
1.3HEC H |O| ⊙ R ⊞ lau pitch35 (incl 3 persons)

LAON
Aisne

France

CM 22 r J-P-Timbaud ☎23232907

Apr–Oct.
1.3HEC H ⊙ G ⊞ lau |O| A8 V5 5 5

LARNAGOL *Lot*

Ruisseau de Treil ☎65312339

15 May–15 Sep.
3HEC H |O| ⊙ G P ⊞ lau R A20 Vn/c 20 20

LARUNS
Pyrénées-Atlantiques

Gaves ☎59053237

On the bank of the Gave d'Ossan. Some pitches reserved for caravans.

1 km S.
All year.
2HEC H ⊙ ⊞ lau |O| P A10 pitch20

LARUSCADE
Gironde

Relais du Chaven ☎57686305

On well-kept meadow edged by a strip of forest. Some traffic noise.

6.5 km NW on N10 near Km20.3.
Jun–15 Sep.
3.5HEC H ⊙ G P ⊞ lau |O| A13 V5 10 10

LATTES
Hérault

See also **MONTPELLIER**

Eden ☎67682968

Jun–Sep.
6HEC H |O| ⊙ G P ⊞ lau pitch70 (incl 2 persons)

Lac des Rêves ☎67501546

Individual pitches. Alongside lake.

On the road between Pérols and Lattes.
Etr–Oct
33HEC ◇ H |O| ⊙ P ⊞ lau pitch60

LAURENS
Hérault

Oliveraie ☎67902436

900 m from village centre.
All year.
4HEC H |O| ⊙ G P ⊞ lau pitch54–77 (incl 2 persons)

LAVANDOU (LE)
Var

St-Pons ☎94710393

1 km SW.
15 Mar–Sep.

2.5HEC lau pitch35–46 (incl 3 persons)

LAVELANET
Ariège
CM ☎61015554
Partly shaded site next to municipal Sports Centre and pool.
Turn off D117 SW of Lavelanet.
All year.
2HEC lau **A**9 pitch10

LE Each name preceded by 'Le' is listed under the name that follows it.

LECTOURE
Gers
Lac des Trois Vallées ☎62688233
This country-side site is part of a large park and lies next to a lake. It has spacious marked pitches.
3 km SE on N21.
Etr–Sep.
40HEC lau pitch65 (incl 3 persons)

LÉON
Landes
Lou Puntaou ☎58487430
In oak wood with separate sections for caravans.
Turn off N652 in village and continue towards lake for 1.5 km on D142.
Jun–15 Sep.
15HEC lau

LÉPIN-LE-LAC See **AIGUEBELETTE (LAC D')**

LES Each name preceded by 'Les' is listed under the name that follows it.

LESCAR
Pyrénées-Atlantiques
Terrier rte du Pont du Gave ☎59810182
On meadowland split in two with pitches surrounded by hedges in foreground.
From Pau take N117 towards Bayonne for approx. 6.5 km, then turn left onto D501 towards Monein to site towards bridge.
All year.
4HEC lau **A**10 pitch19

LESCONIL
Finistère
Dunes ☎98878178
On slightly sloping recently landscaped ground.
Access via D53, turning S in Plobannalac. Signposted.
Etr–Sept.
1.1HEC lau **A**12 **V**6 pitch15

LESPARAT See **PÉRIGUEUX**

LEUCATE
Aude
CM Cap Leucate ☎68400137
Beside sea. Divided into pitches. Open air cinema.
May–Sep.
8HEC lau

LÉZIGNAN-CORBIÈRES
Aude
CM Pinède ☎68270508
Well-kept terraced site, with numbered pitches and tarred drives, decorated with bushes and flower beds.
Signposted from N113.
Mar–Nov.
3.6HEC lau

LILIAN See **SOULAC-SUR-MER**

LIMERAY
Indre-et-Loire
Launay ☎47301682
6 km NE of Amboise on N152.
Apr–Sep.
1.5HEC lau **A**13 pitch14–17

LIMEUIL See **BUGUE (LE)**

LIMOGES
Haute-Vienne
CM de la Vallée de l'Aurence ☎55384943
On level ground, divided by hedges.
Beside River Vienne.
All year.
3HEC lau

LION D'ANGERS (LE)
Maine-et-Loire
CM Frénes ☎41953156
NE on N162.
5 Jun–15 Sep.
2HEC lau **A**6 **V**3 3 3

LION-SUR-MER
Calvados
Roches av de Blagny ☎31972115
NW on D514.
Apr–Sep.
1.3HEC lau

LISIEUX
Calvados
CM 9 r de la Vallée ☎31620040
N on road D579 to Pont l'Évêque.
Apr–Sep.
1HEC lau

LIT-ET-MIXE
Landes
CM Cap de l'Homy ☎58428347
Undulating dunes in pine woodland next to a broad beach.
S on D652, turn W and continue through pine forest for 1 km.
Jun–Sep.
6HEC lau

Univers rte des Lacs ☎58428337
A level site in an old park. Rarely crowded.
On southern outskirts of town towards Léon.
Jun–15 Sep.
10HEC lau **A**14 pitch16

LIVERS-CAZELLES
Tarn
Rédon ☎63561464
4 km SE of Cordes on D600.
Apr–15 Oct.
1HEC lau pitch30 (incl 1–3 persons)

LOCHES
Indre-et-Loire
CM rte de Châteauroux ☎47590591
S on N143. Access from r Quintefol.
Etr–Sep.
3HEC lau

LOCQUIREC
Finistère
Bellevue ☎98788080
Terraced site on hill with fine sea view.
4 km W on D64.
25 Jun–5 Sep.
0.8HEC lau

LONDE-LES-MAURES (LA)
Var
Forge ☎94668265
Level meadow with good sanitary facilities.
Turn off N98 into village, at traffic lights turn N for 1 km to site on outskirts of village.
Jun–Sep.
3HEC lau **A**12 pitch15

Miramar rte de la Plage Miramar ☎94668058
2.5 km S of N98.
June–15 Sep.
3HEC lau pitch38 (incl 2 persons)

Moulières ☎94668238
Well tended level meadowland in quiet location. 1 km from the sea. ➔

On western outskirts towards the coast.
Jun–Sep.

3HEC lau s

Pansard ☎94668322

Beautiful, wide piece of land, beside beach and divided into pitches.

Turn off N98.
Apr–Sep.

6HEC s lau pitch54 (incl 3 persons)

Val Rose ☎94668136

4 km NE on N98.
Jun–Sep.

2.4HEC P lau A12 pitch17

LONGEVILLE
Vendée

Jarny Océan ☎51334221

Subdivided well tended meadow, with a holiday complex of the same name where shopping facilities are provided. 800 m to sea via forest path.

Turn off D105 about 3 km S of Longeville.
Jun–Sep.

2HEC s

At **CONCHES (LES)** (4 km S)

Dunes av de la Plage ☎51333293

Well-kept site amongst sand dunes in pine forest.

6 km S of Longeville on D105.
Apr–Oct.

2HEC P lau s A16 pitch70–96

Fief du Bonaire ☎51333109

Well-kept site with special asphalt drives and children's playground. 600 m to sea. ***Entrance permitted only if camper holds an International Camping Carnet or is prepared to take out an insurance.***

From village 700 m towards the sea.
20 May–15 Sep.

1.6HEC P lau s pitch90–100 (incl 3 persons)

France

LONS-LE-SAUNIER
Jura

CM Marjorie ☎84242694

Clean, tidy site with tent and caravan sections separated by a stream. Caravan pitches (80 sq m) are gravelled and surrounded by hedges. Heated common room with TV, reading area, kitchen. Swimming pool free to campers.

Near swimming stadium on outskirts of town.
All year.

4.5HEC lau P A9 pitch9–12

LOPIGNA See **CORSE (CORSICA)**

LOUAN
Seine-et-Marne

Cerclière ☎64008014

500 m NE on D131.
Mar–Oct.

10HEC lau P

LOUANNEC See **PERROS-GUIREC**

LOUARGAT
Côtes-du-Nord

At **ST-ELOI** (5 km N)

Cleuziou ☎96431490

Apr–Oct.

3.5HEC P A18 pitch34

LOURDES
Hautes-Pyrénées

Arrouach quartier Biscaye ☎62942575

Situated on D940 Soumoulou road.
All year.

4HEC lau P A7 V4 4 4

Belle-Vue 45 av A-Marqui ☎62942240

On level meadow.

1 km from village centre, at fork junction to Tarbes turn off N21.
Etr–Oct.

1HEC lau P

Domec rte de Julos ☎62940879

Off N21 Tarbes road N of town centre.
Etr–Oct.

2HEC lau LP A7 pitch9

Prat 22 av A-Béguère N640 ☎62940153

On level ground, asphalt drives.

Off N21 Tarbes road near stadium.
Jul–Oct.

2HEC lau LP

Sarsan av J-Moulin ☎62944309

Off the N21 in the direction of the secondary school.

15 Jun–15 Sep.

1.8HEC lau A10 pitch10

Scierie 64 av A-Marqui

400 m from town centre. Off N21 Tarbes road.
Apr–Sep.

1HEC lau P A7 pitch10

Theil No 23 ☎62943633

Quiet site on several levels. Bathrooms available.

Turn off N640 in village and follow signposts.
All year.

1HEC lau

LOURMARIN
Vaucluse

Hautes Prairies rte de Vaugines ☎90680289

On gently sloping meadow with trees.

Access is from motorway exit 'Cavaillon' onto the D973 to Cadenet, then onto the D943 to Lourmarin, 0.5 km on D56 to site.
All year.

2.7HEC P lau A11 V8 8 8

LOUVIERS
Eure

Bel Air St-Lubin 32401077

Small site near a forest.

Mar–Oct.

2.5HEC H G P lau A11 pitch15

LUCHON

Haute-Garonne

Beauregard av de Vénasque 61793074

On level meadow.

Off N125.
Mar–30 Oct.

3HEC H lau LP A9 Vn/c 10 A10

LUDE (LE)

Sarthe

CM rte du Mans 43946770

400 m from town centre, direct from N307
Etr–Sep.

4.5HEC H lau |O| P A5 V4 4 A4

LUGRIN

Haute-Savoie

Vieille Église 50760195

On rising meadow with good views.

Etr–Oct.

1.5HEC H G R lau |O| LP A10 V4 8 A8

LUMIO See **CORSE (CORSICA)**

LUNEL

Hérault

Bon Port 67711565

Access via D24.
All year.

5HEC H |O| G P lau pitch48 (incl 3 persons)

LUSIGNAN

Vienne

CM Vauchiron 49433008

500 m NE on N11.
15 Apr–Oct.

4HEC H R lau A5 V3 4 A4

LUTTENBACH

Haut-Rhin

Amis de la Nature 89773860

Site on a long strip of land, divided into pitches next to disused factory and ruined house.

From Munster follow D10 for 1 km.
All year.

6.5HEC H |O| G lau A8 V4 4 A4

LUYNES

Indre-et-Loire

CM Granges 47556085

S of town off D49.
Jun–15 Sep.

0.8HEC H G lau |O| P A7 pitch7

France

LUZ-ST-SAUVEUR

Hautes-Pyrénées

Bergons 62929077

600 m E on D618 Barèges road.
All year.

1HEC H G lau |O| P A8 pitch9

Pyrénées International rte de Lourdes 62928202

1.3 km NW on N21.
Jun–Sep.

4HEC H |O| G lau A12 pitch11

MÂCON

Saône-et-Loire

CM 85381622

Divided into pitches. Water sports centre and pool nearby.

2 km N on N6.
15 Mar–15 Nov.

5HEC H |O| G lau P A9 V5 7 A7

MAGNAC-BOURG

Haute-Vienne

CM Écureuils rte de Limoges 55008028

N on N20.
Etr–Sep

1.3HEC H lau |O| A6 pitch6

MAÎCHE

Doubs

Derrière St-Michel 81641256

1 km S on D422.
All year.

2HEC H lau |O| R

MAISNIL-LÈS-RUITZ

Pas-de-Calais

Parc d'Olhain 21279480

1.5 km S.
Mar–Oct.

3HEC H |O| G lau P

MAISONS-LAFFITTE See **PARIS**

MALAUCÈNE

Vaucluse

Lignol 90652278

Well-kept site at edge of village, partly terraced and subdivided.

Well signposted from village.
Apr–14 Sep.

2HEC H G lau |O| A10 V6 7 A7

At **BEAUMONT-DE-VENTOUX** (2 km NE)

Mont Serein 90634202

All year.

0.6HEC H (in summer)

MALBUISSON

Doubs

Fuvettes 81693150

Mainly level site with some terraces, gently sloping towards lake.

500 m S on D437.
All year.

5HEC H |O| G R L lau

MALLEMORT

Bouches-du-Rhône

Durance et Lubéron 90574336

2.5 km on D23c, 200 m from Canal.
Apr–Sep.

5HEC H P lau |O|

MAMETZ

Pas-de-Calais

Château de Mametz 21390631

All year.

10HEC H |O| G R P lau A10 pitch20

MANDELIEU

Alpes-Maritimes

Cigales av de la Mer 93492353

S on N7.
Mar–Dec.

2HEC H |O| G lau S pitch97 (incl 2 persons)

Plateau des Chasses 93492593

Terraced land, on hill in a park.

Turn off N7 at km 4.2 and continue uphill for 1.2 km.
Apr–Sep.

4HEC H |O| G lau pitch100–124 (incl 5 persons)

Roc Fleuri rte de Pégomas 93930871

Beautiful well-kept site in orchard. Partly sloping.

N of town on D109.
Apr–20 Sep.

2HEC H |O| G lau pitch53 (incl 2 persons)

MANDRES-AUX-QUATRE-TOURS

Meurthe-et-Moselle

CM 83231731

Apr–Oct.

1HEC H G R lau A5 V1 5 A2

MANOSQUE

Alpes-de-Haute-Provence

CM Ubacs av de la Repasse 92722808

1.5 km W off D907, rte d'Apt.
All year.

4HEC H P lau |O|

MARANS
Charente-Maritime
CM Bois Dinot rte de Nantes ☎46011051
500 m N of village on N137, Nantes road.
All year.
6HEC ◆ ◇ H ⊙ G R P ⊞ lau |O| A5 pitch6

MARCILLAC-LA-CROISILLE
Corrèze
Lac ☎55278138
Beside a lake with good facilities for water sports.
Jun–Sep.
3.8HEC ◆ H ⊙ ⊞ lau |O| L A9 pitch8

MARÇON
Sarthe
Lac des Varennes ☎43441372
15 Apr–Sep.
0.4HEC ◆ H |O| ⊙ LR lau G

MAREUIL
Dordogne
Etang Bleu ☎53609270
Jul–Aug.
4HEC ◆ ◆ H |O| ⊙ G ⊞ lau L A12 pitch14–24

MARIGNY
Jura
Pergola ☎84257003
Terraced site
S of Marigny off D27.
Apr–Oct.
6HEC ◆ H |O| ⊙ G L ⊞ lau pitch80 (incl 3 persons)

MARSEILLAN-PLAGE
Hérault
Charlemagne ☎67219249
Apr–10 Oct.
5HEC ◆ H |O| ⊙ G R P ⊞ lau S pitch90 (incl 3 persons)
Grillon des Mers ☎67941683
Jun–Oct.
0.7HEC ◆ H ⊙ |O| S
Hippocampe ☎67219267
Etr–Oct.
2.3HEC ◆ H |O| ⊙ G R P ⊞ lau S pitch106 (incl 4 persons)

MARTRAGNY
Calvados
Château de Martragny Bretteville L'Orgueilleuse ☎31802140
In village turn NE and continue for 0.8 km
May–15 Sep.
8HEC ◆ H ⊙ G P ⊞ lau A19 pitch25

France

MASSEUBE
Gers
CM ☎62660175
500 m E on D27.
Jun–Sep.
6HEC ◆ H |O| ⊙ P ⊞ lau A6 V4 7 4

MASSIAC
Cantal
CM Allagnon av de Courcelles ☎71230393
0.8 km W on N122.
May–Sep.
2.5HEC ◆ H ⊙ ⊞ lau |O| P A8 V5 7 7

MATHES (LES)
Charente-Maritime
Beauséjour ☎46224005
Apr–15 Sep.
7HEC ◆ H ⊙ G R ⊞ lau |O| S A13 V4 9 9
Estanquet ☎46224732
15 May–15 Sep.
6HEC ◆ H |O| ⊙ G R P ⊞ lau pitch56 (incl 3 persons)

MAULÉON-LICHARRE
Pyrénées-Atlantiques
Salson rte de Tardets ☎59281879
1.5 km S on D918 Tardets–Sorholus rd.
Jun–Sep.
1HEC ◆ H ⊙ G R ⊞ lau |O| A9 V3 8 8

MAUPERTUS-SUR-MER
Manche
Anse du Brick ☎33543357
Terraced site in dense wood.
200 m from beach.
Apr–Sep.
7HEC ◆ ◆ H |O| ⊙ G ⊞ lau S A10 pitch11

MAUREILLAS
Pyrénées-Orientales
Bruyères rte de Céret ☎68832664
NW off D618 to Céret.
Etr–15 Oct.
4HEC ◆ H ⊙ G R P ⊞ lau |O| A15 Vn/c 25 15
CM Congo rte de Céret ☎68832321
1 km W on N618.
15 May–Sep.
0.8HEC ◆ H ⊙ ⊞ lau |O|
Val Roma Park ☎68831972
2.5 km NE on N9.
May–Sep.
3.8HEC ◆ ◆ H |O| ⊙ G RP ⊞ lau A20 pitch29

MAURS
Cantal
At **ST-CONSTANT** (4.5 km SE by N663)
Moulin de Chaules rte de Calvinet ☎71491102
Etr–25 Sep.
3HEC ◆ H |O| ⊙ G P ⊞ lau pitch39 (incl 2 persons)

MAUSSANE-LES-ALPILLES
Bouches-du-Rhône
CM Romarins rte de St-Rémy-de-Provence ☎90973360
Very clean, well-kept site completely divided into pitches.
On N outskirts of town. Well signposted.
15 Mar–15 Oct.
3HEC ◆ H ⊙ ⊞ lau

MAUVAISVILLE See **ARGENTAN**

MAXILLY See **EVIAN-LES-BAINS**

MAYENNE
Mayenne
Raymond Faugué rte de Brives ☎43042101
800 m from town centre on N12.
All year.
1.8HEC ◆ H ⊙ G ⊞ lau P

MAZION See **BLAYE**

MÉAUDRE
Isère
Buissonnets ☎76952104
200 m from village centre.
All year.
2HEC ◇ H ⊙ G R Ⓟ ⊞ lau |O| P pitch37 (incl 2 persons)

MÉDIS
Charente-Maritime
Clos Fleuri ☎46056217
25 Jun–8 Sep.
3HEC ◆ H |O| ⊙ G R ⊞ lau

MEGÈVE
Haute-Savoie
Ripaille ☎50214724
All year.
1HEC ◇ H |O| ⊙ G R P ⊞ lau A23 pitch37

MELUN
Seine-et-Marne
Belle Étoile Chemin de Halage ☎64394812
Pleasant grassy site with two central blocks.
At La Rochette, on left bank of River Seine,

1 km from the town.
Mar–Jan.
3.5HEC lau A12 pitch13

MEMBROLLE-SUR-CHOISILLE (LA)
Indre-et-Loire
CM 47412040
On level meadow in sports ground beside River Choisille.
North of village on N138 Le Mans road.
May–Sep.
1.5HEC lau A6 pitch5

MENDE
Lozère
Sirvens rte du Puy 66651693
3 km NE of N88.
2.4HEC lau
Tivoli 66650038
All year.
2HEC lau

MÉOUNES-LES-MONTRIEUX
Var
Aux Tonneaux 94339834
Site in wooded area, divided into pitches.
200 m S of village off N554.
All year.
2.5HEC lau A8 pitch8
Domaine de Belvoir rte de Signes 94908974
Apr–Dec.
6HEC lau

MESCHERS-SUR-GIRONDE
Charente-Maritime
Côte de Beauté Plage de Suzac 46052693
Hilly terrain with mixed woodland between the road and the sea. Broad sandy beach.
On the D25 to Plage de Suzac, halfway between St-Georges and Meschers.
Apr–Sep.
4HEC

France

lau
Escale 46027153
Apr–Oct.
2HEC lau

MESLAND
Loir-et-Cher
Parc du Val de Loire 54702718
Apr–20 Sep.
8HEC lau A18 pitch29

MESNIL-ST-PÈRE
Aube
Voie Colette 25412715
Grassland, with trees, ornamental shrubs and flower beds. Slightly sloping, with a man-made lake nearby.
About 5 km from Mesnil-St-Père; signposted from centre.
15 Mar–15 Oct.
4HEC lau pitch24 (incl 2 persons)

MESQUER
Loire-Atlantique
Beaupré 40425236
On road between Mesquer and Quimiac. Entrance signposted.
20 Jun–10 Sep.
0.6HEC lau

MESSANGES
Landes
Moisan rte de la Plage 58481119
15 May–Sep.
4HEC lau pitch37 (incl 2 persons)
Vieux Port 58482200
2.5 km SW via D652.
Apr–Sep.

30HEC lau
pitch67–82 (incl 3 persons)

MESSERY
Haute-Savoie
Relais du Léman 50947111
May–Sep.
2.6HEC lau A15 pitch15

METZERAL
Haut-Rhin
At **MITTLACH** (3 km SW)
CM 89776377
Situated in forested area in small village, very quiet.
From Munster follow signs for Metzeral then Mittlach D10vi.
Apr–Oct.
3HEC lau A10 V3 3 3

MEURSAULT
Côte-d'Or
CM Grappe d'Or r de 11 Novembre 80212248
Clean terraced site.
700 m NE on D111b.
Apr–Sep.
4.5HEC lau A9 V6 10 10

MEYMAC
Corrèze
CM Garenne 55952280
NE on D30
May–Sep
4.5HEC lau A9 pitch9

MÉZOS
Landes
Sen Yan 58426005
Jun–15 Sep.
8HEC lau

MIÉLAN
Gers

Lac ☎62675176

On slightly sloping, partially uneven ground adjoining the leisure and water sports centre.

2.5 km NE via N21 rte d'Auch.
All year.

2.5HEC H L lau A9 pitch12

MIGENNES
Yonne

CM Leo Lagrange 15 r G-Bovin ☎86801763

Apr–Oct.

1.8HEC H lau R

MILLAC
Lot

Millac ☎53297236

Etr–Sep.

2HEC H lau R

MILLAU
Aveyron

Millau-Cureplat ☎65601575

On E bank of river near Pont de Cureplat.
Apr–15 Oct.

5HEC H RP lau pitch40 (incl 2 persons)

Millau Graufesenque rte de Nant ☎65601133

1 km E on D591 next to River Dourbe.
Jun–Sep.

5HEC H lau P

Millau-Plage ☎65601097

Level site with many pitches on bank of River Tarn. Landing stage for small boats. Individual wash basins.

Etr–25 Sep.

3HEC H RP lau pitch40 (incl 3 persons)

MIMIZAN
Landes

CM Lac av de Woolsack ☎58090121

Level site with pine trees on west bank of Étang d'Aureilhan.

Access by D87 Mimizan–St-Eulalie road.
Apr–Oct.

8HEC H L lau

At **MIMIZAN-PLAGE** (6 km E by D626)

CM de la Plage bd de l'Atlantique ☎58090032

Apr–Sep.

16HEC H lau S

Marina ☎58091266

In mixed woodland. 300 m from beach.

Take D626 from Mimizan to Mimizan Plage. Well signed from paper mill.
May–Sep.

9HEC H P lau S pitch75–85 (incl 2 persons)

MIRANDOL
Tarn

Clots ☎63769278

Situated in the Viaur valley.

5.5 km N via D905, rte de Rieupeyroux.
Etr–15 Oct.

7.5HEC H RP lau A11 V5 6 5

MIREMONT
Puy-de-Dôme

Confolant ☎73799276

7 km NE via D19 and D19E.
15 Jun–15 Sep.

2.8HEC H L lau A9 pitch13

MIRIBEL-LES-ÉCHELLES
Isère

Bourdons ☎76552853

400 m from vil[illegible]e cen[illegible]e
All year.

2HEC H lau

MITTLACH See **METZERAL**

MOISSAC
Tarn-et-Garonne

CM l'Ile de Bidounet ☎63322996

Clean tidy site beside River Tarn; subdivided by hedges.

Signposted from village.
Apr–Sep.

2HEC H lau P

MOLIÈRES
Dordogne

Grande Veyière ☎53225421

Apr–15 Nov.

4.5HEC H P lau A13 pitch17

MOLIETS-PLAGE
Landes

Cigales ☎58485118

On undulating ground in pine trees.

300 m from beach.
15 Apr–Sep.

23HEC H lau S A12 pitch14

Saint Martin ☎58485230

May–15 Oct.

18HEC H sP lau A12 Vn/c 14 11

MOLSHEIM
Bas-Rhin

CM ☎88381167

Tree studded site on level, well tended grassland.

May–Sep.

1.7HEC H P A5 V3 3 3

MONCEAUX-SUR-DORDOGNE See **ARGENTAT**

MONCHAUX-LES-QUEND See **QUEND-PLAGE-LES-PINS**

MONCRABEAU
Lot-et-Garonne

CM Moulat ☎53654328

On D219, 200m from D930.
Jul–Aug.

1.3HEC H lau P A7 pitch6

MONFLANQUIN
Lot-et-Garonne

CM Coulon ☎53364736

1.5 km SW on D124.

4.5HEC H lau P

MONISTROL-SUR-LOIRE
Haute-Loire

Beau Séjour chemin de Chaponas ☎71665390

Adjacent to N88.
10 Apr–Oct.

1.5HEC H lau P A9 V4 8 8

MONNERVILLE
Essonne

Bois de la Justice ☎64950534

Feb–Nov.

5.5HEC H P lau A18 V9 18 9

MONTALIVET-LES-BAINS
Gironde

CM ☎56093345

Level site in pine forest.

700 m from sea. Access via av de l'Europe.
Jun–Sep.

26HEC H lau S A12 pitch17–26

MONTAUBAN
Tarn-et-Garonne

Alsace rte de Paris ☎63032410

1 km N off N20.
15 Mar–15 Sep.

France

1HEC H lau

MONTAUBAN-DE-LUCHON
Haute-Garonne

Lanette ☎61790038

On gently sloping ground surrounded by pastures.

1.5 km E of Luchon. Off D27.
All year.

4.3HEC H lau P pitch57 (incl 3 persons)

MONTBARD
Côte-d'Or

CM r M-Servet ☎80922160

NW via rte de Laignes.
All year.

2.5HEC H lau P A6 V4 6 4

MONTBLANC
Hérault

Rebau ☎67985078

Divided into pitches and surrounded by vineyards.

From Pézenas follow N113; in La Bégude de Jordy turn off main road and drive 2 km on D18 towards Montblanc.
Mar–Oct.

2HEC H P lau pitch50 (incl 1–2 persons)

MONT-DE-MARSAN
Landes

CM ☎58750473

On slightly sloping, wooded land, next to a park. Lunchtime siesta 11–13.00 hrs.

2.5 km E on D1. Signposted.

2HEC H lau P

MONTÉLIMAR
Drôme

Deux Saisons ☎75018899

From bank of River Roubion.

From town centre follow D540 across Pont de la Libération; then first turning right into chemin des Alexis.
15 Feb–Nov.

1.5HEC H P lau R A10 Vn/c 10 10

MONTENDRE
Charente-Maritime

CM Forêt ☎46492017

May–Sep.

5HEC H lau LP

MONTESQUIOU
Gers

Château le Haget ☎62649580

In grounds of Château.

May–Sep.

12HEC H P lau A20 V5 20 20

MONTFERRAT
Isère

At **PALADRU** (2 km SW)

CM ☎76313167

Site divided into pitches. 150 m from lake.

10 km S of Les Abrets on N75 and D50.
15 Apr–15 Sep.

1.8HEC H L

MONTGEARD
Haute-Garonne

Parc de la Thesauque ☎61813467

New site on terraced grassland in rural area about 100 m from lake shore.

A61 exit Villefranche-de-Lauragars about 6 km on N622 towards Auterive.
All year.

2HEC H lau L pitch44 (incl 3 persons)

MONTGIVRAY
Indre ➤

CM Solange Sand r du Pont 54483783

A pleasant, riverside site in the grounds of a château.
15 Mar–15 Nov.

1HEC H lau A5 Vn/c 5 5

MONTHERME
Ardennes

Port Diseur r A-Compain 24530121

Situated on the confluence of Rivers Meuse and Semoy.

Apr–Sep.

2.5HEC H R lau

MONTIGNAC
Dordogne

Castillanderie 53507679

Apr–Oct.

15HEC H L lau A15 Vn/c 15 15

MONTLIS (LES)
Loir-et-Cher

CM 54704754

1 Jun–15 Sep.

1HEC H lau A12 pitch8

MONTLOUIS-SUR-LOIRE
Indre-et-Loire

CM Peupliers rte de Tours 47508190

On level meadow.

1.5 km W on N751, next to swimming pool near railway bridge.
Mar–15 Oct.

6HEC H P lau A7 V7 7 7

MONTLUÇON
Allier

Mas 70293161

4.5 km W of town on N145 on banks of Étang de Sault.
All year.

2HEC H lau L

MONTMAUR
Hautes-Alpes

Mon Repos 92581139

Generally well-kept site on wooded terrain with shaded pitches.

1 km E on D937 and D994.
Apr–15 Oct.

1.2HEC H lau

MONTMERLE-SUR-SAÔNE
Ain

CM Sud 74693440

Site S off rte de Trévoux.
28 May–Oct.

6HEC H lau R

France

MONTMORILLON
Vienne

CM Allochon av F-Tribot 49910233

All year.

0.9HEC H lau P

MONTOIRE-SUR-LE-LOIR
Loir-et-Cher

CM Reclusages av des Reclusages 54850253

On banks of River Loir.

15 Apr–15 Oct.

3HEC H lau P

MONTPELLIER
Hérault

See also **LATTES**

Floréal rte de Palavas 67929305

On level ground surrounded by vineyard.

500 m off Autoroute A9, exit Montpellier-Sud. From town centre follow road for Palavas (D986).
Etr–Sep.

1.6HEC H lau P pitch38 (incl 1–2 persons)

MONTPEZAT
Alpes-de-Haute-Provence

Coteau de la Marine 92744333

A pleasant wooded site, providing easy access to the Verdon gorges.

Mar–15 Dec.

10HEC H RP lau pitch84–94 (incl 3 persons)

MONTREUIL-BELLAY
Maine-et-Loire

Airotel Nobis 41523366

Apr–Sep.

3.1HEC H lau P

MONTREUIL-SUR-MER
Pas-de-Calais

CM 21060728

N of town on N1.
All year.

2HEC H lau P pitch32 (incl 2 persons)

MONTREVEL-EN-BRESSE
Ain

Base de Plein Air et de Loisirs 74308052

Entrance closed between 22.00 & 07.00 hrs.

0.5 km E on D28.
May–Sep.

17HEC H

L lau A9 pitch21

MONT-ST-MICHEL
Manche

Gué de Beauvoir 33600923

4 km S of Abbey on D976 Pontorson road.
Etr–Sep.

1HEC H lau R

Mont-St-Michel 33600933

2 km S of Abbey near 'X' roads. D976/D275.
Apr–Oct.

4HEC H lau A10 V6 9 7

MONTSAUCHE
Nièvre

Plage du Midi 86845197

From Salieu (on N6) follow D977. From town centre follow D193 to Les Sultons, then 1 km to site.
Etr–Sep.

3HEC H L lau A12 V6 7 7

MONTSOREAU
Maine-et-Loire

Isle Verte 41517660

On D947 between road and river.
May–Sep.

3HEC H lau A5 V3 3 3

MOOSCH
Haut-Rhin

Mine d'Argent r de la Mine d'Argent 89823066

1.5 km SW. Access difficult for large caravans.
May–Sep.

3HEC H LP lau A7 Vn/c 6 6

MORGAT
Finistère

Bouis 98261253

Divided into hedge-lined pitches.

15 Jun–15 Sep.

2HEC H lau pitch15

MORTEROLLES-SUR-SEMME See **BESSINES-SUR-GARTEMPE**

MOUCHARD
Jura

Halte Jurassienne 84378392

All year.

0.45HEC H lau A9 V5 6 6

MOURIÈS
Bouches-du-Rhône

Devenson 90475201

Terraced site amongst pine and olive trees in Provençal countryside.

Turn off N113 at La Samatane and continue N towards Mouriès. Site is in N part of village.

Etr–Sep.
3.5HEC H G P lau

MOUSTERLIN
Finistère

Grand Large Pointe de Mousterlin ☎98560406

1.5 km N on D134.
15 May–15 Sep.
6HEC H G S lau A11 V5 15 15

Kost-ar-Moor ☎98560416

On meadow divided into pitches.

300 m from headland off D134.
Apr–Sep.
5.50HEC H G lau S A7 V5 9 9

MOUTCHIC See **LACANAU-OCÉAN**

MOUTIERS-EN-RETZ (LES)
Loiré-Atlantique

Collet ☎40214092

Extensive terrain by sea with groups of trees and open areas of grass and sand.

2.5 km in the direction of Le Collet.
Jun–Sep.
15HEC H G SP lau A12 V10 15 15

MOUTONNE (LA)
Var

Holiday Giavis ☎94388743

Apr–Sep.
5HEC H G R lau A20 pitch35

MOYAUX
Calvados

Colombier ☎31636308

Well-kept site on grounds of manor house.

3 km NE on D143.
May–15 Sep.
5HEC H G P lau A22 pitch35

MULHOUSE
Haut-Rhin

France

CM de l'Ill av P-de-Coubertin ☎89062066

In park beside canal opposite swimming pool.

From town centre follow SP for 'Fribourg & Allemagne'. At Ile Napoléon follow campsite signposts.
Apr–Aug.
5HEC H G lau P

MUNSTER
Haut-Rhin

CM Parc de la Fecht ☎89773108

Almost in town centre within park-like area surrounded by high walls and trees.

Access on D417, 200 m after entering Munster town centre by swimming pool.
15 May–Sep.
4HEC H lau P A8 V4 4 4

MURAT
Cantal

CM de Stalapos ☎71200183

On hilly meadow in valley. Children may paddle in nearby stream.

Well signposted from village.
Jun–Sep & 15 Dec–15 Apr.
5HEC H

MUROL
Puy-de-Dôme

Plage ☎73886027

Busy site beside lake. Caravan section divided into pitches; terraced area for tents. Asphalt drive. Cinema.

1.2 km from centre of village. Turn off into allée de Plage before entering village and follow signposts.
May–Sep.
7HEC H G L lau A10 pitch14

Pré-Bas ☎73886304

15 Jun–15 Sep.

2HEC H lau L A10 pitch15

At **GROIRE** (2 km E)

Groire ☎73886193

Clean, well managed site owned by Germans.

1 km SE on D146.
May–15 Sep.
1.5HEC H L

MÛRS-ERIGNÉ See **PONTS-DE-CÉ (LES)**

MUS
Gard

International Club ☎66350706

2 km N on N113.
All year.
1HEC H R lau pitch50 (incl 3 persons)

MUSSIDAN
Dordogne

CM Le Port ☎53812009

15 Jun–15 Sep.
0.4HEC H G lau P A10 pitch4

MUY (LE)
Var

Cigales ☎94451208

Hilly terrain with Mediterranean pine trees, many terraces and some large boulders.

Exit 'Draguignan' off A8 onto N7. 0.8 km to site. Well signposted.
Jun–15 Sep.
10HEC H G P lau A15 V9 12 12

Sellig rte d'Aix-en-Provence ☎94451171

1.5 km W on N7.
All year.
1.8HEC H R P lau

MUZILLAC
Morbihan

Relais de l'Océan rte de Damgan ☎97416648

2.5 km W via D20. ➔

15 Jun–15 Sep.
1.7HEC ◆ H ⊙ ⊞ lau

NAGES
Tarn

Rieu Montagne Lac du Laouzas ☎63374052

20 Jun–Aug.
3HEC ◇ H ⊙ G R ⊞ lau L pitch80 (incl 4 persons)

NANS-LES-PINS
Var

Sainte Baume ☎94789268

Etr–Oct.
5HEC ◆ H ⊙ G LP ⊞ lau pitch63–87 (incl 3 persons)

NANT
Aveyron

Val de Cantobre ☎65622548

Large variety of recreational facilities.

4 km N of Nant, towards Millau; next to the Dourbie river, and off D591n.
15 May–21 Sep.
6HEC H ⊙ P ⊞ lau

NANTES
Loire-Atlantique

CM Val du Cens bd du Petit Port 21 ☎40744794

On modern well kept park. Separate sections for caravans and tents.

In N part of town near Parc du Petit Port. From town centre follow Rennes road (N137) then signs to camp site.
All year.
8HEC H (Jul–Aug) ⊙ ⊞ lau P A7 Vn/c 34 10

NANTUA
Ain

Signal ☎74750209

The site within a sports ground.

SW opposite Nantua railway station.
15 Jun–Aug.
1HEC H

NAPOULE (LA)
Alpes-Maritimes

Azur-Vacances ☎93499112

Site with many long terraces, on edge of mountain slope in mixed woodland.

Turn inland 200 m after fork at railway station and continue 600 m.
25 Mar–Sep.
7HEC ◆ H ⊙ G ⊞ lau s pitch53 (incl 2 persons)

NARBONNE
Aude

Languedoc ☎68652465

Situated behind the Montlaur supermarket.

France

All year.
2.7HEC H ⊙ G R P ⊞ lau A13 pitch16–24

Relais de la Nautique Anse des Galères ☎68904819

For access take 'Narbonne Sud' exit from Autoroute A9.
May–15 Oct.
16HEC ◇ H ⊙ G R P ⊞ lau

At **NARBONNE-PLAGE** (15 km E on D168)

CM de la Côtes des Roses rte de Gruissan ☎68498365

3 km SW.
Apr–Oct.
15HEC ◇ H ⊙ G ⊞ lau Ls pitch37–48 (incl 2 persons)

CM Falaise ☎68498077

W of Narbonne Plage, 400 m from beach.
Apr–Sep.
7HEC H ⊙ G ⊞ lau s pitch41–54 (incl 2 persons)

NEMOURS
Seine-et-Marne

ACCCF ☎64281062

On well-kept meadow. Clean sanitary installations.

200 m from N7.
Mar–Oct.
4HEC ◇ H ⊙ G R R ⊞ lau

NENON
Jura

Marronniers ☎84706071

Partly sloping site on the edge of extensive woodland near an old château. Access difficult for caravans in places.

May–Sep.
3HEC H ⊙ G P ⊞ lau

NESLES-LA-VALLÉE
Val-d'Oise

Parc de Séjour de l'Étang ☎34706289

Level site near a small lake.

Take D64 to outskirts of town and continue for 300 m.
Mar–Oct.
5HEC H ⊙ ⊞ lau

NEUF-BRISACH
Haut-Rhin

Vauban ☎89725425

500 m from town centre near swimming pool, old town fortifications and adjacent to Rhine-Rhône Canal.

All year.
4HEC ◆ H ⊙ G R P ⊞ lau

NEUVÉGLISE
Cantal

Belvédère du Pont de Lanau ☎71235050

5 km S on D921.
Jun–6 Sep.
3.5HEC H ⊙ G P ⊞ lau pitch70 (incl 2 persons)

NEUVIC
Corrèze

At **ANTIGES** (2 km N)

Centre Président-Queuille Lac de la Triouzoune ☎55958118

2 km NE off N682.
Apr–Sep.
1.6HEC H ⊙ G L ⊞ lau A8 V3 5

NEUVILLE (LA)
Nord

Leu Pindu ☎20865087

N on D8.
All year.
1HEC H ⊙ ⊞ lau A11 pitch11

NÉVEZ
Finistère

Deux Fontaines ☎98068191

Mainly level site, subdivided into several fields.

700 m from Ragunes Beach.
May–Sep.
4.5HEC H ⊙ G ⊞ lau s A12 V5 15 15

NIBELLE
Loiret

Nibelle rte de Boiscommune ☎38322355

Level site in the clearing of an oak woodland.

Access via D921 turning off to Nibelle in an easterly direction. Signposted.
Mar–Nov.
6HEC H ⊙ G R ⊞ lau pitch71 (incl 3 persons)

NIELLES-LÈS-BLÉQUIN
Pas-de-Calais

Peupliers ☎21396806

2.5 km NE via D202, rte d'Affringues.
Apr–Oct.
1.5HEC H ⊙ G ⊞ lau A9 V5 10 10

NÎMES
Gard

Domaine de la Bastide rte de Générac ☎66380921

4 km S via Nîmes-Ouest exit from A9 and the Boulevard Péripherique Sud.

All year.
5HEC H (summer) (summer) lau
P

NOIRMOUTIER (ÎLE DE)
Vendée
BARBÂTRE
Onchères ☎51398131
In quiet setting on sand dunes. ***Only Camping Carnet holders admitted.***
S of village on D95.
Apr–Sep.
10HEC H lau s A10 Vn/c 10 10

NONTRON
Dordogne
At **ABJAT** (15 km NE)
Moulin de Masfrolet ☎53568270
2.4 km N.
15 May–15 Sep.
12HEC H P lau

NOTRE-DAME-DE-MONTS
Vendée
Beauséjour ☎51588388
2 km NW on D38.
Etr–Sep.
1HEC H lau s pitch30–52
Bois Soret ☎51588401
Etr–Sep.
2.5HEC H sP lau
Grand Jardin ☎51588776
Jun–Sep.
2HEC H lau s
pitch51–60 (incl 3 persons)
Pins ☎51588375
Totally divided meadow site under pines and some low deciduous trees.
On D38. Signposted locally.
15 Apr–15 Sep.
2.7HEC H

France

NOUAN-LE-FUZELIER
Loir-et-Cher
CM Grande Sologne ☎54887022
On N20 Orléans-Vierzon road.
Mar–15 Nov.
10HEC H lau P

NOUE (LA) See **RÉ (ILE DE)**

NOUVION-EN-THIÉRACHE (LE)
Aisne
Marlemperche ☎23970154
1.5 km E on N43 then turn onto D965.
15 Mar–15 Oct.
3HEC H lau A7 V6 14 14

NOYAL-MUZILLAC
Morbihan
Moulin de Cadillac ☎97670160
15 Jun–15 Sep.
1.3HEC H lau A6 V3 5 5

NOYELLES-SUR-MER
Somme
Aux Haies de Nolette ☎22232408
Apr–Oct
1HEC H lau

NYONS
Drôme
CM av de la Digue ☎75262239
Situated on bank of river on level meadow with fruit trees. Sports ground and golf course in town.
All year.
1.1HEC H lau RP pitch30 (incl 3 persons)
Sagittaire ☎76276439
Well-kept site divided by hedges.

S of town on D538 road to Vaison-La-Romaine.
15 Mar–Oct.
6HEC H R lau

OBERNAI
Bas-Rhin
CM rte d'Ottrott ☎88953848
Partly terraced site, situated in park.
W on D426 towards Ottrott.
Mar–Oct.
3HEC H lau P A6 V4 4 4

OLÉRON (ILE D')
Charente-Maritime
BOYARDVILLE
Signol ☎46470122
Etr–15 Sep
5HEC H s

CHÂTEAU-D'OLÉRON (LA)
Airotel Domaine de Montravail av de la Libération ☎46476182
Leisure centre area.
Signposted from town centre.
All year.
4HEC H lau s
pitch60 (incl 3 persons)
Brande ☎46476237
15 Mar–15 Nov.
3HEC H R sP lau pitch43 (incl 2 persons)

COTINIÈRE (LA)
Tamaris ☎46471051
About 150 m from sea. Level site in pleasant olive grove.
W side of island, N of town.
Apr–Sep.
2.5HEC H lau s
pitch46 (incl 3 persons)

DOMINO
International Rex ☎46765597
Etr–15 Sep. ➔

10HEC H G s lau pitch60 (incl 2 persons)

Montlabeur ☎46765222

W of town on D734.
15 May–Sep.

7HEC H G R lau s pitch57 (incl 3 persons)

ST-DENIS-D'OLÉRON

Phare Ouest ☎46479000

15 Jun–15 Sep.

4HEC H G R s lau pitch33 (incl 3 persons)

Soleil Levant ☎46478303

Quiet site beside sea.

1 km from village adjacent to D734.
All year.

7HEC H G R s pitch36 (incl 3 persons)

ST-GEORGES-D'OLÉRON

Désirade ☎46765443

26 Jun–1 Sep

3HEC H lau pitch40 (incl 2 persons)

Gros Joncs les Sables Vigniers ☎46765229

Quiet location on undulating land in the midst of lovely pine woodland.

On tourist route from La Cotinière about 5 km NW in the direction of Domino. 1 km SW of St-Georges d'Oléron.
15 Mar–15 Oct.

3HEC H G R lau s pitch64 (incl 3 persons)

Suroît ☎46470725

5 km SW of town.
Etr–Sep.

5HEC H G s lau

Verebleu La Jousselinière ☎46765770

15 May–15 Sep.

6HEC H P lau pitch55 (incl 3 persons)

France

OLIVET

Loiret

CM Olivet r du Pont Bouchet ☎38635394

Site lies partly on shaded peninsula, partly on open lawns beside river.

2 km E. Signposted from village.
Etr–15 Oct.

0.8HEC H lau P A7 V5 5 A5

OLLIÈRES-SUR-EYRIEUX (LES)

Ardèche

Domaine des Plantas ☎75662153

Games room, discothèque and other leisure activities.

May–Sep.

27HEC H G R lau

OLLIERGUES

Puy-de-Dôme

Chelles ☎73955416

5 km from town centre.
15 Mar–Oct.

3.6HEC H G lau A9 V6 7 A7

OLONNE-SUR-MER

Vendée

Loubine rte de la Mer ☎51331292

N via D87/D80.
May–15 Sep.

5HEC H G R P lau s pitch75–95 (incl 3 persons)

Moulin de la Salle ☎51959910

May–Sep.

3HEC H lau pitch80 (incl 3 persons)

Sauveterre ☎51331058

3 km W on D80.
Jun–15 Sep.

2HEC H G lau s

ONDES

Haute-Garonne

CM Peupliers rte de Grenade ☎61828113

SW of the village, beside the River Garonne.
15 May–Sep.

2.5HEC H lau R

ONDRES

Landes

Lou Pignada ☎59453065

Turn off the N10 in the village onto rte de la Plage.
Etr–Sep.

2HEC H G R lau Ls A11 Vn/c 25 A16

ONESSE-ET-LAHARIE

Landes

CM Bienvenu ☎58073049

500 m from village centre on D38.
15 Jun–15 Sep.

1.5HEC H lau A9 V6 9 A9

OPIO See **GRASSE**

ORAISON

Alpes-de-Haute-Provence

CM Oliviers ☎92787652

15 Jun–15 Sep.

2HEC H lau G R P A5 V7 7 A4

ORGON

Bouches-du-Rhône

Vallée Heureuse ☎90730278

A quiet transit site in a rocky valley.

1.5 km from the village on the N7. Access is past a non-working quarry.
All year.

4HEC H G P lau A10 V7 10 A10

ORLÉANS

Loiret

At **ST-JEAN-DE-LA-RUELLE**

CM Gaston-Marchand rte de Blois ☎38883939

On 80 m wide strip of meadow on bank of Loire.

2.5 km from town towards Blois.
Apr–Sep.

2.5HEC H lau RP

ORNANS
Doubs

Chanet ☎81622344

1.5 km SW on D241. Follow green signs.
All year.

1.5HEC H lau RP A7 V2 8 7

OROUET See **ST-JEAN-DE-MONTS**

ORPIERRE
Hautes-Alpes

Princes d'Orange ☎92662253

The site lies on a meadow with terraces.

Etr–15 Nov.

20HEC H lau P pitch62 (incl 3 persons)

ORVILLERS-SOREL
Oise

Château de Sorel ☎44850274

Divided into pitches. Local tradesmen supply provisions.

Leave route A1 at N17, turn right and continue 400 m.
Feb–15 Dec.

4HEC H lau pitch35 (incl 2 persons)

OUISTREHAM-RIVA-BELLA
Calvados

CM Duport ☎31931348

W of village near harbour.

4.5HEC H

OUSSE
Pyrénées-Atlantiques

Sapins ☎59817421

On N117.
All year.

1HEC H lau A8 pitch14

PALADRU See **MONTFERRAT**

PALAIS (LE) See **BELLE-ILE-EN-MER**

PALAMINY See **CAZÈRES**

PALAVAS-LES-FLOTS
Hérault

Palavas ☎67680128

1 km towards Maguelone.
May–18 Sep.

6HEC H

Roquilles 267 bis, av St-Maurice ☎67680347

An attractive site 50 m from the sea.

May–17 Sep.

14HEC H lau S

PALMYRE (LA)
Charente-Maritime

Airotel Parc de la Côte Sauvage Phare de la Coubre ☎46224018

Well laid out site; some sections under pine woods. Adjacent to beach. Near lighthouse.

4.5 km NE on D25. Site entrance hidden down stone track.
May–15 Sep.

12HEC H S lau pitch75 (incl 3 persons)

Bonne Anse Plage ☎46224090

Only Camping Carnet holders admitted.

An extensive, gently undulating site in a pine wood, 200 m from the beach.

2 km NW on D25 towards the lighthouse. Signposted.
25 May–5 Sep.

18HEC H lau S A18 Vn/c 20 20

Charmettes ☎46225096

Etr–Sep.

28HEC H P lau pitch90–105 (incl 6 persons)

Joyeux Faune rte de la Palmyre ☎46224229

1.5 km NE on D141 E Les Mathes road.
Jun–Sep.

5HEC H lau pitch42 (incl 2 persons)

PAMIERS
Ariège

Ombrages ☎61671224

NW on D119 beside river.

1.5HEC H lau RP A5 V2 5 5

PARAY-LE-MONIAL
Saône-et-Loire

Pré Barret bd Dauphin Louis ☎85810505

Well signposted from outskirts of town.
All year.

0.7HEC H lau P A7 V6 4 4

PARCEY
Jura

Bords de Loue ☎84710382

A quiet site on the River Loue.

1.5 km from the centre of the village via N5. Signposted.
15 Apr–15 Sep.

10HEC H R lau A10 pitch12

PARENTIS-EN-BORN
Landes

Arbre d'Or rte du Lac ☎58784156

1.5 km W off D43.
15 Jun–15 Sep.

4.5HEC H P lau A11 pitch18

Si rte de l'Étang ☎58784227

2.5 km W.

2HEC H

At **GASTES** (7.5 km SW)

Réserve ☎58097596

A level site in pine woods on S shore of the Étang de Biscarosse.

Turn off D652 2 km S of Gastes.
15 Mar–Oct.

27HEC G R L lau A10–14 pitch30–40

PARIS

Seine

Paris-Ouest-Bois-de-Boulogne allée du Bord de l'Eau ☎45061498

On right bank of Seine. Often closes by midday in summer due to overcrowding.

France

Access from ring road.
All year.

8.5HEC G lau

At **CHAMPIGNY-SUR-MARNE** (12 km SE)

Tremblay bd des Alliés ☎42833824

Site normally full during peak season. Good transportation into city. Reserved mainly for International Camping Carnet holders. Sanitary installations often overcrowded in morning and evening.

Take N4 and turn left 350 m after Joinville bridge.
All year.

8HEC G R lau P

At **CHOISY-LE-ROI** (14 km SE)

Paris Sud ☎448909230

Signposted.
15 Feb–15 Nov.

7.5HEC G lau P A13–14 pitch13

At **MAISONS-LAFFITTE** (16 km W)

Airotel International r Johnson, Ile de la Commune ☎39624327

A well-kept site in a residential area on the banks of the Seine. Modern installations,

heated in cold weather.

For access, 8 km N of St-Germain-en-Laye; alternatively follow N308 from Porte Champerret or from Colombos-Ouest exit of Autoroute A86.

All year.

6HEC lau **A**7 **V**7 10 5

PATORNAY

Jura

Moulin 84483121

Access is NE via N78, rte de Clairvaux-les-Lacs.

May–15 Sep.

5HEC H P lau pitch55–75 (incl 3 persons)

PAYRAC

Lot

Panoramic 65379845

15 Feb–15 Nov.

1.5HEC H lau P **A**7 pitch7

Pins rte de Cahors 65379632

A well-managed site, partly in forest, partly on meadowland. Sheltered from traffic noise.

S of village off N20.

Etr–Sep.

4HEC H P lau **A**18 pitch18

PEISEY-NANCROIX

Savoie

CM Glières rte des Lanches 79079265

15 Jun–15 Sep.

2HEC H lau **A**6 pitch9

PÉNESTIN-SUR-MER

Morbihan

Airotel-Inly 99903509

15 May–15 Sep.

30HEC H P lau S

France

Cenic 99903314

In a forested area 2 km from the sea.

15 Apr–Sep.

4.2HEC H lau

Iles 99903024

The site lies beside the beach. Paddling pool for children.

3 km S on D201.

Apr–Sep.

2HEC H S lau **A**14 pitch41

PENNAUTIER See **CARCASSONNE**

PENTREZ-PLAGE

Finistère

Tamaris 98265395

Level site divided into pitches.

200 m from beach.

Etr–Sep.

2HEC H lau S **A**7 **V**4 8 8

PENVINS See **SARZEAU**

PÉRIGUEUX

Dordogne

Barnabe-Plage 53534145

Signposted from N89, 2 km E of town centre.

All year.

1.2HEC H R lau **A**10 **V**6 8 8

At **LESPARAT** (4 km E on N89)

Isle 53535775

15 May–15 Sep.

3HEC H RP lau **A**12 pitch10

PÉROLS

Hérault

Airotel l'Estelle rte de Lattes 67500082

800 m SE of town on D132.

All year.

6HEC H P lau pitch59 (incl 2 persons)

PERROS-GUIREC

Côtes-du-Nord

Claire Fontaine r du Pont Hélé 96230355

1.2 km SW of town centre, 800 m from Trestraou beach.

15 Jun–15 Sep.

3HEC H lau S **A**10 **V**5 13 8

At **LOUANNEC** (3 km SE)

CM 96231178

Well situated site next to the sea. Take away food, games room.

1 km W.

15 Jun–15 Sep.

5HEC H S lau **A**8 **V**5 8 6

At **PLOUMANACH** (2 km NW)

Ranolien 96232113

The site is divided into pitches by hedges; separate sections for caravans.

500 m from the village.

All year.

10HEC H SP lau

PETIT-PALAIS

Gironde

Pressoir Queyrai 57697325

Etr–Sep.

2.5HEC H P **A**12 **V**n/c 18 18

PEYRAUD

Ardèche

Château 75340104

2 km S of the Serrières Bridge on N86.

May–Sep.

1.5HEC H lau R

PEYREMALE See **BESSÈGES**

PEZOU

Loir-et-Cher ➤

CM ☎54234069

15 May–8 Sep.

1HEC H lau

PEZULS

Dordogne

Forêt ☎53227169

In extensive grounds on the edge of the forest.

600 m off D703. 3 km from the village centre.
Apr–Sep.

12HEC H P lau A14 pitch14

PHALSBOURG

Moselle

CM Vieux Château r de la Manutention ☎87241372

Site within walls of ancient Castle.

E on rte de Saverne.
Apr–Oct.

1.2HEC H lau A6 V5 4 4

PIERREVAL

Seine-Maritime

Malmaison ☎35349153

In the grounds of an old Château.

1 km from N28 via D122 or D15.
Etr–Sep.

2.5HEC H P lau A13 pitch13

PIEUX (LES)

Manche

Grand Large Anse de Sciotot ☎33524075

In unspoilt landscape.

3 km from the town centre on D117.
May–18 Sep.

2.6HEC H sP lau A12 pitch15

Ranch Le Rozel ☎33524009

Natural area amongst dunes with some bushes. Some pitches within sight of the sea. Long, broad, sandy beach.

S of Les Pieux, towards Le Rozel.
Signposted.

France

Etr–Sep.

4HEC H s lau A10 V6 6 6

PIRIAC-SUR-MER

Loire-Atlantique

Mon Calme rte de Nororet ☎40236077

On open meadow.

On D99.
May–Sep.

1HEC H lau s A10 pitch12

Parc du Guibel ☎40235267

Etr–Sep.

10HEC H lau s A12 V8 9 9

Pouldroit ☎40235091

A modern site on a large field. Divided into pitches.

500 m E on D52.
Jun–15 Sep.

10HEC H lau s A16 V11 12 12

Rio Barre rte de Mesquer ☎40235148

On level field.

2 km E on D52.
15 Jun–15 Sep.

3HEC H lau s

PLAGNE-MONTCHAVIN

Savoie

CM ☎79078323

All year

1HEC H lau P A11 pitch10

PLÉNEUF-VAL-ANDRÉ

Côtes-du-Nord

CM Monts-Colleux r Jean Lebrun ☎967295109

300 m from town centre on N786.
Etr–Sep.

4.5HEC H lau A8 V3 3 3

PLESTIN-LES-GREVES

Côtes-du-Nord

Haye rte de St-Efflam ☎96356253

3 km E on D786.
Jun–Sep.

4.5HEC H lau s A11 V8 10 10

PLEUBIAN

Côtes-du-Nord

Port la Chaine ☎96229238

Grassy site divided by hedges. View of sea

2.5 km N on D20.
Jun–8 Sep

4.7HEC H s lau A12 V6 12 12

PLOËRMEL

Morbihan

Belles Rives rte de Taupont ☎97740122

2 km from village centre, beside the lake.
Apr–Oct.

3HEC H L lau A6 pitch7

Kergo ☎97568066

15 Jun–15 Sep.

2.5HEC H A10 V5 12 12

PLOMODIERN

Finistère

Iroise plage de Pors-ar-Vag ☎98815272

Apr–Sep.

2.2HEC H lau s A7 V4 8 8

PLONÉVEZ-PORZAY

Finistère

International de Kervel ☎98925154

The best site in the region. Ideal for families. 800 m from the sea.

SW of the village on the D107 Douarnene road for 3 km, then towards coast at 'x' roads.
May–15 Sep.
7HEC ◆ H lau P s A17 V8 20 20

Treguer-Plage ☎98925352
Jun–15 Sep.
5.8HEC ◇ H lau s A6 V3 7

PLOUEZOCH
Finistère
Baie de Térénez ☎98672680
Etr–Sep.
2HEC H lau s A13 V5 16

PLOUGASNOU
Finistère
Trégor ☎98673764
Numbered grassy pitches. Surrounded by hedge.
Jun–Sep.
1HEC H lau s A5 V3 pitch6

PLOUGASTEL-DAOULAS
Finistère
Clé des Champs rte de la Pointe d'Amorique ☎98403614
1.2 km from town centre towards Pointe d'Amorique.
15 Jun–15 Sep.
1.5HEC H lau

PLOUGONVELIN
Finistère
Bertheaume ☎98483237
Terraced site above bay.
Apr–Sep.
2.5HEC ◇ H s lau

PLOUHA
Côtes-du-Nord

France

At **TRINITÉ (LA)** (2 km NE)
Domaine de Keravel ☎96224913
Etr–15 Oct.
5HEC H P lau s A18 V8 16 11

PLOUHARNEL
Morbihan
CM Sables Blancs ☎97523715
5 km SW on D768.
Apr–Sep.
18HEC ◇ H s lau A7 V4 4 4

Lande ☎97523148
22 Jun–8 Sep.
1HEC H lau A9 V4 10 10

PLOUHINEC
Morbihan
Moténo rte du Magouër ☎97367663
On slightly sloping ground, subdivided into several fields in a rural area.
All year.
3.8HEC ◆ H lau s A12 V5 8 8

PLOUMANACH See **PERROS-GUIREC**

POËT-CÉLARD (LE) See **BOURDEAUX**

POILLY-LES-GIEN
Loiret
Bois du Bardelet ☎38674739
Access via D940 SW of Gien.
15 Feb–15 Dec.
2HEC H P lau A12 V10 10 5

POINTE-ST-JACQUES See **SARZEAU**

POIX-DE-PICARDIE
Somme

Bois de Pêcheurs ☎22901171
Apr–Sep.
1.6HEC H lau P

PONS
Charente-Maritime
Talbot ☎46940486
Quietly situated on the edge of a small village next to a farm.
From Pons take D732 westwards towards Royan. The site is 2.5 km on the left. Alternatively from exit 26 of the Autoroute A10 and turn towards Pons. Site is 800 m on right.
Dec–Oct.
1.6HEC H lau A7 pitch12

PONTAILLAC See **ROYAN**

PONTARLIER
Doubs
CM ☎81391973
Surrounded by hedges and divided by a public road. Hardstandings for caravans. Lunchtime siesta 12–14.00 hrs.
Follow signs from railway station.
All year.
1.4HEC H lau P A7 V3 3 3

PONT-AVEN
Finistère
Roz Pin ☎98060313
The site covers a large area, well wooded. Good leisure facilities.
Signposted from main road.
May–Sep.
18HEC ◆ ◇ H lau

PONT-DE-RHODES See **FRAYSSINET**

PONT-DU-GARD
Gard
International les Gorges du Gardon rte de Uzès ☎66228181
1 m from aqueduct on D981 Uzès road.
Mar–15 Oct. ➔

3.5HEC H R lau

Pont-du-Gare rte de Uzès 66370300

100 m from the aqueduct on D981 Uzès road.
Mar–15 Sep.

2HEC H lau R

Sousta 66371280

500 m from the aqueduct on D981 Uzès road.
Apr–Nov.

12HEC H PR lau pitch50 (incl 2 persons)

Valive 66228152

All year.

3HEC H P lau R pitch39 (incl 2 persons)

PONT-L'ABBÉ
Finistère

Écureuil 98870339

15 Jun–15 Sep.

3HEC H lau A9 V5 10 10

PONT-L'ÉVÊQUE
Calvados

CM r de Beaumont 31641503

May–Sep.

1.7HEC H lau

Cour de France 31641738

On undulating ground within a leisure complex.

Turn off D48 (Pont l'Évêque–Lisieux) S of the A13 and follow signs 'Centre Loisirs'.
Apr–Sep.

6HEC H lau L

PONT-RÉAN See **RENNES**

PONT-ST-MAMET
Dordogne

Lestaubière 53829815

On wooded pasture in the grounds of Lestaubière Castle.

Off N21.
15 May–15 Sep.

5HEC H P lau L A15 V9 9 9

PONTS-DE-CÉ (LES)
Maine-et-Loire

AT **MÜRS-ERIGNÉ** (4 km SW on N160 and D751)

CM Varennes 41911859

May–15 Oct.

2.5HEC H lau P

PORDIC
Côtes-du-Nord

Madières rte de Vau Madec 96790248

France

1500 m from village on St-Brieuc road (D786).
Jun–Sep.

2HEC H lau S

PORGE (LE)
Gironde

CM de Grigne 56265488

Signposted from D107.
May–Sep.

46HEC H lau S A12 V6 21 20

PORNIC
Loire-Atlantique

Patisseau 40821039

15 Jun–15 Sep.

4HEC H P lau A15 V5 15 15

PORNICHET
Loire-Atlantique

Bugeau 40610202

A well-kept site divided into pitches and set away from the main road.

Jun–Sep.

2HEC H lau S A13 pitch16

Forges 40611884

Jun–Aug.

1.7HEC H lau A7 V6 7 7

PORT-DE-PILES
Vienne

Bec des Deux Eaux 47650271

Etr–Sep.

2.5HEC H P lau A8 pitch8

PORTEAU (LE) See **TALMONT-ST-HILAIRE**

PORTEL (LE) See **BOULOGNE-SUR-MER**

PORT GRIMAUD See **GRIMAUD**

PORT-LE-GRAND See **ABBEVILLE**

PORT-MANECH
Finistère

St-Nicolas 98068975

Divided into hedge-lined pitches.

May–Sep.

3HEC H lau S A12 V4 13 13

PORTO See **CORSE (CORSICA)**

PORTO VECCHIO See **CORSE (CORSICA)**

PORT-SUR-SAÔNE
Haute-Saône

CM Maladière 84915132

15 May–15 Sep.

3HEC H lau R A7 V4 6 5

POTELLE
Nord

Pré Vert 27490947

Apr–Sep.

2HEC H lau L A8 pitch17

POUANCÉ
Maine-et-Loire

CM Roche Martin r des Étangs 41924397

On the edge of a lake.

15 May–15 Sep.

1HEC H L lau

POUGUES-LES-EAUX
Nièvre

CM Chanternes 86688618

On N7 approx. 7 km N of Nevers.
Apr–Oct.

1.4HEC H lau P A6 V5 5 5

POUILLY-SOUS-CHARLIEU
Loire

CM rte de Marcigny 77608067

N on D482. 800 m from town centre.
Etr–Sep.

2HEC H lau A6 V3 3 3

POULDOU (LE)
Finistère

Quinquis 98399240

100 m from village centre.
Jun–7 Sep.

3.5HEC H lau A12 V4 10 10

POULLAN-SUR-MER See **DOUARNENEZ**

PRADEAUX (LES)
Puy-de-Dôme

Château La Grange Fort 73710593

Parklike area surrounding an old château on the bank of the River Allier.

Turn off D996 at Parentignet and continue S on the D34 for about 3 km.
Mar–1 Dec.

15HEC H P lau R A9 Vn/c 17 17

PRADET (LE)
Var

Airotel Mauvallon chemin de la Gavaresse 94217828

A well-kept site amidst young trees divided into pitches.

Turn off the N559 in Le Pradet and take the D86 for 2.5 km towards sea.
Seasonal.

1HEC H

lau S

Pin de Galle ☎94211591

Etr–15 Oct.

1HEC H lau S

Vigneraie ☎94985334

A level site, sub-divided into pitches.

Turn off N599, 1.5 km outside town.
Jun–5 Sep.

0.6HEC H

PRAT-ET-BONREPAUX

Ariège

CM Pont du Bugot ☎61966162

On D117n.
May–Oct.

0.4HEC H lau A6 V5 6 5

PRATS-DE-MOLLO-LA-PRESTE

Pyrénées-Orientales

CM Can Nadal ☎68397089

0.8 km W on D115a.
Apr–Oct.

0.8HEC H

PRAYSSAC

Lot

VVF ☎65224198

2 km E on D911, rte de Cahors.
Jun–Sep.

3HEC H lau RP

PRÉ-EN-PAIL

Mayenne

CM Alain Gerbault ☎43030054

Apr–Sep.

1.3HEC H lau P

PROISSANS See **SARLAT-LA-CANÉDA**

PROPRIANO See **CORSE (CORSICA)**

PUGET-SUR-ARGENS (LE)

Var

Bastiane ☎94455131

Hilly site divided into numbered pitches in pine and oak wood. Individual washing cubicles. Meals to take away.

Access from N7.
All year.

3.5HEC H P lau pitch59 (incl 2–3 persons)

Aubrèdes ☎94455146

Situated on undulating meadowland.

Leave Autoroute A8 at exit Puget-sur-Argens, then site is 150 m. If approaching from Fréjus on N7 turn right before Puget, cross motorway and follow road towards Lagourin.
Apr–Sep.

3.8HEC H P lau A15 pitch21

Haute Vernèdes ☎94455192

Hilly site.

Turn right off N7 just before motorway bridge. Well signposted.
Apr–Sep.

5HEC H P

PUY (LE)

Haute-Loire

CM Bouthezard pl de l'Hôtel-de-Ville ☎71095509

From the town centre follow sign for Clermont-Ferrand; at traffic lights by Church of St-Laurent, turn right following 'camping' signpost, site is 500 m on left of road.
Apr–15 Oct.

1HEC H lau pitch30 (incl 4 persons)

At **BRIVES-CHARENSAC** (4.5 km E)

Audinet ☎71091018

SE on N88.
May–Oct.

3HEC H R lau

PUYBRUN

Lot

France

Sole ☎65385237

May–Sep.

2.5HEC H R P lau R A12 pitch12

PYLA-SUR-MER

Gironde

Dune rte de Biscarrosse ☎56227217

A beautifully situated and quiet site partly on terraced sandy fields. Opposite a dune of over 100 m in height, which separates the site from the sea.

Follow the road towards Pilat-Plage.
Etr–Sep.

6HEC H P lau S pitch60–76 (incl 2 persons)

Panorama ☎56221044

Partially terraced site amongst dunes, on the edge of the 100 m high 'Dune de Rilet'. Views of the sea from some pitches.

On the D218. Signposted.
Apr–Oct.

15HEC H S lau A15 V20 25 15

Petit Nice rte de Biscarrosse ☎56227403

Sandy terraced site, mainly suitable for tents; in parts sloping steeply in pine woodland. Paths and standings are strengthened with timber. 220 steps down to the beach.

6 km S on D112.
Apr–Sep.

4HEC H S lau

Pyla ☎56227456

May–Sep.

8HEC H SP lau pitch89 (incl 4 persons)

QUEND-PLAGE-LES-PINS

Somme

At **MONCHAUX-LES-QUEND** (3.5 km E by D102E)

Roses ☎22277617

Well-kept site with trees and hedges surrounding individual pitches. Only recommended site in area. ➤

Turn off D940 at Quend, site 500 m on left of D102.
Etr–Sep.
4.6HEC lau |O| R

QUERRIEN
Finistère
Ty Nadan 98717547
All year.
3HEC |O| G P lau

QUIBERON
Morbihan
CM Bois d'Amour rte de la Pointe du Conguel 97501352
1.5 km SE.
15 May–Sep.
3.5HEC G

Conguel 97501911
15 Jun–8 Sep.
1.5HEC lau |O| s A6 V4 4 4

QUILLAN
Aude
CM Sapinette 68201352
Access W via D79, rte de Ginoles.
1.2HEC G lau |O| A11 11 11

QUIMPER
Finistère
Orangerie de Lanniron 98906202
2.5 km from town centre via D34.
May–15 Sep.
4HEC G P lau |O| A17 V6 20 20

RAGUENÈS-PLAGE
Finistère
Raguenès-Plage r des Iles 98068069
On field with good views. Asphalt drives 400 m from beaches.
2.5 km SW of Pont Aven.
Etr–Sep.
5HEC G lau |O| s A16 V6 22 22

France

RAMATUELLE
Var
Croix du Sud 94798084
Terraced site in beautiful pine forest divided into pitches with view of sea. Minimum stay 8 days.
3 km NE of town, 80 m N of D93.
May–Sep.
2.5HEC |O| G lau s A14 pitch28

Tournels rte de Camarat 94798054
Lovely views to Pampelonne Bay from part of the site. 1 km to beach.
Access from D93 Croix-Valmer-St-Tropez road, follow the signs to 'Cap Camarat'.
All year.
20HEC |O| G lau s A15 27–46 19

RAMBOUILLET
Yvelines
CM Etang d'Or 30410734
From railway station follow road SE for 1.3 km passing Camping Pont Hardy.
All year.
5HEC G R lau P A5 V3 3 3

RANSPACH-SUR-WESSERLING
Haut-Rhin
Bouleaux 89826470
On a long stretch of grassland subdivided by flowerbeds and hedging.
Adjacent to N66 Bâle road between St-Amarin and Wesserling.
Etr–Sep.
1.75HEC G P lau

RÉ (ILE DE)
Charente-Maritime
ARS-EN-RÉ
Dunes 46294141
1.5 km NW on N735.
Apr–Sep.
2HEC G lau |O| s pitch41 (incl 3 persons)

Soleil 46294062
On level, shaded meadow.
Signposted from the N735 shortly before reaching Ars.
All year.
2HEC |O| G lau s pitch54 (incl 3 persons)

BOIS-PLAGE-EN-RÉ (LE)
Antioche 46092386
In quiet area among dunes.
2 km SE of village towards the beach.
15 Jun–15 Sep.
3HEC G lau s

Gros Jonc 46092338
May–Oct.
2.5HEC |O| G sP lau pitch64 (incl 3 persons)

Interlude rte de Gros-Jonc 46091822
Mar–Oct.
3.6HEC |O| G R lau s pitch64 (incl 3 persons)

COUARDE-SUR-MER (LA)
Océan rte d'Ars 46298770
3 km NW on N735.
Etr–Sep.
6HEC |O| G lau s pitch59 (incl 3 persons)

NOUE (LA)
Grenettes 46302247
Site in two sections in pine forest separated by hedging.
1.5 km W of village off D201. Approach is via narrow track.
Mar–Nov.
7HEC |O| G R lau s

ST-CLÉMENT-DES-BALEINES

Plage ☎46294262
Meadow subdivided by hedges, close by lighthouse. Access to sea via sand dunes. Mobile shop during peak season.
NW on D735.
2.4HEC

ST-MARTIN-DE-RÉ

CM Ste-Thérèse ☎46092196
At foot of ramparts.
2HEC

REDOUTE-PLAGE
Hérault

Mimosas ☎67909292
Leave A9 at exit Béziers Est and continue towards coast via N112 and D37.
Jun–Sep.
7HEC lau

Sablons rte de Portiragnes ☎67909055
Large site subdivided into fields by fences. Beside beach. Night club and discothèque.
0.5 km N on D37.
Apr–Oct.
12HEC lau

RÉGUSSE
Var

Lacs du Verdon ☎94701795
Stony meadowland with bushes and trees in a quiet secluded location.
2.4 km NE of Régusse. Signposted.
Apr–15 Oct.
14HEC lau A19 Vn/c 29 18

REIMS
Marne

Airotel de Champagne av Hoche ☎26854122
Approaching from north, turn off on outskirts of town towards Châlons-sur-Marne. Well signposted.
Etr–Sep.
5HEC (summer only) lau A12 V2 12 12

REMOULINS
Gard

Soubeyranne rte de Beaucaire ☎66370321
S on D986.
Apr–15 Sep.
5.5HEC lau

RENAGE
Isère

CM Verdon ☎76914802
5 km N of Tullins on D45.
May–Sep.
2HEC lau pitch22 (incl 2 persons)

France

RENNES
Ille-et-Vilaine

CM Gayeulles ☎99369122
Apr–15 Oct.
3.6HEC lau
At **PONT-RÉAN** (12 km SW)

Base Nautique ☎99527260
Apr–15 Sep.
1HEC lau

RHINAU
Bas-Rhin

Ferme des Tuileries ☎88746045
Approach from Germany via ferry across River Rhine.
Apr–Sep.
0.4HEC (Jul–21 Aug) A7 pitch7

RIA
Pyrénées-Orientales

Bellevue ☎68964896
Beautifully situated terraced site. Very well kept. Beside former vineyard.
2 km S on N116, take road to Sirach, turn right and continue 600 m up drive which is difficult for caravans.
May–Sep.
2.2HEC lau A12 pitch12

RIBEAUVILLE
Haut-Rhin

CM Pierre-de-Coubertin ☎89736671
Site lies next to school and sports ground.
Well signposted from town centre.
Apr–Dec.
3.5HEC lau A10 V5 5 5

RICHARDAIS (LA)
Ille-et-Vilaine

CM ☎99885080
In village centre beside River Rance and church. Clean, quiet site.
3 km from sea.
All year.
3HEC lau

RIQUEWIHR
Haut-Rhin

Inter Communal ☎89479008
Extensive site overlooking vineyards. Camping Carnet required.
2 km E on D16. Turn W off N83 (Colmar-Strasbourg) at Ostheim.

Apr–Oct.
4HEC lau A10 V5 5 5

RISCLE
Gers

CM Pont de l'Adour ☎62697245
On the River Adour.
Jul–Aug.
2.5HEC lau A4 pitch8

RIVIÈRE-SUR-TARN
Aveyron

Peupliers rte de Millau ☎65598517
2 km SW, beside River Tarn.
Etr–Oct.
1.50HEC lau

Peyrelade ☎65600848
Jun–15 Sep.
4HEC lau A13 V12 12 12

ROANNE
Loire

CM r des Gravière ☎77716753
All year.
2.5HEC lau

ROCAMADOUR
Lot

Relais du Campeur l'Hospitalet ☎65336328
On D36.
Etr–15 Oct.
1.7HEC lau A12

ROCHE-BERNARD (LA)
Morbihan

CM Patïs ☎99906013
On banks of River Vilaine.
100 m from village centre.
All year.
1HEC lau A10 V5 10 10

ROCHE-CHALAIS (LA)
Dordogne

Gerbes ☎53914065
Site on banks of River Dronne.
Off D674 in village centre. Signposted.
All year.
3HEC lau A5 V2 4 4

ROCHEFORT-MONTAGNE
Puy-de-Dôme

Domes Les Quatre-Routes de Nébouzat ☎73871406
15 May–15 Sep.
1HEC lau pp25

ROCHE-LEZ-BEAUPRÉ See **BESANÇON**

ROCHELLE (LA)
Charente-Maritime

CM Port Neuf bd A-Rondeau ☎46438120

W on N22, off bd A-Rondeau.
All year.

1.5HEC H lau s

At **AYTRÉ** (5.5 km S on N137)

Richelieu 73 rte de la Plage ☎46441924

On beach.

All year.

1HEC H G lau s pitch39

ROCHELONGUE-PLAGE See **AGDE**

ROCHETAILLÉE See **BOURG-D'OISANS (LE)**

RODEZ
Aveyron

CM Layoule ☎65670952

Clean, tidy site in valley below town, completely divided into pitches.

NE of town centre. Well signposted.
All year.

3HEC H G R lau P pitch40 (incl 3 persons)

ROMILLY-SUR-SEINE
Aube

Cerisiers ☎25249398

E of town, 250 m from N19 Troyes road.
28 Jun–Aug.

0.7HEC H G R lau A5 V3 5 A5

ROMORANTIN-LANTHENAY
Loir-et-Cher

Tournefeuille ☎54761660

Etr–Sep.

1.5HEC H G P lau

ROQUEBRUNE-SUR-ARGENS
Var

Blavet ☎94454004

All year.

2HEC H G lau pitch58 (incl 3 persons)

Moulin des Iscles ☎94457074

On bank of River Argens.
All year.

1.5HEC H G R lau L pitch44–55 (incl 3 persons)

Pêcheurs ☎94457125

Etr–Sep.

3HEC H G R LRP lau

Lei Suves ☎94454395

4 km N via D7.
All year.

7.4HEC H G R P lau A14 pitch20

ROQUE-D'ANTHÉRON (LA)
Bouches-du-Rhône

Domaine les Iscles ☎42504425

1.8 km N via D67c.
All year.

10HEC H G R P lau

Silvacane ☎42504054

Level gravelled ground with 100 sq m pitches. Heated common room with TV. Water sports centre and stables nearby. Site in wood on slopes of hill.

All year.

3HEC H R P lau

ROQUE-GAGEAC (LA)
Dordogne

Beau Rivage ☎53283205

On banks of River Dordogne.

Between D703 and river.
All year.

6HEC lau A12 pitch15

Butte ☎53283028

In very attractive setting around country estate on steep bank of River Dordogne.

Halfway between Vitrac and Cénac off D703.
Mar–Nov.

4HEC lau pitch55 (incl 2 persons)

ROQUETTE-SUR-SIAGNE (LA)
Alpes-Maritimes

Panoramic quartier St-Jean ☎93472266

All year.

1.3HEC lau pitch50–60 (incl 3 persons)

St-Louis ☎93422667

Level meadow with some terraces on the slopes of a hillock.

Access is via the D9 Cannes–Pegomas road, 5 km from the sea.
Apr–Sep.

5HEC lau

ROSIERS-SUR-LOIRE (LES)
Maine-et-Loire

Val de Loire ☎41519433

Etr–31 Oct.

2HEC lau

ROUFFIGNAC
Dordogne

Cantegrel ☎53054151

1.5 km N via D31, rte de Thenon.
Apr–Oct.

50HEC lau pitch70 (incl 3 persons)

ROUGEMONT
Doubs

At **BONNAL** (3.5 km N on D18)

Val de Bonnal ☎81869087

May–Sep.

5HEC lau

ROYAN
Charente-Maritime

At **PONTAILLAC** (2 km NE on D25)

Clairfontaine allée des Peupliers ☎46390811

300 m from beach.
Jun–7 Sep.

3HEC lau pitch87 (incl 3 persons)

Source Vaux-sur-Mer ☎46391051

1 km N on D141.
All year.

2.5HEC lau pitch44 (incl 3 persons)

France

ROYÈRE-DE-VASSIVIÈRE
Creuse

Masgrangeas ☎55647165

On shore of Lake Vassivière.

5 km S of Royère by D8/D3.
Etr–Oct.

2.2HEC lau pitch50 (incl 3 persons)

RUAUX
Vosges

CM Fraiteux ☎29660071

May–Sep.

0.8HEC lau A6 V3 3 3

RUE
Somme

CM Carolines rte de Quend ☎22274771

All year.

1HEC lau

Garenne de Moncourt ☎22250693–22250107

On D85 towards Montreuil-sur-Mer.
Apr–1 Nov.

3HEC lau A9 V5 5 5

RUPPIONE-PLAGE See **CORSE (CORSICA)**

RUYNES-EN-MARGERIDE
Cantal

CM Petit Bois ☎71234226

0.5 km SW on D13, rte de Garabit.
Signposted.
All year.

1HEC lau A7 V6 6 6

SAÂCY-SUR-MARNE
Seine-et-Marne

CM les Usages ☎60237581

All year.

1.6HEC lau

SABLES-D'OLONNE (LES)
Vendée

Baie de Cayola rte de la Corniche ☎51323209

4 km SW of town centre.
Jun-Sep.

4HEC lau

CM Roses r des Roses ☎51951042

Etr–Oct.

2HEC lau A15 pitch32

Fosses Rouges ☎51951795

3 km SE towards La Pironnière.
20 Apr–15 Sep.

3.5HEC lau

Trianon ☎51953050

May–Sep.

10HEC lau

SADIRAC
Gironde

Bel Air ☎56230190

Country site.

Beside D671.
Apr–Sep.

3HEC lau A9 pitch8

SAILLAGOUSE
Pyrénées-Orientales

Cerdan ☎68047046

On meadow with some terraces. Hot meals served during peak season.

15 Apr–Sep.

0.8HEC lau A13 pitch12

ST-AIGNAN-SUR-CHER
Loire-et-Cher

CM Cochards ☎54751559

On beautiful meadowland, completely surrounded by hedges.

1 km from bridge on D17 towards Selles.
15 Mar–15 Oct.

4HEC lau A7 pitch7

ST-AMAND-LES-EAUX
Nord

Mont des Bruyères ☎27485687

Mar–Nov.

3.5HEC lau

ST-AMAND-MONTROND
Cher

CM Roche off chemin de la Roche ☎48960936

1.5 km SW near river and canal.
Apr–Sep.

4HEC lau A5 V3 4 4

ST-AMANS-DES-COTS
Aveyron

Tours ☎65448856

Jun–Sep.

8HEC lau pitch60 (incl 3 persons)

ST-AMBROIX
Gard

Fumades Domaine des Fumades ☎66857078

Apr–Sep. ➤

13HEC H P lau

ST-ANDIOL
Bouches-du-Rhône

St-Andiol 90950113

Well situated in village centre. Divided into pitches.

All year.

1HEC H P lau A12 pitch16

ST-ANTONIN-NOBLE-VAL
Tarn-et-Garonne

Trois Cantons 63319857

Divided into pitches, partly on sloping ground within an oak forest. Separate section for teenagers.

8.5 km NW near D926. Signposted.
Etr–15 Oct.

20HEC H P lau A17 Vn/c 17 17

ST-ARNOULT See **DEAUVILLE**

ST-ASTIER
Dordogne

Pontet 53541422

Access E via D41, rte de Montanceix.
May–15 Sep.

3.5HEC H R lau P A8 V4 8 8

ST-AUBIN-SUR-MER
Seine-Maritime

CM Mesnil 35830283

2 km W on D68.
Apr–Oct.

2HEC H lau s A15 V8 15 12

ST-AVRE
Savoie

Bois Joli 79562082

Well-kept site with pitches and individual washing cabins.

Etr & 15 Jun–15 Sep.

3HEC H R lau

ST-AYGULF
Var

Eurocamping 94812525

Well-kept site divided into pitches.

3 km NE on D7.
Apr–Sep.

5.5HEC H lau s pitch48 (incl 3 persons)

Paradis des Campeurs 94969355

2.5 km towards Gaillarde-Plage.
20 Mar–Sep.

1.7HEC H lau s

St-Aygulf 270 av Salvarelli 94812014

Access to beach via underpass.

France

Inland from N98 at Km881.3 N of town. Entrance on right of av Salvarelli.
Jun–20 Sep.

35HEC H lau s

ST-BRÉVIN-LES-PINS
Loire-Atlantique

CM Courance 100-110 av du Ml-Foch 40272291

S off D305, in pine forest, by sea.
All year.

4.7HEC H P s

ST-BRÉVIN-L'OCÉAN
Loire-Atlantique

Hameau Gîtes de la Pierre Attelée 40278032

Extensive, well screened terrain made up of 3 sites, 2 of which are open all year.

500 m from the sea. 2 km on D213 toward Pornic.

2.6HEC H R lau s

ST-BRIAC
Ille-et-Vilaine

Emeraude 99883455

Well-kept site in pleasant quiet situation and divided in pitches.

Turn left off D786 and continue for 0.8 km.
Etr–Sep.

2.5HEC H lau s

ST-CAST
Côtes-du-Nord

CM Mielles 964187018

500 m NE on coast.
May–15 Sep.

2HEC H lau sP A7 V3 4 4

ST-CÉRÉ
Lot

CM quai-A-Salesse 65381237

200 m SE on D940
Apr–Sep.

3.5HEC H lau R

ST-CLÉMENT-DES-BALEINES See **RÉ (ILE DE)**

ST-CONSTANT See **MAURS**

ST-COULOMB
Ille-et-Vilaine

Chevrets La Guimorais 99890190

On Lupin Bay near Chevrets beach.

3 km NW.
Apr–Sep.

7HEC H

R lau s A
pitch46 (incl 2 persons)

ST-CYBRANET
Dordogne

Bel Ombrage 53283414

Quiet holiday site in wooded valley.

15 May–15 Sep.

5HEC H PR lau A14 pitch14

Céou 53283212

Terraces on farmland on slopes of a hill, on both sides of D57. Rustic style snackbar with fireplace. Radios forbidden.

1 km S of village.
May–Sep.

2.5HEC H lau RP A22 pitch27

ST-CYPRIEN
Dordogne

CM Garrit rte de Berbiguières 5329205

1.5 km S on D48.
Apr–Oct.

1.2HEC H lau R

ST-CYPRIEN-PLAGE
Pyrénées-Orientales

Cala Gogo Les Capellans 68210712

4 km S towards Les Capellans.
Jun–Sep.

11HEC H R sP lau A23 pitch35

CM Laurent Baudru 68210020

Level site with drives, some asphalted, beside coast road. Enormous block of flats obstructs view of sea.

All year.

20HEC H s

ST-CYR
Vienne

Parc de Loisirs 49625722

15 Apr–Sep

5.4HEC H LR lau A16 pitch20

ST-CYR-SUR-MER
Var

Baumelles 94262127

Terraced sloping site about 50 m away from the sea.

Leave the N559 on the church square before St-Cyr towards La Madrague, then take the D87 for 1.8 km to the entrance of the site.
Feb–Nov.

8HEC H lau s

ST-CYR-SUR-MORIN
Seine-et-Marne

Choisel Courcelles-la-Roue 6023849

2 km W via D31.
Mar–Nov.
3.5HEC H |O| ⊞ lau A20

ST-DENIS-D'OLÉRON See **OLÉRON (ILE D')**

ST-ELOI See **LOUARGAT**

ST-ÉMILION
Gironde
Barbanne 57247580
Mar–Nov
4.5HEC H |O| ⊞ lau A13 pitch17

ST-ÉTIENNE-DE-VILLERÉAL
Lot-et-Garonne
Ormes 53366026
0.9 km S off D255.
Apr–Sep.
10HEC H |O| ⊞ lau A17 pitch22–28

ST-ÉTIENNE-DU-BOIS
Ain
CM Sevron rte de Bourg-en-Bresse 74305065
500 m S of village on N83 by river.
Apr–Oct.
0.7HEC H ⊞ |O| A5 V3 3 3

France

ST-ÉVARZEC
Finistère
Kermoen 98948062
Children's playground and fishing facilities on site.
Jul–Aug.
2HEC H ⊞ lau |O| A8 V3 7 7

ST-FARGEAU
Yonne
CM Calanque 86740455
6 km SE. N of Lac du Boudon.
15 Mar–Oct.
6HEC H ⊞ lau |O|

ST-FERRÉOL
Alpes-de-Haute-Pyrénées
Salvan 61835595
Apr–Oct.
3.5HEC H ⊞ lau |O| A7 V3 7 7

ST-FIACRE See **CROZON**

ST-FLORENT See **CORSE (CORSICA)**

ST-FLORENT-LE-VIEIL
Maine-et-Loire
CM 41785039
On D752.
Jun–Sep.
3.5HEC H ⊞ lau |O|

ST-FLOUR
Cantal
CM Orgues av Dr-Mallet 71602250
On gently sloping meadow.
On W edge of village beside D926 at signpost for Murat.
Etr–Oct.
1.8HEC H ⊞ lau A7 V4 5 5

ST-GABRIEL-PLAGE See **CAMIERS**

ST-GENIES
Dordogne
Bouquerie 53288237
N of village on D704.
Etr–Sep.
5HEC H |O| ⊞ lau

ST-GENIEZ-D'OLT
Aveyron
Marmotel 65704220
Grassy site on River Lot.
On D19 about 2 km NW of St-Geniez-d'Olt.

15 Jun–10 Sep.
3HEC H RP lau pitch53 (incl 2 persons)

ST-GEORGES
Pas-de-Calais
Route Fleurie ☎21419068
Apr–Oct.
1.2HEC H R P lau G A7 V7 7 7

ST-GEORGES-DE-DIDONNE
Charente-Maritime
Bois Soleil 2 av de Suzac ☎46050594
Pitches lie on different levels. Direct access to the beach.
2.5 km S of town on Meschers road (D25).
Apr–Sep.
10HEC H G P lau s pitch60–78 (incl 3 persons)
See advertisement page 187.
Ideal Camping No. 1 ☎46052904
May–15 Sep.
8HEC H G lau s pitch52 (incl 3 persons)

ST-GEORGES-D'OLÉRON See **OLÉRON (ILE D')**

ST-GEOURS-DE-MAREMNE
Landes
Bon Accueil ☎46573212
3 km SW off N10.
Jun–Sep.
10HEC H lau

ST-GERMAIN-SUR-AY
Manche
Aux Grands Espaces ☎33071014
On slightly sloping ground among dunes. Children's play area. Lunchtime siesta 12.30–14.30 hrs. 500 m from sea.
Leave D650 W of town and follow signs 'Plage' on D306.
May–Sep.
11HEC H G lau s A11 pitch13

ST-GERVAIS-LES-BAINS
Haute-Savoie
Dômes de Miage les Bernards ☎50934596
2 km S on D902.
Apr–Sep.
2.3HEC H G R lau P pitch31 (incl 2 persons)

ST-GILDAS-DE-RHUYS
Morbihan
Menhir ☎97452288
3.5 km N.
Jun–20 Sep.
3HEC H G P lau s A12 pitch23

ST-GILLES-CROIX-DE-VIE
Vendée
Ormes 26 r H-Raimondeau ☎51061509
15 Jun–15 Sep.
2HEC H G
Pas Opton ☎51551198
Well tended garden-like site in rural surroundings.
Off D754 Nantes road.
25 May–12 Sep.
4HEC H G R lau pitch72–95 (incl 3 persons)

ST-GIRONS
Ariège
Parc de Palétès ☎61660679
3 km SE on D33.
All year.
2HEC H G R lau A9 Vn/c 9 9
Pont du Nert ☎61665848
Grassy site without any trees. Between road and woodland.
Approx 3 km SE at the junction of the D33 and the D3.
Jun–Sep.
1.5HEC H R lau R A7 Vn/c 9 7

ST-GIRONS-PLAGE
Landes
Eurosol ☎58479014
On undulating sand-dunes in a pine forest. Special 100 sq m pitches for caravans providing shower, handbasin, electricity and drainage. Shopping centre. 500 m to sandy beach.
Jun–15 Sep.
15HEC H G P lau s pitch78 (incl 3–4 persons)

ST-GUÉNOLÉ
Finistère
International de la Joie r de la Joie ☎98586324
Apr–5 Sep.
5HEC H G lau s

ST-HILAIRE-DE-RIEZ
Vendée
Bois Tordu ☎51543378
5.3 km NW.
21 May–5 Sep.
1.7HEC H G R sP lau pitch64 (incl 3 persons)
Chouans 108 av de la Faye ☎51543490
2.5 km NW.
Apr–Sep.
4HEC H G P lau s pitch58 (incl 3 persons)
Ecureuils 100 av de la Pège ☎51543371
From A11 to Nantes, then via D178 and D753 to St-Hilaire-de-Riez.
May–20 Sep.
3HEC H G P lau s pitch65 (incl 3 persons)
Padrelle ☎51553203
May–15 Sep.
0.5HEC H lau s pitch27 (incl 3 persons)
Plage 106 av de la Pège ☎51543393
On a meadow with trees. Access to beach via dunes.
5.7 km NW.
Etr–15 Sep.
5HEC H G lau s A9 V3 21 12
Prairie chemin des Roselières ☎51540856
Jun–15 Sep.
4HEC H G lau s A10 V4 37 28
Riez à la Vie ☎51543049
Flat site, divided into pitches.
3 km NW.
Jun–15 Sep.
3HEC H G P lau pitch57 (incl 3 persons)
Sapinière ☎51544574
Jun–15 Sep.
3.6HEC H G P lau pitch65 (incl 3 persons)

ST-HILAIRE-LA-FORÊT See **TALMONT-ST-HILAIRE**

ST-HONORÉ
Nièvre
Bains 15 av J-Mermoz ☎86307344
Etr–Oct.
3HEC H G P lau A10 12 12

ST-INNOCENT-BRISON
Savoie
Rolande ☎79353972
Situated on gently sloping terrain.
Signposted from village centre.
May–Sep.
2.5HEC H G lau L pitch42 (incl 2–3 persons)

ST-JEAN-DE-LA-RUELLE See **ORLÉANS**

ST-JEAN-DE-LUZ
Pyrénées-Atlantiques
CM Chibaou Berria ☎59261194

2 km SW of Guèthary. Signposted off N10 towards sea.
Jun–Sep.
4.5HEC H G R s lau A11 pitch16

International d'Erromardie ☎59263426

Site is situated by the sea and consists of several sections divided by roads and low hedges. Take away food.

If approached from N to N10, cross railway bridge and turn immediately right and follow signs.
15 Mar–Oct.
2HEC H s lau A10 pitch17

Iratzia ☎59261489

1 km NE off N10.
15 Mar–15 Oct.
4.2HEC H G R s lau A10 V7 13 13

Itsas Mendi ☎59265650

Set out in semi-circle on terraced field with sea-view.

5 km NE on N10 towards the sea.
Jun–Sep.
6HEC H G P s lau

Tamaris Plage quartier d'Acotz ☎59265590

Site divided into sections by drives and hedges.

Signposted from N10 towards the sea.
Apr–Sep.
2HEC H G R s lau pitch50–60 (incl 2 persons)

At **SOCOA** (3 km SW)

Juantcho ☎59471197

2 km W on D912.
Apr–Oct.
6HEC H G s lau A10 V5 10 10

ST-JEAN-DE-MONTS

Vendée

Abri des Pins ☎51588386

Level grassland site subdivided by hedges, bushes and trees.

4 km N on D38 Notre-Dame-de-Monts road.
May–18 Sep.
3HEC H G P s lau pitch90–100 (incl 3 persons)

Amiaux ☎51582222

On the edge of a forest.

3.5 km NW of D38.
Etr–Oct.
5HEC H G P s lau A12 V5

Aux Coeurs Vendéens près de la Tonnelle ☎51588491

N of town on D38 to Notre-Dame-de-Monts.
Jun–15 Sep.
1.5HEC H G P s lau

Bois Masson ☎51586262

Etr–Sep.
7.5HEC H G P s lau pitch70–130 (incl 3 persons)

Clarys Plage ☎51581024

Jun–10 Sep.
1.7HEC H G P s lau pitch59 (incl 3 persons)

CM Commandant G Dornier ☎51588116

Extensive site amongst dunes with pine trees.

Turn off D38 3 km N.
May–Sep.
25HEC H lau s

Demoiselles ☎51580131

Etr–15 Sep.
15HEC H G R lau sP

Moulins d'Orouet ☎51586715

5 km SE on D38 St-Gilles-Croix-de-Vie road.
Etr–Sep.
2HEC H G lau pitch37 (incl 3 persons)

Pins 166 av Valentin ☎51581742

1.5 km SE off D38 to St-Gilles-Croix-de-Vie.
Jun–Aug.
2.5HEC H G lau s

Traite ☎51581982

5 km SE on D38 St-Gilles-Croix-de-Vie road.
15 May–25 Sep.
0.8HEC H G R lau s

At **OROUET** (6 km SE)

Yole chemin des Bosses ☎51586717

Jun–5 Sep.
5HEC H P lau s

ST-JEAN-DU-GARD

Gard

Sources ☎66853803

900 m NE on D50, rte de Mialet.
Apr–15 Sep.
2HEC H G RP lau A10 V4 9 9

ST-JEAN-PLA-DE-CORTS

Pyrénées-Orientales

Deux Rivières rte de Mavreillas ☎68832320

Jun–Sep.
8.5HEC H G R RP lau A17 pitch14

ST-JORIOZ

Haute-Savoie

International du Lac d'Annecy ☎50686793

15 Jun–5 Sep.
2HEC H G P lau pitch55 (incl 2–3 persons)

ST-JULIEN-DES-LANDES

Vendée

Fôret ☎51056201

NE on D55, rte de Martinet.
15 May–15 Sep. ➤

5HEC H P lau pitch80 (incl 3 persons)

Garangeoire ☎51386539

2 km N of the village.
20 May–5 Sep.

6HEC H P lau pitch80 (incl 3 persons)

ST-JULIEN-EN-BORN
Landes

Fleurie Lette ☎58427409

On undulating ground in a pine wood.
15 Apr–15 Sep.

12.5HEC H lau A9 V4 20 A9

ST-LAURENT-DU-VAR
Alpes-Maritimes

Lou Pistou ☎93310544

Small site with many terraces. No motor caravans. Advanced booking required.

500 m SW, access via N7 and D2209.
Jun–Aug.

0.6HEC H lau s

Magali ☎93315700

Level meadowland site.

Turn off N7 onto D2209 near the industrial zone.
20 Mar–Sep.

1.2HEC H R lau pitch53 (incl 3 persons)

ST-LAURENT-DU-VERDON
Alpes-de-Haute-Provence

Farigoulette ☎92744162

15 May–15 Sep.

1.1HEC H P lau L pitch55 (incl 2 persons)

ST-LÉGER-DU-BOURG-DENIS
Seine-Maritime

Aubette 23 r du Vert Buisson ☎35084769

All year.

0.8HEC H R lau A6 pitch8

ST-LÉONARD-DE-NOBLAT
Haute-Vienne

CM Beaufort ☎55560279

Pleasant surroundings.

Access from the D39.
15 Jun–15 Sep.

1.5HEC H R lau P

ST-LÉON-SUR-VÉZÈRE *Dordogne*

Paradis ☎53507264

Situated on the river bank in the picturesque Vézère valley.

S of village off D706 Les Eyzies road.
21 Mar–15 Oct.

4.5HEC H R RP lau A18 pitch31

At **TURSAC** (7 km SW)

Vézère Périgord ☎53069631

0.8 km NE on D706.
Etr–Sep.

3.5HEC H P lau

ST-LUNAIRE
Ille-et-Vilaine

Far West rte de St-Briac-sur-Mer ☎99463398

Turn off D786 towards St-Briac at end of village, site is on left. 100 m from the sea.
Whit–5 Sep.

5HEC H lau s A14 V5 8 A8

Longchamp rte de St-Briac-sur-Mer ☎99463184

Completely enclosed site at foot of hill, beside church. Rear of site laid out in terraces.

Turn off D786 towards St-Briac at end of village. Site 100 m from the sea.
20 Jun–10 Sep.

2.5HEC H lau s A14 V5 8 A8

ST-MALO
Ille-de-Vilaine

Houbarderie ☎99818529

31 Mar–15 Sep.

5HEC H lau P A16 V11 21 A16

At **ST-SERVAN-SUR-MER** (3 km S)

Cité d'Aleth ☎99816091

On peninsula near N137.
All year.

8HEC H lau s A6 V5 5 A5

ST-MALÔ-DU-BOIS
Vendée

Plein Air de Poupet ☎51923332

From village take D72 for 1 km, then take left fork and follow signs. Site on bank of River Sèvre Nantaise.
May–Sep.

2.75HEC H R lau A5 V3 5 A5

ST-MARC See **ST-NAZAIRE**

ST-MARCAN
Ille-et-Vilaine

Balcon de la Baie ☎99802295

10 km NW of Pontorson on D797.
15 Jun–15 Sep.

2.6HEC H lau A6 V3 3 A3

ST-MARTIAL-DE-NABIRAT See **GOURDON**

ST-MARTIN-DE-CRAU
Bouches-du-Rhône

Crau ☎90471709

All year.

3HEC H R P lau

ST-MARTIN-DE-RÉ See **RÉ (ILE DE)**

ST-MAURICE-SUR-MOSELLE
Vosges

Deux Ballons ☎29251126

1 km W on N66.
All year.

4HEC H R P lau A11 V6 6 A6

ST-MICHEL-CHEF-CHEF
Loire-Atlantique

Thar-Cor 43 av du Cormier, Tharon Plage ☎40278281

Subdivided by trees and flowerbeds. Tent campers accommodated in orchard with no parking facilities. Well equipped children's play area. Lunchtime siesta 12.00–13.00 hrs.

Signposted from D213 (St-Nazaire-Pornic).
Etr–15 Sep.

3HEC H lau s A14 V6 15 A15

ST-MICHEL-DES-LOUPS See **JOULLOUVILLE**

ST-MICHEL-EN-GRÈVE
Côtes-du-Nord

Capucines ☎96357228

On D786 Lannion-Morlaix road.
15 May–2 Sep.

4HEC H P lau A16 pitch21

ST-NAZAIRE
Loire-Atlantique

At **ST-MARC** (5 km SW)

CM Eve ☎40919045

Large, well-kept site on gentle slope. Divided into pitches. Access to sea.

On D292.
15 May–15 Sep.

7.2HEC H s lau

ST-OMER
Pas-de-Calais

Château du Ganspette ☎21934393

11.5 km NW on N43 and D207.
Apr–Sep.

8HEC H

At **CLAIRMARAIS** (4.5 km NE by D928 and D209)

Clairmarais ☎21383480

Grassy, rather tough site. Ideal for overnight stays.

Apr–Oct.
3HEC ⊙ ⊞
lau P

ST-OURS
Puy-de-Dôme
Bel Air 73887214
1 km SW on D941.
Jun–15 Sep.
2HEC ⊙ ⊞
lau A6 V4 5 5

ST-PAIR-SUR-MER
Manche
Château de Lez-Eaux 33516609
Situated in grounds of an old Château. Bank, TV and reading room. Fishing available.
7 km SE via D973 rte d'Avranches.
Etr–15 Sep.
4HEC ⊙
P ⊞ lau

Ecutot 33506494
Situated in an orchard 1 km from the sea.
Mar–Sep.
3HEC ⊙
⊞ lau s A12
pitch10

Mariénée 33500571
2 km from sea; situated in grounds of old farm.
2 km S of town on D21.
Apr–Sep.
1.2HEC ⊙ ⊞
lau sP A9 pitch7

ST-PALAIS
Pyrénées-Atlantiques
CM Ur-Aide 59657201
On meadow divided into pitches. Near sports complex.
15 Jun–15 Sep.
2HEC ⊙ ⊞ lau
P A9 Vn/c 16–19 12

ST-PALAIS-SUR-MER
Charente-Maritime
Côte-de-Beauté la Grande-Côte
46222059
Situated facing sea.
N of town on road to La Palmyre (D25).
20 Jun–10 Sep.
1HEC ⊙ ⊞ lau
s

Deux Plages 41 av des Acacias
46231142
500 m from beaches.
All year.
3HEC ◆ ⊙
⊞ lau s

Logis 22 r des Palombes 46232023
Situated 300 metres from the sea.
2.5 km NW on D25.
Jun–15 Sep.
20HEC ◇
⊙ ⊞ lau s

France

Ormeaux av de Bernezac 46382801
2.5HEC ◆ ⊙
⊞ lau s

Puits de l'Auture la Grande Côte
46232031
Situated at the edge of a forest facing the sea.
2 km NW on D25 La Palmyre road.
Etr–Sep.
5HEC ⊙
⊞ lau s A18 V7
13 13

ST-PAUL-EN-FORÊT
Var
Parc 94761535
Quiet, fairly isolated site surrounded by woodland.
3 km N on D4.
All year.
5HEC ⊙
P ⊞ lau A16
18 18

ST-PÉE-SUR-NIVELLE
Pyrénées-Atlantiques
Goyetchea 59541959
0.8 km N on rte d'Ahetze.
15 Jun–6 Sep.
2HEC ◆ ⊙ ⊞
lau A9 pitch16
At **IBARRON** (2 km W)
Ibarron 59541043
2 km W on D918.
Etr–Sep.
2.8HEC ◆ ⊙
A8 pitch17

ST-PÉREUSE
Nièvre
Manoir de Bezolle 86844255
Situated in grounds of a manor house. Well-kept site divided by hedges.
At 'X' roads of D11 and D978.
All year.
7HEC ◆ ◇
⊙ P ⊞ lau
pitch45–61 (incl 2 persons)

ST-PÈRE-SUR-LOIRE See **SULLY-SUR-LOIRE**

ST-PHILIBERT-SUR-MER
Morbihan
Vieux Logis 97550117
Beautiful, well-kept site divided by hedges.
2 km W.
Etr–15 Sep.
1.5HEC ◆ ⊙
⊞ lau A12 V5
13 13

ST-PIERRE-COLAMINE
Puy-de-Dôme
Ombrage 73967787
300 m from D978.
15 Dec–15 Sep.
2HEC ⊙
P ⊞ lau A9 V4
9 9

ST-PIERRE-DE-CHARTREUSE
Isère
Martinière rte de Grenoble 76886036
In pleasant position surrounded by mountains.
2 km SW.
15 Jun–15 Sep.
1.5HEC ⊙
⊞ lau P A10 V5
10 10

ST-PIERRE-LAFEUILLE
Lot
Quercy-Vacances 65368715
On N20. 12 km N of Cahors.
15 May–15 Sep.
2.8HEC ⊙
P ⊞ lau

ST-PIERRE-QUIBERON
Morbihan
Park-er-Lann 97502493
1.5 km S on D768.
15 May–15 Sep.
2.5HEC ⊙
⊞ lau s

ST-PONS-LES-MÛRES See **GRIMAUD**

ST-PRIEST-DE-GIMEL
Corrèze
Étang-de-Ruffaud 55212665
On hilly wooded ground beside lake. Common room with TV.
2.5 km N on D53.
Jun–Sep.
5HEC ⊙ L
⊞ lau

ST-PRIM
Isère
Bois des Sources 74849511
Apr–Sep.
3.5HEC ◆ ⊙

ST-QUAY-PORTRIEUX
Côtes-du-Nord
Bellevue 68 bd du Littoral 96704184
Site adjacent to the sea.
800 m from town centre.
May–15 Sep.
3HEC ⊙ sP
⊞ lau A10 V4 9
9

ST-QUENTIN-LA-POTERIE See **UZÈS**

ST-RAPHAËL
Var ➔

Beauséjour-les-Tasses ☎94950367

400 metres from the sea. Slightly hilly site in pinewoods. Suitable for small caravans and tents.

2 km E of town off N98.
15 May–Sep.

1.6HEC H lau S pitch42–52 (incl 2 persons)

Douce Quiétude 3435 bd J-Baudino ☎94955550

Meadowland site in quiet location in attractively hilly countryside.

Approach from Agay Plage past Esterel Camping in direction of Valescure.
Jun–Sep.

10HEC H G P lau

Royal ☎90920121

Level site divided by walls and hedges. Ideal bathing for children. Bar and dance hall next to site.

On N98 towards Cannes.
Mar–Oct.

2HEC H G S lau A14 11 11

ST-RÉMY-DE-PROVENCE

Bouches-du-Rhône

Pégomas ☎90920121

Well-tended grassland with young trees and bushes. Divided into several fields by high cedars providing shade.

500 m E of village. Well signposted.
Mar–Oct.

1.5HEC H G R P lau

ST-RÉMY-SUR-AVRE

Eure-et-Loir

Pré de l'Église ☎37489387

Follow N12 from town centre.
10 Apr–15 Sep.

0.6HEC H lau A9 pitch14

ST-SAUVEUR-LE-VICOMTE

Manche

CM Vieux Château ☎33215153

NE of village on D2.
15 Jun–15 Sep.

2HEC H lau R

ST-SERVAN-SUR-MER See **ST-MALO**

ST-SEURIN-DE-PRATS

Dordogne

Plage ☎53586107

0.7 kms on D11 alongside the Dordogne.
Jun–15 Sep.

5HEC H G RP lau pitch55 (incl 2 persons)

ST-SORLIN-EN-VALLOIRE

Drôme

Château de la Pérouze ☎75317021

France

2.5 km SE via D1.
Apr–Sep.

14HEC H G R P lau A14 Vn/c 13 10–13

ST-SYMPHORIEN-SUR-COISE

Rhône

Intercommunale de Hurongues ☎788484429

3.5 km W on Chazelles-sur-Lyon road (D2).
25 Mar–6 Oct.

4HEC H G P lau

ST-THIBÉRY

Hérault

Tane ☎67778429

Jun–Sep.

3HEC H P lau R pitch46 (incl 2 persons)

ST-THURIAL

Ille-et-Vilaine

Ker-Landes ☎99613995

The site is situated in the middle of pine trees near an old market town.

200 m W next to the lake.
All year.

2HEC H G lau A10 V4 8 8

ST-USTRE See **INGRANDES**

ST-VALÉRY-EN-CAUX

Seine-Maritime

CM ☎35970507

On narrowly terraced slopes of hill with asphalt drives and fine views. Steep approach with sharp bends not very suitable for caravans (13%).

Access from D925 (Dieppe road).
All year.

2HEC H lau S

ST-VALÉRY-SUR-SOMME

Somme

Croix l'Abbe ☎22608146

Situated in a picturesque and historic area of the town. 400 m from the sea.

W of town at junction D2/940.
15 Mar–15 Oct.

3HEC H P lau

Domaine du Château de Drancourt ☎22269345

Apr–Sep.

5HEC H G R P lau A16 V5 20

ST-VALLIER-DE-THIEY

Alpes-Maritimes

Parc des Arboins ☎93426389

Pleasantly situated terraced site on hillside with some oak trees.

Entrance at Km V36 on N85.
All year.

4.5HEC H G R P lau pitch30–64 (incl 2–4 persons)

ST-YVI

Finistère

CM Bois de Pleuven ☎98947047

4 km from town on N165.
Etr–Sep.

12HEC H G P lau A8 V4 14 14

STE-CATHERINE-DE-FIERBOIS

Indre-et-Loire

Parc de Fierbois ☎47654335

Beside artificial lake; good bathing area.

Follow D101 off N10, 1.5 km SE.
15 May–7 Sep.

6HEC H G L lau pitch85 (incl 3 persons)

STE-CÉCILE-PLAGE See **CAMIERS**

STE-EULALIE-EN-BORN

Landes

Bruyères chemin Laffont ☎58097001

Jun–Sep.

3HEC H G P lau L A12 V4 16 16

STE-FOY-DE-BELVÈS See **BELVÈS**

STE-FOY-LA-GRANDE

Gironde

CM ☎57461384

500m from town centre.
All year.

1HEC H lau P A7 V5 10 8

STE-MARIE

Pyrénées-Orientales

At **TORREILLES** (4 km NW on D11)

Dunes de Torreilles ☎68283032

At the sea, with direct access to beach.

All year.

16HEC H G R SP lau pitch146 (incl 5–6 persons)

Mar-I-Sol ☎68280407

Jun–Sep.

6HEC H G R SP lau

STE-REINE-DE-BRETAGNE

Loire-Atlantique

Château du Deffay ☎40016384

Situated in the beautiful Parc de Brière providing fishing, walking and horse riding. Games and TV rooms.

4.5 km W on D33 rte de Pontchâteau.
15 May–15 Sep.

3HEC H P lau A38 15

SAINTES
Charente-Maritime

CM 46930800

1 km on D128.
15 May–Sep.

2.7HEC H P lau A7 V3 5 5

STES-MARIES-DE-LA-MER
Bouches-du-Rhône

Clos du Rhône 90978599

Jun–Sep.

8HEC H G sP lau A21 pitch21

SALAVAS
Ardèche

Chauvieux 75880537

NE off D579.
May–15 Sep.

1.8HEC H G lau R pitch49 (incl 2 persons)

SALINS-D'HYÈRES (LES)
Var

Port Pothuau 94664117

Completely divided into pitches.

6 km E of Hyères on N98 and D12.
Apr–Oct.

6HEC H G R P lau s pitch53 (incl 3 persons)

SALLANCHES
Haute-Savoie

Mont Blanc Village 50584367

2 km SE off D13.
20 Mar–15 Sep.

6.5HEC H G lau L A12 V9 9 9

SALLE-EN-BEAUMONT (LA)
Isère

Champ-Long 76304181

15 Jun–Oct.

2HEC H P lau L pitch40 (incl 2 persons)

SALLES
Gironde

Val de l'Eyre 56884842

SW on D108, rte de Lugos.
15 Apr–15 Oct.

13HEC H G lau R

France

SALLES-CURAN
Aveyron

Beau Rivage rte des Vernhes 65463332

3.5 km N via D993n and D243.
15 Jun–Sep.

2HEC H G L lau

Genêts 65463534

On the edge of a lake.

7 km W via D577.
Jun–15 Sep.

1.2HEC H G L lau

SALES
Pyrénées-Orientales

International de Roussillon rte de Narbonne 68386072

On level ground divided into pitches.

1.5 km N on N9, next to motel.
All year.

2HEC H lau

SAMOIS-SUR-SEINE
Seine-et-Marne

Base de Plein Air 64246345

All year.

3HEC H R lau A6 6 6

SAMPZON
Ardèche

Soleil Vivarais 75396756

On several levels beside River Ardèche. Good base for canoeing.

From Vallon drive towards Ruoms on D579 for 5 km and cross bridge over River Ardèche.
Etr–Sep.

8HEC H G R lau

SANARY-SUR-MER
Var

Mogador 94741058

Situated 800 metres from the sea. The site, divided into pitches by hedges, is well managed and very well kept.

2 km NW on N559 turn off at Km 15 and take next left.
Apr–Oct.

2.7HEC H G P lau s pitch31

Val d'Aran 94295618

Well-equipped terraced site, divided into pitches with pine trees.

From Bandol E on N559 turn onto N559B and continue 2 km N then turn right and drive uphill.
All year.

9HEC H G R P lau

SANCHEY
Vosges

Lac de Bouzey 29824941

On sloping meadow, divided into pitches.

Near reservoir.
All year.

2HEC H G R lau L A10 pitch11

SARE
Pyrénées-Atlantiques

Goyenetche 59542171

1HEC H G R lau A8 V3 10 10

SARLAT-LA-CANÉDA
Dordogne

Grottes de Roffy 53591561

Apr–15 Sep.

6HEC H G P lau

Maillac Ste-Nathalène par Sarlat 53592212

7 km NE on D47.
15 Jun–15 Sep.

4HEC H G P lau

Moulin du Roch rte des Eyzies 53592027

10 km NW via D704–D6–D47.
May–Sep.

7HEC H G P lau pitch46–94 (incl 2–3 persons)

Pérlères 53590584

Very well kept terraced site in wooded valley.

1 km N of town on D47.
Etr–Sep.

11HEC H G P lau pitch67–96 (incl 2–3 persons)

At **CARSAC AILLAC** (7 km SE by D704a)

Aqua Viva 53592109

Site has wooded terraces.

Etr–Sep.

9HEC H G LP lau A13 pitch15

At **PROISSANS** (6 km NE)

Val d'Ussel 53592873

Off D704 or D56.
18 Apr–Sep.

6HEC H G P lau

SARTÈNE See **CORSE (CORSICA)**

SARZEAU
Morbihan

Kersial 97417559

3 km SW.

May–Oct.
1.5HEC H lau

At **PENVINS** (7 km SE by D198)

Madone ☎97673330

Situated 400 metres from the sea. Extensive sites on edge of village near old country estate. Divided into several sections.

15 May–15 Sep.
7HEC H lau S A12 pitch20

At **POINTE-ST-JACQUES** (5.5 km S)

CM St-Jacques ☎97417929

On beach protected by dunes. Well kept site with asphalt drives.

15 Apr–Sep.
10HEC H S lau A7 pitch8

SASSETOT-LE-MAUCONDUIT
Seine-Maritime

Trois Plages ☎35274011

Mar–Oct.
4HEC H lau A12 Vn/c 13 A13

SAUGUES
Haute-Loire

CM ☎71778062

15 Jun–15 Sep.
3HEC H lau LP A10 Vn/c 7 A7

France

SAUJON
Charente-Maritime

Chênes Médis ☎46067096

15 Jun–15 Sep.
4HEC H lau pitch34 (incl 3 persons)

SAULIEU
Côte-d'Or

CM Perron ☎80641619

1 km NW on N6.
All year.
8HEC H lau P

SAUMUR
Maine-et-Loire

CM Ile d'Offard ☎41674500

On island in the middle of the Loire near municipal stadium.

All year.
4HEC H (Jun–Sep) (Jun–Sep) (Jun–Sep) P lau A10 V6

SAUVETTERRE-DE-BÉARN
Pyrénées-Atlantiques

CM Gave av de la Gare ☎59385330

Turn left before bridge on St-Palais road.
Jun–Sep.
1.5HEC H R lau

SAUVETERRE-LA-LÉMANCE
Lot-et-Garonne

Moulin du Pérlé ☎53716726

In a wooded valley.

E of town off D710.
Apr–Sep.
2HEC H L lau A18 pitch21

SAUZON See **BELLE-ILE-EN-MER**

SAVENAY
Loire-Atlantique

CM Lac ☎40723176

1 km E of lake.
May–Sep.
2HEC H lau P

SAVERNE
Bas-Rhin

CM ☎88913565

Apr–Sep.
0.24HEC H lau P

SAVINES-LE-LAC
Hautes-Alpes

Chaumettes ☎92442016

A shaded terraced site 300 m from the lake.

All year.

1HEC lau

SCHIRMECK
Bas-Rhin

Schirmeck ☎88970161

1.5 km NE. Beside Strasbourg road and railway, on level ground.
All year.

2.6HEC lau A8 V4 4 4

SCIEZ
Haute-Savoie

Chalet du Port ☎50726272

On bank of Lake Léman (Lake Geneva).

May–Sep.

0.3HEC lau

Songy-Plage rte du Port ☎50726248

On meadow with tall poplar trees. Boat moorings 100 m.

1.5HEC lau

SÉEZ
Savoie

Reclus rte de Bourg-St-Maurice. ☎79070575

NW on N90.
All year.

1.9HEC lau

SEIGNOSSE
Landes

Chevreuils ☎58433280

In a pine forest.

On D79 rte de Hossegor.
Jun–15 Sep.

8HEC lau A12 pitch17

CM ☎58433030

France

Very clean and tidy site.

25 May–Sep.

16HEC lau A10 V3 10 10

Oyats ☎58433794

Level site, subdivided into fields and surrounded by woodland. Separate section for young people. Children's play area.

Turn off D79 in N outskirts towards Plage des Casernes.
May–Sep.

15HEC lau

At **SEIGNOSSE-LE-PENON** (5 km W)

Forêt ☎58433020

Jun–15 Sep.

6HEC lau pitch45 (incl 3 persons)

SEIX
Ariège

Haut Salat ☎61668178

Very clean, well kept site beside stream. Big gravel pitches for caravans. Common room with TV.

0.8 km NE on D3.
3 Jan–20 Sep & 20 Oct–20 Dec.

2.5HEC lau A12 pitch12

SÉLESTAT
Bas-Rhin

CM Cigognes r de la 1er DFL ☎88920398

May–15 Oct.

0.7HEC lau

SÉRIGNAN-PLAGE
Hérault

Camargue ☎67321964

Situated on the edge of a wide sandy beach.

15 Mar–15 Oct.

4HEC lau pitch50 (incl 2 persons)

Clos Virgile ☎67322064

Situated 400 metres from the beach, the site is level meadowland with big pitches and has two clean, well kept sanitary blocks.

May–20 Sep.

5HEC lau pitch55–67 (incl 2 persons)

Gabinelle ☎67395087

15 Jun–15 Sep.

3HEC lau pitch59 (incl 2–3 persons)

Grand Large ☎67323884

Apr–Sep.

3.5HEC lau

Sérignan-Plage ☎67323533

May–Sep.

10HEC lau

SERQUES
Pas-de-Calais

Serco Prix ☎21385940

N on N43.
All year.

0.2HEC lau

SERRES
Hautes-Alpes

Barillons ☎92670116

Well-laid out with terraces.

1 km SE on N75.
May–25 Sep.

3HEC lau pitch41 (incl 3 persons)

Domaine des 2 Soleils ☎92670133

Well-kept terraced site in Buëch Valley.

S of town off N75. Signposted.
May–Sep.

26HEC

lau pitch70 (incl 3 persons)

SERRIERA See **PORTO** under **CORSE (CORSICA)**

SÈTE
Hérault

Castellas 67532624

3 km E of Marseillan-Plage on N108.
Jun–13 Sep.

1HEC H s lau

SEURRE
Côte-d'Or

Piscine 80204538

From town centre follow N73 W for 600 m in the direction of Beaune.
15 May–15 Sep.

2HEC H P lau

SEYNE-SUR-MER (LA)
Var

Buffalo Parc 94747208

This site is modelled on a Wild West village. Level pitches for caravans; wooded terraces for tents. 800 m from the sea.

Turn off D16 (Six-Fours-la-Plage-Les-Sablettes road).
All year.

4HEC H lau s

Fontanettes quartier Lery 94947507

Turn off D63 approx 6 km W of Toulon and follow signposts.
All year.

1HEC H lau

Pins 94940689

100 m from the sea.
2 Apr–Oct.

0.8HEC H lau s pitch60 (incl 3 persons)

Union Col d'Artaud 94948610

Terraced site on steep slope which is best suited for tents.

Turn off N559 onto D216 between Km22 and Km23.
Mar–Oct.

1.5HEC H lau

SEYSSEL
Ain

International de Seyssel 50592847

A quiet site on steep, terraced meadowland, with individual washbasins and clean sanitary installations.

1 km SW off Culoz road.
Jun–Sep.

1HEC H lau RP

SÉZANNE
Marne

France

CM 26805700

1.5 km W on D239, rte de Launat.
Etr–10 Oct.

1HEC H P lau A4 V2 2 A2

SIGEAN
Aude

CM 68482004

On the outskirts of the village near the Municipal Sports Stadium.
15 Jun–15 Sep.

1.4HEC H lau

SILLÉ-LE-GUILLAUME
Sarthe

Privé du Landereau Le Grez 43201269

All year.

2.5HEC H lau L A8 V4 3 A2

SILLÉ-LE-PHILIPPE
Sarthe

Château de Chanteloup 43275107

Set partly in wooded clearings and open ground. Good sanitary installations.

17 km NE from Le Mans on D301.
27 Jun–Aug.

20HEC H P lau

SIORAC-EN-PÉRIGORD
Dordogne

At **COUX-ET-BIGAROQUE**

(2.5 km NW by D710/D703)

Clou 53316332

Separate section for dog owners.

Access via D703 (Le Bugue-Delve road)
Apr–Sep.

3HEC H P lau A15 pitch18

Faval 53316044

1 km E of village on D703, near junction with D710.
Apr–15 Oct.

2.2HEC H P lau R A15 pitch18–25

SIREUIL See **EYZIES-DE-TAYAC (LES)**

SISTERON
Alpes-de-Haute-Provence

CM de la Baume 92611969

Pleasant site on east bank of river with fine view of town and castle.

Over bridge and follow D951 upstream for 400 m.
May–Sep.

3HEC H

SIX-FOURS-LES-PLAGES
Var

International St-Jean 94875151

Site with pitches, separated by hedges and reeds. Well managed, and lies just below the Fort Six Fours.

Access from N559 and D63 via chemin de St-Jean.
Mar–Oct.

3HEC H lau

Playes 94255757

Terraced site on north side of town. Trees abound in this excellent location.

Access from N559 and D63 via chemin de St-Jean.
Mar–Sep.

1.5HEC H lau sP A11 V6 16 A16

SOCOA See **ST-JEAN-DE-LUZ**

SOLLIÈS-TOUCAS
Var

Oliviers 94289539

Recreational facilities.

On D554, rte de Belgentier.
10 Jun–5 Sep.

2.5HEC H sP lau

SORBO See **CORSE (CORSICA)**

SORGUES
Vaucluse

Montagne 90833666

10 km NE of Avignon on N7.
Apr–Oct.

2HEC H P lau A6 V3 5 A5

SOSPEL
Alpes-Maritimes

Domaine St-Madeleine 93041048

All year.

3HEC H P lau A11 V7 10 A10

SOUILLAC
Lot

Domaine de la Paille Basse 65378548

6.5 km NW off D15 Salignac-Eyvignes road.
15 May–15 Sep.

8HEC H P lau A21 pitch35–44

SOULAC-SUR-MER
Gironde

Airotel Palace rte de l'Amelie 56098022

Well-kept site on sand dunes. Individual pitches, asphalt drives.

1 km S from village centre. Access is via D1 and D101.

Apr–Sep.
16HEC lau
A16 Vn/c 45 35

Arros r V-Hugo ☎56098651

In a meadow. Near swimming pool by sand dunes.

mid Apr–Sep.
1HEC lau

Genêts ☎56098579

2 km NE on D101E2.
Etr–Sep.
4.5HEC lau

Océan ☎56097610

3.5 km S.
15 Jun–15 Sep.
8HEC lau
pitch38

Sables d'Argent rte de l'Amelie ☎56598287

1.5 km SW of village.
Jun–15 Sep.
2.5HEC lau

At **AMÉLIE-SUR-MER (L')** (4.5 km S)

Amélie-Plage ☎56098727

In hilly wooded terrain. Lovely sandy beach.

3 km S on the Soulac road.
Mar–Oct.
10HEC lau

At **LILIAN** (4.5 km S)

Pins ☎56098252

S on D101.
Etr–Oct.
3HEC lau

SOUPPES-SUR-LOING
Seine-et-Marne

Municipal Chemin des Mariniers ☎64297263

Apr–Oct.
5HEC lau
pitch35 (incl 2 persons)

SOUSTONS
Landes

Airial ☎58480248

2 km W on D652.
Etr–15 Oct.
12HEC lau A12 Vn/c
24 15

CM ☎58483072

15 Jun–15 Sep.
6HEC lau A10
pitch15–26

France

STRASBOURG
Bas-Rhin

Montagne-Verte 2 r R-Forrer ☎88302546

Site is divided into pitches and lies beside the Charles Frey Stadium.

2.5 km from town centre via N4 and D392.
Mar–Oct.
3HEC lau A8 pitch8

At **ILLKIRCH-GRAFFENSTADEN** (7 km S off N68)

Baggersee ☎88390340

Beside artificial lake. Public bathing area but quiet after 9 pm.

All year.
5HEC lau

SUCÉ-SUR-ERDRE
Loire-Atlantique

CM Papinière ☎40777554

1 km SE on D37, rte de Carquefou.
All year.
1.2HEC lau

SUÈVRES
Loire-et-Cher

Château de la Grenouillère ☎54878037

Completely divided into pitches. Castle now hotel with common room for campers. Each pitch 150 sq m. Separate area for overnight campers.

3 km from village towards Orléans.
May–15 Sep.
11HEC lau pitch80–100 (incl 3 persons)

SULLY-SUR-LOIRE
Loiret

CM ☎38362393

Near Château, adjacent to River Loire.

100 m from town.
Apr–Sep.
2.7HEC lau A7 V4
5 5

At **ST-PÈRE-SUR-LOIRE**

St-Père-sur-Loire ☎38363594

Apr–Sep.
1.8HEC lau A9 V4
9 9

TADEN See **DINAN**

TAIN-L'HERMITAGE
Drôme

CM Lucas rte de Valence ☎75083282

Good overnight stopping place but some traffic noise.

S of town near N7. Turn towards River Rhône at ESSO garage.
15 Mar–Oct.
2HEC lau A5 V3 3 3

TALLOIRES
Haute-Savoie

Lanfonnet ☎50607212

1.5 km SE.
Etr–Sep.
2HEC lau pitch55 (incl 2 persons)

TALMONT-ST-HILAIRE
Vendée

Bois Robert ☎51906124

1.3 km W on D949.
25 Jun–4 Sep.
2.2HEC lau pitch48–55 (incl 3 persons)

At **PORTEAU (LE)** (10 km W by D949)

Joie de Vivre ☎51325527

200 m from the sea.
Jun–Aug.
3HEC lau

At **ST-HILAIRE-LA-FORÊT** (7 km SE)

Batardières ☎51333385

5 May–10 Sep.
1.6HEC lau

TARARE
Rhône

CM rte de Lyon ☎74632680

SE near stadium.
0.7HEC

TARASCON
Bouches-du-Rhône

St-Gabriel ☎90911983

15 Mar–Oct.
1HEC lau A10 V3 6
6

Tatarin rte de Vallabrègues ☎90910146

Site lies on E bank of River Rhône.

Follow signs for 'Vallabrègues'.
15 Mar–Sep.
1HEC lau
A12 12 12

TARASCON-SUR-ARIÈGE
Ariège

CM Pré Lombard r Ariège ☎61056194

700 m S on D23.
All year.
4HEC lau

TAZILLY
Nièvre

Château de Chigy ☎86301080 ➤

15 Apr–Sep.
1HEC H P lau

TELGRUC-SUR-MER
Finistère
Armorique ☎98277733
Quiet, partly terraced site in pine forest. Fine view of the Bay of Douarnenez.
Steep access.
Jun–Sep.
2.5HEC H lau S

Panoramic rte de Trez-Bellec-Plage ☎98277841
Quiet terraced site with numbered pitches. Slipway for boats.
W on D887 and then S on D208.
15 May–15 Sep.
4HEC H lau S A12 V6 13 13

TERRASSON-LA-VILLEDIEU
Dordogne
CM ☎53500281
500 m E.
Jun–Sep.
0.8HEC H lau P

TESTE (LA) See **HUME (LA)**

THENON
Dordogne
Jarry Carrey ☎53052078
In beautiful valley.
4 km SE on D67.
All year.
3HEC H P lau

THIEMBRONNE
Pas-de-Calais
Pommiers ☎21395019
NW on D132.
15 Mar–15 Oct.
1.7HEC H

THIONVILLE
Moselle
CM 6 r du Parc ☎82538375
On the edge of River Moselle, adjacent to the Napoléon Park.
Apr–Sep.
2HEC H lau P A4 V2 2 2

THIZY
Rhône
CM ☎74640529
2 km S on D504, rte de Tarare. Access difficult for caravans (gradient of 18%).
15 May–15 Sep.
0.5HEC H lau A3 V3 3 3

France

THOISSEY
Ain
CM ☎74040297
Situated between two rivers, La Saône and La Chalaronne.
1 km SW on D7.
Etr–Sep.
15HEC H RP lau A8 V4 5–13 5–13

THOLY (LE)
Vosges
Noir Rupt ☎29618127
2 km SE on D417.
15 Apr–15 Sep.
1.2HEC H P lau A13 Vn/c

THONON-LES-BAINS
Haute-Savoie
Morcy ☎50713265
2.5 km W of town.
Etr–10 Sep.
0.7HEC H lau L A10 pitch10

THURY-HARCOURT
Calvados
CM Bord de l'Orne r du Val d'Orne ☎31797078
1 km W on D6 and D166 near river.
15 Jun–15 Sep.
0.6HEC H R lau

Vallée du Traspy ☎31796180
Level meadow site near a small reservoir.
Etr–15 Oct.
1.3HEC H R

TINTÉNIAC
Ille-et-Vilaine
Peupliers ☎99454975
Etr–Oct.
4.5HEC H P lau

TOLLENT
Pas-de-Calais
Val d'Authie ☎21471427
All year.
33HEC H P lau R A10 V6 pitch12

TONNEINS
Lot-et-Garonne
CM Robinson ☎53790228
500 m from town centre on N113 Agen road.
Jun–15 Sep.
0.7HEC H lau P

TONNOY
Meurthe-et-Moselle
Grande Vanné ☎83266236
25 May–Aug.
7HEC H R lau A7 pitch10

TORCY
Seine-et-Marne
Parc de la Colline rte de Lagny ☎60054232
Access via exit 9 on the A104.
15 Mar–15 Oct.
7HEC H lau L A10 pitch26

TORREILLES See **STE-MARIE**

TOULOUSE
Haute-Garonne
CM Rupé chemin du Pont de Rupé ☎61700735
Some noise from nearby shunting yard. Sanitary blocks not very well equipped.
6 km N on N20, rte de Montauban.
Signposted.
All year.
3HEC H lau

TOUQUES See **DEAUVILLE**

TOUR-DE-MARE See **FRÉJUS**

TOURNON-SUR-RHÔNE
Ardèche
CM ☎75080528
Well laid-out site in town centre beside River Rhône.
NW on N86.
Mar–Nov.
1.1HEC H lau P A11 V7 7 7

TOURRETTE-SUR-LOUP
Alpes-Maritimes
Camassade ☎93593154
Quiet site under oak trees and pines with several terraces.
From Vence turn left immediately beyond Tourrette. The last 50 m is narrow and steep and therefore not suitable for large caravans.
All year.
1.8HEC H P lau A12 V9

TOURS
Indre-et-Loire
At **BALLAN-MIRÉ** (8.5 km W on D751)
Mignardière ☎47532649
2.5 km NE.
Apr–Sep.
2.3HEC H P lau

TOUZAC
Lot
Ch'Timi ☎65365236

800 m from Touzac, beside the River Lot.
15 May–Sep.
1.7HEC lau A10 pitch10

Clos Bouyssac ☎65365221

On the fringe of a wooded hillside by the sandy shore of the River Lot. Good for walking.

May–Oct.
7HEC lau A14 V15 15 15

TRANCHE-SUR-MER (LA)
Vendée

Baie d'Aunis r du Pertuis ☎51303736

On level land on sea-shore.

300 m E on D46.
20 Mar–Sep.
2.5HEC lau

Bel ☎51304739

400 m from town centre.
Apr–Sep.
3.5HEC pitch89 (incl 3 persons)

Cottage Fleuri la Grière-Plage ☎51303457

20 Mar–4 Oct.
5HEC lau A14 pitch23

Escale du Pertius ☎51303896

In meadowland by the sea and a lovely sandy beach.

On D46 about 4.5 km in the direction of L'Aiguillon.
15 Apr–15 Sep.
0.6HEC lau

Rouillières ☎51303178

Extensive site by the sea with level ground and pine and poplar trees. Largely subdivided into pitches.

Follow D46 E for 3 km in direction of L'Aiguillon.
May–15 Sep.
15HEC lau

TRÉBEURDEN
Côtes-du-Nord

Amor-Loisirs ☎96235231

Modern site with individual pitches surrounded by hedges. Hardstandings for caravans.

500 m S of the Kernévez road.
mid Mar–mid Sep.
2.2HEC lau A14 V7 11 9

TRÉBONS See **BAGNÈRES-DE-BIGORRE**

TREGUNC
Finistère

France

Pendruc ☎98976628

On level grassland subdivided by hedging. Separate section for young campers.

Access via D783 at Pont-Minaouët S in direction of Plage de Pendruc.
20 Jun–10 Sep.
3.6HEC lau A11 V5 12 12

TRÉLÉVERN
Côtes-du-Nord

CM Port l'Epine ☎96237194

1.5 km NW.
15 May–15 Sep.
3.7HEC lau pp15

TRÉLISSAC
Dordogne

CM ☎53544588

5.5 km E of Perigueux on N21.
15 May–15 Sep.
0.5HEC lau A7 V3 5 5

TRÉPORT (LE)
Seine-Maritime

CM les Boucaniers av des Canadiens ☎35863547

Well-kept site on flat meadow on E edge of village. Sports and games nearby.

Etr–Sep.
5.5HEC lau

International du Golf ☎35863380

1 km W on D940.
Apr–Sep.
5HEC lau A14–16 V7–9 10–12 10–12

TRIMOUILLE (LA)
Vienne

CM rte de Bélâbre ☎49916014

'X' roads D121 and N727, by River Banaize.
15 Jun–Sep.
1HEC

TRINITÉ (LA) See **PLOUHA**

TRINITÉ-SUR-MER (LA)
Morbihan

Baie plage de Kervilen ☎97557342

Several strips of land divided by tall trees.

Signposted in the direction of Kerbihan.
15 May–15 Sep.
2.2HEC lau A19 pitch38

Plage Plage de Kervilen ☎97557328

Divided into pitches and lying behind sand dunes which shield from the wind.

1 km S.
23 May–15 Sep.
3HEC lau A21 pitch35

TURBALLE (LA)
Loire-Atlantique

Falaise ☎40233253

500 m W from village centre on D99 towards Piriac-sur-Mer.
25 Mar–Oct.
2.8HEC (in season) (in season) (in season) lau A14 V7 16 16

Parc Ste-Brigitte Domaine de Bréhet ☎40233042

Site in grounds of old Château. Parkland divided into pitches and surrounded by hedges.

E of village on D99 Guérande road.
Apr–Sep.
10HEC lau

TURCKHEIM
Haut-Rhin

CM quai de la Gare ☎89270200

From Colmar follow N417 to Wintzenheim, then to Turckheim. Before bridge turn left, continue past railway station and stadium.
All year.
2.5HEC lau A8 V4 4 4

TURSAC See **ST-LÉON-SUR-VÉZÈRE**

UCHIZY
Saône-et-Loire

National 6 ☎85405390

Site surrounded by poplar trees on banks of river.

Turn off N6 towards Saône 6 km S of Tournus and continue 0.8 km.
Apr–Sep.
6HEC lau

UGINE
Savoie

Sporting rte d'Annecy ☎79373155

Gently sloping, on well-kept meadowland.

2 km NW on N508 rte d'Annecy.
Etr–15 Oct.
2HEC lau

URBÈS
Haut-Rhin

CM Benelux Bâle ☎89827876

Apr–15 Oct.
3HEC lau

URRUGNE
Pyrénées-Atlantiques

Larrouleta ☎59473784

Hilly meadow with young trees.

1.5 km N of Urrugne on N1 to Spain. ➔

All year.
3HEC ◈ H G P ⊞ lau |O| A6 V6 8 8

USSEL
Corrèze

Centre Touristique de Ponty ☎55723005
2.7 km W on D157, on rte de Tulle/rte de Meymac.
All year.
3.5HEC ◈ H ☉ G Ⓟ ⊞ lau |O| L A9 pitch9

UZÈS
Gard

At **ST-QUENTIN-LA-POTERIE** (4 km NE)

Moulin Neuf ☎66221721
Quiet site on extensive meadowland within an estate.
4 km NE on D982.
Etr–Sep.
4HEC ◈ H |O| ☉ G P ⊞ lau pitch40 (incl 2 persons)

VAISON-LA-ROMAINE
Vaucluse

Moulin de César av C-Geoffray ☎903660078
Site divided into pitches by trees and bushes.
800 m E of village on D151 towards St-Marcellin and river.

France

26 Mar–Oct.
4HEC ◈ H (Jul–Aug) |O| ☉ G R ⊞ lau P A15 pitch10

VAL-DE-VESLE
Marne

CM Val de Vesle ☎26039179
Apr–15 Oct.
◈ H ☉ ⊞ lau G RP A6 V4 4 4

VALENCE
Drôme

CM Centre de l'Epervière ☎75436301
Bordering the Rhône.
Access via exit Valence Sud off A7.
5 Jan–20 Dec.
3.5HEC ◆ H |O| ☉ ⊞ lau P

VALLON-PONT-D'ARC
Ardèche

Arc en Ciel ☎75880465
Etr–Sep.
2.5HEC ◈ H |O| ☉ G R ⊞ lau

Ardechois ☎75880663
In a pleasant situation in the Ardèche Gorge. Good access for caravans and plentiful sporting facilities.
From Vallon take D290 towards St-Martin. Signposted.
Mar–Oct.
5HEC ◆ H |O| ☉ G R ⊞ lau pitch68 (incl 2–3 persons)

Mondial rte des Gorges ☎75880044
Modernised site on the bank of the Ardèche with good sanitary arrangements.
Access from Vallon-Pont-d'Arc D290. 800 m towards Gorge d'Ardèche.
15 Mar–Sep.
4.5HEC ◆ H |O| ☉ G R ⊞ lau pitch53 (incl 2 persons)

Plage Fleurie ☎75880115
Holiday site in unspoilt village beside river.
Take D579 towards Ruoms, turn left after 2.5 km towards Les Mazes.
Etr–Sep.
12HEC ◆ H |O| ☉ G R Ⓟ ⊞ lau pitch49 (incl 2 persons)

Provençal rte des Gorges ☎75880048
On long strip of meadow off D290 at beginning of Ardèche Gorge. Bathing not recommended.

Apr–Oct.

2.5HEC H R lau

VALMONT

Seine-Maritime

Parc de Loisirs de Valmont ☎35298359

Apr–Oct.

3HEC H lau

VALRAS-PLAGE

Hérault

Clos Marin ☎67320272

2 km SW.

15 May–Sep.

2.7HEC H lau s

Lou Village ☎67373379

20 May–15 Sep.

10HEC H lau s

pitch69–75 (incl 3–4 persons)

Occitanie av du Casino ☎67320561

Booking address: Reservations Dept., Hilton International, Enterprise House, 30 Langler Road, London NW10 5TL ☎01-969 2711.

Site on rising ground to the north of town.

All year.

5.6HEC H P lau s

Plage ☎67303637

Jun–mid Sep.

10HEC H lau

Yole ☎67373387

Very comfortable site divided into pitches. Good sanitary installations with individual washing cubicles. Hot water tap. Sailing boats for hire. Riding stables in village.

SW of D37E towards Vendres.

20 May–15 Sep.

20HEC H P lau s pitch86 (incl 2 persons)

VANDENESSE-EN-AUXOIS

Côte-d'Or

Lac de Panthier ☎80330179

France

5 km SE from Pouilly-en-Auxois on A6.

May–Sep.

1.7HEC H L lau A9 pitch11

VARENNES-SUR-ALLIER

Allier

Château de Chezeuil ☎70450010

On well-kept meadow.

3 km NW on N7.

May–Sep.

1.5HEC H P lau A15 pitch10

Plans d'Eau ☎70450155

3 km NW on N7.

Apr–Sep.

4HEC H lau R A13 V4 10 10

VARENNES-SUR-LOIRE

Maine-et-Loire

Étang de la Brèche ☎41512292

4.5 km NW via N152.

May–15 Sep.

7HEC H P lau pitch68 (incl 3 persons)

VARILHES

Ariège

CM Parc du Château rte de Pamiers ☎61607117

N on N20.

All year.

1.3HEC H lau A5 pitch5

VARREDDES

Seine-et-Marne

Ile du Bac rte de Congis ☎64348080

Near the L'Oureq Canal.

Pass through Varreddes and take D121 Congis road for 1 km.

All year.

6HEC H P lau R

VAUX-SUR-MER

Charente-Maritime

Nauzan-Plage av de Nauzan Plage ☎46382913

500 m from the beach.

Apr–Sep.

4HEC H lau s

VEDÈNE

Vaucluse

Flory ☎90310051

Well-kept site on hill. Common room with TV.

From motorway, do not head for Vedène but follow D942 for 600 m.

15 Mar–15 Oct.

6.5HEC H P lau A12 pitch12

VELLES

Indre

Grands Pins ☎54361009

The site has individual pitches and has easy access to the countryside.

7 km S of Châteauroux on N20, Les Maisons Neuves.

Apr–Oct.

5HEC H P lau A7 V7 7 7

VENCE

Alpes-Maritimes

Domaine de la Bergerie rte de la Sine ☎93580936

Well-kept site on hilly land. Pitches near to a wood.

3 km W on D2210.

Mar–5 Nov.

14HEC H lau pitch51–71 (incl 3 persons)

VENDÔME

Loir-et-Cher

Grand Prés r G-Martel ☎54770027

Site lies on a meadow, next to a sports ground. ➤

E of town on right bank of Loire.
All year.
3HEC H G lau P A8 pitch5

VENOSC See **BOURG-D'OISANS (LE)**

VERCLAUSE
Drôme

Riousset ☎75278022
1 km on D94.
All year.
3.5HEC H G R lau PR pitch50 (incl 2 persons)

VERDON-SUR-MER (LE)
Gironde

Cordouan ☎56097142
Clean, pleasant meadowland with some pines and deciduous trees. 1 km to sea.
N of Soulac-sur-Mer via D1.
All year.
4HEC H G lau sP pitch28–31 (incl 2 persons)

Royannais Le Royannais ☎56096112
Level, sandy terrain under high pine and deciduous trees. Near tank depot.
S of Le Verdon-sur-Mer in Le Royannais district on D1.
15 Jun–15 Sep.
2HEC H G R lau s pitch27 (incl 2 persons)

VERMENTON
Yonne

Coullemière ☎86535212
On the N6 S of Auxerre.
15 Apr–Oct.
1.1HEC H R lau G A7 V3 5 5

VERNET-LES-BAINS
Pyrénées-Orientales

Cady ☎68055612
On meadow beside a fast flowing river.
1 km S on D116, rte de Casteil.
Apr–Oct.

France

2HEC H G lau R A15 pitch17

VERRUYES
Deux-Sèvres

Fragnée ☎49632137
1 km NE via rte de St-Lin.
Apr–15 Oct.
1HEC H G lau L A8 V4 pitch6

VEZAC
Dordogne

Deux Vallées ☎53295355
Apr–Sep.
3HEC H G P lau R

VIAS
Hérault

Air Marin Farinette ☎67940681
Jun–15 Sep.
7HEC H G R P lau s pitch88 (incl 4 persons)

Bourricot ☎67216427
3 km S on D137; at Vias look for Farinette-Plage and in 100 m before beach turn right.
Apr–17 Sep.
2HEC H G lau sR pitch61 (incl 2 persons)

Californie Plage ☎67940088
Very tidy site completely divided into pitches beside sea.
S on D137 past bridge over Canal du Midi turn right and follow signposts.
Apr–Sep.
5.7HEC H G s lau pitch90 (incl 3–4 persons)

Carabasse Farinette Plage ☎67216401
Clean modern well-kept site.
2 km S.

May–20 Sep.
20HEC H G P lau s pitch103 (incl 4 persons)

Farret ☎67216445
On level meadow beside flat sandy beach; ideal for children.
Etr–Sep.
8HEC H G sP lau pitch80 (incl 4 persons)

France Floride ☎67940180
Tidy site on seashore.
3.5 km SW.
Jun–15 Sep.
2.6HEC H G lau s

Gal Soleil ☎67940198
On level land near sea. Divided into pitches.
Cross Canal du Midi, S of town, then turn W.
All year.
5HEC H G R P lau s pitch60 (incl 2 persons)

Méditerranée ☎67909907
Jun–15 Sep.
10HEC H G R s lau pitch58 (incl 2 persons)

Ondines ☎67940153
Etr–15 Sep.
3.5HEC H G Ps lau

Petit Mousse ☎67490431
28 Mar–Sep.
5HEC H G R s lau pitch46

Salisses ☎67216407
Level grassy site, divided into pitches.
2 km S and 500 m from sea.
Apr–Sep.
7HEC H G R P lau s pitch83 (incl 2 persons)

VICHY
Allier

At **BELLERIVE** (3 km W)

Acacias r C-Decloître ☎70323622

Well-managed site, sub-divided into numbered pitches by hedges. Clean sanitary installations. Library, billiard room. Water sports are available nearby on lake.

From Vichy turn left after bridge beside ESSO garage and follow river for 500 m.
25 Mar–20 Oct.

2.5HEC ◆ H ⊙ G R RP ⊞ lau |O| **A**15 **V**8 12 12

Beau Rivage r C-Decloître ☎70322685

Neat meadowland with marked out pitches. Well kept sanitary installations. TV.

Watch for turning over bridge onto left bank of River Allier.
Apr–Oct.

1.5HEC ◆ H |O| ⊙ G P ⊞ lau **A**16 pitch20

CM 61 av d'Hauterive ☎70323011

Apr–Oct.

1HEC ◆ H ⊙ ⊞ lau |O| P

VICO See **CORSE (CORSICA)**

VIC-SUR-CÈRE

Cantal

CM av des Tilleuls ☎71475104

On level meadow with tarred drives. Large common room with open fireplace.

May–Sep.

4HEC ◆ H ⊙ ⊞ lau |O| P **A**9 **V**4 4 4

Pommerale ☎71475418

2 km SE.
Jun–10 Sep & 20 Dec–15 Apr.

1.7HEC ◆ H |O| ⊙ G P ⊞ lau

VIELLE-ST-GIRONS

Landes

Col Vert ☎58429406

Quiet site on lakeside in sparse pine woodland. Small natural harbour in the mouth of a stream.

Turn off D652 on N side of village and continue towards lake.

France

Etr–Sep.

24HEC ◆ H |O| ⊙ G R L ⊞ lau **A**16 **V**4 21 **V**21

Eurosol ☎58429014

Jun–15 Sep.

17HEC ◆ H |O| ⊙ G R P ⊞ lau S

VIGAN (LE)

Gard

Val de l'Arre rte de Ganges ☎67810277

2.5 km E on D999.
Apr–Sep.

4HEC ◆ H ⊙ G R ⊞ lau |O| pitch7 (incl 2 persons)

VILLARS-COLMARS

Alpes-de-Haute-Provence

Haut-Verdon ☎92834009

On D908 bordering river.
20 Jun–10 Sep.

3.5HEC ◆ H |O| ⊙ G R RP ⊞ lau **A**20 **V**10 10 10

VILLARS-LES-DOMBES

Ain

CM Autières ☎74980021

Clean and tidy park-like site divided into plots and pitches. Part reserved for overnight campers. Clean, modern sanitary installations.

SW off N83.
11 Apr–5 Oct.

4.5HEC ◆ H |O| ⊙ G ⊞ lau P **A**8 **V**4 8 8

VILLECROZE

Var

Cadenières ☎94706031

A terraced site with games for children.

On the D560.
All year.

6.5HEC ◆ H |O| ⊙ G R P ⊞ lau

VILLEDIEU-LES-POÊLES

Manche

CM Pré de la Rose r des Costils ☎33610244

Etr–Sep.

2HEC ◆ H ⊙ G ⊞ lau |O| **A**8 **V**3 8 8

VILLEFRANCHE-DE-PANAT

Aveyron

Cantarelles ☎65464035

On level grassland by Lac de Villefranche-de-Panat.

On the D25 about 3 km N of Villefranche-de-Panat.
May–Sep

2.5HEC ◆ H |O| ⊙ G L ⊞ lau **A**13 pitch12

VILLEFRANCHE-SUR-SAÔNE

Rhône

CM Plage rte de Riottier ☎74653348

3.5 km SE by River Saône.
27 Apr–29 Sep.

1.2HEC ◆ H |O| ⊙ G ⊞ lau

VILLENAVE-D'ORNON

Gironde

Gravières ☎56870036

S towards the river off chemin de Macau.
All year.

4.5HEC ◆ H |O| ⊙ G R ⊞ lau

VILLENEUVE-DE-BERG

Ardèche

Pommier ☎75948281

Holiday site in beautiful setting with terraces divided into pitches. Common room. Library.

On winding private road off N102, 2 km from village.
16 May–12 Sep.

10HEC ◆ H |O| ⊙ G P ⊞ lau **A**19 **V**11 7 7

VILLENEUEVE-LOUBET-PLAGE
Alpes-Maritimes

Avenc ☎93732990

NE via N7 and av des Baumettes.
Feb–Oct.

1.4HEC lau pitch40–50 (incl 2 persons)

Hippodrôme ☎93200200

Divided into two by a busy road. 0.4 km from the sea.

Turn right off the N7 at ATLAS furniture store.
All year.

0.8HEC lau pitch41–81 (incl 2 persons)

Orée de Vaugrenier ☎93335730

2 km S.
15 Mar–Oct.

0.9HEC lau pitch105 (incl 4 persons)

Panorama ☎93209153

Small terraced site mainly for tents 0.8 km from the sea.

About 500 km from the Nice–Cannes Autoroute.
All year.

1.1HEC lau pitch35–42 (incl 2 persons)

Parc des Maurettes ☎93209191

Terraced site in a pine forest.

Access from Autoroute exit Antibes (A8 Nice–Toulon) to N7. Continue 4 km in direction of Nice. Turn left after Vaugrenier Park and proceed for 1 km.
10 Jan–15 Nov.

2HEC (Apr–Oct) (Apr–Oct) lau S pitch30–86 (incl 2 persons)

Sourire ☎93209611

15 Mar–Oct.

8HEC P lau pitch44–72 (incl 2 persons).

Vieille Ferme bd des Groules ☎93334144

Site lies in Vaugrenier Park. Level meadow, terraced site for tents. Used by package tours. 150 m from sea.

All year.

2.2HEC P lau S pitch60–92 (incl 2–3 persons)

VILLENNES-SUR-SEINE
Yvelines

Club des Renardières ☎39758897

Site for caravans only, in beautiful hilly park laid out with hedges, lawns and flower beds. Fully divided into completely separated pitches.

Follow D113 to Maison Blanche turn right and continue 3 km.
All year.

7HEC lau A13 pitch59

VILLEROUGE-LA-CRÉMADE
Aude

Pinada ☎68436182

In pleasant rural surroundings on edge of forest.

600 m NW on D106.
Jun–Sep.

4.5HEC P lau A10 V8 15 V14

VILLIERS-HELON
Aisne

Castel des Biches ☎23960499

Attractive site in grounds of old castle.

Turn off the N2 onto the D2 between Soissons and Villers-Cotterêts and continue to 7 km via Longport.
Apr–Oct.

5HEC lau pitch38–50 (incl 2 persons)

VILLERS-ST-PAUL
Oise

Garenne ☎44710996

No tents.

1.8HEC P lau

VILLERS-SUR-MER
Calvados

Ammonites ☎31870606

4 km SW on rte de Cabourg and D163 towards Auberville.
May–20 Sep.

3.3HEC sP lau A20 pitch23

VILLERVILLE
Calvados

Bruyère ☎31982439

Mar–Oct.

4HEC P

At **ÉQUEMAUVILLE** (6 km E)

Briquerie ☎31892832

Apr–Oct.

5HEC lau

VILLES-SUR-AUZON
Vaucluse

Verguettes rte de Carpentras ☎90618818

Jun–Sep.

2HEC P lau A17 V8 13 13

VINEUIL
Loir-et-Cher

Châteaux ☎54788205

Level site on left bank of River Loire with modern buildings. Boating. Bathing not recommended.

From Blois drive towards St-Dye. After modern bridge continue towards 'Lac de Loire' for 1.5 km.
Mar–Dec.

7HEC (Jun–Sep.) (Jun–Sep) (Jun–Sep) P lau pitch25–40 (incl 2 persons)

VITRAC
Dordogne

Soleil Plage ☎53283333

4 km E on D703, turn by 'Camping Clos Bernard'.
Apr–Oct.

5HEC RP lau A12 pitch14

VITROLLES
Bouches-du-Rhône

Europa ☎42870036

3 km SW on N113 rte de Salon de Provence.
All year.

2HEC L lau A8 Vn/c 10 8

VIVIERS
Ardèche

Rochecondrie Loisirs ☎75527466

N of town on N86.
All year.

4HEC P lau

VIVIERS-DU-LAC See **AIX-LES-BAINS**

VIZILLE
Isère

CM ☎76681239

Apr–15 Oct.

2.3HEC lau P

VOGÜÉ
Ardèche

Domaine de Cros d'Auzon ☎75377586

2.5 km via D579 bordering the river.
Jun–15 Sep.

2HEC lau RP pitch52 (incl 2 persons)

VOIRON
Isère

CM Porte de la Chartreuse ☎76051420

On level terrain with some trees, divided into pitches. Much traffic noise from nearby N75. Clean and modern sanitary installations.

Access is NW of town next to the ESSO garage.
Mar–Oct.

1.8HEC lau P

VOLONNE
Alpes-de-Haute-Provence

Hippocampe rte Napoléon ☎92640506

Several strips of land, interspersed with trees, and running down the edge of lake. Surrounded by fields and gardens.

On S edge of town. 2 km E of N85.
Apr–Sep.
4HEC H G P lau pitch45–72 (incl 2 persons)

VOREY
Haute-Loire

Pra de Mars ☎71034086
Apr–Sep.
5HEC H G R lau A5 V3 13 3

WASSELONNE
Bas-Rhin

CM rte de Romanswiller ☎88870008
1 km W on D224.
Apr–Oct.
2HEC H G P lau A10

WIHR-AU-VAL
Haut-Rhin

Route Verte 13 r de la Gare ☎89711010
15 Apr–15 Oct.
0.8HEC H G lau

XONRUPT/LONGEMER
Vosges

Eau-Vive ☎29630737
2 km SE on D67A next to Lac de Longemer.
All year.
1HEC H G lau A8 V6 6 6

Jonquilles ☎29633401
2 km SE on D67A beside Lac de Longemer.
Apr–15 Oct.
4HEC H G R L lau pitch34 (incl 3 persons)

YSSINGEAUX
Haute-Loire

CM Choumouroux ☎71590113
800 m S of town off rte de Puy.
15 Jun–15 Sep.
0.8HEC H R lau P A5 V3 3 3

GERMANY

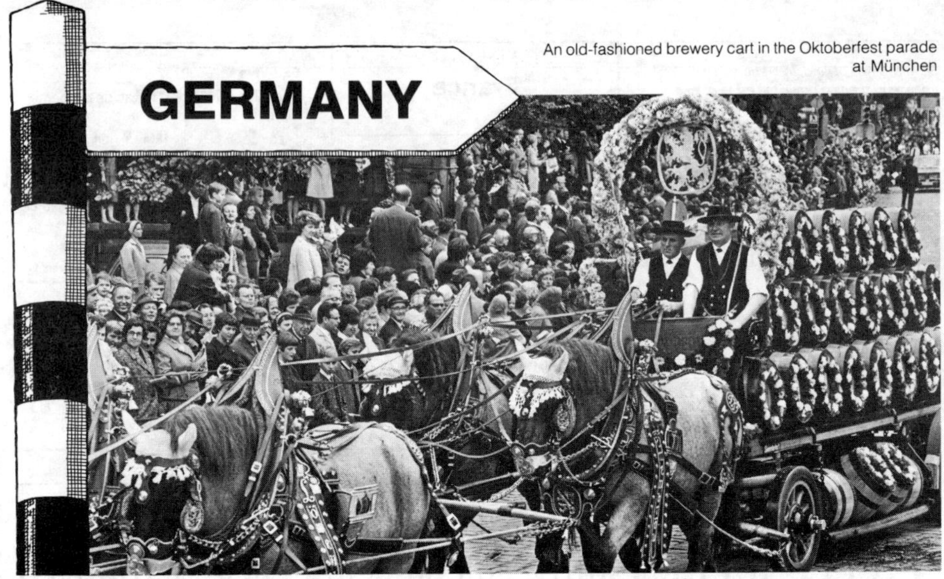

An old-fashioned brewery cart in the Oktoberfest parade at München

The Federal Republic of Germany (West Germany), with its fairytale castles and ancient towns, is a country offering legend and tradition amongst its many attractions. The German Federal Republic is bordered by nine countries: Austria, Belgium, Czechoslovakia, Denmark, German Democratic Republic, France, Luxembourg, Netherlands and Switzerland. It is a country of forests, rivers and mountains. The Rhine Valley boasts magnificent cliffs and woods whilst the Black Forest has some fine valley scenery with countless waterfalls and gorges.

The climate is temperate and variable but Germany enjoys hotter summers than Britain.

HOW TO GET THERE

If you use one of the short-crossing Channel ferries and travel via Belgium, the Federal Republic of Germany is just within a day's drive. The distance from Calais to Köln (Cologne) is just under 260 miles. By driving through northern France and entering Germany near Strasbourg, the journey usually takes two days. This entry point is also used if travelling by the longer Channel crossings: Cherbourg, Caen, Dieppe, or Le Havre to southern Germany. The distance from Le Havre to Strasbourg is 425 miles, a journey which will take at least one or two days. The longer-crossing car ferries operating across the North Sea to the Netherlands can be an advantage if visiting northern Germany. Alternatively, it is possible to use the ferry operating between Harwich and Hamburg.

GENERAL INFORMATION

(see also *Things you need to know*, pages 33–64)

Boats

(see page 33)

British Embassy/Consulates

(see also page 57)

The British Embassy is located at *5300 Bonn 1* Friedrich-Ebert-Allee 77 ☏(0228)234061, but the Embassy has no consular section. There are British Consulates in Berlin, Dusseldorf, Frankfurt/Main, Hamburg and Munich; there are British Consulates with Honorary Consuls in Bremen, Frieburg, Hanover, Nuremberg and Stuttgart.

Camping

There are over 2,000 sites throughout the Federal Republic. Camping is restricted and advanced booking is necessary on the smaller of the East Friesian islands and on Heligoland, because the sites are primarily reserved for organised youth groups or families. The season extends from May to September, but some sites are open all year. Cars are not allowed on Heligoland.

International camping carnet is necessary on some sites and generally recommended when camping in the Federal Republic. Some campsites will allow a reduction in the advertised charge to the holders of a camping carnet. See page 37 for further information.

Off-site camping Permission to camp off an official campsite must be obtained from the landowner or local police. Overnight parking at parking places is tolerated, unless otherwise indicated, provided nearby campsites and hotels are fully booked. However, caravans must remain connected to the towing vehicle. Make sure you do not contravene local regulations.

Currency including banking hours

(see also page 57)
The unit of currency is the Deutsche Mark (*DM*) divided into 100 *Pfennigs*. At the time of going to press £ = *DM* 2.91. Denominations of bank notes are *DM* 5, 10, 20, 100, 500, 1,000; standard coins are *DM* 1, 2, 5 and *Pfennigs* 1, 2, 5, 10, 50. There are no restrictions on the amount of foreign or German currency that a bona fide tourist may import or export.

Most banks are open from Monday to Wednesday and Friday, 08.30–12.00hrs and 14.00–15.30hrs, and on Thursday 08.30–12.00hrs and 14.00–17.30hrs; closed on Saturdays. Exchange offices of the Deutsche-Verkehrs-Kredit-Bank are located at the most important railway stations, road and rail frontier crossing points, and are generally open from early morning until late at night.

Foodstuffs

(see also page 60)
Visitors resident in Europe and entering from an EEC country may import duty-free 1,000g of coffee or 400g of coffee extract and 200g of tea or 80g of tea extract bought duty and tax paid; a reduced allowance applies if bought duty-free, entering from a non EEC country or a non-resident of Europe. Visitors under 15 years of age do not qualify for the duty-free concessions on coffee. Visitors may also import up to 30kg of meat and meat products per person, but meat from Portugal, Spain, Turkey, USSR and non-European countries is strictly forbidden.

Medical treatment

(see page 60)

Shopping hours

Generally these are: *food shops* from Monday to Friday 07.00–13.00hrs and 14.00–18.00hrs, Saturdays 07.00–13.00hrs; *department stores* from Monday to Friday 09.00–18.30hrs, Saturdays 09.00–14.00hrs. Some close for lunch between 13.00 and 15.00hrs.

Tourist information

(see also page 63)
The UK office of the German National Tourist Office is in London at 61 Conduit Street, W1R 0EN, ☎01-734 2600 (recorded message service Monday to Friday 10.00–13.00hrs and 14.00–17.00hrs). In the Federal Republic there are regional tourist associations – (DFV) whilst in most towns there are local tourist offices, usually situated near the railway station or town hall. Any of these organisations will be pleased to help tourists with information and hotel and other accommodation. The offices are usually open 08.30–18.00hrs but in larger towns 20.00hrs.

Visitors' registration

(see page 63)

MOTORING

(see also *Things you need to know*, pages 33–64)

Accidents

(see also page 46)
☎112 for **fire**, ☎110 for **police** and **ambulance** in most areas.
You are generally required to call the police when individuals have been injured or considerable damage has been caused. Not to give aid to anyone injured will render you liable to a fine. Callboxes with two luminous red stripes, installed alongside certain roads, contain an emergency telephone which can be used without inserting money. By lifting the receiver and pulling the emergency lever you are automatically connected with fire or police.

Breakdowns

(see page 48)

Dimensions and weight restrictions

Private **cars** and **trailers** or **caravans** are restricted to the following dimensions – height: 4 metres; width: 2.50 metres; length: 12 metres. The maximum permitted overall length of vehicle/trailer or caravan combination is 18 metres.

A fully laden trailer without an adequate braking system must not weigh more than 50% of the towing vehicle. A fully-laden trailer with an adequate braking system must not weigh more than the towing vehicle.

NORTH SEA
BALTIC SEA
DK
PL
D
NL
DDR
Tinnum
Glücksburg
Langballigau
Falshöft über Kappeln an der Schlei
Oehe-Draecht
Schönhagen
Lürschau bei Schleswig
Loose
Kleinwaabs
Haddeby
Langholz über Eckernförde
Elisabeth Sophienkoog (Island of Nordstrand)
Schöbull
Schönberg
Dänschendorf (Island of Fehmarn)
Burg (Isle of Fehmarn)
Meeschendorf (Island of Fehmarn)
Wulfen (Island of Fehmarn)
Fehmarnsund (Island of Fehmarn)
Tönning
Horst
Heikendorf bei Kiel
St-Peter-Ording
Delve
Preetz
Süssau
Grube
Plön
Grömitz
Dersau
Eutin-Fissau
Neustadt
Malente-Gremsmühlen
Stocksee
Scharbeutz
Büsum
Tellingstedt
Bad Segeberg
Wittenborn
Lübeck
Dorum
Wingst
Dornumersiel
Esens-Bensersiel
Wremen
Klint-bei-Hechthausen
Wittmund
Burhave
Bremerhaven
Hamburg
Büchen
Harsefeld
Zeven
Brietlingen-Reihersee
Bleckede
Leer
Zwischenahn (Bad)
Egestorf
Lüneburg
Melbeck
Tarmstedt
Weener
Elisabethfehn
Bremen
Gartow
Friesoythe
Hatten
Stelle
Wolterdingen
Soltau
Wietzendorf
Suderburg
Bassum
Hermannsburg
Meppen
Wietze-Wieckenberg
Haselünne
Engehausen
Winsen-Aller
Lembruch-Dümmersee
Celle
BERLIN
Wilsum
Lingen
Bissendorf
Ehlerhausen
Gifhorn
Wolfsburg
Dahrenhorst
Hannover
Peine
Osnabrück
Minden
Helmstedt
Borlefzen
Tecklenburg
Kalletal-Varenholz
Rinteln
Wolfenbüttel
Lengerich
Herford
Hameln
Salzhemmendorf
Holle
Ladbergen
Eimke
Lemgo
Sassenbergbei Warendorf
Pyrmont (Bad)
Barntrup
Bodenwerder
Goslar
Harzburg (Bad)
Gandersheim (Bad)
Dülmen
Stukenbrook
Horn-Bad Meinberg
Holzminden
Clausthal-Zellerfeld
Altenau
Wissel
Lüdinghausen
Osterode
Braunlage
Haldern
Schloss Neuhaus
Uslar
Northeim
St Andreasberg
Gahlen
Hardegsen
Walkenried
Trendelburg
Oberweser
Mülheim
Essen
Niederbergheim
Diemels
Warburg
Dransfeld
A7
A1
A24
A27
A28
A29
A30
A2
A3
A43
A44
E26
E30
E51
75
207
213
65

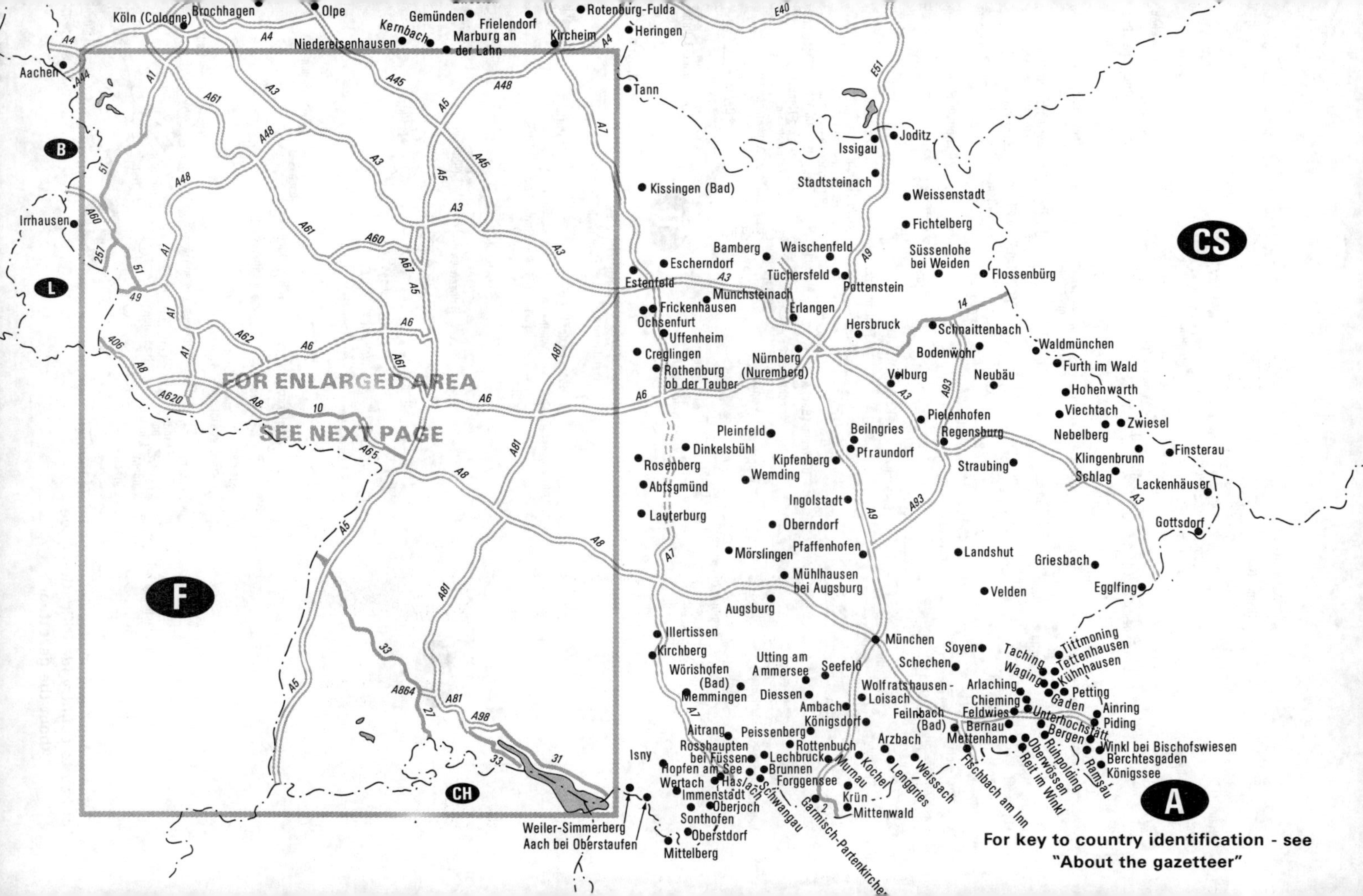

Köln (Cologne)
Brochhagen
Olpe
Gemünden
Frielendorf
Rotenburg-Fulda
Heringen
Kernbach
Niedereisenhausen
Marburg an der Lahn
Kircheim
Aachen
Tann
Irrhausen
Joditz
Issigau
Stadtsteinach
Weissenstadt
Fichtelberg
Kissingen (Bad)
Bamberg
Waischenfeld
Süssenlohe bei Weiden
Flossenbürg
Escherndorf
Tüchersfeld
Pottenstein
Estenfeld
Münchsteinach
Frickenhausen
Ochsenfurt
Erlangen
Hersbruck
Schnaittenbach
Uffenheim
Creglingen
Nürnberg (Nuremberg)
Waldmünchen
Bodenwöhr
Furth im Wald
Rothenburg ob der Tauber
Velburg
Neubäu
Hohenwarth
Viechtach
Zwiesel
Pielenhofen
Regensburg
Nebelberg
Pleinfeld
Beilngries
Pfraundorf
Finsterau
Dinkelsbühl
Rosenberg
Kipfenberg
Straubing
Klingenbrunn
Schlag
Lackenhäuser
Wemding
Abtsgmünd
Ingolstadt
Lauterburg
Oberndorf
Gottsdorf
Mörslingen
Pfaffenhofen
Landshut
Griesbach
Mühlhausen bei Augsburg
Velden
Egglfing
Augsburg
Illertissen
München
Soyen
Tittmoning
Taching
Tettenhausen
Kirchberg
Utting am Ammersee
Seefeld
Schechen
Waging
Kühnhausen
Wörishofen (Bad)
Wolfratshausen - Loisach
Arlaching
Petting
Memmingen
Diessen
Chieming
Gaden
Ainring
Ambach
Feldwies
Unterhochstätt
Piding
Königsdorf
Feilnbach (Bad)
Bernau
Bergen
Aitrang
Peissenberg
Mettenham
Winkl bei Bischofswiesen
Rosshaupten bei Füssen
Rottenbuch
Arzbach
Berchtesgaden
Lechbruck
Königssee
Isny
Hopfen am See
Brunnen
Murnau
Kochel
Lenggries
Weissach
Fischbach am Inn
Oberwössen
Ruhpolding
Ramsau
Reit im Winkl
Wertach
Haslach
Forggensee
Immenstadt
Schwangau
Krün
Oberjoch
Mittenwald
Sonthofen
Garmisch-Partenkirchen
Weiler-Simmerberg
Aach bei Oberstaufen
Oberstdorf
Mittelberg
FOR ENLARGED AREA
SEE NEXT PAGE
CS
B
L
F
CH
A
E40
E51
A1
A3
A4
A5
A6
A7
A8
A9
A44
A45
A48
A60
A61
A62
A65
A67
A81
A93
A98
A620
A864
10
14
27
31
33
49
51
257
406
For key to country identification - see
"About the gazetteer"

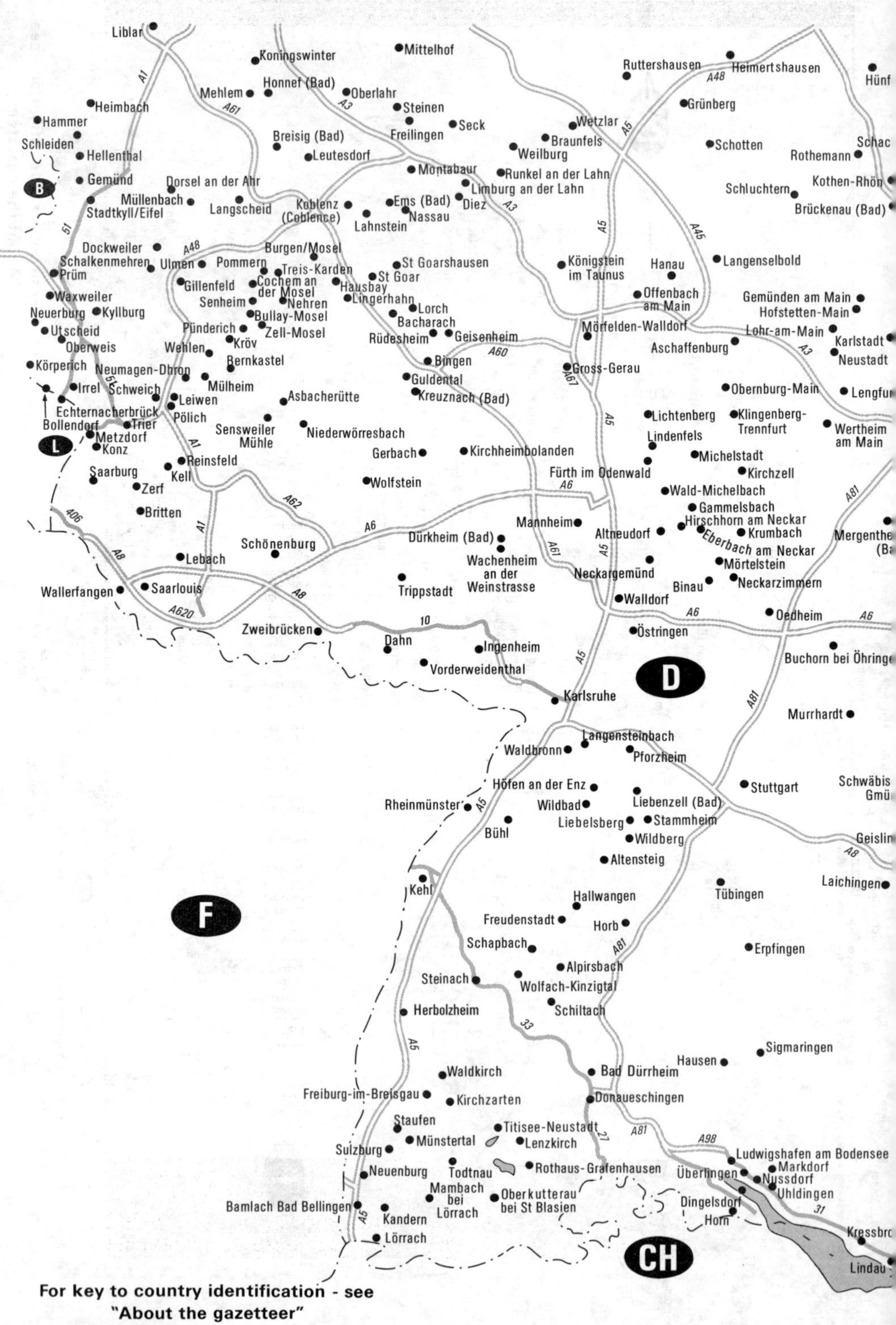

For key to country identification - see "About the gazetteer"

Driving Licence

(see also page 33)
A valid UK or Republic of Ireland licence is acceptable in the Federal Republic. The minimum age at which a visitor may drive a temporarily imported car or motorcycle is 17 years.

Lights

(see page 50 also *Headlights* page 41)

Motoring clubs

(see also page 61)
The principal German motoring clubs are the *Allgemeiner Deutscher Automobil Club* (ADAC) and the *Deutscher Touring Automobil Club* (DTC) who have offices in the larger towns, and the ADAC also has offices at major frontier crossings. The head office addresses are *8000 München 70* Am Westpark 8 ☎(089)76760 and *8000 Müchen 60* Amalienburgstrasse 23 ☎(089)8111048 respectively.

Passengers

(see also page 51)
Children under 12 are not permitted to travel in a vehicle as front seat passengers when rear seating is available.

Petrol

(see page 61)

Roads

The *Bundesstrassen* or state roads vary in quality. In the north and in the touring areas of the Rhine Valley, Black Forest, and Bavaria, the roads are good and well graded. A comprehensive motorway (Autobahn) network dominates the road system and takes most of the long-distance traffic.

Traffic at weekends increases considerably during the school holidays which are from July to mid September. In order to ease congestion, heavy lorries are prohibited on all roads at summer weekends, and on all Sundays and public holidays.

Seat belts

(see page 52)

Speed limits

Car
Built-up areas
*50 kph (31 mph)
Other roads
100 kph (62 mph)
Motorways/Dual carriageways
*130 kph (80 mph)

Car/caravan/trailer
Built-up areas
50 kph (31 mph)
Other roads
80 kph (49 mph)
Motorways/Dual carriageways
80 kph (49 mph)

*If signposted, otherwise recommended maximum speed.

Outside built-up areas, motor vehicles to which a special speed limit applies, as well as vehicles with trailers with a combined length of more than 7 metres (23ft), must keep sufficient distance from the preceding vehicle so that an overtaking vehicle may pull in. Slow moving vehicles must allow a line of following vehicles to pass. If necessary the driver must stop at a suitable place to allow this.

Warning triangle

The use of a warning triangle is compulsory in the event of accident or breakdown. The triangle must be placed on the road about 100 metres (109 yds) behind the vehicle to warn following traffic of any obstruction. Vehicles over 2,500kg (2tons 9cwt 24lb) must also carry a yellow flashing light.

Although the warning triangle sold by the AA does not correspond exactly to the type prescribed for Germany, it is legally acceptable for use by a *bona fide* tourist. See also *Warning triangles/Hazard warning lights* page 54.

Prices are in German Marks (Deutschmarks)

Abbreviations:
pl Platz
str Strasse

AACH BEI OBERSTAUFEN
Bayern (☎08386)

Aach ☎363

A terraced site with beautiful views of the mountains. Sauna, solarium, kitchen, TV room, games room.

From Oberstaufen follow B308 for 7 km towards the Austrian border.
All year.
2HEC ▥ ◇ ⋒H |O| ⊙ G R ⊞ lau R A6 V1 5 5

AACHEN
Nordrhein-Westfalen (☎0241)

Passtrasse ☎155495

Municipal site in town centre near the Kurplatz. Becomes very full during the peak season.

May–Sep.
1.5HEC ▥ ◆ ⋒H |O| ⊙ R ⊞ lau A4 V3 5 3

ABTSGMÜND
Baden-Württemberg (☎07963)

At **POMMERTSWEILER** (6 km N)

Hammerschmiede-See ☎369

A terraced site in a wooded setting beside the lake. Partly divided into pitches with concrete paths.

From Abtsgmünd travel for 3 km then turn N to Pommertsweiler, site signposted.
All year.

5HEC ◆ H G R L lau **A**4 **V**4 4 4

AFFOLDERN See **EDERTAL**

AINRING
Bayern (☎08654)

At **FELDKIRCHEN** (3 km SE)

Berger ☎8487

On a gently sloping meadow with two terraces, on the edge of woodland.

Turn left at ARAL filling station in Feldkirchen, and continue for 1.5 km.
All year.

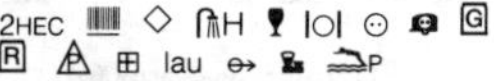

AITRANG
Bayern (☎08343)

Elbsee 3 ☎248

On the E shore of the lake with good bathing facilities. Section reserved for campers with dogs.

Take B12 from Marktoberdorf travel for 11 km then turn N to Aitrang.
All year.

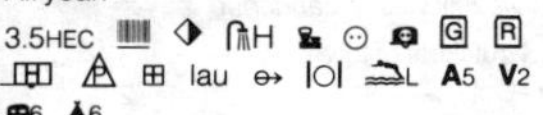

ALPIRSBACH
Baden-Württemberg (☎07444)

Wolpert ☎6313

On level land beside the River Kinzig.

1 km N of town below B294.
20 May–20 Sep.

1HEC ◆ H G lau **A**5 **V**4 4 4

ALTENAU
Niedersachsen (☎05328)

Okertalsperre ☎702

On a long stretch of grassland at the S end of the Oker Reservoir. Lunchtime siesta 13.00–15.00 hrs.

Signposted from B498 (Oker–Altenau road).
All year.

3HEC ◆ H G R L lau

Polstertal ☎(05323)5582

A terraced site in a wood with a lake nearby.

2 km from the Altenau–Clausthal–Zellerfeld road. Signposted.
All year.

1.7HEC ◆ H G R L lau **A**4 pitch8

ALTENSTEIG
Baden-Württemberg (☎07453)

Schwarzwald ☎8415

Parkland site of motor sport club Altensteig beside the River Nagold. Separate section for dog owners.

Germany

On road to Garrweiler 1 km from Altensteig.
All year.

5HEC ◆ H G R R lau **A**5 pitch6

ALTNEUDORF
Baden-Württemberg (☎06228)

Steinachperle ☎467

The site lies in the narrow shady valley of the River Steinach. Lunchtime siesta 13.00–15.00 hrs.

The entrance to the camp lies next to the Gasthaus zum Pflug, on the outskirts of Altneudorf.
Etr–Sep.

AMBACH
Bayern (☎08177)

Hirth ☎546

Beautifully situated site completely divided into pitches. Two summer curling rinks.

S of village between Starnberg–Seeshaupt road and lake.
All year.

3HEC ◆ H G R L

ARLACHING
Bayern (☎08667)

Kupferschmiede ☎446

On meadowland. Partially gravel.

On Seebruck-Traunstein road.
Apr–Sep.

2HEC ◆ H R lau L **A**5 pitch7

ARZBACH
Bayern (☎08042)

Arzbach Alpenbadstr 20 ☎8408

Almost level site with fine views of the mountains.

9 km S of Bad Tolz on road running parallel to west bank of river.
All year.

1.5HEC ◇ H P

ASBACHERHÜTTE
Rhineland-Pfalz (☎06786)

Harfenmühle ☎7076

A quiet site, beautifully situated in Fischbach Valley. Level grassland, partly terraced.

3 km NW off the B327 towards Kempfeld.
All year.

3.3HEC ◆ ◇ H G R R lau **A**5 **V**2 5 5

ASCHAFFENBURG
Hessen (☎06188)

At **KARLSTEIN-GROSSWEIZHEIM**

Freizeitgebiet Grossweizheim ☎5094

The site lies between a pine forest and an extensive gravel pit lake.

From town follow B8 towards Hanau, at N end of Grossweizheim, turn right.
All year.

24HEC ◇ H G lau L **A**4 **V**4 4 4

ASCHHAUSEN See **ZWISCHENAHN (BAD)**

ATTENDORN
Nordrhein-Westfalen (☎02722)

Biggesee-Waldenburg ☎3527

Generously terraced recreational site on the northern shore of the Bigge Reservoir, with adjoining public bathing area. Private sunbathing area. Lunchtime siesta 13.00–15.00 hrs.

From Attendorn follow road towards Heldren. Shortly after the railway turn right and follow the signs to the site, about 1.5 km on.
All year.

6.5HEC ◆ H G R lau LP **A**7 **V**4 8 8

Hof Biggen Finnentroper Str 131 ☎5961

Well-equipped terraced site, surrounded by woodlands. Lunchtime siesta 13.00–15.00 hrs.

Follow Attendorn road to Ahauser Reservoir. Entrance near 'Haus am See' inn.
All year.

10HEC ◇ H G R lau **A**5 **V**2 5 3

AUGSBURG
Bayern (☎0821)

Augusta ☎707575

Hard standings for caravans. Separate section for residential caravans.

Leave E11 by Augsburg–Ost exit. Continue N towards Neuburg and turn right after 400 m.
All year.

5HEC ◆ H

BACHARACH
Rheinland-Pfalz (☎06743)

Sonnenstrand ☎1752

A beautifully situated site on grassland beside the Rhine with some high trees.

The turn off from B9 into the site can be difficult for caravans coming from the north, due to one way traffic.
All year.

1.2HEC ◆ H G R lau **A**5 **V**4 4 4

BAD Each name preceded by 'Bad' is listed under the name which follows it.

Germany

BALHORN
Hessen (☎05625)

Erzeberg ☎5274

Site lies on meadowland on slightly sloping ground above the village. Lunchtime siesta 13.00–15.00 hrs.

On B450 between Istha and Fritzlar.
All year.

4HEC lau P

BAMBERG
Bayern (☎0951)

At **BUG** (5 km S)

Insel ☎56320

The site lies on the bank of the River Regnitz, S of Bamberg.

If approaching from the S, leave motorway at Bamberg exit, take B505 and then B4 towards Bamberg. If approaching from N, drive through Bamberg on B4 and leave it at Nürnberg exit.
All year.

5HEC R lau A5 V4 4 2–4

BAMLACH BAD BELLINGEN
Baden-Württemberg (☎07635)

Lug Ins Land ☎1820

Level terrain and a terrace on S outskirts of the town. Silence required at midday and at night. No admittance after 21.00 hrs.

2 km S of the spa Bad Bellingen. Via Karlsruhe–Basel motorway, exit Kleinkems. Turn left after continuing for 200 m then continue N for 4 km.
All year.

3HEC lau R A5 pitch11–23

BANNWALDSEE See **SCHWANGAU**

BARKHAUSEN See **MINDEN**

BARNTRUP
Nordrhein-Westfalen (☎05263)

Schwimmbad ☎2221

This well-kept site lies next to an open-air swimming pool, which is covered over in autumn and winter.

Barntrup lies on B66, near to junction with B1. Approach signposted from Barntrup.
All year.

2.4HEC P lau A5 V2 pitch6

BARTHOLOMÄ See **LAUTERBURG**

BASSUM
Niedersachsen (☎04241)

At **GROSS-RINGMAR**

Gross-Ringmar Dorfstr 15 ☎5292

On level meadow with trees. Situated approx. 200 m from the edge of the village.

Turn off B51 approx. 3 km SW of Bassum.
All year.

10HEC LP lau A4 pitch10

BAUMBERG
Nordrhein-Westfalen (☎02173)

Bürgel ☎63623

On a long stretch of unshaded land in a protected area beside the River Rhine, surrounded by poplars and bushes. Lunchtime siesta 12.00–15.00 hrs.

From Düsseldorf take B8 to Benrath (10 km). Continue towards Baumberg for approx. 5 km.
Apr–Sep.

5HEC

BEILNGRIES
Bayern (☎08461)

Beilngries ☎8406

Modern, well-tended municipal site on grassland with trees in the Altmühl.

Access via A9/E6 (München–Nürnberg) road exit Altmühital about 18 km NE turn right, off B299 towards Landshut.
25 Dec–Oct.

2.8HEC RP lau A5 pitch7

BERCHTESGADEN
Bayern (☎08652)

Allweglehen ☎2396

A terraced site at the foot of the Untersalzberg Mountain surrounded by bushy woods. There is a steep and narrow asphalt access road with passing places. A truck is available for towing caravans. The camp is closed between 12.30 and 14.30 hrs and from 21.00 hrs.

For access, take the B305, and drive approx 3.5 km towards Schellenberg.
All year.

1.4HEC P lau

BERENBROCK See **LÜDINGHAUSEN**

BERGEN
Bayern (☎08662)

Wagnerhof Campingstr 11 ☎8557

Level site.

Access from München–Salzburg motorway, Bergen exit. Turn right at saw mill just before entering town.
All year.

3HEC lau P A5 pitch8

BERLIN (☎030)

At **KLADOW**

DCC Else-Eckert-Platz Krampnitzer Weg 111–117 ☎2979

All year.

lau L A6 pitch5

At **WANNSEE**

Kohlhasenbrück Neue Kreisstr ☎8051737

Very pleasantly situated site on shore of Lake Griebnitz, owned by Deutscher Camping Club. Bathing area. Most of site taken up by residential campers.

From Wannsee railway station, drive through Königstr, past Rathaus, through Chausseestr, Kohlhasenbrückerstr, and Kreisstr.
Apr–Sep.

8.2HEC L

BERNAU
Bayern (☎08051)

At **FELDEN** (3 km N)

Chiemsee-Süd ☎7540

Level meadowland shaded by trees, on lake shore.

Leave the A8/E11 (München–Salzburg) at exit Felden, continue W towards lake.
May–Sep.

2HEC lau L

BERNKASTEL
Rheinland-Pfalz (☎06531)

Kueser Werth ☎8200

Grassy site near Mosel and boating marina, with view of Castle Landshut.

On S outskirts of town.
Apr–Oct.

2.1HEC lau P A4 V2 6 4–6

BETTINGEN See **WERTHEIM AM MAIN**

BINAU
Baden-Württemberg (☎06263)

(9 km NW of **NECKARZIMMERN** adjacent to River Neckar).

Trailer ☎669

Located on the banks of the Neckar. Good leisure facilities.

Off B37 (Heidelberg–Heilbron) road on right bank of Neckar.
All year.

3HEC R P lau A5 V4 4 3

BINGEN
Rheinland-Pfatz (☎06721)

At **TRECHTINGSHAUSEN** (8 km NW)

Marlenort ☎6133

The site is divided into two sections by the Moorgenbach brook, and lies on meadowland, in a beautiful setting directly next to the River Rhine and at the foot of two castles (Burg Reichenstein and Burg Rheinstein).

From Bingen follow road B9 to the NW for about 8 km. Entry for caravans is 500 m on at the railway station. Both approaches can be difficult for caravans. Busy railway – care needed at level crossing.
All year.

2HEC lau A5 V2 4 4

BINGUM MARINA See **LEER**

BISSENDORF
Niedersachsen (☎05402)

Erholungszentrum ☎8547

Site lies on level meadowland at a lake, near the motorway and the airport. Lunchtime siesta 13.00–15.00 hrs. Separate section for transit campers near the noisy motorway.

From motorway exit Langenhagen/ Kaltenweide follow signs to site S of Bissendorf.
15 Mar–15 Nov.
8HEC H L lau

BLECKEDE
Niedersachsen (☎05852)

Alt-Garge (ADAC owned) am Waldbad 23 ☎(05854)311

A modern site surrounded by tall trees, lying at the SE end of Alt-Garge next to a heated swimming pool in the woods. The camp has its own gas-filling station. Archery butts. Lunchtime siesta 13.00–14.30 hrs.

5 km SE of Bleckede.
All year.
6HEC H R lau P

BLIESDORF See **NEUSTADT (Schleswig-Holstein)**

BODENWERDER
Niedersachsen (☎05533)

Himmelspforte ☎4938

Site on grassland, with a fruit orchard, next to River Weser. Good possibilities for water sport. Separate section and common room for young campers.

Cross River Weser and turn right towards Rühle. Site is in about 2 km.
All year.
5HEC H R P lau

Rühler Schweiz ☎2827

The site lies on well-kept meadowland by the River Weser.

From the Weser Bridge in Bodenwerder and follow road for 4 km towards Rühle.
All year.
5HEC H G P lau

BODENWÖHR
Bayern (☎09434)

Ludwigsheide ☎523

Slightly sloping meadowland on S banks of Hammersee.

Apr–Sep.
1.1HEC H G R L lau

Welchselbrunn Ludwigsheide 50 ☎523

Gently sloping meadowland on S banks of Hammersee. Shade in section above access road. Under same management as Ludwigsheide.

Signposted.
Apr–15 Oct.

Germany

1.4HEC H G R L lau

BÖHL See **ST-PETER-ORDING**

BOLLENDORF
Rheinland-Pfalz (☎06526)

Altschmiede ☎375

The site lies at a farm, on a long stretch of meadowland next to the River Sauer. It is situated partly on level ground and partly on slightly sloping ground.

From Bitburg on road B257 to Echternacherbrück, then for 7 km in NW direction to Bollendorf. At end of village take road towards 'Köperich', 1.5 km to site. Final section is narrow.
Apr–Oct.
3HEC H R

BÖMIGHAUSEN
Nordrhein-Westfalen (☎05632)

Barenberg ☎1044

Beautifully terraced site at Neerdar reservoir.

Access from B251 between Korbach and Brilon.
All year.
2HEC H G R L

BORLEFZEN
Nordrhein-Westfalen (☎05733)

Borlefzen ☎80008

Apr–Oct.
36HEC H G R L lau A6 Vn/c 4 4

BRAUNFELS
Hessen (☎06442)

Braunfels ☎4366

A terraced site surrounded by a forest of pine and deciduous trees. Separate meadow for touring campers. Lunchtime siesta 12.30–14.30 hrs.

Access from Köln–Frankfurt motorway, exit 'Limburg', then B49 towards town.
15 Mar–Oct.
1.6HEC H G R lau P A5 V3 7 5–7

BRAUNLAGE
Niedersachsen (☎05520)

Ferien vom Ich ☎413

Quiet site, partly on different levels, near woodland inn 'Onkel Fred's Hütte'.

2 km from town centre on B27 towards Lauterberg.
All year.
5.2HEC H G R lau P A4 V3 4 3

At **ZORGE** (14 km S)

Waldwinkel ☎(05586)1048

A site on different levels, surrounded by high trees, 200 m from an open-air woodland pool in Kunzen Valley.

14 km from Braunlage on the B4 to Zorge. Closed Nov.
1HEC H R lau P

BREISIG (BAD)
Rheinland-Pfalz (☎02633)

Rheineck ☎95645

A quiet, well-kept site on a level meadow in Vinxtbach Valley.

From Koblenz follow B9 NW to Bad Breisig, then turn left, cross railway and continue for 400 m.
All year.
5HEC H G R lau P A4 V2 3 3

BREITENBACH
Bayern (☎08026)

At **SCHLIERSEE**

Lido ☎6624

The site lies on the NW shore of the lake, amid beautiful scenery. Divided into two sections by a stream.

SW of village off the B307.
May–15 Oct.
1HEC H R L

BREMEN
Bremen (☎0421)

Freie Hansestadt Bremen Bennigsenstr 2–6 ☎212002

Situated in a Nature Reserve 700 m from lake.

Access from autobahn A27 exit University Bremen.
26 Mar–2 Nov.
5.8HEC H R lau L A6 pitch8

BREMERHAVEN
Bremen (☎0471)

Spadener See Seeweg 2 ☎801022

Level grassland close to a lake and adjoining a holiday and leisure complex (under development).

From A27 (Bremerhaven–Cuxhaven) take exit 'Bremerhaven–Überseehafen' in direction of Spaden.
All year.
10HEC H G L lau

BRIETLINGEN-REIHERSEE
Niedersachsen (☎04133)

Reihersee 1 ☎3671

Divided into pitches by hedges and pine trees. Private bathing area.

At car park, 2 km beyond Brietlingen, turn E towards Reihersee and continue for 800 m.
All year. ➔

6.2HEC lau LR

BRINGHAUSEN See **EDERTAL**

BRITTEN
Saarland (06872)
AZUR Saar Reiterhof Girtenmühle 3879
The site lies on a slightly sloping, open meadowland, set around the main building. The lower section is bordered by the Loscheimer Bach (Brook).
1 km off the main B268.
All year.
2HEC H lau P A5 pitch7–8

BROCHHAGEN
Nordrhein-Westfalen (02266)
Wiesengrund 8978
Well-kept site in peaceful surroundings. Lunchtime siesta 13.00–15.00 hrs.
From Köln follow road B55 E to Engelskirchen. Then go N towards Lindlar and Brochhagen.
All year.
3.5HEC H lau R

BROCHTERBECK See **TECKLENBURG**

BRUCHHAUSEN See **OLSBERG**

BRUCHKÖBEL See **HANAU**

BRÜCKENAU (BAD)
Bayern
At **OBERZELL** (6 km NW)
Terrassencamping Kringelweg (06664)512
Beautifully situated, terraced site on slightly sloping meadowland.
From Würzburg–Fulda motorway A7/E70 leave at exit Bad Brückenau/Volkers, then N on B27 towards Fulda as far as Speicherz, then left to Oberzell.
Apr–Oct.
H

BRUNNEN FORGGENSEE
Bayern (08362)
Brunnen Seestr 81 8273

Germany

Situated on E shore of Lake Forggensee.
From Füssen follow B17 to Schwangau, then continue N on minor road.
6 Dec–5 Nov.
2HEC H L lau A7 pitch6

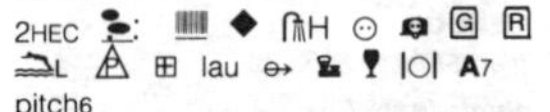

BÜCHEN
Schleswig-Holstein (04155)
Waldschwimmbad 5360
On gently sloping grassland. Lunchtime siesta 13.00–15.00 hrs.
From Lauenburg or Mölln follow road to Büchen then follow signposts to site.
All year.
1.6HEC H lau P

BUCHHORN BEI ÖHRINGEN
Baden-Württemberg (07941)
Seewiese 61568
7 km S of Öhringen via Pfedelbach.
All year.
3HEC H L lau P A5 V2 2 2

BUG See **BAMBERG**

BÜHL
Baden-Württemberg (07223)
Adam Campingstr 1 23194
On level grassland, by lake.
1 km from the Bühl exit of the A5/E4–E11 (Karlsruhe-Basel) in direction of Lichtenau.
All year.
17.5HEC H L lau A7 V4 4 4

BULLAY-MOSEL
Rheinland-Pfalz (06542)
Moselstrand International 22921
On level meadow on right bank of the Mosel, next to the football ground. Fine view.
Access via B49 Cochem-Alf, then over the bridge and through the village.
Signposted.
Apr–Oct.
1.6HEC H lau RP A5 V5 5 5

BURG (Island of Fehmarn)
Schleswig-Holstein (04371)
At **KLAUSDORF** (5 km NW)
Klausdorf 2549
A grassy site with sea views. Divided into pitches. Sandy beach. Lunchtime siesta 12.30–14.30 hrs.
From Burg turn off the main road 2.5 km before Klausdorf onto a narrow asphalt road.
Apr–Sep.
4HEC H lau

BÜRGEL See **OFFENBACH AM MAIN**

BURGEN/MOSEL
Rheinland-Pfalz (02605)
Burgen 2396
A well maintained site with individual pitches set on level meadow with trees by the River Mosel. Site is broken up by shrubs and flower beds.
On the B49 (Kloblenz–Treis).
Apr–15 Oct.
4HEC H RP lau A5 V3 4 2–4

BURHAVE
Niedersachsen (04733)
Burhave III 888
A municipal site between dyke and the sea.
From Nordenham on coastal road NW to Burhave then right to site.
May–Sep.
3.1HEC H lau S

BÜSUM
Schleswig-Holstein (04834)
Nordsee Nordseestr 90 2515
Situated immediately behind the high dyke. The site is divided into two and surrounded

by tall bushes. Lunchtime siesta 12.30–14.00 hrs.
Apr–15 Oct.
3.5HEC lau A5 pitch9

BUXHEIM See **MEMMINGEN**

CELLE
Niedersachsen (05141)
Silbersee 31223
Site lies on level meadowland in woodland near a lake and the railway line. Firm site management. Unaccompanied teenagers not admitted. Lunchtime siesta 13.00–15.00 hrs.
From Celle, follow road B191 towards Uelzen. After 4 km turn left onto minor road towards site.
All year.
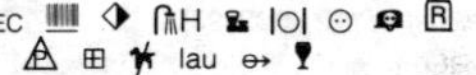
lau

CHIEMING
Bayern (08664)
Chieming Möwenplatz Haupstr 3 361
Small site on shore of lake, with gravelly terrain.
5 km S of Chieming.
Apr–Sep.
1.1HEC lau A6 pitch7

CLAUSTHAL-ZELLERFELD
Niedersachsen (05323)
Prahljust 1300
The site lies on slightly sloping grassland in an area of woodland and lakes.
Follow road B242 SE from outskirts 2 km in direction of Braunlage, then turn right to site in 1.5 km.
All year.
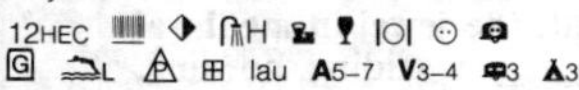
lau A5–7 V3–4 3 A3

Waldweben 1712
Holiday village with individual pitches in open meadow and coniferous woodland by three small lakes.
Signposted from B241 in direction of Goslar.
All year.
4.5HEC A4 V3 3 A3

COBLENCE See **KOBLENZ**

COCHEM AN DER MOSEL
Rheinland-Pfalz (02671)
Freizeltzentrum 4409
Site lies on level meadowland with trees. On right bank of the Mosel, downstream from the swimming pool and sports ground.
In town cross the Mosel bridge, turn sharp right, follow signs 'Wellenbad' along riverside road for 1 km.
end Mar–15 Oct.
1.4HEC lau A4 V3 4–5 A4–5

Germany

Schausten 7528
The site consists of two sections. The lower part is set on a meadow with fruit trees, situated in the narrow valley between the Endertbach (brook) and a hillside. The upper part is terraced and lies between vineyards. There are fine views.
In town, at the Mosel bridge, turn off road B49 towards Mayen, then 1 km to site – narrow entrance to site.
Etr–Oct.
1HEC lau A4 V2 5–6 A4–6

At **LANDKERN** (7 km N)
Altes Forsthaus Hauptstr 2 8701
The partly terraced site lies near woodland in the valley below Landkern.
From motorway A48 (Eifel motorway) leave at exit Kaisersesch, go S to Landkern, then follow signs to site.
All year.
6HEC lau A3 V3 4 A4

COLOGNE See **KÖLN**

CREGLINGEN
Baden-Württemberg (07933)
AZUR-Münstercamping 321
A site completely divided into pitches, lying on the S outskirts of Münster. Children's playground. Individual washing cubicles.
If approaching from Bad Mergentheim or from Rothenburg/Tauber, take the 'Romantic road' up to Creglingen. Then turn S and drive 3 km up to Münster.
All year.
6HEC lau A6 pitch8–9

DAHN
Rheinland-Pfalz (06391)
Büttelwoog 5622
Site lies in a magnificent pine forest, partly surrounded by steep hills and rocks. Section reserved for young people with tents. Lunchtime siesta 12.00–14.00 hrs.
From Pirmasens follow B10 up to Hinterweidenthal then S on B427 to Dahn.
All year.
3HEC lau A7 pitch7

DAHRENHORST
Niedersachsen (05173)
Irenensee 7583
A lakeside site on meadowland, partly surrounded by woods, with separate sections for tourers, statics and residentials. Lunchtime siesta 13.00–15.00 hrs.

From Burgdorf follow road B188 for about 15 km towards Uetze.
All year.
120HEC lau

DÄNSCHENDORF (Island of Fehmarn)
Schleswig-Holstein (04372)
Fehmarnbelt 445
The site lies at the north western tip of the island.
Access via the B207/E4, turn left after the Fehmarnsund Bridge and drive through Landkirchen, Lemkendorf, Dänschendorf and Altenteil up to the dyke.
Apr–Sep.
7.5HEC lau

DELLIEHAUSEN SOLLING See **USLAR**

DELVE
Schleswig-Holstein (04836)
Eldertal (04803)1058
Meadow site with bushes and trees beside the River Eider.
All year.
3HEC lau

DERNEBURG See **HOLLE**

DERSAU
Schleswig-Holstein (04526)
Seeblick 563
Grassy site enclosed by hedging at W end of Grosser Plöner See.
Apr–15 Oct.
3.2HEC lau

DIEMELSEE-HERINGHAUSEN
Nordrhein-Westfalen (05633)
Seeblick Arnold 388
The fenced-in site lies next to the Diemel-Stausee (reservoir) at the Craststätte Seeblick.
From Brilon follow road B7 eastwards to Messinghausen, here turn off main road and follow road to Diemel-Stausee (8 km).
All year.
3HEC lau A3 pitch6

DIESSEN
Bayern (08807)
St-Alban 7305
Clean site next to St-Alban, lakeside with private bathing beach and reserved section for residential campers. Good sanitary installations also used by the public.
From München follow B12 towards Landsberg/Lech. Near Greifenberg turn left, proceed via Utting to St-Alban.
Etr–Sep.
0.6HEC A5 pitch11

DIEZ
Rheinland-Pfalz (06432) ➤

Ochsenwiese ☎2122

On a meadow on the left bank of the River Lahn, below Schloss Oranienstein.

From N leave motorway A3 at Diez exit (from S at Limburg-Nord exit) then continue on B54 for approx 7 km.
Apr–Oct.

7HEC lau A4 V4 4 2–4

DINGELSDORF
Baden-Württemberg (☎07533)

Fliesshorn ☎5262

At a farm, on meadowland with fine trees.

In town turn off Staad-Dettingen road and follow signs to NW for 1.3 km.
Apr–Sep.

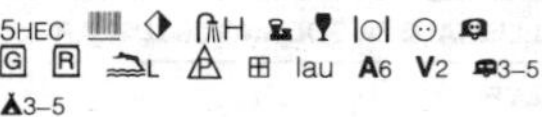

5HEC lau A6 V2 3–5 3–5

DINKLESBÜHL
Bayern (☎09851)

Romantische Strasse ☎7817

Terraced site with some hedges and trees. Separate field for young people. Good sporting facilities.

Signposted.
All year.

9HEC lau A5 pitch5–10

Germany

DOCKWEILER
Rheinland-Pfatz (☎06595)

LUBA-Freizeit-Part ☎400

LUBA Caravan and Holiday Village. A terraced site with individual pitches and two small lakes.

From A48 motorway (Eifel autobahn) leave at exit 'Mehren/Daun', then follow B421 for 18 km via Daun.
All year.

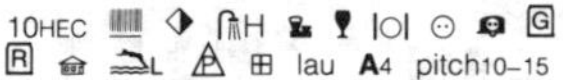

10HEC lau A4 pitch10–15

DONAUESCHINGEN
Baden-Württemberg (☎0771)

Riedsee ☎5511

Level meadow on lakeside.

Turn off A81 at exit 'Geisingen' and continue 13 km on B31 towards Pfohren, then turn left and continue for 1 km.
All year.

8HEC lau A5 pitch9

DORNUMERSIEL
Niedersachsen (☎04933)

SC Nordsee ☎351

Municipal site beside the sea, opposite Langeoog island, between dyke and bathing beach.

From Essens take B210 for 4 km then travel W 10 km.
15 Apr–Sep.

3HEC lau

DORTMUND
Nordrhein-Westfalen (☎0231)

Hohensyburg Syburger Dorfstr 69 ☎774374

Terraced site on hilly grassland near Weitkamp inn.

All year.

11.5HEC lau A5 V3 6 5–10

DORSEL AN DER AHR
Rheinland-Pfalz (☎02693)

Stahlhütte ☎438

Site with individual pitches, on meadowland with trees near River Ahr.

Off B258 (Aachen-Koblenz) road.
All year.

5HEC lau A4 Vn/c 8 8

DORUM
Schleswig-Holstein (☎04742)

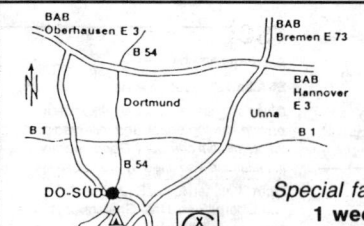

Kransburger See Kransburger Str 1 ☎8160
All year.
23HEC lau pitch15–20

DRANSFELD
Niedersachsen (☎05502)

SC Hohen Hagen ☎2147
Well laid out municipal site. Lunchtime siesta 13.00–15.00 hrs.

S of town off Hohen Hagen road.
All year.
12HEC lau

At **LÖWENHAGEN** (5 km NW)

Löwenhagen ☎2157
The site lies on a long stretch of meadowland beside the River Nieme, in a well wooded area, at the Gasthaus Spiessmühle.

Follow the B3, Kassel-Göttingen to the outskirts of Dransfeld, then turn NW and continue via Imbsen to Löwenhagen.
All year.
2HEC

DÜLMEN
Nordrhein-Westfalen (☎02594)

Tannenwiese Borkenbergestr 217 ☎4795
The site lies on meadowland in a well wooded country area, near the gliderdrome. Lunchtime siesta 12.30–14.30 hrs.

Take the B51 from Recklinghausen towards Münster as far as Hausdülmen, then follow signpost 'Segelflugplatz Borkenberge'.
Mar–Oct.
3.7HEC lau A4 V2 4 4

DÜNNWALD See **KÖLN (COLOGNE)**

Germany

DÜRKHEIM (BAD)
Rheinland-Pfalz (☎06322)

AZUR–Knaus ☎61356
Lakeside site on level meadow between vineyards, adjoining a sportsfield. Lunchtime siesta 12.00–15.00 hrs.

Access from E outskirts of town. Turn N at railway viaduct, near JET petrol station.
Feb–20 Nov.
13HEC lau A6 pitch8–9

DURLACH See **KARLSRUHE**

DÜRRHEIM (BAD)
Baden-Württemberg (☎07706)

Sunthausersee ☎712
All year.
8HEC lau A7 Vn/c 9 5

DÜSSELDORF
Nordrhein-Westfalen (☎0211)

Unterbacher See Kleiner Torfbruch 31 ☎8992038
Site on sloping grassland.

From Düsseldorf B326 to 'Erkrath' exit. Turn left by Unterbacher lake.
Etr–15 Sep.
4.5HEC lau pitch18

EBERBACH AM NECKAR
Baden-Württemberg (☎06271)

Eberbach ☎1071
On slightly sloping meadow on left bank of the river. Separate field for young people. Some traffic noise and liable to flooding when river is high. Lunchtime siesta 13.00–15.00 hrs.

For access head for the sportsground after crossing bridge from town centre.
Apr–Sep.
0.9HEC lau

ECHTERNACHERBRÜCK
Rheinland-Pfalz (☎06525)

GC Echternacherbrück ☎340
Local authority site on long flat stretch of grassland with young trees, beside the river.

Access via Bitburg on B257/E42, close to Luxembourg frontier.
Apr–Sep.
10HEC lau

EDERTAL
Hessen

At **AFFOLDERN**

Edertaler Hof Hamfurther Str 21 ☎(05623)2094
A lakeside site on a level meadow next to Affoldern See. Partly divided into individual pitches.

For access, follow the B485 Bad Wildungen-Baldeck road to Mehlen, then turn off towards Affoldern.
All year.
3HEC lau

At **BRINGHAUSEN**

Linge ☎(05623)4889
Terraced site by the River Eder.

From Bad Wildungen take the B485 to Mehlen then turn left to Bringhausen. ➤

Apr–Sep.

1.1HEC H G R L A4 V2 3–5 A2–4

At **MEHLEN**

Ideal (05623)2190

The site lies on level meadowland and is bordered by the river and a sports ground.

From Bad Wildungen follow road B485 to Mehlen and to the site next to the River Eder.
15 Apr–15 Oct.

2.5HEC H R lau A4 pitch5

At **REHBACH**

Rehbach Strandweg 9 (05623)2049

Site lies on the lake (Eder Stausee), and is situated just E of Bringhausen.

From Bad Wildungen go N to Mehlen, then turn towards the lake and Rehbach.
Apr–Sep.

1HEC H G lau L A5 pitch5–8

EGESTORF
Niedersachsen (04175)

AZUR-Camping Lüneburger Heide 661

Modern site on wooded heathland on the edge of the Lüneburger Heath Nature Reserve 2 km S of town on slightly sloping terrain with asphalt internal roads.

Access via Hamburg-Hannover motorway A7/E4 Egestorf or Evendorf exits.
All year.

17HEC H G R P lau A6 pitch8–9

EGGLFING
Bayern (08537)

Max 356

On meadow divided into pitches and 1 km from spa baths Bad Füssing.

Take B12 to Tutting and then turn off towards Egglfing and the national frontier.
All year.

2.5HEC H G R lau A5 pitch7

EHLERHAUSEN
Niedersachsen (05085)

Waldsee Rotweg 3 7115

All year.

10HEC H G L A4 Vn/c 5 A5

EIMKE
Niedersachsen (05262)

Eimke im Extertal 3307

Extensive, partly terraced site on slightly sloping meadowland with two ponds.

From Dortmund–Hannover motorway (A2/E8) take 'Bad Eilsen' exit and follow B238 S. 1 km beyond Rintein, turn left and continue for 18 km along Extertal-Barntrup road.
All year.

5HEC H G lau L A4 pitch5–7

Germany

ELISABETHFEHN
Niedersachsen

Elisabethfehn Hauptstr 35 (04499)1202

The site lies on level, grassy ground, surrounded by hedging. Lunchtime siesta 13.00–15.00 hrs.

From Cloppenburg N on B72 to Strücklingen. Then follow the 'Barssel' road for approx 3 km.
15 Mar–Oct.

1.8HEC H G P lau

ELISABETH SOPHIENKOOG (Island of Nordstrand)
Schleswig-Holstein (04842)

Elisabeth-Sophienkoog 8534

On meadowland behind the North Sea dyke. Lunchtime siesta 12.00–14.00 hrs.

Access via Husum to Island of Nordstrand.
Apr–Sep.

1.7HEC H R lau

EMS (BAD)
Rheinland-Pfalz (02603)

Bad Ems 4679

Level grassy site with isolated trees by the River Lahn.

On E outskirts on B260.
Apr–Oct.

1.4HEC H G P lau A6 pitch3–7

ENGEHAUSEN
Niedersachsen (05071)

Freizeitpark 2164

Useful as a transit site, lying only 500 m from Autobahn A7/E4. Situated on the Aller and surrounded by pine trees.

For access, leave autobahn A7 at service area Allertal and follow road towards Celle.
Apr–Oct.

5.5HEC H G R lau R A6 9

EPPSTEIN See **KÖNIGSTEIN IM TAUNUS**

ERLANGEN
Bayern (09131)

Naturfreunde Wöhrmühle 6 28499

Site lies on meadowland on an island in the River Regnitz.

Well signposted from outskirts of town.
All year.

1HEC H P A5 Vn/c 8 A5

Rangau (09135)8866

Long stretch of land behind the sportsground and next to the Dechsendorfer Weiher Lake in nature reserve.

Leave Motorway (A3/E5 Nürnberg-Würzburg) at exit Erlangen-West.
Apr–Sep.

1.8HEC H R lau LP A5 pitch7

ERPFINGEN
Baden-Württemberg (072103)

AZUR Rosen Camping Erpfingen
(07128)466

Extensive site on a hill.

Access from Reutlingen on B312 in south easterly direction to Grossengstingen, then S on Schwabische Albstr (B313) for 3.5 km to Haid, then turn right to Erpfingen. Site on W outskirts.
All year.

9HEC H G R P lau A5–6 pitch8–9

ESCHERNDORF
Bayern (09381)

Escherndorf 889

Site lies on meadowland by the River Main, next to the ferry station (River Ferry Norhheim). Lunchtime siesta 13.00–15.00 hrs.

Site can be reached from motorway A7/E70 via exit Würzburg Estenfeld and follow road E towards 'Volkach'.
Apr–Oct.

1.5HEC H G R R lau

ESCHWEGE
Hessen (05651)

Fluss und Mineralbad Torweise 4–5
3871

In grounds of mineral swimming pool at the foot of the Leuchtberg with Bismarck Tower.

From B27 E take B452 or B249 to Eschwege then follow signs.
Apr–Sep.

1HEC H P lau A4 V3 5–12 A5–12

ESENS-BENSERSIEL
Niedersachsen (04971)

Bensersiel 3088

Well-managed, extensive leisure centre with harbour, good fish restaurant and reading room. Swimming pools have sea water and artificial waves.

Takes B210 NE from Aurich to Ogenbargen then via Esens.
14 Apr–15 Sep.

10HEC H lau LP

ESSEN
Nordrhein-Westfalen (0201)

At **WERDEN** (10 km S)

Bahnhof Werden 492978

Several fields divided by bushes and surrounded by thick hedges. Lunchtime siesta 13.00–15.00 hrs.

From centre of Essen towards Werden, then

turn towards railway station and follow signposts.
All year.
4HEC ◇ H |O| ⊙ G R s lau

ESTENFELD
Bayern (☎09305)
Estenfeld Maidbronner Str 38 ☎228
On meadowland next to sportsground.
From motorway A7/E70 leave at exit 'Würzburg/Estenfeld' and continue S on B19 for 1 km.
Mar–Oct.
0.5HEC ◆ H |O| ⊙ R ⊞ lau A5 pitch5

EUTIN-FISSAU
Schleswig-Holstein (☎04521)
Prinzenholz ☎5281
Terraced lakeside site divided by trees and bushes. Mobile shop.
N of town take Malente road and turn right after 2 km.
May–Sep.
1.5HEC ◆ H ⊙ R ⊞ lau |O| L A4 Vn/c 7 7

FALSHÖFT ÜBER KAPPELN AN DER SCHLEI
Schleswig-Holstein (☎04643)
Seehof ☎693
A partly sheltered site beside the Baltic Sea, near a lighthouse.
Leave B199 at Gelting and travel N for 5 km.
Apr–Oct.
2HEC ◇ H ⊙ R s ⊞ lau

FEHMARN (ISLAND OF) See **BURG, DÄNSCHENDORF, FEHMARNSUND, MEESCHENDORF, WULFEN**

FEHMARNSUND (Island of Fehmarn)
Schleswig-Holstein (☎04371)
Miramar ☎3220
A family site on meadowland situated at the southern end of the island.
Turn off the B207/E4 at the first turning after the Sundbrücke (bridge) and drive towards Svendorf.
20 Mar–Sep.

Germany

8HEC ◆ ◇ H |O| ⊙ G R s ⊞ lau A5 pitch12

FEILNBACH (BAD)
Bayern (☎08066)
Tenda Reithof 2 ☎533
Well organised site on level grassland with pitches laid out in circles and hardstandings for tourers near the entrance.
Leave München–Salzburg motorway (A8/E11) at 'Bad Aibling' exit and continue S for 4 km on unclass road.
All year.
14HEC ◆ H |O| ⊙ R P ⊞ lau R

FELDEN See **BERNAU**

FELDKIRCHEN See **AINRING**

FELDWIES
Bayern (☎08642)
Rödigries ☎470
In meadowland between motorway and Chiemsee.
From Feldwies exit of München–Salzburg motorway (A8/E11) drive NW, cross a stream and continue for 0.5 km passing the Madl Boatyard.
Closed 26 Oct–Nov
4.5HEC ◆ ◇ H |O| ⊙ G R L ⊞ lau A5 pitch5–8

FICHTELBERG
Bayern (☎09272)
Fichtelsee ☎270
Gently sloping meadow amid pleasant woodland 100 m from Lake Fichtelsee.
From A9/E6 Bad Berneck exit, take B303 to the Fichtelsee Leisure Centre turning.
20 Dec–Oct.
2.3HEC ◆ H |O| ⊙ ⊞ lau G P A5 pitch6

FINSTERAU
Bayern (☎08557)
Nationalpark-Ost ☎1415
Terraced site on edge of extensive woodland area at entrance to National Park.
N of Freyung towards the frontier.
All year.
4HEC ◆ H |O| ⊙ R ⊞ lau A5 pitch7

FISCHBACH AM INN
Bayern (☎08034)
Inntal ☎2869
On level grassland near a small forest lake.
Off B15 S of town.
Apr–Oct.
1.2HEC ◆ H |O| ⊙ G R L ⊞

FLOSSENBURG
Bayern (☎09603)
Gaisweiher ☎644
A terraced site on well-kept meadowland. It is beautifully situated, and has a splendid view of the nearby castle.
B15 to Neustadt, follow road E through Floss, turn N towards the Gaisweiher Lake.
All year.
8HEC ◆ H |O| ⊙ G R L lau A4 pitch6

FORNSBACH See **MURRHARDT**

FREIBURG-IM-BREISGAU
Baden-Württemberg (☎0761)
Breisgau ☎(07665)2346
Extensive level grassland site on outskirts of town. Section reserved for campers with dogs.
500 m E of autobahn exit 'Freiburg Nord'.
All year.
6.5HEC ◆ H |O| ⊙ G R ⊞ lau L A6 V4 4 4

Ferien & Kurbad Mösle-Park Waldseestr 77 ☎72938
On outskirts of town near 'Busse's Waldschänke' inn.
Turn right after town hall across railway and follow Waldseestr towards Littenweiler.
20 Mar–Oct. ➔

0.7HEC lau P A6 V3 4 A3–4

At **ST-GEORGEN** (4 km SW)

St-Georg Basler Landstr 62 ☎43183

Access to site is in built-up area off B3/B31 at FANAL garage.
All year.

0.6HEC lau P A6 V3 6 A4

FREILINGEN

Rheinland-Pfalz (☎02697)

SC Freilingen ☎282

Local authority site at Lake Postweiher. Lunchtime siesta 13.00–15.00 hrs.

0.5 km from village to the right of B8 Freilingen–Altenkirch road.
All year.

7.5HEC L lau

At **MAXSAIN** (4 km SW)

Klingelwiese ☎(02626)5043

On a meadow beside a woodland lake.

Leave A3/E5 motorway (Köln–Frankfurt) at 'Ransbach/Baumbach' exit and continue via Mogendorf and Selters to Maxsain. Site lies 2 km further on.
All year.

15HEC lau L

FREUDENSTADT

Baden-Württemberg (☎07441)

Langenwald ☎2862

The site consists of several sections and lies next to a former mill beside the River Forbach.

4 km W of Freudenstadt below the B28

Germany

(Freudenstadt–Strasbourg).
May–Sep.

12HEC lau A5 V3 4 A4

FRICKENHAUSEN

Bayern (☎09331)

Azur-Knaus Park Frickenhausen ☎3171

On level meadow in a small poplar wood beside River Main. Lunchtime siesta 13.00–15.00 hrs.

On N bank of Main 0.5 km E of Oshsenfurt.
All year.

4HEC P lau A5–6 pitch8–9

FRIELENDORF

Hessen (☎05684)

SC Sendberg ☎7090

Well kept municipal site next to a swimming pool. Lunchtime siesta 13.00–15.00 hrs.

10 km S of Homberg on B254.
All year.

3HEC lau P A4 pitch6

FRIESOYTHE

Niedersachsen (☎04493)

Heidehof ☎235

Beautiful site, partly divided into pitches, next to the Restaurant Heidehof. Lunchtime siesta 13.00–15.00 hrs.

From B72 continue SW towards. Gehlenberg/Lorup for approx 14 km.
All year.

6HEC

FULDATAL-KNICKHAGEN

Hessen (☎0661)

Fulda-Freizeitzentrum ☎(05607)340

All year.

3.2HEC P lau A4 V2 5 A4

FÜRTH IM ODENWALD

Hessen (☎06253)

Tiefertzwinkel Krumbacherstr 21 ☎5804

Pleasantly landscaped site in beautiful setting next to the municipal open-air swimming pool. Lunchtime siesta 13.00–15.00 hrs.

Feb–Nov.

5HEC lau P A5 Vn/c 5 A3–5

FÜRTH IM WALD

Bayern (☎09973)

SC Einberg ☎1811

Municipal site in Dabergerstr, near swimming pool.

NE of Cham on B20.
All year.

3.3HEC P A2 V2 2 A2

GADEN

Bayern (☎08681)

Schwanenplatz Am Schwanenpl 1 ☎281

Site lies on a meadow, divided into sections, beside one of Bavaria's warmest lakes, Waginger See. Separate section for dog owners.

For access drive from Traunstein to Waging, then turn right towards Gaden.
May–Sep.

3.8HEC L lau A5 pitch9

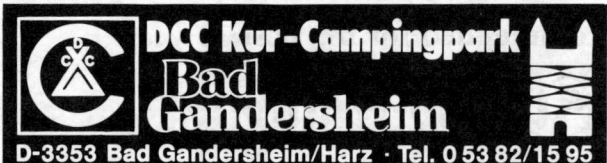

GAHLEN
Nordrhein-Westfalen (☎02853)

Hohen Ufer ☎2480

Site on level meadowland next to Lippe–Seiten canal.

Access from Wesel on country roads via Hünxe and Gartrop. On approach to Gahlen turn left towards Schermbeck.
All year.

2.7HEC

GAMMELSBACH
Baden-Württemberg (☎06068)

Freienstein Neckartalstr ☎1306

The site lies just off the B45 in a landscaped preservation area. It is terraced and divided into pitches. Lunchtime siesta 13.00–15.00 hrs.

Mar–Oct.

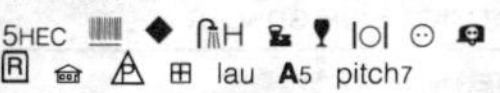

5HEC lau A5 pitch7

GANDERSHEIM (BAD)
Niedersachsen (☎05382)

DCC Kur-Campingpark ☎1595

On level meadow, divided in two by a brook beside a public park. Good sporting facilities. Separate section for young people.

Access from Hannover–Kassel motorway via exit Soesen.
All year.

9HEC lau P A5 pitch10

GARBSEN See **HANNOVER**

GARMISCH-PARTENKIRCHEN
Bayern (☎08821)

Zugspitze ☎3180

In beautiful setting at the foot of the Zugspitze between the road and the Loisach.

On the B24 towards the Austrian frontier.
All year.

3.6HEC lau L

GARTOW
Niedersachsen (☎05846)

SC Waldbad ☎488

Situated in woodland with adjoining meadow.

NE on A493 from Lüchow.
Apr–Oct.

1.5HEC P lau

GEISENHEIM
Hessen (☎06722)

Geisenheim ☎8515

Level grassland site.

Between B42 road and River Rhine.
Mar–Oct.

3HEC lau R A4 V3 5 A4

GEISLINGEN
Baden-Württemberg (☎07331)

Längental ☎62774

Germany

Municipal site on pleasant meadowland at N of town.
Apr–Sep.

0.7HEC lau

GEMÜND
Rheinland-Pfalz (☎06524)

Ourtal ☎832

All year.

0.4HEC R lau A3 V2 4 A2–4

GEMÜNDEN
Rheinland-Pfalz (☎06453)

Aumühle Auestr 26 ☎7501

Well kept meadowland site next to the municipal 'Freibad' (swimming pool) in the valley of the River Wohra. Lunchtime siesta 13.00–15.00 hrs.

From road B3 (Marburg–Fritzlar) turn N in Halsdorf.
All year.

2HEC P lau

GEMÜNDEN AM MAIN
Bayern (☎09351)

SC Saalebrücke ☎8574

This municipal site lies a short distance off the main road bordering the River Fränkische Saale. It is in the grounds of a sports field and has a swimming pool. Individual washing cubicles with curtains for the ladies.

Access signposted off main B26 road.
Mid Apr–15 Oct.

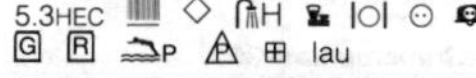

5.3HEC P lau

GERBACH
Rheinland-Pfalz (☎06361)

AZUR-Camping Pfalz ☎8287

Lunchtime siesta 13.00–15.00 hrs.

Access from A8/E12 motorway at junction Enkenbach–Hochspeyer. Then N on B48 via Rockenhausen and at Dielkirchen continue E for 4.5 km to Gerbach.
All year.

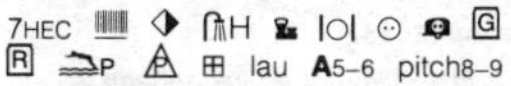

7HEC P lau A5–6 pitch8–9

GIFHORN
Niedersachsen (☎045371)

At **ISENBÜTTEL** (8 km SE)

Tankumsee ☎(05374)1254

Site adjacent to lake (Tankumsee) surrounded by heathland. Separate section for campers close to entrance.

All year.

3HEC lau Ls A4 V2 7 A2

At **RÖTGESBÜTTEL** (8 km S)

Glockenheide ☎(05304)1581

Tranquil site in heathland. Lunchtime siesta 13.00–15.00 hrs.

In Rötgesbüttel turn left, then turn left again after level crossing.
All year.

5HEC A5 V3 3 A3

GILLENFELD
Rheinland-Pfalz (☎06573)

GC Feriedorf Pulvermaar Schwalbenweg 6 ☎311

Partly terraced municipal site on a slightly sloping meadow at Pulver Maar, surrounded by woods.

From motorway A48 (Eifel autobahn) leave at exit Mehren/Daun, continue S on B421 and take the first turning into Gillenfeld. On near side of village turn off towards Pulver Maar.
May–Sep.

3HEC lau L A3 V2 8 A3

GIROD See **MONTABAUR**

GLÄSERKOPPEL See **PREETZ**

GLÜCKSBURG
Schleswig-Holstein (☎04631)

Schwennau ☎2670

A watercourse divides the site into two sections which are linked by a bridge.

In town centre make for Postplatz, then Hindenburgplatz, Collenburger Strasse. Schwennau–Strasse direct onto the site which lies adjacent to the Flensburger Förde.
All year.

1HEC sP A4 V5 5 A5

GLÜDER See **SOLINGEN**

GOSLAR
Niedersachsen (☎05321)

Sennhütte ☎22498

In woodland adjacent to the Hotel Sennhütte.

3 km S on B241 Clausthal–Zellerfeld road.
All year.

2HEC lau s A4 V3 4 A4

At **HAHNENKLEE** (13 km S on road B241 at turn-off to Hahnenklee)

Kreuzeck ☎(05325)2570

In the forest beside a lake. Terraces and a separate section for dog-owners.

Beside Café am Kreuzeck at the junction of the B241 and the Hahnenklee road.
All year.

5HEC lau LP A6 pitch9

At **WOLFSHAGEN** (11 km W on unclass road off B82) ➤

SC Krähenberg ☎(05326)4088

Situated in a quiet valley.

S off the B82 between Langelsheim and Astfeld.
All year.

6.5HEC G P lau

GOTTSDORF
Bayern (☎08593)

AZUR-Ferienzentrum Bayerwald ☎444

Extensive terrain in quiet location.

All year.

12HEC R P lau A6 pitch8–9

GRIESBACH (BAD)
Bayern (☎08532)

Kur-und Feriencamping Dreiquellenbad ☎1550

1 km S of Griesbach Spa, on the Karpfham–Schwaim road.
All year.

2.5HEC

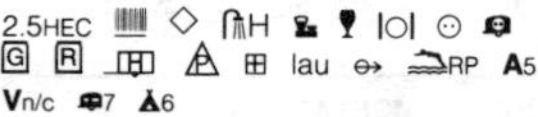

G R lau RP A5 Vn/c 7 6

GRÖMITZ
Schleswig-Holstein (☎04562)

Ahoi ☎8586

This large site, divided by bushes, is 500 m from a sandy beach. Washrooms are closed at night.

Apr–15 Oct.

5HEC G R lau S A5 pitch12

Hohe Leuchte ☎8655

Situated behind a dyke on a level meadow with trees. There is direct access to the beach.

Apr–Sep.

3.7HEC lau S A6 pitch12

Porta del Sol Mittelweg ☎7141

Level meadow divided by isolated trees and shrubs. 600 m to beach.

Apr–Sep.

5HEC R lau L

GROSS-GERAU
Hessen (☎06152)

Niederwaldsee ☎2981

Clean and well laid out site in bird reserve beside Lake Niederwald. Lunchtimes siesta 13.00–15.00 hrs.

Germany

Off B44.
All year.

12HEC G R lau A5 Vn/c 6 6

GROSS-RINGMAR See **BASSUM**

GRUBE
Schleswig-Holstein (☎04365)

Rosenfelder Strand Textil Aegidienstr 29 ☎412

Excellently managed family site beside the sea with a 1 km long beach. Divided into separate fields by rows of bushes. Children's playground in woodland between site and sea. Strict observance of lunchtime siesta 13.00–15.00 hrs.

Take the B207/E4 from Lübeck and drive N to Lensahn, then E to Grube.
Apr–Sep.

20HEC G R S lau A5 pitch11

GRÜNBERG
Hessen (☎06401)

Spitzer Stein ☎6553

Beautifully situated site at a forest swimming pool.

From the Frankfurt–Kassel motorway (A5) leave at Homberg junction. Campsite is 8 km S.
All year.

4HEC G R lau P A4 pitch5

GRUNDMÜHLE BEI QUENTEL
Hessen (☎05602)

Quentel-Grundmühle ☎3659

A forest camp site with a sunny location. Lunchtime siesta 13.00–15.00 hrs.

From Melsungen follow road B83 to Röhrenfurth. Here turn right towards 'Furstenhagen' and follow road via Eiterhagen to Quentel.

2HEC P

GULDENTAL
Rheinland-Pfalz (☎06707)

Guldental ☎633

Site lies in a valley of the Guldenbach Valley. Some terraces are reserved for tourers and there is a lake suitable for bathing.

From Bad Kreuznach N on road B48 to Langenlonsheim, and on nearside turn left to Guldental.
All year.

7HEC R P A4 pitch7

HADDEBY
Schleswig-Holstein (☎04621)

Haddeby ☎32450

Clean, tidy site beside River Schlei.

From Schleswig follow B76 towards Eckernförde.
Mar–Oct.

3.5HEC G R L lau A6 Vn/c 10 10

HAGEN See **LENGERICH**

HAHNENKLEE See **GOSLAR**

HALDERN
Nordrhein-Westfalen (☎02857)

Erich Neuhaus ☎500

On meadowland at the 'Hagener-Meer'.

Access via B8 (West-Emmerich) via Rees to Halden-Sonsfeld.
All year.

2HEC LR

Strandhaus Sonsfeld ☎2247

On meadowland at the 'Hagener-Meer' next to B8 and railway line.

All year.

1.5HEC G R L A3 V4 4 4

HALLWANGEN
Baden-Württemberg (☎07443)

Königskanzel ☎6730

In an elevated position in the centre of the Black Forest.

Via B28 from Freudenstadt.
All year.

4HEC G R lau A5 V3 4 3–4

HAMBURG
Land Hamburg (☎040)

Anders Kieler Str 650 ☎5704498

Useful transit site on a level meadow.

All year.

2HEC G lau P

City-Camp Kieler Str 620 ☎5705121

The site lies behind an inn and a filling station and is divided into two sections by a hedge.
All year.
1HEC H lau P A5 V4 8–12 5–12

HÄMELERWALD See **PEINE**

HAMELN
Niedersachsen (05158)
Waldbad Pfedeweg 2 2288
A grassy terraced site on the edge of woodland beside a public swimming pool.
Follow 'swimming pool' signs from Havelstorf.
Apr–Oct.
2.8HEC H lau P A3 pitch7

HAMMER
Nordrhein-Westfalen (02473)
Hammer 8115
In a quiet secluded valley.
Apr–Oct.
2HEC H L A3 V3 5 3

HANAU
Bayern
At **BRUCHKÖBEL**
SC Bärensee (06181) 12306
Lakeside site with touring and residential sections. Lunchtime siesta 12.00–15.00 hrs.
Take B40 to NE of town as far as the Erlensee turning, then follow signposts.
All year.
38HEC H lau L A5 V4 4 4
At **KAHL AM MAIN** (9 km SE)
Freigericht-Ost (06188) 2013
Extensive site on the lakeshore with public swimming facilities.
Take B8 to Kahl, then turn off at ARAL petrol station.
All year.
20HEC H L

HANNOVER
Niedersachsen
At **GARBSEN** (10 km W)
Blauer See (05137) 71021
On a small lake beside the Garbsen service area on Hannover–Bielefeld motorway A2/E8.
Apr–Oct.
4.4HEC H lau L pp9
At **ISERNHAGEN** (16 km NE)
Parksee Lohne (05139) 88260
In recreation area by a lake. On the flight approach path for Hannover Langenhagen airport. Separate section for tourers.
From motorway exit 'Kirchhorst' follow

Germany

Altwarmbüchen road to Isernhagen.
Apr–Sep.
16HEC lau L
At **LAATZEN** (7 km S)
Birkensee (0511) 529962
On a meadow beside a wooded lake. Nearest site to Hannover Fair. Lunchtime siesta 13.00–15.00 hrs.
From Laatzen exit of Hannover–Kassel motorway continue W on B443 for 200 m, then turn left for 400 m.
All year.
8.2HEC H L lau L A5 V2 5 5

HARDEGSEN
Niedersachsen (05505)
Ferienpark Solling 2272
Terraced site in forested area. Separate field for touring pitches. Lunchtime siesta 13.00–15.00 hrs.
In town take 'Waldgebiet Gladeberg' road.
All year.
2.8HEC H lau P

HARLESIEL See **WITTMUND**

HARSEFELD
Niedersachsen (04164)
SC Harsefeld 5357
Level local authority site surrounded by bushes and trees. Heated open air swimming pool nearby. Lunchtime siesta 13.00–5.00 hrs.
Apr–Sep.
1.5HEC H lau P A2 V2 2 2

HARZBURG (BAD)
Niedersachsen (05322)
Wolfstein 3585
Long, terraced site on edge of woodland.
500 m from town on B6 towards Eckertal.
All year.
20HEC H lau A6 pitch7
At **ORSTEIL GOTTINGERODE**
Harzar 81215
On outskirts of village next to main road. Terraced site with separate touring field. Lunchtime siesta 13.00–15.00 hrs.
On the B6 between Bad Harzburg and Goslar.
All year.
8HEC H P lau A4 V4 4 4

HASELÜNNE
Niedersachsen (05961)
Hase-Ufer Andruper Str 1 1331
Beside the River Hase in an attractive area E of the town.
Signposted from Andrup.
All year.
10HEC H lau L A5 Vn/c 6 6

HASLACH
Bayern (08361)
Feriencenter Wertacher Hof 770
Well-kept site on Lake Grüntensee.
Access road near the Wertach–Haslach railway station.
10 Jan–Oct.
3HEC H lau L A6 pitch9

HATTEN
Oldenburg (06746)
Freizeitzentrum (04482) 677
All year.
2.8HEC H lau P A4 Vn/c 7–16 7–12

HATTINGEN
Nordrhein-Westfalen (02324)
Ruhrbrücke Ruhrstr 6 80038
Grassy site by small Ruhr dam near a restaurant.
N of town.
Apr–Oct.
1.6HEC H R lau A4 V2 6 5–6

HAUSBAY
Rheinland-Pfalz (04482)
At **PZALZFELD-HAUSBAY**
Schinderhannes (06746) 1674
Terraced site on S facing slope, broken up by trees and shrubs beside a small lake. Separate section for young people. Lunchtime siesta 13.00–15.00 hrs.
E of B327. 29 km S of Koblenz.
All year.
30HEC H R lau A5 pitch10
See advertisement page 226

HAUSEN
Baden-Württemberg (07579)
Wagenburg 559
On meadowland between the railway bank and the Danube.
From Hausen drive towards Beuron. Entrance through subway.
15 Apr–15 Oct.
1.2HEC H R lau A5 V4 4 4

HEIKENDORF BEI KIEL
Schleswig-Holstein (0431)
Möltenort 241316 ➔

Terraced site by the Kieler Förde. 15 km NE of Kiel to W of road B502.

Approach to site is via a narrow, winding road.
Apr–Sep.
2HEC H R s lau A5 pitch8–10

HEIMBACH
Nordrhein-Westfalen (02446)

Gut Habersauel 437

Pitches for tourers are near site entrance but unmarked. Terraces are for statics only. Lunchtime siesta 13.00–15.00 hrs.

From railway station turn towards Hausen Nideggen. Site lies in a loop of the River Rur.
All year.
15HEC H R RP

Rurthal-Burg Blens 3377

Site with individual pitches on meadowland beside the River Rur.

From Düren follow road S via Nideggen and Abenden to Blens, then cross bridge and turn left.
All year.
7HEC H G R RP lau A4 V3 4 A4

HEIMERTSHAUSEN
Hessen (06635)

Heimerstshausen 206

Near swimming pool in extensive, grassy, wooded valley. Lunchtime siesta 13.00–15.00 hrs.

From Kassel–Frankfurt motorway take Alsfeld–West exit, then continue via Romrod and Zell.
Apr–Sep.
3.6HEC H G R lau P A5 V4 4 A4

HEINSEN See **HOLZMINDEN**

HELLENTHAL
Nordrhein-Westfalen (02482)

Hellenthal 500

On extensive meadowland.

Germany

0.5 km S of town.
All year.
7HEC H G R P lau A5 pitch10

HELMSTEDT
Niedersachsen (05351)

Waldwinkel Maschweg 46 37161

In an orchard next to the Gasthaus Waldwinkel.

Signposted from autobahn exit 'Helmstedt'.
All year.
2HEC H lau P A4 V4 4 A4

HEMELN
Niedersachsen (05544)

Hemeln 1414

Well-kept site on N outskirts of village, beside the River Weser.

15 Apr–15 Oct.
1.2HEC H R lau A4 V3 3 A3

At **REINHARDSHAGEN-VAAKE** (2 km W)

Ahletal 408

Well kept municipal site about 500 m from River Weser, adjacent to a leisure centre with an indoor swimming pool. Lunchtime siesta 13.00–15.00 hrs.

From autobahn Kassel–Hannover leave at 'Hann–Münden' exit. Then follow B80 N along W bank of Weser to Reinhardshagen–Vaake then turn left.
All year.
4.5HEC H R P lau A4 Vn/c 5 A3–5

HERBOLZHEIM
Baden-Württemberg (07643)

Herbolzheim 1460

All year.
1.7HEC H G R P lau A7 pitch4–6

HERFORD
Nordrhein-Westfalen (05221)

Elisabethsee 33411

All year.
6HEC H lau A5 pitch4

HERINGEN
Hessen (06624)

Werra 1211

Municipal site on slightly sloping ground at the swimming pool. Lunchtime siesta 13.00–15.00 hrs.

All year.
0.7HEC H (summer only) P lau A3 pitch4

HERMANNSBERG
Niedersachsen (05052)

Örtzetal 3072

Site lies on meadows on the E bank of the River Örtze, set in unspoilt woodlands of the Lüneburg Heath. Boat landing stage. Lunchtime siesta 13.00–15.00 hrs.

From the B3 Celle–Soltau road turn off in Bergen and follow road NE towards Hermannsburg, then continue towards Eschwege.
All year.
H lau G A4 V2 5 A3

HERSBRUCK
Bayern (0915)

At **HOHENSTADT** (6 km E)

Pegnitzgrund Bahnhofweg 6 1500

Quiet holiday site in forest region of River Pegnitz.

About 6 km E of Hersbruck.
1.5HEC H G R R A4 pitch7

HIRSCHHORN AM NECKAR
Hessen (06272)

Odenwald-Zeltplatz 809

Extensive site in wooded valley. Divided by River Ülfenbach and hedges.

Turn off B37 towards Wald-Michelbach and continue for 1.5 km.

Apr–Oct.
7HEC H P lau A5 V11

HÖFEN AN DER ENZ
Baden-Württemberg (☎07081)

Quellgrund ☎5226

Well maintained municipal site on grassland between the B294 and the River Enz.

Access from Pforzheim on the B294 in SW direction to the 'Quelle' inn with entrance to ARAL petrol station at entrance to Höfen, then turn right.
All year.
3.6HEC H lau P

HOFGEISMAR
Hessen (☎05671)

SC Parkschwimmbad ☎1215

Municipal site, subdivided by hedges. Next to a swimming pool. Lunchtime siesta 13.00–15.00 hrs. Mobile shop.

All year.
1.2HEC H P lau

At **LIEBENAU-ZWERGEN** (9 km W)

Terrassen-Camping Wärmetal ☎(05676) 246

A terraced, south facing site, with magnificent scenery. 300 m from a swimming pool.

Access from B83, at Hofgeismar turn W towards Liebenau, alternatively from B7 turn N at Obemeiser towards Liebenau.
All year.
3HEC H lau P A5 pitch6

HOFSTETTEN-MAIN
Bayern (☎09351)

Schönrain ☎8645

Slightly sloping, partly terraced meadowland E of River Main. Lunchtime siesta 13.00–15.00 hrs.

From Gemunden/Main along the left bank of the River Main about 3 km downstream. Turn left off B26 through Hofstetten to site.
Apr–Sep.
5HEC H P lau A5 pitch5–6

HOHENSTADT See **HERSBRUCK**

HOHENWARTH
Bayern (☎09946)

Fritz-Berger-Comfort ☎367

Meadowland in the valley of the Weissens Regens with views of the mountain range and town above.

Access from Cham on the B85 S to Miltach and continue via Kötzing to Hohenwarth.
All year.
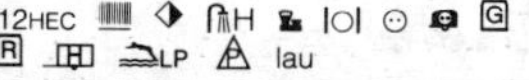
12HEC H LP lau

HOLLE
Niedersachsen (☎05062)

At **DERNEBURG** (2 km NW on unclass road)

Germany

Seecamp-Derneburg ☎565

A terraced lakeside site on a hill slope with a southerly aspect. Separate towing field. Useful transit site near autobahn.

From the motorway, leave at exit 'Derneburg' and continue to road B6.
Apr–15 Sep.
8HEC H L lau A4 V2 4 4

HOLZMINDEN
Niedersachsen

At **HEINSEN** (8 km N)

Weserbergland Weserstr 66 ☎8733

Meadowland site on the bank of the Weser.

From Holzminden follow the B83 N to Heinsen.
15 Mar–Oct.
2.8HEC H P lau

At **SILBERBORN** (9 km SE)

Silberborn ☎(05536) 664

A grassy site in Solling/Vogler woodland nature park, on the outskirts of Silberborn. Special sanitary installations for children. Lunchtime siesta 13.00–15.00 hrs.

From Holzminden or Höxter drive towards Neuhaus/Solling and continue 4 km E in direction of Dassel.
All year.

2.7HEC H P lau A5 V2 6 5

HONNEF (BAD)
Nordrhein-Westfalen (☎02224)

At **HONNEF-HIMBERG (BAD)** (7 km E)

Jilieshof ☎8896

All year.
2HEC H P A5 pitch7

HOPFEN AM SEE
Bayern (☎08362)

Hopfensee ☎7431

In quiet situation beside lake. Private beach. Ski-ing lessons.

4 km N of Füssen.
15 Dec–Oct.
5HEC H L lau L A8 pitch12–14

HORB
Baden-Württemberg (☎07451)

Schüttehof ☎3951

Situated on flat mountain top.

Access from Horb in direction of Freudenstadt. 1.5 km beyond the town boundary turn towards stables and site, and onward for 1 km.

All year.
5.5HEC H P lau

HORN-BAD MEINBERG
Nordrhein-Westfalen (☎05255)

Eggewald ☎236

Site lies in well wooded countryside.

Access via road B1. In Horn-Bad Meinberg turn off main road at the Waldschlosschen and follow the 'Altenbeken' road for about 8 km up to Kempen.
All year.
2HEC H lau A4 pitch5

HORN-BODENSEE
Baden-Württemberg (☎07735)

Horn ☎685

Large and well-manage municipal site with a pleasant beach.

In Horn turn off the Radolfszell-Stein am Rhein road and head towards the lake.
Apr–Sep.
7HEC H lau L

HORST
Schleswig-Holstein (☎04836)

Eldercamping ☎611

A quiet, pleasantly landscaped site on the banks of River Eider. Lunchtime siesta 13.00–14.00 hrs.

From Heide drive NE to Süderheistadt, then via Hennstedt to the site on the nearside of Horst.
Apr–15 Oct.
2.5HEC H RP lau

HÖSSERINGEN See **SUDERBURG**

HÜNFELD
Hessen (☎06652)

SC Forsthaus St-Hubertus ☎2922

Municipal site in mixed woodland.

For access B27 from Hünfeld to the turning to Shlitz, turn right then 2 km to site.
May–Sep.
1.7HEC H

HUTTEN See **SCHLÜCHTERN**

ILLERTISSEN
Bayern (☎07303)

Illertissen ☎7888

Partially terraced site with plenty of trees.

Turn off towards Dietenheim at the ARAL filling station and continue along road for 1.5 km. Site on left hand side of road.
Apr–15 Oct.
3HEC H P lau A5 V4 3 3

IMMENSTADT
Bayern
Buchers

Site in meadow on sloping bank of Alpsee. ➤

From Immenstadt/Allgau follow B308 Lindau road westward. 2 km turn right at fork for Bühl 0.5 km on.
May–Sep.

1.5HEC H G R LP lau A4 V2 4 3

At **MISSEN** (9 km NW)

Wiederhofen (08320) 481

In lovely mountainous area.

Access from Immenstadt direction, Isny to Missen. Turn left along winding road to Wiederhofen, left again and continue 1.5 km downhill.
Closed May & Sep.

1.2HEC H G R P lau

INGENHEIM
Rheinland-Pfalz (06349)

SC Klingbachtal 6278

Municipal site lies on level meadowland at the edge of the village, next to the sports ground.

8 km S of Landau via B38. Final approach well signposted.
All year.

1.5HEC H G R lau P

INGOLSTADT
Bayern (0841)

Auwaldsee 68911

Near to Auwaldsee, this site lies in a beautiful setting beside the München–Ingolstadt motorway.

Access via the Ingolstadt–Süd exit off the A9/E6 (Müchen–Nürnberg motorway).
Apr–Sep.

10HEC H R G L

IRREL
Rheinland-Pfalz (06525)

Nimseck 3.4

Site on long grassy strip in wooded valley on the bank of River Nims.

Approach from Bitburg via B257/E42 in SW direction. At the turn-off from the bypass to Irrel, turn left.
Apr–Oct.

8HEC H G R P lau A6 V1 10 10

IRRHAUSEN
Rheinland-Pfalz (065502)

Irsental 753

Terraced site in very pleasant surroundings of a nature reserve.

From Prüm follow road B410 SW via Lünebach and Arzfeld to 2 km beyond Irrhausen, then turn left to site.
All year.

1.5HEC H lau

ISENBÜTTEL See **GIFHORN**

ISERNHAGEN See **HANNOVER**

Germany

ISNY
Baden-Württemberg
At **RIEDHOLZ** (6 km S)

Sonnenbuckel (08383) 383

Terraced site in attractive setting by the Eistobel Nature Reserve. Lunchtime siesta 13.00–15.00 hrs.

Access from Isny, travelling S. Turn left 2 km beyond Maierhöfen and follow signs.
Closed Oct and Nov.

1.5HEC H G R P lau A6 Vn/c 5–6 4–6

ISSIGAU
Bayern (09293)

Schloss Issigau 7173

About 5 km W off A9 E6 (München–Berlin) road via the Berg/Bad Steben exit.
All year.

0.6HEC H lau

JODITZ
Bayern (09295)

Auensee 381

Municipal site on partly terraced meadowland above lake.

Leave München–Berlin motorway at Berg–Bad Steben exit and drive E for 4 km.
All year.

4HEC H G lau L A3 V1 5 1–4

JUNGHOLZ See **WERTACH**

KAHL AM MAIN See **HANAU**

KALBERSCHNACKE
Nordrhein–Westfalen (02763)

Gut Kalberschnacke 6171

Terraced site above Lister Reservoir in wooded area.

Turn off A45 autobahn at Wegringhausen exit and continue NE for approx 4 km.
All year.

10HEC H G lau L A6 V3 6 3–5

KALIFORNIEN See **SCHÖNBERG**

KALLETAL-VARENHOLZ
Nordrhein-Westfalen (05755)

Ost/Weser/Freizeit-Zentrum 444

Extensive site in Weser recreation area near River Weser N of Schloss Varenholz. Separate field and common room for young campers.

Leave A2/E8 motorway at Exter exit then continue via Vlotho towards Rintein.
All year.

12HEC H G lau L A6 pitch5–10

KANDERN
Baden-Württemberg (07626)

Terrassen Beim Schwimmbad 7874

Terraced site above open-air swimming pool.

15 Mar–15 Oct.

2.2HEC H G R lau P A5 pitch6–8

KARLSRUHE
Baden-Württemberg (0721)

At **DURLACH** (8 km SE)

Azur Türmbergblick Tiegener Str 40 44060

On level ground amongst orchards. Lunchtime siesta 12.30–15.00 hrs.

Access via Karlsrühe–Dürlach exit on A5/E4. Signposted.
All year.

3HEC H G R lau P A6 pitch6

KARLSTADT
Bayern (09353)

Karlstadt 1268

Site lies on meadowland beside River Main.

15 Apr–Sep.

1.3HEC H G lau P

KARLSTEIN-GROSSWEIZHEIM See **ASCHAFFENBURG**

KASSEL
Hessen (0561)

SC 22433

Site lies within the town on bank of River Fulda, next to DLRG station.

Approaching from Frankfurtstr (B3) follow Damaschkestr as far as Giessenallee then 300 m S to site. From motorway leave at 'Kassel–Mitte' exit.
Apr–Sep.

1.4HEC H R

KEHL
Baden-Württemberg (07851)

Freundschaft 2603

Park-like site divided into separate sections for young campers, transit and holiday campers. Lunchtime siesta 13.00–15.00 hrs

Turn left at the Rhine dam on the outskirts of the town.
Apr–15 Oct.

2.3HEC H G R lau P A4 pitch9

KELL
Rheinland-Pfalz

Freibad Hochwald (06589) 844

On meadow on slightly sloping wooded hillside, near a public open-air swimming pool. ***Advance booking necessary in high season.***

2 km from B407 towards Trier.
All year.

KERNBACH
Hessen (☎06420)

Kernbach ☎7494

Site lies on level meadowland at the River Lahn. Lunchtime siesta 13.00–14.30 hrs.

From Marburg on B3 N to Cölbe, then follow road B62 W to Kernbach, and then turn left to site. Alternative approach from Marburg via Marbach (Behringwerke) and Caldern to Kernbach.
All year.

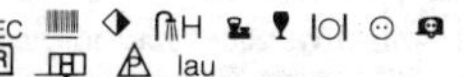

KESSENHAMMER See **OLPE**

KIPFENBERG
Bayern (☎08465)

AZUR-Camping Almühltal ☎588

All year.

4.5HEC lau **A**5 pitch8–9

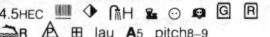

KIRCHBERG
Baden-Württemberg (☎07354)

Christophorous ☎663

Completely enclosed, clean site. From time to time there is noise from the military airfield nearby.

Leave motorway A7 (Ulm–Memmingen) at exit Illereichen Allenstadt to town centre, then towards the railway station.
All year.

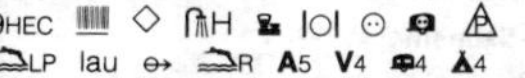

KIRCHBERG (Hessen) See **NIEDENSTEIN**

KIRCHESOHL See **OLPE**

KIRCHHEIM
Hessen (☎06628)

Seepark Kirchheim ☎1525

This terraced site, with individual pitches, is part of an extensive and well equipped leisure and recreation centre.

Germany

All year.

7HEC lau

KIRCHHEIMBOLANDEN
Rheinland-Pfalz (☎06352)

Vogelgesang ☎3463

Beside a swimming pool. Lunchtime siesta 12.30–13.30 hrs.

Access from B40 towards Rockenhausen.
Apr–Sep.

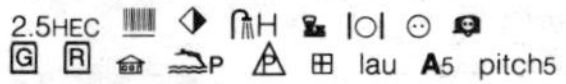

KIRCHZARTEN
Baden-Württemberg (☎07661)

Kirchzarten ☎39375

Extensive site with trees providing shade.

About 8 km E of Freiburg im Breisgau off the B31.
All year.

5.6HEC lau **A**6–8 pitch8

KIRCHZELL
Bayern (☎09373)

AZUR-Camping Odenwald ☎566

In natural terraced meadowland in wooded hilly country. No admission after 21.30 hrs. Lunchtime siesta 13.00–15.00 hrs.

From Amorbach follow the Eberbach road for 5 km. Site 1 km from town.
All year.

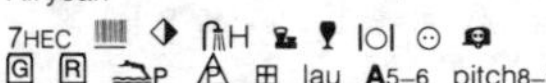

KISSINGEN (BAD)
Bayern (☎0971)

Bad Kissingen Euerdorferstr 1 ☎5211

In park beside River Saale. Lunchtime siesta 13.00–15.00 hrs.

Access near the southern bridge over the Saale.
Apr–15 Oct.

1.6HEC lau

KLAUSDORF See **BURG (Island of Fehmarn)**

KLEINWAABS
Schleswig-Holstein (☎04352)

Ostee Heide ☎2530

Divided into pitches and pleasantly landscaped. Large games room for teenagers. Lunchtime siesta 13.00–14.30 hrs.

All year.

20HEC lau **A**4 pitch15

KLINGENBERG-TRENNFURT
Bayern (☎09372)

Aqua ☎2390

On level meadow beside the River Main. Lunchtime siesta 13.00–15.00 hrs.

Access from Miltenberg road (B469) at Trennfurt exit.
15 Mar–Sep.

7HEC lau

KLINGENBRUNN
Bayern (☎08553)

Nationalpark ☎727

For access, leave the B85, which runs from Cham to Passau, approx. 12 km SE of Regen near Kirchdorf turn off E and drive about 6 km towards Klingenbrunn.
All year.

5HEC lau **A**5 **V**2

KLINT-BEI-HECHTHAUSEN
Niedersachsen

Geesthof Geesthofer Weg 37 ☎(04774)512

On dry meadowland next to the River Oste, in quiet setting with trees. Lunchtime siesta 13.00–15.00 hrs.

In Hechthausen leave road B73 and drive W towards 'Lamstedt' for about 3 km.
All year

5.5HEC lau pitch12–15

KNICKHAGEN See **MÜNDEN**

KOBLENZ (COBLENCE)
Rheinland-Pfalz (☎0261)

At **WINNINGEN** (9 km SW)

Ziefuhrt ☎(02606)356

Site lies on level wooded meadowland.

From Koblenz follow road B416 for 11 km towards Trièr. Access to site at the Schwimmbad (swimming pool).
May–Sep.

7HEC ◑ ⋒H |O| ⊙ Ⓖ Ⓡ ≋R ⊞ lau ⊖→ ≋P **A**6 pitch6

KOCHEL
Bayern (☎08851)

Kesselberg ☎464

Off the road beside the lake.

From town take B11 southwards until the turning for the Walchensee power station. Site on right of road.
Apr–20 Sep.

1.5HEC ◇ ⋒H |O| ⊙ Ⓡ ⊞ lau ⊖→ ≋L

KÖLN (COLOGNE)
Nordrhein-Westfalen (☎0221)

At **DÜNNWALD** (NE of Köln)

Waldbad P-Baum-Weg ☎603315

In a wood near an open-air pool and park. Lunchtime siesta 13.00–15.00 hrs.

From B51 (Köln–Mülheim) follow Berliner Str to Dünwald. The turn right and continue via Leuchterstr.
All year.

2.2HEC ◑ ⋒H ⊙ Ⓡ ⊞ ⊖→ |O| ≋P

At **POLL** (6 km SE)

SC Poller Fischerhaus Weidenweg 46 ☎831966

Local authority site on right bank of Rhine below motorway bridge.

Access S across Deutzer bridges, along Siegburger Str via swing bridge, A-Schuttle-Allee and Wiedenweg.
May–mid Oct.

2HEC ◆ ⋒H |O| ⊙ Ⓖ Ⓡ ⊞ lau **A**5 **V**4 4 3–4

At **RODENKIRCHEN**

Berger ☎392421

Mar–Nov.

6HEC ◑ ⋒H |O| ⊙ Ⓖ Ⓡ ⊞ lau ⊖→ ≋P **A**5 pitch5

KÖNIGSDORF
Bayern (☎08179)

Königsdorf ☎442

Unspoilt site in natural setting in meadowland. A number of individual pitches for tourers. Lunchtime siesta 12.30–14.30 hrs.

Off B11, 2 km S of town just beyond the edge of the forest.
All year.

8.6HEC ◑ ◇ ⋒H |O| ⊙ Ⓖ Ⓡ ⊞ lau **A**5–6 **V**3 3 3

KÖNIGSSEE
Bayern (☎08652)

Grafenlehen ☎4140

A terraced site on Königsee–Ache.

From Berchtesgaden turn right at the Königsee car park and continue for 300 m.
All year.

3HEC ◇ ⋒H |O| ⊙ lau

Mühlleiten ☎4584

All year.

1.5HEC ◇ ⋒H |O| ⊙ Ⓖ Ⓡ ⊞ lau **A**7 **V**3 3 3

KÖNIGSTEIN IM TAUNUS
Hessen

At **EPPSTEIN** (8 km SW)

Hubertushof ☎7000

In the Taunus landscape preservation area.

Follow B455 from Königstein.
All year.

3HEC ◑ ⋒H ⊙ Ⓖ Ⓡ ⊞ lau ⊖→ |O| **A**6 **V**4 4 4

KÖNIGSWINTER
Nordrhein-Westfalen (☎02223)

Holstein Pleiserhohenstr 12 ☎(02244)3222

All year.

4HEC ◆ ⋒H |O| ⊙ Ⓡ ≋P ⊞ lau ⊖→ |O| **A**5 **V**3 4 3–4

KONZ
Rheinland-Pfalz (☎06501)

Saarmündung ☎2577

On a level meadow near the confluence of Rivers Mosel and Saar.

From B51 (Trier–Saarburg) turn off at the Saarbrücke (bridge).
Apr–Oct.

1.2HEC ◆ ◑ ⋒H |O| ⊙ Ⓡ ⊞ lau ⊖→ ≋RP **A**3 **V**3 3 3

KÖRPERICH
Rheinland-Pfalz (☎06566)

Eifellux-Ferienpark ☎8474

On a level meadow beside the sportsground and swimming pool (price reduction for campers).

From Bitburg on road B50 towards Vianden. Site lies near the Luxembourg frontier.
All year.

3.6HEC ◑ ◆ ⋒H |O| ⊙ Ⓖ ⊞ lau ⊖→ ≋P **A**4 **V**4 4 4

At **OBERSGEGEN** (2 km N)

Reles-Mühle ☎8741

In rural surroundings next to a farmhouse, set on a level meadow at a brook with trees and bushes.

From Bitburg on road B50 towards Vianden. Site lies near the Luxembourg frontier.
All year.

1HEC ◑ ⋒H ⊙ Ⓖ ⊞ lau ⊖→ |O|

KOTHEN-RHÖN
Bayern (☎09748)

Rhönperle ☎450

Partly terraced, partly level meadowland at lake behind Gasthof Rhönperle. Lunchtime siesta 12.30–14.30 hrs.

From A7/E70 (Würzburg–Kassel motorway) take Bad Brückenau/Volkers exit then follow B27 towards Fulda.
All year.

2.5HEC ◑ ⋒H |O| ⊙ Ⓖ Ⓡ ≋L ⊞ lau **A**4

KRESSBRONN
Baden-Württemberg (☎07543)

Gohren am See ☎8656

A large site beside the lake. It has an older section divided by many hedges reserved for residential campers, and a newer section with fewer bushes.

3 km from Kressbronn. Well signposted from B31.
Etr–15 Oct.

38HEC ◑ ⋒H |O| ⊙ Ⓖ Ⓡ ≋L lau **A**7 pitch7

KREUZNACH (BAD)
Rheinland-Pfalz (☎0671)

SC Salinental ☎27304

Near municipal swimming pool, adjoining a public park on the banks of a canal.

From town centre S on B48 then turn left off bridge over River Nahe.
All year.

1.1HEC ◑ ⋒H ⊙ Ⓖ ⊞ lau ⊖→ |O| ≋P **A**5 pitch5

KRÖV
Rheinland-Pfalz (☎06541)

AEGON-Ferienpark Mont Royal ☎9234

On ridge of a hill. Adjoining fields for caravans and tents.

Access from town centre via mountain road leading to Kövenich.
Apr–Oct.

10.3HEC ◇ ⋒H |O| ⊙ Ⓖ Ⓡ ≋P ⊞ lau pitch15–30

KRUMBACH
Baden-Württemberg (☎06287)

Odenwalk ☎1485

Site lies on a long stretch of open meadowland in a wooded valley. Lunchtime siesta 13.00–15.00 hrs.

Situated about 6 km W of the Mosbach–Buchen road B27.
All year.

4HEC G R P lau A6 Vn/c 4 4

KRUN
Bayern (08825)

Tennsee 714

15 Dec.–2 Nov.

5.2HEC H G R lau LP A9 pitch14

KÜHNHAUSEN
Bayern (0868)

Stadler 8037

Level meadow on lake with private beach.

2 m E shore of Lake Waginger.
May–Sep.

0.6HEC H L

KYLLBURG
Rheinland-Pfalz (06563)

SC Kyllburg 2007

Local authority site on a long, level stretch of meadow beside the River Kyll.

On S outskirts of town. Approach can be difficult.
Apr–Oct.

9HEC H G P lau A2 V2 3 3

LAATZEN See **HANNOVER**

Germany

LACKENHÄUSER
Bayern (08583)

Knaus-Camping-Park 311

Extensive site with woodland parks, waterfalls. Siesta 13.00–15.00 hrs. Many health resort facilities. Garden chess. Curling. Open-air theatre. Indoor table tennis. Ski-lift.

All year.

19HEC H G R P lau A6 pitch8–9

LADBERGEN
Nordrhein-Westfalen (05485)

Waldsee 1816

Site lies at the inn, near the bathing area of the lake.

2 km N. From motorway leave at 'Ladbergen' exit following road towards Saerbeck/Emsdetten and after 100 m turn right.
All year.

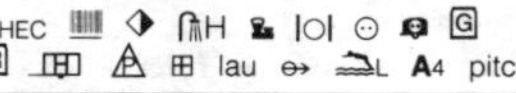

5HEC H G R lau L A4 pitch5

LAHNSTEIN
Rheinland-Pfalz (02621)

Burg Lahneck 2765

Level grassland site with sunny aspect and terraces which provide shade. Situated next to Lahneck Castle. Pleasant view of the Rhine Valley.

From Koblenz (8 km distance) follow road B42. In Lahnstein, leave main road and follow signs (Burg Lahneck), 1.5 km to site.
Apr–Sep.

1.8HEC H G P A4 V3 5 4–5

See advertisement page 232

LAICHINGEN
Baden-Württemberg (07333)

Heidehof 6408

Well-cared for site on hillside with some high firs. Asphalt roads. Separate section outside enclosure for overnight campers.

Leave Ulm–Stuttgart motorway at Merkingen exit, then continue S via Machtolsheim to camp 2 km S.
All year.

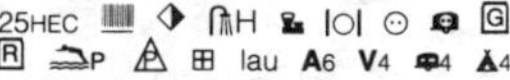

25HEC H G R P lau A6 V4 4 4

See advertisement page 232

At **WESTERHEIM** (5 km NW)

Westerheim 6197

In forest area on a hillock.

Access from the A8/E11 (Stuttgart–München) via limited motorway exit after Mülhausen exit and after the tunnel. From München direction take limited exit after Merklingen exit and before tunnel.
All year. ➤

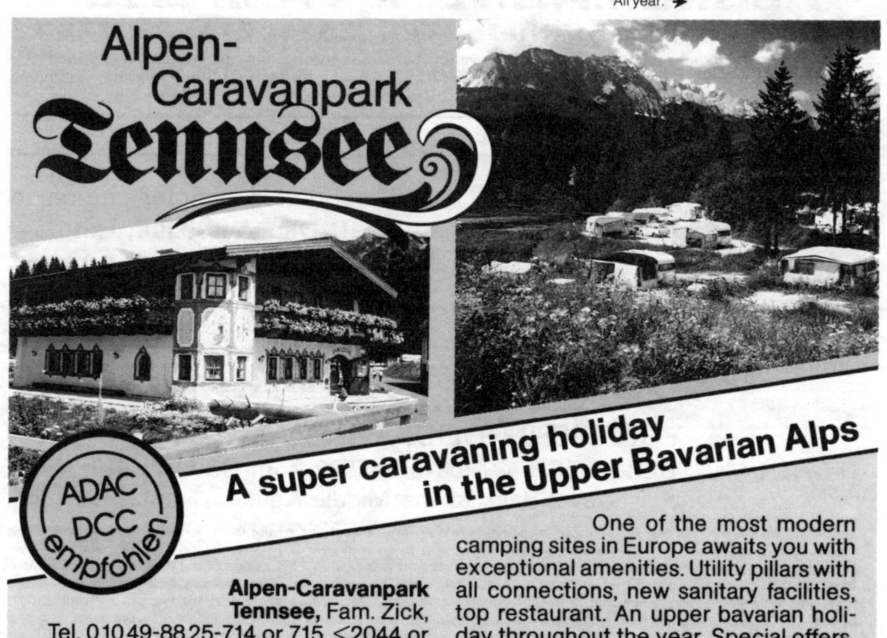

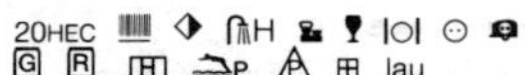

LANDKERN See **COCHEM AN DER MOSEL**

LANDSBERG
Bayern (☎08191)

Romantik am Lech ☎47505

Level site with some terraces on right bank of the Lech. Lunchtime siesta 13.00–15.00 hrs.

S towards Gut Pössing.
All year.

7.3HEC H R lau A5 pitch9

LANDSHUT
Bayern (☎0871)

SC Landshut ☎53366

Municipal site on banks of the Isar, mainly grassy with some trees.

Access via B11 by-pass, exit Landshut Ost, then signposted.
Apr–Sep.

0.4HEC H lau

LANGBALLIGAU
Schleswig-Holstein (☎04636)

Langballigau ☎308

Level grassland site between the Baltic and inland lake.

Germany

Leave B199 Flensburg to Kappeln road at Langballig and travel N for 3 km.
Apr–Oct.

3HEC H lau sL A4 6

LANGENSELBOLD
Hessen (☎06184)

GC Kinzigsee ☎3589

Lakeside site on level meadowland. Lunchtime siesta 13.00–15.00 hrs.

On road B40 between Hanau and Gelnhausen.
Apr–Sep.

6HEC H lau L

LANGENSTEINBACH
Baden-Württemberg (☎07202)

Karlsbad ☎5664

Site on level meadow.

On the Ettlingen–Pforzheim road S of motorway.
Jan–Oct.

3.5HEC H lau P A4 pitch7

LANGHOLZ ÜBER ECKERNFÖRDE
Schleswig-Holstein (☎04352)

Langholz ☎2542

A holiday site surrounded by a belt of trees situated at a wide natural beach, at the mouth of the Eckernförde Bay.

From the Eckernförde take the B203 towards the NE to the turn off for Langholz, then turn right and continue 3 km to site.
Apr–Sep.

1.8HEC H s lau

LANGSCHEID
Nordrhein-Westfalen (☎2655)

Falklay-Mühle ☎1852

A terraced site with individual pitches, in the Nette Valley, next to the Falklay Mill. Beautiful views of the wooded hillsides.

From Mayen go N towards 'Kempenich' past the Riedener Mühlen, then 2 km to site.
All year.

5HEC H

LAUTERBURG
Baden-Württemberg (☎07365)

Hirtenteich ☎296

This site lies on gently sloping terrain, near the Hirtenteich recreation area.

Turn off the B29 (Aalen–Schwäbisch Gmünd) in Mögglingen and drive S for approx 5 km.

All year.
2.5HEC H P lau A4 pitch6

At **BARTHOLOMÄ** (3 km S)

Feriendorf Amalienhof ☎(07173)7542

Level site on high plateau of eastern Alps, partially surrounded by tall trees.

All year.
4.2HEC H G R lau A5 6 6

LEBACH
Saarland (☎06881)

SC Dillingerstr 81 ☎2764

Local authority site. Grassland, slightly sloping on edge of wood.

Take B269, entrance 750 m from sports field.
All year.
3.2HEC H G R P lau A4 6 6

LECHBRUCK
Bayern (☎08862)

DCC Stadt Essen Oberer Lechsee ☎8426

Terraced site, very tidy and well maintained on Oberen Lech lake. Separate section for dog owners. Closed 13.00–15.00 hrs and 22.00–07.00 hrs.

Signposted from town centre.
All year.
15HEC H G R L lau P A5 Vn/c 10 5

LEEDEN See **TECKLENBURG**

LEER
Niedersachsen (☎0491)

At **BINGUM MARINA**

Marina Bingum ☎4421

On B75, over Ems bridge, 200 m W of river.
Mar–15 Nov.
4HEC H G R lau R

LEIWEN
Rheinland-Pfalz (☎06507)

AEGON–Ferienpark Sonnenberg ☎3039

Germany

Extensive terraced site in one of the largest wine growing areas of this district. Lies above the River Mosel.

Access from main B53 (Mosel Valley road), cross the River Mosel at Thornich then via Leiwen to site.
Apr–Oct.
2.3HEC H G R lau P pitch15–30

LEMBRUCH-DUMMERSEE
Niedersachsen (☎05447)

Gotker Tiemann Tiemannshof 2 ☎264

The site lies on extensive meadowland beside Lake Dummersee. Divided into two sections by a ditch. Separate section for young campers.

Turn off from the B51, the Osnabrück–Diepholz road, the approach to the site is signposted.
All year.
10HEC H L

LEMGO
Nordrhein-Westfalen (☎05261)

Freibad Regenstorstr ☎14858

The site lies by the swimming pool.

Apr–Oct.
1HEC H R lau P

LENGERICH
Nordrhein-Westfalen (☎05481)

At **HAGEN** (3 km NE)

Teutoburger-Wald-See ☎4847

Lakeside site in pleasant surroundings. Separate sections for touring campers on open meadow. Lunchtime siesta 13.00–15.00 hrs. Large open play areas for children. Archery butts.

From Lengerich follow road towards Osnabrück. In 3 km on an 'S' bend, turn right and follow camp signs.

All year.
20HEC H L lau

LENGFURT
Baden-Württemberg (☎09395)

Main-Spessart-Part ☎1079

Site lies partly on terraced meadowland and partly on the E slopes of the Main Valley. Lunchtime siesta 12.30–14.00 hrs. Possibilities for water sports, nearby private mooring on the River Main.

From Frankfurt–Würzburg motorway A3/E5 leave at exit Marktheidenfeld. N to Altfeld then E for 6 km to Lengfurt. Site lies at NW edge of village.
All year.
6.5HEC H G lau P A5 V3 4 4

LENGGRIES
Bayern (☎08042)

Isar ☎8361

On partly wooded land between B13 and River Isar.

On B13 from Bad Tolz to Sylvenstein Stausee.
All year.
1.6HEC H G R lau

LENZKIRCH
Baden-Württemberg (☎07653)

Kreuzhof ☎700

Grassland near former farm below the Rogg Brewery on the B315.

Access from Freiburg on the B31 to Titisee, continue on the B317 towards Schaffhausen junction then take the B315 via Lenzkirch, site is some 2 km from centre.
All year.
2HEC H G R P lau R

LEUN See **WETZLAR**

LEUTESDORF
Rheinland-Pfalz (☎02631)

Leutesdorf ☎73508

Site lies on level terrain next to River Rhine, near the Rhein Westerwald Nature Reserve. ➔

Access from Koblenz via the B42 and Neuwied, continue about 7 km to Leutesdorf. Final approach by very narrow lane and across the railway line.
All year.

2HEC H R lau

LIBLAR
Nordrhein-Westfalen (☏02235)

Liblarer See ☏3899

This site lies at Lake Liblar, with its own bathing area.

Access SW from Cologne on the B265 (for approx 15 km) 1 km before Liblar turn left towards the lake.
All year.

9.5HEC H G L lau

LICHERODE See **ROTENBURG-FULDA**

LICHTENBERG
Hessen (☏06166)

Odenwald Idyll ☏8577

In quiet and beautiful setting. Lunchtime siesta 13.00–15.00 hrs.

Access from Darmstadt and Gross-Bieberau.
All year.

1.5HEC H R P A2 A4

LIEBELSBERG
Baden-Württemberg (☏07053)

Erbenwald ☏7382

Pleasant site on edge of wood.

Approach via Calw on the B463 for about 6 km travelling S, then turn right and shortly before Neubulach continue N about 2 km.
All year.

6.5HEC H G R P lau A5 pitch6

LEIBENAU-ZWERGEN See **HOFGEISMAR**

LIEBENZELL (BAD)
Baden-Württemberg (☏07052)

Bad Liebenzell ☏40460

Municipal site with trees near tennis courts. Divided by hedges and internal asphalt roads.

Approach from Pforzheim on the B463 about 19 km S. Turn left 500 m before Bad Liebenzell to site on the banks of the Nagold.
Closed Nov.

3HEC H G lau P A7 V8 8 A8

Germany

LIMBURG AN DER LAHN
Hessen (☏06431)

SC ☏22610

A municipal site on the banks of the River Lahn, sometimes affected by noise from the nearby railway line.

Access via the Limburg–Nord motorway exit; then through Welburger Str, the link road to Verbindungsstr, Offenheimer Weg, Westerwaldstr, Seilerbahn and Am Schwimmbad.
May–15 Oct.

2.5HEC H G R lau P A4 V2 4 A4

LINDAU
Bayern (☏08382)

At **OBERREITNAU** (5 km N)

Gitzenweiler Hof ☏5475

A large site, partly divided into pitches and lying on rather hilly ground. Small lake and facilities for boating.

For access, turn off the B12 which runs from Lindau to Munich, approx 5 km N of Lindau and drive W through Rehlings, and a further 1.5 km to the site.
All year.

13HEC H R P lau A6 V3 5 A5

At **ZECH** (4 km SE)

Lindau-Zech Fraunhoferstr 20 ☏72236

Site lies on meadowland with trees, reaching down to the lake. Very large sanitary blocks. Common room, reading room, field for ball-games and a separate common room for young people.

From Lindau, take the B31 towards Bregenz and turn right (signposted) just before the level crossing. The site is 500 m further down the road.
16 Apr–20 Oct.

5.5HEC H G L lau S A7 Vn/c 7 A7

LINDENFELS
Hessen (☏06255)

Terassencamping Schlierbach ☏630

Site is fenced and lies on sloping terrain. Lunchtime siesta 13.00–15.00 hrs.

From Bensheim–Michelstadt road B47, turn off in Lindenfels and go SW to Schlierbach.
Closed Dec.

4.2HEC H G R lau P A5 pitch6

LINGEN
Niedersachsen (☏0591)

Emswiesen ☏3008

The site lies in the grounds of the railway sports club.

From Lingen follow road towards 'Nordhorn'. After crossing the River Ems turn right.
Apr–Oct.

1HEC H G R R lau A3 V2 2 A2

LINGERHAHN
Rheinland-Pfalz (☏06746)

Mühlenteich ☏533

Site lies on slightly sloping meadowland, divided into sections by a group of trees. Isolated situation at the edge of woodland and adjoining the forest swimming pool (free entry for campers). Lunchtime siesta 13.00–15.00 hrs. Trout fishing.

Access is from Koblenz–Bingen motorway A61 via exit 'Pfalzfeld' – or for caravans, an easier approach would be via exit 'Laudert'.
All year.

15HEC H G R P lau A4 pitch8

LOHR-AM-MAIN
Bayern (☏09352)

Forellenhof Brunnenwiesenweg 38 ☏2865

Site lies on meadowland on an artificial lake.

From town centre follow B26 towards Aschaffenberg then turn off left between SHELL and ARAL garages.
All year.

1.5HEC H R L lau A5 V2 4 A3–4

LOOSE
Schleswig-Holstein (☏04358)

Gut Ludwigsburg ☏1068

This partly wooded holiday site lies between an inland lake and the sea. 100 m long private beach. It is divided into pitches.

From Eckernförde, head towards Klein-Wabbs up to Gut Ludwigsburg, then follow a dirt track for 2 km.
Apr–Sep.

10HEC H G lau L A4 pitch10

LORCH
Hessen (☏06726)

Suleika ☏9464

Well laid out terraced site in Rhine Valley. Separate car park for users of the smaller pitches.

From Assmannshausen take B42 for 3 km towards Lorch then turn right into the Bodental–access to site through railway underpass. Approach for larger caravans – turn right 1 km before Lorch.
All year.

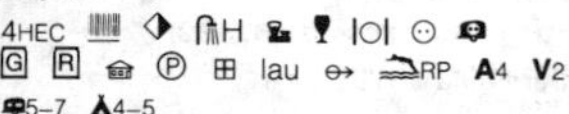

LÖRRACH
Baden-Württemberg (☎07621)

SC Im Grütt ☎82588

Level, grassy site near frontier.

From motorway exit Lörrach on B316 then via Freiburger Str and bridge over the Wiesse and turn left after 100 m.
Apr–Oct.

LÖWENHAGEN See **DRANSFELD**

LÜBECK
Schleswig-Holstein (☎0451)

At **RATEKAU** (10 km N)

Waldklause ☎(04504)3833

Divided by trees and shrubs. Noise from E4 (B207) partially absorbed by wood and motel.

Access from Lübeck–Puttgarden motorway exit Ratekau.
Apr–Oct.

1.2HEC H lau A6 8–9

LÜDINGHAUSEN
Nordrhein-Westfalen (☎02591)

At **BERENBROCK** (4 km NW)

Kanalküste ☎5677

On meadowland between canal and railway line. Lunchtime siesta 13.00–15.00 hrs.

From Dülmen follow B474 towards Seppenrade. 1 km before Seppenrade turn left and continue for 1 km.
All year.

3HEC H lau A5 V1 6 5

LUDWIGSHAFEN AM BODENSEE
Baden-Württemberg (☎07773)

See Ende ☎5366

Meadowland with tall trees W of town, between railway and lake.

Access via Stuttgart-Singen-Lindau motorway. In Ludwigshafen turn off in direction of Radolfzell.
May–Sep.

2.6HEC H L lau A8 V5 5 5

LÜGDE-ELBRINXEN See **PYRMONT (BAD)**

LÜNEBURG
Niedersachsen (☎04131)

Germany

Rote Schleuse ☎791500

In woodland clearing. Lunchtime siesta 12.30–14.30 hrs.

S of town off B4. Signposted.
All year.

2HEC H lau R A4 V4 4 3

LÜRSCHAU BEI SCHLESWIG
Schleswig-Holstein (☎04621)

Lürschau am See ☎4052

N of Schleswig off B76.
15 May–15 Sep.

0.8HEC H lau L A3 V3 3 3

MALENTE-GREMSMÜHLEN
Schleswig-Holstein (☎04523)

Schwentine Wiesenweg 14 ☎4327

A park-like setting with tall bushes, at a small river within the village of Malente.

17 km NW of Eutin.
Apr–Sep.

2.5HEC H R A5 V2 7 7

MAMBACH BEI LÖRRACH
Baden-Württemberg (☎07625)

Wiesengrund ☎7600

On B317. The site can be seen from the road.
20 Mar–20 Oct.

6HEC H lau P A4 V2 3–4 2–4

MANNHEIM
Baden-Württemberg (☎0621)

At **NECKARAU** (5.5 km S)

SC Strandbad ☎856240

A municipal site in the grounds of a park beside the Rhine. At high water the site can get flooded.

From motorway exit 'Mannheim' to Neckaraul/Neuostheim motorway, via the Freudenheim Bridge, then drive through Morchfeldstr, Friedrichstr, Rheingoldstr, Franzosenweg and Strandbadweg to the camp.
Apr–Sep.

0.9HEC H lau RP

At **NEUOSTHEIM**

Neckar Seckenheimer Landstr 191 ☎412536

The site lies directly next to road B37, and the tramline Mannheim-Heidelberg, near the power station, in between the suburbs of Neuostheim and Seckenheim.
Apr–Sep.

2.7HEC H RP A3 pitch6

MARBURG AN DER LAHN
Hessen (☎06421)

GC Lahnaue am Krummbogen ☎21331

Municipal site on level meadowland next to the 'Sommerbad' (swimming pool) in the W part of this 'Town on the River Lahn'.
All year.

1HEC H lau P

MARKDORF
Baden-Württemberg (☎07544)

Wirtshof ☎2325

All year.

4HEC H lau A6 pitch8

MAXSAIN See **FREILINGEN**

MEESCHENDORF (Island of Fehmarn)
Schleswig-Holstein (☎04371)

Europa ☎2419

The site lies in grassland in the S part of the island, divided by asphalt-gravel paths and rows of trees with its own sandy beach.

Approach from the B207/E4 towards Burg to Meeschendorf.
15 Apr–Sep.

5.7HEC H lau

Südstrand ☎2189

Site stretches up to public footpath along the beach. Narrow, difficult approach road.

From town, head towards Südstrand.
Apr–Sep.

9HEC H S lau A4 pitch13

MEHLEM
Nordrhein-Westfalen (☎0228)

Genlenau ☎344949

The site lies opposite the Drachenfels.
All year.

1.8HEC H R lau A4 V3 4 3–5

MEHLEN See **EDERTAL**

MELBECK
Niedersachsen (☎04134)

Melbeck ☎7311

Extensive site in woodland on the banks of the Ilmenau. Centre of site free of trees and reserved for tourers.

On B4, 9 km from Lüneburg.
All year.

3HEC H RL lau

MEMMINGEN
Bayern (☎08831)

At **BUXHEIM** (5 km NW)

AZUR-Camping am See ☎71800

Terraced site beyond public bathing area.

Leave Ulm-Kempten motorway at Memminger Kreuz then right to Buxheim.
All year.

2HEC H L lau

MEPPEN
Niedersachsen (☎05931)

SC Bleiche an der Meppen ☎16411

Level, grassy terrain between open air and indoor pool next to the River Ems. Lunchtime siesta 13.00–15.00 hrs.

From Lingen N on road B70, alongside the Dortmund-Ems canal.
Apr–Sep.

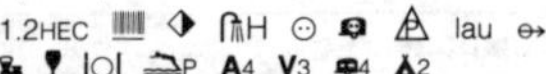

MERGENTHEIM (BAD)
Baden-Württembeg (☎07931)

Willingertal ☎2177

Site lies on a meadow between high green bank and wooded hillside.

From Bad Mergentheim follow B19 S towards Stuttgart, then left towards Wachbach after 2 km, then left to Gastätte.
All year.

METTENHAM
Bayern (☎08649)

Zellersee ☎217

Terraced site, mainly under trees, with bathing facilities.

All year.

METZDORF
Sauer (☎06501)

Alter Bahnhof ☎12626

In delightful wooded surroundings beside the Sauer. Divided into fields by paths, bushes and shrubs. Touring pitches are mainly near the river. Separate field for young people.

Access from Trier on B49, then N on B418 for approx. 6 km.
All year.

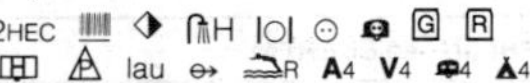

MICHELSTADT
Hessen (☎06061)

Odenwaldparadies ☎74152

Site in partly fenced in and lies next to the station and swimming pool in the NE part of town.

Site is well signposted from the by-pass road of Michelstadt.
May–Sep.

1.2HEC ◇ H lau P

MINDEN
Nordrhein-Westfalen (☎0571)

At **BARKHAUSEN** (5 km S)

SC Porta Westfalica ☎72743

Site next to the River Weser, near the bridge.

From Minden follow road B61 S for 5 km to Barkhausen.
Apr–Sep.

2HEC H lau

Germany

MISSEN See **IMMENSTADT**

MITTELBERG
Vorarlberg (☎08329)

Vorderboden ☎5696

In fine situation at the head of the Kleinwalsertal Valley. One of the highest sites in the area.

Access from Oberstdorf, turn towards Breitach approx 2.5 km beyond Mittelberg.
Jun–18 Oct.

1HEC H G R lau A5–7 pitch7–8

MITTELHOF
Rheinland-Pfalz (☎02742)

Eichenwald ☎1643

In oakwood, mainly divided into pitches.

From Siegen follow B62 towards Wissen. Turning to site approximately 4 km NE of Wissen.
All year.

10HEC H G lau A4 V4 4 3

MITTENWALD
Bayern (☎08823)

Isarhorn ☎5216

In a loop of the River Iser with many pines. Lunchtime siesta 13.00–15.00 hrs.

3 km N to the W of B2 (Garmisch–Partenkirchen–Mittenwald road).
Closed Nov–15 Dec.

7.5HEC H G R R lau A6–7 7–8

MONTABAUR
Rheinland-Pfalz (☎02602)

At **GIROD** (4 km E)

Eisenbachtal ☎(06485)766

Situated in the 'Nassau' nature valley.

From motorway exit 'Montabaur' follow the B49 towards Limburg, in 6 km turn right. From motorway exit 'Diez' follow B49 towards Montabaur in 5 km turn left.
All year.

2.5HEC H G R lau A4 pitch6

MÖRFELDEN-WALLDORF
Hessen (☎06105)

Arndt-Mörfelden ☎22289

Well laid out site in two sections near motorway. Lunchtime siesta 13.00–15.00 hrs.

Well signposted 0.3 km from Langen/Morfelden exit on A5/E4 Frankfurt–Darmstadt motorway.
All year.

4.2HEC H G R lau A5 V3 4–6 3

MÖRSLINGEN
Bayern (☎09074)

Jägerhütte ☎4024

6 km N of Dillengen.
All year.

1HEC H G lau L A3 Vn/c 10 5

MÖRTELSTEIN
Baden-Württemberg (☎06262)

Germania ☎1795

Site is in Mörtelstein, 5 km W of Obrigheim. Site lies between the left bank of the River Neckar and a wooded hillside.

Follow road B292 W towards 'Sinsheim' to just beyond Obrigheim, then N on a narrow, steep road into the Neckar Valley.
Apr–Sep.

0.8HEC ◇ ◆ H G R R lau

MÜHLAHAUSEN BEI AUGSBURG
Baden-Württemberg (☎07733)

Ludwigshof am See ☎(08027)1077

Clean site with small lake away from motorway, near restaurant of the same name. Separate section for residential pitches.

1.5 km from Augsburg Ost exit towards Neuberg.
Apr–Oct.

11HEC ◆ H G R L lau A5 V4 4–8 4–8

Ryssel-Camping am See ☎(08207)316

On level grassland with own swimming facilities on lakeside.

2 km N in direction of Neuburg..
May–Oct.

4HEC H G R L lau

MÜLHEIM
Rheinland-Pfalz (☎06534)

Mülheim ☎8057

Near Mülheim–Lieser bridge over the Mosel.

Access from Bernkastel, 5.5 km along B53 towards Trier.
Apr–Oct.

2.5HEC H G lau R A4 6 4

MÜLHEIM AN DER RUHR
Nordrhein-Westfalen (☎0208)

Entenfangsee ☎(0203)760111

Extensive site near lake. Touring pitches near railway line. Adventure playground. Lunchtime siesta 13.00–15.00 hrs.

From motorway exit Duisburg–Wedau, continue towards Bissingheim to lake.
All year.

14HEC H G R lau L A4 Vn/c 8 8

MÜLLENBACH
Rheinland-Pfalz (☎02692)

Nürburgring ☎224

All year.

30HEC H A4 Vn/c 12 8–12

MÜNCHEN (MUNICH)

Bayern (☎089)

Langwieder See Eschenriederstr 119 ☎8141566

Site in well-tended grassland totally enclosed by a very high hedge about 50 m from lakeshore.

Follow München–Augsburg motorway for 5 km then leave at exit for Rasthaus Langwiedersee.

Apr–15 Oct.

0.8HEC H G R lau L A5 V3 5 4

Nord-West Dachauerstr 571 ☎1506936

On level meadow, well shaded. Lunchtime siesta 13.00–15.00 hrs.

Signposted.

All year.

40HEC H G R P L A5 V4 6–7 5–7

At **OBERMENZING**

München-Obermenzing Lochhausener Str 59 ☎8112235

Park-like site near motorway. Shop closed in winter and no campers accepted after 5 Oct.

Approx 1 km from the end of Stuttgart–München motorway.

15 Mar–Oct.

5HEC H G R lau A5 V4 8 8

At **THALKIRCHEN**

SC München-Thalkirchen Zentralländstr 49 ☎7231707

15 Mar–Oct.

5HEC H G R lau P

MÜNCHSTEINACH

Bayern (☎09166)

Bad ☎750322

Level, long stretch of grassland with isolated bushes and trees. Lunchtime siesta 13.00–15.00 hrs. Pool also open to public.

All year.

4HEC H G R P lau A4 V3 3 3

MÜNDEN

Niedersachsen (☎05541)

Zella im Werratal ☎31310

Beautiful site on left bank of River Werra near motel and restaurant of the same name.

7 km from town towards Laubach.

Apr–Sep.

2.5HEC H R lau A5 pitch6

At **KNICKHAGEN** (5 km SW)

Fulda-Freizetzentrum ☎(05607)340

Slightly sloping site surrounded by woods in a beautiful and quiet situation. Lunchtime siesta 13.00–15.00 hrs.

From the B3 Kassel–München road turn off towards 'Knickhagen' and follow signs to site.

All year.

3.2HEC H R P lau

MÜNSTERTAL

Baden-Württemberg (☎07636)

Münstertal ☎353

Level, grassy site in pleasant situation with fine views. Lunchtime siesta 13.00–15.00 hrs.

Leave Karlsruhe–Basel motorway at Bad Kroningen exit and continue SE via Stauffen to W outskirts of Untermünstertal.

All year.

3.9HEC H G R P lau

MURNAU

Bayern (☎08841)

Halbinsel Burg ☎9870

In pleasant situation beside Lake Staffel.

1.5 km SW of Seehausen.

10 May–Sep.

3.5HEC H G R L lau A5 V4–5 4–9 2–4

MURRHARDT

Baden-Württemberg (☎07192)

At **FORNSBACH** (6 km E)

Waldsee ☎6436

The site lies near Lake Waldsee. Asphalt paths and pitches, with gravel surface.

Drive through Murrhardt towards Fornsbach and the camp, which is on the eastern shore of the lake.

All year.

2HEC H G R L lau A4–5 V3–4 3–4 3–4

NASSAU

Rheinland-Pfalz (☎02604) ➔

Auf der Au ☎4442

Level, grassland site, with some trees situated in a bend of the River Lahn below Nassau Castle. Lunchtime siesta 13.00–15.00 hrs.

Follow the River Lahn from Lahnstein to Nassau or take the B417 from Limburg.
Apr–Oct.

pitch7

NEBELBERG
Bayern (☎09922)

Waldhof ☎1024

Partially terraced site on the Schwarzachback.

Turn off the B85 to Regen then N to Langdorf and continue NE.
All year.

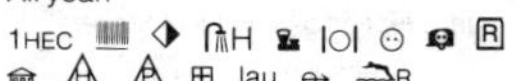

NECKARAU See **MANNHEIM**

NECKARGEMÜND
Baden-Württemberg (☎06223)

Friedensbrücke ☎2178

Campsite lies on the left bank of the River Neckar below the Frieden's Bridge.

Apr–Sep.

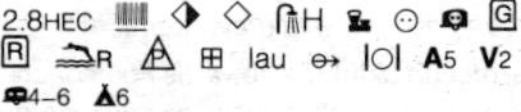

Haide ☎2111

The site is well situated beside the River Neckar and a short distance from the road above.

From Heidelberg on B37 to Schlierbach, over bridge and turn right.
Apr–Oct.

2.6HEC H G R lau RP A5 V2 5 A4

Unterm Dilsberg ☎72585

Beside the Lido.

From Neckargemünd towards Rainbach-Dilsberg turn left about 300 m after Rainbach to site. Difficult access for caravans due to narrow road through village and 17% gradient.
Apr–Sep.

3HEC H R lau

NECKARZIMMERN
Baden-Württemberg (☎06261)

See also **BINAU**

Cimbria ☎2562

Site lies on level meadowland on the bank of the River Neckar.

Access to the site is signposted from road B27.
Apr–Oct.

3HEC H G R R lau A5
pitch6

Germany

NEHREN
Rheinland-Pfalz (☎02673)

Nehren ☎4612

On level terrain beside the River Moselle. Separate section for teenagers. Lunchtime siesta 13.00–15.00 hrs. Liable to flood at certain times of the year.

Turn off the B49 Cochem–Alf road in Nehren.
Apr–15 Oct.

3.5HEC H A5 pitch8

NEUBÄU
Bayern (☎09469)

Seecamping Seestr 4 ☎331

Meadowland site along lakeshore.

Access from Schwandorf on the B85 in direction of Cham.
Closed Nov.

5HEC H G R L lau A5 5 A5

NEUENBURG
Baden-Württemberg (☎07631)

Dreiländer Camping und Freizeitpark ☎9576

An excellent site, very extensive, providing many entirely separate pitches.

Access via Karlsruhe–Basel motorway A5/E4, take the Müllheim/Neuenburg exit, then about 3 km to site.
May–Oct.

20HEC H G R P P lau P A5 V4 6 A6

At **STEINENSTADT** (9 km S)

Vogesenblick ☎(07635)1846

Small, well tended grassland site in orchard.

Access via A5/E4 exit.
Müllheim–Neuenberg', Neuenberg turn off for site 9 km.
Apr–Oct.

0.5HEC H lau

NEUERBURG
Rheinland-Pfalz (☎06564)

Neuerburg ☎2660

Site divided by hedges, close to an open-air pool with a smaller lake for inflatable boats.

Access via the B50 (Bitburg–Vianden). At Sinspett turn N and continue to site on N outskirts (7 km).
Apr–Oct.

2HEC H G lau P A4 V3 5 A5

NEUMAGEN-DHRON
Rheinland-Pfalz (☎06507)

Neumagen-Dhron ☎5249

Level grassland site between the River Mosel and the village.

From Trier follow road B53 towards 'Bernkastel–Kues', cross the River Mosel, then turn right and under the railway.
Apr–15 Oct.

2.5HEC H R A3 V3 5–6 A3–5

NEUOSTHEIM See **MANNHEIM**

NEUSTADT
Bayern (☎09393)

Main-Spessart-Camping-International ☎639

Beautifully situated site along the River Main. Watersports, including water skiing. Lunchtime siesta 12.00–14.00 hrs.

Access from Frankfurt–Würzburg motorway A3/E5, leave at Marktheidenfeld exit, and follow road towards Lohr.
Apr–Sep.

5.6HEC H G R P lau

NEUSTADT
Schleswig-Holstein (☎04561)

Klebitzberg ☎3358

Grassy site, surrounded by hedges and divided into fields, on ground sloping up from the beach.

Access from Neustadt towards Pelzerhaken, 3rd site on the right.
Apr–Sep.

7.2HEC H S

Strande am Strande 25 ☎4188

The site is divided into small sections and slopes down to the sea. Narrow sandy beach.

Access from Neustadt towards Pelzerhaken, first site on the right after leaving Neustadt.
Apr–Sep.

4.5HEC H R lau S A6 pitch10

Südstrand ☎7238

Pleasant, well cared for site on grassland, sloping down a broad stretch of sandy beach.

Access from Neustadt 2 km towards Pelzerhaken, 4th site on right.
Apr–Sep.

10HEC H G R lau S A5
pitch10

At **BLIESDORF** (7 km NE)

Walkyrien ☎587

Site lies on meadowland above steeply sloping shore. Path gives access to beach 200 m away. Lunchtime siesta 13.00–15.00 hrs.

Take the Lübeck–Puttgarden motorway, leave at the 'Neustadt/Nord Gromnitz' exit and continue on road 501 to centre of Bliesdorf, then follow signs.
Apr–Sep.

5.5HEC H G R lau L

NIEDENSTEIN
Hessen (☎05624)

At **KIRCHBERG** (4.5 km S)

Wiesnthalsmühle ☎363

Grassy site, fenced off in woodland area, close to inn of same name.

From Fritzlar take B450 N to Riede, turn right and continue for 2 km towards Kirchberg, then branch left for 1.5 km.
Signposted.
All year.

5HEC H |O| R P lau A4 V4 4 4

NIEDERBERGHEIM
Nordrhein-Westfalen (☎02925)

Niederbergheim ☎1842

Site lies on a meadow surrounded by woodland to the E of the Möhne Dam.

From the Möhne Dam follow the B516 E to Niederbergheim, here turn S towards Hirschberg. 2 km to site.
All year.

4HEC H G R lau A4 V1 5 5

NIEDEREISENHAUSEN
Hessen

Hinterland ☎(06464)7564

Lunchtime siesta 13.00–14.30 hrs.

Follow signs to 'Schwimmbad'.
All year.

2HEC H |O| R lau P A4 pitch5

NIEDERWÖRRESBACH
Rheinland-Pfalz (☎06785)

Fischbachtal ☎7372

On level grassland in Fischbach valley. Lunchtime siesta 12.00–14.00 hrs.

6 km N of Fischbach towards Herrsteij.
All year.

1.7HEC H |O| G R lau A5 V6

NORDSTRAND (ISLAND OF) See **ELISABETH SOPHIENKOOG**

NORTHEIM
Niedersachsen (☎05551)

Sultmer Berg ☎51559

Grassland site with views of surrounding hills. Lunchtime siesta 13.00–15.00 hrs.

Germany

Follow B3 from town centre.
All year.

5HEC H |O| G R lau L A4 V4 4 2

NÜRNBERG (NUREMBERG)
Bayern (☎0911)

SC Volkspark Dutzendteich Hans-Kalb-Str 56 ☎408416

Well-kept municipal site in beautiful situation in a forest next to a stadium with a swimming pool.

Leave A9 Munich motorway at Nürnberg-Fischbach exit, and continue towards the stadium.
May–Sep.

2.7HEC H |O| G R lau LP A5 V4 8 4

NUSSDORF
Baden-Württemberg (☎07551)

Denz ☎4151

Narrow stretch of land, partly sloping, between the old lakeside road and the shore.

4 km from Überlingen.
Apr–Sep.

1HEC H |O| G R L A5 V4 7 5–8

Nell ☎4254

Site within orchard between farm of same name and the lakeside promenade. Small private beach.

Under railway bridge, then turn right.
25 Mar–15 Oct.

0.6HEC H G R lau |O| L A4 V3 5 5

OBERJOCH
Bayern (☎08324)

Bergheimat ☎7108

One of Germany's highest sites. Terraced, with beautiful views.

Above the road from Oberjoch to the frontier.
All year.

1HEC H |O|

OBERKUTTERAU BEI ST-BLASIEN
Baden-Württemberg (☎07672)

Waldfrieden ☎1403

Grassy, slightly sloping terrain between River Alb and Waldfrieden Inn. Lunchtime siesta 13.00–14.00 hrs.

Turn off Waldshut–Schluchsee road (B500) at Häusern towards St-Blasien. Turn sharp left at Mercedes garage just before 'St-Blasien' signpost and continue for 3 km.
All year.

2HEC H |O| lau L

OBERLAHR
Rheinland-Pfalz (☎02685)

Lahrer Herrlichkeit ☎7326

Holiday site with leisure park in wooded surroundings. Lunchtime siesta 13.00–15.00 hrs.

From motorway A3 (Frankfurt–Köln) leave at exit 'Neuwied/Altenkirchen' then 5 km on B256 towards Altenkirchen.
All year.

6.8HEC H |O| G R lau RP A5 V4 5 4

OBERMENZING See **MÜNCHEN (MUNICH)**

OBERNBURG-MAIN
Bayern (☎06022)

River Range ☎1215

Site lies next to the River Main.

2 km S of Obernburg by B469.
May–Sep.

2.5HEC H |O| G R R lau A3 Vn/c 4 4

OBERNDORF
Bayern (☎09002)

Donau-Lech ☎4044

Apr–Oct.

5HEC H |O| G R L lau P A5 pitch10

OBERREITNAU See **LINDAU**

OBERSGEGEN See **KÖRPERICH**

OBERSTDORF
Bayern (☎08322)

Oberstdorf im Steinach 6 ☎6525

Level grassland site with fine mountain views.

800 m N of town centre near railway line.
All year.

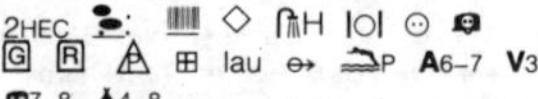

OBERWEIS
Rheinland-Pfalz (☎06527)

SC Oberweis ☎426

Local authority site on long, level stretch of meadow beside River Prüm and sports ground.

From Bitburg take B50 towards Vianden (Luxembourg).
15 Mar–15 Oct.

OBERWESER
Hessen (☎05572)

Oberweser Gieselwerder ☎391

Located by outdoor swimming pool on banks of the River Weser.

Apr–Oct.

Oberweser-Oedelsheim ☎1322

Site lies next to the indoor swimming pool, by the River Weser and at the N edge of the village. Lunchtime siesta 13.00–14.30 hrs.

From Karlshafen follow road B80 to Gieselwerder, cross the River Weser, then 3 km up river.
Apr–Oct.

OBERWÖSSEN
Bayern (☎08640)

Litzelau ☎8704

Almost level meadowland surrounded by forested slopes.

Take B305 from Bernau exit on München–Salzburg motorway and continue through Marquartstein and Unterwössen.
All year.

2.5HEC ◆ ⋔H ▪ ▼ |O| ⊙ Ⓖ Ⓡ ⊞ lau ⇔ ≏L A5–6 pitch5–8

OBERZELL See **BRÜCKENAU**

OCHSENFURT
Bayern (☎09331)

Polisina ☎3081

Terraced site at edge of wood.

From town centre follow road towards Markbreit and in 2 km turn off under railway and continue uphill.
All year.

2HEC ◆ ⋔H ⊙ ⊞ ⇔ ▪ ▼ |O| ≏P A5 Vn/c 8 5

ODERSBACH See **WEILBURG**

OEDHEIM
Baden-Württemberg (☎07136)

Hirschfeldpark ☎5353

Extensive site with lakes near River Kocher.

Turn left off B27 shortly before village.
Apr–Sep.

30HEC ◆ ⋔H ▪ |O| ⊙ Ⓖ ≏L ⊞ lau

OEHE-DRAECHT
Schleswig-Holstein (☎04642)

Oehe-Draecht ☎6124

Grassy site, divided into pitches, on sandy ground behind a sea dyke.

From Kappeln follow B199, turn towards Hasselberg and follow signs 'Strand'.
Apr–Sep.

6HEC ◆ ◇ ⋔H ▪ |O| ⊙ Ⓖ Ⓡ ⊞ lau ⇔ ≏S A4 pitch9

OFFENBACH AM MAIN
Hessen (☎0611)

At **BÜRGEL**

Wassersportverein G-Becker Str 400 ☎862949

In attractive location beside River Main. Lunchtime siesta 13.00–15.00 hrs.

N of B43 (Offenbach–Hanau).
All year.

5HEC ◆ ⋔H ▪ |O| ⊙ Ⓡ ⊞ lau

OLPE
Nordrhein-Westfalen (☎02761)

At **KESSENHAMMER**

Biggesee Kessenhammer ☎61352

Long, narrow partly terraced site in quiet woodland setting on E shore of Bigge-Reservoir. Lunchtime siesta 13.00–15.00 hrs.

A45 exit Olpe continue B54 to Olpe eastwards on B55 and turn off at exit Rhode.
All year.

2.5HEC ◆ ◆ ⋔H ▪ ⊙ Ⓡ ≏L ⊞ lau ⇔ ▼ |O| A7 V4 7 7

At **KIRCHESOHL**

Biggesee Kirchesohl ☎5180

Terraced site on SE shore of Bigge-Reservoir. Lunchtime siesta 13.00–15.00 hrs.

Exit Olpe A45 and continue in direction of Bigge-Reservoir (Stausee).
May–Aug.

1.3HEC ◆ ⋔H ▪ ⊙ ≏L ⊞ lau ⇔ ▼ |O| A7 V4 7 7

At **SONDERN**

Biggesee–Sondern Sonderner Kopf ☎65250

Exit Olpe A45 in direction of Attendorn. In 6 km turn off for Bigge-Reservoir (Stausee).
All year.

6.7HEC ◆ ⋔H ▪ ⊙ Ⓖ Ⓡ ⊞ lau ⇔ ▪ ▼ |O| ≏L A7 V4 8 8

OLSBERG
Nordrhein-Westfalen (☎02962)

At **BRUCHHAUSEN** (7 km SE)

Bruchhauser Steine ☎3000

The site lies on meadowland next to a brook. Lunchtime siesta 13.00–15.00 hrs.

From Meschede follow road B7 for 13 km eastwards, then turn off to 'Bigge' and continue via 'Olsberg' and 'Elleringhausen' to 'Bruchhausen' and finally follow signs for 'Skigebiet Sternrodt'.
All year.

1.8HEC ◆ ⋔H |O| ⊙ Ⓖ Ⓡ ⊞ lau ⇔ ▪ |O| A4 V2 6 3–5

ORSTEIL GOTTINGERODE See **HARZBURG (BAD)**

OSNABRÜCK
Niedersachsen (☎0541)

Niedersachsenhof Nordstr 109 ☎77226

The site lies on a gently sloping meadow bordering a forest, near a converted farmhouse with an inn.

On outskirts of town 5 km from town centre NW on B51/65 towards Bremen, turn right and continue 300 m.
All year.

3.6HEC ◆ ⋔H ▼ |O| ⊙ Ⓖ ⊞ lau A5 Vn/c 6 6

OSTERODE
Niedersachsen (☎05522)

Sösestausee ☎3319

Terraced site on edge of woodland and by reservoir.

Follow road B498 from Osterode towards Altenau and after 3 km turn right to the site.
All year.

10HEC ◇ ⋔H ⊙ Ⓖ Ⓡ ≏LR ⊞ lau ⇔ |O| A5 pitch7

ÖSTRINGEN
Baden-Württemberg (☎07259)

Kraichgau Camping Wackerhof ☎361

A modern terraced site. Lunchtime siesta 13.00–15.00 hrs (except Saturdays).

From motorway exit 'Kronau/Bad-Schönborn' follow road B292 to Östringen.
15 Mar–15 Oct.

2.5HEC ◆ ⊙ Ⓡ ⊞ lau ⇔ |O| A4 pitch5

PEINE
Niedersachsen

At **HÄMELERWALD** (8 km NW)

Waldsee ☎(05175)4767

Near a woodland lake and a railway line. Lunchtime siesta 13.00–15.00 hrs.

From motorway A2/E8 (Hannover–Braunschweig) leave at exit 'Hamelerwald' and follow road S.
All year.

5HEC H R L lau

PEISSENBERG
Bayern (08803)

Ammertal 2797

Leave B2 at S end of Weilhelm and follow road towards Peissenberg. In centre of Peissenberg turn left for Wortherstrasse and Boderstrasse.
All year.

3.5HEC H P lau R

PETTING
Bayern (08686)

Hainz am See 287

Very clean and well-maintained site on W shore of lake. Asphalt interior roads.

On the Waging–Petting road.
24 May–4 Sep.

2.5HEC H L

PFAFFENHOFEN
Bayern (08441)

SC Warmbad 78148

The municipal site lies on the northern outskirts of the town beside the River Lim.

Take the München–Nürnberg motorway, and leave at Pfaffenhofen exit, or take the B13 which runs from München to Ingolstadt.
May–Sep.

0.9HEC H lau P A4 pitch7

PFALZFELD-HAUSBAY See **HAUSBAY**

PFORZHEIM
Baden-Württemberg (07234)

International Schwarzwald 6517

Site on edge of wood with southerly aspect. Separate fields for residential, overnight and holiday campers.

S through Huchenfeld from Pforzheim to Schellbron (15 km).
All year.

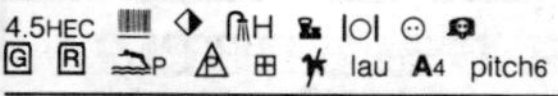

G R P lau A4 pitch6

PFRAUNDORF
Bayern (08461)

Kratzmühle 525

Terraced site, divided into pitches, on a wooded hillside overlooking the River Altmühl.

In village turn off to Kratzmühle.
All year.

9.8HEC H G R lau LR A6 Vn/c 6 5

PIDING
Bayern

Germany

Staufeneck (08651)2134

In beautiful and quiet situation beside River Saalach.

Leave motorway A8/E11 (München–Salzburg) via exit Bad Reichenhall road for 2.5 km and then turn right.
15 Mar–Oct.

2.7HEC H R R lau P A6 pitch7

PIELENHOFEN
Bayern (09409)

Naabtal 373

The site is well-situated beside the River Nab, and has a special section for overnight visitors.

Access from the Nittendorf turn off from A3/E5 Nürnberg–Regensburg N via Etterzhausen.
All year.

5HEC H G R R lau A5 pitch6

PLEINFELD
Bayern (09144)

Waldcamping Badstr 11–13 1921

Closed Nov.

14HEC H G R lau P A5 pitch8

PLÖN
Schleswig-Holstein (04522)

Ruhleben 5375

Generously laid out site on meadowland on the shores of Lake Plön. Next to a farm of the same name.

Access from Plön on the B76 towards Eutin, turn right at the edge of the town, then continue for 400 m.
Apr–Sep.

10HEC H G L lau A5 Vn/c 8 4–8

Spitzenort 2769

A pleasantly situated site with hedges on the shore of Lake Plön. Surrounded by water on three sides, it is ideal for water sports.

Access from Plön on B430 towards Neumünster.
Apr–Sep.

4.5HEC H G R L lau

PÖLICH
Rheinland-Pfalz (06507)

Pöllcher Held 3175

The level grassland site lies next to the sports ground, between the road and the River Mosel, and is surrounded by vineyards.

From Trier follow B53 to Pölich, continue for a further 1 km down river, then turn right.
15 Apr–15 Oct.

1.2HEC H G

POLL See **KÖLN**

POMMERN
Rheinland-Pfalz (02672)

Pommern 2461

The site lies on level meadowland on the left bank of the River Mosel. Fine views along the valley.

About 8 km E of Cochem and just outside Pommern on the B49.
Apr–Oct.

4HEC H G R RP lau A4 V3 5 5

POMMERTSWEILER See **ABTSGMÜND**

POTTENSTEIN
Bayern (09243)

Bärenschlucht 206

The site lies on unspoilt meadowland in the narrow Püttlach valley and is surrounded by the rocky hills of the Fränkische Schweiz range.

From the München–Berlin motorway leave at the Pegnitz exit and drive W for 10 km on the B470 towards Forchheim.
All year.

5HEC H G R lau P A6 V2 4 4

PREETZ
Schleswig-Holstein (04342)

Kirchsee Kahlbrook 25 82265

A quiet site, surrounded by bushes S of Preetz at Lake Kirch and split into three sections.

About 300 m from the B76. Turn off at Schellhorn sign.
Apr–Oct.

2HEC H G R lau L

At **GLÄSERKOPPEL**

Lanker See 81513

Situated on a gently sloping lakeside meadow.

Access SE from Preetz on B76 for 4 km. From here follow signposts. The last 500 m are on a dirt track.
Apr–Oct.

5HEC H R L lau A4 pitch6

PRÜM
Rheinland-Pfalz (06551)

Waldcampingplatz 2481

Site lies on both sides of the River Prüm and is surrounded by woods. Divided into three sections of level meadowland.

Situated at the NW of Prüm.
All year.

4.5HEC H G R P lau A4 V3 5 2–6

Germany

PÜNDERICH
Rheinland-Pfalz (☎06542)

Marienburg ☎2877

Site, divided into pitches, lies on level meadowland with trees between River Mosel and the village. Fine view of castle.

From B43 in the village follow signs towards the Mosel.
Apr–Oct.

1HEC ◇ |O| ⊙ lau

PYRMONT (BAD)
Niedersachsen (☎05281)

International ☎8772

Site partially flat grassland, partially terraced with large building in the middle. Some tall trees, many bushes and flowers.

E from town centre to Dak–Kurcenter, then turn left toward Friedensthal.
All year.

At **LÜDGE-ELBRINXEN** (3 km S)

Eichwald ☎(05283)335

Pleasantly situated grassy site near woodland and pool.

S of Lüdge in direction of Rischenau to Elbrinxen.
All year.

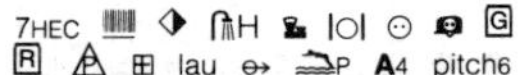

RAMSAU
Bayern (☎08657)

Simonhof ☎284

Long, slightly sloping stretch of meadow, partially shaded.

All year.

1HEC |O| ⊙ lau A5 V2 6 5

RAMSBECK
Nordrhein-Westfalen (☎02905)

At **VALME** (3 km S)

Valmetal ☎253

Well-kept terraced site in the narrow valley of the River Valme. Only a few pitches for touring campers during the winter.

From Meschede follow B7 for 9 km eastwards to Bestwig, then turn S and continue via Heringhausen to Ramsbeck and Valme.
All year.

3HEC ⊙ R lau

RATEKAU See **LÜBECK**

RECHBERG See **SCHWÄBISCH GMÜND**

REGENSBURG
Bayern (☎0941)

Dunnerkell Weinweg 40 ☎26839

The municipal site lies on the western outskirts of the town, and the right bank of the Danube. Has a special section reserved for caravans.

Access via the western by-pass, and over the Pfaffenstein Bridge.
Mar–Oct.

2.6HEC |O| ⊙ lau RP A5 pitch4–7

REHBACH See **EDERTAL**

REINHARDSHAGEN-VAAKE See **HEMELN**

REINSFELD
Rheinland-Pfalz (☎06503)

AZUR Camping Hunsrück Parkstr 1 ☎1021

Well-maintained grassy site on slight incline partially on edge of woodland. Separate pitches are arranged in circular groups, providing small camping communities, each of which has its own sanitary block.

Access via the B52 or B407.
All year.

20HEC |O| ⊙ P lau A6 Vn/c 9 4

REIT IM WINKL
Bayern (☎08640)

St-Sebastian ☎8911

On long stretch of natural terrain beside River Lofer.

Just off B305 towards Ruhpolding.
All year.

1.5HEC |O| ⊙ R lau P A5–7 pitch5–7

Seegatterl ☎8582

Well-kept site. Lunchtime siesta 13.00–15.00 hrs.

In village turn left and continue on Deutsche–Alpenstrasse towards Ruhpolding.
All year.

3.2HEC |O| ⊙ lau L A5–7 V2–3 6–8 4

RHEINMÜNSTER
Baden-Württemburg (☎07227)

At **STOLLHOFEN**

Friezeitcenter Oberrhein ☎2500

Modern leisure complex next to Rhine.

All year.

36HEC |O| ⊙ L lau A5–8 pitch8–10

RIEDHOLZ See **ISNY**

RINTELN
Niedersachsen (☎05751)

Doktor-See ☎2611

In a beautiful situation by a recreation area and beside the Doktor See bathing beach. Section for touring campers. Lunchtime siesta 13.00–15.00 hrs.

In town turn down stream at the River Weser bridge and continue along the left bank for 1.5 km.
All year.

15HEC |O| ⊙ L lau A5 Vn/c 6 6

RODENKIRCHEN See **KÖLN (COLOGNE)**

ROSENBERG
Baden-Württemberg (☎07963)

Hüttenhof ☎203

Flat meadow on include in quiet woodland area, next to large farm.

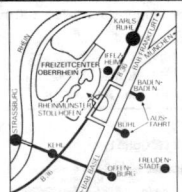

From Ellwangen 3 km N towards Crailsheim, turn W towards Adelmannsfelden and continue for 8 km to turn off to N at Gaishardt.
All year.
3HEC H G R lau

ROSSHAUPTEN BEI FÜSSEN
Bayern (☎08367)

Warsitzka ☎406

A well-kept site with good installations.

From Fussen follow road B16 for 10 km towards Rosshaupten. About 2 km before the village and before the bridge turn right.
All year.

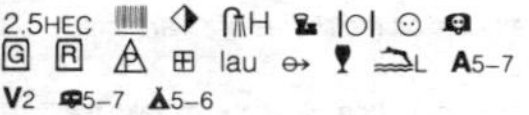

2.5HEC H G R lau L A5–7 V2 5–7 5–6

ROTENBURG-FULDA
Hessen (☎06623)

SC ☎5556

SE of town on River Fulda, follow 'DCC' signs.
May–Sep.
0.7HEC H G R lau P A3 V3 4 3–4

At **LICHERODE** (10 km NW)

Alte Mühle ☎(05664)8141

In beautiful wooded valley. Lunchtime siesta 13.00–15.00 hrs.

From motorway A7/E4 (Kassel–Frankfurt) take 'Raststätte–Hasselburg' exit, follow road towards Wichte then turn off towards Licherode.
Mar–Oct.
2HEC H G R LP lau

RÖTGESBÜTTEL See **GIFHORN**

ROTHAUS-GRAFENHAUSEN
Baden-Württemberg (☎07748)

Schwarzwälder Speckhulsli ☎392

Site made up of several large terraces on an incline.

Leave B500 (Waldshut road) and follow road towards Rothaus/Grafenhausen 3 km to site.
All year.
2.5HEC H lau G

ROTHEMANN
Hessen (☎06659)

Rothemann ☎2285

A small, well-kept site surrounded by a hedge, lies next to the main Fulda road.

Germany

From Fulda follow road B27 for 10 km towards Bad Brückenau; can also be reached from the Kassel–Würzburg motorway leaving at exit Fulda Sud, then 3 km along B27 towards Bad Brückenau.
Apr–Oct.
0.6HEC H G R P lau A4 V4 3 3

ROTHENBURG OB DER TAUBER
Bayern (☎09861)

Detwang ☎6191

Etr–Oct.
1.5HEC H G R lau A5 pitch7–8

Tauber-Idyll Detwang 28A ☎3177

The well-kept site lies on a meadow scattered with trees and bushes, on the outskirts of the N suburb of Detwang and next to the River Tauber.

Access from all main roads is well signposted. The best route is from Nordinger Str (B25) heading W along the River Tauber in the direction of Bad Mergentheim.
Etr–20 Oct.
5HEC H G R lau A5 pitch7

ROTTENBUCH
Bayern (☎08867)

Terrassencamping am Richterbichl ☎422

Several pleasant terraces with good views.

On S outskirts on B23.
1.2HEC G R lau A6 6 6

RÜDESHEIM
Hessen (☎06722)

Langut Ebental ☎2518

On meadowland surrounded by woodlands. Ponies and carriages for hire. Private sports plane for pleasure flights.

N towards Presberg. Steep approach road to Ebental. Signposted.
1 May–15 Nov.
1HEC H G R lau A5 Vn/c 10 10

Rüdesheim ☎2528

Near the open-air swimming pool and the River Rhine.

May–Sep.
2.8HEC H G P lau A5 V4 6 5–7

RUHPOLDING
Bayern (☎08663)

Ortnerhof ☎1764

Well-kept site at the foot of the Rauschberg Mountain, opposite the cable-car station.

Off Deutsche Alpenstr.
All year.
2.4HEC H G lau A6–7 V2 3 3

RUNKEL AN DER LAHN
Hessen (☎06482)

Bleiche ☎2395

On road from Limburg.
Apr–Sep.
2HEC H G R R lau

RUTTERSHAUSEN
Hessen (☎06406)

Lahnblick ☎1510

Level grassland site on the Lahn with simple but clean sanitary installations.

For access, turn off the B3 Giessen–Marburg road N of Lollar and head W.
15 Apr–15 Oct.
H R RP P A4 V2 3 3

SAARBURG
Rheinland-Pfalz (☎06581)

AEGON-Ferienpark Warsberg ☎2037

Open site in quiet situation on top of a hill. Chairlift (700 m) leads down to the town.

At N end of the town leave the B51 'Trier' road and follow signs 'Ferienpark Warsberg' 3 km uphill on good road.
mid Mar–mid-Nov.
27HEC H G R P lau pitch15–30

Leukbachtal ☎2228

Municipal site on level meadows on both sides of the Leuk-Bach (brook).

Leave Saarburg on road B51 towards Trassen, then after crossroads, turn left off the B51.
15 Apr–Oct.
3HEC H G R lau P A4 V5 7 7

Waldfrieden Im Fichtenheim 4 ☎2255

Site lies next to the Café Waldfrieden on unspoilt, slightly rising meadowland in woods.

S of town leave B51 and follow road towards Wincheruigen. 200 m to site.
All year.

0.8HEC H lau P A3 Vn/c 8 A6–8

SAARLOUIS
Saarland (☎06831)

SC Dr Ernst Dadder ☎3691

A municipal site, divided into pitches, and set on a level meadowland with tall trees. Lunchtime siesta 13.00–14.30 hrs.

Turn off road B51 in suburb of Roden, cross new bridge over the River Saar and continue to site, beyond sport hall.
All year.

2HEC H lau P

ST-ANDREASBERG
Niedersachsen (☎05582)

Erikabrücke ☎1431

Open site next to B27 NE of Oderstausee. Off B27 from Bad Lauterberg towards Braunlage.
All year.

5.5HEC H LR A4 V3 4 A4

ST-GEORGEN See **FREIBURG-IM-BRIESGAU**

ST-GOAR
Rheinland-Pfalz (☎06741)

Friedenau ☎368

On level, narrow stretch of meadowland at Gasthaus Friedenau.

Leave B9 in St-Goar and continue through railway underpass towards Emmelshausen for approx 1 km.
Apr–Nov.

0.8HEC H lau RP A6 V5 5 A4–5

ST-GOARSHAUSEN
Rheinland-Pfalz (☎06771)

Loreleystadt ☎2592

Municipal site on level meadow beside the Rhine. Near a sportsfield and opposite Rheinfels Castle.

Access via B42.
15 Mar–Oct.

2HEC H lau A5 V4 5 A3–8

ST-PETER-ORDING
Schleswig-Holstein (☎04863)

At **BÖHL** (1 km SE)

Kniese Böhler Landstr 185 ☎676

Family site near sea dyke, separate fields for tourers and static, divided by high hedge.

Apr–15 Oct.

Germany

1.5HEC H lau S

SALZHEMMENDORF
Niedersachsen (☎05186)

Ferienland Humboldtsee ☎348

Extensive, partially terraced site with lake suitable for bathing. Separate touring field. Lunchtime siesta 13.00–15.00 hrs.

Access from Hameln on B1 to Hemmendorf. Turn right via Salzhemmendorf to Thüste. Then right again to Wellensen.
May–Sep.

10HEC H L lau A4 V1 5 A2–5

SASSENBERG BEI WARENDORF
Nordrhein-Westfalen (☎02583)

Eichenhof Feldmark 3 ☎1585

The site lies at a working gravel-pit lake. For touring campers there are only two small meadows, remainder of the site used by residential campers. Lunchtime siesta 13.00–14.30 hrs.

Site lies about 3 km beyond Sassenberg, turning W off the B476 Versmold road.
Mar–Oct.

10HEC H L lau

SCHACHEN
Hessen (☎06654)

Hochrhön ☎322

Lies 1.5 km from the Kneipp (hydrotherapeutic) Spa area of Gersfeld.

2 km N of Gersfeld.
All year.

3HEC H LP A4 pitch6

SCHALKENMEHREN
Rheinland-Pfalz (☎06592)

Schneider ☎2318

Terraced lakeside site on meadowland at the Schalkenmehrener Maar (water-filled crater). Towing help for caravans.

From A48 (Eifelautobahn) leave at 'Mehren/Daun' exit and follow B42 to Mehren. Turn off to the SW.
All year.

1HEC H LP A5 Vn/c 10–15 A5–8

SCHAPBACH BEI WOLFACH
Baden-Württemberg (☎07839)

Allsehof ☎203

The site lies on well-kept ground with several terraces and is separated from the road by the River Wolfach.

In Wolfach turn off the B924 at the Kinzighbrücke and drive N for about 8 km to Schapbach. Site is 1 km N of village.
All year.

1.8HEC H lau P A7 pitch6–7

SCHARBEUTZ
Schleswig-Holstein (☎04503)

Seepferdchen Pönitzer Chausee ☎72348

Grassland site broken up by shrubs.

300 m from the sea, off the road to Pönitz.
Apr–Sep.

4HEC H S

SCHECHEN
Bayern (☎08039)

Erlensee ☎1695

The site lies on the shores of an artificial lake.

If approaching from Rosenheim, take the B15 for approx 10 km N of Rosenheim towards Wasserburg and turn right upon entering Schechen.
All year.

5HEC H L lau A6 V3 7 A5–7

SCHILTACH
Baden-Württemberg (☎07836)

Schiltach ☎659

The site lies on meadowland on the banks of the River Kinzig and is well placed for excursions.

15 May–15 Sep.

0.3HEC H RP A3 V4 4–5 A3–5

SCHLAG
Bayern (☎09928)

Hirtenwiese ☎1396

A terraced site surrounded by a tall forest.

For access take the B85 S for 8 km. SE from Regen.
All year.

1.5HEC H lau

SCHLEIDEN
Nordrhein-Westfalen (☎02445)

Schafbachmühle ☎(02485)268

The site is terraced and well-managed.

Access via the B258 from Schleiden towards Monschau. After 2 km turn right at the Weyermühle (mill), and drive on for a further 2.5 km.
All year.

8HEC H lau A5 V3 5 A5

Schleiden Dreffenbachtal ☎7030

Site lies in hilly, well-wooded country.

On the B258 to Monschau, 1 km to site.
All year.

5.5HEC H lau P

SCHLIERSEE See **BREITENBACH**

Germany

SCHLOSS NEUHAUS
Nordrhein-Westfalen (☎05254)

Waldsee ☎7372

Site lies on level meadowland next to a wood and a small lake. Lunchtime siesta 12.30–14.00 hrs.

From N edge of Schloss Neuhaus, leave the B68 and follow signs 'Waldfriedhof', then 2 km to site.
All year.

10HEC H P

SCHLÜCHTERN
Hessen (☎06661)

At **HUTTEN** (8 km E)

Hutten Heiligenborn ☎2411

Site lies at Heiligenborn and has a pleasant southerly aspect. Lunchtime siesta 13.00–15.00 hrs.

Approach from Fulda on B40 towards Frankfurt to Flieden for 19 km, then turn left via Rückers to Hutten (8 km).
All year.

4HEC H G R lau P A5 pitch5–7

SCHNAITTENBACH
Bayern (☎09622)

SC Naturbad ☎1011

Gently sloping well tended municipal site in rural area close by large open-air swimming pool, available to campers free of charge.

Follow signs 'Naturbad'.
All year.

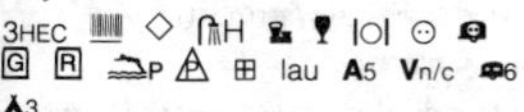

3HEC H G R P lau A5 Vn/c 6 A3

SCHOBÜLL
Schleswig-Holstein (☎04841)

Seeblick ☎3321

Beautifully situated beside the sea and divided into two sections.

Turn off the B5 on the northern outskirts of Husum, and drive towards Insel Nordstrand for 4 km up to Schobüll.
Apr–15 Oct.

3.4HEC H G R lau sP A5 pitch8

SCHÖNBERG
Schleswig-Holstein (☎04344)

At **KALIFORNIEN** (5 km N)

California ☎9591

Family site behind the dyke, divided by numerous hedges.

Access through Schönberg, follow road to Kalifornien, then left at the dyke. Turn left and continue by rough track for 800 m to site.
Apr–Sep.

8HEC H R lau s A5 pitch8–10

SCHÖNENBERG
Saarland (☎06373)

Ohmbachsee ☎6233

Terraced site on sloping ground above E bank of the Ohmabachsee. Separate field for young people. Lunchtime siesta 13.00–15.00 hrs.

Signposted.
All year.

7.8HEC H G R P lau L A6 pitch10

SCHÖNHAGEN (Niedersachsen) See **USLAR**

SCHÖNHAGEN
Schleswig-Holstein (☎04644)

Seestern ☎305

Well kept site beside the sea. Its grassy plots are separated by trees and bushes.

From Eckernförde follow a concrete road through Karby to the site 5 km beyond.
Apr–Sep.

2.5HEC H G R s lau A4 pitch11

SCHOTTEN
Hessen (☎06044)

SC Nidda-Stausse ☎1418

Access via B455.
All year.

2.2HEC H lau L A4 Vn/c 6 A6

SCHWÄBISCH GMÜND
Baden-Württemberg

At **RECHBERG** (6 km S)

Schurrenhof ☎(07165)8190

The site lies in a beautiful setting on the edge of a forest, and has a lovely view of the surrounding countryside.

Drive S on the B29 from Schwäbisch Gmünd, through Strassdorf and Rechberg, and towards Reichenbach on the B10. Then turn towards Schurrenhof.
All year.

2.5HEC H G R P lau A5 pitch6

SCHWANGAU
Bayern (☎08362)

At **BANNWALDSEE** (4 km NE)

Bannwaldsee ☎81001

Meadow gently sloping towards lake.

Turn off the B17 about 4 km NE of Schwangau, in westerly direction towards lake.
All year.

12HEC H G R L lau A6–7 pitch7–8

SCHWEICH
Rheinland-Pfalz (☎06502)

Schweich ☎3099

On level meadowland on the Mosel, next to a marina.

Access via A48 (Eifelautobahn) exit 'Schweich' in direction of Trier. Continue through Schweich, turning left just before the Mosel bridge.
15 Apr–15 Oct.

3.5HEC H G R lau P A3 Vn/c 4

SECK
Rheinland-Pfalz (☎02664)

Weiherhof ☎8555

Site lies on level meadowland next to a small lake in a wooded nature reserve. Special section reserved for young people. Many bathers at weekends.

Take the B255 from Rennerod and drive to Hellenbahn-Schellenberg. Then turn S and continue for approx 2 km.
Apr–Sep.

10HEC H G L P lau A4–5 Vn/c 5–7 A5–7

SEEFELD
Bayern (☎08152)

Strandbad Pilsensee Graf Toerringstr 11 ☎7232

S towards Pilsensee.
All year.

15HEC H G lau L

SEEFELDEN See **UHLDINGEN**

SEGEBERG (BAD)
Schleswig-Holstein (☎04551)

Seeblick ☎81729

The site is very well laid out, divided into pitches, and has a lawn for sun-bathing which gently slopes down to a narrow gravel beach.

Take the B432 towards Ostsee (Baltic Sea) and turn right 300 m after Klein Rönnau.
25 Mar–8 Oct.

10HEC H G R lau L A5 pitch8

SENHEIM
Rheinland-Pfalz (☎02673)

Internationaler Holländischer Hof ☎4660

On level meadowland, divided into pitches beside the River Mosel which has boat-mooring facilities.

Access from Cochem on the B49 in direction of Zell as far as Senhals, then over the bridge and turn left.
15 Apr–15 Oct.

3HEC H G R lau A5 pitch8

SENSWEILER MÜHLE
Rheinland-Pfalz (☎06786)

Bauernhof Bundestr 422 ☎395 ➔

On extensive grassland beside the Idar, partially terraced, in rural area near a farm. Views of wooded range of hills. Next to Camping Oberes Idartal. Separate section for youth groups.

From Idar-Oberstein follow road B422 for about 10 km to the NW. Site lies between Katzenloch and Allenbach.
All year.

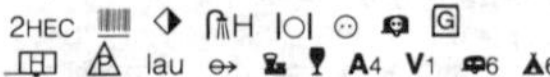
2HEC ◆ ⋔H |O| ⊙ G lau A4 V1 6 A6

Oberes Idartal ☎309

Site lies by a farm on the Idar, set on several small meadows and partly on terraced terrain next to Camping Sensweiler Mühle. Blockhouse with facilities for spit-roasting.

From Idar-Oberstein follow road B422 for about 10 km to the NW. Site lies between Katzenloch and Allenbach.
All year.

2.8HEC ◆ ◆ ⋔H ⊙ G R R lau |O|

SIGMARINGEN
Baden-Württemberg (☎07571)

SC ☎106223

On right bank of Danube by town hall.
May–Sep.

0.8HEC ◇ ⋔H ⊙ R lau |O| RP A3 V3 3 A3

SILBERBORN See **HOLZMINDEN**

SOLINGEN
Nordrhein-Westfalen (☎02122)

At **GLÜDER**

Waldcamping Glüder ☎44448

Site on level terrain surrounded by woodland on banks of the River Wupper.

Access via Cologne-Kamen Autobahn exit Burscheid, via Hilgen and Witzhelden to

Germany

Glüder or from Solingen on B229/B224 in direction of Witzhelden via Burg Hohenscheid.
All year.

2HEC ◆ ⋔H |O| ⊙ R

SOLTAU
Niedersachsen (☎05191)

Waldpark-Camp Scandinavia ☎2293

Heathland site in pine forest. Useful transit site 1 km from motorway (from which there is some noise). Separate section for young campers. Lunchtime siesta 13.00–15.00 hrs.

Access from the Soltau Ost (East) motorway exit then 1 km on the B209/71 towards Lüneberg.
All year.

22HEC ◆ ⋔H |O| ⊙ G R P lau pitch13–26 (incl 2 persons)

SONDERN See **OLPE**

SONTHOFEN
Bayern (☎08321)

Iller ☎2350

Site lies on the shore of the River Iller (too dangerous for swimming) near a swimming pool.

1 km on the B19 towards Obersdorf, before the bridge over the River Iller.
Closed Nov–20 Dec.

1.6HEC ◆ ⋔H |O| ⊙ G lau P pitch23–28

SOYEN
Bayern (☎08071)

Soyen-See Seestr 28 ☎3860

Partly terraced site on eastern shore of Lake Soyen. Several pitches for tourers near entrance.

From B15 between Wasserburg and Haag.
Apr–Oct.

1HEC ◇ ⋔H |O| L

STADTSTEINACH
Bayern (☎09225)

Stadtsteinach ☎6600

Terraced site on SE facing slope with a view over the town and surrounding hills. Lunchtime siesta 13.00–15.00 hrs.

Access via Badstr.
All year.

12HEC ◆ ⋔H ⊙ G lau P A5 Vn/c 7 A3 (per person)

STADTKYLL/EIFEL
Rheinland-Pfalz (☎06597)

AEGON Ferienpark Wirftal ☎608

Extensive, level grassland beside the upper of two small reservoirs, approx 1 km outside the town.

Access S from Euskirchen on the B51, through Blankenheim and towards Stadtkyll.
All year.

6HEC ◆ ⋔H |O| ⊙ G R lau P pitch21–33

STAMMHEIM
Baden-Württemberg (☎07051)

Obere Mühle ☎4844

The site is divided into two sections by the access road, and sub-divided into pitches.

Off B296 almost 3 km S of Calw.
All year.

2.5HEC H lau P A7
pitch7

STAUFEN
Baden-Württemberg (☎07633)

Belchenblick ☎7045

Well kept site on level ground.

Access from motorway exit Bad Krozingen/ Staufen and continue 4 km SE..
Closed 11 Nov–14 Dec.

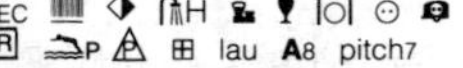
1.8HEC H P lau A8 pitch7

STEINACH
Baden-Württemberg (☎07832)

Kinzigtal ☎87122

Site on level meadowland with tall trees, situated next to the municipal heated swimming pool.

Signposted from Steinach.
All year.

4HEC H lau P A6 V4 4
4

STEINEN
Hessen (☎02666)

Hofgut Schönerlen ☎207

Beautiful and quiet site at Lake Hausweiher, has a special section reserved for residential campers. Young campers under 18 years old not accepted unless with adults.

Take the B8 Limburg-Altenkirchen road. In Steinen turn left to the site.
All year.

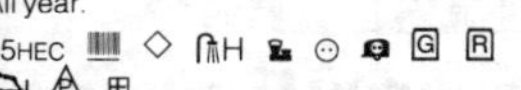
15HEC H L

STEINENSTADT See **NEUENBERG**

STELLE
Niedersachsen (☎04174)

Steller See ☎(04206)250

Delmenhorst-Ost exit off motorway. Site 300 m.
Apr–Sep.

4HEC H L A4 V2 5 5

STOCKSEE
Schleswig-Holstein (☎04526)

Ruh dich Aus ☎608

Terraced site with bushes on the Stocksee.

Access N from Bad Segeberg towards Blunk and Damsdorf for 18 km.
Apr–Sep.

2.5HEC H L
lau

STOLLHOFEN See **RHEINMÜNSTER**

STRAUBING
Bayern (☎09421)

SC Straubing Dammweg 17 ☎12912

Municipal site N of town on left bank of Danube.

Germany

Situated 200 m from the B20 Straubing-Cham road.
May–15 Oct.

4HEC H
lau pitch12–20 (incl 2 persons)

STUKENBROCK
Nordrhein-Westfalen (☎05257)

Furlback am Furlbach 33 ☎3373

Extensive site, partly on level, open meadow and partly in woodland. Separate section for dog owners. Old barn is used as a common room for young campers. Lunchtime siesta 12.30–14.30 hrs.

From the Dortmund–Hannover motorway (A2/E73) leave at exit 'Bielefeld/ Sennenstadt' then follow B68 for about 12 km towards Paderborn. At Km44.2 turn off main road then 400 m to site.
Apr–Oct.

9HEC H
lau A4 V3 4 3–4

STUTTGART
Baden-Württemberg (☎0711)

Canstatter Wasen ☎556696

Level site with tall poplar trees alongside the River Neckar. Lunchtime siesta 12.30–14.00 hrs.

Access from Bad Cannstatt near sports stadium.
Apr–Oct.

1.7HEC H
lau P A6 V3
5–8 4–5

SUDERBURG
Niedersachsen (☎05826)

At **HÖSSERINGEN** (5 km SW)

Hardausee ☎676

Grassland site without firm internal roads. Statics have individual pitches and outbuildings. Separate field for tourers.

Approach from Uelzen S on B4. In 9 km turn right, continue via Suderburg to site on the right just before Hösseringen.
All year.

10HEC H
lau L

SULZBURG
Baden-Württemberg (☎07634)

Alte Sägemühle ☎8550

Quiet holiday site in beautiful situation, surrounded by woodland. Partly terraced, the site is divided into two sections by the approach road.

From autobahn exit 'Bad Krozingen' and B3 to Heitersheim. Here turn E for site in 6 km.
All year.

2.8HEC H P

SÜSSAU
Schleswig-Holstein (☎04365)

Minigolf ☎284

The site lies on bushy meadowland behind a dyke next to the Süssauer beach.

Access from Neustadt N to Lensahn, then E to Goube, and then to Süssau. From there, follow the signposts to the site, 1 km away.
Apr–Sep.

3HEC H s
lau A5
pitch11

SÜSSENLOHE BEI WEIDEN
Bayern (☎09602)

Süssenlohe ☎4404

Large meadow of former farm beside the Süssenlohe Weiher.

Access from Altenstadt/Waldnaab on the B22 about 1 km towards Erbendorf then turn left.
Apr–Oct.

10HEC H
lau L A4 pitch5

TACHING
Bayern (☎08681)

GC Taching ☎9548

Moorland meadow.

Off the Waging–Tittmoning road, 3 km towards lake.
Apr–15 Oct.

2HEC H L
lau

TANN
Hessen (☎06682)

Ulstertal Dippach 4 ☎8292

Terraced site on slightly sloping meadowland. 3 lakes nearby for fishing.

Leave the Bischofsheim–Tann road B278 in Wendershausen and go SE to Dippach.
All year.

2.4HEC H
lau A4
pitch5

TARMSTEDT
Niedersachsen (☎04283)

Rethbergsee ☎422

Level site on a grand scale. Lunchtime siesta 13.00–15.00 hrs.

About halfway between Bremen–Lilienthal and Zeven.
All year.

10HEC H
lau L A5
Vn/c 6 6

TECKLENBURG
Nordrhein-Westfalen (☎05405)

At **BROCHTERBECK** (6 km W)

Bocketal Im Bocketal 12 ☎(05455) 1760

The site lies next to the Otte estate, on the southern slopes of the Teutoburg Forest. There is a separate section for tourists, on a meadow next to the road.

Access from Brochterbeck by-pass on Lengerich to Ibbenbüren road.
All year. ➔

1.5HEC ⬛ ◆ ⋒H ⬛ |O| ⊙ ⬛ R ⛺ ⊞ lau A4 pitch5

At **LEEDEN** (12 km E, also E of motorway)

Truma-Campingpark ☎1007

Site lies on undulating meadowland, with asphalted roads. Four separate buildings. Separate section for dog owners. Lunchtime siesta 13.00–15.00 hrs.

From A1–E3 Bremen–Munster motorway leave at Lengerich/Tecklenburg exit, then via Lengerich to Leeden (10 km).
All year.

30HEC ⬛ ⋒H ⬛ |O| ⊙ ⬛ G R P ⛺ ⊞ lau

TELLINGSTEDT
Schleswig-Holstein (☎04838)

Tellingstedt ☎657

Divided by a row of high shrubs.

Off B203 towards the swimming pool.
May–15 Sep.

0.8HEC ⬛ ◆ ⋒H ⊙ ⬛ ⛺ ⊞ lau ⬛ ⬛ ▼ |O| G P

TETTENHAUSEN
Bayern (☎08681)

Gut Horn ☎227

Quiet site, divided into pitches on lake shore, sheltered by forest. Lunchtime siesta 13.00–14.00 hrs.

SE on Wagingersee.
All year.

5HEC ⬛ ◆ ⋒H ⬛ ⊙ ⬛ G R ⬛ ⬛ L ⛺ ⊞ lau A5 pitch7

Germany

GC Tettenhausen ☎1622

Between lake and Tettenhausen–Waging road.

Access from Waging towards Tittmoning, turn right after 3 km.
Apr–Sep.

1.3HEC ⬛ ⬛ ◆ ⋒H ⬛ ▼ |O| ⊙ ⬛ G L ⛺ ⊞ lau A5 V1 ⬛7 ⛺7

THALKIRCHEN See **MÜNCHEN (MUNICH)**

TINNUM (Island of Sylt)
Schleswig-Holstein (☎04651)

Südhorn ☎3607

Well-kept site divided into pitches.

Well signposted from railway unloading ramp. No road connections between the island and the mainland-rail from Niebüll to Westerland.
All year.

1.7HEC ⬛ ◇ ⋒H ⬛ ▼ |O| ⊙ ⬛ G R ⬛ ⬛ ⛺ ⊞ ⬛ lau ⬛ S A6 V3 ⬛10 ⛺6–9

TITISEE-NEUSTADT
Baden-Württemberg (☎07651)

Bankenhof ☎(07652) 1351

From Titisee village follow signs 'Campingplatz'. Access road to site closed 22.00–06.00 hrs.
All year.

3.5HEC ⬛ ◆ ◆ ⋒H ⬛ ▼ |O| ⊙ ⬛ G R ⛺ ⊞ lau ⬛ LRP A5 V5 ⬛4 ⛺4

Bühlhof ☎(07652) 1606

In pleasant situation on hillside above lake. Lunchtime siesta 13.00–14.30 hrs.

Well signposted.
Closed 15 Dec–Oct.

6HEC ⬛ ◆ ⋒H ⬛ ⊙ ⬛ G R ⛺ ⊞ lau ⬛ ▼ |O| LP A5–6 pitch9–10

Sandbank ☎8243

On terrain rising from lakeside, upper part terraced, landscaped with trees.

Access from Titisee, N bank of lake, turn into old Feldbergstr. At SW end of lake turn left and continue along narrow private road through Camping 'Bankenhof' (closed 22.00–06.00 hrs) to the site about 700 m on SE bank of lake.
Apr–20 Oct.

3HEC ⬛ ◆ ◆ ⋒H ⬛ |O| ⊙ ⬛ G R ⬛ ⬛ L ⛺ ⊞ lau A5–6 pitch10

Weiherhof ☎1468

Mainly level site with trees, bordering on lake shore for about 400 m.

Signposted from Titisee.

15 May–15 Sep.
2HEC H lau A6 V5 6 A6

TITTMONING
Bayern (08683)

Seebauer 541
On meadow with a few terraces. Near a farm, beside a lake.

3 km NW towards Burghausen.
All year.
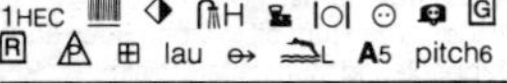
1HEC H lau L A5 pitch6

TODTNAU
Baden-Württemberg

Hochschwarzwald (07671) 1288
Terraced site, partially grassland, by ski-lift.

6 km NW of Todtnau.
Closed 21 Apr–May.

2.5HEC H lau A6 Vn/c 7 A4–7

TÖNNING
Schleswig-Holstein (04861)

Lilienhof Katinger Landstr 5 439
Well-maintained site in the woodland grounds of an old manor house next to a quiet country road.

Leave B202 at far end of Tönning, then 2 km W towards Welt.
All year.
2.3HEC H lau A5 V3 5 A6

TRECHTINGSHAUSEN See **BINGEN**

TREIS-KARDEN
Rheinland-Pfalz (02672)

Mosel-Boating-Center 2613
An extensive, level site on a grassy island in the Mosel next to a yacht marina.

Turn off the B49 in Treis onto the southern coastal road.
15 Apr–15 Oct.
2.5HEC H lau RP A5 pitch7

TRENDELBURG
Hessen (05675)

Trendelburg 301
Site located at the foot of the castle, subdivided on the banks of the River Diemel. Covered tennis court.

Access from Kessel N via Hofgeismar (B83) to Trendelburg cross the bridge and turn sharp left, down to the site.
All year.
1.5HEC H R lau P A4 4

TRIER
Rheinland-Pfalz (0651)

SC Monaise 86210

Germany

Municipal site on level meadow under high trees in former Schloss Park on banks of the Mosel.

From town follow B49 along left bank of the Mosel 5 km up river towards Zewen.
Apr–Oct.
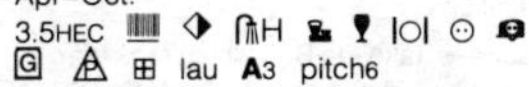
3.5HEC H lau A3 pitch6

Trier-City Luxemburger Str 81 86921
Level site owned by the Rowing Club Treviris, on left bank of the Mosel divided by an asphalt road.

It lies between the Romer bridge and Adenauer bridge on road towards Luxembourg.
15 Mar–15 Nov.
1.8HEC H R lau A5 V7 7 A4–5

TRIPPSTADT
Rheinland-Pfalz (06306)

Sägmühle 1215
The site lies in a wooded valley beside the Sägmühle Lake (Saw Mill Lake). It consists of several unconnected sections, some of them terraced. Lunchtime siesta 12.30–14.00 hrs.

14 km S of Kaiserslautern.
All year.
8HEC H L lau A5

TÜBINGEN
Baden-Württemberg (07071)

Tübingen 23343
A quiet site, well situated on the left bank of the River Neckar.

For access from the town centre, cross the Neckar Bridge, then turn right and drive S through Uhlandstr or Bahnhofstr to next bridge. Cross bridge and drive upstream to the Rappenberghalde hill.
All year.
2HEC H lau P

TÜCHERSFELD
Bayern (09242)

Fränkische Schweiz 440
Access from motorway A9/E6, leave at exit 'Pegnitiz' then 12 km W on B470 towards Forchheim.
Apr–Sep.
2HEC H R lau A6 V3 4 A4

ÜBERLINGEN
Baden-Württemberg (07551)

SC Bahnhofstr 57 64583
The sites lies on the western outskirts of the town, between the railway line and the road on one side, and the concrete shore wall on the other. It is divided into several sections by low wooden barriers and has a very small beach. No individual youths under 18.

Apr–10 Oct.
3HEC H L lau P A6 pitch10–12

UFFENHEIM
Bayern (09842)

SC Uffenheim 670
Access from Würzburg, follow B13 SE. On entering Uffenheim turn right, then 500 m to site.
15 May–15 Sep.
0.5HEC H P

UHLDINGEN
Baden-Württemberg (07743)

At **SEEFELDEN** (1 km W)

Seeperle
This site has some large trees along the shore of the lake. 50 m-long boat landing stage. It is one of the few camps that does not reserve its best pitches for residential campers.

Turn off B31 at Oberuhldingen and head towards Seefelden. Site 1 km.
Etr–15 Oct.
0.7HEC H L lau R A5 V5 5 A5

ULMEN
Rheinland-Pfalz (02676)

Jungfernweiher 684
Site lies in an industrial area to the N of the Ulmener Maar, at the small lake.

From motorway A48 (Eifel autobahn) leave at exit Ulmen, then N to Ulmen railway station and continue towards 'Berenbach'. After 1 km turn right and follow signs to site.
All year.
2HEC H lau R

UNTERHOCHSTÄTT *Bayern* (08664)

Sporte-Ecke 500
Small site between road and lake, private shore.

1 km S of Chieming.
Apr–Sep.
1.2HEC H lau L A6 V2 7 A5–6

USLAR
Niedersachsen (05573)

At **DELLIEHAUSEN SOLLING** (8 km NE)

Bergsee Bergseestr 1 1217
Well-kept site on meadow beside lake, in Solling nature reserve. Separate section for young campers. Lunchtime siesta 13.00–15.00 hrs. Mobile shop.

Access from motorway exit Nörten-Hardenberg, take the B446 and then the B421 via Hardegsen to Volpriehausen, then right to Delliehausen (2.5 km).
All year. ➔

1HEC lau LP A7 pitch8

At **SCHÖNHAGEN** (6 km W)

SC Schönhagen ☏2811

Local authority site in meadow by woodland pool.

From motorway Hannover–Kassel leave at exit 'Norten–Hardenberg', then along road B446 and B241 via Hardegsen and Uslar to Schönhagen. Continue on road B497 towards Neuhaus and within 2 km turn right, and follow signs to the site.
Apr–Oct.

4.5HEC P

UTSCHEID
Rheinland-Pfalz

Michelbach ☏(06564)2097

A municipal site at the Michelbach, surrounded by meadows and woods, 50% individual pitches.

From the B50 Bitburg–Vianden road turn N in Sinspelt. Then continue via Niederraden to Utscheid.
All year.

1.2HEC lau A2 V2 5 5

UTTING AM AMMERSEE
Bayern (☏08806)

Freizeitgelände ☏7245

Municipal site separated from lake which offers private bathing facilities. Separate site for residentials.

Turn off the B12, München–Landsberg road. Turn left before Greifenberg, and continue 5 km to site.
Etr–15 Oct.

6HEC lau L A4 V4 6–7 5–6

VALME See **RAMSBECK**

VELBURG
Bayern (☏09182)

Hauenstein ☏454

A well-appointed site, lies on several terraces and is completely divided into individual pitches. All with electric points.

From motorway A3 Nürnberg–Regensburg leave at exit Velberg, then continue through village towards the S following signs Naturbad.
All year.

5HEC lau L A4 V2 4 3

VELDEN
Bayern (☏08086)

Lain ☏319

Very quite site, partially terraced, and level meadowland on Lake Erlensee.

All year.

8HEC lau L A4 pitch4

Germany

VIECHTACH
Bayern (☏09942)

Knaus-Camping-Park ☏1095

Site on slightly undulating meadow, divided by rows of trees. The site has modern installations.

For access, take the B85 which runs from the junction with the road towards Freibad Viechtach, and follow the signposts.
Closed Nov–4 Dec.

8HEC P lau A6 pitch8–9

VINKRATH BEI GREFRATH
Nordrhein-Westfalen (☏02158)

SC Waldrieden ☏3855

Municipal site, within nature reserve.

From Grefrath N towards Wankum after 3 km. Turn left.
Apr–15 Oct.

3HEC lau A4 V4 5 3–5

VORDERWEIDENTHAL
Rheinland-Pfalz (☏06398)

Bethof ☏244

Terraced site at the 'Naturefreudhaus' (hostel belonging to Friends of Nature). Separate tent area for the young.

From Bad Bergzabern follow road B427 for 7 km westwards, after Birkenhördt turn right, then 1.5 km to site.
Apr–Oct.

1.2HEC lau A4 pitch6

WACHENHEIM-AN-DER-WEINSTRASSE
Rheinland-Pfalz (☏06322)

Burgtal Waldstr ☏2689

The site lies in a long valley surrounded by woodland, within the area of a lake with swimming facilities.

From motorway junction Ludwigshafen go to Bad Dürkheim, turn left and follow road B271 (Deutsche Weinstrasse) for 2 km towards 'Neustadt'.
All year.

1HEC lau P A3 V1 5 5

WAGING
Bayern (☏08681)

Strandcamping Lido ☏552

Extensive, level grassland site divided in two by access road to neighbouring sailing club. The site lies near the Strandbad and Kurhaus bathing area and spa, and the Casino. There is a Kneipp (hydrotherapeutic) pool in the camp.

Follow the signposts leading to the Strandbad bathing area.
All year.

18HEC L lau A5–6 pitch7

WAISCHENFELD
Bayern (☏09202)

Steinerner Beutel ☏359

The site lies on a meadow beside the River Wiesent. The camp has a footbridge leading to the heated swimming pool across the river.

Leave the motorway A9/E6 (Munich/Berlin) at either Bayreuth-Nord or Sud exit and follow B22 westwards to Donndorf–Eckersdorf. Then turn off to Obernsees and via Truppach and Munkenfels to site.
All year.

2.2HEC PR lau

WALDBRONN
Baden-Württemberg (☏07243)

Albgau Herrenalbstr 2 ☏61069

Extensive meadowland adjacent to the little Alb river.

Near the Neurod Inn and the infrequent Ettingen–Herrenalb railway.
Closed 16 Oct–14 Nov.

3.6HEC lau

WALDECK
Hessen (☏05634)

Hohe Pappel ☏484

The site, with some terraced individual pitches, lies on the northern shore of the Eder-Stausee (reservoir), on the Schied peninsula.

From Korbach follow road B251 to Sachsenhausen, then turn S via Nieder-Werbe to Halbinsel Scheid.
15 Mar–Oct.

1HEC lau LP A5 pitch7

WALDKIRCH-SIENSBACH
Baden-Württemberg (☏07681)

Elztalblick ☏7433

All year.

1HEC lau P

WALD-MICHELBACH
Hessen (☏06207)

Schöner-Odenwald ☏2237

The site is split into two sections and lies partly on sloping ground, bordered by woodland. Lunchtime siesta 13.00–15.00 hrs.

From Beerfelden on road 45 turn W, then via Affolterbach to Wald-Michelbach. Alternatively, from Mörlenbach on road B38 turn SE to Wald-Michelbach. The turn off for the site lies in the village centre.
Closed Oct.

2.5HEC lau P

WALDMÜNCHEN
Bayern (☏09972)

SC Perlsee ☎1469

A municipal, terraced site, lying between pine woodland and Perlsee.

From Waldmünchen follow the road towards trhe railway station, and 100 m short of the station turn right in a northerly direction (Perlenseestr). Continue for 1.5 km to the site.
All year.

4.5HEC ... H ... L ... lau **A**5 pitch6

WALKENRIED
Niedersachsen (☎05525)

AZUR-Knaus Ellricher Str 7 ☎778

Closed Nov–15 Dec.

5.5HEC ... H ... P ... lau **A**6 pitch8–9

WALLDORF
Baden-Württemberg (☎06227)

Walldorf-Astoria Schwetzinger Str ☎9195

The site lies near a swimming pool in the woods. Separate section for dog owners.

For access, take the Karlsruhe to Mannheim motorway, leaving it at the Walldorf exit.
15 Apr–15 Oct.

2HEC ... H ... P **A**4 **V**4 4 4

WALLERFANGEN
Saarland (☎06831)

GC Blauwald ☎60591

Follow signs from B406.
Apr–Sep.

4.8HEC ... H ... lau ... P

WANNSEE See **BERLIN**

WARBURG
Nordrhein-Westfalen (☎05641)

Eversburg ☎8668

Site lies next to restaurant of the same name on the SE outskirts of the town.

All year.

1HEC ... H ... lau ... P **A**3 **V**2 5 5

WASSERFALL
Nordrhein-Westfalen (☎02905)

Wasserfall ☎332

Terraced site, surrounded by woodland, next to leisure centre 'Fort Fun'. Little room for touring campers during the winter.

Germany

About 10 km E of Meschede, between Bestwig and Nuttlar, turn S off the B7. Drive past Gevelinghausen and up to Wasserfall.
All year.

0.75HEC ... H ...

WAXWEILER
Rheinland-Pfalz (☎06554)

AEGON-Ferienpark im Prümtal ☎427

Site lies on level terrain and is divided into pitches, with a separate field on the opposite side of the River Prüm. Near swimming pool. Lunchtime siesta between 13.00–15.00 hrs.

From N end of Waxweiler, turn off towards the River Prüm.
Apr–Oct.

3HEC ... H ... lau ... P pitch15–30

WEENER
Niedersachsen (☎04951)

Weener am Erholungsgebiet 4 ☎1740

A municipal site, pleasantly landscaped and set inside a leisure centre with swimming pool and harbour. Lunchtime siesta 13.00–15.00 hrs.

From the main road B75 (E35) from Leer towards the Dutch frontier and turn off in the centre of Weener and follow signs to site.
Apr–Oct.

3.5HEC ... H ... lau ... PR **A**4 pitch6

WEHLEN
Rheinland-Pfalz (☎06531)

Schenk ☎8176

A site in the Mosel valley, partly set on terraces. The site approach can be difficult for caravans due to the steep gradient.

From Bernkastel-Kues follow B53 for 4 km NW towards 'Koblenz' reaching Wehlen turn right.
Etr–Oct.

1HEC ... H ... lau ... RP **A**5

WEILBURG
Hessen (☎06471)

At **ODERSBACH**

Odersbach ☎7620

In attractive setting beside the River Lahn, next to a public swimming pool. Lunchtime siesta 12.00–14.00 hrs.

On S outskirts of town.
Apr–Oct.

5HEC ... H ... RP ... lau ... **A**4 **V**3 4 3

WEILER-SIMMERBERG
Bayern (☎08381)

Alpenblick ☎3447

Clean facilities on this site belonging to the Deutsche Alpenstrasse.

Access from the B308 in Weiler.
Signposted.
Jan–Sep.

2.5HEC ... H ... L ... lau ... **A**6 pitch8

WEISSACH
Bayern (☎08022)

Wallberg ☎5371

This well-kept site lies on a level meadow with a few trees beside a stream.

For access take the B318 from Gmund to Tegernsee, drive through Bad Wiessee, and on to Weissach, approx 9 km further on.
All year.

2.5HEC ... H ... lau ... LR

WEISSENSTADT
Bayern (☎09253)

Weissenstädter See ☎288

This municipal site is in close proximity to a swimming pool and a lake, so offering numerous sports facilities.

1 km NW of the town.
All year.

1.7HEC ... H ... lau ... LP **A**4 **V**3 3 3

WEMDING
Bayern

AZUR Wemding ☎(09092)1356

All year.

9HEC ... H ... L ... lau **A**5–6 pitch8–9

WERDEN See **ESSEN**

WERTACH
Bayern (☎08365)

Grüntensee Grünterseestr 41 ☎375

A modern site beside Lake Grünten.

If approaching from Kempten, turn right entering Nesselwang, and follow the signposts. ➔

All year.

3.5HEC lau

At **JUNGHOLZ** (5 km SE)

Jungholz ☎882

Terraced site.

About 100 m from the Austrian frontier.
All year.

3.3HEC lau

WERTHEIM AM MAIN

Baden-Württemberg (☎09342)

Wertheim ☎5719

Site lies on a level, long stretch of meadowland on the banks of the River Main next to a swimming pool. Lunchtime siesta 12.00–14.00 hrs.

Follow road towards 'Miltenberg', and in 1 km turn right at the ARAL petrol station and head towards the site.
Apr–Sep.

5HEC RP lau A6 pitch7–8

At **BETTINGEN** (5 km E)

Wertheim-Bettingen ☎7077

Motorway Frankfurt–Würzburg, exit Wertheim, 1 km.
Apr–Oct.

7.5HEC lau

WESTERHEIM See **LAICHINGEN**

WETZLAR

Hessen (☎06473)

At **LEUN** (11 km W)

Bergcamping ☎501

Terraced meadowland site on hillside with southerly aspect. Lunchtime siesta 13.00–15.00 hrs.

From Wetzlar follow B429 'Limburg' road 1 km westwards to Leun.
Apr–Sep.

0.8HEC A3 V3 3 2–8

WIETZENDORF

Niedersachsen (☎05196)

Südsee ☎345

This site is beautifully situated in a forest beside lake.

Leave the Hannover–Hamburg motorway at the Soltau–Süd exit, and take the B3 for 2 km towards Celle. At the underpass in Bokel, turn left and drive on for approx 4 km towards Wietzendorf.
All year.

55HEC L lau pitch22–34

WIETZE-WIECKENBERG

Niedersachsen (☎05146)

An der Alten Wietze ☎2379

A very quiet site at the edge of the nature reserve 'Südheide'. Lunchtime siesta 13.00–15.00 hrs.

Germany

From motorway A7/E4 (Hannover–Hamburg) leave at exit Schwarmstedt, then follow the B214 'Celle' road to Wietze. Here, turn right and continue for 2 km to site.
Apr–Oct.

2.8HEC lau

WILDBAD

Baden-Würtemberg (☎07081)

AZUR-Camping Schwarzwald
☎(07055)1795

Long narrow site with some terraces, set between the River Enz and the wooded hillside. Separate section for young campers.

Access is from Pforzheim along B294 via Calmbach southwards.
All year.

2.5HEC lau A5 pitch7–8

Kleinenzhof ☎3435

All year.

6HEC R lau A6 pitch7

WILDBERG

Baden-Württemberg (☎07054)

Wildberg Calw ☎458

All year.

3.5HEC P lau A6 Vn/c 5 5

WILSUM

Niedersachsen (☎05945)

Wilsumer Berge ☎1029

An extensive generously laid out site under Dutch ownership. Parts of the site adjoin a large lake. The separate section for touring campers has its own sanitary building.

From Nordhorn follow road B403 via Uelsen to Wilsum. On nearside of Wilsum turn right.
Apr–Sep.

75HEC L lau

WINDEBRUCH

Nordrhein-Westfalen (☎02358)

Seeblick ☎381

Terraced site on large meadow near the forest on the western shore of the Lister reservoir, which is for residential campers only. For touring campers there are individual pitches next to the main road. Lunchtime siesta 13.00–14.00 hrs.

Access as for Gut Kalberschnacke (listed under Kalberschnacke) which lies on the opposite reservoir shore.
All year.

4HEC lau A5 V3 5 5

WINGST

Niedersachsen (☎04778)

Knaus Camping-Park Wingst ☎7044

This modern comfortable site extends over several terraces, above a small artificial lake on the northern edge of an extensive forested area. Lunchtime siesta 13.00–15.00 hrs. Municipal recreation centre across the road.

Turn off the B73 between Stade and Cuxhaven, about 3 km S of Cadenberge.
All year.

9HEC lau P A5–6 pitch8–9

WINKL BEI BISCHOFSWIESEN

Bayern (☎08652)

Winkl ☎7572

In meadow between the B20 and edge of woodland.

From Bad Reichenhall to Berchtesgaden about 8 km.
All year.

1.2HEC lau

WINNINGEN See **KOBLENZ (COBLENCE)**

WINSEN-ALLER

Niedersachsen (☎05143)

Auf der Hude

Site lies on meadowland at the River Aller. Watersports available. Lunchtime siesta 13.00–15.00 hrs.

From Celle go NW to Winsen.
All year.

3HEC P lau

WISSEL

Nordrhein-Westfalen (☎02824)

Wisseler See ☎6613

Well-kept municipal site with modern equipment beside Lake Wissel. There is a separate car park next to the open-air swimming pool. This pool belongs to the camp. The washrooms are closed during lunchtimes and at night.

From Kleve, take the B57 towards Xanten. After about 9 km, turn left and drive a further 3 km towards Wissel.
Seasonal.

6HEC lau L A6 V3 7 7

WITTENBORN

Schleswig-Holstein (☎04554)

Weisser Brunnen ☎1757

A lakeside site consisting of several sections, hilly in parts, next to Lake Mözen. A public road, leading to the lake, passes through part of the site.

Turn off B206 at Km23.6 towards lake.
Apr–15 Oct.

6HEC lau L A4 pitch8

WITTMUND
Niedersachsen (☎04462)
At **HARLESIEL** (16 km N)
Harlesiel ☎(04464)8046
Level, subdivided grassland site between dyke and sandy beach. Shop and leisure facilities near the site entrance.
May–15 Sep.
14.9HEC H ⊙ R sP

WITZENHAUSEN
Niedersachsen (☎05542)
Werratal ☎1465
The site lies on a meadow between the outskirts of Witzenhausen and the banks of the Werra.
For access, leave Hannover–Kassel motorway at Werratal. 10 km on B80 to Witzenhausen. From market place follow signs.
All year.
2.2HEC H ⊙ G R |O| R

WOLFACH-KINZIGTAL
Baden-Württemberg (☎07834)
Wolfach Schiltacherstr ☎6100
Site lies on narrow well-kept meadowland between the River Kinzig and the small Kinzig Canal, opposite a swimming pool.
Situated at the SE end of Wolfach off the B294.
All year.

6HEC H |O| ⊙
G R ⓟ lau P A5 pitch6

WOLFENBÜTTEL
Niedersachsen (☎05331)
SC Wolfenbüttel ☎2538
Municipal site next to heated swimming pool. The sanitary installations of the swimming pool can be used by campers.
From Wolfenbüttel follow B4 to the signposted turn-off to 'Hallenbad Campingplatz'.
15 May–Aug.
10HEC H |O| ⊙
P A3 V2 3 3

WOLFRATSHAUSEN-LOISACH
Bayern (☎08171)
SC Wolfratshausen ☎78795
Municipal site, level grassland by a tributary of the River Loisach.
From Wolfratshausen follow road S towards 'Autobahn' then turn left to site.
All year.
0.6HEC H |O| ⊙
R lau

WOLFSBURG
Niedersachsen (☎05361)
Allersee ☎63395
The site lies next to the Allerwiesen House belonging to the Friends of Nature.
It is well kept and has many trees, and is close to the lake.

Germany

All year.
1.5HEC H ⊙ R
lau |O| L A5 pitch6

WOLFSHAGEN See **GOSLAR**

WOLFSTEIN
Rheinland-Pfalz (☎06304)
SC Königsberg ☎7543
Municipal site, beside small River Lauter next to open air swimming pool.
Site lies at S end of Wolfstein to the right of B270 from Kaiserslautern.
All year.
1.4HEC H |O| ⊙ G
R lau P A4 pitch6

WOLTERDINGEN
Niedersachsen (☎05191)
Auf dem Simpel ☎3651
The site lies in the Lüneburg Heath area in a very quiet setting of the main road. Densely wooded terrain. Separate section for touring campers. Lunchtime siesta 13.00–15.00 hrs.
From Soltau head N on the B3 for about 4 km towards 'Hamburg'. At the junction for Wolterdingen turn right and continue towards 'Harber'. Approach road is signposted.
All year.
4HEC H |O|
⊙ R P lau A5 pitch7

WÖRISHOFEN (BAD)
Bayern (☎08247)
Kur Gottfried-Daimler-Str ☎5446
Level grassy site.
Site lies at the N end of Kneipp-Spa Wörishofen.
Apr–15 Oct.
1HEC H |O| ⊙ R
lau P

WREMEN
Niedersachsen (☎04705)
SC Wremer Tief ☎288
The municipal site lies next to public bathing beach which lies at the estuary of the River Aussenweser-Wremertief. The ground is liable to flooding by high tides.
From A27 motorway (Bremen/Cuxhaven) leave at exit Debstedt and follow road W via Sievern and Wremen.
May–Sug.
10HEC H |O|
P lau R

WULFEN (Island of Fehmarn)
Schleswig-Holstein (☎04371)
Wulfener Hals ☎4250
Meadowland site beside the Baltic Sea and an inland lake (Burger Binnensee). 1700 m long private beach.

Turn off B207/E4 (Vogelfluglinie) after the 'Sundbrücke' and follow roads towards 'Avendorf', then 'Wulfen' and 'Wulfener Hals'.
Mar–3 Nov.
31HEC H |O| ⊙
G R sP lau
A4–5 pitch8–14

ZECH See **LINDAU**

ZELL-MOSEL
Rheinland-Pfalz (☎06542)
Mosella ☎41241
Divided into plots and screened from the road by fruit trees. Site lies on strip of grassland on the left bank of the River Mosel, opposite town.
From road B53 (Koblenz-Trier) turn off in Zell-Kaimt, and follow signs to site.
Apr–Oct.
1HEC H |O| ⊙ G
R R A4 pitch6

ZERF
Rheinland-Pfalz (☎06587)
Rübezahl ☎814
Meadowland site in natural grounds on wooded hillside.
Leave Zerf S on B268 towards Saarbrücken then turn towards Oberzerf 2.5 km to site from turning. From Saarburg, follow B407 beyond Vierherrenhorn, turn right and follow track for 60 m.
All year.
2HEC H ⊙ G R
P lau |O| A5
pitch5

ZEVEN
Niedersachsen (☎04281)
Sonnenkamp Zeven ☎2876
The site lies mainly on open terrain, on the outskirts of the town, opposite the swimming pool. For touring campers there is an open meadow near the entrance. Lunchtime siesta 13.00–15.00 hrs.
From Zeven town centre follow road for 'Freibad' (swimming pool).
May–Sep.
8HEC H |O| ⊙ R
lau P

ZIERENBERG
Hessen (☎05606)
Freizeitzentrum Zierenberg ☎3966
A municipal site on a level meadow next to a river. Hydro-therapeutic pool on site.
From Kassel-Dortmund motorway leave at exit Burghasungen/Zierenberg.
All year.
3.5HEC H |O| ⊙ R
ⓟ lau

ZORGE See **BRAUNLAGE**

ZWEIBRÜCKEN
Rheinland-Pfalz (☎06332)
Zweibrücken ☎46844
All year. ➔

ZWESTEN
Hessen (☎05626)

Waldcamping ☎379

Site in bend of River Schwalm. Lunchtime siesta 13.00–15.00 hrs. For touring campers there is also an overflow site outside the actual campsite.

Access from Kassel in SW direction via Fritzlar to Zwesten.
All year.

3.2HEC H lau A4 pitch6

Germany

ZWIESEL
Bayern (☎09922)

AZUR-Ferienzentrum Bayerischer Wald ☎1847

A modern site. Clean sanitary installations.

All year.

16HEC H G lau P A6 pitch8–9

ZWISCHENAHN (BAD)
Niedersachsen (☎04403)

At **ASCHHAUSEN**

Lönskrug ☎4034

Site lies next to the 'Graststätte Lönskrug' (inn).

From Oldenburg follow road B75 towards Leer. On nearside of Bad Zwischenahn turn right towards Wiefelstede.
All year.

0.7HEC H L

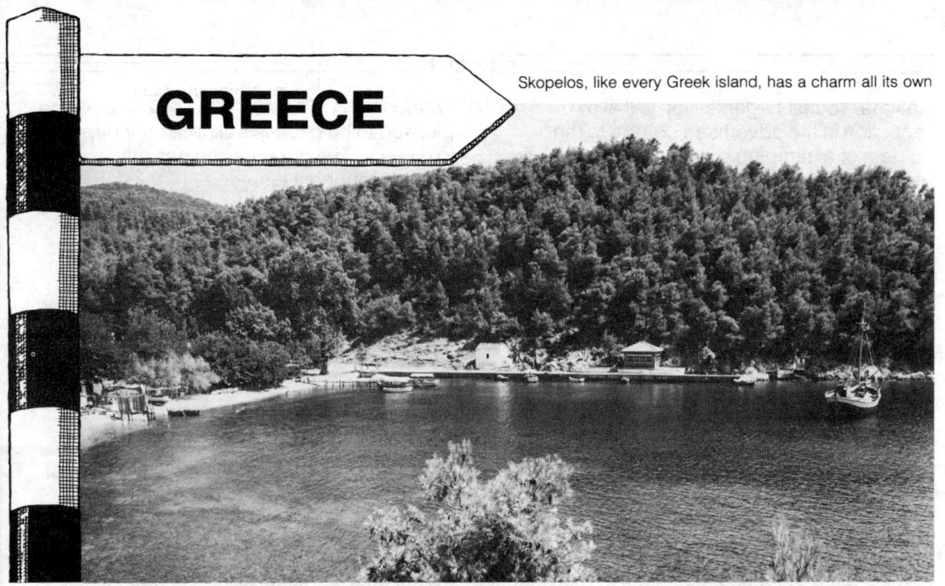

Skopelos, like every Greek island, has a charm all its own

Greece, a country rich in history and art, offers many attractions to the tourist, ranging from archaeology to water sports. Greece is bordered by four countries: Albania, Bulgaria, Turkey and Yugoslavia. The countryside is still largely unspoilt. Northern Greece is mountainous, Mount Olympus being one of the highest and most famous peaks. The fertile central plains area is said to contain over six thousand species of wild flowers. The islands of the Aegean Sea, among them Crete and Rhodes, are very popular holiday areas. In the extreme south the Peloponnesian peninsula combines the best aspects of Greek scenery and is dominated by the Taygetos Mountains and the great plains of Argolis.

The climate is predominantly maritime and the seasons are regular and predictable with very hot, dry summers. Modern Greek is the official language but English and French are useful second languages. English will be spoken in larger towns and resort areas and is quite widely understood.

HOW TO GET THERE

The usual and most direct route for the motorist is through Belgium, Federal Republic of Germany, (Köln/Cologne and München/Munich), Austria, Salzburg, and Yugoslavia, Belgrad (Belgrade). The alternative route is via France, Switzerland, Italy (Milano and Trieste), and Yugoslavia. The third way of reaching Greece is to drive to southern Italy and use the direct ferry services. The distance to Athinai (Athens) is just under 2,000 miles and would normally require four or five overnight stops.

GENERAL INFORMATION

(see also *Things you need to know*, pages 33–64)

Boats

(see page 33)

British Embassy/Consulates

(see also page 57)

The British Embassy is located at *10675 Athinai* 1 Ploutarchou Street ☎(01)7236211; information section *10562 Athinai* 2 Karageorgi Servias Street ☎7236211 ext 246. There is a British Consulate with Honorary Consul in Salonika; there are British Vice-Consulates in Kriti and Kérkira; British Vice-Consulates with Honorary Consuls in Patras, Rhodes and Samos.

Camping

There are numerous campsites throughout the country, most of them privately-owned. Some sites are open all year, but the main season is from April to October. The National Tourist Organisation provides camping information, see under *Tourist Information* for address. *International camping carnet* not compulsory but recommended. Campsites run by the

National Tourist Organisation will allow a reduction in the advertised charge to the holders of a camping carnet. See page 37 for further information.
Off-site camping and parking of caravans at archaeological sites, on the beach, in woods and in public places is prohibited. A limited stay (at the maximum one night) is however permitted by public highways, in rest areas or parking areas, provided that Greek regulations appertaining to the maintenance of hygiene are adhered to. Parking where it is prohibited or where it interferes with the free flow of traffic will result in the caravan being towed away by the police and this will be strictly enforced.

Currency including banking hours

(see also page 57)
The unit of currency is the Greek Drachma (*Dr*) divided into 100 *Lepta*. At the time of going to press £ = *Dr* 217. Denominations of bank notes are *Dr* 50, 100, 500, 1,000, 5,000; standard coins are *Dr* 1, 2, 5, 10, 20, 50. The maximum amount of Greek currency which may be taken into or out of Greece is *Dr*3,000 in notes of *Dr*50 and *Dr*100 denominations. There are no formalities concerning the import and export of foreign currency not exceeding the equivalent of US$500. However, if the amount is in excess of this it must be declared to the Currency Control Authorities upon arrival.

Banks are open from 08.00–14.00hrs Monday to Friday. Some foreign exchange offices are open in the afternoon.

Foodstuffs

(see also page 60)
Visitors from EEC countries may import duty-free 1,000g of coffee and 200g of tea; a reduced allowance applies in respect of visitors from non EEC countries. Up to 10kg of foodstuffs may be imported for the journey to your campsite.

Medical treatment

(see page 60)

Shopping hours

Generally shops and stores are open from 08.00–15.00hrs on Monday, Wednesday and Saturday; on Tuesday, Thursday and Friday from 08.00–14.00hrs and 17.30–20.30hrs.

Tourist information

(see also page 63)
The National Tourist Organisation of Greece has an office at 195–197 Regent Street, London W1R 8DL ☎01-734 5997 who will be pleased to help tourists before their departure to Greece. The organisation has offices in main towns throughout Greece.

Visitors' registration

(see page 63)

MOTORING

(see also *Things you need to know*, pages 33–64)

Accidents

(see also page 46)
Fire in Athinai ☎199. In other cities the numbers are given in the local telephone directories. **Police** in Athinai and most big cities ☎100; elsewhere local telephone directories should be consulted. **Tourist Police** ☎171. **Ambulance** in Athinai ☎166; in other cities consult local telephone directories.

In the case of accidents in which private property is damaged or persons injured the police should be called. They should also be called to minor incidents that cannot be settled amicably on the spot. Your own insurance company should be informed as well as the Motor Insurers Bureau in Athinai. The Motoring Club (ELPA) should also be informed, preferably at their Head Office.

Breakdowns

(see page 48)

Dimensions and weight restrictions

Private **cars** and towed **trailers** or **caravans** are restricted to the following dimensions – height: 4 metres; width: 2.50 metres; length (including any coupling device); up to 2,500 kg 8 metres, over 2,500 kg 10 metres. The maximum permitted overall length of vehicle/trailer or caravan combination is 18 metres.

Trailers without brakes may have a total weight of up to 50% of the unladen weight of the towing vehicle and of the driver whose weight is considered equal to 70 kg. The maximum permitted total weight of trailer and towing vehicle must not exceed 3,500 kg.

Driving Licence

A valid UK licence is acceptable in Greece. The minimum age at which a visitor may drive a temporarily imported car or motorcycle (over 50cc) is 17 years. However, an International Driving Permit is required by the holder of a licence issued in the Republic of Ireland. See

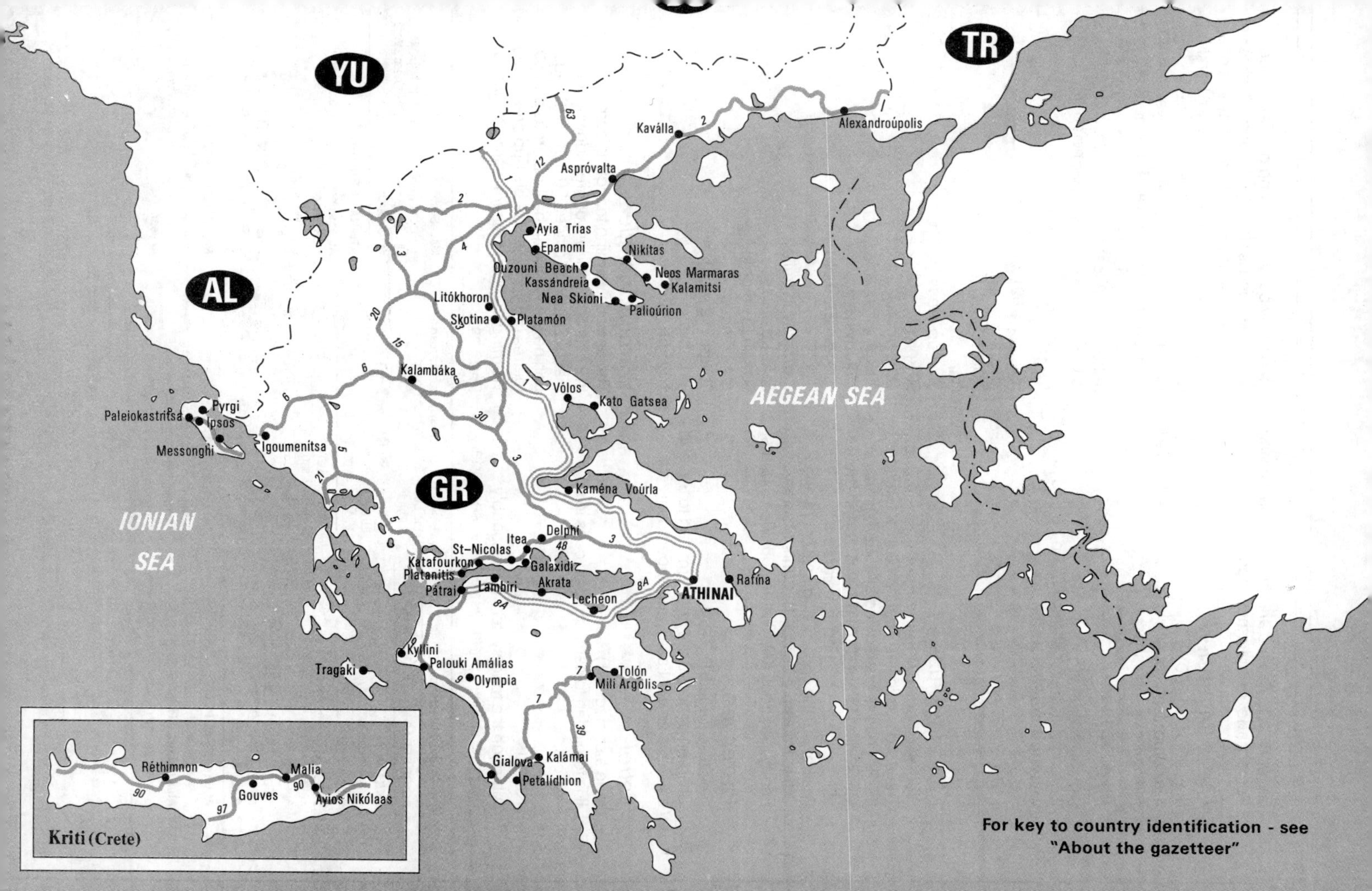
YU
TR
AL
GR
Alexandroúpolis
Kaválla
Aspróvalta
Ayia Trias
Epanomi
Nikitas
Ouzouni Beach
Neos Marmaras
Kassándreia
Kalamitsi
Nea Skioni
Palioúrion
Litókhoron
Skotina
Platamón
Kalambáka
Vólos
Kato Gatsea
AEGEAN SEA
Pyrgi
Paleiokastritsa
Ipsos
Messonghi
Igoumenitsa
Kaména Voúrla
IONIAN SEA
Delphi
Itea
St-Nicolas
Katafourkon
Galaxidi
Platanitis
Akrata
Pátrai
Lambiri
Lecheon
Rafína
ATHINAI
Kyllini
Palouki Amálias
Tragaki
Olympia
Tolón
Mili Argolis
Gialova
Kalámai
Petalidhion
Réthimnon
Malia
Gouves
Ayios Nikólaas
Kriti (Crete)
For key to country identification - see "About the gazetteer"

under *Driving licence and International Driving Permit* page 33 for further information.

Fire extinguisher

(see also page 50)
It is compulsory for all vehicles to be equipped with a fire extinguisher.

First-aid kit

(see also page 50)
It is compulsory for all vehicles to be equipped with a first-aid kit.

Lights

(see page 50 also *Headlights* page 41)

Motoring clubs

(see also page 61)
The *Automobile and Touring Club of Greece* (ELPA) has its head office at *11527 Athinai* 2 Messogion Street ☏(01)779 1615, and branch offices are maintained in major towns throughout the country and on Kérkira and Kriti. Office hours are 08.30–19.30hrs Monday to Friday; Saturday and Sunday 08.30–13.00hrs.

Passengers

(see also page 51)
Children under 10 are not permitted to travel in a vehicle as front seat passengers.

Petrol

(see also page 61)
It is **forbidden** to carry petrol in cans in a vehicle.

Roads

Although the road system is reasonably comprehensive, surfaces vary and secondary roads may be poor. On long drives, a good average speed is between 30 and 40 miles an hour. The islands are best visited by sea or air. Only the larger islands – Kriti (Crete), Kérkira (Corfu) and Rodhos (Rhodes) – have reasonably comprehensive road systems. Roads on the smaller islands are generally narrow and surfaces vary from fairly good to rather poor. A leaflet entitled *'Road Conditions in Greece'* is available to AA members.

Seat belts

(see page 52)

Speed limits

Car
Built-up areas
50 kph (31 mph)
Other roads
80 kph (49 mph)
Motorways
100 kph (62 mph)

Car/caravan/trailer
Built-up areas
50 kph (31 mph)
Other roads
80 kph (49 mph)
Motorways
100 kph (62 mph)

Warning triangle

The use of a warning triangle is compulsory in the event of accident or breakdown. The triangle must be placed 20 metres (22 yds) behind the vehicle in built-up areas and 50 metres (55 yds) outside built-up areas. See also *Warning triangles/Hazard warning lights* page 54.

Prices are in Drachmae

AGIOS SERAFIM See **KAMÉNA VOURLA**

AKRATA
Peloponnese (☏0696)

Krioneri ☏31405

At Krathion, 3 km W of Akrata on Corinth–Patrai road.
Apr–Oct.

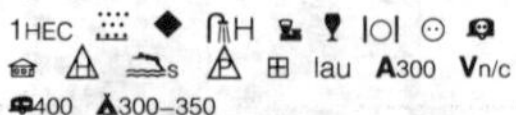
1HEC lau **A**300 **V**n/c 400 300–350

ALEXANDROÚPOLIS
Thrace (☏0551)

Alexandroúpolis ☏28735

A large site on a meadow with concrete pitches.

Between Thessaloniki–Istanbul road and the beach to the W of the town.
All year.

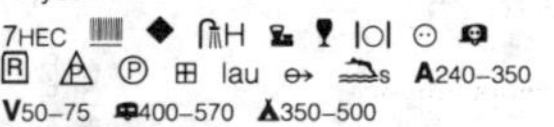
7HEC lau **A**240–350 **V**50–75 400–570 350–500

ASPRÓVALTA
Thessaly (☏0397)

EOT ☏22249

Apr–Oct.
50HEC

Europe ☏22319

Small, well-kept site divided into four fields between the coast road and the sea.

Signposted from village; 3 km towards Kaválla.
May–Sep.
1.3HEC lau **A**250 **V**250 280 250

ATHÍNAI (ATHENS)

Athens Leoforos Athion 198, Peristeri ☏5814114

6.5 km W of city.
All year.
1.4HEC **A**350 **V**150 350 150

Nea Kifissia ☏8016435

16 km N of Athens. Signposted from Aharnes exit on Athens–Lamia motorway.
All year.

Greece

2.2HEC H P

AYIA TRIAS

Thessaly (☎0392)

Akti Thermaikou ☎51360

A modern site in a park-like setting, divided into pitches and planted with a variety of trees. Adjoining the site is a fine public bathing area with a long sandy beach.

On main road 25 km S of Thessaloniki, follow road S past airport and continue for 10 km.
All year.

20HEC H G s **A**240–350 **V**50–75 300–470 250–400

AYIOS NIKÓLAOS See **KRÍTI (CRETE)**

CORFU See **KÉRKIRA**

CRETE See **KRÍTI**

DELPHÍ

Central Greece (☎0265)

Chrissa ☎82050

On a hill overlooking the sea.

7 km along the Delphi-Itea road.
All year.

1.8HEC H G R P lau **A**270 **V**170 200 170

Delphi ☎82363

A spacious site on a small plateau with fine views of the Parnassus mountain range and the Gulf of Corinth.

3 km along the Delphi–Amfissa road at Km172.
All year.

2HEC H G P lau

EPANOMÍ

Macedonia (☎0392)

EOT ☎41379

A modern site by the sea. All pitches on well tended grass with hard-standing for caravans. Divided by bushes, trees and flowering shrubs. Broad flat beach.

All year.

10HEC H G R P s **A**240–350 **V**50–75 400–570 350–500

GALAXIDI

Galaxidi (☎0265)

Galaxidi ☎41530

A peaceful site, situated 50 m from the sea.

20 May–20 Sep.

1.5HEC H R s lau **A**220 **V**120 300 200

GIALOVA

Peloponnese (☎0723)

Navarino Beach ☎22761

All year.

1.7HEC H G R lau s **A**250 **V**100 250 200

GOUVES See **KRÍTI (CRETE)**

IGOUMENÍTSA

Epirus (☎0665)

Sole Mare ☎22158

South near ferry.
All year.

0.5HEC H G P lau s **A**225 **V**225 450 225–450

IPSOS See **KÉRKIRA (CORFU)**

ITÉA

Central Greece (☎0265)

Ayannis ☎32555

The site stretches over several terraces and is scattered with small olive trees and strengthened by stone walls. There are fine views over the Gulf of Corinth.

3 km E on Uferstr.
Apr–15 Oct.

3HEC H lau s

Kaparellis ☎32330

All year.

3.3HEC H G R lau s **A**300 **V**100 300 200–300

KALAMBÁKA

Thessaly (☎0432)

International Rizos ☎22954

On main road towards Trikala.
All year.

1.2HEC H G P

Metéora Garden ☎22727

1 km from town on slope opposite Metéora rocks.

All year.

1.2HEC H G R P lau R **A**300 **V**230 230 230

Vrachos-Kastraki ☎23134

The site lies at the foot of a rock formation.

Situated in a small village, 3 km N of town on the Metéora road.
All year.

2HEC H G R P

KALÁMAI (KALAMATA)

Peloponnese (☎0721)

Patista ☎29525

Site in an orange and lemon grove.

Situated at end of Navarinostr, 3 km from town centre.
All year.

2.3HEC H G R lau s

KALAMÍTSI

Macedonia (☎0375)

Kalamitsi ☎41410

On well-tended meadowland with pitches divided by trees. Shade is provided by roof and matting. Situated in a bay surrounded by cliffs with a broad sandy beach.

Approach from Thessaloniki via Kassándria peninsula to Sithonia peninsula. Kalamitsi is located on the most southerly point.
May–Sep.

6HEC H G R P lau s **A**420 **V**n/c 540 460

KAMÉNA VOÚRLA

Thessaly (☎0235)

Apollon ☎22486

The site is on level ground with olive trees, set between the beach and the main road.

S on road to Lamia.
Apr–15 Oct.

0.8HEC H s **A**200 **V**100 150 100–200

EOT ☎22053

Apr–Oct.

3HEC H s

At **AGIOS SERAFIM**

Venezuela ☎(0235) 41692

May–Oct.

1.6HEC H G s lau **A**250 **V**80 250 200

KASSÁNDREIA
Macedonia (0374)

Sani 31229

Situated beside a beach in a lovely valley surrounded by pine trees. The site is completely fenced and has asphalt standings for caravans.

From Thessaloniki S, past the airport towards Néa Moundania and onto Kassándra peninsula. Well signposted. Turn off road then continue 9 km.
15 Apr–Sep.

10HEC ◆ H |O| ⊙ G R ⊞ lau s

KATO GATSEA
Thessaly (0423)

Hellas 22267

The site lies in an olive grove on sloping ground between the road and the beach.

10 km W of Volos.
All year.

3.5HEC ◆ H |O| ⊙ G R ⊞ s A250 V200 250 200

KATAFOURKON
Central Greece (0642)

Straitis Beach 51123

15 Apr–15 Oct.

2.5HEC ◆ H |O| ⊙ G s Ⓟ ⊞ A340 V160 350 230–340

KAVÁLLA
Central Macedonia (051)

EOT Akti Kaválla 227151

A coastal site with a short ramp at the entrance.

Take the coast road through Akti Kavália on the W outskirts of Kavália and continue for approx 4 km.
All year.

3.5HEC ◆ H |O| ⊙ G R ⊞ lau s A240–350 V50–75 400–570 350–500

Irini 229785

Site on meadowland with young poplars set between the coast road and the beach. The site is divided into several sections one being for campers with dogs.

Access is from the eastern end of town at the FINA petrol station. Well signposted.
All year.

2.4HEC ◆ H |O| ⊙ G R s Ⓟ ⊞ lau A360 500 450

Greece

KÉRKIRA (CORFU)
Kérkira (0661)

IPSOS

Ipsos 93243

15 km N towards Ipsos from ferry.

1.5HEC ◇ H |O| sR

Karoussades 31394

Situated in an olive grove, 600 m from village fronting onto main road.

15 May–15 Oct.

6.5HEC ◆ H |O| ⊙ G R s ⊞ lau

MESSONGHI

Sea Horse 55364

20 km S of Kérkira on E coast of the island.
May–mid Oct.

5HEC ◆ H |O| ⊙ G P ⊞ lau s A350 Vn/c 250 200–250

PALEOKASTRITSA

Paleokastritsa 41204

On W coast of the island.

1.6HEC H

PYGRÍ

Paradise 93557

Signposted.
May–15 Oct.

5HEC H |O| ⊙ s A250 V160 190 130–190

KRÍTI (CRETE)
Kriti

AYIOS NIKÓLAOS

Gournia Moon (0842) 93243

15 Apr–Oct.

2HEC H |O| ⊙ G L ⊞ lau s

GOUVES

Creta (0879) 41400

On well maintained, slightly sloping meadowland. Separated from the beach by the access road.

16 km E of Iraklion. Turn towards sea as signposted and continue for approx. 2 km along narrow, stony lane.
May–Sep.

2HEC ◇ H |O| ⊙ s A200–260 V150–180 230–270 140–170

MALIA

Malia (0897) 31460

In an attractive bay adjoining a large beach. Lunchtime siesta 13.00–5.00 hrs.

Apr–Oct.

40HEC ◆ H |O| ⊙ G R s ⊞ lau

RÉTHIMNON

Arcadia Missiria (0831) 28825

4 km E Réthimnon adjacent to the sea shore.
All year.

1.4HEC ◆ H |O| ⊙ G R s ⊞ lau A300 V150 300 250

Elizabeth (0831) 28694

A quiet family site.

3 km E.
20 May–20 Oct.

3.5HEC ◆ H |O| ⊙ G s ⊞ lau A300 V150 300 250

KYLLINI
Peloponnese (0761)

EOT Camping Kyllini 96278

Apr–Oct.

9.5HEC ◆ H |O| ⊙ R Ⓟ ⊞ lau s A400 V80 640 560

LAMBIRI
Peloponnese (0691)

Tsoli's 31469

A level site with a terraced section set aside for tents under pine trees. Fine views over the Bay of Corinth. Beach accessible via steps. Some noise from road and railway.

Along the old coastal road from Patras.
19 Apr–Sep.

1.7HEC ◆ H |O| ⊙ G R s ⊞ lau

LECHEON
Corinth (0741)

Blue Dolphin 25766

Site on level ground near to the sea, with its own private beach.

6 km W of Corinth.
May–15 Oct.

4HEC ◆ H |O| ⊙ G s ⊞ lau

LITÓKHORON
Macedonia (0352)

Gritsa 61295

Turn off Thessaloniki–Athens road about 15 km S of Katerini towards the sea, across the railway and along a track for 1.2 km.
May–Sep.

1.8HEC ◆ H lau A380 V80 600 530

Mitikas ☎61275

200 m from the sea.

About 15 km S of Katerini, turn in direction of Gritsa Beach. Site on the right beyond railway line.
May–Oct.

◆ H lau A300 V100 150 100

At **PLÁKA LITÓKHORON**

Apollon ☎22109

A pleasant, nearly level site, shaded by fruit and poplar trees.

1 km from railway underpass.
May–Sep.

Minerva ☎22178

A nearly level, partly wooded site with a private beach.

20 km S of Katerini turn towards the sea 1 km to Pláka Beach. Well signposted.
May–Sep.

3HEC ◆ H lau A650 V116

Olympos Beach ☎22112

Partly shaded meadow site on top of 10 m cliffs. Steps to pebble beach. Near a railway which is sometimes noisy.

20 km S of Katerini turn off to Pláka Beach. Entrance to site immediately after crossing railway.
Apr–Sep.

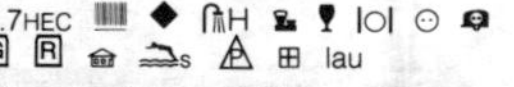

Olympios Zeus ☎22115

Extensive site with broad beach. Separate sections for camping and bungalows. A section of site is shaded and has individual pitches.

Well signposted.
15 Apr–15 Oct.

MALIA See **KRÍTI (CRETE)**

MESSONGHI See **KÉRKIRA (CORFU)**

MILI-ARGOLIS
Peloponnese (☎0751)

Learna-Beach ☎47520

Apr–10 Oct.

1.7HEC ◆ H lau

NEA SKIONI
Chalkidiki (☎0374)

Greece

Anemi Beach ☎71276

A new camp, alongside the beach.

May–Sep.

2.2HEC ◆ H lau A280–400 V60–80 320–450 280–400

NEOS MARMARAS
Macedonia (☎0371)

Areti ☎71430

Mainly even grassland with varied trees and bushes. Additional shade provided by roof-matting.

About 10 km s, turn off the Neos Marmaras–Porto Koufos road towards the sea and continue 4 km on very poor road.
May–15 Oct.

◆ H lau A350 V175 175 175

NIKÍTAS
Macedonia (☎0375)

Mylos ☎22042

A family site which is terraced and shaded by trees and sunshade roofs. A minimum stay of one week applies.

2 km W of Nikitas.
May–Sep.

2HEC ◇ H

OLYMPIA
Peloponnese (☎0624)

Diana ☎22314

Near the Olympic Games Museum.
All year.

5HEC ◆ H lau A300 V200 350 250–350

OUZOUNI BEACH
Macedonia (☎0373)

Ouzouni Beach ☎23394

May–10 Oct.

1.6HEC ◆ H lau A400 pitch650

PALEOKASTRITSA See **KÉRKIRA (CORFU)**

PALIOÚRION
Macedonia (☎0374)

Xenia ☎92206

On a long stretch of grassland with sand dunes, trees and bushes. Situated in a bay with a natural harbour.

2.5 km from village next to Xenia Hotel.
May–Sep.

20HEC ◆ H lau A345 V95 320 285

PALOUKI AMÁLIAS
Peloponnese (☎0662)

Paradis ☎22721

The site lies on level ground, stretching down to a sandy beach.

From Patras follow road 9 to Pygos to about 2 km beyond Amálias, then turn W.
May–15 Oct.

25HEC ◆ H lau A270 V110 400 300

PÁTRAI (PATRAS)
Peloponnese (☎061)

EOT ☎424131

A modern site with some concrete pitches for caravans.

1.5 km from Agyia, 5 km from Patrai.
All year.

3HEC ◆ H lau

PETALÍDHION
Peloponnese (☎0722)

Eros Beach ☎31208

Pleasant terraced site with a private beach.

0.5 km S of village.
May–Sep.

22HEC ◆ H lau

PLÁKA LITÓKHORON See **LITÓKHORON**

PLATAMÓN
Macedonia (☎0352)

Castle ☎41252

The site lies below an old Venetian castle and is shaded by poplar trees. Lunchtime siesta 13.00–15.00 hrs.

Leave Thessaloniki–Athens road at the beginning of a short mountainous section, turn towards the sea and continue for 600 m.
15 Apr–15 Oct.

4HEC ◆ H lau

Hellas ☎41490

A large site with old trees and flower beds.

5 km SW. Approach road has gradients of 12% and 17%.
May–28 Sep.

6HEC ◆ H lau A300 V105 450 385

Poseidon Beach ☎41654

Level site by the sea with a large, sandy, private beach.

Leave Thessaloniki–Athens road at beginning of short mountainous section, and continue towards the sea for 600 m.
15 Mar–Oct.

2.8HEC ◆ H lau

PLATANITIS
Central Greece (☎0634)

Platanitis Beach ☎31555

15 May–3 Sep. ➔

8HEC ◆ H ! |O| ⊙
Ⓖ Ⓡ s ⊞ lau A250
V200 200 200–300

RAFÍNA
Attica (☎0294)

Cococamp ☎23413

The site is divided into many sections by plants and is near the rocky coast with winding steps leading to the sea.

All year.

1.2HEC ◆ H Ⓖ
Ⓟ ⊞ lau ! |O| s

Rafína ☎23118

On several small terraces, set in a pinewood some 2 km from sea.

On road to Marathon near MOBIL petrol station.
May–Oct.

4.5HEC ◆ H Ⓡ
Ⓟ ⊞ ! |O| A250 V100 150
150

RÉTHIMNON See **KRÍTI (CRETE)**

ST-NICOLAS
Central Greece (☎266)

Doric ☎31722

15 Apr–Oct.

2HEC ◆ H ! |O| ⊙
Ⓖ Ⓡ Ⓟ ⊞ lau s

SKOTINA
Macedonia (☎0352)

EOT Camping Olympou ☎91263

Well-maintained meadowland site with small pine woodland on a narrow but long beach. Ample space for campers. Some hard-standing pitches, surrounded by hedges.

Greece

1 km S of tollbooth turn towards the sea and continue for 800 m on an asphalt road.
Apr–Oct.

6.5HEC ◆ H ! |O| ⊙
s Ⓟ ⊞ lau

TOLÓN
Peloponnese (☎0752)

Lido I ☎59489

Small site 50 m from sea, shade provided by roof matting. Separated from beach by road.
Apr–Oct.

0.8HEC ◆ H ! |O| ⊙ Ⓖ
Ⓡ ⊞ lau s

Lido II ☎59396

12 km from town towards Nauplia.
May–10 Oct.

2HEC ◆ H ! |O| ⊙
Ⓖ Ⓡ Ⓟ ⊞ lau
s A400 V150 400 250

Stars ☎59226

The site comprises three sections with a few narrow terraces. Shade is provided by sunshade roofs. A good centre for excursions.

200 m from the beach.
All year.

4.5HEC ◆ H ! ⊙
⊞ lau |O| s

Swiss ☎59223

Turn right in Nauplia and continue for 12 km.

0.5HEC ◇ H
P

Xeni II Beach ☎59338

Small site by sea on Tolón–Nauplia road.
Mar–Oct.

0.7HEC ◆ H ! |O| ⊙
Ⓖ Ⓡ Ⓟ ⊞ lau
s

TRAGAKI
Zákynthos (☎0695)

Zante ☎24754

The camp is sited in a high open place surrounded by trees with good shade and exceptional views all round. There is a large private beach.

15 May–15 Oct.

2.6HEC ◆ H ! |O| ⊙
Ⓖ Ⓡ s ⊞ lau A200–300 V80–100 150–250 150–250

VÓLOS
Thessaly (☎0421)

Pefkakia ☎38357

Set among tall pines on a hill above the sea. Steps to beach.

Approach from Vólos 1.7 km towards Lamia, turn towards the sea in the direction of Pefkakia and continue 1.5 km on a winding road.

6HEC ◆ H |O|
sR

Picturesque Greece: donkeys go where cars cannot

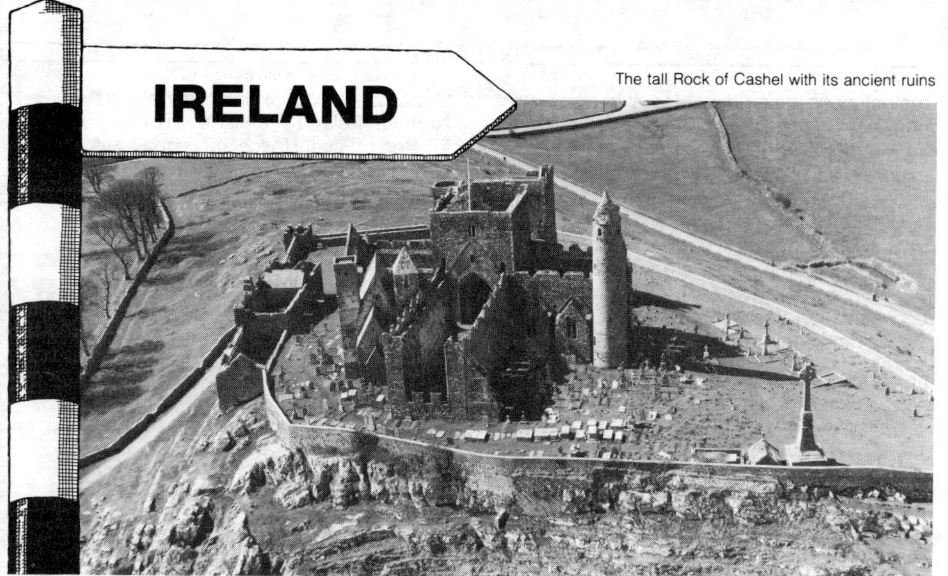

The tall Rock of Cashel with its ancient ruins

Ireland, which provides some of Europe's most varied scenery, lies in the North Atlantic ocean separated from Great Britain by the Irish Sea. The soft beauty of the lakes and rivers of the interior have a quiet fascination all of their own. In sharp contrast the magnificent Atlantic coastline offers sandy beaches, rugged cliffs, miniature fjords and secluded bays warmed by the Gulf Stream.

The country has a temperate climate with warm summers and cool winters. In general climatic conditions are very similar to those prevailing in Britain. The traditional tongue is Gaelic, but English is the principal language. Gaelic is still spoken however, although it will be heard mainly in the west of the country.

HOW TO GET THERE

Car-carrying ferry services operate from Britain to both the Republic and the Northern Counties. The services to the Republic are Fishguard to Rosslare; Holyhead to Dun Laoghaire; Holyhead to Dublin; Liverpool to Dublin. To the north the services are from Cairnryan to Larne; Stranraer to Larne; Liverpool to Belfast. There are also services to and from France, Le Havre and Cherbourg to Rosslare and Roscoff and Le Havre to Cork.

GENERAL INFORMATION

Politically, Ireland is divided into two, the Republic which is a sovereign independent state and Northern Ireland which forms part of the United Kingdom. Motoring conditions and regulations in the North are almost the same as in Great Britain and therefore the *Country information section* will apply only to the Republic except where some notes concerning the North are considered necessary. The information should be read in conjunction with the general content of *Things you need to know* pages 33–64, with special reference to *Rule of the Road*, page 52.

British Embassy/Consulate

(see also page 57)
The British Embassy together with its consular section is located at 31–33 Merrion Road *Dublin 4* ☎01-695211.

Camping

There are numerous campsites throughout the country, most of which are open from May to September.
International camping carnet not compulsory. Generally no reductions in campsite charges are given to the holders of a camping carnet. See page 37 for further information.
Off-site camping is permitted, but permission should be obtained from the landowner before doing so.

Currency including banking hours

(see also page 57)
The unit of currency is the Irish Pound or Punt (*IR£*) divided into 100 *Pence*. At the time of going to press £ = *IR£* 1.10. There is no

restriction on the amount of foreign and Irish currency or travellers cheques which may be imported, but large amounts which are to be re-exported should be declared on entry. Visitors and residents leaving the Irish Republic may only export up to *IR*£100 in Irish currency and up to *IR*£500 in foreign currency, together with the imported amount declared on entry.

Banks are open from Monday to Friday between 10.00–12.30hrs and 13.30–15.00hrs. Dublin banks remain open on Thursday until 17.00hrs; in other parts of the country most banks have one late opening evening but this varies from town to town.

Foodstuffs

(see also page 60)
Visitors may import small quantities of foodstuffs for personal use without an import licence or payment of duty. However, the import of meat or poultry, meat or poultry products or milk or milk products, in tins or otherwise, and fresh vegetables is prohibited.

Medical treatment

(see page 60)

Shopping hours

Generally shops are open from 09.00–17.30hrs Monday–Saturday with some supermarkets open until 21.00hrs on Thursday or Friday. Most shops have one early closing day each week and this is usually 13.00hrs on Wednesday or Saturday.

Tourist information

(see also page 63)
The Irish Tourist Board has an office at 150 New Bond Street, London W1Y 0AQ ☎01-493 3201 and regional offices at 6–8 Temple Row, Birmingham B2 5HG ☎021-236 9724; 28 Cross Street, Manchester M2 3NH ☎061-832 5981 and 19 Dixon Street, Glasgow G1 4AJ ☎041-221 2311. In Northern Ireland the Irish Tourist Board has offices at 53 Castle Street, Belfast BT1 1GH ☎227888 and 40 Foyle Street, Londonderry BT48 6AR ☎369501. In the Republic the Irish Tourist Board offices are located at Baggot Street, Dublin ☎01-765871; tourist information 747733.

The Northern Ireland Tourist Board has an office at 11 Berkeley Street, London W1 ☎01-493 0601 and a regional office at PO Box 26, Sutton Coldfield, West Midlands ☎021-353 7604. In the Republic of Ireland the Northern Ireland Tourist Board has an office situated in Clery's Department Store, O'Connell Street, Dublin ☎786055. In Northern Ireland the Northern Ireland Tourist Board offices are located at River House, 48 High Street, Belfast BT1 2DS ☎231221; tourist information 246609.

Visitors' registration

(see page 63)

MOTORING

(see also *Things you need to know*, pages 33–64)

Accidents

(see also page 46)
Fire, police, ambulance ☎999.

Breakdowns

If your car breaks down, try to move it to the side of the road so that it obstructs traffic flow as little as possible. The AA's Breakdown Service is available to members on terms similar to those in Britain. Patrols operate throughout the country and their services are complemented by garages.

Dimensions and weight restrictions

Private **cars** and towed **trailers** or **caravans** are restricted to the following dimensions – height: no restriction; width: 2.50 metres; length: 12 metres. The maximum permitted overall length of vehicle/trailer or caravan combination is 18 metres.

Trailers without brakes may weigh up to 762kg or may have a total weight up to 50% of the towing vehicle.

Driving Licence

(see also page 33)
A valid UK licence is acceptable in the Republic of Ireland. The minimum age at which a visitor may drive a temporarily imported car or motorcycle (exceeding 150 cc) is 17 years.

Lights

(see page 50 also *Headlights* page 41)
As the rule of the road in the Republic is drive on the left, the general advice regarding adjustment of headlights for driving on the right should be ignored.

Motoring club

The Automobile Association has its regional headquarters in the Republic of Ireland at 23 Suffolk Street *Dublin* ☎01-779481 and an AA Centre at 9 Bridge Street *Cork* ☎(021)505155.

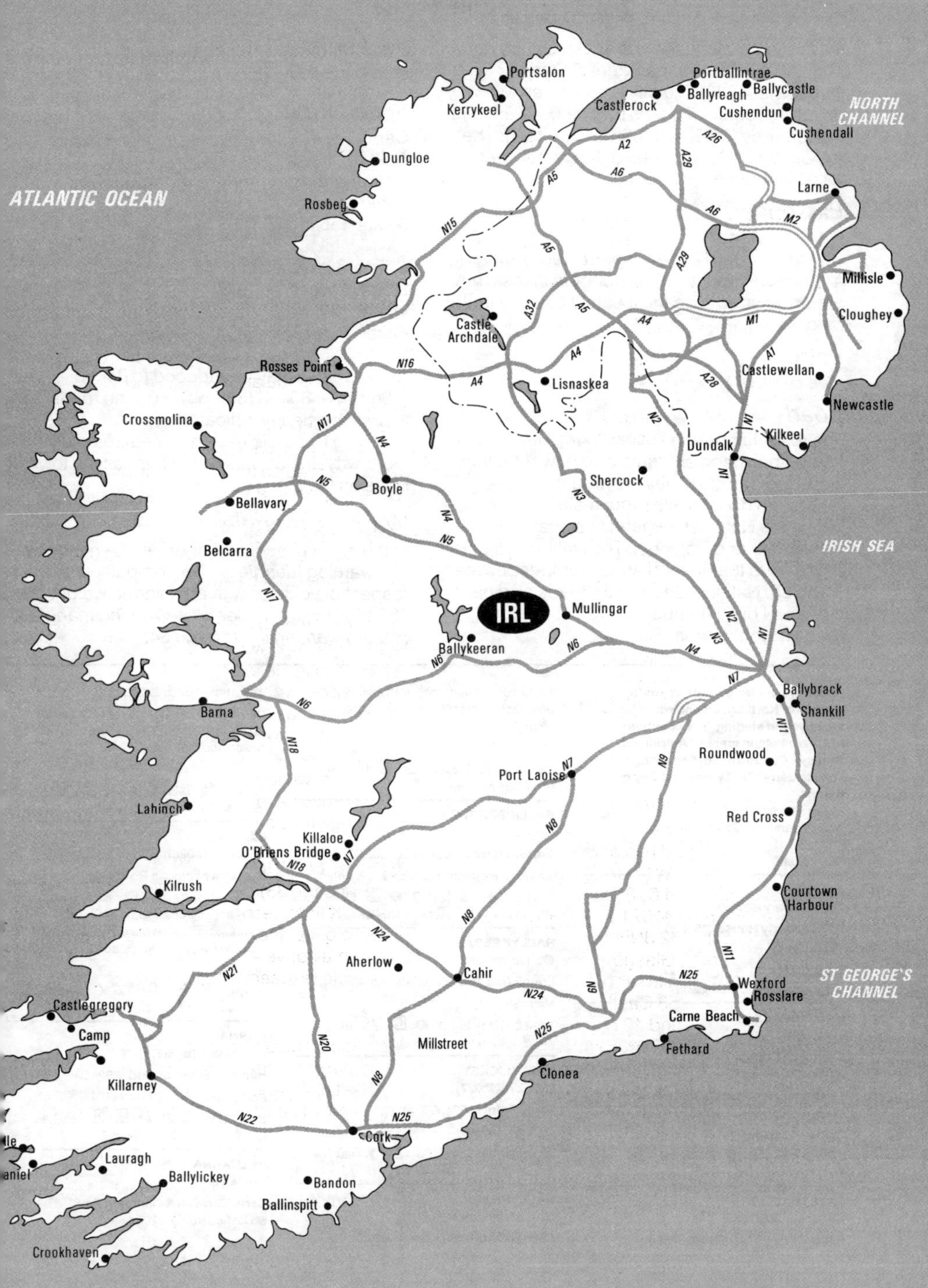

For key to country identification - see "About the gazetteer"

In Northern Ireland there is an AA Centre at 108–110 Great Victoria Street *Belfast* ☎(0232)244538. The offices are open Monday to Friday 09.00–17.00hrs and 09.00–12.00hrs on Saturday (09.30–13.00hrs in Belfast). The AA Centre in Cork closes for lunch between 13.00–14.00hrs.

Passengers

(see also page 51)
Children under 12 are not permitted to travel in a vehicle as front seat passengers unless they are using special seats or safety belts suitable for children.

Petrol

(see page 61)

Roads

The road numbering system in the Republic of Ireland has been changed and new direction signs are gradually being brought into use. Roads are divided into three main categories. These are National Primary, National Secondary and Regional. The National Primary roads have the prefix N and a number between 1 and 25. National Secondary roads also have a prefix N but a number above 50. Regional roads have the prefix R.

Seat belts

(see page 52)

Speed limits

Car
Built-up areas
48 kph (30 mph)
Other roads
88 kph (55 mph)*

Car/caravan/trailer
Built-up areas
48 kph (30 mph)
Other roads
56 kph (35 mph)
*Speed limits may be reduced to 64kph (40mph) or 80kph (50mph) on some roads, but this will be clearly indicated.
Note The Republic has only one stretch of motorway, the 5 miles which bypass the town of Naas on the N7.

Warning triangle

In the event of accident or breakdown the use of a warning triangle is only compulsory in respect of vehicles with an unladen weight of 1524kg (1½ tons). See also *Warning triangles/Hazard warning lights* page 54.

Prices are in Irish pounds or punts, except for Northern Ireland when prices are in pound sterling. The counties of Northern Ireland are: Co. Antrim, Co. Armagh, Co. Down, Co. Fermanagh, Co. Londonderry, Co. Tyrone and City of Belfast.

Abbreviations:

Av	Avenue	Sq	Square
Pl	Place	St	Street
Rd	Road	m	Miles

AHERLOW
Co. Tipperary (☎062)
Ballinacourty House ☎56230
7 May–12 Sep.
1.8HEC ⋔H ⊙ G ⊞ lau pitch6 (incl 2 persons)

BALLYBRACK
Co. Dublin
Cromlech Cottage Killiney Hill ☎Dublin(01)826882
Level grass site amidst various trees and bushes, near sea, beach and mountains.
28 Mar–13 Sep.
2.2HEC ⋔H ⊙ G

BALLYCASTLE
Co. Antrim (☎02657)
Silver Cliffs 21 Clare Rd ☎62550
Part level site with trees and bushes, adjacent to River Glenshesk and beach ¼ m W of town.
Mar–mid Oct.
2HEC ⋔H ⊙ G R lau pitch5 (incl 2 persons)

BALLINSPITTLE
Co. Cork
Garrettstown House ☎Cork(021)778156
Jul–Aug. Restricted service Jun & Sep.
3.2HEC ⋔H ⊙ G R lau pitch6 (incl 2 persons)

BALLYKEERAN
Co. Westmeath
Lough Ree ☎Athlone(0902)72145
May–Sep.
1.6HEC ⋔H ⊙ G ⊞ lau pitch7 (incl 2 persons)

BALLYLICKEY
Co. Cork (☎027)
Eagle Point ☎50630
16 May–18 Sep.
8.1HEC ⋔H ⊙ lau pitch7–8 (incl 2 persons)

BALLYREAGH
Co. Londonderry
Carrick-Dhu 12 Ballyreagh Rd ☎Portrush (0265)823712
Part level, part sloping, grass site set in downland within the urban area close to sea, beach and main road.
Apr–Sep.
1.2HEC ⋔H ⊙ G R lau pitch5 (incl 2 persons)

BANDON
Co. Cork (☎023)
Murray's Kilbrogan Rd ☎41232
Part level, part sloping, grass and gravel site with various trees and bushes, set in meadowland within the urban area and close to river and main road.
Apr–Sep.
0.8HEC ⋔H ⊙ G R lau pitch5 (incl 2 persons)

BARNA
Co. Galway (☎091)
Hunters' Silver Strand ☎92452
Apr–Aug.
8HEC ⋔H ⊙ G R lau pitch5 (incl 2 persons)

BELCARRA
Co. Mayo
Carra Caravan & Camping Park ☎Castlebar(094)32054
Jul–Aug.

0.2HEC lau pitch4 (incl 2 persons)

BELLAVARY
Co. Mayo (☎094)

Carrowkeel ☎31004
May–15 Sep.
6HEC

BOYLE
Co. Roscommon (☎079)

Lough Key Forest Park ☎62212 (outside opening times (044)48761
A level and grassy site in woodland 2½ m E of town on N4.
31 Mar–9 Apr & 2 May–2 Sep.
5.5HEC lau pitch4–6 (incl 2 persons)

CAHERDANIEL
Co. Kerry (☎0667)

Wave Crest ☎5188
Apr–28 Sep.
1.8HEC lau pitch5 (incl 2 persons)

CAHIR
Co. Tipperary (☎052)

The Apple Moorstown ☎41459
15 Jun–15 Sep.
1.4HEC lau **A**2–3

CAMP
Co. Kerry

Seaside ☎Tralee(066)30161
All year. Restricted service Oct–May
7.4HEC lau pitch5 (incl 2 persons)

CARNE BEACH
Co. Wexford

Carne Beach ☎Wexford(053)31131
Mainly level and grass site with sand, gravel and bushes. Near to sea, beach and main road.
20 May–11 Sep.
3.2HEC lau pitch6 (incl 2 persons)

CASTLE ARCHDALE
Co. Fermanagh

Castle Archdale ☎Irvinestown(03656)21333
Level, grass site with trees and bushes, set in woodland close to a lake.
Apr–Sep.
4.8HEC lau pitch5 (incl 2 persons)

CASTLEGREGORY
Co. Kerry

Anchor ☎Tralee(066)39157
Mainly level, grass site with mature trees and bushes, set in mountainous meadowland close to sea and beach.
Etr Thu–Sep.

Ireland

2HEC lau pitch6–7 (incl 2 persons)

CASTLEROCK
Co. Londonderry (☎0265)

Castlerock ☎848381
Level grass site with bushes, set in meadowland, adjacent to sea, beach and River Bann estuary.
Etr–Oct.
1.2HEC lau pitch5 (incl 2 persons)

CASTLEWELLAN
Co. Down (☎03967)

Castlewellan Forest Apply to: Ministry of Agriculture, Forestry Division, Castlewellan ☎78664
Neatly maintained touring site forming part of country park but also convenient for town centre. Camping area is screened by trees.
2.8HEC lau pitch2–5 (incl 2 persons)

CLONEA
Co. Waterford (☎058)

Casey's ☎41919
Situated 3½ m from Dungarvan with direct access to the beach.
21 May–4 Sep.
1.6HEC lau pitch6 (incl 2 persons)

CLOUGHEY
Co. Down

Silver Bay Ballyspurge ☎Portavogie(02477)71321
A level, sandy and grassy site with mature trees and bushes, near to sea and beach.

CORK
Co. Cork (☎021)

Cork City Togher Rd ☎961866
Level, grass and gravel site with mature trees. 2½ m from city centre.
All year.
0.8HEC lau pitch5 (incl 2 persons)

COURTOWN HARBOUR
Co. Wexford

Courtown ☎Gorey(055)25147
Apr–Oct.
1.4HEC lau pitch7 (incl 2 persons)

Parklands Ardamine ☎Gorey(055)25202
Mainly level grass site with mature trees and bushes; access to sea and beach. No tents.
Apr–Oct.
1.2HEC lau pitch6 (incl 2 persons)

CROOKHAVEN
Co. Cork

Barley Cove ☎Skibbereen(028)35302
Level, grass gravel site with trees and bushes set among sand dunes. Adjacent to sea and beach.
14 May–10 Sep.
2HEC lau pitch6–8 (incl 2 persons)

CROSSMOLINA
Co. Mayo

Hiney's Mullinmore St ☎Ballina(096)31202
Mar–Oct.
1.4HEC lau pitch4 (incl 2 persons)

CUSHENDALL
Co. Antrim (☎02667)

Cushendall ☎71699
Level, grass site, adjacent to sea, beach and main road.
mid Mar–mid Oct.
0.4HEC lau

CUSHENDUN
Co. Antrim (☎026674)

Cushendun 14 Glendun Rd ☎254
Level grass site with trees and bushes; adjacent to sea, beach, river and hills.
Mar–7 Oct.
0.2HEC lau pitch5 (incl 2 persons)

DUNDALK
Co. Louth (☎042)

Gyles Quay Riverstown PO, Gyles Quay ☎76262
28 May–3 Sep.
lau pitch6 (incl 2 persons)

DUNGLOE
Co. Donegal (☎075)

Dungloe Carnmore Rd ☎21350
May–Sep.
1HEC lau pitch4 (incl 2 persons)

FETHARD
Co. Wexford

Ocean Island Booley Hill ☎Waterford(051)97148
Etr–Sep.
0.8HEC pitch5 (incl 2 persons)

KERRYKEEL
Co. Donegal

Rockhill ☎Letterkenny(074)50012
Level grass site, set in meadowland, adjacent to Mulroy Bay.
Apr–9 Sep.
0.8HEC lau pitch5 (incl 2 persons)

KILKEEL
Co. Down (☎06937)

Leestone Leestone Rd ☎62567

Part-level, part-sloping grass site set in hilly country, with access to sea, river and beach and main road. 1 m from town on A2 Newcastle road.

Etr–Oct.

0.4HEC H G R lau pitch5 (incl 2 persons)

KILLALOE
Co. Clare

Lough Derg ☎Limerick(061)76329

On level ground in the Shannon valley by the shore 3½ m N of Killaloe on the L12.

6 May–24 Sep.

1.8HEC H G R lau pitch7 (incl 2 persons)

KILLARNEY
Co. Kerry (☎064)

Beech Grove Fossa (3m NW) ☎31727

Etr–Sep.

1.2HEC H G lau pitch5–7 (incl 2 persons)

Fossa ☎31497

A level grassy site with mature trees and bushes, near lake and woodland 2½m from town on N70.

Etr–Sep.

2.8HEC H G R lau pitch7 (incl 2 persons)

White Bridge Ballycashseen ☎31590

A grass site set in woodlands and mountains on banks of River Flesk. 1 m E of Killarney, 300 yds off Killarney–Cork road.

17 Mar–Sep.

1.4HEC H lau pitch6 (incl 2 persons)

KILLORGLIN
Co. Kerry (☎066)

West's Killarney Rd ☎61240

All year.

1HEC H G R P lau pitch6 (incl 2 persons)

KILRUSH
Co. Clare

Aylevarroo ☎(065)51102

Level grass site, set in meadowland adjacent to beach, river and Shannon estuary, 2 km from Kilrush.

14 May–4 Sep.

3HEC H G lau pitch5–6 (incl 2 persons)

LAHINCH
Co. Clare (☎065)

Lahinch ☎81424

Situated south of village near sandy beach. If approaching from Ennistymon, pass through village, turn left then right opposite church.

May–Sep.

Ireland

20HEC H G lau pitch7 (incl 2 persons)

LARNE
Co. Antrim (☎0574)

Curran 131 Curran Rd ☎72313

Apr–Sep.

1.2HEC H lau

LAURAGH
Co. Kerry

Creveen Lodge Healy Pass Rd ☎Killarney(064)83131

Situated on the Healy Pass road, 1 m SE of Lauragh.

Etr–Sep.

0.8HEC H G lau pitch5 (incl 2 persons)

LISNASKEA
Co. Fermanagh (☎03657)

Lisnaskea ☎21040

Apr–Oct.

1.6HEC H lau pitch4 (incl 2 persons)

MILLISLE
Co. Down (☎0247)

Sea View Ballycopeland ☎861248

Mainly a static caravan site, there is ample space for touring vans in a quiet area. Set on a hillside, overlooking the Irish Sea.

Apr–Oct.

1.2HEC H G lau

MULLINGAR
Co. Westmeath (☎044)

Lough Ennel ☎48101

Level, grass and gravel site set in wood and meadowland. Access to Lough Ennel.

Apr–Sep.

3.2HEC H G R lau pitch6 (incl 2 persons)

NEWCASTLE
Co. Down (☎03967)

Newcastle Tullybrannigan Rd ☎22351

Part level, part sloping, grass site with mature trees and bushes near sea, beach and river. Set amid hills, mountains, moorland and woodland. 1 m W of Newcastle on A2. No tents.

Mar–Nov.

1.2HEC H G R pitch3 (incl 2 persons)

Tollymore Forest Park ☎22428

Part level, part sloping, grass site with various trees and bushes. Set in woodland countryside, adjacent to River Shimma and Tollymore Forest. 2 m W of Newcastle on B180.

All year.

3HEC H lau

O'BRIENS BRIDGE
Co. Clare (☎061)

Shannon Cottage ☎377118

Apr–Sep.

0.4HEC H G lau S pitch6 (incl 2 persons)

PORTBALLINTRAE
Co. Antrim

Ballintrae ☎Bushmills(02657)31478

A level grassy site near to sea and beach.

Apr–Sep.

0.6HEC H lau pitch4–5 (incl 2 persons)

PORTLAOISE
Co. Laoise (☎0502)

Kirwans Mountrath Rd ☎21688

Small, clean site, well situated for touring. On the Dublin–Limerick road.

Apr–Sep.

0.6HEC H G R lau pitch5 (incl 2 persons)

PORTSALON
Co. Donegal

Knockalla ☎(074)53130

Situated in the foothills of Knockalla Mount, overlooking the sea and beach.

Apr–15 Sep.

1HEC H G R lau pitch6 (incl 2 persons)

RED CROSS
Co. Wicklow

Johnson's Ballintim ☎Wicklow(0404)8133

Etr–16 Sep.

0.8HEC H G R lau pitch5 (incl 2 persons)

River Valley ☎Wicklow(0404)8647

A flat grassy site set in a picturesque valley, off the N11 Dublin–Arklow road.

15 Mar–22 Aug.

3.2HEC H G R lau pitch5 (incl 2 persons)

ROSBEG
Co. Donegal

Tramore Beach ☎(075)51106

Part level, part sloping, grass and sand site set in hilly country with access to sea, beach and main road.

Etr–Sep.

2HEC H R pitch7 (incl 2 persons)

ROSSES POINT
Co. Sligo

Greenlands ☎Sligo(071)77113

26 May–6 Sep.

1.6HEC H R lau pitch4–5 (incl 2 persons)

ROSSLARE
Co. Wexford

Burrow Holiday Park
☎Wexford(053)32190

Mar–Nov.

1.2HEC H |O| G R lau pitch7 (incl 2 persons)

ROUNDWOOD

Co. Wicklow

Roundwood ☎Dublin (01)818163

Part level, part sloping grass site with trees and bushes, set in mountains and woodland, adjacent to Vartry river, 12 m from Bray.

Apr–Sep.

2HEC H G R lau pitch5–6 (incl 2 persons)

SHANKILL

Co. Dublin

Shankill ☎Bray (01)820011

A grassy site with mature trees and bushes, situated S of village on main road.

All year.

2.4HEC H G R lau pitch6 (incl 2 persons)

SHERCOCK

Co. Cavan

Lakelands ☎Dundalk (042)69206

Mainly level grass and gravel site amidst young trees and bushes. Set in hilly country, close to lake and main road.

Etr & 28 May–27 Aug.

1.2HEC H |O| G R lau pitch6 (incl 2 persons)

WATERVILLE

Co. Kerry

Pine Grove ☎Tralee(0667)4185

Apr–Sep. Restricted service Oct–Mar.

7.4HEC H G R lau pitch7 (incl 2 persons)

Waterville Spunkane ☎(0667)4191

Situated on elevated ground overlooking Ballinskelligs Bay, 300 yds off main Cahirciveen-Waterville road, N70, ½ m from village.

All year.

1.7HEC H G P lau pitch6–8 (incl 2 persons)

WEXFORD

Co. Wexford (☎053)

Ferrybank ☎24378

A level and grassy site with bushes near sea, beach and river. N side of bridge.

Etr–Aug.

4HEC H |O| R P lau pitch6 (incl 2 persons)

The scenic twin lakes of Glendalough in County Wicklow

ITALY & SAN MARINO

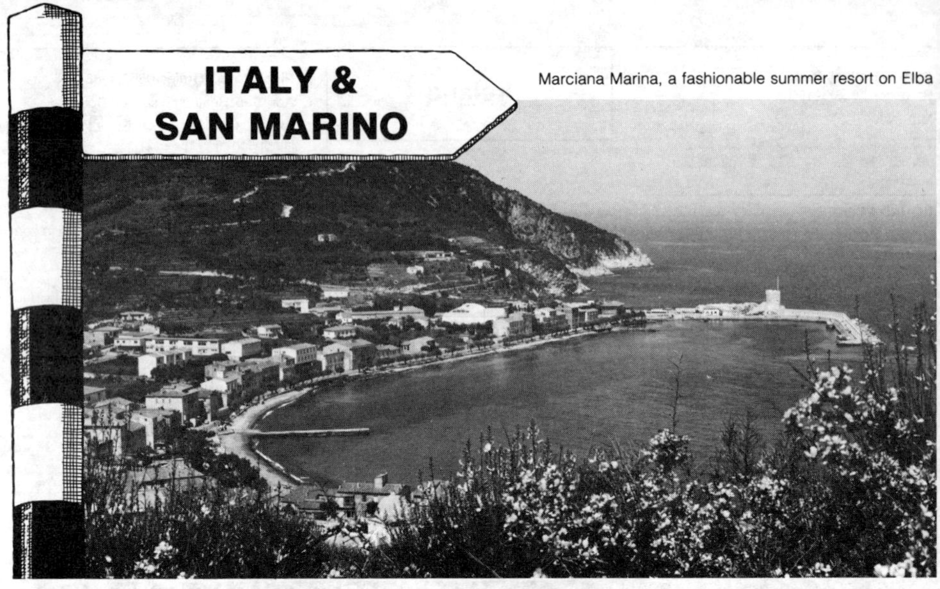

Marciana Marina, a fashionable summer resort on Elba

Italy, with its many beautiful cities and rich architectural heritage, is bordered by four countries: Austria, France, Switzerland and Yugoslavia. The approaches are all dominated by mountains. The lakes of the north present a striking contrast with the sun-parched lands of the south and there is some beautiful countryside in the central Appenines. There are fine, sandy beaches on both the Mediterranean and Adriatic coasts.

The north has a Continental climate whilst the south has an almost African climate with extremely hot summers. The language is Italian, a direct development of Latin. There are several dialect forms such as Sicilian and Sardinian, but the accepted standard is from Florence. German is spoken to a small extent near the Austrian frontier.

HOW TO GET THERE

Although there are several ways of getting to Italy, entry will most probably be by way of France or Switzerland. The major passes, which are closed in winter, are served by road or rail tunnels. The distance from the Channel ports is approximately 650–700 miles, requiring one or two night stops. Rome is 360 miles further south. Car-sleeper services operate during the summer from Boulogne, Brussels, 's-Hertogenbosch or Paris to Milan.

GENERAL INFORMATION

(see also *Things you need to know.* pages 33–64)

Boats

(see page 33)

British Embassy/Consulates

(see also page 57)

The British Embassy together with its consular section is located at *00187 Roma* Via xx Settembre 80A ☎4755441/4755551. There are British Consulates in Florence, Genoa, Milan, Naples and Venice; there are British Consulates with Honorary Consuls in Cagliari (Sardinia) and Trieste.

Camping

The Assessorati Regionali per il Turismo (ART) and the Ente Provinciale per il Turismo (EPT) have regional and provincial information offices and can provide details of campsites within their locality. In northern Italy, especially by the lakes and along the Adriatic coast, sites tend to become very crowded and it is advisable to book in advance during the season which extends from May to the end of August.

International camping carnet although not generally compulsory it is required on certain sites. Some campsites will allow a reduction in the advertised charge to the holder of a camping carnet. See page 37 for further information.

Off-site camping is permitted provided the landowner's permission has been obtained, but is strictly prohibited in state forests and national parks. In built-up areas if parking is allowed the towing vehicle must remain connected to the trailer or caravan and the corner steadies must not be used.

Currency including banking hours

(see also page 57)
The unit of currency is the Italian Lira (*Lit*). At the time of going to press £ = *Lit* 2,110. Denominations of bank notes are *Lit* 1,000, 2,000, 5,000, 10,000, 50,000, 100,000; standard coins are *Lit* 5, 10, 20, 50, 100, 200, 500. The maximum amount of Italian currency which may be taken into or out of Italy is *Lit*400,000. There are no restrictions on the amount of foreign currency that may be imported and amounts up to *Lit*5,000,000 may be exported without formality. However, in order to export amounts in excess of *Lit*5,000,000 it is necessary to declare the amount on entry using the special form (V2) obtainable at frontier Customs posts. This form is then shown to the Customs when leaving Italy. Most banks are open from Monday to Friday 08.30 to 13.00hrs and from 15.30 to 16.30hrs.

Fiscal receipt

In Italy the law provides for a special numbered fiscal receipt (ricevuta fiscale) to be issued after paying for a wide range of goods and services including meals and accommodation. This receipt indicates the cost of the various goods and services obtained and the total charge after adding VAT. Tourists should ensure that this receipt is issued as spot checks are made by the authorities and both proprietor and consumer are liable to an on-the-spot fine if the receipt cannot be produced.

Foodstuffs

(see also page 60)
Visitors resident in Europe and entering from an EEC country may import duty-free 1,000g of coffee or 400g of coffee extract and 200g of tea or 80g of tea extract; a reduced allowance applies for non residents of Europe or if entering from a non EEC country.

Medical treatment

(see also page 60)

Shopping hours

Generally *food shops* are open Monday to Saturday 08.00–13.00hrs and 16.00–20.00hrs, but close at 13.00hrs on Thursday. Most *other* shops are open Monday to Saturday 09.00–13.00hrs and 16.00–19.30hrs, but only open at 16.00hrs on Monday.

Tourist information

(see also page 63)
The Italian State Tourist Office (ENIT) has an office in London at 1 Princes Street, W1R 8AY ☎01-408 1254. It will be pleased to assist you with any information regarding tourism. In Italy there are three organisations: the *Ente Nazionale Italiano per il Turismo* (ENIT) with offices at the frontiers and ports; the *Assessorati Regionali per il Turismo* (ART) and the *Ente Provinciale per il Turismo* (EPT) who will assist tourists through their regional and provincial offices. The *Aziende Autonome di Cura Soggiorno e Turismo* (AACST) have offices in places of recognised tourist interest and concern themselves exclusively with matters of local interest.

Visitors' registration

(see page 63)

MOTORING

(see also *Things you need to know*, pages 33–64)

Accidents

(see also page 46)
Fire, police, ambulance (Public emergency service) ☎113.

Breakdowns

(see page 48)

Dimensions and weight restrictions

Private **cars** and towed **trailers** or **caravans** are restricted to the following dimensions – **car** height: 4 metres; width: 2.50 metres; length: with one axle 6 metres, with two or more axles 12 metres. **Trailer/caravan** height: 4 metres; width: 2.30 metres; length: with one axle 6 metres, with two axles 7.50 metres. The maximum permitted overall length of vehicle/trailer or caravan combination is 18 metres.

Trailers with an unladen weight of over 750kg or 50% of the weight of the towing vehicle must have service brakes on all wheels.

Driving Licence

(see also page 33)
A valid Republic of Ireland or green UK* licence is acceptable in Italy if accompanied by an official translation which may be obtained free from the AA. The minimum age at which a

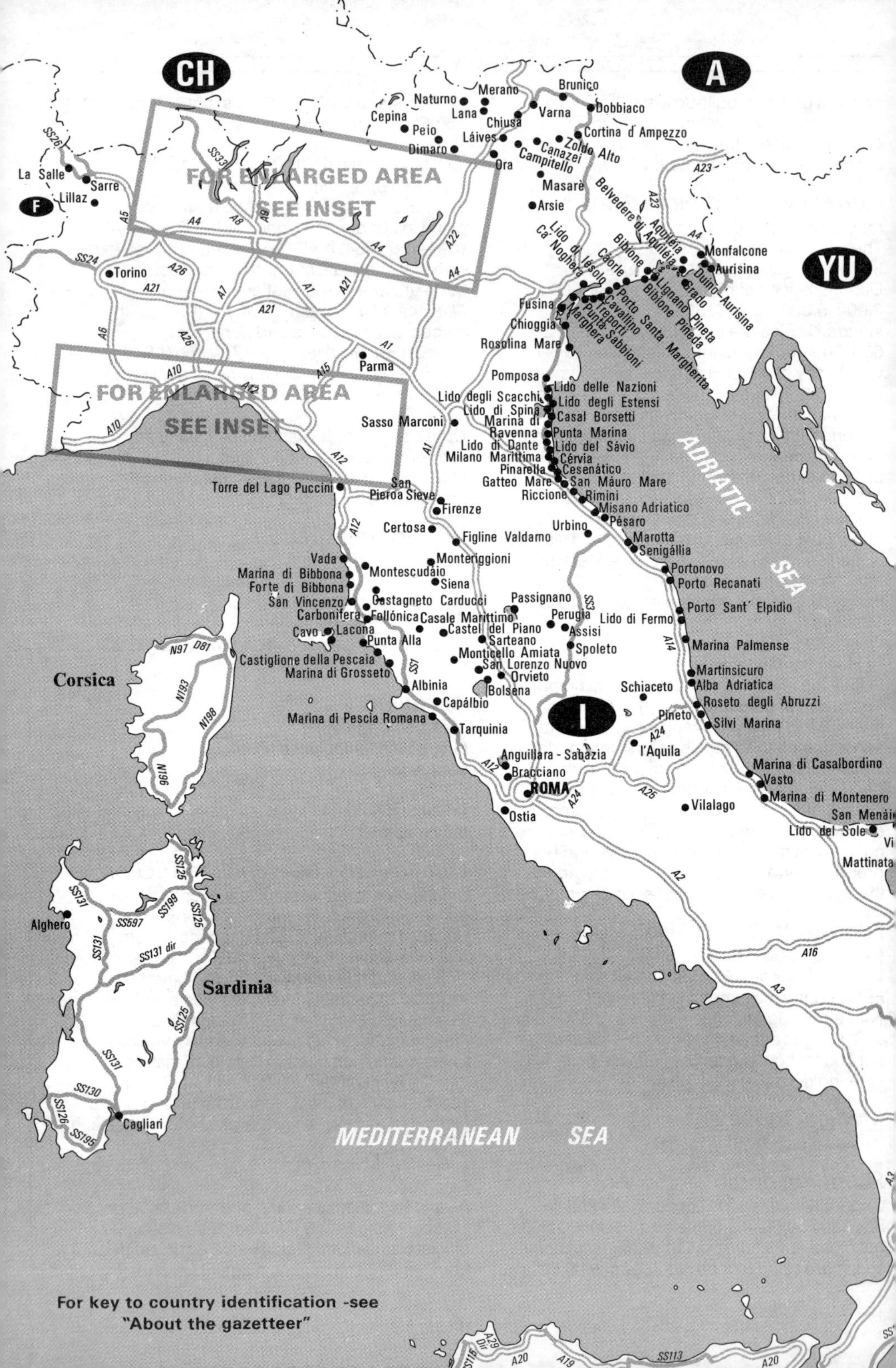

For key to country identification -see "About the gazetteer"

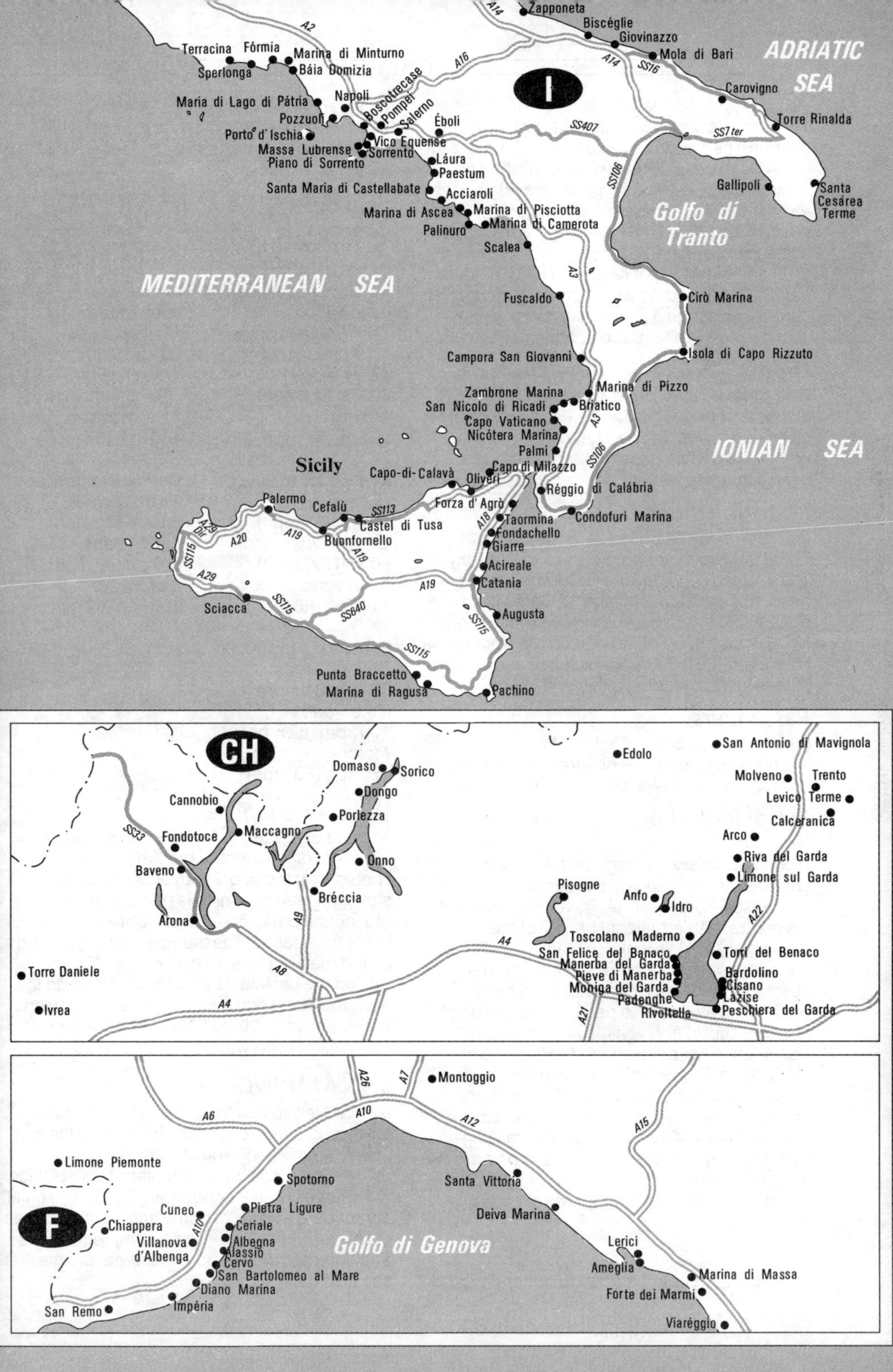

ADRIATIC SEA
MEDITERRANEAN SEA
IONIAN SEA
Golfo di Tranto
I
Zapponeta
Biscéglie
Giovinazzo
Mola di Bari
Carovigno
Torre Rinalda
Gallipoli
Santa Cesárea Terme
Terracina
Fórmia
Marina di Minturno
Sperlonga
Báia Domizia
Maria di Lago di Pátria
Napoli
Pozzuoli
Boscotrecase
Pompei
Salerno
Éboli
Porto d'Ischia
Vico Equense
Massa Lubrense
Sorrento
Piano di Sorrento
Láura
Paestum
Santa Maria di Castellabate
Acciaroli
Marina di Ascea
Marina di Pisciotta
Palinuro
Marina di Camerota
Scalea
Fuscaldo
Cirò Marina
Campora San Giovanni
Isola di Capo Rizzuto
Zambrone Marina
Marina di Pizzo
San Nicolo di Ricadi
Briatico
Capo Vaticano
Nicótera Marina
Palmi
Sicily
Capo-di-Calavà
Capo di Milazzo
Oliveri
Réggio di Calábria
Palermo
Cefalù
Forza d'Agrò
Castel di Tusa
Taormina
Condofuri Marina
Buonfornello
Fondachello
Giarre
Acireale
Catania
Sciacca
Augusta
Punta Braccetto
Marina di Ragusa
Pachino
A14
A2
A16
SS16
SS407
SS7 ter
SS106
A3
SS113
A18
A19
A20
A29
A29 Dir
SS115
SS640
CH
Edolo
San Antonio di Mavignola
Domaso
Sorico
Molveno
Trento
Cannobio
Dongo
Levico Terme
Calceranica
Porlezza
Maccagno
Arco
Fondotoce
Riva del Garda
Baveno
Onno
Limone sul Garda
Pisogne
Anfo
Idro
Bréccia
Arona
Toscolano Maderno
San Felice del Banaco
Torri del Benaco
Manerba del Garda
Pieve di Manerba
Bardolino
Moniga del Garda
Cisano
Padenghe
Lazise
Rivoltella
Peschiera del Garda
Torre Daniele
Ivrea
SS33
A9
A8
A4
A21
A22
Montoggio
A26
A7
A10
A6
A12
A15
Limone Piemonte
Spotorno
Santa Vittoria
Cuneo
Pietra Ligure
Deiva Marina
F
Chiappera
Ceriale
Villanova d'Albenga
Albegna
Golfo di Genova
Lerici
Alassio
Ameglia
Cervo
San Bartolomeo al Mare
Marina di Massa
Diano Marina
Forte dei Marmi
Impéria
San Remo
Viaréggio

visitor may drive a temporarily imported car is 18 years. However, visitors under 21 years are not permitted to drive vehicles which have a top speed in excess of 180 kph (112 mph). The minimum ages at which visitors may ride temporarily imported motorcycles are 17 (not exceeding 125cc), 18 (between 125cc–350cc) and 21 (exceeding 350cc).

*The translation is not required by the holder of a pink UK licence. The UK licensing authorities cannot exchange a green licence for a pink licence purely to facilitate continental travel.

Lights

(see page 50 also *Headlights* page 41)
Full beam headlights can be used only outside cities and towns. Dipped headlights are compulsory when passing through tunnels even if they are well lit.

Motoring clubs

(see also page 61)
There are two motoring organisations in Italy. The *Touring Club Italiano* (TCI) which has its head office at 20122 Milano 10 Corso Italia ☏(02)85261 and the *Automobile Club d'Italia* (ACI) whose head office is at *00185 Roma 8* Via Marsala ☏(06)49981. Both clubs have branch offices in most leading cities and towns.

Passengers

(see also page 51)
It is recommended that children do not travel in a vehicle as front seat passengers.

Petrol including petrol coupons

(see page 61)
A concessionary package of Italian petrol coupons and motorway toll vouchers may be purchased from most AA Travel Agencies and AA centres. An additional benefit of the package is a free breakdown and replacement car concession, but see also *Breakdowns* page 00 for details of the 5-Star Service. The package is available to personal callers only and a passport and vehicle registration document must be produced at the time of application. Further information may be obtained from any AA Centre. The package **cannot** be purchased inside Italy but may be obtained from ACI offices at main crossing points and also many ACI offices in port areas if arriving by ship.

It is **forbidden** to carry petrol in cans in a vehicle.

Roads

Main and secondary roads are generally good and there are an exceptional number of bypasses. Mountain roads are usually well engineered; see pages 70–79 for details of mountain passes.

Seat belts

(see page 52)

Speed limits

Vehicles not exceeding 8 tonnes

up to 599cc
Built-up areas
*50 kph (31 mph)
Other roads
80 kph (49 mph)
Motorways
90 kph (56 mph)

from 600cc to 900cc
Built-up areas
50 kph (31 mph)
Other roads
90 kph (56 mph)
Motorways
110 kph (68 mph)

from 901cc to 1300cc
Built-up areas
50 kph (31 mph)
Other roads
100 kpm (62 mph)
Motorways
130 kph (80 mph)

over 1300cc
Built-up areas
50 kph (31 mph)
Other roads
110 kph (68 mph)
Motorways
140 kph (87 mph)

Car/caravan/trailer
Built-up areas
50 kph (31 mph)
Other roads
80 kph (49 mph)
Motorways
100 kph (62 mph)

Warning triangle

The use of a warning triangle is compulsory in the event of accident or breakdown. They should be used to give advance warning of any stationary vehicle which is parked on a road in fog, near a bend, on a hill at night when the rear lights have failed. The triangle must be placed on the road not less than 50 metres (55 yds) behind the vehicle. Motorists who fail to do this are liable to an administrative fine of between *Lit*5,000 and *Lit*20,000. See also *Warning triangles/Hazard warning lights* page 54.

SAN MARINO

A small Republic with an area of 23 sq miles and a population of 21,500. Situated in the hills of Italy near Rimini. The official information office in the UK is the Italian State Tourist Office at 1 Princes Street, London W1R 8AY. The chief attraction is the city of San Marino on the slopes of Monte Titano. Its laws, motoring regulations and emergency telephone numbers are the same as Italy.

Prices are in Italian Lire
Abbreviation: pza piazza

ACCIAROLI
Salerno (☎0974)

Ondina via Nationale Km35/V ☎904040

Delightful seaside site, full of flowers. Lunchtime siesta 14.00–16.00 hrs.

Turn off towards the sea at Km35/VII.
Apr–Nov.

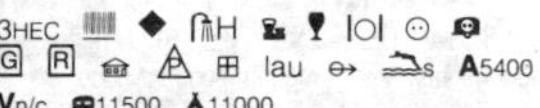
3HEC H |O| G R lau s A5400 Vn/c 11500 A11000

Terrazza a Mare ☎904064

Site on numerous terraces between coast road and the sea. Lemon, olive and fig trees, shade also provided by sunshade roofing. Siesta 14.30–16.30 hrs.

Turn off SS267 at Km35/VII seawards and continue 800 m.
May–Oct.

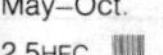
2.5HEC H |O|

G R s P lau A3100 pitch15500

At **AGNONE CILENTO** (6.5 km N)

Calù

In quiet location by the sea. Shade provided by roof matting; sandy terrace.

Access at Km33 of the coastal road near last house on a bend. Last 300 m very poor road and difficult for caravans.

2.2HEC H |O| s

ACIREALE See **SICILIA (SICILY)**

ADRIANO (LIDO) See **PUNTA MARINA**

ALASSIO
Savona (☎0182)

Monti e Mare ☎43036

In an attractive situation among olive trees.

Turn off SS1 at Km619.5.
Apr–10 Oct.

7HEC H |O| G R lau s

ALBA ADRIATICA
Teramo (☎0861)

Spiaggia Argento ☎77365

Site on longish strip of land, shade between housing and hotels. Siesta 14.00–16.00 hrs.

Next to Hotel Boston. Signposted from beach road.
May–Sep.

0.7HEC H |O| G R lau s

At **TORTORETO (LIDO)** (4 km S)

Salinello ☎786306

Well-tended meadowland site with numerous rows of poplars. Private beach, siesta 14.00–16.00 hrs.

On southern outskirts, signposted from Km405 of the SS16.
Jun–15 Sep.

12HEC H |O| G R s lau

Italy

Welcome ☎786341

The site has two sections, one for tents and the other for caravans, separated by a railway. Shade provided by sunshade roofs. No unaccompanied teenagers.

Access is via motorway exit San Benedetto de Tronto from A14 (Ancona–Pescara). Follow SS16 to southern end of village and branch off main road.
15 Apr–Sep.

6HEC H |O| G R s P lau pitch6000–12000 (incl 2 persons)

ALBENGA
Savona (☎0812)

Bella Vista ☎540213

1 km from Km613.5 on SS1.
May–Sep.

0.6HEC H |O| lau |O| s A4000 V3500 4500 A3000–4500

Dei Fiori ☎52339

The site which lies between Camping Roma and coast road, consists of two sections, and is completely divided into pitches. Shade is provided by trees and straw mat roofs.

Approach as for Camping Roma.
Etr–Sep.

2HEC H |O| G s P lau

Delfino via Aurelia 23 ☎51998

N from Alàssio on SS1.
Apr–Sep.

1.2HEC H |O| G lau s A3500–4750 V3500–4750 3500–4750 A3500–4750

Piccolo Paradiso ☎51734

This site, on level, well shaded meadowland, is planted with grape vines and trees. Separated from its private beach by a railway embankment through which there is an underpass.

Inland off road to Ceriale.
Apr–Sep.

1HEC H |O| s lau A4750 V4750 4750–9500 A4750

Roma via Aurelia ☎52317

The site is divided into pitches and laid out with many flower beds.

N of bridge over Centa, turn left.
15 Apr–Sep.

0.8HEC H |O| G R lau sR

At **CÉNESI**

Villaggio Turistico Versolmar ☎20671

Modern terraced site. 7 km to sea, bus service available.

Off the A10 (Genova–San Remo) exit Albengo seawards then immediately right across the bridge and continue in direction of Cénesi following signs.
All year.

12HEC H |O| R P

ALBINIA
Grosseto (☎0564)

Acapulco ☎870165

Set on hilly terrain in pine woodland.

Take coast road from via Aurelia at Km155.
15 May–15 Sep.

2HEC H |O| G R P s A5200 pitch6100–9000

Africa ☎870482

In undulating terrain in pine woodland.

Turn seawards at Km153/VIII of the via Aurelia and continue to site in 100 m.
May–Sep.

10HEC H |O| G P lau s

Gabbiano ☎870202

Site in pine woodland and open meadowland with sunshade roofing.

Turn off SS1 at Km155.
Etr–15 Sep.

3HEC H |O| G R s P lau

Hawaii ☎870164

The site lies in a pine forest on rather hilly ground.

Turn off via Aurelia at Km154/V and drive towards the sea.
May–Sep.

4HEC H |O| G P lau s A5340 Vn/c 9000 A6050–9000

International Argentario ☎870302

Set in a pine forest on the shores of the Bay of Porto S. Stefano. Mooring facilities.

Apr–Sep.

5HEC H |O| G R P P lau s

Oasi ☎870482

The site lies in a meadow and a pine wood.

Turn off via Aurelia at Km152/VI and drive towards the sea.

8HEC H |O| G P lau s

Strand ☎870304

Site lies in pine wood and grassland, equipped with roof matting to provide shade. One section of the site has wooden bungalows. Private beach.

Access from via Aurelia, at Km153/III turn seawards.
Etr–Sep.

4HEC H |O| G R s lau A3300–5200 V1400–2700 5500–9000 A5500–9000

Voltoncino ☎870158

Undulating terrain in pine woodland and on grass. ➤

Turn seawards at Km153/VII of the via Aurelia and continue to site in 100 m.
15 May–15 Sep.

7HEC ⓖ ⓟ ⊞ lau A4690 Vn/c 8800 A8800

ALGHERO See **SARDEGNA (SARDINIA)**

AMEGLIA
Le Spezia (☎0187)

Garden ☎65557

On SS432 near Bocca de Magra, opposite Gulf petrol station.
All year.

1HEC ◇ H ⊞ lau R

ANFO
Brescia (☎0365)

Palafitte ☎809051

Pleasant site divided into plots, sloping towards the lake where there are some trees.

Access as for Pilù, then turn right.
May–12 Sep.

2HEC ◆ H ⓖ R LP ⊞ lau A4000
pitch8000

Pilù via Bersaglio Il Lago d'Idro ☎809037

Well-maintained, slightly sloping site subdivided by trees and rows of shrubs on pebble beach from which is it separated by narrow public footpath.

On southern outskirts; well signed.
Apr–Sep.

2.5HEC ◆ H ⓖ

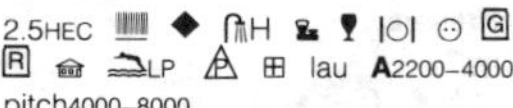

R LP ⊞ lau A2200–4000
pitch4000–8000

ANGUILLARA-SABAZIA
Roma (☎06)

Parco del Lago ☎3046602

Alongside Lake Bracciano, off the Trevignano road.
May–15 Oct.

3.2HEC ◆ H ⓖ R L lau A4250 Vn/c 5100 A5100

AQUILA (L')
Abruzzo (☎0862)

Italy

Funivia del Gran Sasso ☎606163

Jul–15 Sep & Nov–Apr

0.7HEC H R ⓟ ⊞ lau A3500 V1000 5000 A4000

AQUILÉIA
Udine (☎0431)

Aquiléia via Gemina 10 ☎91042

Well-maintained park-like site situated in quiet area.

400 m E of village centre.
15 May–15 Sep.

3.2HEC ◆ H ⓖ R P ⊞ lau

ARCO
Trento (☎0464)

Arco ☎517491

On right bank of River Sarca, in quiet park-like terrain in small woodland and on open meadow.

6 km from Lake Garda. Access via SS45 bis (Trento–Riva) turn off at Km118/VII.
Mar–4 Nov.

3.6HEC ◆ H ⓖ R RP ⊞ lau A4000
pitch6000

ARONA
Novara (☎0322)

At **DORMELLETTO** (5 km S)

Lago Azzurro via E-Fermi 5 ☎497197

S of Arona off SS Sempione 33.
All year.

2.5HEC H ⓖ LP ⊞ lau A3800 V2800 5000 A5000

Lago Maggiore ☎497193

Well-maintained site divided into plots, pleasantly landscaped by the lakeside.

Access from SS33, well signposted.
15 Mar–15 Oct.

5HEC H ⓖ R L ⊞ lau A5000
pitch6500–8200

Lido ☎497047

Site on bank of the lake, with some trees.

Turn off the SS33 at Km60/VII and the IP petrol station, then about 250 m towards the lake turn off past the Evinrude ship yard.
Apr–Sep.

4HEC ◆ H ⓖ R LP ⊞ lau
A3000–5000 Vn/c 5000–8000 A5000–8000

Smeraldo via Cavour 103 ☎497031

Well-landscaped site, divided into plots and situated in woodland by lakeside.

Access from SS33.
Mar–Nov.

2.4HEC ◆ H ⓖ R L ⊞ lau A5000
pitch8200

ARSIE
Belluno (☎0439)

Gajole Loc Soravigo ☎58505

Access from SS50 bis.
Apr–Sep.

1.4HEC H ⊞ lau L A2200 V1400 2000 A1800

ASCEA (MARINA DI)
Salerno (☎0974)

Villággio delle Palem ☎971036

A modern site by gravel beach. The camp has original 'Truli' chalets.

Take coast road SS267 and drive 50 m S of Paestum.

8HEC H sP ⊞

ASSISI
Perugia (☎075)

Fontemaggio Eremo Carceri 8 ☎812317 (winter) 813636 (summer)

This terraced site is scattered with olive trees and has a beautiful view of surrounding countryside.

It lies just off the road that climbs up to the hermitage of St Francis of Assisi. Short, steep approach.
All year.

10HEC H lau A3600 V1500 4500 3500

AUGUSTA See **SICILIA (SICILY)**

AURISINA
Trieste (040)

Imperial 200459

Access via SS14 in Sistiana–Aurisina direction.
Jun–Sep.

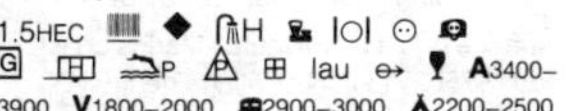
1.5HEC H G P lau A3400–3900 V1800–2000 2900–3000 2200–2500

BÁIA DOMIZIA
Caserta (0823)

Báia Domizia 930164

Part of this extensive seaside site is laid out with flower beds. No children under 3 and no radios allowed.

Turn off the SS7 (qtr) at Km6/V, then 3 km seawards.
24 Apr–Sep.

30HEC H G RP lau A7500 V3400 9900 9900

BARDOLINO
Verona (045)

Rocca 7211300

Subdivided site in slightly sloping grassland broken up by rows of trees. Separated from the lake by a public path (no cars). Part of site on the other side of the main road is terraced amongst vines and olives with lovely view of lake.

Below the SS249 at Km40/IV.
May–Sep.

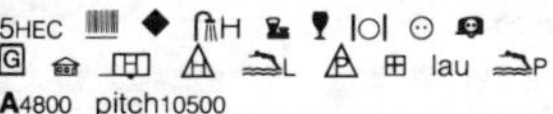
5HEC H G L lau P A4800 pitch10500

BAVENO
Novara (0323)

Tranquilla 24878

Site lies on terrace above lake and village.

W of lake on SS33.
All year.

2HEC H G R P

Italy

BELVEDERE DI AQUILÉIA
Udine

Belvedere Pineta 91007

Situated on hilly ground in groves of pine and deciduous trees, next to lagoon beach.

On road 352 turn left at Km34/VII and continue 1.2 km.
May–Sep.

H sP

BIBBONA (MARINA DI)
Livorno (0586)

See also **FORTE DI BIBBONA**

Capannino 600252

Well tended park site in pine woodland with private beach.

On via Aurelia by Km272/VII turn towards sea.
May–15 Sep.

3HEC H R s P lau

BIBIONE
Venezia (0431)

Villaggio Turistico Internazionale 43231

Mostly sandy terrain under pine trees. Some meadowland with a few deciduous trees. Wide sandy beach. Tennis court.

Access is well signed along approach roads.
2 May–27 Sep.

13HEC H G R sP lau A6000 pitch15000

BIBIONE PINEDA
Venezia (0431)

Capalonga 43597

Between a lagoon and the sea, the site is generously laid out in pitches with plants and trees. During peak periods, no children under 2 yrs allowed in the camp.

May–Sep.

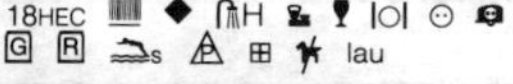
18HEC H G R s lau

Lido 43180

Sandy terrain along private beach of several hundred metres. Shade provided by mixed woodland and medium trees. Separate section for tents and caravans. No advanced bookings.

Well signposted.
15 May–15 Sep.

8HEC H G s lau A300–5500 V4000 8000–13000 8000–13000

BISCEGLIE
Bari (080)

Batteria 950009

The site lies off the SE beach road in the levelled grounds of an old fortress on 12 m-high cliffs.

For access, leave the SS16 at Km765/O, turn towards the sea, and then continue for 0.5 km to the site, which is enclosed by walls.
May–15 Sep.

2.2HEC H G s lau

BOLSENA
Viterbo (0761)

Chez Vous 98203

Situated within a garden by a villa.

At Km3.5.
Mar–Sep.

1HEC H lau L

BOSCOTRECASE
Napoli (081)

Vesúvio via Ugo Foscolo 56 8581367

The site lies on two terraces in the grounds of the Hotel Vesúvio.

About 150m to the right of the main Vesúvius road.
Apr–Sep.

1.2HEC H G

BRACCIANO
Roma (06)

Roma Flash Sporting via Settevene Palo Km19,800 9023669

Apr–Sep. ➔

5.5HEC H lau A4100 Vn/c 4900 Å4200

BRÉCCIA
Como (☎031)

International ☎501636
On a level meadow near the motorway. Lunchtime siesta 13.30–15.30 hrs.
Off A9 Como–Milan motorway.
Apr–16 Oct.
2.5HEC H G R P lau A3500 V2200 3500 Å3500

BRIATICO
Catanzaro (☎0963)

Dolomiti ☎391355
The site is in a delightful setting on two terraces planted with olive trees. It lies by the road and 150 m from railway.
Turn off road 522 between Km17 and Km18 and head towards the sea.
Jun–Sep.
18HEC H G R Ⓟ lau s A6400 V3000 7200 Å7200

Squalo 33 ☎391084
In a former olive grove near the sea. The beach consists of small bays and isolated rocks. There are some reed huts and wigwams.
Located between SS522 and the coastal road.
4HEC H s

BRUNICO-BRUNECK
Bolzano (☎0474)
At **RASUN** (10 km E)

Italy

Corones ☎46490
Very quiet site surrounded by trees with woodland.
Turn off SS49 about 10 km E of Brunico towards Rasun-Antholz and onwards 1.2 km.
All year.
2HEC H G R P lau pitch14500–17500 (incl 2 persons)

BUONFORNELLO See **SICILIA (SICILY)**

CAGLIARI See **SARDEGNA (SARDINIA)**

CALCERANICA
Trento (☎0461)

Al Pescatore ☎723062
The site consists of several sections of meadowland, inland from the lake shore road to Lago di Caldonazzo. Well maintained with private beach.
Jun–15 Sep.
4HEC H G lau L A4000 pitch6400

Fleiola ☎723153
Site is divided into sectors beside lake.
Apr–Sep.
1.2HEC H G L lau A4000 pitch5000

CAMEROTA (MARINA DI)
Salerno (☎0974)

Happy ☎932326
The site lies on a park-like hill sloping down to the sea and is scattered with olive trees.
1 km N of village just off the coast road.
May–Sep.
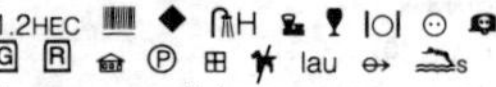
1.2HEC H G R Ⓟ lau s
A6000–11000 pitch7000–12000

Isola ☎93223
Lies on several terraces in an olive grove. Pleasant bathing area with sandy beach.
Entrance is just off Palinuro–Marina coast road (SS562) 1 km N of village near ESSO petrol station.
2.3HEC H G s

Pineta ☎931771
The site is divided into pitches amongst shrubs and pines. Wide beach stretching for several kilometres.
Jun–Sep.
3HEC H R s Ⓟ lau pitch35000 (incl 4 persons)

CAMPITELLO DI FASSA
Trento (☎0462)

Miravalle ☎62002
Signposted.
Closed Apr–14 May & Oct.
2HEC H lau

CAMPORA SAN GIOVANNI
Cosenza (☎0982)

Principessa ☎46047
Modern motel with camp site annexed to it, lying 150 m from the sea and a fine sandy beach.

2 km S and 100 m inland from Campora on SS18.
All year.
1HEC lau S A3800
V2800 4500 4000

CANAZEI
Trento (0462)
Marmolada 61660
Grassland site extending to the river, part of it in spruce woodland.
Located on S outskirts on the right of the road to Alba Penia.
All year.
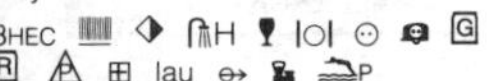
3HEC H lau P

CANNOBIO
Novara (0323)
Campagna via Nazionale 22 70100
Turn off SS34 to Locarno at Km35/V on N outskirts of village. W of lake on road 21.
Apr–15 Oct.
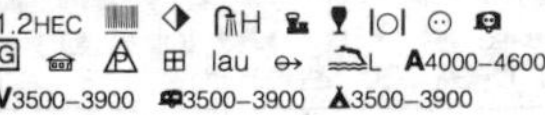
1.2HEC H lau L A4000–4600
V3500–3900 3500–3900 3500–3900
Gelsi 71318
Pleasantly landscaped site on meadowland at side of lake.
Access from the SS34 at Km35/V.
Mar–Oct.
0.6HEC H L lau A4400 V3850
3850 3850
International Paradis 71227
A level site on the bank of a lake.
Access from the SS34 at Km35/V.
Apr–Oct.
1.2HEC H L lau A4500
pitch7800
Riviera 71360
A grassy site with poplar and pine trees. It is divided into pitches next to Camping dei Gelsi.
For access, turn off the SS34 at Km35/II, N of the river bridge and towards the lake.
Apr–15 Oct.
2.2HEC H L lau
Valle Romantica 7249
A pleasant site with trees, shrubs and flowers. Internal roads are asphalted and a mountain stream provides bathing facilities.
1.5 km W off road to Malesco.
Apr–Sep.
5HEC H R lau L

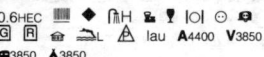

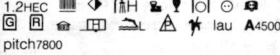

CA'NOGHERA
Venezia (041)
Alba d'Oro 964112
Access from SS14.
Mar–Oct.
7HEC H P lau

Italy

CÁORLE
Venezia (0421)
Falconera via dei Casoni 84282
Level site partially on sandy meadowland under tall poplars on the Porto di Falconera.
E on riverside road to Pizzeria Capri, then turn seawards.
15 May–15 Sep.
2.9HEC H lau S A2700–5000
pitch4300–7700
San Francesco 89333
This generously laid-out site, on level lawns with shady poplars, lies in the midst of a holiday village.
Follow signs from Cáorle for access.
15 Apr–Sep.
30HEC H SP lau A3000–7000 pitch5500–16000
Sole 81908
Bungalow village and site on beach under pines.
Approach travelling E along the riverside road.
May–Sep.
2HEC H S lau

CAPÁLBIO
Grosseto (0564)
Chiarone 890101
Partially hilly terrain with dunes and bushes by the sea with lovely beach. Roof matting provides shade.
Turn off via Aurelia at Km124 or Km120 towards the sea, 5 km over level crossing.
May–15 Sep.
5.7HEC H S lau

CAPO DI CALAVÀ See **SICILIA (SICILY)**

CAPO DI MILAZZO See **SICILIA (SICILY)**

CAPO VATICANO
Catanzaro (0963)
Quattro Scogli 63126
The site is in a quiet sandy bay surrounded by rocks.
Drive from San Nicolo di Ricardi to Capo Vaticano.
All year.
1.2HEC H S lau A6000
V3000 7000 4000–8000

CARBONIFERA
Livorno (0565)
Pappasole 20414
Landscaped area inland off the coastal road.
Apr–15 Oct.

14HEC H SP lau A5550–7150
V2050–2800 6250–5750 4800–8600

CAROVIGNO
Brindisi (0831)
At **SPECCHIOLLA (LIDO)**
Pineta al Mare 968057
Site in pine woodland with sandy beach and some rocks.
E of Bari–Brindisi road at Km31.5.
All year.
5.5HEC H lau S A4450
pitch6250

CARRUBA See **ACIREALE** Under **SICILIA (SICILY)**

CASALBORDINO (MARINA DI)
Chieti (0823)
S. Stefano 918118
Level terrain, below road, within agricultural area, adjoining railway line. Open air disco. Lunchtime siesta 14.00–16.00 hrs.
Exit off Vastro–Nord of A14 (Percara–Bari) and continue north via SS16 to Km498.
All year.
2.5HEC H lau S
A2800–4500 pitch6500–10500

CASAL BORSETTI
Ravenna (0544)
Adria 445217
The site lies in a field behind the Ristorante Lugo.
Turn off the motorway at the Ravenna exit or take the SS309 (Romea) Km 13 N of Ravenna.
May–20 Sep.
4.4HEC H lau SP
A5000 pitch8300
Florida 445105
On level meadowland, separated from the sea by dunes and pines, subdivided by various bushes and trees. Private beach with guarded area where boats may be left.
4 km on via Romeo at Km14.
25 May–10 Sep.
2.7HEC H lau S
Reno 445213
Meadowland in sparse pine woodland and separated from the sea by dunes.
Turn off SS309 at Km8 or 14.
25 Apr–Sep.
3.3HEC H lau S A4350
pitch7300
At **ROMEA (MARINA DI)** (4 km S)
Romea 446311
Site in meadowland, sparse poplars and a few pines. Near the sea and a wide sandy beach.
Turn off SS309 at Km8 or Km11.
May–15 Sep.

4HEC

CASALE MARITTIMO
Pisa (☎0586)

Valle Gaia ☎681236

Site amongst pines and olive trees in a quiet rural location.

In Southern Cecina turn off the SS1 inland. Site about 9 km from the coast.
4 Apr–Oct.

4.2HEC lau A5000 V2000 6000 6000

CASTAGNETO CARDUCCI
Livorno (☎0565)

Climatico le Pianacce ☎763667

Terraced site on slopes of mountain in typical Tuscany landscape, enhanced by site landscaping. Pleasant climate due to height.

Turn off via Aurelia at Km344/VIII in direction of Castagneto Carducci/Sassetta. In 3.2 km to left in direction of Bolgheri, in 500 m turn right towards mountains.
15 Mar–15 Oct.

9HEC lau

CASTEL DEL PIANO
Grosseto (☎0564)

Amiata ☎955107

A grassland site with a separate section for dog owners.

Off the Arcidossa road, SS323, on the outskirts of the town at Km25.
All year.

4HEC lau A3500–5000 Vn/c 5300–7500 3200–5550

CASTEL DI TUSA See **SICILIA (SICILY)**

CASTELFUSANO (LIDO DI) See **OSTIA**

CASTIGLIONE DELLA PESCAIA
Grosseto (☎0564)

Maremma Sans Souci ☎933765

The site, in an area of natural beauty, is divided into individual naturally screened pitches and lies on hilly ground in a pine forest by the sea.

On SS322 towards Punta Ala/Follónica, turn off at Km21 and drive 1 km towards the sea.
Apr–Sep.

10HEC lau

Santa Pomata ☎941037

Site in hilly woodland terrain with some pitches amongst bushes. Flat clean sandy beach.

Turn off the SS322 at Km20, then in direction of Le Rocchette 4.5 km NW and continue towards the sea for 1 km to site on left.
Mar–Oct.

7HEC lau A3600–6600 pitch5600–10200

Italy

CATANIA See **SICILIA (SICILY)**

CAVALLINO
Venezia (☎041)

Europa via Faustra 332 ☎968069

On grassland reaching to the sea, with some poplars. Lunchtime siesta 13.00–15.00 hrs.

Well signposted on Punta Sabbioni road.
May–Sep.

10HEC lau A35000–55000 pitch8000–13000

Garden Paradiso ☎968075

An attractive, pleasantly laid-out holiday site. Lunchtime siesta 13.00–15.30 hrs.

On road to Cavallino.
7 May–24 Sep.

13HEC lau A5800 pitch16800

Holiday ☎968178

A site with poplars next to the sea.

15 May–20 Sep.

2HEC lau A1350–4000 3800–9000 3800–9000

Joker via Fausta 318 ☎968019

Between coastal road and the sandy beach with tall poplars. Partially subdivided.

May–Sep.

4.4HEC lau

Residence ☎968027

Well laid out site on level grassland, by a sandy beach. Lunchtime siesta 13.00–15.00 hrs.

Signposted.
Apr–21 Sep.

8HEC lau A3900–5800 8500–12500 7500–11500

Sant' Angelo via F-Baracca 63 ☎968882

All year.

7HEC lau

Silva via F-Boracca ☎968087

The site lies on sand and grassland and is located between road and beach, divided by a vineyard. The section of site near the beach is quiet.

10 May–15 Sep.

3HEC lau A3000–4000 Vn/c 8000–12000 7000–11000

Union-Lido Litorale del Cavallino ☎968080

This site lies on a long stretch of land next to a 1 km-long beach. Separate section for tents and caravans. ***Minimum stay during peak period is one week.***

May–Sep.

60HEC lau A5200–6700 pitch6000–15500

Villa al Mare ☎968066

Level site divided into plots behind the lighthouse.

10 Apr–Sep.

2HEC lau A2200–4400 pitch5000–10500

CAVO See **ELBA (ISOLA D')**

CEFALÚ See **SICILIA (SICILY)**

CÉNESI See **ALBENGA**

CEPINA
Sondrio (☎0342)

Stelvio ☎950349

The site lies partly in meadowland and partly in pine forest which slopes down towards the valley.

Near Km98/VII off the SS38, S of Bormio.
All year.

2.8HEC lau

CERIALE
Savona (☎0182)

Ali Baba via Magnone ☎90182

May–Sep.

2HEC lau

Baciccia via Torino 19 ☎90743

An orderly site, lying inland off the via Aurelia.

Entrance 100 m W of Km613/V.
All year.

1.2HEC lau A3200–5500 V2500–5000 3500–6000 3200–5500

CERTOSA
Firenze (☎055)

Internazionale Firenze ☎2020445

A terraced site on the wooded slopes of a small valley.

On narrow road to Christofano by Km292 just N of junction with Autostrada at the Firenze–Certosa exit.
Apr–15 Oct.

6HEC lau A4500 V3000 5000 3000

CÉRVIA
Ravenna (☎0544)

Adriatico via Pinarella 30 ☎72346

Level meadowland site with plenty of shade, pleasantly landscaped with olives, willows, elms and pine trees.

Located shortly before Pinarella di Cérvia. Access via Via Caduti per le Liberta (SS16) 600 m from sea.
15 May–15 Sep.

3.4HEC lau A3100–4400 pitch7000–8000

CERVO
Imperia (183)

Lino 400087

A seaside site shaded by grape vines, which is clean and well managed. There is a knee-deep lagoon suitable for children.

Turn off via Aurelia at Km637/V near the railway underpass and follow via Nazionale Sauro towards sea.
Apr–15 Oct.

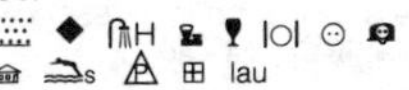

1.1HEC s lau

Mare 400130

The seaside site is laid out with flowerbeds and is shaded by grape vines. It is divided into pitches. Lunchtime siesta 12.00–15.00 hrs.

For access, turn off the main road to Km637/VII at the Sterio bridge, and drive 200 m towards the sea.
Apr–15 Oct.

10HEC H lau s

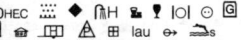

CESENÁTICO
Forlì (0547)

Camping Motel via Cavour 1 82748

400 m from sea, a subdivided park-like terrain in between local housing, partially surrounded by bushes and grape vines.

N of town off SS16 at Km178.
May–Sep.

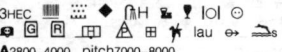

3HEC H lau s A2800–4000 pitch7000–8000

Cesenático via Mazzini 182 81344

The site stretches over an area of land belonging to the Azienda di Soggiomo e Turismo.

1.5 km N at Km178 turn off the SS16 towards the sea.
Apr–Sep.

18HEC H lau s A4000 pitch10500

Zadina 82310

Very pleasant terrain in dunes on two sides of a canal.

15 May–15 Sep.

Italy

10HEC H s lau A4000 Vn/c 8000 A7000

CHIAPPERA
Cuneo (0171)

Campo Base 44068

All year.

1HEC H lau R A2500 Vn/c 3600 A3600

CHIAVERANO See **IVREA**

CHIOGGIA
Venezia (041)

Miramare via A-Barbarigo 490610

Longish site reaching as far as the beach, clean and well-maintained.

Access from Strada Romeo (SS309) in direction of Chiòggia Sottomarina, turn right on reaching beach and continue 500 m.
May–20 Sep.

3.6HEC H s lau A5000 pitch5000–9500

Villaggio Turistico Isamar 498001

The site lies on level grassland at the mouth of the River Etsch. Shade is provided by high poplars. Good beach.

Access via the SS309. Caravans are advised to approach via Km84/VIII near the Brenta village.
16 May–19 Sep.

16HEC H sP lau A6500 pitch11500–15500

CHIUSA-KLAUSEN
Bolzano (0472)

Gamp via Gries 22 47425

The site lies next to the Gasthof Gamp, between the Brenner railway line and the motorway bridge, which passes high above the camp.

Access from the motorway exit and the SS12 is well signposted.
All year.

0.8HEC H P

CIRÒ MARINA
Catanzaro (0962)

Punta Alice 31160

The site lies on meadowland amidst lush Mediterranean vegetation and borders a fine gravel beach, some 50 m wide.

2 km from town. From SS106 (Strada Ionica) turn off at Km290 seaward to Cirò Marina. Pass through village and follow beach road for 1.5 towards lighthouse.
Apr–Sep.

5HEC H s lau A4900 V2300

CISANO
Verona (045)

Cisano 7210061

Partly terraced site beside Lake Garda.

AFFI exit on Brenner–Verona motorway, access 4 km further.
Apr–Sep.

13HEC H LP lau A3700–4800 pitch7300–10500

CLASSE (LIDO DI) See **MILANO MARITTIMA**

COMO (LAGO DI) See **DOMASO, DONGO, ONNO, SÓRICO**

CONDOFURI MARINA
Réggio Calábria (0965)

Salinella 784097

This site lies on gently sloping, partly terraced meadowland, and is shaded by olive trees.

It lies just off SS106 at Km40 on western outskirts of the village.
Jun–Sep.

0.8HEC H lau s

CORTINA D'AMPEZZO
Belluno (0436) ➤

Cortina via Campo 2 ☎2483

The site lies amongst pine trees, several hundred metres away from the edge of town, off the Dolomite road towards Belluno.

Turn off road and drive 1 km to the campsite which is situated by a small river.
All year.

4.5HEC P lau A4600–5300 pitch6900–10000

Dolomiti ☎2485

This site is beautifully situated on grassland with pine trees in a hollow, not far from the Olympic ski-jump.

For access, follow the directions for Camping Cortina. The camp is then 500 m further on 2.7 km S of Cortina.
15 May–Sep.

5.4HEC P lau

Olympia ☎5057

A very beautiful site set in the centre of the magnificent Dolomite landscape.

It lies N of town off the SS51 towards Toblach at Km107.2
All year.

4HEC lau R A5300 pitch10000

Rochetta ☎5063

In beautiful wooded surroundings.

Access S from Cortina via SS51.
Jun–20 Sep.

2.5HEC lau A5300 pitch10000

CUNEO
Cuneo (☎0171)

Turistico Comunale Bisalta San Rocco Castagnaretta ☎491334

Italy

All year.

4HEC P lau A3050 pitch4400

DANTE (LIDO DI)
Ravenna (☎0544)

Classe ☎494021

Level meadowland in grounds of former farm.

Access from the SS16 turning towards the sea at Km154/V and continue 9 km to site.
May–Sep.

7HEC P lau S A4300 pitch6500

DEIVA MARINA
La Spezia (☎0187)

Costa Bella ☎815948

All year.

1HEC lau A7000 Vn/c 7500 6500

DIANO MARINA
Imperia (☎0183)

Diana ☎495302

400 m NW of road to Imperia.
All year.

3HEC lau S pp10000

DIMARO
Trento (☎0463)

Dolomiti di Brenta Rovina ☎94332

Turn off SS42, at Km173.5
All year.

3HEC lau A5000 Vn/c 8500 8500

DOBBIACO-TOBLACH
Bolzano (☎0474)

Lago di Dobbiaco ☎72294

Extensive grassland, spruce woodland with splendid view of lakeside. Sanitary blocks are modern and restaurant is rustic style.

Access from Km181 off the SS51 Dobbiaco (Toblach)–Cortina road.
All year.

4.5HEC L lau

Olympia ☎72147

This extensive site lies next to Hotel Olympia. Part of the camp lies in a wood of tall pine trees.

At Km56/V of the SS49 through the Puster Valley.
All year.

4.5HEC P lau A5000 pitch4000

DOMASO
Como (☎0344)

Gardenia ☎96262

N at Case Sparse.
Apr–Sep.

2HEC LR lau A3350 V2800 3350 3350

DONGO
Como (☎0344)

Miralago ☎81736

By lake.

150 m from Km15.

Apr–Sep.
0.8HEC H L Ⓟ lau A3200 V2200 3200 3200

DORMELLETIO See **ARONA**

DUINO-AURISINA
Trieste (☎040)
At **SISTIANA**
Marepinetá ☎299264
May–15 Sep.
10HEC H P lau s 5500 pitch10000

ÉBOLI
Salerno (☎0828)
Paestum ☎691003
Sandy, meadowland site in tall poplar wood by river mouth. Steps and bus service to private beach, 600 m from site.
Access from the Litoranea at Km20 from the road fork to Santa Cecilia and continue for 0.3 km. Signposted.
10 Apr–18 Sep.
8HEC H  lau sP

EDOLO
Brescia (☎0364)
Adamello ☎71694

Italy

1.5 km W of SS39.
All year.
1.2HEC H P lau R A4500 V2500 4800 3400–4800

ELBA (ISOLA D')
Livorno (☎0565)
CAVO
Paguro's ☎949966
Very quiet extensive site in a natural valley partially terraced 0.6 km from the sea.
1 km S in Velle di Baccetti.
May–Sep.
3.5HEC H Ⓟ lau s A7150 V2200 7700 7700

LACONA (7 km W of Porto Azzurro)
Stella Mare ☎964007
Terraced site with level pitches on a hillside peninsula overlooking the Gulf of Lacona. Plenty of shade provided by pines and deciduous trees. Lovely views. Steep steps and paths to the beach.
Turn left 100 m beyond the turn off for Camping Lacona and past this site to the Stella Mare.

Apr–Sep.
3.5HEC H lau s A7700 V2200 8200 8200

OTTONE
Rosselba Le Palme ☎966101
Apr–Oct.
8HEC H sP lau A5600–7600 V2200 6100–8100 6100–8100

ESTENSI (LIDO DEGLI)
Ferrara (☎0533)
Mare e Pineta ☎330194
Extensive site on slightly hilly ground under pines and deciduous trees, providing shade. Near the beach and has numerous mobile homes.
2 km SE of Port Garibaldi.
15 May–15 Sep.
16HEC H lau sP

FERMO (LIDO DI)
Ascoli Piceno (☎0734)
At **SANTA MARIA A MARE**
Gemma ☎49211
The site lies near the Porto San Giórgo motorway exit of the A14 at Santa Maria a Mare. In fields bordering a gravel beach. ➔

May–15 Sep.

3HEC lau

FIGLINE VALDARNO
Firenze (055)

Norcenni Girasole 959666

Terraced site on partial slope. Separate section for young people.

3 km W of village. Take Valdarno motorway exit and drive N for 15 km.
All year.

11HEC lau A4800 V2200 4300 3900

FIRENZE (FLORENCE)
Firenze (055)

Parco Communale viale Michelangelo 80 6811977

A municipal site near the city centre. It is terraced and lies below the viale Michalengelo, and is scattered with olive trees.

The access is well signposted.
15 Mar–Oct.

4HEC lau

FLORENCE See **FIRENZE**

FOIANA See **LANA**

FOLLÓNICA
Grosseto (0566)

Riva del Butteri via delle Collacchie 86088

A site on level meadowland with trees. Car park under sunshade roofing.

2.5HEC lau S

Tahiti 60255

Site lies amongst dunes and level terrain, separated from the sea only by the beach road. Shade in the parking area is provided by roof matting. Internal asphalt roads.

Access via SS1 via Aurelia, seawards at Km232/V across railway line then turn left to the site.
May–Sep.

4.5HEC lau S

At **PUNTONE** (5 km S on S322)

Piper 86037

Site in meadowland with young trees by the sea with private beach.

Access at Km6/IV of SS322.

2.5HEC S

FONDACHELLO See **SICILIA (SICILY)**

FONDOTOCE
Novara (0323)

Lido Toce 496087

On E of lake.
Jun–Sep.

20HEC lau L A4200 V3400 4000 4000

FÓRMIA
Latina (0771)

Gianola 270223

Situated in a narrow grassland area near a little stream and trees amidst agricultural land. Pleasantly sandy beach edged by rocks.

Access via Roma–Naples road, from S Croce 800 m.
All year.

4HEC lau sR
pitch20000 (incl 2 persons)

FORTE DEI MARMI
Lucca (0584)

Internazionale della Versilia 83664

Site in level meadowland under poplars. Bus service during season to sea 1.5 km away.

Access via road to Forte dei Marmi from Aurelia across motorway bridge, on left hand side.

4HEC

FORTE DI BIBBONA
Livorno (0586)

See also **BIBBONA (MARINA DI)**

Acrobaleno via dei Cavalleggeri 600296

Level site in sandy terrain with young trees. Separate section for dog owners.

400 m from the sea. Approach from SS1 (Aurelia) to Forte di Bibbona turn right and continue 300 m to site.
Etr–Sep.

3HEC lau S

Capanne 600064

Site is situated on level tidy grassland amongst peach and olive trees.

Access from Km273 via Aurelia travelling in inland direction.

6HEC sP lau

Esperidi 600196

Site stretching to the sea with pines and other coniferous trees.

Turn off via Aurelia, at Km727.7.
Apr–Sep.

7HEC S lau A5500 V2000 5500 5500

Forte 600155

Level site, grassy sandy terrain.

24 Apr–15 Sep.

8HEC lau S

FUSCALDO
Cosenza (0982)

Lago 85239

Site lies below road in olive grove.

Turn off SS18, at Km307.
Jun–15 Sep.

2HEC lau S

FUSINA
Venezia (041)

Fusina 969055

On level grassland beside the Venice Lagoon.

Access via SS 309 Venezia exit.
7HEC

GALLICO See **RÉGGIO DI CALÁBRIA**

GALLIPOLI
Lecce (0833)

Vecchia Torre 261083

This well-kept and clean site lies amidst sand dunes in a pine wood. Small size pitches.

5 km N of Gallipoli and 200 m S of hotel Rivabella at seaward side of coast road.
May–Sep.
8HEC lau s **A**4500 **V**2500 6500 6500

GATTEO MARE
Forli (0547)

Rose 86213

Turn off SS16, at Km186.
15 May–20 Sep.
5HEC lau s **A**3200–4500 pitch7800

GIARRE See **SICILA (SICILY)**

GIOVINAZZO
Bari (080)

Freddo 931112

Site in level terrain by the sea, mainly under sunshade roofing. Siesta 14.00–16.00 hrs.

Italy

Turn off the SS16, 20 km N of Bari at Km784,300.
May–15 Sep.
3.2HEC s lau

GRADO
Gorizia (0431)

Europa 80877

In level terrain under half grown poplars. Partially in shade in pine forest.

On road to Monfalcone.
26 Mar–Sep.
22HEC sP lau **A**3100–6000 pitch6000–9600

Punta Spin 80732

The site lies on sandy grassland with many bungalows. About half the pitches in shade of pine woodland. Separate car park.

Off the Grado Monfalcone–Trieste road.

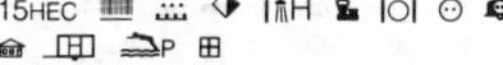

15HEC P

Tenuta Primero 81371

The site lies in extensive level grassland between the road and the dam, which is 2 m high along the narrow and level beach.

Tennis court.

Access from Monfalcone road. Signposted.
20 May–15 Sep.
20HEC sP lau **A**5800–6800 pitch7000–8500

GROSSETO (MARINA DI)
Grosseto (0564)

Rosmarina via della Colonne 37 36319

A modern site situated in a pine wood and close to the sea.

Apr–Sep.
1.4HEC lau s **A**3900–6600 pitch2600–7600

IDRO
Brescia (0365)

AZUR Idro Rio Vantone 83125

The site lies at the mouth of the river of same name beside Lake Idro. Subdivided into pitches (separate pitches for youths) on grass and woodland at the foot of strange rock formations.

Approach from Idro direction of Vantone, well signed from there.
All year.
4HEC L lau **A**2700–4500 **V**1600–3000 2100–6100 2000–3700

Vantone Pineta ☎83347

On eastern shore of lake. Grassland enclosed by rush and willow fencing. Part of site in small woodland on bank of stream.

Approach from Idro and follow signs for Camping Idro Rio Vantone.
All year.

2.2HEC lau A4300 pitch8500

IÉSOLO (LIDO DI)
Venezia (☎0421)

At **IÉSOLO PINETA** (6 km E)

Turistico Europa ☎961183

From Venezia via Cavallino on coast road to Cortellazzo.

3HEC

At **PORTO DI PIAVE VECCHIA** (8 km S)

Internazional ☎971826

Site on sandy beach and also on far side of coast road.

W opposite ESSO filling station.
May–Sep.

7.5HEC lau A5500 V3500 7500 5500

IMPÉRIA
Impéria (☎0183)

Wijnstok via Poggi 2 ☎64986

W of village, at Km650.95 turn off via Aurelia inland towards Poggi, then right to site.
All year.

10HEC lau

ISCHIA (ISOLA D')
Napoli (☎081)

PORTO D'ISCHIA

Internazionale ☎991449

Well-landscaped site, situated on hill terraces, scattered with tall pine trees and surrounded by walls. A large part of the camp is occupied by tents and bungalows for hire.

Lies on the left of the Barano road about 900 m from the port of Ischia and 500 m from the sea.
Apr–15 Oct.

3HEC lau

ISOLA DI CAPO RIZZUTO
Catanzaro (☎0962)

Oasi ☎791628

The site lies in an isolated situation, above a wide red sand beach which can be reached by a winding road.

Turn off coast road (N106) and drive 5 km towards sea.
1 Jun–20 Sep.

14HEC lau

IVREA
Torino (☎0472)

At **CHIAVERANO** (5 km N)

Laghi ☎(0125)422065

The site lies partly in a hollow in hilly terrain, with some terraces. It is about 0.4 km from the lake.

The approach from Turin is well signposted.
May–Oct.

20HEC lau

JÉSOLO (LIDO DI) See **IÉSOLO (LIDO DI)**

LACONA See **ELBA (ISOLA D')**

LÁIVES-LEIFERS
Bolzano (☎0471)

Steiner ☎950105

The site lies behind the Gasthof Steiner, the AGIP petrol station and a bungalow estate.

Off the SS12 on the northern outskirts of the village.
10 Mar–4 Nov.

2HEC lau A4500–5000 pitch8500–11000

LANA
Bolzano (☎0473)

Schlosshof ☎51469

The site is situated in an orchard.

Access from Merano via the SS238 to Lana. Then continue towards Bolzano through Lana–Mitterlana for 1 km, then follow signs. Alternatively if coming from Bolzano turn off SS38 in Burgstall/Postall towards Lana.

1.3HEC

At **FOIANA**

Arquin ☎51187

This site lies in a quiet orchard, is very well-kept and is divided into pitches.

If approaching from Merano, take the SS238 and drive to Lana-Mitterlana. If approaching from Bolzano, turn off the SS38 in Burgstall/Postall and take the road to Lana, then turn left.
15 Mar–30 Oct.

0.4HEC lau

Völlan ☎58056

The terraced site is in a rather isolated situation, surrounded by wooded hill slopes.

If approaching from Merano, take the SS238 and drive S until 3 km beyond Lana, then turn right and drive towards Völlan. Steep approach. Towage for caravans provided.
Mar–Oct.

0.5HEC lau A3500 V1500 3500 3500

LÁURA
Salerno (☎0828)

Hera Argiva ☎851193

Site in sandy terrain in eucalyptus grove by the sea.

Signposted from Km88/VIII SS18.
Apr–Oct.

10HEC lau

Nettuno ☎843197

Lying on hilly ground near its own private beach amongst bushes and pine trees.

Turn off SS18 at Km91/VII or Km95 and drive towards sea for 2 km.
All year.

7HEC lau

LAZISE
Verona (☎045)

Parc via Sentieri ☎7580127

Well-kept, lakeside site off main road.

If approaching from Garda, the site is on S side of Lazise just after turning for Verona.
Apr–15 Oct.

4HEC lau A3300–5200 pitch6500–10500

Quercia ☎7580051

The site is divided into many large sections by tarred drives and lies on terraced ground that slopes gently down to the lake. There is a large private beach.

For access, turn off the main road SS49 at Km31/8 and drive for 400 m.
Apr–Sep.

12HEC lau A5000–6650 pitch10000–16000

LERICI
La Spezia (☎0187)

Gianna ☎966411

Turn left by Km2.9 on Lerici-Tellaro road.
mid Apr–Sep.

2HEC lau

LEVICO TERME
Trento (☎0461)

Jolly ☎706934

The site is divided into plots and lies on the lakeside with its own pool.

15 May–15 Sep.

2.5HEC lau A4000 pitch5300

LIDO Each placename beginning with 'Lido' or 'Lido di' is listed under the name that follows it.

LIDO DI CASTELFUSANO See **OSTIA**

LIDO DI IÉSOLO See **IÉSOLO (LIDO DI)**

LIDO TORTORETO See **ALBA ADRIATICO**

LIGNANO PINETA
Udine (☎0431)

Italy

Pino Mare ☎428512

On mouth of River Tagliamento on undulating terrain in a natural pine forest.

10 May–20 Sep.

16HEC H lau G R s A6000 V5200 6000 4700

LILLAZ

Aosta (☎0165)

Salasses ☎74252

Pleasant site surrounded by mountains, grassland and conifers. The site lies at the end of the Val di Cogne.

Entrance to site before Camping al Sole.
May–Sep.

1.5HEC H G R lau A3800 V1500 3500 3500

LIMONE PIEMONTE

Cuneo (☎0171)

Luis Matias ☎927565

This tidy site offers winter facilities and skiing lessons are provided by the owner. Fishing is also available.

It lies to the N of the town, off the Limone-Nice road.
All year.

1.5HEC H G R Ls lau A4100 pitch5250

LIMONE SUL GARDA

Brescia (☎0365)

Nanzel ☎954155

Well managed site, with low terraces in olive grove.

Access from Km101.2 (Hotel Giorgiol).
Apr–15 Oct.

0.7HEC H G L lau A4200 V3000 4500 4500

MACCAGNO

Varese (☎0332)

AZUR Park via Corsini 3 ☎560203

By the lake.

In village turn off SS394 at Km43/III towards lake and after 500 m turn right.
All year.

1.2HEC H G L lau A3000–4700 V1800–3300 2300–3900 2300–3800

MAGGIORE (LAGO) See **ARONA, BAVENO, CANNOBIO, FONDOTOCE, MACCAGNO**

MANERBA DEL GARDA

Brescia (☎0365)

Rio Ferienglück ☎653450

Follow SS572 Desenzano-Salo road, turn off between Km8 and 9, site 4 km N.
May–Sep.

3HEC H G R lau L

Zocco ☎53605

The site consists of several, terraced sections. The section below the maintenance/supply building lies on a sloping olive grove and is somewhat obstructed by bungalows.

500 m S of Gardonicino di Manerba.
Apr–20 Sep.

5HEC H G lau L

MARGHERA

Venezia (☎041)

Jolly Piscine ☎920312

The site lies on meadowland scattered with poplars.

For access, turn off the Autostrada in Venezia in the direction of Chioggia on the SS309 and continue for 10 m.
Apr–Oct.

3.6HEC H G lau P A5000 pitch10000

MARINA Each placename beginning with 'Marina' or 'Marina di' is listed under the name that follows it.

MAROTTA

Pesaro (☎0721)

Club Cesano ☎96322

This site is near the sea. In corner of meadow (about 200 × 50 m) with gravel paths, very clean and tidy. Situated between the railway line and a holiday village. Parking area providing shade.

Approach via SS16 at Km267/V before bridge across the Cesano or the Autostrada A14. Exit Senigallia 8 km in northerly direction to the site.
May–Sep.

1HEC H G R lau s A5100 pitch9200

MARTINSICURO

Ascoli Piceno (☎0861)

Villa Elena ☎72368

Protected from noise, surrounded by houses and vineyards. Flat sandy beach. Clean site on a well-kept meadow.

Access from the SS16 via the coast road Villa Rosa-Martinsicuro.
15 Apr–Sep.

2.5HEC H G R lau s

MASARÈ

Belluno (☎0437)

Alleghe ☎723737

Several terraces on a wooded incline below a road.

10 Dec–20 Apr & 15 Jun–15 Sep.

2HEC H G R P lau L A4000–5000 V2000–3000 4000–4500 2500

MASSA LUBRENSE *Napoli* (☎081)

Villaglo Conca Azzurra ☎8789666

Terraced site on right of road under olive trees. It has steep private roads and own bathing beach. Not suitable for caravans.

4 km beyond Sorrento and 1 km before reaching Masse Lubrense.
Apr–Oct.

2.8HEC H G R lau sP

Villa Lubrense via Partenope 31 ☎8771255

All year.

3HEC H G R lau s A5000 V3000 6000 3500–6000

MASSA (MARINA DI)

Massa Carrara (☎0585)

Caletella ☎22777

Site on level meadowland partially under high deciduous trees providing shade.

Turn inland off the SS328 at FINA filling station about 600 m in direction of Pisa. 800 m from the sea.
May–Sep.

2.2HEC H G P lau s

Citta di Massa ☎241225

Sandy meadowland.

On the land side of coastal road.
May–Sep.

3.6HEC H G lau s A3000 V3000 10000 10000

Giardino ☎241605

Site in pine woodland and on two meadows, shade provided by roof matting.

On the island side of the SS328 to Pisa.
May–Sep.

2.7HEC H lau s A3500 V3000 10000 10000

See advertisement on page 288

MATTINATA *Foggia* (☎0884)

Degli Ulivi ☎4000

This well-kept grassland site lies in an old olive grove.

Off SS89, 0.6 km N of turning to Mattinata.
Jun–Sep.

2HEC H G R lau s

Europa ☎4452

Gently sloping meadowland in sparse olive grove near the sea. Siesta 13.00–16.00 hrs.

Access from coast road.
May–15 Sep.

1.3HEC H P lau s A3000–4200 V1600–2200 3600–5000 2800–4000

Villaggio Turistico San Lorenzo ☎4152

The site is situated above the coast road in direction of Viesta. Bungalows for hire.

Jun–Sep.

5HEC H G R lau s

Italy

MELILLI See **AUGUSTA** under **SICILIA (SICILY)**

MERANO-MERAN
Bolzano (☎0473)
Merano via Piave 44 ☎31249
This site stretched over a number of fields with little or no shade.
Etr–Oct.
1.5HEC H R lau P

MILANO MARITTIMA
Ravenna (☎0544)
Villaggio Turistico Romagna ☎949326
Level and flat site with young trees.
Access via the SS16 (Strada Adriatica) turn off beyond Milano Marittima and follow signs.
9 May–10 Sep.
3.6HEC H G s lau A3700–4950 Vn/c 8300 6300

At **CLASSE (LIDO DI)** (8 km N)
Pineta Ramazzotti ☎494207
In uneven grassy and sandy terrain with wild olive trees separated from the sea by dunes and a narrow strip of pines.
Turn off towards the sea at Km154/V SS16 and continue for 9 km to site.
May–15 Sep.

4HEC H G R s lau

MILO See **GIARRE** See **SICILIA (SICILY)**

MINTURNO (MARINA DI)
Latina (☎0771)
Golden Garden ☎680167
Secluded quiet site within agricultural area by the sea.
Access from the SS7 across river bridge (Garigliano) and continue 4.6 km changing direction. Last km sandy field track.
All year.
14HEC H G R s lau pitch16200–22900 (incl 2 persons)

MIRAMARE DI RIMINI See **RIMINI**

MISANO ADRIATICO
Forlì (☎0541)
Misano Adriatico via Litoranea Sud 6 ☎614330
May–Sep.
6HEC H G R s lau

MOLA DI BARI
Bari (☎080)
Caloria ☎644897
Site in meadowland enclosed by wall.
In southern outskirts below the busy SS16 at Km824/VII.
25 May–10 Sep.
0.8HEC H G P lau s A5000 V2750 4500 4000

MOLVENO
Trento (☎0461)
Spiaggia-Lago di Molveno via Lungolago 27 ☎586978
All year.
3HEC H G lau LP A4000–5300 pitch5000–8500

MONFALCONE
Gorizia (☎0481)
Panzano Lido via Bagni 171 ☎74202
15 May–15 Sep.
13HEC H G R s lau A5000 pitch8000
Albatros ☎40562
Level site by the sea with young poplars.
Access from Monfalcone in direction of Marine Julia for 5 km. Adjoining bungalow village.
Apr–Sep.
4HEC H P

MONIGA DEL GARDA
Brescia (☎0365)
Fontanelle via del Magone ☎502079
Apr–Sep.
4HEC H G L lau A5000 pitch10000
Rose ☎502031
This site lies on gently sloping ground with a few terraces.
Turn off main road at Km7.5 near Ristorante La Pergola and drive down to lake for 1 km.
Mar–Oct.
2.2HEC H G L lau A3700–4200 pitch8200–9000
Sereno ☎52080
Well-maintained and appointed site with good lakeside and swimming facilities.
Turn off SS572D-S at Km13/VII or (better for caravans) 13/IV.
Apr–Sep.
6HEC H G R L lau

MONTENERO (MARINA DI)
Campobasso (☎0873)
Costa Verde ☎52144
This seaside site lies E of San Salvo Marino.
Leave the coast road, SS16, at Km525/VII and continue by a farm road for 300 m to the site.
15 May–15 Sep.
10HEC H G R s lau

MONTERIGGIONI
Siena (☎0577)
Piscina Luxor Quies ☎743047
Lies on a flat-topped hill, partly in an oak wood, partly in meadowland.
Turn off via Cassia (SS2) at Km239/II or Km238/IX and continue for further 2.5 km, crossing railway line.
6 Jun–Aug.
1.3HEC H G lau P A4900 V2200 2600 2200

MONTESCUDÁIO
Livorno (☎0586)

Montescudáio ☎683477

This modern site is situated on a hill and is completely divided into individual pitches, some of which are naturally screened. Children under 2 years are not accepted.

From Cecina (on SS1, via Aurelia) follow road to Guardistallo for 2.5 km.
15 May–15 Sep.

25HEC lau A3900–5700 Vn/c 6900–7200 6200–7200

MONTICELLO AMIATA
Grosseto (☎0564)

Lucherino ☎992975

15 Jun–15 Sep.

lau A4000 Vn/c 5500 3500

MONTOGGIO
Genoa (☎010)

Castello del Fiesch ☎938812

All year.

20HEC lau

NÁPOLI (NAPLES)
Napoli (☎081)

Complesso Turistico Averno via Domitiana ☎8662323

Access via Tangenziale 16 km W of Napoli to site 4 km W of Pozzuoli.
All year.

7HEC lau

NATURNO-NATURNS
Bolzano (☎0473)

Wald ☎87298

The site lies on gently rising ground, in a forest of pine and deciduous trees.

For access, turn off the SS38 near the Gasthof Alderwirt in the village, and drive 0.8 km S over the railway line.
25 Mar–Oct.

0.2HEC lau

NAZIONI (LIDO DELLE)
Ferrara (☎0533)

Tahiti ☎39500

Pleasantly laid out site 650 m from sea. Has own private beach accessible via a miniature railway. Lunchtime siesta 13.30–15.30 hrs.

Turn off SS309 near Km32.5 then 2 km to site. Signposted.
15 May–20 Sep.

3HEC lau A3300–5100 pitch5900–9500

NICÓTERA MARINA
Catanzaro (☎0963)

Sabbia d'Oro ☎81545

Italy

Lies on level ground amidst farmland 100 m from a beautiful lonely beach.

Turn off SS18 at Km453/VII and continue 15 km.
Jun–Sep.

2.6HEC lau A4900 V2500 6800 5700

OLIVERI See **SICILIA (SICILY)**

ONNO
Como (☎0341)

Jost al Meigone ☎581373

May–Oct.

1HEC lau A7000 V6000 6000

ORA-AUER
Bolzano (☎0471)

Wasserfall ☎810150

Sloping site in front of the Gasthaus Wasserfall, between wooded rocky hills and the River Schwarzbach.

For access turn off Fleimstralstrasse (SS48) E of the bridge over the River Schwarzbach and drive N for 300 m.
15 Mar–3 Nov.

1HEC lau A3800–4600 V3800–4600 3800–4600 3800–4600

ORVIETO
Terni (☎0744)

Orvieto Lago di Corbara ☎950240

Turn off SS448 at Km3.770.
Etr–Sep.

1.3HEC lau

OSTIA
Roma (☎06)

At **CASTELFUSANO (LIDO DI)**

Capitol ☎5662720

Widespread site scattered with pine trees, lying about 5 km from sea.

On the Via di Castelfusano. From Roma follow Via Cristoforo Colombo towards the sea and at Km26 turn right.
All year.

8HEC lau A4600 V1700 3400 2250

OTTONE See **ELBA (ISOLA D')**

PACHINO See **SICILIA (SICILY)**

PADENGHE
Brescia (☎030)

Cá ☎917106

The site lies in a park-like setting on terraced ground. Coaches are not welcome.

For access, turn off the road along Lake Garda, 1.5 km N turn for Padenghe, and drive down a very steep road towards the lake.
15 Mar–15 Oct.

2HEC lau A4400 V4400 4400 4400

Campagnola ☎917623

Turn off SS572 at Km17.7.
15 May–Sep.

5HEC A4600–6000 pitch7400–8900

Valtenesi ☎917123

The site lies in a beautiful, quiet setting on terraces that slope down to the lake.

Turn off road along Lake Garda, 1.5 km N of turning for Padenghe, and drive down a steep road to lake and in 150 m turn right into site after the AGIP petrol station.
Apr–15 Oct.

6HEC lau A4800 pitch9000

PAESTUM
Salerno (☎0828)

Apollo via Principe di Piemonte ☎71374

Seaside site with eucalyptus and pine trees.

May–Sep.

1.5HEC lau A3500 pitch11000

Marepineta ☎843023

Site in undulating terrain under pines extending down to the wide sandy beach.

Approach via Battipáglia exit of the A3.
15 Apr–Sep.

8HEC

Villaggio Athena ☎843505

Site in level terrain partially undulating in pine woodland and shade. By the sea, private well tended beach.

Approach from the SS18, turn towards the sea at the antique temple, 1 km from Paestum.
Apr–Sep.

3HEC A3800 Vn/c 10000 8000

Villaggio dei Pini ☎811030

The site lies on hilly ground in a pine forest beside clean and sandy beach.

Turn off via Tirrenia at Km95/IX and continue 1 km.
All year.

3HEC lau

Ulisse ☎851095

Seaside site in quiet setting with many flower beds.

Access from the SS18, turn right at the antique temple and head towards the sea.
All year. ➔

4HEC H s

PALERMO See **SICILIA (SICILY)**

PALINURO
Salerno (0974)

Degli Olivi 931045

The site slopes gently down from the local road to the steep coast and is scattered with olive trees.

Turn off SS18 at Km113 and drive to outskirts of village then turn right and drive towards sea.
Jun–Sep.

2.2HEC H s lau

PALMENSE (MARINA)
Ascoli Piceno (0734)

Paradiso 30110

Near Km363 on SS16.
May–Sep.

3HEC H s lau

Villagio Verde Mare 53167

Extensive level grassy terrain with poplars of medium height, divided into two by a stream.

At Km363 on N16.
30 May–Sep.

14HEC H sP lau
A4300–5000 pitch12000

PALMI
Réggio Calábria (0966)

Sant'Elia 22177

On the Monte Elia Plateau.

Jun–Sep.

1.5HEC H lau

San Fantino 46306

Site on several terraces with lovely views of the bay of Lido di Palmi. 200 m to the beach. Siesta 13.00–16.00 hrs.

Turn off road SS18 seawards N of Palmi.
All year.

4HEC H lau s

PARMA
Parma (0521)

Cittadella via Passo Buole 7 581546

Apr–Oct.

0.4HEC H lau P A3800 V4500 4500
4500

PASSIGNANO
Perugia (075)

Gestione Camping Plougler Sport
827403

200 m from SS75 bis at Km33.5 (Del Trasimeno).
Apr–Oct.

3.3HEC H L lau

Kursaal 827182

The site is situated between the road and the lake, near the villa of the same name.

Access from SS75, Arezzo to Perugia road, from Km35.2.
Apr–15 Oct.

3HEC H LP lau A3900
V1650 5050 4050

PÁTRIA (MARINA DI LAGO DI)
Napoli (081)

International Marina Lago Pátria
8677016

Somewhat undulating terrain under deciduous trees.

Access by the bridge at Km43/V of the SS7.
All year.

5HEC H lau

PEIO
Trentino (0463)

Val di Sole 73177

The site lies on terraced slopes at the foot of the Ortier mountain range.

400 m off SP87.
Jun–Sep & Dec–Apr.

4.5HEC H lau A4000 pitch6300

PERUGIA
Perugia (075)

Il Rocolo 798550

8 km W of SS75.
Jun–Sep.

2.4HEC H lau A3700 V1600 5000
4000

PÉSARO
Pésaro (0721)

Marinella via Adriatica 244 55795

Access is through railway underpass from Km244 of SS16.
Apr–Sep.

1.5HEC H lau s

PÉSCHICI *Foggia* (0884)

Centro Turistico San Nicola 94024

Terraced site in lovely situation by the sea, in a bay enclosed by rocks. Can become overcrowded.

Turn off coast road Péschici–Vieste, follow signs along winding road to site in 1 km.
Apr–15 Oct.

10HEC H
lau s A4500–8000
V3000–4500 5800–10000 4800–9000

Manacore 94050

Meadowland with a few terraces in attractive bay, surrounded by wooded hills.

Turn off the coastal road (Péschici–Vieste) towards the sea in a wide U bend.
Apr–15 Sep.

15HEC H lau s A7000
V3000 9000 7000

Parco degli Ulivi 94208

In the midst of century-old olive grove. Modern security devices, equipment and services. Open-air cinema. Self contained village.

Follow signs to Peschici from autostrada A14.
15 May–30 Sep.

120HEC H lau sP A4500–6000 V2000 7000–8500 7000–8500

PESCHIERA DEL GARDA
Verona (045)

Bella Italia 7550138

Extensive lakeside site.

Turn off Brescia road between Km276.2 and Km275.8 and head towards lake.
May–Sep.

15HEC H L lau A5500
pitch11000

Gasparina 7550775

The site lies at Hotel Gasparina and is very clean and well kept. There is a lawn for sunbathing and a concrete quay.

Turn off main road at Km59.9 and drive towards lake for a further 1.4 km.
Apr–20 Sep.

5HEC H L

PESCIA ROMANA (MARINA DI)
Viterbo (0766)

Amici del Camping 830250

A quiet, pleasantly situated site behind dunes. Clean wide beach.

Turn off via Aurelia seawards at Km118.5. After 4.3 km turn right and continue on sandy tracks 900 m.
Etr–Sep.

2.7HEC H lau sP

PIANO DI SORRENTO
Napoli (081)

Pini 8786891

Subdivided site mainly under orange trees and vines between the road to Sorrento and a deep gorge on the seaward site.

Access at Km23/11 of the SS145, 1 km from the sea.
Apr–Sep.

3HEC H P lau s

PICCIOLA BY PONTECAGNANO See **SALERNO**

PIETRA LIGURE
Savona (019)

Mare 645450

The site lies in the village in front of some residential buildings. The beach can be reached by crossing road and railway.

Just off via Aurelia at Km604/V.
May–Sep.

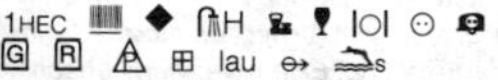

1HEC lau s

PIEVE DI MANERBA
Breccia (0365)

Sanghen 651048

Seasonal.

7HEC lau LP A5100 pitch9800

PINARELLA
Ravenna (0544)

Pinarella viale Abruzzi 52 987408

Subdivided terrain surrounded by houses. Partially shaded, some young poplars. Private beach.

May–15 Sep.

1.8HEC lau s A4700 Vn/c 8000 7000

Safari viale Titano 130 987356

The site is divided into several sections. Only families are accepted.

7 May–11 Sep.

2.4HEC lau s A3400–4750 7300–8300 6300–7300

PINETO
Téramo (085)

International 930639

Site on level terrain with young poplars. Sunshade roofing on the beach.

Turn off SS16 at Km431.2 and continue under railway underpass. Adjoining railway line.
May–Sep.

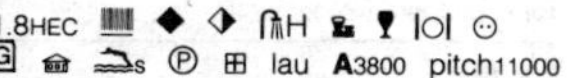

1.8HEC s lau A3800 pitch11000

PISCIOTTA (MARINA DI)
Salerno (0974)

Villággio Lido Paradiso 973232

Terraced site by the sea, under olive trees. Long wide sand and gravel beach. Open air discotheque.

Follow coastal road S and at sign, turn off.
7 Jun–13 Sep.

7HEC s lau A2600–6500 pitch7300–12500

PISOGNE
Brescia (0364)

Eden 8050

The site lies on eastern lake shore with tall trees and a level beach.

Turn off SS510 at Km37/VII, over railway line and towards lake.
All year.

1.8HEC lau L A4800 pitch11000

Italy

PIZZO (MARINA DI)
Catanzaro (0963)

Pinetamare 264067

N of town.
15 Jun–Sep.

11HEC lau sP A7000 V1500 8000 4500

Torre 231489

This site lies on level ground near the sea and a long, fine, sandy beach. Shade is provided by trees and straw mat roofs.

2.5 km off the motorway exit Pizzo or 2 km N of village off the coast road.
15 Jun–15 Sep.

3HEC lau s

POMPEI
Napoli (081)

Spartacus via Plinio 8614901

Site is on a level meadow with orange trees.

Lies near the motorway exit, Scafati–Pompei and access is from the main Napoli road, opposite Scari di Pompei near an IP petrol station.
All year.

11HEC lau A3600–4500 V2000 2900–3500 1600–2000

POMPOSA
Ferrara (0533)

International Tre Moschettleri 88376

Camp site set beneath pine trees next to sea.

Signposted from SS309.
Apr–Sep.

1HEC s lau

Vigna Sul Mer 380216

Well tended meadowland under poplars. Well signposted from entrance to Lido.

Private beach of 1 km beyond the dunes.
May–20 Sep.

14HEC s lau A3200–4500 V2000–3000 6000–8000 6000–8000

PORLEZZA
Como (0344)

Paradiso 61027

The site lies in meadowland on the north-eastern lake shore.

S from SS340.
Apr–Sep.

4.6HEC L lau

PORTO D'ISCHIA See **ISCHIA (ISOLA D')**

PORTO DI PIAVE VECCHIA See **IÉSOLO (LIDO DI)**

PORTONOVO
Ancona (071)

Comunale la Torre 801038

Situated near an old church and a watch tower.

From Ancona follow Panorama road, turn off after tunnel and drive 9 km towards Portonovo, then drive down steep hill towards sea.
Jun–15 Sep.

2HEC lau s

PORTOPALO See **PACHINO** under **SICILIA (SICILY)**

PORTO PINO See **CAGLIARI** under **SARDEGNA (SARDINIA)**

PORTO RECANATI
Macerata (071)

Bellamare 976628

On the S side of the mouth of the Musone.

Access from the Autostrada exit Ancona Sud via the SS16 turn to S bank at Km324.
May–Sep.

5HEC s lau A4600 9700 7500

PORTO SANTA MARGHERITA
Venezia (0421)

Pra'delle Torri 89063

Extensive site on flat ground.

3 km W at edge of beach.
May–Sep.

50HEC s lau

PORTO SANT'ELPÍDIO
Ascoli Piceno (0734)

Holldays International Lungomare Triéste 993309

The site lies in beautiful meadowland.

Turn off SS16 at Km347.3 and drive 0.4 km towards sea.
May–Sep.

10HEC sP lau A2700–5800 Vn/c 7000–14500 5000–10000

Mimose 993379

Site with modern installations next to sandy beach.

At Km 351/V of the SS16.
May–Sep.

3.3HEC sP lau A3000–5500 pitch7000–13500

Querce 991587

Terraced site with splendid view out to sea, sited in pleasant landscape, surrounded by fields. Set out like a garden.

Well-signposted from entrance into Porto Sant'Elpidio. →

4HEC ◆ lau
s

Risacca ☎991423

Clean, well-kept site on level meadowland, with some trees and surrounded by fields.

Turn off main SS16 N of village, follow road seawards under railway (narrow underpass maximum height 3 m), then 1.2 km along field paths to site. Caravan access is 400 m further S along SS16, then under railway and along field paths to site.
May–Sep.

7HEC ◆ s lau
A4600 pitch11600

POZZUOLI
Napoli (☎081)

Vulcano Solfatara ☎8673413

Clean and orderly site situated in a deciduous forest near the crater of the extinct Solfatara volcano.

Leave Nuova via Domiziana (SS7 qtr) at Km60/1 (at about 6 km short of Naples) and turn inland through stone gate.
Apr–15 Oct.

5HEC ◆ P lau s A4400–5050 V3000–3200 4900–5200 3500–4200

At **VARCATURO (MARINA DI)** (12 km N)

Partenope ☎5091076

Partially undulating terrain in woodland of medium height.

Turn sewards for 300 m at Km45/II of the SS7 (via Domiziana).
May–Sep.

8HEC ◆ lau s A4900–5500 V3300–3800 5500–5900 3900–4700

PUNTA ALA
Grosseto (☎0564)

Báia Verde ☎921220

The site lies partly in a pine forest and partly in open meadowland. It is divided into pitches. There is a wide range of amenities. Strict observance of the resting periods.

29HEC ◆
s

Puntala ☎922294

Level site near beach divided into plots, partially hilly in mixed woodland with mature trees and some shrubs. Rest periods strictly enforced. ***Minimum stay 6 days in peak season.***

Access from Follonica via SS322, turn sharp right at Km11/VI (clearly signed) and continue along asphalt road for another 2 km to the site.
Apr–Oct.

30HEC ◆
s lau

PUNTA BRACCETTO See **SICILIA (SICILY)**

PUNTA MARINA
Ravenna (☎0544)

Italy

At **ADRIANO (LIDO)** (4.5 km S)

Adriano via dei Campeggi 7 ☎437230

300 m from the sea. A pleasantly landscaped site amidst the dunes of the Punta Marina.

On SS309 via Lido Adriano to Punta Marina.
15 Apr–15 Sep.

14HEC ◆
lau
sP A4400 pitch7500

Coop 3 via dei Campeggi 8 ☎437353

300 m to the sea. Level site under isolated high pines and poplars. Across flat dunes to the beach.

Signposted.
May–Sep.

7HEC ◆
lau s

PUNTA SABBIONI
Venezia (☎041)

Marina di Venézia ☎966146

Extensive, well-organised and well maintained holiday centre, extremely well appointed, with ample shade by trees. A section of the site is designated for dog owners, caravans and tents.

Access from the coastal road, turn seawards about 500 m before the end then continue along narrow asphalt road. Well signposted approach.
Apr–Sep.

80HEC ◆
s lau
A3000–5500 pitch8000–16000

Miramare via Fausta ☎966150

Site next to the sea.

Apr–Sep.

1.8HEC ◆
lau s A4100
7500 6500

PUNTONE See **FOLLÓNICA**

RAGUSA (MARINA DI) See **SICILIA (SICILY)**

RASUN See **BRUNICO-BRUNECK**

RAVENNE (MARINA DI)
Ravenna (☎0544)

Internazionale Piomboni ☎430230

Site on slightly undulating mainly sandy terrain with pines and poplars. Separate section for tents. Lunchtime siesta 14.00–16.00 hrs. No reservations.

Access is 1 km S from town centre off coast road.
May–Sep.

5HEC ◆
s lau

RÉGGIO DI CALÁBRIA
Réggio Calábria (☎0965)

At **GALLICO** (10.7 km N)

Paradiso ☎371866

Level, totally subdivided site with view of Straits of Messina. All pitches provided with sunshade roofing. Extensive sandy beach.

At Km527.300 of SS18 turn seawards 1 km.
15 Jun–Sep.

2HEC ◆
sP lau

RICCIONE
Forlì (☎0541)

Adria via Torino 29 ☎602256

The site is situated on flat grassland amongst young poplars. Approach signposted from southern outskirts. The section of the site between road and beach has been closed by the local authorities.

May–20 Sep.

5.6HEC
s

Fontanelle ☎615449

On southern outskirts separated from beach by coast road. Underpass to public beach.

Turn off SS16 between Km216 and 217.
May–20 Sep.

5.8HEC ◆
s lau

Riccione via Marsala ☎615400

About 300 m from sea. Extensive flat meadowland, with poplars of medium height.

From SS16 turn seawards on the S outskirts of the town and continue for 200 m. Alternative access from coast road, turn inland on S outskirts at sign and continue for 700 m.
May–Sep.

6.7HEC ◆
P lau s A3100–4900 pitch6500–9200

RIMINI
Forlì (☎0541)

At **MIRAMARE DI RIMINI** (6.8 km S)

Maximum ☎32602

Site in three sections, separated by public road with guarded entrances. Low dense trees provide much shade.

Signposted from southern outskirts. Near airport. Southern section has best sanitary facilities. However, shopping facilities are only in the final section.

3.6HEC

At **VISERBELLA**

Belverdere ☎720960

Pleasant site with numerous trees, in quiet rural location about 400 m from the sea.

Access from SS16 turning off at Km197 and continue to site in 300 m.

4.5HEC ◆
lau s

Italy

RIVA DEI TARQUINI See **TARQUINIA**

RIVA DEL GARDA
Trento (☎0464)

Bavaria via Rovereto 100 ☎552524
Apr–Oct.
0.6HEC H lau L **A**4500 pitch6300

RIVOLTELLA
Brescia (☎030)

San Francesco ☎9110245
This well-kept site is divided into many sections by drives, vineyards and orchards and has a private gravel beach.
At Km268 on SSNII.
Apr–Sep.
8.5HEC H L lau

ROMA (ROME)
Roma (☎06)

Flaminio ☎3279006
An extensive site, which lies in a quiet valley on narrow terraces on a hill.
From ring road follow via Flaminia, SS3, for 2.5 km towards city centre.
Apr–Oct.
10HEC H P lau **A**6100

Happy ☎6422401
A new site situated in the N of town.
2 m SS2 Cassia–Bis, 1 km from 'Grande Raccordo Anulare'.
15 Mar–Oct. ➤

2.5HEC ▥ ◆ ⋔H ▪ ▼ |O| ⊙ G
⚠ ⊞ lau

Nomentano ☎6100296

Mar–Oct.

2.5HEC ▥ ◆ ⋔H ▪ ▼ |O| ⊙ ▪
G ⌂ ⚠ ⊞ lau

Roma via Aurelia 831 ☎6223018

The site lies on terraces on a hill near the AGIP Motel. All kinds of excursions can be arranged.

From ring road follow SS1 (via Aurelia) for 1.5 km towards town centre turn off to site at Km8/11.
All year.

3.2HEC ▥ ◆ ⋔H ▪ ▼ |O| ⊙ ▪
G ⚠ lau A5750 V2500 ▪5050 Ʌ2500

See advertisement on page 293

Roman River via Tibernia ☎6913079

Modern site on level ground beside the Tiber.

N of city. Signposted from ringroad.

2HEC ▥ ⁝⁝⁝ ◇ ⋔H ▪ |O| ⊙ ▪
≈P

Salaria via Salaria 2141 ☎6917642

May–Oct.

1.7HEC ▥ ◆ ⋔H ▪ ▼ |O| ⊙ ⌂
▭ ⚠ ⊞ lau A4500 V2000 ▪4500
Ʌ2500

See advertisement on page 293

Seven Hills via Cassia 1216 ☎3765571

Italy

Partly terraced, set in a small valley. 2.5 km NE of outer ring road.

20 Mar–Oct.

5HEC ▥ ◆ ⋔H ▪ ▼ |O| ⊙ ▪
G R ⌂ ≈P ⚠ ⊞ lau

Tiber via Tiberina ☎6910733

On level grassland, shaded by poplars beside the Tiber.

N of city. Signposted from ringroad.
Mar–Oct.

5HEC ▥ ◆ ⋔H ▪ ▼ |O| ⊙ ▪
G R ⌂ ▭ ⚠ ⊞ lau A5600
V2900 ▪4800 Ʌ2900

ROMEA (MARINA DI) See **CASAL BORSETTI**

ROSETO DEGLI ABRUZZI
Teramo (☎085)

Eurocamping 'Roseto' ☎8993179

A meadow site at the S end of the beach road.

Leave the SS16 within the town, then continue for 500m to the site.
All year.

5HEC ▥ ◆ ⋔H ▪ ▼ |O| ⊙ G
R ⌂ ▭ ≈P ⚠ ⊞ lau ⊖ ≈S
A4700 V3700 ▪5200 Ʌ5200

ROSOLINA MARE *Rovigo* (☎0426)

Rosapineta ☎68033

The site lies in the grounds of an extensive holiday camp. Pitches for caravans and tents are separate.

Take Strada Romea towards Ravenna and drive to the bridge over the River Adige. Continue for 800m, then turn off, cross bridge and head towards Rosolina Mare and Rosapineta (approx 8 km).
14 May–17 Sep.

7HEC ⁝⁝⁝ ◈ ⋔H ▪ ▼ |O| ⊙ ▪
G R ⌂ ▭ ≈sP ⚠ ⊞ lau
A4800 Vn/c ▪8400 Ʌ6300

SALERNO *Salerno* (☎089)

At **PICCIOLA BY PONTECAGNANO** (15 km S)

Isola Verde ☎203030

Site on the right bank of river mouth between the coastal road to Paestum and the sea. Sunshade roof matting.

May–Sep.

10HEC ▥ ⁝⁝⁝ ◇ ⋔H ▪ |O| ⊙ ▪
≈

SALLE (LA) *Aosta* (☎0165)

Mont Blanc ☎861183

A grassy site on sloping ground, provided with flat terraces; lovely views of Mont Blanc and Grivola.

Take road towards La Salle from Aosta-Courmayeur road.
All year.

SAN ANTONIO DI MAVIGNOLA

Trento (☎0465)

Faé ☎57178

Situated in famous winter skiing region of Madonna di Campiglio. Good base for climbing in Brenta mountain range. On four gravel terraces, and alpine meadow in hollow next to SS239.

15 Jun–Sep & Dec–Apr.

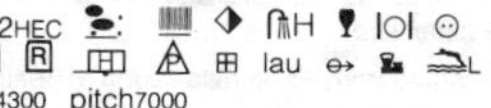

A4300 pitch7000

SAN BARTOLOMEO AL MARE

Imperia (☎0183)

Rosa via al Santuario 4 ☎400473

200m from sea. The site is in the village. Well-kept and in a quiet situation. Straw roofs provide some shade.

Signposted in the village.
All year

1.8HEC H P lau s
pitch1500–23000 (incl 3 persons)

SAN FELICE DEL BANACO

Brescia (☎0365)

Italy

Europe-Silvella ☎651095

Two sites under same management separated only by the joint approach road. The beach is situated about 80 m below.

Signposted.
Apr–Sep.

8.4HEC H LP lau A3700–5100
pitch8900–9800

Fornella ☎62294

May–20 Sep.

5.4HEC H L lau A3700–4600 pitch8000–10000

Ideal Molino ☎62023

The site lies in a beautiful, quiet setting on terraces that slope down to the lake and has a 400 m-long beach, with private landing stage. Although the approach roads are steep, with bends, they are not very difficult, except for large caravans.

Signposted.
15 May–15 Sep.

1.7HEC H L lau A5800
pitch10600–12200

SAN LORENZO NUOVO

Viterbo (☎0763)

Patrizia ☎77483

The site is situated in meadowland, on terraces above lake.

At Km 118/VIII turn off via Cassia and drive 0.3 km towards lake.
20 May–15 Sep.

2HEC H L lau A3500
V1900 2800 2000–2800

SAN MÁURO MARE

Forli (☎0541)

Green ☎46929

Site lies in well-kept grassland with poplars and plane trees by the railway.

About 300 m from the sea.
May–Oct.

1.2HEC H lau s
A3800 pitch6000

At **SAVIGNANO SUL RUBICONE**

Rubicone ☎46377

An extensive, level site divided into two sections by a narrow canal. It extends to the beach.

Situated about 0.8km from the road fork at Km 187/O off SS16 (Strada Adriatica).
15 May–Sep.

10HEC H s lau A3700–5200 pitch4600–9200

Italy

SAN MENÁIO
Foggia (☎0884)

Calanella ☎98046

15 May–15 Sep.

10HEC lau A3200–5800 V2000–3000 4500–7000 3000–5500

Valle d'Oro ☎91580

Site in olive grove surrounded by wooded hills with some terraces.

Turn off the SS89 onto SS528 and to site at Km1.800.2 km from the sea.
All year.

3HEC lau

SAN NICOLO DI RICARDI
Catanzaro (☎0963)

Agrumento ☎63175

The access road leads over a dusty field track, then on to a steep ramp with large, wide bends. Because the trees are very close together, the pitches are rather narrow. Lying in a lemon grove beside the sea, this site looks more like a garden. Beautiful beach. Excursions by boat can be arranged.

15 May–Sep.

Costa Verde ☎63090

Shade is provided throughout by roof matting. 3 km N by beach.

Access via dusty and uneven lane through field with concrete ramps.
Seasonal.

1.8HEC lau A3500–6500 V3500 4500–7500 4500–7500

Torre Ruffa Robinson ☎63185

A level site beside the sea with a fine sandy beach. Shade is provided by fruit trees and rush mat roofs.

The site is signposted from the coast road towards Ricadi.
15 May–15 Oct.

3.5HEC lau A3000–5500 Vn/c 7000–14000 5000–11500

SAN PIERO A SIEVE
Firenze (☎055)

Mugello Verde via Masso Rondinaio 2 ☎848511

Terraced site in wooded surroundings. Lunchtime siesta 14.00–16.00 hrs.

Leave motorway at exit 18 and follow signs.
All year.

12HEC RP lau A5500 V3000 6000 4000

SAN REMO
Imperia (☎0184)

San Remo via Tiro a Volo 3 ☎60635

All year.

2HEC lau

SAN VINCENZO
Livorno (☎0565)

Park Albatros ☎702414

This site lies amongst beautiful, tall pine trees. 1 km from sea.

Turn off SP23 beyond Piombino at Km7/III and drive 600 m inland.
28 Jun–11 Nov.

11.4HEC lau A4200–6000 V900–1250 5100–7300 V5100–7300

SANTA CESÁREA TERME
Lecca (☎0836)

Scogliera ☎944216

1 km S on SS173.
All year.

8.5HEC lau LP A4200–5600 V2400–3000 4200–6000 4200–6000

SANTA MARIA A MARE See **FERMO (LIDO DI)**

SANTA MARIA DI CASTELLABATE
Salerno (☎0974)

Trezene ☎065013

The site is partly divided into pitches and consists of two sections lying either side of the access road. Pitches between road and fine sandy beach are reserved for touring campers.

Apr–Oct.

2.5HEC lau

SANTA VITTORIA
Gènova (☎0185)

Santa Vittoria ☎409204

The site lies on meadowland in a wide valley at the foot of a pine-covered mountain. A very clean site.

2 km inland from via Aurelia. North of Sestri Levante and the motorway.
All year.

20HEC lau
pitch18000–30000

SARDEGNA (SARDINIA) (☎079)

ALGHERO

Mariposa ☎950360

The site lies among sand dunes and is scattered with pine and eucalyptus trees.

From harbour 1 km towards Lido S Giovanni turn left and cross first bridge.
Apr–Oct.

4HEC lau

CAGLIARI

At **PORTO PINO**

Sardegna ☎(0781)96813

On sand dunes in a pine forest beside a wide, shady beach.

6 km from Sant Anna Arresi towards Porto Pino.
15 May–Sep.

1HEC lau

At **SANT' ANTIOCO**

Tonnara ☎83803

May–Sep.

9HEC lau A5500–6500 9000–10000 7000–8000

SARRE
Aosta (☎0165)
International Touring ☎57061
4 km W of Aosta on SS26.
15 May–20 Sep.
5.5HEC H P lau

SARTEANO
Siena (☎0578)
Piscine via del Bagno Santo 29 ☎265531
The site lies 8 km S of Chianciano Terme; 6 km from Chiusi/Chianciano Terme motorway (A1) exit.
Apr–Sep.
10HEC H P lau **A**5300 **V**2000 5500 5500

SASSO MARCONI
Bologna (☎051)
Piccolo Paradiso ☎842680
Pleasant site with plenty of trees.
Leave A1 autostrada (Milano-Roma) at town exit and continue towards Vado for 2 km. Signposted.
Mar–Dec.
6.5HEC H lau RP **A**3500–4750 pitch5750–8900

SAVIGNANO SUL RUBICONE See **SAN MÁURO MARE**

SÁVIO (LIDO DEL)
Ravenna (☎0544)
Nuova International ☎949014
Well tended meadowland with high poplars.
Turn E off the main road in the village at Km168/IV then drive 4.5 km towards sea.
15 May–10 Sep.
5HEC H P lau s

SCACCHI (LIDO DEGLI)
Ferrara (☎0533)
Florenz ☎380193
Site with sand dunes extending to the sea.
Turn off the Strada Romea in the direction of Lido degli Scacchi, and continue along an asphalt road to the sandy beach.
15 May–15 Sep.
6HEC H s lau **A**4000 pitch7100

SCALEA
Cosenza (☎0985)
Gabbiano ☎20563

Italy

Lies S of the Gulf of Policastro between the coast road and the sea, and 1 km S of village.
10 Jun–10 Sep.
3HEC H s lau **A**6300 **V**6300 6300 6300

SCIACCA See **SICILIA (SICILY)**

SCHIANCETO
Macerata (☎0737)
Monte Prata Castel Sant'Angelo Sul Neva ☎98124
On large, level terrace with some trees on an incline. Fine mountain views. Signposted from Castel Sant' Angelo.
15 Jun–15 Sep.
5.5HEC H lau **A**3500 **V**n/c 3500 3500

SENIGÁLLIA
Ancona (☎071)
Summerland via Podesti 236 ☎62933
On SS16.
Jun–15 Sep.
2.2HEC H lau s **A**3000–4500 pitch7500–8800

SICILIA (SICILY) (☎095)

ACIREALE
Internazionale la Timpa via Floristella 25 ☎894420
The site is on eight terraces in a magnificent setting on top of the cliffs. Difficult for caravans. The beach can only be reached by means of a lift.
Turn off SS114 and drive towards Riporto and the sea for 1.4 km along winding road.
All year.
16HEC H lau s **A**4500 **V**3500 7500 5000

At **CARRUBA** (10.2 km N)
Praiola ☎964366
In idyllic location, very quiet.
5 km S of Riposto by the sea between orchards. 6 km from A18 exit Giarre.
25 Mar–Sep.
2.2HEC H lau s **A**4500 **V**3000 8000 8000

At **MELILLI** (15 km SW)
Mirage ☎(091)959059
Level site on the SS14. Young poplars and pines. Disco in cellar. Siesta 14.00–16.00 hrs. Bus service.
Turn seawards at Km124 on the SS114, 4 km from the sea.
All year.
4HEC H s lau

BUONFORNELLO
Himera ☎940240
The site is in a rural setting by the sea.
All year.
5HEC H lau s

CAPO DI CALAVÁ
Paradiso
Level site in olive grove on extreme point sloping steeply down to the sea with lovely view.
Mar–Oct.
2HEC H lau

CAPO DI MILAZZO
Cirucco ☎9284845
All year.
2HEC H lau s

CASTEL DI TUSA
Scoglio ☎34345
A terraced site. No shade on the gravel beach.
Turn off SS113 at Km164, 2 km W of Castel di Tusa.
15 Jun–15 Sep.
1.5HEC H lau s **A**4500 **V**2500 7000 5000

CATANIA
Ionio ☎491139
On a clifftop plateau. Access to beach via steps. Lunchtime siesta 14.00–17.00 hrs.
Turn off SS14 N of town towards sea.
All year.
1.2HEC H s lau

CEFALÙ
Sanfilippo Contrada Ogliastrillo ☎20184
Slightly terraced site in olive grove, surrounded by vineyards. Views of the sea.
3 km W signposted from coastal road. ➤

Apr–Sep.

1.5HEC H s lau

FONDACHELLO

Mokambo ☎938731

Level terrain, thickly wooded in parts not directly next to the sea.

For access leave A18 (Messina–Catánia) at Giarre exit, through Giarre and via Máscali to Fondachello on coast.
Apr–Sep.

1.4HEC H lau s A3800 V2300 4900 A3300

GIARRE

At **MILO** (11 km E)

Mareneve ETNA ☎951396

Site in hilly terrain with lovely view of the sea.

Approach from the A18 exit Giarre direction Venerina and Milo about 10 km.
All year.

1.5HEC H P lau A5100 V3250 8650 A8650

OLIVERI

Marinello ☎33000

Apr–Oct.

5HEC H s lau A3000–3800 V1800–2200 5000–6500 A2000–3000

PACHINO

At **PORTOPALO** (6.6 km SE)

Capo Palssero ☎(0931)842333

Site slightly sloping towards the sea with view of fishing harbour of Portopalo. Discotheque.

Turn S on 115 in Noto or Iolspica in direction of Pachino.
15 Feb–Nov.

3.4HEC H lau s A4000–4500 V2000–2500 5500–6000 A5500–6000

PALERMO

Internazionale Trinacria ☎(091)530590

Lying on level ground near a large rock, the site is separated from a rocky beach by an asphalt road.

12 km NW of Palermo. Turn off SS113 at Km273/1 and drive 1 km towards the sea.
All year.

4.2HEC H lau s A6500

PUNTA BRACCETTO

Bala del Coralli ☎(0932)911336

Italy

Level site with numerous olive trees, acacias and eucalyptus trees. Siesta 14.00–16.00 hrs.

From Marina di Ragusa follow coast road in direction of Punta Braccetto.
All year.

4HEC H s lau

Rocca del Tramonti ☎918054

The site lies in a quiet setting on rather barren land near a beautiful sandy bay surrounded by cliffs.

From Marina di Ragusa 10 km W on coast road to Punta Braccetto.
Etr–15 Oct.

3HEC H s lau A3000 V2500 6500 A4500–6500

RAGUSA (MARINA DI)

Bala del Sole Lungomare A-Doria ☎39844

Well tended level site. Pitches provided with roofs of straw matting.

All year.

5HEC H s lau

International Villa Nifosi ☎39118

Site set in gently sloping terrain on edge of village.

N off road from Ragusa. 200 m from sea.
May–Sep.

3HEC H lau sP A4000 V2500 6000 A4000–6000

SCIACCA

Gioventu ☎(0925)25962

Site in long terrain, with access to public beach which is suitable for children. Siesta 14.00–17.00 hrs.

Turn off SS115 at Km115, 3 km W of Sciacca in direction of sea and to site in 100 m.

0.7HEC H s

TAORMINA

At **CALATABIANO** (5.2 km SW)

Castello de San Marco ☎641181

In lemon grove by an old castle. 9 km S of Taormina.

Turn off SS114 between Calatabiano and Fiumefreddo in direction of the sea and continue for 1 km.
All year.

4HEC H lau s A4600 V3100 6500 A5500

SIENA

Siena (☎0577)

Slenc Colleverde via Scacciapensieri 47 ☎280044

Apr–Oct.

4HEC H P lau A6500 pitch3100

SILVI MARINA

Teramo (☎085)

Europe Garden ☎930137

Terraced site in olive grove with lovely coastal views.

Turn off SS16 in Silvi onto SS553 and continue on winding road for 2 km.
May–15 Sep.

4.5HEC H P lau s A4300 pitch11000

SISTIANA See **DUINO-AURISINA**

SOLE (LIDO DEL)

Fóggia (☎0884)

Adria ☎97174

Level grassland site with some old trees.

On the Rodi Gargánico road. Signposted.
Jun–Sep.

1.4HEC H s lau

SORICO

Como (☎0344)

Grande Quiete ☎84041

Well-maintained quiet site by the side of the lake.

Near the 'Ristorante Mera' and the bridge across the Mera. Access via the SS340d at Km27 near the road fork Splugen/Sondrio/Como. Turn towards the lake and continue along an uneven lane for 2.2 km.
All year.

1.9HEC H L A4000 V2300 5000 A3500–4500

Lac de Como ☎84035

The well-kept site lies on the right of the River Mera as it flows into Lake Como.

Turn off the SS340d at Km25 near TOTAL petrol station and drive 200 m towards lake.
All year.

1.7HEC H L lau

Torre ☎84106

Site on grassland sloping towards the lake with some trees.

Access via the SS340 at Km24.1 (TOTAL filling station). Turn towards the lake and continue for 200 m.

1.8HEC fìH lau L

SORRENTO

Napoli (☎081)

Campogalo via Capo 39 ☎8781444

Lies on terraces scattered with olive trees.

2 km from town centre and 400 m beyond the turning from the SS145 on road towards Massa Lubrense and 50 m from sea.
Mar–Oct.

7HEC fìH lau sP

International Camping Nube d'Argento ☎8781344

The site lies on narrow terraces just off a steep concrete road between the beach and the outskirts of the town.

Access is rather difficult for caravans.
All year.

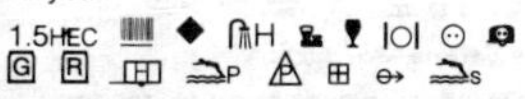

1.5HEC fìH P s

Santa Fortunata via Capo ☎8781444

Extensive site lying on terraces in a shady olive grove with many small, secluded pitches.

1 km from town and 50 m from sea.
Mar–Oct.

12HEC fìH lau sP A5000–7000 V2000–35000 ⛟5000–7000 ⛺3000–4500

SPECCHIOLLA (LIDO) See **CAROVIGNO**

SPERLONGA

Latina (☎0771)

Nord-Sud via Flacca ☎54255

1 km from town towards Gaera.
Apr–Oct.

4.5HEC fìH lau s pitch22800 (incl 2 persons)

SPINA (LIDO DI)

Ferrara (☎0533)

Spina via Del Campeggio ☎330179

Widespread site on level meadowland and on slightly hilly sand dune terrain. Separate section for dog owners.

Off SS309. Signposted.
16 May–15 Sep.

24HEC fìH P lau s A4500 V4000 ⛟6800 ⛺2800

SPOLETO

Perugia (☎0743)

Il Girasole ☎51335

All year.

Italy

2HEC fìH P lau A3450–3850 V1500–1700 ⛟4600–5300 ⛺3700–4200

SPOTORNO

Savona (☎019)

Rustia via G-Verdi 22 ☎745042

Part of site is in an orchard at the foot of a hill.

Apr–Sep.

1.4HEC fìH lau s A4300 V3200 ⛟4700 ⛺4700

TAORMINA See **SICILIA (SICILY)**

TARQUÍNIA

Viterbo (☎0766)

At **RIVA DEI TARQUINI** (9 km NW)

Riva dei Tarquini ☎814028

Site in tall pine woodland by the sea.

Turn seawards at Km102/II via Aurelia to site in 3 km.
Jun–Sep.

5.4HEC fìH Ps

TERRACINA

Latina (☎0773)

Blue via Badino Km4,350 ☎730727

The site is divided into plots on even grassland, with roof matting providing shade on mouth of the River Badino. The tenting section is located in pine woodland. Berthing facilities for boats in river mouth. Football pitch.

May–Sep.

4.5HEC fìH sR lau pitch14000–28800 (incl 2 persons)

TORINO (TURIN)

Torino (☎011)

Riviera sul Po corso Moncalieri 422 ☎638706

On a stretch of land between Corso Moncalieri and the river.

On E bank of Po about 3 km SE of Torino.
All year.

0.7HEC fìH P

TORRE DANIELE

Torino (☎0125)

Mombarone ☎757907

13 km N of Ivrea on SS26. Very close to river.
All year.

1.3HEC fìH lau R A3000 V1000 ⛟3000 ⛺3000

TORRE DEL LAGO PUCCINI

Lucca (☎0584)

Europa ☎341524

Site in pine and poplar woodland.

On the land side of the viale dei Tigli, coming from Viareggio.
Apr–Sep.

5.5HEC fìH lau s A2600–4700 V1600–2900 ⛟3150–4750 ⛺3150–4750

Italia ☎341504

The site is divided into pitches and lies in meadowland planted with poplar trees.

Inland from the Viareggio road (viale dei Tigli).
May–15 Sep.

9HEC fìH lau s

Lago via G-Puccini273 ☎341513

The site, which is planted with poplar trees, lies in level meadowland beside Lake Massaciuccoli.

1 km E on road No. 1.
All year.

2HEC fìH lau L A3500–4500 V2000–2500 ⛟3500–4500 ⛺3000–4000

TORRE RINALDA

Lecce (☎0832)

Torre Rinalda ☎652161

On an extensive level meadow, separated from the sea by dunes. Discotheque. Lunchtime siesta 13.30–16.00 hrs.

Access via SS613 (Brindisi–Lecce) exit Trepuzzi then coastal road for 1.5 km.
Jun–Sep.

23HEC fìH sP lau A3000–5500 V2500–4500 ⛟4300–6500 ⛺2000–4000

TORRI DEL BENACO

Verona (☎045)

Olivetl ☎7225522

Rising terrain amongst olive trees and vines. Footpath to lake about 50m.

At Km48.2 behind the Hotel 'S Faustino'.
Mar–Sep.

0.7HEC fìH L

TORTORETO (LIDO) See **ALBA ADRIATICO**

TOSCOLANO MADERNO

Brescia (☎0365)

Toscolano ☎641584

Walled site reaching down to lake. Within the grounds of a former monastery (built 1700) which has been made into a bar/restuarant.

Access via the SS45, at Km77.5 turn towards the lake then left.
Apr–Sep.

5.4HEC fìH L lau A3300–5100 pitch8200–11000

TRENTO (TRENTINO)

Trento (☎0461) ➤

Trento Lungadige Leopardi ☎25162

Municipal site on left bank of River Adige, 300 m above S Giorgio bridge.

For access, follow signposts from the SS12 (Brenner–Verona road) in northern part of town and drive towards Riva on Lake Garda.
Apr–Sep.

11HEC ◆ H lau

TRÉPORTI
Venezia (☎041)

Cá Pasquali Littorale del Cavallino, via Treporti ☎966110

Sandy, meadowland site with poplar and pine trees.

Access from Cavallino-Punta Sabbioni coast road, along an asphalt road for 400 m.
May–25 Sep.

9HEC ◆ H s lau

Cá Savio via Cá Savio ☎966017

A level site along the edge of the sea with private, sandy beach. Separate pitches for caravans and tents.

From Cá Savio, at traffic lights, turn towards the sea and continue for 500 m to the beach.
May–Sep.

28HEC ◆ H s lau A2200–4700 Vn/c 4000–12000 A4000–12000

Flori ☎966448

The site stretches over a wide area of sand dunes and pine trees with separate sections for caravans and tents.

May–Sep.

10HEC ◆ H sP lau A7300 pitch24000

Mediterráneo ☎966721

Slightly hilly grassland site with trees and sunshade roofs. Lunchtime siesta 13.00–15.00 hrs.

Well signposted.
2 May–Sep.

17HEC ◆ H sP lau

TURIN See **TORINO**

URBINO
Pesaro (☎0722)

Pineta ☎4710

Etr–15 Sep.

2.2HEC ◆ H lau A3350–4300 V1700–2100 6000–8000 A4800–5150

VADA
Livorno (☎0586)

Flori ☎770096

Level grassland surrounded by fields. Shade provided by roof matting.

Access from the SS1 S of Vada, after 1.5 km turn right and continue for 500 m.
Apr–15 Oct.

Italy

15HEC ◆ H P lau s A5800 V2350 7000 A7000

Pineta via di Pietrabianca 1 ☎788524

The site lies on grassy and sandy terrain with some reed mat roofs and lies inland from the access road in a pine grove. Private beach.

Etr–10 Oct.

1.5HEC ◆ H lau s A3800–4800 V1800–2000 4600–5800 A2700–5800

Rifugio del Mare ☎770091

Site lies in extensive grassland with young trees about 400 m from the sea. Shade, at present, only provided by roof matting.

Access via the SS1, turn right S of Vada and continue on gravel road past Camping del Fiori to the coast road, then left and continue for 500 m to the site.
May–Sep.

5.5HEC ◆ H P lau s A5800 V2350 7000 A7000

VARCATURO (MARINA DI) See **POZZUOLI**

VARNA-VAHRN
Bolzano (☎0472)

Löwenhof ☎23216

Site lies on gently sloping ground, near to Gasthof of same name.

S on SS12 (Brennerstrasse) from Vipiteno.
All year.

0.5HEC H PR lau

VASTO
Chieti (☎0873)

Europa ☎59802

Site on level terrain by the road with poplars.

At Km 522 of road SS16.
15 Mar–Sep.

2.3HEC ◆ H lau

Grotta del Saraceno ☎50213

Site in olive grove on steep coastal cliffs with lovely views. Steep path to beach. Siesta 14.00–16.00 hrs.

Turn off SS16 at Km512.200.
Jun–15 Sep.

12HEC ◆ H lau s A5500 V3000 9900 A9900

VIARÉGGIO
Lucca (☎0584)

Paradiso via dei Tigli ☎392005

Site with tall pine trees and firm terrain.

2.5 km S, turn off via Aurelia at Km354/V onto via Comparini towards the sea to site in 600 m.

May–Sep.

6HEC ◆ H lau s A3000–4500 V2000–3000 4000–5000 A4000–5000

Viaréggio ☎391012

The site lies in a poplar wood.

1.5 km S of town. At Km354/V head towards coast.
Apr–15 Sep.

2HEC ◆ H lau s A2900–4200 Vn/c 3200–4800 A3200–4800

VILALAGO
L'Aquila (☎0864)

I Lupi ☎740100

All year.

7HEC ◇ H lau L A4000 pitch8500

VICO EQUENSE
Napoli (☎081)

Selano Spiaggia Marina Aequa ☎8798165

About 200 m from the sea.

Apr–15 Oct.

2.2HEC ◆ H lau s

Bála Serena ☎8799255

Due to the steep and narrow site roads only cars and tents are accepted in the camp. The site is scattered with olive trees and has a magnificent view of the Gulf of Naples and Mount Vesuvius.

Lies off the coast road between Vico Equense and Sorrento.
Apr–Oct.

2HEC H P

Sant' Antonio ☎8799261

Apr–Sep.

1HEC ◆ H lau s A5500 V2000 5500 A4000

VIESTE
Foggia (☎0884)

Bala degli Aranci ☎787025

The site is partially level and terraced with poplars and olive trees.

N of village.
Jun–Sep.

11HEC ◆ H sP lau A2700–5800 pitch5300–9100

Bala Turchese ☎78587

1 km N of Vieste on Strada Panoramica towards Peschici.
15 May–Sep.

4HEC ◆ H s lau A4000–6600 V2500 4000–8000 A4000–8000

Canzone del Mare ☎76124

Site under orange trees with some terraces.

700 m N on coast road.
Jun–Sep.

1.7HEC ◆ H lau s

Capo Vieste ☏76326

The site lies on a large area of unspoilt land, planted with a few rows of poplar and pine trees. It is by the sea and has a large bathing area.

Off coastal road to Peschici about 7 km beyond Vieste.
May–25 Sep.
6HEC ◆ H lau A3500–5800 V1400–2000 4500–7500 4500–7500

Centro Vacanze Crovatico ☏76487

Site with poplars in a bay with lovely sandy beach surrounded by wooded hills. Siesta 14.00–16.00 hrs.

At Km9 on coast road Vieste–Peschici.
May–10 Oct.
48HEC ◆ H lau

Diomedee ☏76472

Level meadowland site with poplars, by the sea.

5 km on coast road.
3.5HEC H s

Eden Garden ☏78696

A fairly level site, in an olive grove, situated about 200 m from the sea.

From town, follow the well-signposted road to Lido di Portonuovo.
Jun–15 Sep.
2.5HEC ◆ H lau s A8000

Girarrosto ☏78106

2 km S of Vieste, amongst reeds, vineyards and agricultural land. Section of site adjoins beach.

Approach via coast road 0.3 km S of filling station.
Jun–Sep.
3HEC ◆ H lau s

Holiday Village ☏76138

The site lies on level terrain in a large bay, surrounded by rocks between the coastal road and the sea.

Italy

Jun–Sep.
5.5HEC ◆ H s lau A3000–6000 V2500–4000 4000–7500 4000–7500

Porticello ☏76125

The site lies in a long, sandy bay which is bordered on one side by rocks.

5 km on coast road to Peschici and then turn right.
16 Apr–Sep.
2.5HEC ◆ H s lau A2500–6000 Vn/c 4500–5500 4500–5500

Vieste Marina ☏76471

Level site adjacent to the coast road.

5 km N of Vieste, signposted.
Jun–15 Sep.
5HEC ◆ H lau s A2500–6000 V1400–2500 3800–8000 3800–8000

Village Punta Lunga ☏76031

A terraced site including two sandy bathing bays, a rocky peninsula and the village of Vieste.

2 km N of Vieste, signposted from coast road.
15 Apr–Sep.
6HEC ◆ H s lau A5500 V2000 7000 7000

VILLANOVA D'ALBENGA
Savona (☏0182)

C'era una Volta ☏580461

Holiday centre set on a hill overlooking the surrounding area. Disco. Tennis court.

15HEC ◇ H P lau

VISERBELLA See **RIMINI**

ZAMBRONE MARINA
Catanzaro (☏0963)

Bianca Spiággia ☏392009

The site looks like a garden and is planted with lemon and orange trees. It lies beside sea and magnificent beach.

Turn off SS522 at KM25/V, pass under the road and railway line.
10 Jun–25 Aug.
5HEC ◆ H s lau

ZAPPONETA
Foggia (☏0884)

Ippocampo ☏23894

In grounds of a holiday village.

Jun Sep.
1.5HEC ◆ H lau s

ZOLDO ALTO
Belluno (☏0437)

Pala Favera ☏78155

Site with some woodland, at the foot of Monte Pelmo.

15 Jun–20 Sep & Dec–Apr.
5HEC ◆ H lau R A4000–5000 Vn/c 4000–4500 2500–3000

San Marino

Prices are in Italian Lire.

Della Murata ☏991299

A terraced site on Monte Titano, below the firing range.

About 2 km from the town centre. On route of Strada-Panoramico from Rimini.
All year.
4HEC ◆ H lau

Echternach on the River Sûre is a busy tourist centre

Luxembourg, the tiny Grand Duchy only 999 square miles in size, offers a wide range of facilities to the visitor. Entirely landlocked, it is bordered by three countries: Belgium, France and the Federal Republic of Germany. One third of the country is occupied by the hills and forests of the Ardennes, while the rest is taken up by the wooded farmland and, in the south-east, the rich wine-growing valley of the Moselle.

The Grand Duchy enjoys a temperate climate, the summer often extending from May to late October. The official languages are French and German, but most of the people speak Luxembourgeois as an everyday language. Tourists will find, however, that English is also widely understood and spoken.

HOW TO GET THERE

Luxembourg is easily approached through either Belgium or France, Luxembourg City is just over 200 miles from Oostende or Zeebrugge, about 260 miles from Boulogne, Calais or Dunkerque, and is therefore within a day's drive of the Channel coast.

See page 99 for location map

GENERAL INFORMATION

(see also *Things you need to know*, pages 33–64)

Boats

(see page 33 and *Customs regulations* page 57)

British Embassy/Consulate

(see also page 57)

The British Embassy together with its Consular Section is located at *Luxembourg Ville* 14 Boulevard Roosevelt ☎29864/66.

Camping

There are over 100 officially recognised campsites throughout the country. Most of them are open from April to October, but some function throughout the year. A booklet containing details of campsites is obtainable from the National Tourist Office (B.P.1001, L-1010 Luxembourg). All campsites open to the public must be authorised by the Minister of Tourism.

International camping carnet not compulsory but recommended. Very few campsites will allow a reduction in the advertised charge to the holders of a camping carnet. See page 37 for further information.

Off-site camping is permitted but permission must always be obtained from the authorities in the case of public land and the owner in respect of private land before camping or parking a caravan. It is prohibited to camp on the shores of the lake (dam) of Esch/Sûre.

Currency including banking hours

(see also page 57)
The unit of currency is the Luxembourg Franc (*LFr*) divided into 100 *Centimes*. At the time of going to press £ = *LFr*61.70. Denominations of bank notes are *LFr*50, 100, 1,000; standard coins are *LFr*1, 5, 10, 20 and *Centimes* 25, 50. There are no restrictions on the amount of foreign or local currency which can be taken into or out of the country, but because of the limited market for Luxembourg notes in other countries, it is advisable to change them before leaving. Belgian currency is also used in Luxembourg.

Banks are open Monday to Friday from 08.30/09.00–12.00hrs and 13.30/14.00–16.30/17.00hrs.

Customs regulations

A *Customs Carnet de Passages en Douane* is required for all temporarily imported boats unless entering and leaving by water. See also *Customs regulations for European countries* page 57 for further information.

Foodstuffs

(see also page 60)
Visitors entering from an EEC country may import duty-free 1,000g of coffee or 400g of coffee extract and 200g of tea or 80g of tea extract; a reduced allowance applies if entering from a non EEC country. Visitors under 15 years of age do not quality for the duty-free concession on coffee.

Medical treatment

(see page 60)

Shopping hours

While some shops are closed on Monday mornings, the usual hours of opening for *food shops* are: from Monday to Saturday 08.00–12.00 hrs, 14.00–18.00hrs. *Supermarkets* open from 09.00–20.00hrs but close at 18.00hrs on Saturdays.

Tourist information

(see also page 63)
The National Tourist Office in London is at 36–37 Piccadilly (entrance Swallow Street), W1V 9PA ☏01-434 2800 (recorded message service out of office hours). In Luxembourg the Office National du Tourisme (National Tourist Office), local authorities, and tourist information societies (*Syndicat d'Initiatives*) will be pleased to assist you with information regarding tourism.

Visitors' registration

(see page 63)

MOTORING

(see also *Things you need to know*, pages 33–64)

Accidents

(see also page 46)
Fire, police, ambulance ☏012-Civil Defence emergency service (*Secours d'urgence*).

Breakdowns

(see page 48)

Dimensions and weight restrictions

Private **cars** and towed **trailers** or **caravans** are restricted to the following dimensions – height: 4 metres; width: 2.50 metres; length: 12 metres. The maximum permitted overall length of vehicle/trailer or caravan combination is 18 metres.

The weight of a caravan must not exceed 75% of the weight of the towing vehicle.

Driving licence

(see also page 33)
A valid UK or Republic of Ireland licence is acceptable in Luxembourg. The minimum age at which a visitor may drive a temporarily imported car or motorcycle is 17 years.

Lights

(see page 50 also *Headlights* page 41)

Motoring club

(see also page 61)
The *Automobile Club du Grand-Duché de Luxembourg* (ACL) has its head office at *8007 Bertrange* 13 Route de Longwy ☏450045. ACL office hours are 08.30–12.00hrs and 13.30–18.00hrs from Monday to Friday; closed Saturday and Sunday.

Passengers

(see also page 51)
Children under 10 are not permitted to travel in a vehicle as front seat passengers when rear seating is available.

Petrol

(see page 61)

Roads

There is a comprehensive system of good main and secondary roads.

Seat-belts

(see page 52)

Speed limits

Built-up areas	*Other roads*	*Motorways*
60kph	90kph	120kph
(37mph)	(56mph)	(74mph)

All lower signposted speed limits must be adhered to. There are no special speed restrictions imposed on vehicle/trailer combinations.

Warning triangle

The use of a warning triangle is compulsory in the event of accident or breakdown. The triangle must be placed on the road about 100 metres (109yds) behind the vehicle to warn following traffic of any obstruction. See also *Warning triangles/Hazard warning lights* page 5

Prices are in Belgian Francs

Abbreviations:
r rue
rte route

BERDORF

Belle Vue 2000 r de Consdorf 15A ☎79635

Jun–11 Sep.

4.5HEC H G R lau

Parc Martbusch Rischette Emile ☎79545

All year

3HEC H G R P lau

BOURSCHEID-PLAGE

Bel-Air ☎90019

A clean, well-kept site, partly on meadowland and partly on terraces.

The entrance lies to the N of CR308.
Apr–Sep.

10HEC H L A100 160 160

Bourscheid r du Château ☎90377

The site is partly on meadowland and partly on terraces and surrounded by rows of shrubs.

Entrance off N side of CR308 at KM21.
Apr–Oct.

1.2HEC H R A80 120 120

BOUS/REMICH

Source rte de Luxembourg 47 ☎698332

Mar–Oct.

0.5HEC H G

CLERVAUX

Officiel de Clervaux Klatzewe 33 ☎92042

Situated next to the sports stadium, between the La Clervé stream and the railway in a forested area. Trains only run during the day and there is little noise. Separate field for tents.

0.5 km SW from the village.
Apr–Oct.

3HEC H G P lau

COLPACH

Colpecher Dall r Haupstr 1 ☎61227

All year.

1.6HEC H P

CONSDORF

Bel Air Burgkapp ☎79353

The site is divided into pitches and lies on level meadowland in the forest area of 'Petite Suisse Luxembourgeoise'.

On W outskirts of village. Turn right off E42.6 km S of Echternach.
Apr–15 Sep.

1.9HEC H G R P lau A100 pitch130

DIEKIRCH

Op der Sauer rte de Gilsdorf ☎808590

500 m from town centre on Larochette road near the sports stadium.
All year.

6HEC H L lau A100 pitch100

Sûre rte de Gilsdorf ☎809425

In a pleasant situation, 200 m from the town centre.

Access from the Gilsdorf road.
Apr–Sep.

4HEC H G R lau

DILLINGEN

Benelux chemin de la Fôret 2 ☎86267

A terraced, grassland site partially in an orchard and divided into pitches.

Off N10, turn right before reaching the church.
Apr–Nov.

1.8HEC H G R lau A85 pitch100

ECHTERNACH

Alferweiher Alferweiher 1 ☎72271

May–15 Sep.

4HEC H G P lau A110 pitch140

Officiel rte de Diekirch 5 ☎72272

15 Mar–15 Oct.

2.5HEC H R R

ENSCHERANGE

Val d'Or ☎92691

All year.

2.2HEC H R R A65 V60 60 60

ERMSDORF

Klein Zwitserland ☎87450

Etr–Oct.

1.2HEC H R A45 pitch190

ESCH-SUR-ALZETTE

Gaalgebierg ☎541069

A level park-like grassland site with lovely trees on a hillock.

SE along N6 from the town centre in the direction of Dudelange as far as the motorway underpass. Then turn right and follow the steep climb uphill.
All year.

2.5HEC H R lau pitch340

GREVENKNAPP

Loos ☎63141

An extensive, slightly sloping grassy site on the edge of a large woodland area on the Helperknapp–Berg.

Approach from Mersch via N8 to Grevenknapp turn-off. Continue to site via CR115.
Apr–Sep.

5HEC H G P lau A100 pitch160

HALLER

Relax r Henerecht 6 ☎86748

All year.

1.5HEC H P lau

HEIDERSCHEID

Fuussekaul rte de Bastogne 2 ☎89659

A level grassland site with a large subdivision of pitches on a plateau adjoining a woodland area.

Turn off the N15 (Ettelbruck–Wiltz/ Bastogne) S of Heiderscheid in a westerly direction.
All year.
30HEC lau A110 pitch160

INGLEDORF

Gritt r du Pont ☎802018

On southern bank of River Sûre between Ettelbruck and Diekirch. In beautiful country setting ideal for fishing.

21 Mar–26 Oct.
5HEC lau

LAROCHETTE

Kengert ☎87186

On gently sloping meadow.

Take the N8 towards Mersch, then the CR119 towards Nommern and turn right after approx. 2 km.
Mar–7 Nov.
4.5HEC lau pitch540 (incl. 4 persons)

LINTGEN

Waldesruh ☎328484

May–15 Oct.
3HEC

Luxembourg

MERSCH

Um Krounebierg r des Quatre Vents ☎328578

A clean, well-kept site on five terraces, split into sections by hedges.

Approx 0.5 km W of village church.
15 Apr–25 Sep.
3.5HEC lau

MERTERT

Mertert r du Parc ☎7481745

15 Apr–15 Oct.
2HEC

MONDORF-LES-BAINS

Mondorf-les-Bains rte de Burmerange ☎660746

Set on a hill, divided into pitches with plenty of trees

SE of town to the N of the CR152 (Schengen road) at Km 15.
All year.
11HEC A80 pitch100

NOMMERN

Bell Vue r Principale 3 ☎87868

Mar–15 Nov.
2HEC lau

Europe Nommerlayen ☎87878

A terraced site in wooded surroundings.

Mar–8 Nov.
12HEC lau pitch480 (incl 4 persons)

See advertisement on page 306

REISDORF

Rivière rte de la Sûre 21 ☎86398

The entire site is divided into pitches and lies on a field near the church.

Between the River Sûre/Sauer and Km9.5 off the N19, 10 km E of Diekirch.
Apr–Oct.
1.1HEC

Sûre r de la Sûre 23 ☎86509

Apr–Oct.
2.1HEC

REMICH

C M Europe ☎698018

A level grassland site on the edge of town with a separate section for young campers. ➔

Access 200 m S of the E42 between the banks of the Mosel to the W and Remich.
May–20 Sep.
1.5HEC H lau

REULER

Rellerweiler ☎92160
25 Mar–Sep.
1.6HEC H G lau

SCHWEBSANGE

Port ☎60460
Apr–15 Oct.
2.3HEC H G R R lau A70 pitch80

SEPTFONTAINES

Simmerschmelz ☎307072
All year
2.5HEC H G R P lau A90 pitch120

STEINFORT

Luxembourg

Steinfort rte de Luxembourg ☎39727
All year.
3.5HEC H G lau A80 pitch170

TROISVIERGES

Walensbongert Grand rue 33 ☎97141
In a gently sloping grassy area with tarred drives and some terraced pitches. Next to a sports field and a swimming pool.
On S outskirts of the village by the CR337.
Mar–Oct.
3HEC H P lau

VIANDEN

Deich ☎84375
23 Mar–Sep.
3HEC H R

Moulin rte de Bettel ☎84501
On Bettel–Vianden road beside the river.
27 May–Aug.
2.8HEC H R A85 pitch90

At **WALSDORF** (2 km SW)

Romantique ☎84464
A terraced grassland site.
W of Diekirch–Vianden road, access from the N17 and CR354.
All year.
6HEC H G

WALDORF See **VIANDEN**

WILTZ

Kaul ☎95359
In a valley, surrounded by trees.
2 km NW of Clervaux road. Turn left at Grummelscheid 6 sign, then right.
May–Sep.
6.5HEC H P lau A80 pitch100

NETHERLANDS

A pastoral scene in the province of Limburg

The Netherlands is bordered by two countries, Belgium and the Federal Republic of Germany. A fifth of this flat, level country criss-crossed by rivers and canals lies below sea-level. The areas reclaimed from the sea, known as *polders*, are extremely fertile. The landscape is broken up by the forests of Arnhem, the bulbfields in the west, the lakes in the central and northern areas, and the coastal dunes which are the most impressive in Europe.

The climate is generally mild and tends to be damp. The summers are moderate with changeable weather and are seldom excessively hot. The language, Netherlandish or Dutch, is fairly guttural and closely allied to the low German dialect. One form of the Dutch language is spoken in the northern districts of Belgium and is known as Flemish. Other dialect forms exist throughout the Netherlands.

HOW TO GET THERE

There are direct ferry services to the Netherlands. Services operate from Harwich to the Hook of Holland, Hull to Rotterdam (Europort) and Sheerness to Vlissingen (Flushing); the sea journey can take between 7 and 14hrs depending upon the port of departure. Alternatively one of the short Channel crossings can be used, and then the Netherlands can be easily reached by driving through France and Belgium. The distance from Calais to Den Haag is just over 200 miles and is within a day's drive.

GENERAL INFORMATION

(see also *Things you need to know*, pages 33–64)

British Embassy/Consulate

(see also page 57)
The British Embassy is located at *2514 ED Den Haag* Lange Voorhout 10 ☎(070)645800, but the Embassy has no consular section. The British Consulate is located at *1075 AE Amsterdam* Koningslaan 44 ☎(020)764343.

Camping

There are some 800 officially recognised and classified campsites throughout the Netherlands. It is not generally possible to book sites in advance. Coastal sites tend to be crowded in June and July when many of the Dutch take their holidays. Local tourist information offices (VVV) can provide detailed information about sites in their area. The camping season is generally from April to September, but some sites are open all year.

Hire of equipment is possible in a few of the larger sites, but arrangements should be made well in advance of your holiday.

International camping carnet is not compulsory but may be requested on certain campsites; generally it is recommended when camping in the Netherlands. Few campsites will allow a reduction in the advertised charge to the holders of a camping carnet. See page 37 for further information.

Off-site camping is not possible outside organised sites. Overnight stops are not permitted.

Currency including banking hours

(see also page 57)
The unit of currency is the Dutch Guilder or Florin (*Fls*) divided into 100 *Cents*. At the time of going to press £ = *Fls* 3.29. Denominations of bank notes are *Fls* 5, 10, 25, 50, 100, 250, 1,000; standard coins are *Fls* 1, 2.50 and *Cents* 5, 10, 25. There are no restrictions limiting the import of currency. All imported currency may be freely exported, as well as any currency exchanged in, or drawn on an account established in, the Netherlands.

Banks are open 09.00–15.00hrs from Monday to Friday, but closed on Saturday. At all ANWB offices money can be exchanged 08.45–16.45hrs from Monday to Friday and 08.45–12.00hrs on Saturday. There are exchange offices at the principal railway stations (*eg* Amsterdam, Arnhem, Eindhoven, Den Haag, Hook of Holland, Maastricht, Rosendaal, Rotterdam, Utrecht and Venlo).

Firearms

Dutch laws concerning the possession of firearms are the most stringent in Europe. Any person crossing the frontier with any type of firearm will be arrested. The law applies also to any object which, on superficial inspection, shows any resemblance to real firearms (*eg* children's toy plastic imitations, etc). If you wish to carry firearms, real or imitation, of any description into the Netherlands, seek the advice of the Netherlands Consulate.

Foodstuffs

(see also page 60)
Visitors from EEC countries may import duty-free 1,000g of coffee or 400g of coffee extract and 200g of tea or 80g of tea extract bought duty and tax paid; a reduced allowance applies if bought duty-free. Visitors under 15 years of age do not quality for the duty-free concessions on coffee.

Medical treatment

(see page 60)

Shopping hours

Generally food shops are open 08.00–18.00hrs Monday–Saturday. Most food shops close for one half day per week, but this varies according to location. Most other shops including department stores are open from 13.00–17.30hrs on Monday, from 09.00–17.30hrs Tuesday-Friday, from 09.00–16.00hrs Saturday.

Tourist information

(see also page 63)
The Netherlands Board of Tourism, 25–28 Buckingham Gate, London SW1E 6 LD ☏01-630 0451 will be pleased to assist you with any information regarding tourism and it has branch offices (VVV) in all towns and large villages in the Netherlands.

There are three types of these branch offices: Travel Offices giving detailed information about the whole of the Netherlands; Information Offices giving general information about the Netherlands and detailed information about their own region; and Local Information Offices giving detailed information about the locality.

Visitors' registration

(see page 63)

MOTORING

(see also *Things you need to know*, pages 33–64)

Accidents

(see also page 46)
Police and **Ambulance** Amsterdam and Den Haag, ☏222222; Rotterdam ☏141414, **Fire** Amsterdam ☏212121, Den Haag ☏222333, Rotterdam ☏292929. Numbers for other towns are in the front of the local telephone directories. If necessary, contact the Police Emergency Centre ☏(03438)14321.

Breakdowns

(see page 48)

Dimensions and weight restrictions

Private **cars** and towed **trailers** or **caravans** are restricted to the following dimensions – height: 4 metres; width: on 'A' roads* 2.55 metres, on 'B' roads* 2.20 metres; length**: with 2 axles 12 metres. The maximum permitted overall length of vehicle/trailer or caravan combination is 18 metres.
Maximum weight for caravan/luggage trailers without brakes 750kg or 75% of weight of towing vehicle; with brakes 100% of weight of towing vehicle.

*'A' roads are main roads, 'B' roads are secondary roads. 'B' roads are indicated by signs bearing the capital letter 'B', roads which do not have these signs may be considered 'A' roads.

**Trailers with single axle and manufactured before 1967–10 metres, after 1967–8 metres.

For key to country identification - see "About the gazetteer"

Driving licence

(see also page 33)
A valid UK or Republic of Ireland licence is acceptable in the Netherlands. The minimum age at which a visitor may drive a temporarily imported car or motorcycle is 18 years.

Lights

(see page 50 also *Headlights* page 41)

Motoring club

(see also page 61)
The *Koninklijke Nederlandsche Toeristenbond* (ANWB) has its headquarters at *2596 EC Den Haag* Wassenaarseweg 220 and offices in numerous provincial towns. Offices are usually open between 08.45 and 16.45hrs Monday to Friday and 08.45 and 12.00hrs on Saturday. Traffic information can be obtained from the ANWB 24hrs a day ☎(070)313131.

Passengers

(see page 51)
Children under 12 are not permitted to travel in a vehicle as front seat passengers with the exception of children under 4 using a safety seat of approved design and children over 4 able to wear a safety belt.

Petrol

(see page 61)

Roads

Main roads usually have only two lanes but are well surfaced. The best way to see the countryside is to tour along minor roads, often alongside canals.

Seat-belts

(see page 52)

Speed limits

Car
Built-up areas
50 kph (31 mph)
Other roads
80 kph (49 mph)
Motorways
100 kph (62 mph)

Car/caravan/trailer
Built-up areas
50 kph (31 mph)
Other roads
80 kph (49 mph)
Motorways
80 kph (49 mph)
On motorways there is a minimum speed limit of 70 kph (43 mph) for cars and 60 kph (37 mph) for vehicles with trailers.

Warning triangle

The use of a warning triangle is compulsory in the event of accident or breakdown. The triangle must be used to warn following traffic of any obstruction and also if a parked vehicle is insufficiently illuminated either by its own or street lighting. See also *Warning triangle/ Hazard warning lights* page 54.

Prices are in Dutch Florins (Gulden or Guilder)
Abbreviation:
Str Straat

AALSMEER
Noord-Holland (☎02977)

Amsterdamse Bos Kleine Noorddijk 1 ☎(020)416868

The site is in a park-like setting in the Amsterdam wood. The camp is near the Airport flight path and is subject to noise, depending on the wind direction.

If approaching from The Hague along the motorway, turn at the northern edge of the airport, and head towards Amstelveen. Then follow directions for Aalsmeer. Alternatively, if approaching from Utrecht, leave the motorway at the Amstelveen exit, and drive towards Aalsmeer, passing through Bovenkerk.
Apr–Oct.
5.3HEC H A7 pitch16

AFFERDEN
Limburg (☎08853)

Hengeland Hengeland 10 ☎1355

On slightly hilly heathland, near a farm.

To the N of the town, about 1 km E of the N95.
All year.
10HEC H P pitch25

Klein Canada ☎1223

All year.
10HEC H P lau pitch32

ALKMAAR
Noord-Holland (☎072)

Alkmaar Bergerweg 201 ☎116924

The site is well-kept and divided into many sections by rows of trees and bushes.

Lies on the NW outskirts of the town, off the Bergen road.
Apr–Sep.
3HEC H A4 V4 4 A4

AMELAND (ISLAND OF) See **NES**

AMEN
Drenthe (☎05920)

Reservaat Diana Heide ☎89297

An ideal site for relaxation, which lies away from the traffic amongst forest and heathland.

If approaching from Assen along the E35, drive through Ekehaar and Amen and on towards Hooghalen.
15 Mar–Oct.
30HEC H P lau pitch23

AMERONGEN
Utrecht (☎03434)

Ossenberg Dwarsweg 1 ☎(03431)354

4 km NE.
All year.
16HEC H P lau

AMSTERDAM
Noord-Holland (☎020)

See also **AALSMEER**
AYC Ijsbaanpad 45 ☎620916

On SW outskirts near the Olympic Stadium.

15 Mar–Sep.

5.7HEC H G A5 V2 6 3

Vliegenbos Meeuwenlaan 138 368855

This is a tent site for young people.

From main railway station through tunnel, then right and right again at traffic lights, then follow signposts.
Apr–Sep.

2HEC H G lau A5 pitch20

ANNEN
Drenthe (05922)

Hondsrug Annerweg 3 1292

Apr–Oct.

18HEC H G P lau

ARCEN
Limburg (04703)

Maasvallei Dorperheideweg 34 1564

Off the N271.
All year.

9.5HEC H G lau pitch27

Schans 1957

All year

15HEC H G R LP lau pitch32(incl 4 persons)

ARNEMUIDEN
Zeeland (01182)

Witte Raaf Muidenweg 3 1212

A modern well-maintained site in meadowland, divided into sections by rows of shrubs, ideal for sailing and motor boat enthusiasts with yacht marina.

Situated on the Veersmeer, N of the Goes–Vlissingen motorway. From Arnemuiden exit follow signs for about 5 km.
Mar–Oct.

18HEC H G lau pitch27(incl 2 persons)

ARNHEM
Gelderland (085)

Arnhem Kemperbegerweg 771 431600

The site lies on grassland and is surrounded by trees.

NW of town and S of E36.
Mar–Oct.

36HEC H G lau A4 V4

Hooge Veluwe Koningsweg 14 432272

From Apeldoorn exit on E36 drive NW towards Hooge Veluwe.
Apr–Sep.

11HEC H G P lau pitch35

Warnsborn Bakenbergseweg 257 423469

The site is surrounded by woodland and lies on slightly sloping meadowland. Near zoo and open-air museum.

Netherlands

Near the E36 motoway NW of town in the direction of Utrecht. 200 m S of SHELL filling station, continue in W direction for 0.7 km.
Apr–15 Sep.

3.5HEC H G P lau A4 V3 3 3

ASSELT
Limburg (04740)

Maasterras Eind 4 1287

Well-kept site on terrace. Private beach.

W of Swalmen–2.3 km W of the SHELL petrol station on the N273.
All year.

3HEC H G

ASSEN
Drenthe (05920)

Witterzomer Witterzomer 7 55688

A large site with asphalt internal roads, lying in mixed woodland near nature reserve. Separate sections for dog owners. Individual washing facilities for the disabled.

Turn off the E35 at Assen W exit into Europaweg Zuid and continue for 100 m, then turn right. Continue through Witten and follow signs.
All year.

60HEC H G P lau A5 V5 5 5

BAARLAND
Zeeland (01193)

Scheldeoord Landingsweg 1 226

S of town on the coast.
15 Mar–Oct.

10HEC H G P lau pitch30

BAARLE NASSAU
Noord-Brabant (04257)

Heimolen Heimolen 6 8001

1.5 km SW.
All year.

15HEC H G lau A4 V3 4 4

BAARSCHOT See **DIESSEN**

BABBERICH
Gelderland (08364)

Rivo Torto Beekseweg 8 7332

3 km W on E36.
Apr–15 Oct.

3HEC H lau A3 V3 4 4

BEEKBERGEN
Gelderland (05766)

Bosgraaf Kanaal Zuid 444 (05765)1359

Situated on hilly grassland and woodland, but the woodland pitches are mainly used by residential caravans.

For access from the N50, Arnhem–Apeldoorn road, turn N in West Hoeve onto the Loenen road, then follow signs for 2 km.
Apr–Oct.

20HEC H G P lau

Groot Panorama Groot Panorama 36 2707

Apr–Sep.

3HEC H G P lau A5 V4 5 5

Lange Bosk Hoge Bergweg 16 (05765)1252

On level ground in a spruce forest. Divided into pitches.

Turn off the Beekbergen–Loenen road at Km4.3 and drive N. Site about 3.5 km from town.
Apr–Sep.

35HEC H G P lau A4 V4 4 4

Pietersberg 1953

Apr–15 Oct.

2HEC H G P lau A4 V4 4 4

BELFELD
Limburg (04705)

Eekhoorn 1326

On a flat-topped hill covered with trees.

3 km E of village and N95.
Apr–Oct.

14HEC H G lau pitch26

BERG EN TERBLIJT
Limburg (04406)

Oriental Rijksweg 6 40075

On Maastrict–Valkenburg road 3 km from Maastrict.
May–20 Oct.

4.3HEC H G P lau pitch24

BERGIJK
Noord-Brabant (04975)

Paal De Paaldreef 14 1977

Signposted.
Apr–25 Dec.

17HEC H G P lau pitch34(incl 4 persons)

BERKHOUT
Noord-Holland (02295)

Westerkogge 1208

Apr–Sep.

11HEC H G R LP lau A4 V2 4 3–4

BERKUM See **ZWOLLE**

BIDDINGHUIZEN See **DRONTEN**

BLADEL
Noord-Brabant (04977) ➔

Achterste Hoef Troprijt 10 ☎1579

S of town.
All year.

15HEC lau pitch33(incl 4 persons)

BLOEMENDAAL AAN ZEE
Noord-Holland (☎023)

Het Helmgat Zeeweg 97 ☎260820

On sandy ground in a deep valley among the sand dunes with tarred drives.

Apr–Sep.

4HEC lau

BORGER
Drenthe (☎05998)

Hunzedal De Drift 3 ☎34698

The site is clean, well kept and lies NE of the village.

For access, turn off the road towards Buinen, drive 200 m E of the bridge over the Buinen–Schoondoord canal, then head S for a further 1 km.
Apr–Sep.

21HEC lau A4 V4 4 4

Lunsbergen Rolderstr 3 ☎36565

On main road between Emmen and Groningen.
Apr–24 Oct.

23HEC lau pitch26

BORSSELE
Zeeland (☎01105)

Estancia Catalijneweg 47 ☎1568

Clean well-kept site surrounded by trees and hedges.

W of town of N shore of Westerschelde.
All year.

1.9HEC

BOXTEL
Noord-Brabant (☎04110)

Dennenoord Dennendreef 5 ☎1280

Level, grassy site with hedging and groups of trees. Leisure activities organised for adults and young people. Soundproof disco.

Turn off the N2 at Esch in direction of Osterwijk. Follow signs.
Mar–1 Nov.

9HEC lau A3 V3 8 8

BRESKENS
Zeeland (☎01172)

Zeebad Nieuwesluisweg 5 ☎1815

The site lies NW of Breskens below the dyke road to Nieuwesluis and the lighthouse.
15 Mar–Oct.

16HEC lau pitch25

BRIELLE
Zuid-Holland (☎010)

Netherlands

Krabbeplaat Oude Veerdam 4 ☎(01810)2363

On level ground scattered with trees and groups of bushes. It has asphalt drives.

Apr–23 Oct.

25HEC lau

BUSSUM
Noord-Holland (☎02159)

Fransche Kamp Franse Kampweg 3 ☎17751

SW towards Hilverson.
Apr–Oct.

8HEC A4 V4 4 4

BUURSE
Overijssel

't Hazenbos Oude Buurserdk 1 ☎(05426)338

On several meadows, partially surrounded by trees.

All year.

8HEC lau A4 V3 4 4

COCKSDORP (DE) (ISLAND OF TEXEL)
Texel (☎02222)

Sluftervallei Krimweg 102 ☎214

On sand-dunes. It is advisable to book in advance during the peak season.

From the ferry landing stage, drive to the N tip of the island. Just before enterng the village, turn left and head towards Vuurtoren (lighthouse). Turn left again after several hundred metres. The road leads directly to the site.
27 Mar–Oct.

36HEC lau

CROMVOIRT
Noord-Brabant (☎04118)

Vondst Pepereind 13 ☎1431

1 km SE.
All year.

8HEC lau A3 V3 3 3

CULEMBORG
Gelderland (☎03450)

Welborn Rietveldseweg 21 ☎13050

On SW edge of village.
Apr–Sep.

11HEC lau A4 V4 4 4

DELDEN
Overijssel (☎05407)

International De Mors 6 ☎61922

On two grassy terraces at the edge of a wood, to the SE of town.

For access, turn S off the E8, Hengelo to Deventer road, in the E outskirts of town, then take two left turns to Zwemmbad.
Etr–Sep.

6HEC A4 V4 4 4

DELFZIJL
Groningen (☎05960)

Delfzijl Kustweg 13 ☎12870

On coast.

Apr–Sep.

2HEC A3 V3 3 3

DEN Each name preceded by 'Den' is listed under the name that follows it.

DENEKAMP
Overijssel (☎05413)

Papillon Kanaalweg 30 ☎1670

Predominantly a chalet site on meadowland in a tall coniferous and deciduous forest, about 2 km N of Denekamp. It has a few naturally screened pitches.

For access, turn off the E72 towards Nordhorn (Germany), about 0.3 km N of the signposts for Almelo–Nordhorn canal, and drive NE for 1.5 km.
Apr–Sep.

14HEC lau A4 V4 4 4

DIEPENHEIM
Overijssel (☎05475)

Molnhofte Nyhofweg ☎1514

E of town.
May–15 Oct.

3HEC lau A4 V3 4 4

DIESSEN
Noord-Brabant (☎04254)

At **BAARSCHOT** (2 km S)

Kempenbos Westelbeersedijk 6 ☎1567

Apr–25 Oct.

6.5HEC lau pitch28

DIEVER
Drenthe (☎05219)

Hoeve aan de Weg Bosweg 12 ☎(05212)7269

Apr–Oct.

9HEC lau A4 V4 4 4

At **DIEVERBRUG** (2 km SE)

Ellert en Brammert Groningerweg 13 ☎1207

On hilly ground in a forest of conifers and deciduous trees.

0.2 km W of Km22.4 off the E35.
Apr–Oct.

26HEC lau A4 V4 4 4

DOESBURG
Gelderland (☎08334)

Ijsselstrand Eekstr 18 ☎72797

On level meadow with trees and hedges beside the River Ijssel. Separate field for young people. Water sports.

NE across river. Signposted.
All year.

45HEC H G lau A4 V3 6 A5

DOETINCHEM

Gelderland (☎08340)

Wrange Rekhemseweg 144 ☎24852

On the eastern outskirts of the town. It is set in meadowland and surrounded by bushes and deciduous trees.

200 m E of link road between roads to Varsseveld and Terborg.
Apr–Sep.

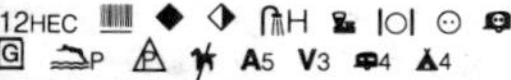

12HEC H G P A5 V3 4 A4

DOMBURG

Zeeland (☎01188)

Domburg Schelpweg 7 ☎1679

On meadowland divided into several sections, with asphalt drives. It is on the inland side of the road, along the dyke, with a belt of shrubs dividing it from the road. 2 tennis courts, small golf course, a children's swimming pool and play garden.

500 m on main road to Westkapelle.
Apr–Oct.

13.5HEC H G Ⓟ lau pitch31(incl 3 persons)

DOORN

Utrecht (☎03430)

Bonte Vlucht Leersumsestraatweg 23 ☎12476

3 km E.
Apr–Sep.

10HEC H G Ⓟ pitch22(incl 4 persons)

Het Grote Bos Hydeparkin 24 ☎13644

Well layed out site on wooded grassland. Varied leisure activities for children and adults.

About 1 km NW of Doorn.
All year.

80HEC H G R Ⓟ lau pitch13–26(incl 2 persons)

DORDRECHT

Zuid-Holland (☎078)

Bruggehof Rijksstraatweg 186 ☎183241

Near Moerdijkbrug.
Apr–15 Oct.

Netherlands

24HEC H G P lau A5 V4 5 A5

DRONTEN

Gelderland (☎03210)

At **BIDDINGHUIZEN** (9 km S)

Flevostrand Strandweg 1 ☎(03202)480

Plots of grassland separated by close belts of shrubs. Own marina.

On the Polder, 5 km S of Biddinghuizen turn right near the Veluwemeer.
Apr–Oct.

10HEC H G Ⓟ lau pitch26

Riviera Spijkweg 15 ☎(03211)1344

Situated on grassland near a forest of deciduous trees and surrounded by shrubs.

On the Polder beside the Veluwemeer, 5 km S of Biddinghuizen turn left.
28 Mar–15 Sep.

30HEC H G P lau pitch30

DWINGELOO

Drenthe (☎05219)

Noordster Noordster 105 ☎7238

3 km S on E35.
All year.

20HEC H G P lau pitch28(incl 2–3 persons)

Torentjeshoek Leeuweriksveldweg 1 ☎1706

Apr–Sep.

4HEC H G A4 V2 3 A3

ECHT

Limburg (☎0475)

Marisheem Brugweg 89 ☎1458

The site is well-kept and lies E of the village.

From town drive approx 2.2 km towards Echterbosch and the border, then turn left.
15 Mar–15 Oct.

10HEC H G P lau pitch32(incl 6 persons)

EERBEEK

Gelderland (☎08338)

Coldenhove Boshoffweg 6 ☎59101

In woodland.

From Apeldorn–Dieren road, drive 2 km SW, then NW for 1 km.
29 Mar–19 Oct.

74HEC H G P lau

Robertsoord Doonweg 4 ☎51346

1 km SE.
All year.

2.5HEC H G lau A3 V3 4 A4

EES

Drenthe (☎05998)

Land van Bartje Buinerweg 8 ☎36162

21 Mar–24 Oct.

40HEC H G lau pitch35

EMMEN

Drenthe (☎05910)

Emmen Angelsloërdijk 31 ☎12018

On several pitches of well-kept meadowland, near an indoor swimming pool.

From village drive towards Angelso for 1.5km, then follow signposts.
May–Aug.

8HEC H G P A5 V5 4 A4

EMST

Gelderland (☎05787)

Wildhoeve Hanendorperweg 102 ☎1324

3.5 km W. Signposted.
All year

10.5HEC H G lau pitch27

ENSCHEDE

Overijssel (☎053)

Aamsveen Lappenpad 250 ☎611547

Apr–Sep.

20HEC H G P lau pitch17

Klein-Zandvoort Keppelerdijk 200 ☎611372

E towards Glanerbrug.
All year

11HEC H G P lau pitch27

EPE

Gelderland (☎05780)

Schaapskool Centrumweg 5 ☎16204

SW of village.
Apr–Sep. ➔

4HEC H lau P A4 V4 4 A4

ERMELO
Gelderland (03417)

Haeghehorst Fazantlaan 4 53185

20 Mar–Oct.

2HEC H lau P A4 V4 7 A7

EXLOO
Drenthe (05919)

Hunzebergen Valtherweg 36 49116

2.5 km SE.
Apr–Oct.

H P lau pitch18–24

FLUSHING See **VLISSINGEN**

GARDEREN
Gelderland (05776)

Hertshoorn Putterweg 68 1529

W on road to Putten.
Apr–20 Oct.

10HEC H lau

GASSELTE
Drenthe (05999)

Berken Borgerweg 23 64255

Part of this site lies in wooded surroundings.

0.5 km SW.
Apr–28 Sep.

5.5HEC H lau A4 V4 4 A4

Hoefslag Achter de Brinken 14 64343

E of town.
28 Mar–21 Oct.

8.5HEC H P lau pitch25

GROEDE
Zeeland (01171)

De Ploeg Voorstr 47 1358

A meadow site on the N outskirts of the village. Vehicles permitted on site only at time of arrival and departure.

Apr–Sep.

3.5HEC H lau

GROENLO
Gelderland (05440)

Kunne Lichtenvoordsweg 68 61260

Wooded with sandy lanes. There is a pleasant bar and a café situated in an old farm.

Netherlands

2 km from old road to Lichtenvoorde.
Apr–Sep.

1.5HEC H P lau pitch19

GROET See **SCHOORL**

GROLLOO
Drenthe (05925)

Berenkuil De Pol 15 242

Partly in a forest and partly on heathland.

On the western outskirts of the village towards Hooghalen. Drive a further 0.8 km along a road which narrows at the end.
Apr–Sep.

35HEC H P lau pitch21

GRONINGEN
Groningen (050)

Stadspark Campinglaan 6 251624

A well-kept site on patches of grass between rows of bushes and groups of pine and deciduous trees. Some of its pitches are naturally screened.

For access from the SW outskirts of the town, take the road towards Peize and Roden.
15 Mar–14 Oct.

7.2HEC H A4 V4 4 A4

HAAG (DEN) (THE HAGUE)
Zuid-Holland (070)

Ockenburg Wijndaelerweg 25 252364

Site lies on the W of town and 500 m from beach. Advance booking not accepted.

For access follow signs towards Kijkduin.
Apr–19 Oct.

46HEC H lau A3 V3 14

HAAKSBERGEN
Overijssel (05427)

Scholtenhagen Scholtenhagenweg 30 12384

The internal site roads are asphalt and there are pony-rides for children.

Turn off by-pass W of town and drive towards Eibergen for 0.7 km, then turn right and follow Zwemmbad singposts.
Apr–Oct.

8HEC H A4 V4 4 A4

t'Stien-Nboer 12610

Mar–Nov.

10.5HEC H lau A4 V4 4 A4

HAAMSTEDE
Zeeland (01115)

Ginsterveld J-J-Boeyesweg 45 1590

Apr–Sep.

14HEC H lau pitch28

HALFWEG
Noord-Holland (023)

Houtrak 382424

Grassy site on several levels subdivided by trees, hedges and shrubs. Separate section for young campers.

Signposted from Spaarwonde exit on A5.
May–1 Sept.

5HEC H L pp6

HARKSTEDE
Groningen (050)

Grunostrand 416371

All year

45HEC H L lau A4 V3 4 A4

HARLINGEN
Friesland (05178)

Zeehoeve Westerzeedijk 45 3465

A well-kept meadow site which is divided into large sections by rows of bushes.

It lies 1 km S of Harlingen near a dyke.
Apr–Sep.

7.5HEC H pitch14

HATTEM
Gelderland (05206)

Leemkule Leemkuilen 6 41945

2.5 km SW.
Apr–20 Oct.

26HEC H P lau pitch28

HEEL
Limburg

Heelderpeel De Peel 13 (04748)1596

This well-maintained site lies in mixed woodland, next to a lake surrounded by forest.

For access, drive 6 km W from Roermond, then turn SW on to the Maaseyk road for 3.5

km to site approach road with sign 'Hotel de Peel'.
Apr–Oct.

HEERDE
Gelderland (☎05782)

Buitencentrum de Koerberg ☎2066
Apr–Oct.
23HEC ◆ H lau

HEILOO
Noord-Holland (☎072)

Heiloo De Omloop 24 ☎331950
One of the best sites in the area. It is divided into many large squares by hedges.
Apr–15 Sep.
4.5HEC H lau pitch25

Klein Varnebroek De Omloop 22 ☎331627
Apr–15 Sep.
4.2HEC H lau pitch23

HELDEN-DORP
Limburg (☎04760)

Heldense Bossen ☎72476
Access via Maastricht via A67/E3 (Venlo–Eindhoven) Signposted.
All year.
20HEC ◆ H P lau pitch31

HELDER (DEN)
Noord-Holland (☎02230)

Donkere Duinen Jan Verfailleweg 616 ☎14731
3 km SW.
Apr–15 Sep.
7HEC H P lau A4 Vn/c 10 10

Noorder Sandt Noorder Sandt 2 ☎41266
A flat, well-maintained site on meadowland, with good sanitary blocks.
Access from the Den Helder to Callantsoog coastal road.
All year.

Netherlands

11HEC H P lau pitch24

HENGELO
Gelderland (☎05753)

Kom-Es-An Handwijzersdijk 4 ☎7242
NE of village in wooded area in the direction of Ruurlo.
Apr–Sep.
6.5HEC H P pitch19

HENGELO
Overijssel (☎074)

Kristalbad-Hengelo Kettingbrugweg 60 ☎916550
SE towards Enschede between canal and road.
15 Apr–15 Sep.
3HEC H P Ⓟ pitch14

HENGSTDIJK
Zeeland (☎01148)

Vogel Meerkoetstr 6 ☎1625
All year.
34HEC H pitch25

HERKENBOSCH
Limburg (☎04752)

Elfenmeer Meinweg 1 ☎1689
Hilly, well maintained site in pine forest beside a small lake
NE off Roermand road.
All year.
34HEC ◆ H P lau pitch28

HERPEN
Noord-Brabant (☎08867)

ENNIA-Herperduin Schaijkesweg 12 ☎1383
Situated in extensive woodland
Access from the 'S-Hertogenbosch–Nijmegen motorway. Take the Ravenstein exit and continue towards Herpen, then in direction Bergheim/Oss.
27 Mar–23 Oct.
26HEC H lau

HEUMEN
Gelderland (☎08896)

Heumens Bos Vosseneindseweg 46 ☎5814481
NW of village, 100 m N of the Wijchen road.
Apr–Sep.
2HEC H P lau A4 pitch18

HILVARENBEEK
Noord-Brabant (☎04255)

Beekse Bergen Beekse Bergen 1 ☎(013)360032
Situated in a holiday centre in the Brabant afforestation on the edge of a safari park. Lake suitable for swimming. Various other facilities.
10 km S of Tilburg.
Apr–26 Oct.
27HEC H lau L A9 pitch10

HOEK
Zeeland (☎01152)

Braakman Middenweg 1 ☎1730
On meadowland between a wood and shrubs
About 4 km W of town and 40 m N of expressway to Breskens.
All year
56HEC H lau pitch28

HOEK VAN HOLLAND
Zuid-Holland (☎01747)

Hoek van Holland Wierstr 101 ☎2801
On grass, surrounded by rows of poplar trees, bushes and paved drives.
If approaching from the N, turn left off the E36, take the Riipstraat and drive to the end of the road.
28 Mar–27 Sep. ➔

7.8HEC pitch22

HOENDERLOO
Gelderland (05768)

Miggelenberg Miggelenbergweg 65 1251

Site situated in sparse, mixed woodland.

For access, turn off the Arnhem to Apeldoorn road at Woesterhoeve and drive W to Hoenderloo and continue for 2.5 km on the Beekbergen road.
27 Mar–23 Oct.

33HEC lau pitch28

Pampel 1760

All year

14.5HEC lau A6 V4 6 6

't Veluws Hof Krimweg 154 777

W of N93.
All year

10HEC lau pitch22

HOEVEN
Noord-Brabant (01659)

Hoeven Oude Antwerpse 81 2570

Between Breda and Rosendaal W of Etten-Leur.
10 Apr–20 Sep.

35HEC lau pitch22

HOLTEN
Overijssel (05480)

Prins Wildweg 2 12272

A holiday complex operated by the Dutch ENNIA Company, in an area of attraction to the rambler. Swimming pool on edge of site.

Access from the E8 Deventer–Almelo road. Take the Holten/Rijssen exit then turn off.
Apr–Sep.

11HEC lau pitch22

HOORN (DEN) (ISLAND OF TEXEL)
Texel (02226)

Loodsmansduin Witteweg 24 203

Extensive site, numerous large and small hollows between some quite high dunes, connected by paved paths. Several sanitary blocks. At the highest part there is a bungalow village in amongst a shopping and administrative complex.

From the ferry drive N towards Den Burg, then turn left at crossroads towards Den Hoorn.
Apr–Sep.

50HEC pitch18

KAATSHEUVEL
Noord-Brabant (04167)

Duinlust Duinlaan 1 72775

In a meadow surrounded by hedges.

Turn off main road 200 m N of village and drive 1.1 km E.
All year.

2.5HEC lau A4 V3 3 3

't Hoekske van Haestrechtstr 22 72794

A flat site divided into plots.

For access turn E off the Tilburg to Waalwijk road at the windmill and drive for 600 m.
Apr–20 Oct.

15HEC lau A4 V3 3 3

KAMPERLAND
Zeeland (01107)

Molenhoek Molenweg 69 1202

On meadowland and is surrounded by tall, bushy hedges.

NW outskirts of village.
15 Mar–Oct.

8HEC lau

Roompot Mariapolderseweg 1 1555

A level, well maintained site with a private beach.

Turn off Kamperland–Wissenkerke road and drive N for 0.5 km.
All year

32HEC lau

Schotsman Schotsmanweg 1 1751

On a large, level meadow beside the Veerse Meer, next to a Nature Reserve. Water sports.

Signposted.
28 Mar–25 Oct.

26HEC lau pitch32(incl 3 persons)

KESTEREN
Gelderland (08886)

Lede en Oudewaard Hogedijkseweg 40 1477

On level meadowland surrounded by bushy hedges and divided into individual pitches. 100 m from private beach and pool.

2 km N of village, turn W off main Rhenen–Kesteren road, and continue for 2.7 km.
All year.

4HEC lau pitch21

KORTGENE
Zeeland (01108)

Paardekreek Havenweg 1 2051

A municipal site next to a canal that flows into the Veerse Meer.

For access, turn off the Zierikzee–Goes trunk road at the CHEVRON petrol station and drive towards Kortgene, continue through the village and drive SW.
Apr–Oct.

9HEC lau pitch23

KOUDEKERKE
Zeeland (01185)

Dishoek Dishoek 2 1348

3 km SW of Koudekerke.
3 Apr–25 Oct.

2.2HEC lau pitch21

Duinzicht Strandweg 7 1397

W on Vlissingen–Westkapelle road.
15 Apr–Sep.

5HEC lau A4 V3 3 3

LAAG-SOEREN
Gelderland (☎08337)

Jutberg De Jutberg 78 ☎220

1 km S.
All year.

20HEC ◆ ◈ H G
P lau pitch26

LAGE MIERDE
Noord-Brabant (☎04259)

Vakantiecentrum de Herterwei
Wellenseind 7 ☎1295

2 km N.
All year.

20HEC ◇ H
P pitch19–37(incl 4 persons)

LATHUM
Gelderland (☎08309)

Honingraat Marsweg 2 ☎59010

Site with modern facilities on an arm of the Ijssel with good boating facilities and its own marina.

For access, turn off the Arnhem–Doesburg road and pass through the village to the site in 1.5 km.
Apr–Oct.

17HEC ◈ H G
LP ⊞ lau pitch22

Mars Marsweg 6 ☎1000

Divided into pitches on level meadowland beside a dammed tributary of River Ijssel.

Turn off Arnhem–Doesberg road N of village and continue W for 1.7 km.
Apr–Sep.

2.5HEC ◈ H G R
A3 V2 3 3

LEEUWARDEN
Friesland (☎058)

At **TIETJERK** (7 km E)

Netherlands

Kleine Wielen de Groene Ster 14 ☎(05118)1660

This municipal site is the best in Friesland. It is completely divided into pitches and lies on grassland beside a lake.

Off the E10 and 4 km E of Leeuwarden, towards Groningen.
Apr–Sep.

6HEC ◈ H G
Ⓟ lau A5 V5 5 5

LOCHEM
Gelderland (☎05730)

Ruighenrode Vordenseweg 6 ☎3151

Site among mixed woodland with tall spruce.

2 km SW of town. For access, turn off the road to Zutphen at Km 10.4 in S direction on the Vorden road for the site in 4.5 km.
All year.

25HEC ◆ H
G P lau A4 Vn/c 12 12

LUNTEREN
Gelderland (☎08388)

Goudsberg Hessenweg 85 ☎2386

The site consists of two sections and is set on grassland in a forest.

Situated 3 km from main road E of village.
Apr–Oct.

25HEC ◆ H
G P lau A4 V4 4 4

LUTTENBERG
Overijssel (☎05724)

Luttenberg Heuvelweg 9 ☎1405

Apr–Sep.

11.9HEC ◈ H
G lau A4 V4 4 4

LUYKSGESTEL
Noord-Brabant (☎04974)

Zwarte Bergen Zwarte Bergen 1 ☎1373

The site is isolated and very quiet, and lies on undulating dune-like ground in a pine forest.

From Eindhoven through Valkenswaard and Bergiejyk. Signposted.
All year.

25.5HEC H G
P Ⓟ ⊞ lau pitch25

MAARN
Utrecht (☎03432)

Laag-Kanje Laan van Laag-Kanje 1 ☎1348

Situated 500 m from the lake.

1 km NE.
Apr–Oct.

30HEC ◈ H R
Ⓟ ⊞ A4 Vn/c 8 8

MAASBREE
Limburg (☎04765)

Ruige Hoek De Ruige Hoek 2 ☎2360

On the E3 just before Venlo, on the border with Germany.
Apr–Sep.

7HEC ◈ H
G P ⊞ lau pitch16(incl 2 persons)

MARKELO
Overijssel (☎05476)

Hessenheem Potdijk 8 ☎1200

Situated near a swimming pool.

3 km NE.
All year. ➔

40HEC H lau P pitch27

MIDDLEBURG
Zeeland (01180)
Ysbaan Koninginnelaan 55 25395
On meadowland surrounded by trees and bushes.
On W outskirts of town.
15 May–15 Sep.
4.2HEC H

MILHEEZE
Noord-Brabant (04924)
Peel Hutten 5 1225
N on road to Boxmeer.
Apr–15 Sep.
11HEC H P lau

NEEDE
Gelderland (05450)
Eversman Bliksteeg 1 1906
Situated in a quiet position, surrounded by trees.
W of town.
Apr–Oct.
1.5HEC H P lau A4 V4 4 4
't Klumpe Diepenheimseweg 38 1780
N of town.
Apr–Oct.
9.7HEC H lau A4 V4 4 4

NES (ISLAND OF AMELAND)
Ameland (05191)
Duinoord J-van Eijckweg 4 2070
Take ferry at Holward, site left off road towards beach.
Apr–Oct.
10HEC H lau A4 V2 5 5

NIEUW-MILLIGEN
Gelderland (05775)
ENNIA Rabbit Hill Grevenhout 21 431
On hilly ground in a forest of coniferous and deciduous trees. Advance booking required for peak season.

Netherlands

From E8 drive 0.3 km S towards Kootwijk then turn E and continue 400 m.
27 Mar–23 Oct.
48.6HEC H P lau pitch32

NIEUWVLIET
Zeeland (01171)
International St-Bavodk 2 1233
On N outskirts, near a windmill on the road leading to the dyke.
Apr–Oct.
3HEC H lau pitch20
Pannenschuur Zeedijk 19 1391
NW of town. Signposted.
All year.
14HEC H P lau pitch26

NIJMEGEN
Gelderland (080)
Kwakkenberg Bosweg 33 232443
On gently sloping meadowland between rows of deciduous trees and groups of bushes.
Situated on E outskirts of town and reached by turning off N53 (Nijmegen–Klef/Kleve) and driving S.
Apr–15 Oct.
4.5HEC H A3 V3 3 3

NOORD SCHARWOUDE
Noord-Holland (02269)
Molengroet 3444
All year.
10HEC H S

NOORDWIJK AAN ZEE
Zuid-Holland (01719)
At **NOORDWIJKERHOUT** (5 km NE)
Club Soleil Kraaierslaan 7 (02523)74225

Signposted.
Apr–Oct.
6HEC H P lau pitch41

NULAND
Noord-Brabant (04102)
Vinkeloord Vinkeloord 1 2966
S of village.
All year.
50HEC H A2-5 pitch28

NUNSPEET
Gelderland (03412)
Vossenberg Groenlaantje 25 52458
Apr–15 Oct.
1HEC H A4 Vn/c 3 3

OISTERWIJK
Noord-Brabant (04242)
Reebok Burg Vd Oeverweg 19 82309
Situated in a large pine forest, hardly fenced off and impossible to overlook. In attractive surroundings with numerous small lakes.
SE of town.
Apr–25 Oct.
21.5HEC H lau A4 V4 5 5

OMMEN
Overijssel (05291)
Calluna Stouweweg 3 (05297)234
NW on left off road to Zwolle.
Apr–Sep.
17HEC H P lau pitch20

ONNEN
Groningen (05906)
Fruitberg Dorpsweg 67 1282
S of the village, and right of the Haren–Zuidlaren road.
Apr–Sep.
4.8HEC H lau A4 V3 3 3

OOSTKAPELLE
Zeeland (01188)
In de Bongerd Brouwerijstr 13 1510

Well-kept in a meadow with hedges and apple trees.

500 m S.
14 Mar–8 Nov.

3.7HEC H G lau pitch21

Ons Bulten Aagtekerkeseweg 2 ☎1813

From church drvie S towards Gapinge, turn W and continue 400 m.
27 Mar–Oct.

6.6HEC H G P lau pitch27(incl 3 persons)

OUDDORP
Zuid-Holland (☎01878)

Groene Welde Oude Nieuwlandseweg 11 ☎1747

A municipal site on flat grassland.

On N outskirts. Signposted.
Apr–Sep.

12HEC H G R lau pitch12–25

Klepperstee ☎1511

On level meadow divided by hedges and trees. Soundproof disco.

Access via A29 (Rotterdam–Willemstad) exit Middelharnis.
Apr–Oct.

38HEC H lau S pitch27

PATERSWOLDE
Drenthe (☎05907)

At **SCHELFHORST**

Schelfhorst Schelfhorst 26 ☎1953

The site lies 8.5 km S of Groningen and about 1 km from the Paterswolder Meer. For access turn off the N43, NW of the village towards Groningen and continue W for 0.6 km.
Apr–Oct.

9HEC H G lau A3 V3 3 3

PETTEN
Noord-Holland (☎02268)

Verzorging Pettemerweg 4 ☎1432

SW towards N9.
15 Apr–15 Sep.

7HEC H G P P lau A4 V4 4 4

PLASMOLEN
Limburg (☎08896)

Eldorado Witteweg 18 ☎1914

S of N271.
Apr–Sep.

Netherlands

6HEC H L P lau A4 V4 5 5

RENESSE
Zeeland (☎01116)

Bremhoeve Hoogenboomlaan 11 ☎1403

Well-kept site belonging to a trade union, but also accepting tourists. The last camping site in Hoogenboomlaan with numbered sections. It is advisable to reserve pitches between 21 Jun and 9 Aug.

29 Mar–24 Oct.

12HEC H P pitch29

International Scharendijkseweg 8 ☎1391

On grassland, between rows of tall shrubs and trees. Between dyke road and main road to Scharendijk on E outskirts of village.

Mar–1 Nov.

3HEC H G V3 4–5 4–5

Oase Roelandsweg 8 ☎1358

Well-kept park like site.

S of village, turn off Haamstede–Scharendijke trunk road at petrol station, take road to Hogezoom, then turn left.
Apr–Sep.

7.5HEC H G lau A6 V5 5 5

Vakantiepark 'Schouwen' Hoogenboomlaan 28 ☎1231

Mar–Oct.

9HEC H G lau

RENSWOUDE
Utrecht (☎08387)

Batterijen Dijkje 1 ☎1130

S before railway.
Apr–Sep.

5HEC H G P lau A3 V4 4 4

RHENEN
Utrecht (☎08376)

Thymse Berg Nieuwe Veenendaalseweg 229 ☎12384

N of town.
Apr–Oct.

7.5HEC H G P P lau A5 Vn/c 5 5

RIJEN
Noord-Brabant (☎01612)

Kampzicht Oosterhoutseweg 13 ☎2664

SW of town.
Mar–Oct.

7HEC H G P P lau A5 V2 3 3

RIJNSBURG
Zuid-Holland (☎01718)

Koningshof Elsgeesterweg 8 ☎26051

Modern site on level meadow.

1 km N.
All year.

6.5HEC H G P lau A3 V3 7 7

RODEN
Drenthe (☎05908)

Leekstermeer Meerweg 13 ☎(05945)12073

On the S shores of the Leekstermeer.

For access, turn off the N13 about 1.6 km SE of Leek (towards Roden) and drive NE. Then take a narrow paved road, and continue for a further 2.7 km.
Apr–15 Oct.

4HEC H P lau

ROELOFARENDSVEEN
Zuid-Holland (☎01713)

Braassem ☎2091

Off highway A4/E10. (Amsterdam–Leiden). Follow signs for Braassemer Meer from Roelofarendsveen exit.
Apr–1 Oct.

2HEC H G R P LP A4 V4 4 4

ROOSENDAAL
Noord-Brabant (☎01656)

Zonneland Turfvaartsestr 6 ☎429

S of town towards the Belgian border.
Mar–26 Oct.

14HEC H G P A4 V4 4 4

ROTTERDAM
Zuid-Holland (☎010)

Kanaalweg kanaalweg 84 ☎159772

Leave motorway by-pass (roads E10/E36) at exit Rotterdam–Centrum, then follow signs.
Apr–Sep.

4HEC H G lau A4 V4 6 6

Netherlands

RUINEN
Drenthe (☎05221)
ENNIA-Wiltzangh Witteveen 2 ☎1227
N of the village in the middle of a coniferous and deciduous forest, and within the grounds of a big holiday village. Advance booking is necessary for the peak season.
For access, drive from Ruinen towards Ansen for 3 km, then turn right and head N.
Apr–23 Oct.
13HEC H G P lau pitch26

RUURLO
Gelderland (☎05735)
't Sikkeler Sikkelerweg 8 ☎(05736)221
4 km SW.
17 Apr–Sep.
8.5HEC H G lau pitch13–19

ST-ANTHONIS
Noord-Brabant (☎08858)
Ullingse Bergen Bosweg 36 ☎1700
W of town.
Apr–20 Oct.
11HEC H G P lau pitch22

ST-MAARTENSZEE
Noord-Holland (☎02246)
St-Maartenszee Westerduinweg 30 ☎1401
Completely surrounded and divided into pitches by hedges, lying on meadowland on the edge of a wide belt of sand dunes.
For access, turn off the Alkmaar to Den Helder road at St-Maartensvlotburg and drive towards the sea. Take the road over the dunes and follow it for about 1.5 km, then turn right and continue for a further 300 m.
27 Mar–15 Sep
4HEC H G lau A5 Vn/c 4 4

ST-OEDENRODE
Noord-Brabant (☎04138)
Rijsingen de Klenehoef Zwembadweg 35 ☎72877
NW towards Boxtel.
All year.
10.5HEC H G P lau A4 pitch9

SCHAESBERG
Limburg (☎045)
Bousberg Paarklaan 8 ☎311213
NW towards Kakert.
Apr–20 Oct.
7.5HEC H G P lau pitch26

SCHELFHORST See **PATERSWOLDE**

SCHIN OP GEUL
Limburg (☎04459)
Schoonbron Valkenburgerweg 128 ☎1209
SE towards Wijlre
Mar–Oct.
9HEC H G P lau pitch22(incl 4 persons)

SCHINVELD
Limburg (☎045)
Brenkberg Bouwbergstr 126 ☎255096
S towards Brunssum.
All year.
2.5HEC H G lau A4 V3 4 4

SCHOORL
Noord-Holland (☎02209)
Elba Omloop 35 ☎1936
On meadowland and divided into pitches by hedges, which provide some shelter from the wind.
For access follow the Bergen road and turn left at the 'Aagtdorp' bus stop.
Apr–Sep.
2.5HEC H G A4 V4 4 4
At **GROET** (4 km NW)
Groede Hargerweg 8 ☎1555
The site consists of a meadow enclosed by hedges.
15 Apr–15 Sep.
3HEC H G P pitch21

SEVENUM
Limburg (☎04767)
Schatberg Midden Peelweg 5 ☎1756
SW towards Eindhoven.
All year.
73HEC H G LP lau A5 V2 2 2

SLUIS
Zeeland (☎01178)
Meldoorn Hoogstr 68 ☎1662
In a meadow surrounded by rows of deciduous trees.
N on the road to Zuidzande.
Apr–Sep.
5.5HEC H G L

SONDEL
Friesland (☎05140)
Sondel Beuckeswijkstr 26 ☎2300
In a dense wood.
Just off the Sondel–Rijs road.
29 Mar–Oct.
6HEC H G P lau

STEENWIJK
Overijssel (☎05210)
Kom Bultweg 25 ☎13736
Split into two sections, lying near a country house, and is surrounded by a beautiful oak forest.
The access road off the Steenwijk–Frederiksoord road is easy to miss.
Apr–15 Oct.
9.6HEC H G L lau A4 V3 5 5

STRAMPROY
Limburg (☎04956)
't Vosseven Lochstr 26 ☎1560
Turn right at the church and continue for 5 km.
Apr–Oct.
10.6HEC H G P lau A5 Vn/c 5 5

TERHORNE
Friesland (☎05668)
Oan'e Poel Buorren 1 ☎373
11 Apr–27 Sep.
1.8HEC H P lau pitch22

TERSCHELLING (ISLAND OF) See **WEST-TERSCHELLING**

TEXEL (ISLAND OF) See **COCKSDORP (DE) & HOORN (DEN)**

TIETJERK See **LEEUWARDEN**

UITDAM
Noord-Holland (☎02903)
Uitdam Zeedijk 2 ☎1433
Apr–Oct.
16HEC H G A4 V5 5 5

UTRECHT
Utrecht (☎030)
Berekuil Ariensla 5 ☎713870
On N outskirts near motorway to Hilversum.
Apr–Oct.
4.5HEC H G P P pitch21

VAASSEN
Gelderland (☎05788)
Bosrand Elspeterweg 45 ☎1343
In castle grounds.
Apr–20 Oct.
0.5HEC H G P lau A5 pitch7

VALKENBURG
Limburg (☎04406)
Europa Couberg 29 ☎13097
SW of town.
Apr–Oct.
9.7HEC H G P lau pitch25

VELSEN-ZUID
Noord-Holland (☎023)
Weltevredem ☎383726
15HEC H lau **pp**7

VENRAY
Limburg (☎04780)
Oude Barrier Maasheseweg 93 ☎82305
NE of town.
Apr–Sep.
9.8HEC H G P lau

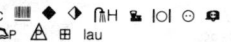

VIERHOUTEN
Gelderland (☎05771)

Saxenheim Plaggeweg 90 ☎283

1.5 km N.
All year.

40HEC ◆ ◈ H |O| ⊙ G P ⊞ lau

VIJLEN
Limburg (☎04455)

Cottesserhoeve Cottessen 6 ☎1352

All year

5.5HEC ◈ H |O| ⊙ G R P lau A4 V2 4 3–4

VLISSINGEN (FLUSHING)
Zeeland (☎01184)

Nolle Woelderenlaan 1 ☎14371

The site consists of five sections near two tennis courts.

All year.

1.7HEC ◈ H |O| ⊙ G Ⓟ lau

VOGELENZANG
Nord-Holland (☎02502)

Vogelenzang 2e Doodweg 17 ☎7014

1 km W.
Apr–15 Sep.

10HEC ◈ H |O| ⊙ G P ⊞

VOORTHUIZEN
Gelderland (☎03429)

Zanderij Hoge Boeschoterweg 96 ☎1343

Apr–Oct.

13HEC ◆ H |O| ⊙ G ⊞ lau

VROUWENPOLDER
Zeeland (☎01189)

Oranjezon Koningin Emmaweg 16 ☎1549

Well kept, between tall, thick hedges and bushes. SW of the village.

For access, drive towards Oostkapelle for approx 1.5 km, then turn N and continue for 300 m.
Apr–Oct.

5.5HEC ◈ H |O| ⊙ G R Ⓟ ⊞ lau

Zandput Vroondijk 9 ☎1651

On level ground behind sand dunes. Separate area for young people.

2 km N.
Apr–Oct.

13HEC ◈ H |O| ⊙ G ⊞ lau

WAPENVELD
Gelderland (☎05206)

Ennerveld Molenweg 2 ☎78552

On partly hilly ground in a dense forest of coniferous and deciduous trees, left off the Wapenveld–Wezep road.

For access turn off the N93 (Zwolle–Apeldoorn) in Wapenveld and drive W for 0.7 km.

All year.

12HEC ◆ H |O| ⊙ G P ⊞ lau

WASSENAAR
Zuid-Holland (☎01751)

Duinrell Duinrell 5 ☎19314

Very well maintained site with additional recreation centre which is free for campers. NW in area of same name. Some noise from aircraft. Toilets for invalids. Area restricted to cars. Naturist beach nearby.

Turn off A44 (Den Haag–Leiden) at traffic lights in Wassenaar. Follow 'Wassenaar dorp' and camping signs.
All year.

25HEC ◆ ◈ H |O| ⊙ G P lau A9 V4 5 5

WEDDE
Groningen (☎05976)

Wedderbergen Molenweg 2 ☎1673

On meadowland divided by deciduous trees and bush hedges.

On the E outskirts of the village take a narrow asphalt road, and drive N for 3.2 km. Then take Spanjaardsweg and Molenweg to the camp.
All year.

24HEC ◆ ◈ H |O| ⊙ G P lau pitch18

WEERT
Limburg (☎04950)

Ijzeren Man Herenvennenweg 60 ☎33202

Well kept with asphalt drives, in a big nature reserve with zoo, heath and forest.

Off E9.
Feb–Sep.

10.5HEC ◆ ◈ H |O| ⊙ G LP Ⓟ lau A4 V4 5 5

WEMELDINGE
Zeeland (☎01192)

Linda Oostkanaalweg 4 ☎1259

On meadowland surrounded by rows of tall shrubs.

Turn opposite bridge in town and continue 100 m, over bridge to camp.
All year.

5HEC ◈ H |O| ⊙ G lau

WESTKAPELLE
Zeeland (☎01187)

Boomgaard Domineeshofweg 1 ☎1377

A flat grassy site.

For access turn off the Middleburg road on the S outskirts of the town, then follow signs.
22 Mar–29 Sep.

4HEC ◈ H |O| ⊙ G lau

WEST-TERSCHELLING (ISLAND OF TERSCHELLING)
Friesland (☎05620)

Cnossen Hoofdweg 8 ☎2321

Several patches of meadowland, left of the road towards Formerum, and right of the forest.

For access, take the ferry from Harlingen.
Mar–Oct.

2.5HEC ◈ H |O| ⊙ G Ⓟ A5 V4 6 6

WEZEP
Gelderland (☎05207)

Heidehoek Heidehoeksweg 7 ☎1382

0.5 km W of railway station.
Apr–15 Oct.

12.5HEC ◆ H |O| ⊙ G ⊞ lau pitch24

WINSCHOTEN
Groningen (☎05970)

Burcht Bovenburen 46 ☎13290

All year.

3.5HEC ◆ ◈ H |O| ⊙ G ⊞ lau A3 V3 4 4

WORKUM
Friesland (☎05151)

It Soal Süderseleane 27 ☎1443

In front of a dyke, beside the sea (Ijsselmeer). It is a good bathing area for children.

SW towards lake.
Mar–Oct.

21HEC ◈ H |O| ⊙ G L ⊞ lau pitch30

ZEEWOLDE
Flevoland (☎03202)

Harderwold Pluvierenweg 7 ☎544

N of the Harderwijk
Apr–25 Oct.

30HEC ◈ H |O| ⊙ G P ⊞ lau pitch28

Zeewolde Dasselaarweg 1 ☎(03242)1246

Apr–Oct.

39.7HEC ◈ H |O| ⊙ G P Ⓟ lau pitch34

ZELHEM
Gelderland (☎08342)

Het Zonnetje Ruurloseweg 30 ☎1455

3 km NE.
All year.

5.5HEC ◆ ◈ H |O| ⊙ G P lau

ZEVENHUIZEN
Zuid-Holland (☎01802)

Zevenhuizen Tweemanspolder 8 ☎1654

Situated NW of the village, this site is surrounded by a wide belt of bushes.

On NW outskirts follow signs for Roerdamp. Site on right of the road beyond a car park.
Apr–Sep.

5HEC ◈ H |O| ⊙ G lau

ZOUTELANDE
Zeeland (☎01186)

Meerpaal Duinweg 133 ☎1300

On meadowland hidden behind bushy hedges at the end of a cul-de-sac.

1 km SE.
Apr–Sep.
1.2HEC lau

ZUIDWOLDE
Drenthe (☎05287)

Netherlands

Ekelenberg Slagendijk 2 ☎1356

SE of town.
All year.
12HEC P lau

ZWOLLE
Overijssel (☎038)

At **BERKUM** (1 km E)

Agnietenberg Haersterveerweg 27 ☎531530

1 km W.
Apr–Sep.
14HEC R lau

Fun on a sailboat at Westwal

NORWAY

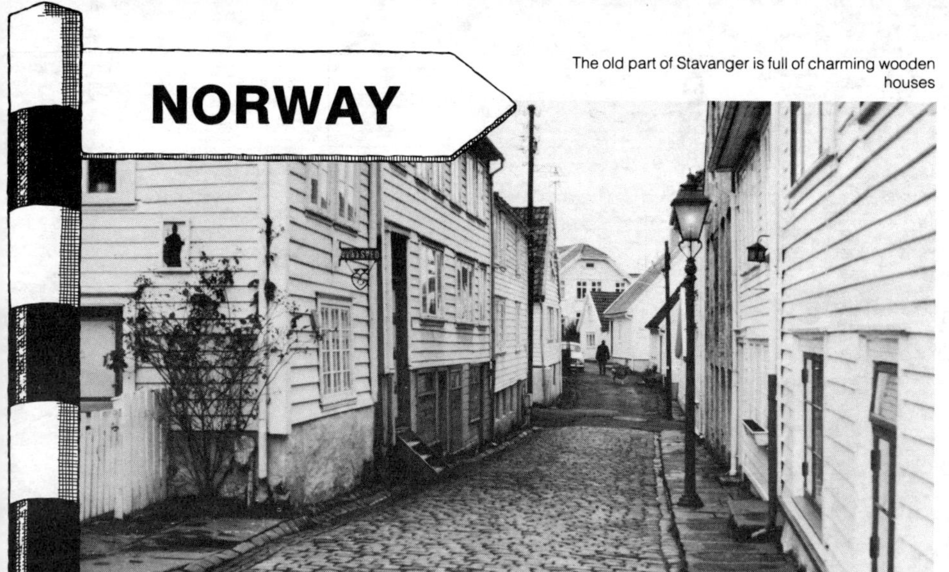

The old part of Stavanger is full of charming wooden houses

The fjords between Stavanger and Trondheim are the most outstanding features of Norway's landscape. Many of them, such as Hardanger, Sogn and Romsdal, are between fifty and a hundred miles long and they are all extraordinarily deep and surrounded by towering mountains. Much of northern Norway is beyond the Arctic Circle and experiences perpetual daylight during the summer. In the south the landscape is less stark, notably the lakes and forest around Telemark.

Despite its northerly position Norway has a favourable climate. The coastal areas have cool summers, but inland temperatures are more extreme with hot summers. Norwegian is the official language and is closely allied to Danish and Swedish and to a lesser degree Dutch, English and German. English is taught in all schools and spoken throughout Norway.

HOW TO GET THERE

Norway can be reached direct by ferry. Services operate from Newcastle to Bergen or Stavanger, or from Harwich to Kirstiansand and Oslo. Crossing times vary between approximately 21 and 36 hours. Another way of reaching Norway is by using one of the short Channel crossings to France or Belgium, then driving through the Netherlands and northern Germany to Denmark, then either using one of the direct ferry links to southern Norway or travelling via Sweden. Crossings from Harwich to Hamburg give a shorter overland journey via Germany and Denmark. The distance from the Channel ports to Oslo via Sweden is about 1,000 miles, and would normally require three overnight stops.

GENERAL INFORMATION

(see also *Things you need to know*, pages 33–64)

British Embassy/Consulates

(see also page 57)

The British Embassy together with its consular section is located at *Oslo 2* Thomas Heftyesgate 8 ☎563890/7. There are British Consulates with Honorary Consuls in Ålesund, Bergen, Harstad, Haugesund, Kristiansund (N), Kristiansand (S), Narvik, Stavanger, Troms and Trondheim.

Camping

Norway has about 700 organised campsites, all of which are officially classified. Sites are found along most main roads and there are some near Oslo, Bergen, Stavanger and Trondheim. The fjord and mountain region of west Norway is generally unsuitable for caravans and a map showing the roads affected is available from the Norwegian Tourist Board (see *Tourist information*). Sites are normally open from 15 June to 25 August, although dates do vary.

Hire Tents are not generally available for hire at sites. Huts (hytter) with accommodation for between two and six people are available on about half of the sites, outside campsites in the central mountain area, in the south, and in the west between Stavanger and Bergen. Details may be obtained from the Norwegian Tourist Board (see *Tourist information*) or Den Norske Hytteformidling, Boks 3207, Oslo 4.

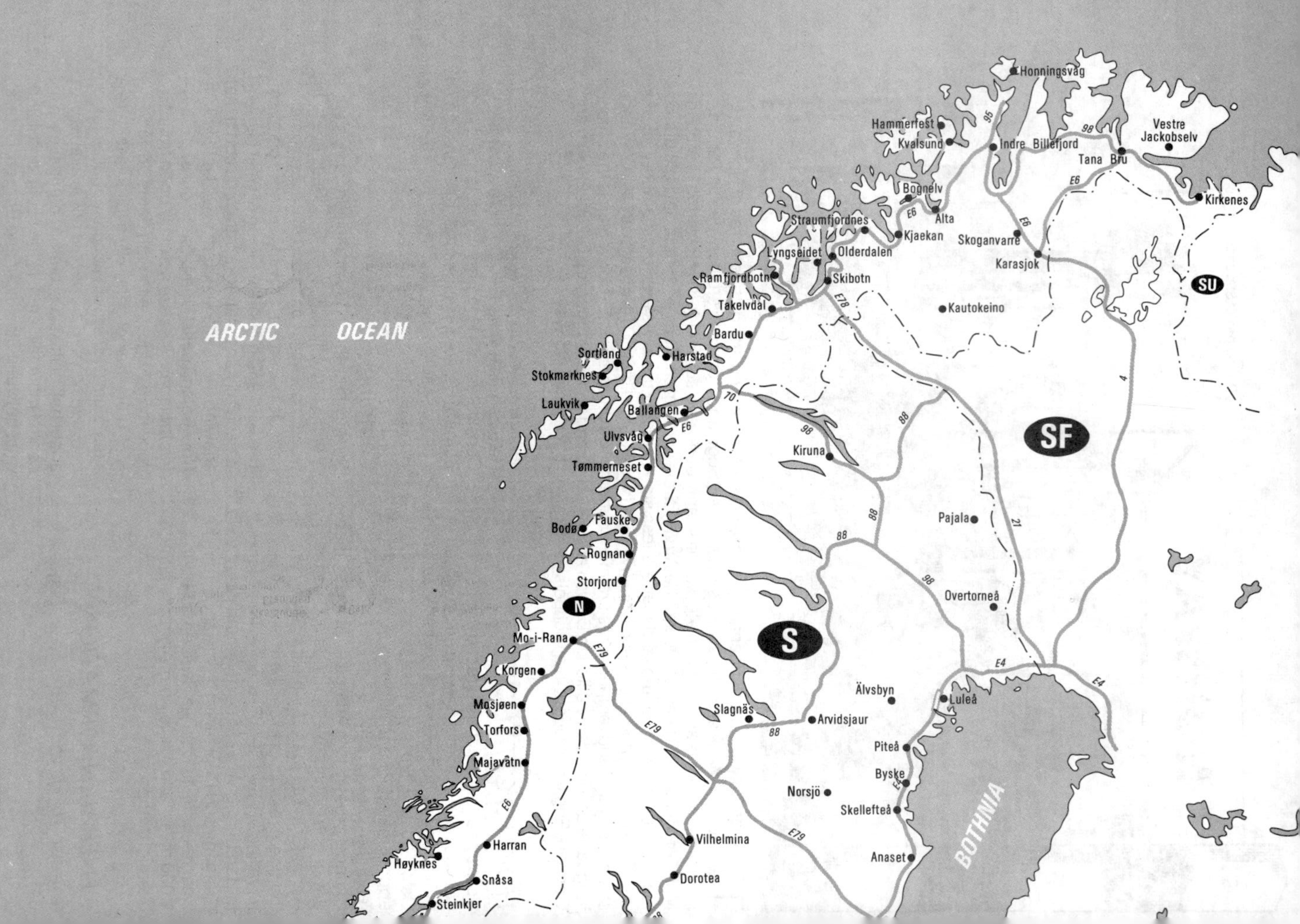
ARCTIC OCEAN
BOTHNIA
N
S
SF
SU
Honningsvåg
Hammerfest
Kvalsund
Indre Billefjord
Vestre Jackobselv
Tana Bru
Kirkenes
Bognelv
Alta
Straumfjordnes
Kjaekan
Skoganvarre
Karasjok
Lyngseidet
Olderdalen
Ramfjordbotn
Skibotn
Kautokeino
Takelvdal
Bardu
Sortland
Harstad
Stokmarknes
Laukvik
Ballangen
Ulvsvåg
Kiruna
Tømmerneset
Pajala
Fauske
Bodø
Rognan
Storjord
Overtorneå
Mo-i-Rana
Korgen
Älvsbyn
Luleå
Mosjøen
Slagnäs
Arvidsjaur
Torfors
Piteå
Majavåtn
Byske
Norsjö
Skellefteå
Harran
Vilhelmina
Anaset
Høyknes
Snåsa
Dorotea
Steinkjer
E6
E78
E79
E4
95
98
88
70
21
4

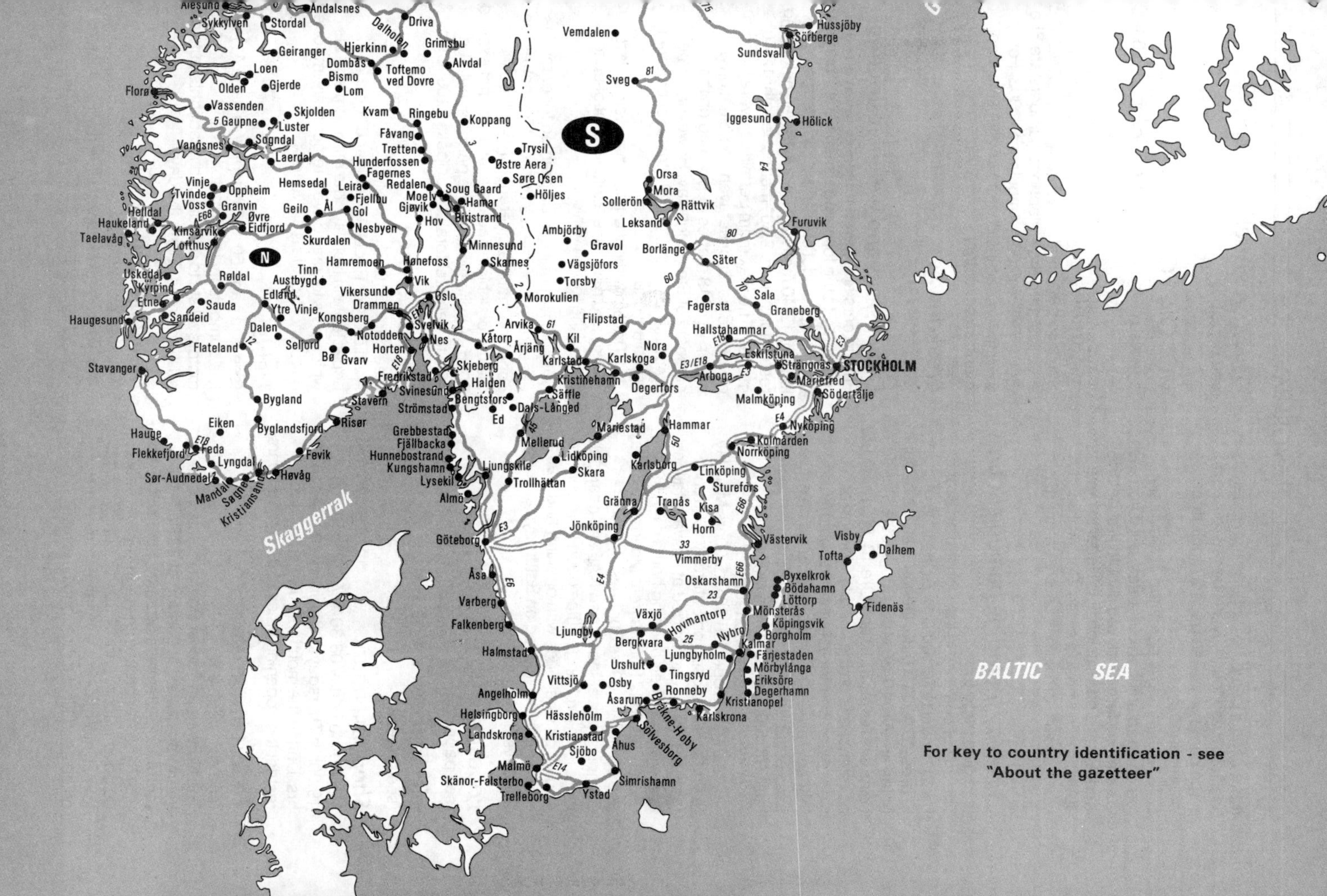

For key to country identification - see "About the gazetteer"

International camping carnet is not generally in use in Norway, but may still be requested on some campsites. See page 37 for further information.
Off-site camping is permitted in mountain regions and uninhabited areas, but if you wish to camp on farmland, you should first get the landowner's permission. It is illegal to have open fires in wooded areas. Remember to stock up with provisions before entering mountain areas.

Currency including banking hours

(see also page 57)
The unit of currency is the Norwegian Krone (*NKr*) divided into 100 *Ore*. At the time of going to press £ = *NKr*10.80. Denominations of bank notes are *NKr*10, 50, 100, 500, 1,000; standard coins are *NKr*1, 5, 10 and Ore 10, 50. There are no restrictions on the import of foreign or Norwegian currency, but it is recommended that any large amounts be declared on arrival in case of subsequent re-exportation. No more than *NKr*5,000 in notes not higher than *NKr*1,000 may be exported.

Banks are open 08.30–15.00hrs Monday to Friday and closed on Saturday. Currency may usually be exchanged at railway stations and airports. Their opening hours vary, but are usually 08.00–21.00hrs from Monday to Friday and 08.00–14.00hrs Sundays. At Bogstad Camping (a well-equipped NAF site near Oslo) there is an exchange office open from June to August on weekends with opening hours as ordinary banks, closed on Saturdays and Sundays.

Foodstuffs

(see page 60)

Medical treatment

(see page 60)

Shopping hours

Monday to Friday 08.30–17.00hrs (09.00–19.00hrs Thursdays). Saturdays 08.30–14.00 hrs. During the month of July some shops restrict their opening times to 09.00–15.00hrs.

Tourist information

(see also page 63)
The Norwegian Tourist Board maintains an information office in London at 20 Pall Mall (entrance St James's Square), SW1Y 5NE ☎01-839 6255 (recorded message service between 09.00–11.00hrs and 14.00–17.00hrs). Local tourist information is available from tourist offices and kiosks throughout Norway.

Visitor's registration

(see page 63)

MOTORING

(see also *Things you need to know*, pages 33–64)

Accidents

(see also page 46)
In Oslo emergency telephone numbers are **Fire** ☎001, **Police** ☎002, **Ambulance** ☎003. For other towns see inside front cover of the local telephone directory.

Breakdowns

(see page 48)

Dimensions and weight restrictions

Private cars and towed trailers or caravans are restricted to the following dimensions – **car** height: no restriction; width: 2.50 metres; length: 12.40 metres. **Trailer/caravan** height: no restriction; width: 2.30* metres; length: 12.40 metres. The maximum permitted overall length of vehicle/trailer or caravan combination is either 15 or 18 metres depending on the category of State Highway. However, some roads are closed to vehicle/trailer or caravan combinations.

Trailers without brakes may weigh up to 750 kg and may have a total weight of up to 50% of the towing vehicle.

*A special permit can be granted for caravans exceeding 2.30 metres but not 2.35 metres, on condition that the difference in width between the motor vehicle and caravan does not exceed 30cm. Applications for the permit should be sent to Vegdirektoratet, Postboks 8109, Oslo 1.

Driving licence

(see page 33)
A valid UK or Republic of Ireland licence is acceptable in Norway. The minimum age at which a visitor may drive a temporarily imported car or motorcycle is 17 years.

Lights

(see also page 50 and *Headlights* page 41)
It is compulsory for all motorists and motorcyclists to use dipped headlights outside built-up areas during the day.

Motoring club

(see also page 61)
The *Norwegian Motoring Club* (NAF) which has its headquarters at *0155 Oslo 1* Storgaten 2

☎(02)429400 has offices or agents in main towns. Office hours are generally 08.30–16.00hrs Monday to Friday and 08.30–13.00hrs on Saturday.

Passengers

(see also page 51)
Children under 12 are not permitted to travel in a vehicle as front seat passengers.

Petrol

(see page 61)

Roads

In southern and eastern Norway, the most important routes have modern surfaces. In the west and north, some road surfaces are oil bound (partly water bound) grit. Vehicles with a high ground clearance are more suitable on mountain roads than those with low ground clearance. As a courtesy to other road users, you should fit mudguard flaps. The roads sometimes have soft verges – a great inconvenience to motor cyclists. Watch for warning signs *Løse Veikanter* and *Svake Kanter*. In the fjord district, and often in other areas, careful and confident driving is necessary although gradients are seldom excessive and hairpin bends can usually be easily negotiated. The region is mainly unsuitable for large vehicles or caravans. There are sometimes ferry crossings and a reasonable touring maximum is 100 to 150 miles a day.

Bergen tollring experiment A pay-and-display toll system has been introduced by the local authorities to help finance improvements to the roads of Bergen. All motorists entering Bergen must now pay *NKr*5 (approximately 50p). However, visiting motorists coming by ferry from Britain to the Skoltegrunnskaien pier will not have to pay any toll on arrival.

Seat-belts

(see page 52)

Speed limits

Car
Built-up areas
50 kph (31 mph)
Other roads
80 kph (49 mph)
Motorways
90 kph (56 mph)
Car/caravan/trailer with brakes
Built-up areas
50 kph (31 mph)
Other roads
80 kph (49 mph)
Motorways
80 kph (49 mph)
Car/caravan/trailer without brakes
Built-up areas
50 kph (31 mph)
Other roads
60 kph (37 mph)
Motorways
60 kph (37 mph)

Warning triangle

The use of a warning triangle is compulsory in the event of accident or breakdown. See also *Warning triangles/Hazard warning lights* page 54.

Prices are in Norwegian Kroner
Abbreviation:
NAF Norges Automobil Forbund

ÅL

Buskerud (☎067)

Sundre ☎81326
Purpose built, well laid out site on meadowland.
1 km SW of Ål, on left bank of the river below the dam.
All year.
3.6HEC lau A8 pitch34

ÅLESSUND

Møre-og-Romsdal (☎071)

Volsdal (NAF) ☎25890
Situated at the edge of the Brei-Heissa-Fjord on extensive meadowland with boulders and trees.
1.5 km E of town centre turn off E69 to fjord.
15 May–Sep.
10HEC lau A8 Vn/c 40 25

At **GÅSEID** (5 km E on E69)

Strandcamping Prinsen ☎35204
Site with private beach on S of E69.
Jun–25 Aug.
30HEC lau A10 pitch45

ALTA

Finnmark (☎084)

Alta River ☎34353
In a level meadow without shade.
5 km S off the Kautokeino road 93, 400 m along the river bank.
All year.
1.1HEC lau

Wisløff ☎34303
Site on meadowland by Alta river.
5 km off road 93.
All year.
3HEC lau A5 pitch40

At **ELVEBAKKEN** (11 km N)

Kronstad (NAF) ☎37360
In uneven woodland with some pitches on grassland adjoining a brook.
Situated about 1 km N on E edge of town left of road 6 to Kirkenes.
Jun–Aug.
3.4HEC lau

Solvang Ungdomssenter NA ☎30477
Located partly in a pine forest and partly on open meadowland. Separated by a fence from the Altafjord.
100 m off the road 6, 6 km N of Alta centre. ➔

1.4HEC H lau sR

ALVDAL
Hedmark (065)
Gjelten Bru (NAF) 87444
5 km NW of Alvdal station, on road RV29 near River Folla.
25 May–25 Sep.
0.8HEC H G R lau A6 pitch30

ÅNDALSNES
Møre-og-Romsdal (072)
Åndalsnes (NAF) 21629
Set in beautiful surroundings.
Access from Dombås, turn left before entering town, cross Rauma Bridge, and immediately turn left into site.
15 May–15 Sep.
6.6HEC H R lau A8 pitch40

ÅROS See **SØGNE**

ÅSEN
Noord-Trøndelag (076)
Gullberget 16151
Grassy site on slight incline on E6 from which it is separated by a villa and a hedge. Partitioned by trees and shrubs.
15 May–1 Sep.
2HEC H lau L A10 pitch30

BALLANGEN
Nordland (082)
Ballangen 28297
100 m from road 6, near the sea.
All year.
8HEC H R sP lau pitch50–60

BARDU
Troms (089)
Setermoen 81558
A beautiful site in a sparse forest.
Off E6 N of Bardu near OPEL Garage.
All year.
30HEC H lau P

BIRISTRAND
Oppland (61)
Stranda (NAF) 84672
Situated on grassy banks of Lake Miosa.
From town drive N on the Lillehammer road for 3 km then turn left, NAF Sign, and continue along road 4 for 500 m. Turn right onto lake road and pass under road 4 to site.
May–Sep.
8HEC H R s lau

BISMO
Oppland
Bismo (062)14024
Situated on road 15, 18 km W of Lom.
All year.

Norway

5HEC H lau G

Skamsar (NAF) (062)14049
Apr–Oct.
1.5HEC H lau pitch50

BØ
Telemark (036)
Beverøya (NAF) 60508
Located on a wooded meadow which stretches down to the river.
1.5 km E of town and 50 m off road 36.
All year.
3HEC H lau

BODØ
Nordland (081)
Bodøsjoen 22902
Situated on the edge of Saltfjord, in close proximity to the military airfield. Beautiful views of rocky coastline, sea and mountains.
Turn off the E80 in E outskirts following signs for 1.3 km.
15 May–Aug.
3HEC H s

BOGNELV
Finnmark (084)
Altafjord (NAF) 32824
Site on slightly sloping meadow and woodland incline separated by a road from the Langfjord.
Situated on road 6.
15 May–1 Sep.
3HEC H lau s A8 pitch35

BYGLAND
Aust-Agder (043)
Bygland (NAF) 35281
Extensive natural meadowland surrounding a farm and sloping towards a lake.
1 km N of the village between road 12 and quiet bay.
20 Jun–1 Sep.
5HEC H lau

BYGLANDSFJORD
Aust-Agder (043)
Neset (NAF) 34255
A beautifully situated site, about 2.5 km N. Swimming facilities and boats for hire.
Between road 12 and E shore of Fjord.
All year.
3.5HEC H L lau A10 pitch40

DALEN
Telemark (036)
Dalen (NAF) 77100

Site located near NUH Hostel, between tributaries of Lake Bandak. Divided in 2 parts, the site lies in meadowland surrounded by woodland.
Over bridge by Tokke Vinje Sparebank.
15 May–Aug.
1.5HEC H lau L

DALHOLEN
Hedmark
Fjellsyn (NAF) (064)93082
On sandy terrain in a sparse pine forest surrounded by some bungalows, a church and a petrol station.
Turn off E6 onto road 29 and continue for 15 km.
All year.
5HEC H lau

DJUPVIK See **OLDERDALEN**

DOMBÅS
Oppland (062)
Faksfall (NAF) 41471
Consists of beautiful meadow and woodland.
The site lies 100 m above the E6, 4.5 km SE of Dombås.
All year.
1.5HEC H lau A5 pitch25

DRAMMEN
Buskerud (03)
Drammen Buskerudreien 97 (NAF) 821798
A terraced site on the left of the River Drammen. It is divided into pitches.
Turn left off the road to Kongsberg about 4 km beyond Drammen and continue for 200 m.
20 May–10 Sep.
3.6HEC H lau A11 pitch42

DRIVA
Sør-Trøndelag (074)
Granmo (NAF) 24147
On level ground between busy road and a shallow river.
50 m E6, S of Oppdal. Well signed from Myøen.
Jun–1 Sep.
H R lau A7 pitch30

Smegarden 24159
S on E6.
All year.
2HEC H R R lau pitch55–60

EDLAND
Telemark
Tallaksbru (NAF) (036)70172
Situated on undulating meadowland on both sides of the Bykle road, close to a bridge of

the same name.

150 m from junction of E76 with road 12.
Jun–Aug.

1.2HEC ◇ H ⊙ R ⊞ lau |O| G sR

EIKEN
Vest-Agder (043)
Eiken 48200
Between a cemetery and the eastern shore of Lake Lygne, partly on a peninsula.
For access turn off road 9 at church.
1.2HEC ◇ H ⊙ G R L ⊞ lau pitch55

ELVEBAKKEN See **ALTA**

ETNE
Hordaland
Etne (NAF) (047)56643
On a level meadow, surrounded by woodland and a small lake. 2 km E of E76 Odda road.
Turn left before MOBIL filling station and continue for 200 m.
May–1 Oct.
8HEC ◆ H ⊙ R ⊞ lau |O| A5 pitch30

FAGERNES
Oppland
Fagernes (NAF) (063)60510
On slightly hilly meadow on Strandafjord, surrounded by hedges and mixed woodland. Situated near bathing facilities.
Turn off E68 W of town and continue for 100 m in direction of lake.
15 May–Sep.
4HEC ◇ H ⊙ L ⊞ lau |O| A12 pitch20–45

FAUSKE
Nordland (081)
Lundhøgda (NAF) 43966
In meadowland on small hillock. Lovely views of Fauske, the fjord and surrounding hills.
Turn left off road 80 to Bodø and drive along the Erikstadveien for 1.6 km.
Jun–Aug.
1.5HEC ◇ H ⊙ ⊞ lau S pitch60

FÅVANG
Oppland
Krekke (NAF) (062)84571
Between the E6 and the river bank, 9.5 km S of Fåvang.

Norway

Jun–Aug.
1.5HEC ◇ H ⊙ L

FEDA
Vest-Agder (043)
Svindland (NAF) 52380
Located by a small, beautiful lake with high rocks.
Situated 13 km E of Flekkefjord and 800 m from the E18.
Jun–Oct.
1HEC ◆ H |O| ⊙ G L ⊞ lau A8 pitch30

FEVIK
Aust-Agder (041)
Bagatell (NAF) 47467
Beneath a 10–15 m high cliff. The site can be reached by turning sharp left on the southern outskirts of the village.
Off the E18 towards Kristiansand drive around the bay and pass Fevik Camping and the fishing harbour.
10 Jun–25 Aug.
2.4HEC ◇ H |O| ⊙ G R S ⊞ lau A10 pitch50

FJELLBU
Oppland (061)
Vasetdansen 64041
Situated in the Tisleidalen valley.
200 m W of Tisleia bridge by main road 49 Leira–Gol.
All year.
50HEC ◇ H |O| ⊙ G R R ⊞ lau pitch35–60

FLATELAND
Aust-Agder (043)
Flateland 36837
On a peninsula and is scattered with pine trees.
The entrance is on road 12, N of junction with road 45.
Jun–Aug.
1.3HEC ◆ H ⊙ R R ⊞ lau A10 pitch33

FLEKKEFJORD
Vest-Agder (043)
Egenes (NAF) 20148
4 km E by Selurvatn, 1.5 km off E18.

Jun–25 Aug.
1HEC ◇ H ⊙ R L ⊞

FLORØ
Sogn-og-Fjordane (057)
Krokane 42220
About 50 m from beach.
Jun–Aug.
6HEC ◆ H ⊙ ⊞ lau S

FREDRIKSTAD
Østfold (032)
At **KONGSTEN**
Fredrikstad (NAF) 20315
Located on eastern banks of the Glomma estuary and next to a swimming pool.
From town centre over bridge then turn right. Alternative approach from E6 Skjeberg road on road 110 to Gamlebyen then turn left.
Jun–Aug.
3HEC ◆ H |O| ⊙ ⊞ lau

FROSTA
Nord-Trøndelag
Frosta (NAF) (07)807354
Situated on meadowland which slopes towards the fjord. Next to a farm.
400 m along road 753, Breiveien–Haugen, close to the Logtun stone church (11th century).
May–Aug.
2HEC ◆ H ⊙ S ⊞ lau

GÅSEID See **ÅLESUND**

GAUPNE
Sogn-og-Fjordane (056)
Sandvik (NAF) 81153
Good views of Jostedalsbreen Glacier. About 50 m from the beach.
On road 55.
15 May–Aug.
2.5HEC ◆ H ⊙ G ⊞ lau S A10 pitch30

GEILO
Buskerud (067)
Solli Turistenter 85201
On a level meadow beside the River Usta.
100 m S of the bridge on road 8.
All year.
2HEC H |O| ⊙ ⊞ lau R pitch60

See advertisement page 332

Norway

GEIRANGER
Møre-og-Romsdal (☎071)

Geiranger (NAF) ☎63120

Situated on level meadowland between access road to holiday complex and the fjord on two sides of a brook.

Turn off at ESSO filling station and continue for 200 m past shops and Hotel Meroks.
20 May–1 Sep.

1.4HEC H lau s A7 pitch30

Vinje (NAF) ☎63017

1.5 km on road 58.
Jun–1 Sep.

1.4HEC H lau s

GJERDE
Sogn-og-Fjordane (☎054)

Gjerde ☎83154

By main road 604, 7.5 km from Nigardsbreen Glacier.
Apr–Nov.

3HEC H lau R A6 pitch16–25

GJØVIK
Oppland (☎061)

Vikodden ☎73233

On slightly sloping ground on the W bank of the Mjosa amidst tall conifers.

Access is via road 33 Minnesund road, then towards lake in Vikodden and continue for 200 m.
All year.

1.8HEC H lau L pitch70

GOL
Buskerud (☎067)

Gol (NAF) ☎74144

On both sides of road 7. The upper section consists of grassland and is surrounded by mountain huts. The lower, old part of the site, stretches down to the Hallingdalselva. This section is approached by an underpass, which is also suitable for caravans.

All year.

1HEC H R RP lau pitch60

Fossheim (NAF) ☎77316

3.3 km W, between road 7 and river.
Jan–Aug.

2.5HEC H G R R lau pitch60–65

GRANVIN
Hordaland (☎05)

Espelandsdalen ☎525167

Close to lake, by main road to Ulvik, 7 km off E68.
All year.

5HEC H lau L A5 pitch35

Granvin ☎525282

On E68.
Jun–Aug.

0.5HEC H lau L pitch55

At **ØVRE GRANVIN** (5 km N)

Seim (NAF) ☎525730

On mainly level meadowland by a stream.

Turn off the E68 NW of Seim and continue for 0.4 km towards Nesheim. Turn off over bridge.
May–Sep.

1HEC H lau L A5 pitch30

GRIMSBU
Hedmark (☎064)

Grimsbu (NAF) ☎93529

The site which is annexed to a motel is well kept and lies on lawns in a scanty wood of birch and pine trees.

Off road 29.
All year.

2HEC H G R lau L pitch60–70 (incl 2 persons)

GVARV
Telemark (☎036)

Teksten ☎64596

Surrounded by forests on a peninsula formed by a loop in the River Böelva.

16 km N of Ulefors off road 36.
15 May–Aug.

5HEC H lau

HALDEN
Østfold (☎031)

Fredriksten (NAF) ☎84032

At the top of the Fredriksten forest mountain, partly in a pine forest and partly on stony ground with a few patches of grass.

On SE outskirts of town separated from road 22 to Sweden by a river.
Jun–Aug.

H lau

HAMAR
Hedmark (☎065)

NAF Hamar ☎24490

A well-kept site amongst pine trees between the Strandvegen and E shore of Lake Mjøsa.

Well-signposted from E6 turn off and drive through Hamar, past railway station.
May–Sep.

2.7HEC H R L lau 70 A35

HAMMERFEST
Finnmark.(☎084)

Storvannet (NAF) ☎11010

Site in sparse, slightly hilly grassland. On eastern bank of small beautifully situated lake of same name.

Access via road 94 from Kvalsund. In harbour area turn right beyond bridge and continue 1 km to the site, at far end of bridge.
20 Jun–20 Aug.

1HEC H lau L

HAMREMOEN
Buskerud (☎067)

Slevika ☎47439

Turn left off road 7.1 km W of town.
All year.

5HEC H Ls lau pitch50–60

HARRAN
Nord-Trøndelag
Harran (NAF) ☎32762
On a level field at the edge of the village towards Crang.
Between the E6 and the River Namsen.
15 May–Sep.
2HEC |O| R lau

HARSTAD
Troms (☎083)
Harstad (NAF) ☎73662
In meadow on a slight incline on bank of Vagsfjord.
About 5 km S turn left off road 83 and continue for 800 m on single track access road.
All year.
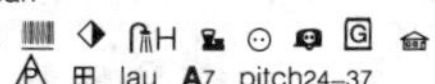
1HEC s lau A7 pitch24–37

HAUGE
Rogaland (☎044)
Amodt (NAF) ☎77171
Situated between a residential area and the River Sokndalselva on a slight slope.
Access on road 44. At church turn on to Flekkefjord road for 1.2 km and continue via Prestbru towards Midland/Titania.
May–Aug.
0.6HEC

HAUGESUND
Rogaland (☎047)
Haraldshaugen (NAF) ☎28077
3 km N of town centre.
Jun–Aug.
3HEC |O| lau s pitch40–65

HAUKELAND
Hordaland (☎05)
Lone (NAF) ☎240820
A busy site within a bungalow complex situated in a hollow on the shore of Lake Haukeland.
On the E68 approx 19 km of Bergen.
All year.
0.5HEC |O| R L lau

HEIMDAL
Sør-Trøndelag (☎07)
Sandmoen (NAF) ☎886135
Situated amidst an extensive leisure area in woodland. The terrain slopes slightly towards the road from which it is separated by a low earth bank.

Norway

10 km S of town centre and 500 m to the right of E6 coming from Oslo.
All year.
5HEC |O| lau A15 pitch50–85

At **LEINSTRAND** (5 km SW)
Øysand ☎870698
Industrial estate behind site.
Access 20 km S of Trondheim on road 65.
15 Jun–15 Aug.
10HEC lau pitch75

HELLDAL
Hordaland (☎05)
Grimen (NAF) ☎102506
Small site on W bank of Lake Grimen. Huts and rooms available.
Near Grimevannel by E68.
All year.
5HEC |O| LR lau

HEMSEDAL
Buskerud (☎067)
Rjukandefoss ☎79174
5 km NW.
0.9HEC

HJERKINN
Oppland (☎062)
Hjerkinn Fjellstue ☎42927
Signposted.
All year.
4HEC |O|

HØNEFOSS
Buskerud (☎067)
Hønefoss (NAF) Ringeriksgtn 20 ☎22903
On a level field stretching alongside a river.
Just off the E68 from Oslo and next to the stadium.
Jun–Aug.
1HEC lau |O| P A10 pitch40

HONNINGSVÅG (ISLAND OF MAGERØYA)
Finnmark (☎084)
Nordkapp (NAF) ☎75113
In stony meadowland on flat hillock within area of natural beauty. Small pond in site area.
8 km in direction of Nordkapp, close by NUH Hostel.
15 Jun–20 Aug.
5HEC |O| R Ls

HORTEN
Vestfold (☎033)
Rørestrand (NAF) ☎73340
Situated on both sides of the access road between the railway and Oslofjord.
For access turn left off road 10 on southern outskirts of town near to a large school and drive across railway towards the fjord.
May–Aug.
1.7HEC G R |O| s A6 V10 60 50

HOV
Oppland (☎061)
Lyngstrand ☎2205858
In a natural forest meadow sloping down to the lovely Randsfjord.
4.5 km N of Hov between road 35 and the Randsfjord.
15 May–Sep.
3HEC lau L

HØVÅG
Aust-Agder (☎042)
Skottevig (NAF) ☎74293
A well tended site situated in a hollow and surrounded by the lovely scenery of rocks, woods and heathland.
Turn off the E18 near the Fjord-Kro and take road 401 towards Høvåg.
May–Sep.
30HEC |O| G sP lau

HØYKNES
Nord-Trøndelag
Namsos (NAF) ☎72896
1.5 km N of Namsen bridge.
3.3HEC |O| L lau pitch35–60

HUNDERFOSSEN
Oppland (☎062)
Hunderfossen (NAF) ☎74165
On ground sloping down to the W bank of the River Lågen.
For access, leave the E6, 13 km N of Lillehammer, cross a narrow bridge, next to the reservoir, over the river and the single railway line.
All year.
|O| R lau P pitch70

Norway

INDRE BILLEFJORD
Finnmark

Stabburselv (NAF) ☎(084)64760

On stony, hilly ground, on the right bank of the river.

200 m upstream from the arched bridge.
Etr–Nov.

1.5HEC lau

KARASJOK
Finnmark

Karasjok (NAF) ☎(084)66135

On a long strip of meadow, 15 m above the left bank of the river.

Approaching from Lakselv turn right off road 96 between SHELL and MOBIL filling stations and continue 700m.
5 Jun–20 Aug.

3HEC lau

KÅTORP
Østfold

Kåtorp (NAF) ☎(02)811391

Uneven grassland on small peninsula in Lake Rödenas adjoining partially rocky coastline.

Jun–Aug.

2.5HEC

KAUTOKEINO
Finnmark

Kautokeino (NAF) ☎(084)56192

On level meadowland on southern outskirts of town.

Turn left off road 93 in direction of Enontekiö.
All year.

1.8HEC lau R

KINSARVIK
Hordaland (☎054)

Harding (NAF) ☎63182

By River Kinso 250 m from the ferry station. On left of road 7 to Geilo and at the NE outskirts of the village.

All year.

1.4HEC P lau S

KIRKENES
Finnmark (☎085)

Kirkenes ☎98028

Jun–Aug.

2.6HEC lau S

KJAEKAN
Troms (☎083)

Navitfoss ☎69743

On naturally hilly terrain with soft woodland soil scattered with boulders and low conifers. Some parts have beautiful view of the fjord.

20 km S on W arm of fjord above road 6.
Jun–Oct.

3HEC lau P

KONGSBERG
Buskerud (☎03)

Lågdalsmuseet (NAF) ☎732228

A mainly level terraced site with some steep approaches. Nearby is a museum of the same name.

Access is via the railway subway to the museum.
Jun–Aug.

1.5HEC lau R

Skavanger (NAF) ☎732031

Situated in a valley with grassy terraces above woodland.

Access is via road 8 to Geilo, 2 km N, turn right 20 m before FINA filling station.
Jun–Aug.

1.5HEC lau R

KONGSTEN See **FREDRIKSTAD**

KOPPANG
Hedmark

Trønnes-Sundfloen (NAF) ☎(064)60726

On several strips on the right bank beyond the huge suspension bridge over the River Glomma.

Access is from road 3, between the ESSO petrol station and the suspension bridge.
All year.

3HEC lau LR

KORGEN
Nordland (☎087)

Korgen (NAF) ☎91136

On level grassland on a bend of the Røssage river.

In the centre of Korgen turn right beyond the church, 700 m off E6.
Jun–Aug.

1HEC R lau A12 pitch40

KRISTIANSAND
Vest-Agder (☎042)

Roligheten ☎94759

A municipal seaside site, situated in the E outskirts of the town. The somewhat undulating site is divided into sections and lies next to the large bathing beach, near the naval barracks.

For access, leave the E18 at the road junction at the E end of the town, then continue for 1.5 km to the site next to the Ungdomsherberge. The approach is signposted after the second traffic signal.
Jun–Aug.

5HEC S A15 pitch20–50

KRISTIANSUND
Møre-og-Romsdal (☎073)

Atlanten ☎71104

In several grassland hollows on rocky hillside next to sports field, and the high school.

At entrance to the town next to Ungdoms Hostel.
Jun–Sep.

4HEC S lau A6 pitch30

KVALSUND
Finnmark (☎084)

Gargo ☎15228

On sloping meadowland reaching down to Repperfjord.

6 km E on road 94, 7.5 km from toll bridge to island of Kvalöya (Hammerfest).
Jun–Aug.

0.7HEC lau S

KVAM
Oppland (☎062)

Brendeløkken (NAF) ☎94184

On a meadow which slopes down to a river.

The approach road to the site is on the N outskirts. Turn right off the E6 Trondheim road, then continue for 300 m and pass under the railway.
5 Jun–25 Aug.

0.9HEC R lau A5 pitch21

KYRPING
Hordaland

Kyrping (NAF) ☎(047)64449

Situated in an idyllic location in the bay of the Akrafjord.

About 2 km off E76.
Apr–Oct.

4HEC S lau pitch50

LAERDAL
Sogn-og-Fjordane

Vindedal (NAF) ☎66190

Access road unsurfaced, narrow and steep.

1.5HEC

LAUKVIK
Nordland (☎088)

Sandsletta (NAF) ☎75257

On a meadow 50 m from the sea.

May–Sep.

2HEC lau Ls pitch50

LEINSTRAND See **HEIMDAL**

LEIRA
Oppland

Leira (NAF) ☎(061)32365

On a level meadow on SW outskirts behind a furniture store.

Turn left off E68 in town centre at BP filling station. Continue towards Gol, on road 49,

across bridge and turn right.
All year.

4HEC H L A12 Vn/c 40 35

LEVANGER
Nord-Trøndelag (☎076)

Mo (NAF) ☎81638

200 m left on the E6 towards Steinkyer on the S outskirts of the village.
Jun–Aug.

0.6HEC H lau

LOEN
Sogn-og-Fjordane (☎057)

Lo-Vik (NAF) ☎77619

On stony terrain, separated from the Innvikfjord by a football ground.

On both sides of road 60, opposite the big Vei Kro and the Motel.
All year.

3HEC H G sP lau A8 pitch35

Sande (NAF) ☎77659

On meadowland in beautiful location on the beach road, beyond guest house.

4.5 km S of Leon. Take Kjenndal road 3 km SE of turning off road 60 in Leon and drive to the hotel which is signposted Kafe–Husrom.
All year.

2HEC H R L lau A10 pitch35

LOFTHUS
Hordaland (☎054)

Lofthus (NAF) ☎61364

In an orchard, above the village and about 400 m above the fjord. Magnificent view of fjord, mountains and glaciers.

For access turn off road 47 N of Ullensvang, to the right then continue uphill for 1.2 km.
15 May–15 Sep.

1.2HEC H G lau sP A8 pitch44

LOM
Oppland (☎062)

Lom (NAF) ☎11220

On grassland which slightly slopes from road to River Bövra.

300 m from fork of roads 15 and 55.
All year.

1HEC H lau s

Nordal (NAF) ☎11010

In the village on undulating meadowland near the Nordal Touring Home. In a built-up area below road 15.

200 m from turning off road 55. Near ESSO filling station.
May–Sep.

3.5HEC H G lau LR pitch65

Norway

LUSTER
Sogn-og-Fjordane (☎056)

Dalsøren (NAF) ☎85436

Extensive, partly sloping meadow, on Lustrafjord.

Next to SHELL filling station below road 55.
May–Oct.

1.7HEC H lau s pitch35

LYNGDAL
Vest-Agder (☎043)

***Kvavik* (NAF)** ☎46132

By main road 43 by Lungdalsfjord, 4 km from E18 and 1.6 km from the town centre.
Jun–Aug.

4HEC H lau

Rosfjord (NAF) ☎45252

On pine covered land divided into sections by 2 m-high banks.

2 km S of village on the right of the Spangereld road and next to the beach.
All year.

8HEC H G s lau A10 pitch55

LYNGSEIDET
Troms

Lyngseidet (NAF) ☎(089)10202

On grassland on the W outskirts close to the motel of the same name.

Access from Tromsø on right below road 91,200 m from the ferry to Olderdalen.
All year.

1.2HEC H lau s A15 pitch30–75

MAGERØYA (ISLAND OF) See **HONNINGSVÅG**

MAJAVATN
Nordland

Sandvik ☎(056)81153

Grassland on slope near school and youth hostel, and facilities of which are used by campers. Views of lake and hilly countryside.

19 km N of Mosjo on E6.
Jun–15 Sep.

2HEC H lau L

MALVIK See **TRONDHEIM**

MANDAL
Vest-Agder (☎043)

Sjøsanden ☎61419

In sparse pine forest adjoining pleasant broad sandy beach.

Turn left in village off E18 to Flekkefjord after the bridge and drive W for 2 km following the signposts.
6 Jun–16 Aug.

5HEC H lau s A6 pitch75

MERÅKER
Nord-Trøndelag (☎07)

Brenna ☎810234

1.5 km E on E75.
All year.

1.5HEC H lau pitch50

Meråker ☎98048

Site on level meadow.

Entrance to site opposite parking area for the ski lift on edge of town on road E75.

1HEC H

MINNESUND
Akershus (☎06)

Storenga (NAF) ☎968352

A well-situated grassland site, sloping down to the Sund, and surrounded by trees. The sanitary installations are in the basement of a residential house. Rooms to let.

Well signposted approach road from the E6 N of the railway bridge.
15 Jun–Aug.

1.4HEC H lau G

MOELV
Hedmark (☎065)

Steinvik ☎67228

Close to the historical 'Stein-Hof' beside Lake Mjøsa.

Turn left off the E6 (Oslo–Trondheim) 1 km S of Moelv and continue for 400 m.
All year.

0.76HEC H G L lau pitch70

MO-I-RANA
Nordland (☎087)

Fågerasen ☎51530

Terraced site with fine views of the fjord and town. Situated next to the Fjelheisen cable railway station, and near the NUH Youth Hostel.

Turn off the E6 on S outskirts of VW garage towards the mountains.
Jun–Sep.
2HEC H lau A7 V30 12 20

Revelen (NAF) ☎31710

Grassland site divided up by internal paths sloping towards the river below the road. Large iron foundry above site.

Turn off E79 in direction of Täraby and continue for 1.5 km to site.
All year.
4.5HEC H R lau

MOROKULIEN
Hedmark (☎066)

Morokullen (NAF) ☎37259

In a pine forest near the Swedish border.

All year.
1.5HEC H lau P pitch40

MOSJØEN
Nordland (☎087)

Kippermoen ☎70314

On a strip of land on the eastern outskirts of the town.

On E of town off road 6 towards Hammarheim. Main approaches are well signposted.
Jun–Aug.
2.5HEC H lau P A6 pitch20–35

NES
Østfold (☎032)

Nes (NAF) ☎70176

On E bank of Oslofjord on N edge of peninsula.

Access is via Moss to Jeløy road (9 km). The site is then signposted.
May–Sep.
2.5HEC H lau A7 pitch45

NESBYEN
Buskerud

Sjong Campingsenter (NAF) ☎(067)73164

3 km N on Hønefoss–Gol road.
May–Sep.
3HEC H

NOTODDEN
Telemark (☎036)

Notodden (NAF) ☎13310

On a meadow with no shade.

Turn off the E76 on W outskirts of the town, and drive towards the airport which lies next to the site.
May–Sep.

3HEC H R A8 lau pitch35

OKSFJORDHAMN See **STRAUMFJORDNES**

OLDEN
Sogn-og-Fjordane (☎057)

Alda (NAF) ☎73138

Near bridge between main road and sea.
May–Sep.
1HEC H s lau

Gytri ☎75934

Near Oldedalen road.
May–15 Sep.
0.4HEC H lau L A5 pitch15–25

OLDERDALEN
Troms

Olderdalen (NAF) ☎(083-09611)42

On a sloping meadow. Difficult approach for caravans when wet.

To the right of the road to Alta (R6). 0.8 km N of the fishing port.
Jun–Aug.
0.7HEC H

At **DJUPVIK** (15 km N)

Lyngenfjord ☎(089)17121

Situated on sparse birch woodland with magnificent views.

9 km N of the ferry, on a knoll off road 6.
Jun–Aug.
1.5HEC H lau s

OPPHEIM
Hordaland (☎055)

Oppheim ☎22452

On E68.
All year.
0.8HEC H lau

OSLO
Oslo (☎02)

Ekeberg (NAF) ☎198568

On the south-eastern outskirts of the town, on a hill high above Oslo and has a magnificent view.

Turn off the E6 and drive towards Hamar, then at railway bridge follow signs.
15 Jun–23 Aug.
7HEC H lau pitch75

Stubljan ☎612706

On a sloping meadow with a few terraces, and is separated from the motorway by a rocky outcrop.

The access road to Oslofjord is via the E road and is about 200 m long. The access to the site is via the motorway exit Hauketo.
Jun–Aug.
2HEC lau s pitch75

ØSTRE AERA
Hedmark (☎064)

Østre Aera (NAF) ☎44911

By road 215.
All year.
6HEC H (22 Jun–Aug) P lau

ØVRE EIDFJORD
Hordaland (☎054)

Garatun ☎65911

An open, slightly sloping grassland site, partly in an orchard at a farm and nursery garden.

From Øvre Eidfjord follow road towards Hjømo. 700 m from road.
20 May–10 Sep.
2HEC H lau

Saebø (NAF) ☎65927

On a meadow that stretches from road 7 to the waters' edge.

The access road is opposite the Eidfjord Gjestgiven.
Jun–Aug.
2HEC H L

ØVRE GRANVIN See **GRANVIN**

RAMFJORDBOTN
Troms

Ramfjord ☎(083)92149

On a meadow, on the shores of the fjord.

Below road E78 about 26 km SE of Tromsø.
Jun–Aug.
2.5HEC H sR lau

REDALEN
Oppland (☎062)

Sveastrand (NAF) ☎81529

Grassy site largely covered with high conifers.

S of village, turn right (13 km N of Gjøvik) off road No. 4 direction Lillehammer and follow signs.
All year.
10HEC H LRs lau pitch70

RINDAL
Møre-og-Romsdal (☎073)

Trøknaholt (NAF) ☎66562

N on road 65.
Apr–Oct.
0.7HEC H R lau A6 pitch30

RINGEBU
Oppland (☎062-86700)

Elstad (NAF) ☎80071

On a slightly sloping meadow at the river bank, and includes many mountain huts. The buildings, sanitary block and maintenance building moderate the traffic noise from E6.

The access to the site is at the signpost Kirknaer 1; 4 km S of Ringebu on E6.
Jun–20 Aug.

4.5HEC H lau R

Skjeggestad (NAF) ☎80063

Between the E6 and the slopes of a mountain 1 km S of the village centre and near the BP petrol station. The entrance is near a small, black wooden church with white doors.
Jun–Sep.

1HEC H lau

RISØR

Aust-Agder (☎041)

Sorlandet (NAF) ☎45080

Above the fjord and surrounded by forest.

Access is from the E18 via road 411 towards Laget, then another 6 km to the site.
15 May–Aug.

6HEC H lau s pitch50–80

ROGNAN

Nordland (☎081)

Rognan (NAF) ☎90136

On flat meadowland on edge of Saltdalofjord.

In town turn left off E6 opposite church.
All year.

0.6HEC H s lau pitch55

RØLDAL

Hordaland (☎054)

Røldal ☎47133

A level, grassy site with no shade. Rows of bungalows alongside the road.

Turn off the E76 in the village, after the SHELL filling station, in the direction of the stave church. The site lies beyond the church.
All year.

4HEC H R A6 pitch25

Norway

Saltvoll (NAF) ☎47245

Near church and farm. In a fairly level meadowland adjoined by woodland on one side and cemetery on the other.

In village turn off E76 after SHELL filling station and continue for 300 m in direction of stave church.
All year.

2.5HEC H lau A6 pitch30

SANDEID

Rogaland

Sandeid (NAF) ☎(047-61)126

Situated on fairly level meadow next to the school.

Located 1 km from town centre on road 514 to Ølen on NW outskirts.
All year.

0.4HEC H lau s

SAUDA

Rogaland (☎044)

Sauda ☎(04)781257

3.5 km from centre of Saudafjord.
All year.

2HEC H lau pitch50–60

SELJORD

Telemark

NES Motell og Camping ☎(036)50153

Off the E76 on the NW shore of Lake Seljord. The sandy beach and the bay are very suitable for children.

Access is indicated by a large signpost near 'Mat-Bui', on the S outskirts of the village.
mid Apr–15 Sep.

3HEC H lau

Sanden (NAF) ☎932

On sloping meadowland by eastern shore of Seljordvatnet.

9 km SE on road V36.

0.8HEC H L

SKARNES

Hedmark (☎066)

Sandgrund ☎63631

All year.

1HEC H R lau pitch45–65

SKIBOTN

Troms (☎089)

Skibotn (NAF) ☎15277

A mainly sandy site with no shade. Fenced off from the Lyngenfjord. Beautiful views of mountains and glaciers.

At N end of town on road E6.
May–Sep.

3.5HEC H lau s A6 pitch27

SKJEBERG

Østfold (☎031)

Høysand (NAF) ☎68125

The site, which slopes towards the sea, lies on either side of a secondary road.

2 km off E6.
Jun–Aug.

1.6HEC H lau s pitch80–90

SKJOLDEN

Sogn-og-Fjordane

Bolstad (NAF) ☎(056)86636

0.5 km N of road 55 and the village centre, near the ridge over the river, where it flows into the fjord.
5 Jun–15 Sep.

4HEC H s

Nymoen ☎(056)86603

On two large terraces, in a splendid setting, overlooking the S shore of the Eidsvatnet.

The entrance is near the BP petrol station, 0.3 km N of the bridge.
15 May–15 Sep.

0.6HEC H lau A7 pitch30

SKOGANVARRE
Finnmark
Skoganvarre ☎(084)64846
Overnight accommodation within the complex of holiday bungalows with the required facilities, on the Orrevatnet.
On road 96 (Lakselv–Karasjok) 26 km S of Lalselv.
All year.
0.8HEC L pitch30–60

SKURDALEN
Buskerud (☎067)
Skurdalen (NAF) ☎88717
On two nicely laid-out terraces with a beautiful view of the surrounding mountains.
Off road 8 in village next to ESSO petrol station.
All year.
6HEC H L lau pitch50

SNÅSÅ
Nord-Trøndelag (☎077)
Vegset ☎52930
Strip of meadowland gently sloping down to the lake shore.
On NW shore of Lake Snåså by road fork E6/763.
May–Sep.

2HEC H lau L pitch35–45

SOGNDAL
Sogn-Fjordane
Stedje (NAF) ☎(056)71012
On road 5 at the centre of Sogndal.
20 May–Aug.
2HEC H lau s A22

SØGNE
Vest-Agder
At **ÅROS** (3 km S)
Åros (NAF) ☎(042)66411
Partially meadow and woodland site with long level sandy beach surrounded by boulders.
Turn off E18, 15 km W of Kristiansand in direction of Vegsbygd onto road 456 and follow signs.
All year.
6HEC H s lau

SØR-AUDNEDAL
Vest-Agder (☎042)
Furuholmen (NAF) ☎(043)56598
On a small peninsula near the harbour and fishing port. Some pitches are on the rock and cannot be reached by car.
Turn off the E18 in Vigeland, from there continue in direction of Lindesnes (road 460) and continue 4 km along river.
Jun–Aug.
2.5HEC H s lau A10 pitch45

Norway

SØRE OSEN
Hedmark
Osensjøen Turistsenter (NAF) ☎(064)54006
An undulating grassy site.
E of Lake Osensjøen on road 25 along a very narrow track with bad surface.
All year.
0.7HEC H L lau

SORTLAND
Nordland
See also **STOKMARKNES**
Sortland (NAF) ☎(088)22578
In a small meadow within the village.
Turn left (from direction of Stokmarknes) off road 19 by the SAAB garage. Alternatively the site is approx 1.5 km S of the bridge linking the island.
May–Sep.
0.3HEC H lau P A8 pitch25–35

SOUG GAARD
Hedmark (☎065)
Soug (NAF) ☎54009
Site on grassy incline, facing S.
2.5 km NW of Hamar, turn off E6 in direction of Korslund.
All year.
3HEC H lau pitch55

STAVANGER
Rogaland (☎045)
Mosvangen (NAF) ☎532971
On sloping meadowland beside Lake Mosvangen. The site is divided into many sections by groups of trees and drives.
Turn left off the E18 from Oslo, after tunnel, take 'Ullandhang' exit and follow signs for 1 km.
Jun–Aug.
1.5HEC H lau s pitch40–65

STAVERN
Vestfold (☎034)
Anvikstranda ☎95927
Off road 301 from Naverfjord towards Nevlunghavn then turn left 7 km SW of Stavern.
May–Aug.
6HEC H lau s pitch75

STEINKJER
Nord-Trøndelag (☎077)
Guldbergaunet (NAF) ☎62045
Well-tended municipal site by the River Ogna.
Turn into road 762 in direction of Ogndal 100 m N of MOBIL filling station and in 1 km turn left to site 300 m beyond football ground.
All year.
4HEC H lau pitch30–60

STJØRDALSHALSEN
Nord-Trøndelag (☎07)
Hognes Gård (NAF) ☎824506
2 km on E76 at Hognes Farm.
Apr–Oct.
2HEC H lau

STOKMARKNES
Nordland
See also **SORTLAND**
Stokmarknes (NAF) ☎(088)52022
In a small meadow surrounded by birch trees at the foot of a steep mountain slope.
1 km S of village off road 19.
Jun–Sep.
1HEC H lau s

STORDAL
Møre-og-Romsdal
Stordal (NAF) ☎(071)78151
On even meadowland and divided in two by a small pine wood, adjoining large assembly shed. Idyllic situation between mountains.
About 400 m E of ferry station.
Etr–Sep.
1.5HEC H lau s pitch55

STØREN
Sør-Trøndelag (☎075)
Støren (NAF) ☎31470
In a park-like setting next to the River Gaula. The sites lies in the S part of the town.
For access turn off the E6 and follow the road towards Folstad, the site is within 0.7 km, across the river bridge and next to the railway line. The approach road is not suitable for caravans.
15 Jun–Aug.
2.5HEC H

STORFJORD
Nordland
Polar (NAF) ☎Rognan 703
On level meadow on woodland incline in pleasant mountain area.
About 300 m beyond the bridge to the right of E6 to Fauske.
1HEC H

STRAUMFJORDNES
Troms
At **OKSFJORDHAMN** (5 km N)
Sandnes (NAF) ☎(083)64915
On a raised plateau and meadowland which slopes gently down towards Straumfjord.
10 km NE of Storslett on the Olderdalen-Alta road (E6).
20 May–5 Sep.

3HEC H s lau A8 pitch25

SVELVIK
Vestford
Homannsberget (NAF) (03)772563
Between a 20 m-high rock and the marshy shores of Drammen Fjord.
1 km S of village off road 319.
May–Aug.
3HEC H lau |O| s

SYKKYLVEN
Møre-og-Romsdal (071)
Sjøbakken (NAF) 51374
1.5 km S on road 60.
May–Aug.
0.4HEC H G lau s

TÆLAVÅG
Hordaland (05)
Tælavåg Hytte (NAF) 337710
On meadowland above a wild and lonely rocky coastline with quiet bays and islands.
15 Apr–15 Sep.
1.3HEC H |O| R lau s

TAKELVDAL
Troms
Takelv (NAF) (089)35114
Divided into sections by groups of birch trees and lies by the river, partly on a terrace. Surrounded by wooded hills, mountains, and meadows.
1 km E of Olsberg to the right of the E6, Narvik-Vollan, road.
Jun–Aug.
2HEC H lau R

TANA BRU
Finnmark (085)
Tana Bru (NAF) 28198
On terraced meadowland sloping towards the left bank of the river.
Left of road 6 towards Kirkenes, just before the suspension bridge.
Jun–Aug.
2.5HEC H |O|

TINN AUSTBYGD
Telemark (036)
Sandviken (NAF) 98173
100 m from lake.
All year.
3HEC H lau LR pitch50–55

TOFTEMO VED DOVRE
Oppland (62)
Toftemo (NAF) 40045
Occupying a wide stretch of land, this site is behind the Toftemo Guesthouse.
About 2 km NW of Dovre between the E6 and the River Lågen.
All year.

Norway

3HEC H |O| P lau R A10 pitch25–40

TØMMERNESET
Nordland
Fjelltun (NAF) (081)72930
Below a mountain, sloping slightly towards Sandnesvatnet.
To the left of road 6 (Bonnåsjoen-Bognes). 6 km N of signpost to Kråkmo.
10 Jun–20 Aug.
1HEC H R lau

Kråkmo (NAF) (081)72922
On meadowland, by the Youth Hostel, separated by road E6 from Fjerdevatnet.
Between E6 and a wooded hillock.
Jun–Aug.
1HEC H LR lau pitch35

TRETTEN
Oppland (062)
Magell (NAF) 76322
A widespread meadow site with asphalt drives. Fishing free of charge for campers.
Jun–Aug.
5HEC H |O| G R L lau

TROFORS
Nordland (087)
Fellingfors 81312
In a grassy valley on the right bank of the River Vefsna. No caravan trailers.
2 km N of the E6/73 road fork by inn of the same name.
Jun–Aug.
0.3HEC H lau R

TRONDHEIM
Sør-Trøndelag (075)
At **MALVIK**
Storsand Gård (NAF) 976360
A terraced site on a peninsula among wooded hills.
12 km E between E6, a railway cutting and fjord.
May–Oct.
10HEC H |O| G s lau

TRYSIL
Hedmark
Klara (NAF) (064)50856
Undulating meadow on Trysil river with view of Trysil mountain.
Access from road 26, 5 km N of Nybergsund to E bank of river.
All year.

5HEC H |O| R lau |O|

TVINDE
Hordaland
Tvinde (05)516919
All year.
1.2HEC H G R lau R A5 pitch40

ULVSVÅG
Nordland
Ulvsvåg (NAF) Hamarøy 2173
Situated in a pleasant bay in a small pine forest.
In village centre turn off at Ulvsvåg-Gjestgiveri.
1.4HEC H |O| s

USKEDAL
Hordaland (054)
Rabben (NAF) 86150
At S end of village past the bridge and church turn towards the fjord.
All year.
1.5HEC H G s lau |O| R

VANGSNES
Sogn-og-Fjordane
Solvang Vangsnes (NAF) (56)96620
In an orchard, on an incline between the ferry station and Fridtjovparken.
Access from quay in direction of Fridtjovdenkmal then continue for 100 m.
15 May–15 Sep.
2.5HEC H lau s

VASSENDEN
Sogn-og-Fjordane (057)
Jolstraholmen (NAF) 27135
Partially on an island in fast flowing river. Between the road and the right bank of the river, above an old picturesque bridge.
Access 6.8 km NE of road fork in Moskog.
All year.
1.8HEC H |O| RP lau A10 pitch35

VESTRE JAKOBSELV
Finnmark (085)
Vestre Jakobselv (NAF) 56064
In meadowland close to a mission building.
500 m from road 98 towards Jakobselvdal.
Jun–Aug.
1HEC H |O| R

VIK
Buskerud
Vik (NAF) (067)39240
N of town 11 km SW of Hønefoss.
Apr–Sep.
7HEC H |O| G L lau pitch75

Norway

VIKERSUND
Buskerud (☎03)

Natvedt (NAF) ☎787355

Situated in meadowland opposite the harbour amidst birch trees.

For access turn off road 35 in Vikersund and continue over the bridge onto road 284 to Sylling then onwards for 2 km along lakeside.
13 May–12 Sep.
2HEC lau pitch35–50

VINJE
Hordaland (☎055)

Myrkdalen (NAF) ☎22735

Meadowland sloping fairly steeply towards the Myrkdalelva. High waterfall about 70 m above.

6 km N of road fork E68 and 570 at Vinge.
Jun–Aug.
0.6HEC lau LR A6 pitch28

VOSS
Hordaland (☎055)

Voss (NAF) ☎511597

Splendidly situated beside Lake Vangs, partly on meadowland and partly in sparse pine forest.

Take E68 towards Kvanndal, turn towards lake and continue 600 m.
All year.
1.2HEC G R lau s

YTRE VINJE
Telemark (☎036)

Groven (NAF) ☎71421

Set on three terraces above a brook and surrounded by trees. Idyllic Telemark scenery.

The site is located 100 m to the right and below road 37 to Sandvika. It is 300 m N of the E76 'X' roads.
20 May–Sep.
8HEC H (20 Jun–10 Aug) lau pitch50

By horse and coach to see the Briksdal glacier

PORTUGAL

Diana's temple at Évora, built by the Romans in ancient times

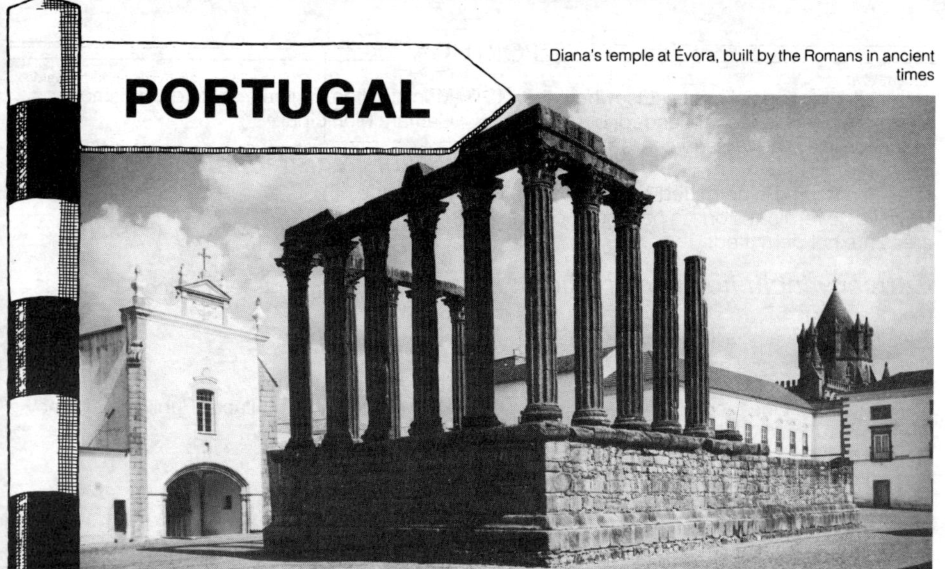

A relatively small country lying in the south western corner of the Iberian peninsula, Portugal's only land frontier is the Spanish border in the east. The country is, perhaps, best known for its five hundred miles of coastline. The Algarve in the extreme south is one of the finest stretches of coastline in Europe, with unique caves and a remoteness which has been conserved by the lack of development in the area. Inland the cool valleys and pastures of the Tagus contrast sharply with the wooded mountain slopes of the Minho area in the north.

Generally the country enjoys a mild climate with the Algarve being very hot in the summer. The language is Portuguese, which was developed from Latin and closely resembles Spanish.

HOW TO GET THERE

The usual approach to Portugal is via France and Spain, entering Spain on the Biarritz to San Sebastian road at the western end of the Pyrénées. The distance from the Channel ports to Lisboa (Lisbon), the capital is about 1,300 miles, a distance which will require three or four night stops. The driving distance can be shortened by using one of the car-sleeper services from Boulogne or Paris to Biarritz, or Paris to Madrid. Alternatively you can ship your vehicle to Spain by the Plymouth to Santander car ferry then travel onwards by road. Santander to Lisboa is about 550 miles and this will require one or two night stops.

See page 349 for location map

GENERAL INFORMATION

(see also *Things you need to know*, pages 33–64)

British Embassy/Consulates

(see also page 57)

The British Embassy together with its consular section is located at *1296 Lisboa Cedex* 35–37 Rua de São Domingos à Lapa ☎661122/47/91. There is a British Consulate in Oporto and British Consulate with Honorary Consul in Portimão.

Camping

Portugal has about 140 campsites most of which are on the coast. There are about 16 Orbitur parks in the country which are privately owned and of a high standard, as indeed are the municipal sites. Orbitur sites are open throughout the year and most of them offer fully equipped bungalows which accommodate four people. A booklet containing details of officially classified sites is produced by the Direccão Geral de Turismo, Palácia Fox, Praça dos Restauradores, Lisbon ☎(01)363314. The Oporto office is at Praça D Joao 125 ☎(02)27556 and Coimbra office is at Largo da Portagem. Otherwise ask for Comissão Municipal de Turismo, Junta de Turismo or Câmara Municipal.

International camping carnet is compulsory on campsites belonging to the Federaçaö Portuguesa de campismo and for camping

clubs offering special prices. Elsewhere the camping carnet is recommended, but no reduction in the advertised charge can be expected.
Off-site camping is permitted but not advisable. However, overnight stops in parking and rest areas are not permitted.

Currency including banking hours

(see also page 57)
The unit of currency is the Escudo (*ESc*) divided into 100 *Centavos*. It is sometimes written with the dollar sign *eg* 1$50 (one escudo fifty centavos). One thousand escudos are known as 1 *Conto*. At the time of going to press £ = *Esc*226. Denominations of banks notes are *ESc* 100, 500, 1,000, 5,000; standard coins are *ESc* 1, 2½, 5, 20, 25, 50 and *Centavos* 50. There are no restrictions on the import of foreign currency, but amounts in excess of *ESc*100,000 must be declared on arrival. It is prohibited to import more than *ESc*50,000 in Portuguese currency. Any amount of foreign currency may be exported provided it was declared on entry, but no more than *ESc*50,000 in Portuguese currency may be exported.

Banks are open Monday to Friday from 08.30–11.45hrs and 13.00–14.45hrs. During the summer currency exchange facilities are usually provided throughout the day in main tourist resorts, at frontier posts, airports and in some hotels.

Foodstuffs

(see page 60)

Medical treatment

(see page 60)

Shopping hours

Shops are usually open Monday to Friday 09.00–13.00hrs and 15.00–19.00hrs and Saturdays 09.00–13.00hrs.

Tourist information

(see also page 63)
The Portuguese National Tourist Office, New Bond Street House, 1/5 New Bond Street (above National Westminster Bank, entrance in Burlington Gardens opposite Burlington Arcade), London W1Y 0NP ☎01-493 3873, will be pleased to assist you with information regarding tourism. An office of the Direccão Geral de Turismo and local information offices will be found in most provincial towns under this name or one of the following: Comissão Municipal de Turismo, Junta de Turismo or Câmara Municipal.

Visitors registration

(see page 63)

MOTORING

(see also *Things you need to know*, pages 33–64)

Accidents

(see also page 46)
Fire, police and **ambulance** Public emergency service ☎115

Breakdowns

(see page 48)

Dimensions and weight restrictions

Private **cars** and towed **trailers** or **caravans** are restricted to the following dimensions – height: 4 metres; width: 2.50 metres; length: 12 metres. The maximum permitted overall length of vehicle/trailer or caravan combination is 18 metres.

There are no weight restrictions governing the temporary importation of trailers into Portugal. However, it is recommended that the following be adhered to – weight (unladen): up to 750kg if the towing vehicle's engine is 2,500cc or less; up to 1,500kg if the towing vehicle's engine is between 2,500cc and 3,500cc; up to 2,500kg if the towing vehicle's engine is more than 3,500cc.

Driving licence

(see also page 33)
A valid UK or Republic of Ireland licence is acceptable in Portugal. The minimum age at which a visitor may drive a temporarily imported car or motorcycle (over 50cc) is 18 years. See also *Speed limits*.

Lights

(see page 50 also *Headlights* page 41)

Motoring club

(see also page 61)
The *Autómovel Club de Portugal* (ACP) which has its headquarters at *Lisboa 1200* Rua Rosa Araújo 24 ☎563931 has offices in a number of provincial towns. ACP offices are normally open 09.00–12.45hrs and 13.00–16.45hrs Monday to Friday; English and French are spoken. Offices are closed on Saturday and Sunday.

Passengers
(see also page 51)
It is recommended that children do not travel in a vehicle as front seat passengers.

Petrol
(see also page 61)

Roads
Main roads and most of the important secondary roads are good, as are the mountain roads to the north-east. A leaflet entitled '*Road Conditions in Spain and Portugal*' is available to AA members.

Seat-belts
(see page 52)

Speed limits
Car
Built-up areas
60 kph (37 mph)
Other roads
90 kph (56 mph)
Motorways
min 40kph (24 mph)
max 120 kph (74 mph)

Car/caravan/trailer
Built-up areas
50 kph (31 mph)
Other roads
70 kph (43 mph)
Motorways
90 kph (56 mph)
There is a minimum speed limit of 40 kph (24 mph) on motorways, except where otherwise signposted. Visitors to Portugal who have held a full driving licence for less than one year are restricted to driving at a top speed of 90 kph (56 mph). They must also display a yellow disc bearing the figure '90' at the rear of their vehicle (obtainable from ACP frontier offices at Valenca, Vilar Formoso and Caia). Leaflets giving details in English are handed to visitors at entry points.

Warning triangles
The use of a warning triangle is compulsory in the event of accident or breakdown. The triangle must be placed on the road 30 metres (33yds) behind the vehicle and must be clearly visible from 100 metres (109 yds). See also *Warning triangles/Hazard warning lights* page 54.

Prices are in Portuguese Escudos
Abbreviation:
r rua

ALBUFEIRA
Algarve (☎0089)
Albufeira ☎53851
All year.

See advertisement page 344

ALCANTARILHA
Algarve (☎082)
Turismovel-Parque Campismo de Canelas ☎32612
All year.
7.5HEC lau sP **A**200 **V**180 240 **A**190

ALCOBAÇA
Estremadura (☎062)
CM ☎(012)42265
Terraced hill site with tall eucalyptus trees overlooking the town. Divided into pitches and partly bordered by hedges and flower beds.
Turn off by-pass (N8) in NE outskirts at large roundabout and turn towards hills at covered market.
All year.

ALJEZUR
Algarve (☎082)
Vale de Telha ☎72444
All year.
6HEC lau sP L **A**140 **V**110 150 **A**115

ALMORNOS
Estremadura
CM de Almornos CCL ☎9273960
In woods from Caneças.
All year.
6HEC P lau

AMARANTE
Douro Litoral (☎055)
Parque dos Frades ☎422133
Long narrow terraced site above river.
Turn right just before the concrete bridge over River Tamega (at Km61) and continue for 160 m.
All year.
0.4HEC R lau **A**60 **V**80 100 **A**50

ANGEIRAS See **MATOSINHOS**

ARGANIL
Beira Litoral (☎035)
CM de Arganil ☎22850
All year.
lau sR **A**130 **V**100 140 **A**130

CALDAS DA RAINHA
Estremadura (☎062)
Orbitur Parque D Leonor ☎22367
Long narrow site on wooded hill.
300 m from N8 on S outskirts.
16 Jan–15 Nov.
4HEC lau **A**320 **V**235 320–460 **A**200–460

CAMINHA
Minho (☎058)
Orbitur Mata do Camarido ☎921295
On undulating sandy ground with trees.
Turn off N13 at Km89.7 and drive W, along the Rio Minho for about 800 m, then turn left
All year.
3HEC lau sR **A**320 **V**235 320–460 **A**200–460

Portugal

CHAVES
Tras-Os-Montes Alto Douro (☎0506)

San Roque ☎22733

Between the Largo de S Roque road and the Rio Tamega. Divided into pitches and scattered with lawns, flower beds, hedges and trees.

From Verin turn right along Largo da Madlena for 150 m and turn right.
All year.

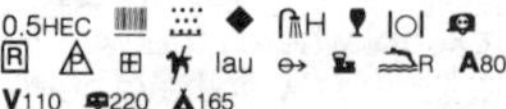

COSTA DE CAPARICA
Estremadura (☎01)

Obitur ☎2900661

1 km N turn right at Km9.9.
All year.

7.2HEC ◆ H lau S A320 V235 320–460 200–460

ÉVORA
Alto Alentejo (☎066)

Orbitur ☎25190

2 km S right of road near Km94.5
All year.

FIGUEIRA DA FOZ
Beira Litoral (☎033)

CM ☎23116

In a sandy depression, on a hill, among pine trees and flower beds. Tennis courts and facilities for volleyball and basketball. Becomes very crowded, sometimes full, during August

Turn left off N109 at Km116, sit 1 km, signposted.

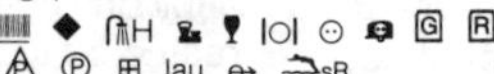

Ⓟ ⊞ lau sR

Orbitur ☎31492

In a pine forest on level sandy ground.

Off the N109 at Km122.1 signed 'Matas Nacionals' 4 km after the village, and drive W for 500 m.
16 Jan–15 Nov.

6HEC ◆ H G ⊞ lau sP A320 V235 320–460 200–460

GUARDA
Beira Alta (☎071)

Orbitur ☎21264

In an enclosed area within a municipal park on top of Guarda Hill.

At Km177, on the NW outskirts of the town, turn left off the N16 Porto road and drive uphill for about 500 m.
16 Jan–15 Nov.

2HEC ◆ H G ⊞ lau P A320 V235 320–460 200–460

GUINCHO
Estremadura

Orbitur ☎2851014

On hilly ground amidst a pine wood in the Parque du Guincho, near the Boca do Inferno.

4 km W of Cascais at Km98, turn right and follow road no 247–6 for 1 km.
All year.

7HEC ◆ H G R ⊞ lau sP A320 V235 320–460 200–460

LISBOA (LISBON)
Estremadura (☎01)

CM Monsanto ☎704413

Park like site on flat hill. Metalled interior roads and pitches.

Turn off motorway at KmV2/111 towards Estoril and follow signposts.
All year.

38HEC ◆ H G P ⊞ lau A180 V120 270 180

MATOSINHOS
Douro Litoral

At **ANGEIRAS** (12 km N)

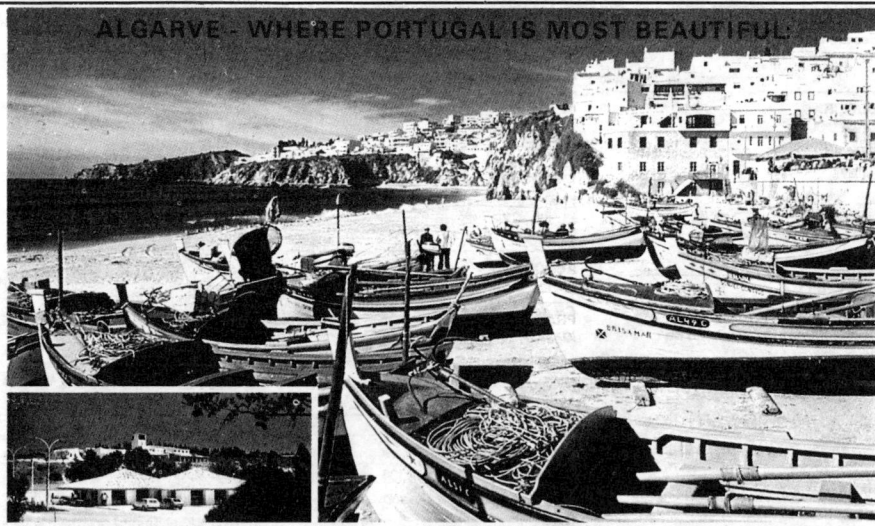

CM Matosinhos ☎9270571

A modern, well-kept site in a pine wood on a hill overlooking the sea.

W off the N13 at the X-roads at Km12.1, E of Vila do Pinheiro and towards the sea for 5 km.
All year.

7.7HEC H s

MONTE GORDO
Algarve (☎081)

CM Monte Gordo ☎44188

2 km from Km154.7 on N125.

4HEC H lau s

NAZARÉ
Estremadura (☎062)

Orbitur Valado ☎51111

300 m E of village, S of road 8–4 Nazaré-Alcobaca.
16 Jan–15 Nov.

7HEC H lau s A320 V235 320–460 200–460

OEIRAS
Estremadura

CM ☎2430330

Between Parque Jardin and station.
2 May–Oct.

1.5HEC H lau s A60 V60 90–120 42–90

OPORTO See **PORTO**

PALHEIROS DE MIRA
Beira Litoral

Orbitur ☎(031)47234

Site lies in a dense forest.

N off the N334 at Km2, towards Videira, opposite a road fork.
16 Jan–15 Nov.

3HEC H lau sR A320 V235 320–460 200–460

PENHA
Minho

Parque de Campismo de Penha ☎414936

Portugal

Terraced site with many grass pitches.

6 km SE.
All year.

1.4HEC H P lau

PENICHE
Estremadura (☎062)

CM ☎72529

On sandy hillock, partly wooded 0.5 km from sea.

2 km E.
All year.

12.6HEC H lau s A60 V60 130 60–100

PORTALEGRE
Alto Alentejo (☎045)

Orbitur-Quinta da Saude ☎22848

3.4 km W.
16 Jan–15 Nov.

2HEC H lau A320 V235 320–460 200–460

PORTO (OPORTO)
Douro Litoral (☎02)

Parque de Campismo de Prelada r Monte dos Burgos ☎62616

Slightly sloping site in park of old manor house.

Well signposted from town centre.

10HEC H

PRAIA DA AREIA BRANCA
Estremadura

CM ☎42199

Level and dusty section for tourers.

3.5 km NW and 200 m from sea.
All year.

2.5HEC H lau s

PRAIA DA LUZ
Algarve (☎082)

At **VALVERDE**

Parque de Turismo Valverde ☎69215

Well-equipped site with children's playground and tennis courts.

Off N125 Lagos–Cape St Vincent road. 4 km from Lagos.
All year.

12.5HEC H P lau s A260 V260 300 280

PRAIA DE SALEMA See **VILA DO BISPO**

QUARTEIRA
Algarve (☎089)

Orbitur ☎35238

A terraced site at the top of a hill.

Off M125 in Almoncil and follow signs to Quarteira. About 500 m before reaching the sea turn left into the camp.
All year.

11HEC H lau sP A320 V235 320–460 200–460

SAN MARTINHO DO PORTO
Estremadura (☎062)

Colina do Sol ☎98763

May–Sep.

8.5HEC H lau s

SÃO JACINTO
Beira Litoral

Orbitur ☎(034)48284

In a dense pine wood seawards from the uneven, paved road from Ovar which runs alongside the lagoon.

1.5 km away from the sea.
16 Jan–15 Nov.

3HEC H lau sR A320 V235 320–460 200–460

SÃO PEDRO DE MUEL
Estremadura (☎044)

Orbitur ☎59168

On a hill amidst pine trees.

Off road No. 242–2 from Marinha Grande at the roundabout near the SHELL petrol

station on the E outskirts of the village and drive N for 100 m.
All year.
7HEC H G R lau s A320 V235 320–460 200–460

SETÚBAL
Estremadura (065)

Toca do Pal Lopes 22475

Divided into pitches, on level land between steep hills and the mouth of the Rio Sado.

Turn SW off N10 in town centre, on outskirts turn left and continue 200 m.
All year.
2.5HEC H G R R lau A60 V60 130 130

SINES
Baixo Alentejo (069)

CM 634011

In a pine wood on the Cabo de Sines peninsula, to the N of the town.

Follow signs from the rua de Marinquez Pompal and past the water tower.
15 Jan–15 Dec.
3.3HEC H G R lau s A75 V113 105–128 60–83

TOMAR
Ribatejo (049)

CM 33750

Well maintained park-like site with tall poplars

Turn off N110 (C–E), turn right before bridge and continue for 200 m.
Apr–Oct.
1.3HEC H G R P lau

Portugal

VAGOS
Beira Litoral

Orbitur Vagueira (034)791618

All year.
10HEC H G R lau s A320 V235 320–460 200–460

VALVERDE See **PRAIA DA LUZ**

VIANA DO CASTELO
Minho (058)

Orbitur Cabedelo 22167

A rather windy site in a pine wood, 0.2 km away from a pleasant beach.

Off the N13 at Km65.4 about 400 m past railway bridge over Rio Lima, and W for 1.8 km.
15 Jan–15 Nov.
3HEC H G R lau sR A320 V235 320–460 200–460

VILA DO BISPO
Algarve

At **PRAIA DE SALEMA** (7.5 km SE)

Quinta dos Caricos (082)65201

All year.
5HEC H G R lau s A250 V250 300 250–325

VILA FLOR
Tras-os-Montes (078)

CM 52350

Woodland area next to the municipal swimming pool and a small lake.

20 km S of Mirandela.
All year.
H G R LRP lau

VILA NOVA DE CACELA
Algarve

Calico (081)95195

Slightly sloping ground under trees in olive grove.

Turn inland off N125 and follow asphalt road for 3 km.
All year.
4HEC H G P lau

VILA REAL
Tras-Os-Montes (059)

Parque Campismo 24724

In the E part of town turn off N2 by GALP petrol station. Site in 300 m near new school.
Feb–Dec.
3HEC H G R R lau

VISEU
Beira Alta (032)

Orbitur Parque do Fontelo 25547

In a dense oak wood, and slopes down from a rocky hill.

Turn right at Km93.2 on N16, site 300 m.
All year.
2.2HEC H G lau A320 V235 320–460 200–460

ZAMBUJEIRA
Alto Alentejo (083)

Zambujeira 95193

All year.
3HEC G R lau P A135 V135 185 160

The imposing main square of Lisbon

SPAIN & ANDORRA

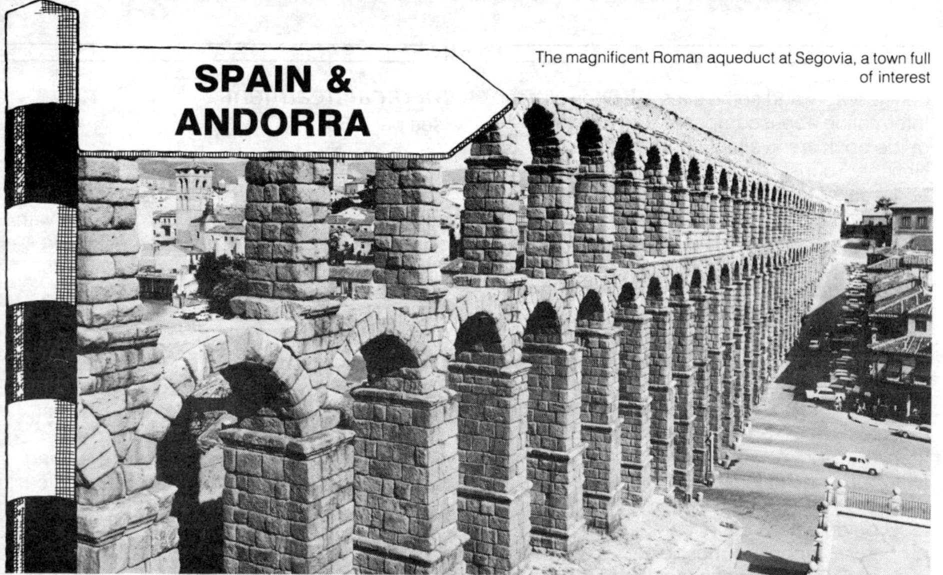

The magnificent Roman aqueduct at Segovia, a town full of interest

Rich in history and natural beauty, Spain is bordered by two countries, France in the north and Portugal in the west. Central Spain is mountainous and barren and the coastline is extremely rocky. Some of the most popular holiday areas in Europe are in Spain, the best known being the Costa Brava, the Costa Blanca, the Costa Dorada and the Costa del Sol. All these regions offer fine, sandy and safe beaches.

Spain has a varied climate; temperate in the north, dry and hot in the south and in the Balearic Islands. The language is Spanish and has developed from the Castilian dialect. Certain words are of Arabic origin and there are many local dialects spoken throughout the provinces.

HOW TO GET THERE

From the Channel ports, Spain is approached via France. The two main routes are at either end of the Pyrénées Mountains, the Biarritz to San Sebastián–Donostia road or motorway at the western end for central and southern Spain or the Perpignan to Barcelona road at the eastern end for the Costa Brava. The distance from Calais to Madrid is about 990 miles and usually requires two or three night stops. It is possible to shorten the road journey by using the car-sleeper services between Boulogne or Paris and Biarritz or Narbonne or Paris to Madrid. There is also a car ferry service from Plymouth to Santander, which takes about 24 hours.

GENERAL INFORMATION

(see also *Things you need to know*, pages 33–64)

Boats

(see page 33)

British Embassy/Consulates

(see also page 57)

The British Embassy together with its consular section is located at *Madrid 4* Calle de Fernando el Santo 16 ☎(91)4190200. There are British Consulates in Alicante, Barcelona, Bilbao, Malaga, Seville and Palma; there are British Consulates with Honorary Consuls in Santander, Tarragona and Vigo. There is a British Vice-Consulate in Algeciras and Ibiza and a British Vice-Consulate with Honorary Consul in Mènorca.

Camping

Sites are numerous on the Costa Brava and elsewhere along the coast, but there are not many inland. They are officially classified according to the facilities and services provided and their classification should be displayed at the site entrance and on any literature. If you intend visiting sites at popular resorts along the coast between late Spring and mid October, it is best to book in advance. Late Spring is recommended, as the intense heat of mid-summer is avoided and sites and roads are less congested. Opening dates vary

considerably and some sites are open all year. Information about campsites and a detailed guide book are available from the Spanish National Tourist Office (see *Tourist Information*) and local tourist information offices.
Hire of equipment is not generally possible, but some campsites have bungalow accommodation.
International camping carnet not compulsory but recommended. Generally campsites will allow a reduction in the advertised charge to the holders of a camping carnet. See page 37 for further information.
Off-site camping is permitted, except in mountain areas, provided there are no more than three tents or caravans and ten campers at any one place and they do not remain for more than three days. However, permission must be obtained before camping on private property. Camps may not be set up within a radius of 150 metres of a main road, or within 100 metres of a national monument. Camp fires within 200 metres of a main road are forbidden.

Currency including banking hours

(see also page 57)
The unit of currency is the Spanish Peseta (*Ptas*) divided into 100 Centimos. At the time of going to press £ = *Ptas*198.75. Denominations of bank notes are *Ptas* 100, 500, 1,000, 2,000, 5,000; standard coins are *Ptas* 1, 5, 25, 50, 100. Visitors may import unlimited amounts of foreign and Spanish currency, but amounts over *Ptas* 100,000 and *Ptas* 500,000 must be declared on arrival. No more than *Ptas*100,000 in Spanish currency may be exported, but there are no restrictions on the export of foreign currency provided the amount does not exceed the sum declared on arrival.

In the summer banks are usually open 08.30–13.30hrs Monday to Friday and 08.30–12.30hrs on Saturday. There are also exchange offices at travel agents which are open 09.00–13.00hrs and 16.00–19.00hrs from Monday to Friday, and 09.00–13.00hrs on Saturday.

Customs regulations

A television set, radio, pocket calculator or tape recorder may be temporarily imported, but only against a deposit of duty and a permit valid for three months issued by the Spanish Customs. See also *Customs regulations for European countries* page 57 for further information.

Foodstuffs

(see page 60)

Medical treatment

(see page 60)

Shopping hours

Generally shops are open Monday to Saturday from 09.00–13.00hrs and 15.00–19.30hrs with a two-hour break for lunch; department stores may open at 10.00hrs and close at 20.00hrs.

Tourist information

(see also page 63)
The Spanish National Tourist Office, Metro House, 57–58 St James's Street, London SW1A 1LD ☎01-499 0901, will be pleased to assist you with information regarding tourism and there are branch offices in most of the leading Spanish cities, towns and resorts. Local offices are normally closed at lunchtime.

Visitors' registration

(see page 63)

MOTORING

(see also *Things you need to know*, pages 33–64)

Accidents

(see also page 46)
Fire, police, ambulance. In all cases ☎091 for **police**, and ☎080 for **fire** service in Madrid and Barcelona; in other towns call the operator.

Bail Bonds

An accident in Spain can have very serious consequences, including the impounding of the car, and property, and the detention of the driver pending trial. A Bail Bond can often facilitate release of person and property, and you are advised to obtain one of these from your insurer, for a nominal premium, together with your Green Card.

A Bail Bond is a written guarantee that a cash deposit of usually up to £1,500 will be paid to the Spanish Court as surety for bail, and as security for any fine which may be imposed, although in such an event you will have to reimburse any amount paid on your behalf.

In very serious cases the Court will not allow bail and it has been known for a minor Spanish court to refuse to accept Bail Bonds, and to insist on cash being paid by the driver. Nevertheless, motorists are strongly advised to obtain a Bail Bond and to ensure that documentary evidence of this (in Spanish) is attached to the Green Card.

Breakdowns
(see page 48)

Dimensions and weight restrictions
Private **cars** and towed **trailers** or **caravans** are restricted to the following dimensions–height: 4 metres; width: 2.50 metres; length: 11 metres. The maximum permitted overall length of vehicle/trailer or caravan combination is 18 metres.

Trailers with an unladen weight exceeding 750 kg must have an independent braking system.

Driving licence
The minimum age at which a visitor may drive a temporarily imported car or motorcycle (over 75cc) is 18 years. An International Driving Permit (IDP) is compulsory for the holder of a Republic of Ireland or green UK driving licence, unless the licence is accompanied by an official Spanish translation stamped by a Spanish Consulate. The IDP is not compulsory for the holder of a pink UK driving licence but, as local difficulties may arise over its acceptance, an IDP is recommended. The UK licensing authorities cannot exchange a green licence for a pink licence purely to facilitate continental travel. See under *Driving Licence and International Driving Permit* page 33 for further information.

Lights
(see also page 50 and *Headlights* page 41)

Motoring club
(see also page 61)
The *Real Autómovil Club de España* (RACE) has its headquarters at *28003 Madrid* Calle José Abascal 10 ☎4473200 and is associated with local clubs in a number of provincial towns. Motoring club offices are normally open from 09.00–14.00hrs only and are closed on Sundays and public holidays. Some, including Madrid, are closed on Saturdays.

Passengers
(see also page 51)
It is recommended that children do not travel in a vehicle as front seat passengers.

Petrol
(see page 61)

Roads
The surfaces of the main roads vary, but on the whole are good. The roads are winding in many places and at times it is not advisable to exceed 30–35mph. Secondary roads are often rough, winding, and encumbered by slow, horse-drawn traffic. Holiday traffic, particularly on the coast road to Barcelona and Tarragona and in the San Sebastian area, causes congestion which may be severe at weekends. A leaflet entitled '*Road Conditions in Spain and Portugal* is available to AA members.

In the Basque area local versions of some placenames appear on signposts together with the national version used in current AA gazetteers and maps. Some local names differ considerably from the national spelling – *eg* San Sabastián = Donostia. In the Catalonia area some local spellings are used exclusively on signposts but most of these are recognisable against the national version – *eg* Gerona = Girona, Lérida = Lleida.

Seat-belts
(see page 52)

Speed limits
Car
Built-up areas
60kph (37mph)
Other roads
*90kph (56 mph) or
**100kph (62mph)
Motorways
120kph (74mph)

Car/caravan/trailer
Built-up areas
60kph (37mph)
Other roads
*70kph (43mph) or
**80kph (49mph)
Motorways
80kph (49mph)

*On ordinary roads
**On roads with more than one lane in each direction, a special lane for slow moving vehicles or wide lanes.

Warning triangles
In the event of accident or breakdown the use of two warning triangles is compulsory for vehicles weighing more than 3,500kg (3 tons 8cwt 100lbs) and passenger vehicles with more than nine seats (including the driver's). The triangles must be placed on the road in front of and behind the vehicle at a distance of 30 metres (33yds) and be visible from at least 100

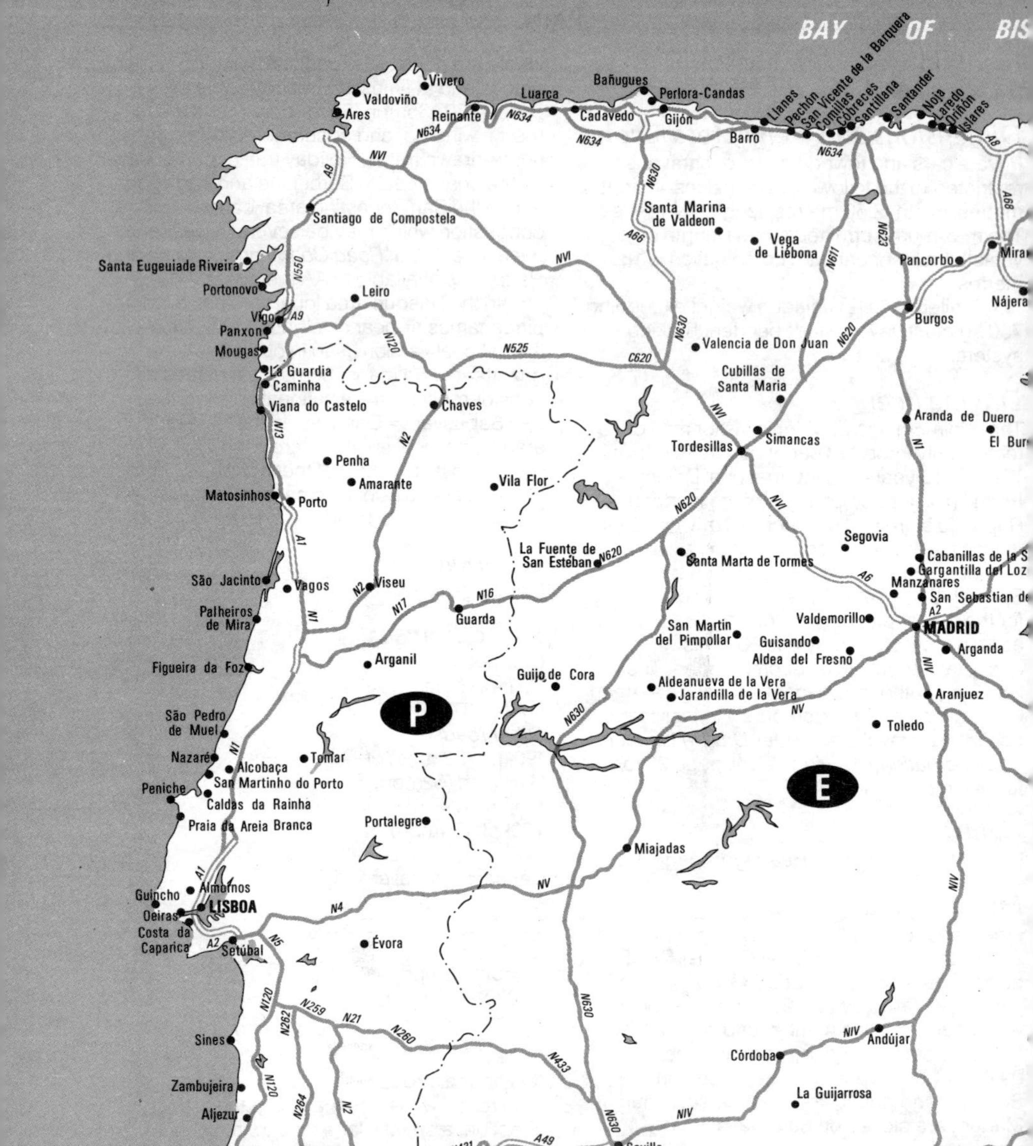
BAY OF BIS
Vivero
Valdoviño
Ares
Reinante
Luarca
Bañugues
Perlora-Candas
Cadavedo
Gijón
Barro
Llanes
Pechón
San Vicente de la Barquera
Comillas
Cóbreces
Santillana
Santander
Noja
Laredo
Oriñón
Islares
Santiago de Compostela
Santa Eugeuiade Riveira
Portonovo
Vigo
Panxon
Mougas
La Guardia
Caminha
Viana do Castelo
Leiro
Chaves
Santa Marina de Valdeon
Vega de Liébona
Pancorbo
Mira
Nájera
Burgos
Valencia de Don Juan
Cubillas de Santa Maria
Aranda de Duero
El Bur
Simancas
Tordesillas
Penha
Amarante
Vila Flor
Matosinhos
Porto
Segovia
La Fuente de San Esteban
Santa Marta de Tormes
Cabanillas de la S
Gargantilla del Loz
Manzanares
San Sebastian de
São Jacinto
Vagos
Viseu
Guarda
Palheiros de Mira
San Martin del Pimpollar
Valdemorillo
Guisando
Aldea del Fresno
MADRID
Arganda
Figueira da Foz
Arganil
Guijo de Cora
Aldeanueva de la Vera
Jarandilla de la Vera
Aranjuez
P
São Pedro de Muel
Toledo
Nazaré
Alcobaça
Tomar
San Martinho do Porto
Peniche
Caldas da Rainha
E
Praia da Areia Branca
Portalegre
Miajadas
Guincho
Almornos
Oeiras
LISBOA
Costa da Caparica
Setúbal
Évora
Sines
Andújar
Córdoba
Zambujeira
La Guijarrosa
Aljezur
Sevilla
Dos Hermanas
Santa Fé
Granada
Vila do Bispo
Alcantarilha
Albufeira
El Rompido
Punta Umbria
Mazagón
La Zubia
Praia da Luz
Quarteira
Vila Real
Monte Gordo
Vila Nova de Cacela
Torre del Oro
Torre del Mar
Adra
Málaga
Castell de Ferro
Puerto de Santa Maria
Chiclana de la Frontera
Puerto Real
Marbella
Fuengirola
Estepona
Golfo de Cadiz
Conil
Tarifa
N634
NVI
A9
N550
N120
N525
C620
N630
A66
NVI
N611
N623
N620
A8
A68
N1
N13
N2
A1
N17
N16
N620
A6
A2
NIV
NV
N630
N4
A2
N5
N120
N262
N259
N21
N260
N433
N264
N2
N431
A49
N630
NIV
A4
N321
N340

For key to country identification - see "About the gazetteer"

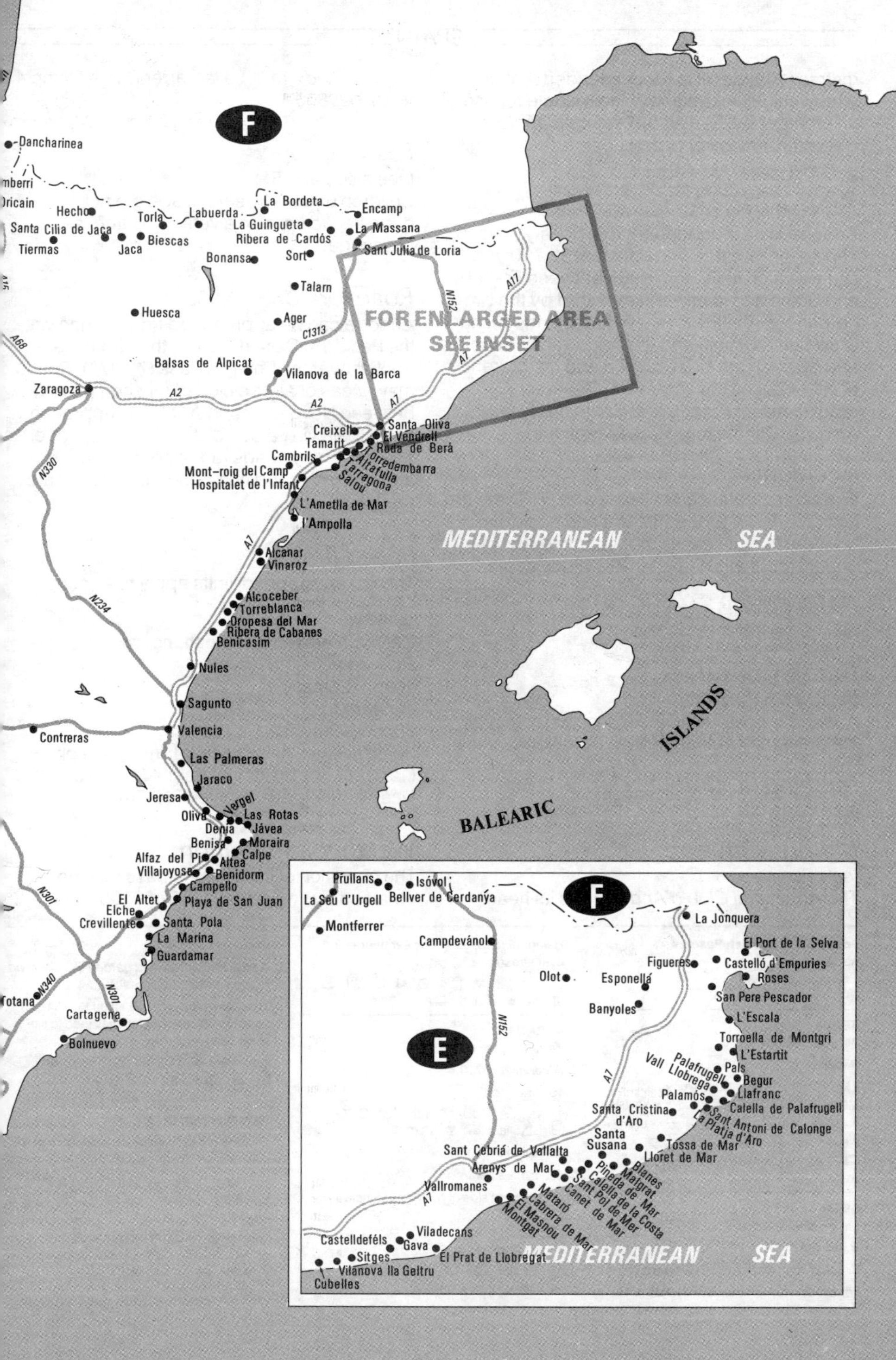
F
Dancharinea
Hecho
Santa Cilia de Jaca
Tiermas
Torla
Jaca
Biescas
Labuerda
La Bordeta
Encamp
La Guingueta
La Massana
Ribera de Cardós
Sant Julia de Loria
Bonansa
Sort
Talarn
Huesca
Ager
C1313
Balsas de Alpicat
Vilanova de la Barca
Zaragoza
A68
A2
N152
A17
A7
FOR ENLARGED AREA SEE INSET
Santa Oliva
El Vendrell
Creixell
Tamarit
Roda de Berá
Cambrils
Torredembarra
Altafulla
Tarragona
Salou
Mont-roig del Camp
Hospitalet de l'Infant
L'Ametlla de Mar
l'Ampolla
N330
Alcanar
Vinaroz
MEDITERRANEAN SEA
N234
Alcoceber
Torreblanca
Oropesa del Mar
Ribera de Cabanes
Benicasim
Nules
Sagunto
Valencia
Contreras
Las Palmeras
Jaraco
Jeresa
Oliva
Vergel
Las Rotas
Denia
Jávea
Benisa
Moraira
Calpe
Alfaz del Pi
Altea
Villajoyosa
Benidorm
Campello
El Altet
Playa de San Juan
Elche
Crevillente
Santa Pola
La Marina
Guardamar
N301
N340
Totana
Cartagena
Bolnuevo
BALEARIC ISLANDS
Prullans
Isóvol
La Seu d'Urgell
Bellver de Cerdanya
Montferrer
Campdevánol
La Jonquera
El Port de la Selva
Figueres
Castelló d'Empuries
Olot
Esponellá
Roses
Banyoles
San Pere Pescador
L'Escala
E
Torroella de Montgri
L'Estartit
Palafrugell
Pals
Vall Llobrega
Begur
Palamós
Llafranc
Santa Cristina d'Aro
Calella de Palafrugell
Sant Antoni de Calonge
La Platja d'Aro
Santa Susana
Tossa de Mar
Sant Cebriá de Vallalta
Lloret de Mar
Arenys de Mar
Blanes
Malgrat
Pineda de Mar
Calella de la Costa
Sant Pol de Mer
Canet de Mar
Vallromanes
Mataró
Cabrera de Mar
El Masnou
Montgat
Viladecans
Castelldeféls
Gava
Sitges
El Prat de Llobregat
Vilanova Ila Geltru
Cubelles

metres (109yds). It is recommended that all other vehicles carry a warning triangle for use in an emergency. See also *Warning triangles/ Hazard warning lights* page 54.

ANDORRA

Andorra is an independent Principality covering 190 sq miles with a population of 32,700. It is situated high in the Pyrénées between France and Spain and jointly administered by the two co-princes (the President of France, the Bishop of La Seu d'Urgell) and the Andorrans. French and Spanish are both spoken and the currency of either country is accepted. General regulations for France and Spain apply to Andorra with the following exceptions.

Accidents

Fire and **ambulance** ☎18 **police** ☎17. There are no firm rules of procedure after an accident; however in most cases the recommendations under *Accidents* on page 46 are advisable.

Breakdowns

(see page 48)

British Consulate

(see also page 57)
Andorra comes within the Consular District of the British Consul-General at Barcelona.

Medical treatment

(see page 60)

Motoring club

(see also page 61)
The *Automobil Club d'Andorra* has its head office at *Andorra la Vella* Carrer Babot Camp 4 ☎(078)20890.

Passengers

(see also page 51)
Children under 10 years of age are not permitted to travel in a vehicle as front seat passengers.

Roads

Andorra can be approached from France via the Pas de la Casa (6,851ft), then from the frontier over the Envalira Pass (7,897ft). Roads may occasionally be closed for short periods between November and April. The approach from Spain via La Seu d'Urgell is always open. The three main roads radiating from the town are prefixed N and numbered; side roads are prefixed V.

Speed limits

The following speed limits apply to Andorra:

Car, car/caravan combinations
Built-up areas
40kph (25mph)
Other roads
70kph (43mph)
Some villages have a speed limit of 20kph (12mph). The maximum height for vehicles where tunnels are involved is 3.5m.

Weather information

The condition of the Envalira pass may be obtained by ringing ☎21166 or 21055.

Prices are in Spanish Pesetas
Abbreviations:

ctra	carretera
Gl	Generalissimo

ADRA
Almeria (☎951)

Habana

2 km W at Km58.3 on N340 (Almeria–Málaga).
All year.

1.5HEC ∴ H ⊙ lau **A**200 **V**200 200 **Å**200

AGER
Lleida (☎973)

Badia ☎435034

Situated in an orchard and vineyard.

For access, turn off the L904 Tremp–Balaguer road, at Km35 near bridge and over stream.

0.5HEC ◆ H ⊙ G R P ⊞ |O|

ALCANAR
Tarragona (☎977)

Alcanar ☎737100

15 Jun–Sep.

1.7HEC ◑ H |O| ⊙ G lau

Alfaques ☎740561

Site slopes gently down to the sea.

On seaward side of N340 to Valencia at Km159.6
Mar–Oct.

2.5HEC ◆ H |O| ⊙ G R lau **A**200–250 **V**200–250 200–250 **Å**125–250

Casas ☎737165

A pleasant subdivided garden-like site in an orange grove on the beach.

Turn seawards off the N340 at Km154 and continue 300 m along access road to site.
May–Sep.

1HEC ◆ H |O| ⊙ G ⊞ lau **A**220–250 **V**220–250 220–250 **Å**200–250

Mare Nostrum ☎737179

Gently sloping towards the sea with pines, olive and deciduous trees.

Turn towards the sea off the N340 at Km58.3.
All year.

1.4HEC ◆ H |O| ⊙ G ⊞ lau **A**200–225 **V**200–225 200–225 **Å**200–225

Spain

ALCOCEBER
Castellón (☎964)

Playa Tropicana ☎410885

On a 500 m long sandy beach 3 km from the village.

For access, leave motorway at exit 44, then drive 3 km N on the CN340 and turn towards the sea at Km109.
Mar–Oct.

3.1HEC lau A420 V380 660 660

ALDEA DEL FRESNO
Madrid (☎91)

Fresno ☎8637299

A well-maintained site totally enclosed by chain link fencing near the Rio Alberche.

1.3 km towards Méntrida.
All year.

6HEC RP A200 V200 200 200

ALDEANUEVA DE LA VERA
Cáceres (☎927)

Yuste ☎560910

Meadowland with dense woodland on a hill above two valleys.

300 m S of C501 at Km49.1
Apr–Sep.

3HEC P lau R A200 V200 200 200

ALFAZ DEL PI
Alicante (☎96)

Hermosa ☎5888823

A sub-divided site, mainly provided with shade by roofing. Part of site in olive grove.

On the landward side of coastal road to Alfaz del Pi-El Abir, opposite bay of Altea.
All year.

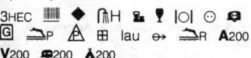

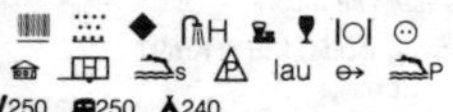

2.3HEC S lau P A230 V250 250 240

Parque Tropical ☎5888588

All year.

2.5HEC P lau A250 pitch950

ALTAFULLA
Tarragona (☎977)

Santa Eulalia ☎650213

On level meadow with poplar trees beside railway embankment.

Access from N340 at Km262.1, continue towards sea for 400 m.
May–Sep.

1.5HEC S

ALTEA
Alicante (☎96)

Cap Blanch

A new site on Albir beach.

All year.

San Antonio ☎5840917

Site with trees and roofing for shade with large pitches between a hillock with pines and beach.

In town turn off N332 (Valencia–Alicante road) towards the harbour in direction of El Abir.
Apr–Sep.

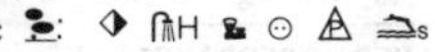

0.4HEC S

ALTET (EL)
Alicante (☎96)

Morant

Enclosed site under olive trees.

7 km S of Alicante.
Jun–Sep.

1.4HEC P

AMETLLA DE MAR (L')
Tarragona (☎977)

Nautic ☎456110

Terraced with pines, palms and olives and has uneven stony ground. Has own beach.

Turn right off N340 (Tarragona–Valencia) at Km20.1, take TV3025 and continue to railway station via flyover and level crossing. Turn right and take third road or left. Access road has 10% gradient.
May–Sep.

5HEC SP lau

AMEYUGO See **MIRANDA DE EBRO**

AMPOLLA (L')
Tarragona (☎977)

Western Camping, Los Daltoners ☎470265

16 Apr–20 Oct.

5HEC lau A250 V250 250 250

ANDÚJAR
Jaén (☎953)

Andúlar ☎500700

A walled, grassland site within the town.

May–Sep.

1.8HEC P

ARANDA DE DUERO
Burgos (☎947)

Costajàn ☎502070

Turn off N1 (Burgos–Madrid) at Km162.1 N of town.
Apr–Oct.

1HEC P

ARANJUEZ
Madrid (☎91)

Soto del Castillo ☎8911395

Site developed into two parts with trees and lawns in large castle park.

Turn off NIV at Km46. In the village 200 m beyond the FIRESTONE petrol station, turn sharp NE and continue for 1 km.
May–Sep.

1.5HEC P

ARENYS DE MAR
Baracelona (☎93)

Marcos ☎7921238

A site with many trees and a pedestrian tunnel leading to the beach.

Seaward side of the N11 near Km666.3 and between the railway line and the road above it.
May–Sep.

0.6HEC R P lau S

ARES
La Coruña (☎981)

Playa el Raso ☎0676

Well tended, partially terraced site above a sandy beach.

Turn off NVI in Cabana N of Puertedueme and follow signs.
15 May–15 Sep.

1.1HEC

ARGANDA
Madrid (☎91)

Arganda ☎8712663

Well maintained site subdivided into several fields by hedging. ➤

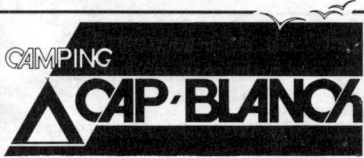

On NIII at Km22.8 N of town.
All year.
10HEC P lau

BAGUR See **BEGUR**

BALSAS DE ALPICAT
Lleida (☎973)

Balsas ctra Osca ☎235954

Site lies within a large leisure complex. Campers have access to sports facilities.

Access via N240 for 6 km towards Huesca and turn off at Km98.5.
Apr–Sep.
2.5HEC lau P A220 V220 220 220

BAÑOLAS See **BANYOLES**

BAÑUGUES
Asturias (☎985)

Molino ☎880785

Meadow with rows of trees by a canal-like stream.

SE, near Avilés-Podes–Luanco road.
15 May–15 Sep.
4.4HEC lau S A230 V180 250 220

BANYOLES
Girona (☎972)

Lago de Bañolas ☎570305

2 km NW, 800 m W of lake.
All year.
2.2HEC P L

Sombrero ☎571133

Well-kept site surrounded by hills and woods, partly on meadowland.

Turn E off C150 near Km20 and turn towards Porqueras.
All year.
4.4HEC P

BARRO
Asturias (☎985)

Sorraos ☎401161

Level meadowland on a rocky bay.

Wel signposted.
Apr–Sep.
1.3HEC S lau A150 V145 200 185

BEGUR
Girona (☎972)

Spain

Bagur ☎623201

A terraced site in a dip.

1.4 km SE of town and right of the road to Palafrugell, 400 m after the turn towards Fornells and Aiguablava.
12 May–Aug.
4HEC P lau A330 V330 330 290–330

Maset Playa de Sa Riera ☎623023

A well-kept terraced site, divided into pitches in a beautiful valley.

3 km N of Begur. If entering from the W, turn left just before reaching the town.
10 Apr–27 Sep.
1HEC lau S A300–360 V300–360 360–450 300–360

BELLVER DE CERDANYA
Lleida (☎973)

Solana del Segre ☎510310

On the River Segre, known for its trout fishing.

All year.
6.5HEC RP lau A270 V270 270 270

BENICASIM
Castellón de la Plana (☎964)

Bonterra ☎300007

Between the railway line and avenida de Barcelona with a number of deciduous trees.

300 m N towards Las Villas de Benicasim.
15 May–Sep.
5HEC P lau S A365 V365 365 365

Tauro ☎301266

On level grassland partially under poplars providing shade on edge of a built up area. 0.4 km to the sea.

Follow coastal road towards El Grao and in 3 km turn right. Signposted.
All year.
1.4HEC P S

BENIDORM
Alicante (☎96)

Armanello ☎5853190

Divided by bushes with large pitches on terraces under olive and palm trees next to a small orange grove.

For access turn off the N332 at Km123.1 N of the town.
15 Mar–Apr & Jul–Sep.
1.8HEC P lau S A260 V260 300 260

Benidorm ☎5860011

Level site with trees and sunshade roofing.

2.5 km from sea, 700 m off N332 at Km117.
Jun–Sep.
0.6HEC A280 V300 300 180–280

Torreta ☎5854668

Terraced site, surrounded by tall buildings. Trees and sunshade roofing.

800 m from sea. Turn off N332 (Valencia–Alicante) at Km123.1 and continue towards town for 300 m.
All year.
2HEC P S

BENISA
Alicante (☎96)

Fanadix ☎730099

Terraced site completely divided into pitches.

10 km E & 400 m from the sea. Access off AV-1445.
All year.
1.5HEC S A225 V225 260 225

BIESCAS
Huesca (☎974)

Edelweiss ☎485084

In meadow with deciduous trees on a hill in a pleasant situation.

Turn right off C138 at Km97.
Jun–Sep.
40HEC lau RP A310 V310 310 310

BLANES
Girona (☎972)

Bella Terra ☎331955

May–Sep.
8HEC S lau A350 V350 350 350

Blanes ☎331591

In a pine forest bordering the beach beyond Camping El Roca.

On left of the Paseo Villa de Madrid coast road towards town.
May–Sep.
2.5HEC lau

Masia ☎331013

50 m inland from Paseo Villa de Madrid coast road.
May–Sep.
6HEC lau

Pinar ☎331083

Divided into two by the coastal road. Partially under pines, partially meadow under poplars.

1 km on Paseo Villa de Madrid coast road.
May–Sep.
7HEC lau A350 V350 450 350

Roca ☎330540

Site with trees beside the coast road.

Next to Camping Solmar.
May–Sep.
2.4HEC

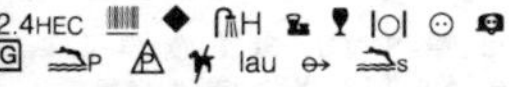

Sabanell ☎331809

Within a pine wood, a section of which is inland and open to the public.

On either side of the Paseo Villa de Madrid road. Off coast road S of Blanes.
Apr–Oct.
3.5HEC lau A385 pitch1200

Sardaña ☎330635

On hilly meadowland; 1 km from sea.

Access off Malgrat road.
Jun–Sep.
1.6HEC

Solmar ☎331331

Surrounded by poplar trees inland from beach road.

Inland from Paseo Villa de Madrid coast road on the way from Blanes.
Apr–mid Oct.
3.8HEC lau A280–350 V280–350 320–400 220–280

Vora Mar av de Madrid ☎330349

Level site with pine trees on sandy beach.

1.5 km from Blanes on seaward side of the Paseo Villa de Madrid coast road.
May–Oct.
1.9HEC

BOLNUEVO
Murcia (☎968)

Bolnuevo ☎594822

All year.
6.5HEC lau A200 V200 200 200

Spain

Garoa Camping Playa de Mazarrón ☎594535

On level ground divided by a footpath and partly bordered by palm trees.

Turn W off N322 in Puerto de Mazarrón at approx Km111 and head towards Bolnuevo. Then take the MU road and drive 4.6 km to site entrance which is 1 km E of Punta Bela.
8HEC A245 V245 245 245

BONANSA
Huesca (☎974)

Ballera

15 Jun–15 Sep.
5HEC lau A245 V245 245 245

BORDETA (LA)
Lleida (☎973)

Prado Verde ☎(973)640241

Level meadowland on River Garona with sparse trees and sheltered by high hedges from traffic noise.

On the N230, Puente de Rey (French border)–Lleida road, at Km199 behind PIRELLI GENERAL filling station.
All year.
1.4HEC lau A245 V245 245 190

BURGO DE OSMA (EL)
Soria (☎975)

Pedriza ☎340806

In an orchard on rising ground.

Turn off N122 (Soria–Aranda de Duero), turn left in town and follow signs.
Jun–Sep.
3HEC

BURGOS
Burgos (☎947)

Fuentes Blancas ☎221016

Apr–Sep.
3.6HEC lau A225 V225 225 175–225

CABINILLAS DE LA SIERRA
Madrid (☎91)

Oremor ☎8439034

Gently sloping farmland with very old trees.

Leave N1 (Burgos–Madrid) at Km5.8 and turn W upon entering the village from the N. Take Madrid road towards Navalafuente and drive for 0.8 km. Site entrance in the S.
All year.
4HEC lau

CABRERA DE MAR
Barcelona (☎93)

Costa de Oro ☎7591234

The beach is reached via a railway underpass.

Lies at Km650 of the N11, on the seaward side, between the road and the railway embankment.
Jun–15 Sep.
1.2HEC lau

CADAVEDO
Asturias (☎985)

Regalina ☎645056

The site has mountain and sea views.

All year.
1HEC lau A200 V190 225 200

CALELLA DE LA COSTA
Barcelona (☎93)

Botanic Bona Vista ☎7692488

Totally subdivided and well tended terraced site on a hillside, beautifully landscaped. Internal roads steep. Access to beach via pedestrian underpass.

Turn off the N11 at Km672 beyond road bridge.
All year.
3HEC lau A275 V275 275 275

Faro ☎7690967

Terraced site on a hillock under deciduous trees with lovely view of Calella and out to sea. Steep internal roads.

For access, travel S before reaching a major left hand bend at Km673.7 to the right of the N11.
May–Sep.
2.5HEC lau A275 V275 275 275

Granja ☎7690856

Level, terraced site 0.7 km from sea.

Inland from N11 near church.
May–Sep.
2.8HEC

CALELLA DE PALAFRUGELL
Girona (☎972)

Moby Dick ☎304807

A terraced site on the slopes of a hill on the southern outskirts of Calella, some distance from the sea.

For access take the Palafrugell–Calella road, then drive through the village.
Jun–Sep.
2.7HEC lau A325–370 V325–370 350–395 350–395

Siesta ☎300016

Partly terraced, on hillside with some trees.

From Palafrugell site lies just before Calella, approx 200 m to right of the wide ➔

asphalt road.
Etr–Sep.

6.4HEC H lau P s

CALONGE See **PALAMÓS** and **SANT ANTONI DE CALONGE**

CALPE
Alicante (96)

Ifach 5830477

Totally subdivided site with roofing providing shade. Narrow beach.

On both sides of Calpe–Benisa road between Km9 and Km10, about 300 m from Ifach rocks.
15 Mar–Oct.

1.5HEC H s lau A260 pitch785

Vinã de Calpe 5831551

Level site with sunshade roofing.

1.5 km towards Benisa and turn inland towards Cometa.
All year.

1.5HEC H P lau

CAMBRILS
Tarragona (977)

Amfora d'Archs ctra Nacional 340 (Valencia–Barcelona) Km233 361211

All year.

5HEC H P lau s

Costa Blanca 361015

Planted with trees and flowering shrubs.

It lies on the Salou coast road.
May–Sep.

3HEC H s lau P A290 V290 290 290

Don Camilo 361490

Divided into pitches, lying on both sides of the coast road.

Drive 2 km N of the town towards Salou and W of the bridge over the river.
May–Sep.

6HEC H sP A225–300 V235–290 235–290 165–290

Llosa 362615

Turn left off N340 from Tarragona just after Km231 SW of town. Cross railway and continue for 500 m towards sea.
May–Sep.

4.5HEC H sP lau

Masia Blanca

Well-kept site on level lawns.

Turn off N340 (B-V) before bridge at Km228.4 and turn seawards to follow signs.
Apr–1 Oct.

1.5HEC H s lau

Playa l'Ardiaca 360913

Spain

Completely divided into numbered pitches and lies on sandy terrain with many poplar trees.

About 2 km S of Cambrils on the N340 Tarragona–Valencia road. Turn seawards at Km228.9, later fork left and continue by a dusty track for 1.2 km to the site by the sea.
Jun–15 Sep.

1HEC H s

Villa Magdalena 360803

Clean site on level meadow.

Entrance off beach road 300 m before Cambrils–Puerto.
Apr–Oct.

2HEC H lau s

CAMPDEVÀNOL
Girona (972)

Moli Serradell 730927

On meadowland with three low terraces next to a small hotel above the River Merdes.

On S outskirts turn off N152 (Barcelona–Puigcerda road) at Km110.5, cross bridge in direction of Baga and continue for 5km.
All year.

1.5HEC H P lau A200 V200 200 170–200

CAMPELLO
Alicante (96)

Costa Blanca 5630670

On almost level ground scattered with old olive and eucalyptus trees. The Alicante–Denia railway line runs behind the camp.

For access turn off the N332 at Km94.2 next to the big petrol station, and drive along a narrow gravel track towards the sea for 0.5 km.
All year.

1.2HEC H P lau s A250 V250 280 250

CANET DE MAR
Barcelona (93)

Globo Roglo 7941142

On level meadowland on a hillside with poplar trees.

Inland off the N11 which runs from Girona to Barcelona at Km667.8.
Jun–1 Sep.

2HEC H P s

Llave 7940400

Divided into pitches, surrounded by walls and hedges and shaded by trees.

To the right of Camping Costa Dorado and right of the NII towards Barcelona.
May–Sep.

1.8HEC H P lau s

CARTAGENA
Murcia (968)

Los Madriles Isla–Plana 594551

All year.

6HEC H P lau s A215 V215 235 235

CASTELLDEFÉLS
Barcelona (93)

Estrella de Mar 6653257

Most of this site lies in a pine forest.

Inland off the C246 motorway at Km16.7.
All year.

9HEC H P

CASTELL DE FERRO
Granada (958)

Palmeras 646130

SW on N340.
Jun–Aug.

3.5HEC H s lau A225 V225 325 300

CASTELLÓ D'EMPURIES
Girona (972)

Internacional-Amberes 450507

On a meadow and has a sheltered pleasure boat harbour 100 m away.

For access, 2 km before Roses turn right and continue for 800 m towards the beach.
15 May–Sep.

8HEC H sP lau A280–365 V280–365 280–365 280–365

Laguna 450553

Flat grassland site by the sea.

Turn right at Km11 Figueres–Roses road in direction of Sant Pere Pescador and continue, last 4 km poorly surfaced lane.
10 May–Sep.

10HEC H sR lau A310–400 V310–400 310–400 310–400

Mas Nou 250575

Etr–1 Oct.

8.5HEC H P lau s A370 V370 370 370

Nautic Almanta 250447

Level meadowland, no shade, good facilities, reaching as far as the sea. Alongside the Rio Fluvia which has been made into a canal. Boating is possible in the canal which flows to the sea.

Turn S at Km11 on C260, approx, halfway along the road and turn E along the track and continue 2.2 km.
15 May–Sep.

14HEC H sP lau

CHICLANA DE LA FRONTERA
Cádiz (965)

Barrosa ☎403605

All year.

2.8HEC ◆ H lau sP A260 V260 260 A260

CÓBRECES

Cantabria (☎942)

Cóbreces ☎725120

15 Jun–15 Jul.

1HEC ◇ H lau s lau

COMILLAS

Cantabria (☎942)

Comillas ☎720074

Level grassland site to the right of the road to the beach.

E on C6316 at Km23.
Jun–Sep.

3HEC ◆ H lau s A250 V250 250 A250

CONIL

Cádiz (☎965)

Conil ☎440306

On a flat hillock 700 m from the sea. Shade is provided by eucalyptus trees.

Well signposted from the N340.
All year.

5HEC H lau s

CONTRERAS

Cuenca (☎96)

Venta de Contreras ☎2186090

All year.

4HEC ◆ H P lau LR A200 V200 200 A125–250

CÓRDOBA

Córdoba (☎957)

CM del Turismo ctra del Brillante ☎2705048

In terraced park off the ctra del Brillante.

N of town, near Km1 on C110. Follow signs to Centro Ciudad and then to site.
All year.

Spain

1HEC H P

CREIXELL

Tarragona (☎977)

Creixell ☎800620

All year.

8HEC ◇ H P lau s

Gavina ☎801503

By a sandy beach with isolated palms and low bushes.

15 km NE of Tarragona. Leave the N340 (Barcelona–Tarragona) at Km267.3 and drive towards the beach for a further 0.8 km.
Apr–12 Oct.

6HEC H s lau

Plana ☎800304

Subdivided on both sides of the railway line. Shade provided by roofing and several trees.

250 m from the N340 (Barcelona–Tarragona), turn seawards at Km269 before reaching town.
May–Sep.

0.7HEC ◆ H lau A250 V250 250 A250

Sirena Dorada ☎801303

Level site shaded by medium poplars. Beach lies across the railway.

Turn off N340 at Km268 and follow signposts.
All year.

7.5HEC ◆ H P lau s

CREVILLENTE

Alicante (☎96)

Palmeras ☎5400188

On N340 at Km45.5

◆ H P lau A250 V250 300 A175–225

CUBELLES

Barcelona (☎93)

Rueda ☎(343)8950207

Level terrain between road and railway. Access to beach by means of an underpass.

The site lies about 1 km N of Cunit near Km52.1 of the C146.
23 May–13 Sep.

6HEC ◆ H P lau s A230–320

See advertisement page 358

CUBILLAS DE SANTA MARTA

Valladolid (☎983)

Cubillas ☎580147

Meadowland with young trees, subdivided by hedges.

Entrance on the right of the N620 from Burgos between Km100 & 101.
All year.

2.5HEC H lau R A230 V230 230 A175–215

DANCHARINEA

Navarra (☎948)

Josenea ☎599011

On gently sloping meadow between the French border and the Spanish Customs.

On the N121 to Pamplona, turn left 100 m after Km80.2. Signposted.
10 Jun–Sep.

2.5HEC ◆ ◇ H lau

DENIA

Alicante (☎96)

Eden del Sol ☎5781253

Large pitches with plenty of spaces for individual campers.

On the land side of the road P1324 Vergel–Denia between Camping les Basetes and Denia. Access to beach across coastal road.
All year.

1HEC H s

Marinas ☎5781446

For access turn off the N332 in Vergel and drive E on the Denia road for 4km. ➔

Turn N, cross the P1324, turn right near the beach and continue for 200 m.
All year.
1.3HEC H G R lau s A250 V250 280 250

DOS HERMANAS
Sevilla (954)

Vilisom 720828
Park-like site with numerous palms and orange trees.
100m W of the NIV at Km554.8.
Feb–Nov.
1.45HEC H G lau P A275 V275 290 275

EJIDO (EL)
Almeria (951)

Mar Azul 481535
Sports and recreational facilities available.
6 km from village.
Apr–Sep.
10HEC H G sP lau A330 V330 330 330

EL Each name preceded by 'El' is listed under the name that follows it.

ELCHE
Alicante (96)

Palmeral Calle Federico Garcia 5422766

Spain

Long narrow site in a palm forest. It has many pitches in recesses between groups of trees.
Off the N340 and continue for 200 m. Signposted.
All year.
1.8HEC H G R P lau

ESCALA (L')
Girona (972)

Escala 770084
Level site, partially under pines.
Within village on the left of the road towards Riells.
Etr–Sep.
1.8HEC H G lau s

Malte playa Riells 770544
An extensive site, lying inland, but near the sea, at a small lake. Partly on a hillock under pine trees.
The access is well signed from the outskirts of L'Escala on the road towards Cala Montgó.
Jun–15 Sep.
6HEC H G L

lau s A370 V370 370 370

Montgó Europ 770866
In a pine wood at the foot of hills, about 400 m from the sea.
For access take the L'Escala–Montgó road which is very dusty and passes between the two sections of the camp.
All year.
12HEC H G P lau s A345 V335 335 335

ESPONELLÁ
Girona (972)

Esponellá 597074
In the Rio Fluvia valley W of Esponellá in a quiet situation on shady meadows and has a number of young pine trees and deciduous trees.
For access leave N11 in Figueres and take the C260 westward to Olot. At road junction S of Cabanellas take road S to Esponellá. 400 m on stony track.
All year.
5HEC H G RP lau A260 V260 260 260

ESTARTIT (L')
Girona (972)

Castell Montgri 758630
On a large terraced meadow in pine woodlands.

100 m N of GE road from Torroella de Montgri and about 0.5 km before L'Estartit on a hillock.
May–Oct.
20.7HEC H P lau s

Estartit ☎758909

In a valley on sloping ground which is rather steep in places. Some terraces, shaded by pine trees.

It is located about 200 m from the church and the road from Torroella de Montgri.
Apr–Sep.
1.5HEC H s A325 V325

Spain

325 280–325

Medes ☎758405

Turn right off GE641 from Torroella di Montgri by Km5 and continue for 1.5 km.
Jun–Sep.
2.6HEC H P lau s A315 pitch750

Molino ☎758629

Divided into several sections of open meadowland near the beach on grassland with young poplars. The reconstructed mill is a landmark.

Approaching from Torroella de Montgri turn right on entering L'Estartit and follow signs.
May–Sep.
5HEC H s lau

ESTEPONA

Málaga (☎952)

Chimenea ☎800437

In a dense forest on level ground.

6 km NE on N340 near Km169.
All year.
3.2HEC H ➤

G sP lau A275 V270 310 A280

FIGUERES
Girona (972)

Fresca 501149

Tourist site in park-like surroundings.

NW outskirts of Figueres.
All year.

1.2HEC H G P lau

FUENGIROLA
Málaga (952)

Calazul Mijas Costa 493219

All year.

4.5HEC H G lau sP A275 V275 275 A275

FUENTE DE SAN ESTEBAN (LA)
Salamanca (923)

Cruce 440130

Useful transit site.

On N620 at Km288.
10 Jun–Sep.

H G lau P A200 V200 225 A200

GARGANTILLA DE LOZOYA
Madrid (91)

Monte Holiday 8693076

Turn off N1 (Burgos–Madrid) at Km69 towards Cotos and continue for 10 km.
All year.

40HEC H G P lau (Jul–Aug) R A200 V200 200 A200

GAVÁ
Barcelona (93)

Albatros 6622031

In a shady pine wood divided into pitches on partly level, partly uneven terrain by the sea.

For access, turn off the C246, dual carriageway at Km15 and drive towards the sea.
27 Mar–27 Sep.

15HEC H G R sP (Jul–25 Aug) lau A340–415 V340–415 340–415 A340–415

Gavá

Turn seaward off C246 Barcelona–Castelldeféls road at Km13.9.
May–Sep.

3HEC H G R s lau

Tortuga Ligera 661229

All year.

9HEC H G R sP lau A340 V340 340 A340

Tres Estrellas 6621116

Completely divided into pitches. Discotheque.

Turn seawards off C246 Barcelona to Castelldeféls road at Km13.2. There is no direct access if coming from Barcelona but it is possible to turn around about 200 m past the site entrance.
15 Apr–Sep.

8HEC H P lau s

GIJÓN
Asturias (985)

Gijón 365755

Bare terrain on rocky plateau above rugged coastal scenery.

Approach via coastal road round the bay.
Jun–Sep.

1HEC H G lau s A200 V175 250 A150–200

GRANADA
Granada (958)

Maria Eugenia 200606

Level meadow between hedging, under deciduous and fruit trees.

3 km W on N342, N of road near Km436.5.

1.2HEC H G P

Sierra Nevada av de Madrid 107 200061

Almost level grassy site, in numerous sections, within motel complex.

N of N323, W of road at Km428.8.
Mar–Oct.

2.3HEC H P lau

Ultimo 123069

In park-like setting divided by hedging.

Turn right off Sierra Nevada road over the Riò Genil Ave Cervantes and follow signs.
All year.

0.5HEC H R P lau

GUARDAMAR DEL SEGURA
Alicante (96)

Mare Nostrum 5728073

Partially terraced meadow with some shade from roofing.

Turn towards the sea off the N332 Alicante–Cartagena road at about Km38.5.
All year.

2HEC H G P lau s

Palm Mar 5728856

Jun–Sep.

1.8HEC H G s lau A275 V275 330 A200–275

GUARDIA (LA)
Pontevedra (986)

Santa Tecla Apartado 10 613011

E off the C550.
Jun–Sep.

8HEC H G R lau A250 V250 250 A250

GUASA See **JACA**

GUIJAROSSA (LA)
Cordoba (957)

Campiña 313348

In a quiet location.

Acess via N4 turn off at Km424 onto C3312 25 km to site.
All year.

0.7HEC H G R P lau A200 V200 200 A150–200

GUIJO DE CORIA
Cáceres (927)

Borbollón

Gently rising meadow under olive trees.

About 700 m from reservoir of same name on the provincial road from Guijo de Coria to Moraleja.
Mar–Sep.

1HEC H

GUINGUETA (LA)
Lleida (973)

Vall d'Aneu 626083

In meadowland on rising ground on both sides of the road, partially in shade. No shade on terrace between road and lake.

On outskirts of town near the by-pass, C147.
Jun–Sep.

0.32HEC H G P lau L A200 V200 200 A200

GUISANDO
Avila (918)

Galayos 370921

Terraced site amid mixed woodland in mountain valley.

Turn off C501 in Avenas de San Pedro towards Guisando, before entering turn right into AV924 and onwards for 1.5 km.
All year.

0.2HEC H P lau

HECHO
Heusca (974)

Selva de Oza 375168

On meadowland, partly covered with pines and deciduous trees and between a dirt track and a mountain stream.

12.5 km NE towards Espata.
Jun–15 Sep.

2HEC H G R A285 V285 315 A285

HOSPITALET DE L'INFANT
Tarragona (977)

Cala d'Oques 823254

Divided in two, level and totally enclosed between a guest house and the pebbly beach, on a hillock.

Turn off the N340 at Km218.1 towards Hospitalet de l'Infant, continue through the town and southwards along the coastal road. Access possible also from Km214.5. All year.

2.5HEC ◆ H |O| ⊙ G s A lau A350 V350 350 A350

HUESCA
Huesca (☏974)

San Jorge ☏221560

Site with sports field surrounded by high walls. Subdivided by hedges, sparse woodland.

From town centre, about 1.5 km along M123 in Zaragoza direction and follow signs. May–Sep.

1HEC ◆ H |O| ⊙ P ⊞ lau A325 V325 325 A325

ICIAR
Guipúzcoa (☏943)

Iclar ☏601394

Enclosed by a stone wall 1 m high. Some noise from commercial vehicles.

On N634 turn right at Km39 behind the restaurant. Jun–Sep.

0.5HEC ◇ H |O| ⊙ ⊞ lau

IGUELDO See **SAN SEBASTIAN**

ISLARES
Cantabria (☏942)

Playa Arenillas ☏863152

In meadowland with some pine trees.

On N634 at Km 155.8 turn N and continue 100 m. The entrance is rather steep. Apr–Sep.

3HEC ◆ H |O| ⊙ G lau s A200 V200 250 A230

ISÓVOL
Girona (☏972)

Bellver ☏510017

On long stretch of land between road and river.

From Puigcerdá turn left off C1313 by Km165.2 about 200 m from Rio Segre bridge. Jun–15 Sep.

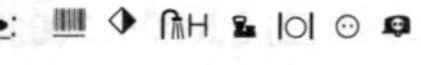

2HEC ◆ H |O| ⊙ s

JACA
Huesca (☏974)

Victoria ☏360323

On level meadow subdivided by rows of tall poplars.

N of C134 at Km18.6. May–Oct.

1HEC ◆ H |O| ⊙ ⊞

At **GUASA**

Peña Oroel ☏360215

Spain

Grassland site with rows of high poplars.

At Km13.8 of the C134 Jaca-Sabiñanigo road. Jun–Sep.

50HEC ◆ H |O| ⊙ G R ⊞ lau A310 V310 310 A310

JARACO
Valencia (☏96)

Dorado ☏2890062

Divided into pitches.

Turn off the N332 Valencia–Denia in Jaraco at Km204 and to site in 4 km. May–Sep.

2HEC ◆ H |O| ⊙ G s

San Vincente ☏2890188

Level subdivided site with some trees.

On leaving Jaraco at Km332 turn off at Km304 (Valencia–Alicante) in the direction of Playa to the site in 3.5 km. All year.

0.5HEC ◆ H |O| ⊙ R ⊞ lau R

JARANDILLA DE LA VERA
Cáceres (☏927)

Jaranda ☏560454

Apr–Sep.

3HEC ◆ H |O| ⊙ G P ⊞ lau A200 V200 200 A200

JÁVEA
Alicante (☏96)

Jávea ☏5791070

1.5 km from the sea. Jun–Sep.

2HEC ◆ H |O| ⊙ G P ⊞

Mediterráneo ☏5791226

Off the carretera de Montañer, completely divided into pitches and scattered with deciduous trees and sunshade roofs.

For access, take the coastal road to Cabo de la Nao and turn inland just before Km1. 25 May–Sep.

1.8HEC ◆ H |O| ⊙ G P ⊞ lau s A280 V280 310 A280

JERESA
Valencia (☏96)

Caudell ☏2890376

A partly enclosed terraced site with sunshade roofing and 2 km from the sea.

5 km NW of Gandia off N332 at Km200.4 All year.

1.5HEC ◆ H |O| ⊙ G P ⊞ lau s

JONQUERA (LA)
Girona (☏972)

Moli de Vent ☏540066

A well-kept site, lying on a hill, 300 m SW of the Spanish frontier station.

Turn off the N11 (French border–Barcelona) at Km782.1 and drive W. 15 May–15 Sep.

0.45HEC ◆ H |O| ⊙ ⊞ lau P A300 V300 300 A300–315

LA Each name preceded by 'La' is listed under the name which follows it.

LABUERDA
Huesca (☏974)

Pena Montanesa ☏500032

15 Mar–15 Oct.

2HEC ◆ H ⊙ G RP ⊞ lau |O| A250 V250 250 A250

LAREDO
Cantabria (☏942)

Carlos V ☏605593

Camp surrounded by walls and buildings on W outskirts of Laredo.

Turn off old N634 at Km171.6 into an avenue and drive towards the sea. Turn left before reaching the beach and drive around the roundabout on the plaza Carlos V. Jun–Aug.

0.52HEC ◆ H |O| ⊙ G ⊞ s A250 V200 250 A230

Laredo ☏605035

In meadowland, part of which is provided with shade by poplars.

Turn off old N634 (Bilbao–Santander) at Km71.6 and drive N towards the sea and beach. Turn left between the tall buildings and a wood and follow a field track for a further 350 m. Jun–Sep.

3.7HEC ◆ H |O| ⊙ G ⊞ sR

LAS Each name preceded by 'Las' is listed under the name which follows it.

LECUMBERRI
Navarra (☏98)

Aralar ☏504011

On two long grassland terraces in hollow above a narrow stream, small section of site on other side of bridge surrounded by hills and woodland.

100 m S turn NW at Km32.8 off N240. 15 Jun–15 Sep.

1.3HEC ◆ H |O| ⊙ P Ⓟ ⊞ lau A250 V225 225 A175–225

LEIRO
Orense (☏988)

Leiro ☏488036

On level meadow in a pine forest in a valley by a stream, behind the football ground. ➔

All year.
1HEC ◆ H lau A275 V275 275
250–275

LLAFRANC
Girona (972)

Kim's 301156

Terraced site with winding drives, lying on the wooded slopes of a narrow valley leading to the sea.

For access, turn right off the Palafrugell–Tamariu road, follow a wide tarred road for 1 km, past the El Paranso Hotel and head towards Llafranc, 0.4 km from sea.
Etr–Sep.
5.3HEC ◆ H ⊙ P ⊞ lau s
A375 V375 395 395

LLANES
Asturias (985)

Brao 400014

Humpy hillside site on three terraces totally enclosed by 2 m-high wall.

0.5 km from the sea. At Km96.2 on N634 turn N for 1.8 km and turn E towards Cue for 200 m.
Jun–15 Sep.
2.7HEC H ⊙ ⊞ lau s A200 V185
235 200

Maria Elena Celorio 400028

Turn off the N634 (direction Celorio) and continue in the direction of the beach. Opposite the fingerpost follow the steep and narrow access road.
Apr–Sep.
3.7HEC ◇ H ⊙ s ⊞ lau A175 V165 215
155–180

Palacio de Garaña 407487

15 Jun–15 Sep.
20HEC ◇ H ⊙ P ⊞ lau s A260
V220 275 240

LLORET DE MAR
Girona (972)

Canyelles 364504

Spain

Near hotel of same name. Small section near the road has level terrain but access is steep to terraces on two slopes of narrow valley.

If approaching from Tossa de Mar, take the GE682. Turn sharp left between Km15 and Km14. 3.5 km NE of Lloret de Mar and near the signpost for Zona Residencial Cala Canyelles. Drive 0.8 km NE. The asphalt access road has many deep potholes.
May–Sep.
10HEC ◆ H ⊙ P ⊞ lau s

Santa Elena Cludad 364009

Brick terraces on a hill with some poplars and pines.

500 m from the sea. For access turn right off the GE682 to Blanes about 1.2 km S of town, between Km10 and 11 and continue for 200 m.
Seasonal.
6HEC H ⊙
⊞ lau s A475 V475 475 475

LUARCA
Asturias (985)

Cantiles 640938

Meadowland beautifully situated high above the cliffs with little shade from bushes. Footpath to bay 70 m below.

At Km308.5 turn off the N634 from Oviedo, turn towards Faro de Luarca beyond the Firestone filling station. In Villar de Luarca turn right and onwards 1 km to site.
All year.
1.8HEC ◆ H ⊙
⊞ lau s A200
V190 255 175–200

MADRID
Madrid (91)

Madrid 2022835

Terraced site on a hill.

N on N1 near Km7.5 turn NE and continue 800 m on poor access road.
All year.
2.5HEC ◆ H ⊙
lau P

Osuna Canillejas Madrid 17 7410510

On long stretch of land, shade being provided by pines, acacias and maple. Some noise from airfield, road and railway.

If approaching from the town centre take N11 road and drive towards Barajas for about 7.5 km. At Km1 in 300 m and after railway underpass turn right.
All year.
2.3HEC ◆ H ⊙
⊞ lau P A275
V275 275 275

MÁLAGA
Málaga (952)

Balneario del Carmen av Pintor Sorolla 290021

4 km E on Malága–Almeria road at Km249.
All year.
15HEC ◆ H
⊙ s ⊞ lau
A320 V320 320 320

MALGRAT
Barcelona (93)

Kufert 7610389

On two terraces in quiet valley, 1.5 km from the sea.

About 200 m to the right of the N11 (La Jonquera–Barcelona) road, turn off immediately after the branch off to Malgrat de Mar at the MOTEL filling station.
All year.
1.5HEC ◇ H
⊙ P ⊞

Naciones Europ 7611153

Level site divided by a small stream. Partially dusty, another part in meadow under high poplars.

Approach road passes through Camping Malgrat de Mar.
May–Sep.
10HEC ◆ H ⊙
⊞ lau sR A270
V270 270 270

Tordera Tordera 20344693

Situated in dense poplar wood.

Access from Malgrat–Blanes coast road at southern end of Tordera river bridge. Turn seawards and follow single lane rough track for 2 km to site.
May–Sep.

3.5HEC H lau

MANZANARES EL REAL
Madrid (91)

Ortigal 8530120

On sloping ground surrounded by meadows, rocks and scattered with young deciduous trees.

Turn off the local road M612 head N along mountain road for further 2.5 km until reaching the edge of the barren rocky region.
All year.

2HEC H P

MARBELLA
Málaga (952)

Buganvilla 831973

All year.

4HEC H P lau s A275 V275 325 225–275

Marbella Playa 833998

On beach with large sports area.

Access is via carretera nacional 340 Cadiz–Málaga Km200.
All year.

5.5HEC H P lau s A300 V300 550 550

MARINA (LA)
Alicante (96)

Internacional 5419051

At Km29 on Alicante–Cartagena road.
All year.

5HEC H P lau s A280 pitch660

MASNOU (EL)
Barcelona (93)

Hispano 5550875

Turn right at Km642.2 off N11 (Girona–Barcelona road).
All year.

0.8HEC H sP lau

Masnou Camilo Fabra 33–35 5551503

It lies inland from the N11 at Km639.8.
All year.

2HEC H P lau s A310 V310 310 310

Spain

MATARÓ
Barcelona (93)

Costa de Levante 7904236

On gently sloping ground, laid out in large terraces with many shady pitches. Swimming pool and tennis courts between road and site.

Off N11 (Girona–Barcelona road) at Km656.9.
May–Sep.

3HEC H P lau s

Playa Sol 7904720

On gently sloping ground rising above the road in several large terraces to the N of town.

At Km657.2 on the right of the N11 (Girona–Barcelona road) which runs from the French border to Barcelona.
15 May–Sep.

2.5HEC H P

MAZAGÓN
Huelva (955)

Playa de Mazagón 376208

Undulating terrain amongst dunes in sparse pine forest. Long sandy beach.

Turn off the N431 Sevilla–Huelva road just before San Juan del Puerto in direction of Moguer and continue S via Palso de la Frontera.
All year.

8HEC H P lau s A225 V225 225 225

MIAJADAS
Cáceres (927)

301 ctra Madrid–Lisboa Km301. 347931

Level meadowland site above the road from which it is separated by a parking area.

On the N-V1E4 at Km301.8.
May–Oct.

0.5HEC H P lau R A175 V175 175 140–175

MIRANDA DE EBRO
Burgos (947)

At **AMEYUGO** (5 km S)

Monumento al Pastor 354079

On slope behind monument, no shade.

On the N1 Vitoria–Burgos road at Km308.
All year.

1.5HEC H lau RP

MONTFERRER
Lleida (973)

Gran Sol 351332

May–Sep.

9HEC H P lau A215 V215 215 215

MONTGAT
Barcelona (93)

Don Quijote 3891016

On a hill, inland from the main road, on the N outskirts of Montgat. Very few trees, but many sunshade roofs.

Access to the sea leads over N11, then through a railway underpass. On N11 at Km638.8.
Jun–Sep.

2.5HEC H P lau s A260 V260 260 260

MONTRÁS See **PALAFRUGELL**

MONT-ROIG DEL CAMP
Tarragona (977)

Els Prats 810027 ➤

CAMPING CARAVANING PLAYA MONTROIG

COSTA DAURADA - MONT-ROIG - TARRAGONA

Free climatised swimming and paddling pools

Reductions:
30 % from 1.4 to 15.6 and from 1 to 30.9.
50 % from 1.10 to 31.2.

For further information and or site reservation please write to:

Camping Caravaning Playa Montroig Apartado 64 - CAMBRILS (Tarragona) SPAIN Tel. (77) 81 06 37

According to ADAC (and its British couterpart AA) one of the «Top European Camp-sites».

Directly by the sea and along a magnificent, 1 km long sand beach. Well-shaded through typically Mediterranean trees and with carefully maintained gardens.

Spacious, luxurious installations of all kinds and a complete animation and sports programme make it your ideal destination for relaxing, comfortable, nature-contact holidays. Open throughout the year.

Our staff speak English and British guests are specially welcome. No dogs. No television sets.

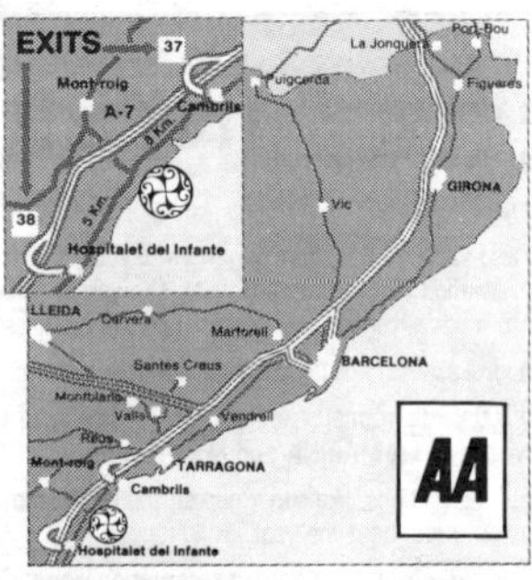

All year.

3HEC |O| lau A275 pitch1100

Marius ☎810684

Pitches are planted with flowers and shrubs. Separate section for dog owners.

For access, leave the N340, Tarragona to Valencia road, at Km224.8 and drive through a 4.9 m-wide railway underpass with a clearance of 3.65 m, then head towards the beach.
Apr–15 Oct.

4HEC |O| G lau A230–330

Miami Playa ☎810920

Partially terraced in pine woodland between the main road and the sea.

To the left of the N340 (Tarragona–Valencia) at Km219.6.
May–Oct.

0.8HEC |O| G R lau
A315 V315 380 315

Miramar ☎811203

Motorway exit 37 or 38. At Km222 on Tarragona–Valencia road (N340) turn off towards the sea.
All year.

4HEC |O| G lau

Oasis Mar Aparado 130 ☎837395

Completely divided into pitches, about 5 km S of Cambrils. Shade is provided by trees.

For access, leave N340 at Km226.7 and turn seawards, then continue on an unsurfaced road for 500 m.
All year.

3HEC |O| G lau A175–350 V175–350
275–550 275–550

Playa Montroig ☎810637

Extensive totally subdivided meadowland site, well shaded by trees. Unfortunately the railway passes right through the site: there is an underpass. TV's are prohibited.

Turn left off the N340 at Km223.5. Use motorway exit 37 or 38.
All year.

30HEC |O| G P lau
A470 V420 750 750

Torre del Sol ☎810486

A level tidy grassland site on two levels, with young poplars and some of medium height between a long stretch of beach and the railway.

For access, turn off the N340, Tarragona to Valencia road at Km224.1 then follow the road towards the sea.
15 Mar–15 Oct.

21HEC |O| G lau A350 pitch1000

MORAIRA

Alicante (☎96)

Buena Vista ☎5744275

Terraced site with pines and eucalyptus

Spain

trees. 0.4 km from the sea. It is more suitable for tents than caravans.

Turn seawards for 100 m at Km2.4, coast road to Calpe E of N332.
All year.

1HEC |O| G lau sP

Moraira

0.5 km from the sea in a pine forest. It is on several terraces and divided into pitches.

It is 1 km S on AP1347, turn W and continue up a hill for 500 m.
15 Jun–15 Sep.

1.5HEC G lau |O| A270
V270 325 270

MOTRICO (MUTRIKU)

Guipúzcoa (☎943)

Altzeta ☎603356

On two sloping meadows, partially terraced. Lovely view of the sea 1 km away.

0.5 km NE on C6212 turn at KmSS56.1.
All year.

1HEC |O| G lau sP

Saturraran ☎601498

In meadow by a narrow stream below the road.

3 km W turn off C6212 at SS60 leave road seawards and continue 200 m over stone bridge.
Jun–Sep.

0.7HEC |O|

MOUGAS

Pontevedra (☎986)

Pedra Rubia ☎355133

In meadowland enclosed by a wall in sterile terrain with views of the mountains. Seawater swimming pool.

Access from Vigo on coastal road C550 to La Guardia at Km67.2 turn off in southerly direction.
Jun–Sep.

2HEC |O| G sP lau A220
V200 220 V220

NÁJERA

Rioja (☎941)

Ruedo ☎360102

Amongst poplars and the area of the bullring, almost no shade.

Turn off the N120 Logroño–Burgos road in Nájera and then continue along the river banks just before the stone bridge across the River Majerilla, then turn left.
Apr–Sep.

1HEC G P lau |O| RP A180
V160 210 210

NOJA

Cantabria (☎942)

Playa Dorada de Ris ☎630830

Level meadowland surrounded by buildings. Not fenced. Section of site near restaurant has no shade.

2 km N of Noja.
Jun–Sep.

1.5HEC |O| G R P lau

Playa Joyel ☎630081

Etr–Sep.

7HEC |O| G R lau A275
V275 275 275

At **PLAYA DE RIS**

Suaces ☎630081

In sandy terrain amongst dunes surrounded by a low wall. Separated from the beach by a large parking area.

Turn N off the N634 in Gama or Beranga towards the sea in the direction of Noja then to site past Camping Playa Dorada.
All year.

0.85HEC |O| G sP lau

NUEVALOS

Zaragoza (☎976)

Laga Park ☎849038

NE towards Alhama de Aragon.
Apr–Sep.

3HEC G P
lau |O| L A300 V300
300 300

NULES

Castellón de la Plana (☎964)

Huertas ☎670817

Clean well-kept site, completely divided into pitches. Few trees but equipped with straw mat roofs. Dancing every Saturday and Sunday.

Turn off N340 at Km47.1 and drive towards sea for 5.3 km. Site about 20 m from the sea.
All year.

2.2HEC |O| G sP lau A310
V310 310 310

OLIVA

Valencia (☎96)

Euro Camping ☎2851753

On a wide sandy beach lying between orange groves and well shaded with poplar and eucalyptus trees.

For access turn off the N332 at Km184.9, 600 m from Oliva. Following signs for camp drive towards the sea for 3.3 km. The access road has narrow stretches and some blind corners so beware of oncoming traffic.
Mar–Oct.

4.3HEC |O| G R P lau
R A275 V275 400 275

Ferienplatz Olé ☎2851180

An extensive site with some pitches amongst dunes. ➔

Turn off the N332 at Km182.4 about 5 km S of Oliva. In about 3 km continue to site on access road partially asphalt, through an orchard.
Mar–Oct.
6.5HEC lau

Kiko ☎2850905

Family holiday camp, divided into pitches, lying between marshland and vineyard. The sea can be reached by crossing a dyke and there are sunshade roofs.

2.2 km on W1065, turn left along camino Pont de Bolo, turn left along camino Azagadar de Carro.
Apr–15 Nov.
1.5HEC lau

OLOT
Girona (☎972)

Tries ☎262405

In woodland with high trees opposite the swimming pool.

Access from the town on the C150 in direction of Girona. On outskirts and before bridge over River Fluvia turn off.
May–Oct.
1HEC lau

ORICAIN
Navarra (☎948)

Ezcaba ☎(948)330315

Gently sloping meadowland and a few terraces on a flat topped hill.

N of Pamplona. Turn off N121 at Km7.3 and drive W towards Berriosuso. Turn right and drive uphill after crossing the bridge over the River Ulzama.
Jun–Sep.
2HEC lau A275 V275 350 275

ORIÑON
Cantabria (☎942)

Oriñon ☎4440246

In a eucalyptus grove and grassland on a bay surrounded by tall steep cliffs.

Turn off the N635 (Bilbao–Santander)

Spain

immediately before reaching Km161 on the Monte Candina and drive along a narrow road down a hill towards the sea for a further 800 m passing Oriñon on the left.
May–Sep.
3HEC lau

ORIO
Guipúzcoa (☎943)

CM Playa de Orio ☎834801

On two flat terraces along cliffs and surrounded by hedges.

Turn off N634 San Sebastian–Bilbao road at about Km12.5 in Orio. Shortly before the bridge over the Rio de Orio turn towards the sea and continue for 1.5 km.
All year.
5.4HEC lau

OROPESA DEL MAR
Castellón de la Plana (☎964)

Almendros ☎310475

Level, subdivided site, surrounded by tall steep cliffs.

Turn off the N634 0.9 km from sea. E of N340 between Km87.2 and Km87.3. Close to sea.
Mar–Sep.
0.8HEC lau A265 V265 265 200–265

Blavamar ☎310347

Sloping site with shade provided by roofing. Individual pitches which are relatively close together.

Turn left off the N340 (Tarragona–Valencia) at Km90.6, a few kms before Oropesa and continue on a stony lane. In 1 km turn right to site along an asphalt access road.
May–Sep.
1.5HEC

Didota
Etr–Sep.

1.7HEC lau A275 V275 275 275

PALAFRUGELL
Girona (☎972)

At **MONTRÁS** (3 km SW)

Relax-Ge ☎301549

Level meadow under poplars and olive trees.

Turn off the C255 at Km38.7. 4 km to the sea.
Jun–Aug.
4HEC lau A300 pitch700

At **PLAYA DE ENSUEÑOS**

Tamarlu playa de Ensueños ☎300422

Terraced site with mixture of high young pines.

Turn towards site at beach parking area and continue 300 m.
May–Sep.
2HEC lau A315–350 V315–350 355–375 315–350

PALAMÓS
Girona (☎972)

Benelux ☎315575

On hilly ground, stretching over an area planted with pine trees and a field planted with poplars.

If approaching from Girona take the C255 and turn east near Km40.5. Take rather narrow partly asphalted road and follow it for a further 1.3 km.
Apr–Sep.
4.6HEC lau

Coma ☎314638

Sloping terraced terrain with young deciduous trees and isolated pines. 0.8 km from the sea.

In N outskirts turn seawards off the C255 near the RENAULT garage.
Apr–Sep.
5.8HEC lau

Internacional Palamos ☎314736
Signposted.
Apr–Sep.
5.2HEC H |O| P lau s A330–375 V330–375 330–375 Å330–375

International Kings ☎317511
Apr–Sep.
8HEC H |O| P lau s A430 V435 525 Å525

Palamós Cala Margardia ☎314296
Apr–15 Oct.
5HEC H |O| sP lau A375 V375 375 Å375

Vilarromá ☎314375
Clean and tidy site, almost completely divided into pitches.
Turn off on the eastern outskirts of Palamós near big petrol station.
May–Sep.

Spain

1.8HEC H |O| lau s A340–360 V330–360 370–390 Å230–260

At **CALONGE** (5 km W)

Cala Gogó de Luxe ☎651564
Terraced site in tall pine woodland and poplars with some good views of the sea. Underpass across to section of site with private beach. Some internal dusty roads.
Access from Palamós 4 km S on coastal road C253, entrance to site on right shortly after Km47.
May–Sep.
16HEC H |O| sP lau A465 V465 550 Å465

Internacional ☎651233

All year.
9.3HEC H |O| P lau s A335–405 V335–405 335–405 Å280–405

PALMERES (LAS)
Alicante (☎96)

Palmeres ctra del Saler
At Km23 on Nazaret–Oliva road.
All year.
H |O| P

PALS
Girona (☎972)

Cypsela ☎636211
Well-kept grassy site in a pine wood.
For access, turn towards the sea N of Pals and follow road towards Playa de Pals, then turn left after Km3.
15 May–Sep.
20HEC H |O| P lau s A440 V440 550 Å550

See advertisement page 368

Inter-Pals ☎623179

Terraced site on gently sloping ground in pine wood.

4.8 km E of Pals between Km4 and Km5 of the GE road to Playa de Pals. 1 km past Cypsela.
Apr–Sep.

4HEC ◆ H lau sP A375 V375 375 375

Mas Patoxas ☎636928

All year.

11HEC ◆ H P lau A310–375 V310–375 310–375 310–375

At **PLAYA DE PALS**

Playa Brava ☎636894

Recently opened site on level terrain adjoining pine woodlands, golf course, rivers and sea.

From N end of village of Pals turn towards sea and Playa de Pals.
15 May–15 Sep.

11HEC H P lau s A220 pitch1400

PANCORBO

Burgos (☎947)

Desfiladero ☎354027

Off N 1 at Km305.2.
All year.

1.3HEC ◆ H RP lau A200 V200 200 200

PANXÓN

Pontevedra (☎986)

Playa de Patas ☎366110

Gently sloping towards the sea in deciduous woodland on edge of built up area.

Turn off the C550 Vigo la Guardia road at Km48.6 in direction of Panjón. Continue on coastal road PO333 to within 3 km of the bay then turn sharp right.
Jul–Aug.

1HEC H lau s

PECHÓN

Cantabria (☎942)

Arenas ☎717188

On numerous terraces between rocks, reaching down to the sea.

Turn off N634 E of Unquera at Km74 towards sea and take road towards S. Difficult for caravans.
Jun–Sep.

12HEC H s

PERLORA-CANDAS

Asturias (☎985)

Perlora ☎870048

On top of a large hill on a peninsula with a few terraced pitches.

Access 7 km W of Gijon, turn off N632 in direction Luanco and continue for 5 km.
All year.

2HEC H s lau

PINEDA DE MAR

Barcelona (☎93)

Bel-Sol ☎7625055

Level site with some trees providing shade.

The access road is at the end of the village. From the S end of the village take the signposted turning for the 'sea' and 'Hotel Taurus'. Continue on this road to the beach promenade, then turn right for the site.
May–Sep.

2.5HEC H lau s

Caballo de Mar ☎7625566

On sandy terrain on both sides of the railway line and scattered with poplars and sunshade roofs.

Access from southern outskirts turning seawards and to the right at beach to site.
All year.

3HEC H lau sP

Camell ☎7623846

Surrounded by deciduous trees next to a small wood owned by the Taurus Hotel.

Turn off the N11 at Km677 and drive along av de los Naranjos in direction of sea.
May–Sep.

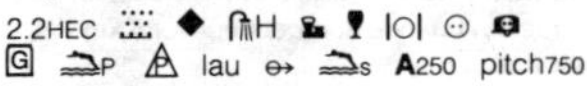
2.2HEC ◆ H lau s A250 pitch750

Enmar ☎7625918

Leave autopista at exit 9 (Lloret and Malgrat) and continue towards Pineda de Mar.
All year.

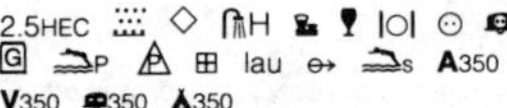
2.5HEC ◇ H P lau s A350 V350 350 350

Euro-Mar ☎7623342

Level, well-kept site near the sea, shaded by trees.

From the N outskirts of the village turn off towards the sea, then continue for 500 m.
May–Sep.

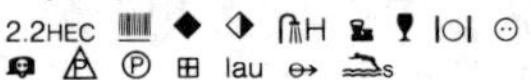
2.2HEC ◆ H Ⓟ lau s

PLATJA D'ARO (LA)

Girona (☎972)

Riembau ☎817123

Level grassland site under poplar trees, in quiet rural area.

Turn off the C253 inland on southern outskirts after the Rio Riudau bridge and continue 0.9 km to site, signposted, and 1 km from sea.
May–Sep.

15.5HEC ◆ H P lau s A235–275 pitch1125–1400

Valldaro ☎817515

Extensive level meadowland under poplars, pines and eucalyptus trees. Some large pitches without shade.

Site lies on the left of the GE662 towards Castell and Santa Cristinia d'Aro at Km4.
All year.

15HEC ◆ H P lau s A300–375 V300–375 300–375 265–375

PLAYA DE ENSUEÑOS See **PALAFRUGELL**

Spain

PLAYA DE PALS See **PALS**

PLAYA DE RIS See **NOJA**

PLAYA DÈ SAN JUAN

Alicante (☎96)

Playa Muchavista ☎5654526

Within high walls, under a few palms and sunshade roofing. Inland from coast road A190 (Campello–Alicante). Narrow beach can be reached by crossing the coastal road.

For access turn off near Km9.2, cross single track railway line, drive on for 400 m then turn right. For better route turn off near Km8.6.
All year.

1.7HEC ◆ H lau s A270 V270 320 225–320

PORTONOVO

Pontevedra (☎986)

Paxariñas ☎723055

Slightly sloping towards a bay, in amongst dunes, with high pines and young deciduous trees. Lovely beach.

All year.

2HEC ◆ H s lau A240 V225 250 250

PRAT DE LLOBREGAT (EL)

Barcelona (☎93)

Cala Gogõ ☎3794600

Long narrow site, on level meadowland party in a pine wood. Five swimming pools.

For access, leave the C246 dual carriageway, Barcelona to Castelldefèls, by crossing the bridge in the direction of the airport, turn left again at the next junction and continue towards the beach.
Well signposted.
Feb–15 Dec.

23HEC ◆ H sP lau A265–375 V265–375 265–375 265–375

PRULLÁNS

Lleida (☎973)

Cerdanya ☎510262

On meadowland rising gently from the road. Some deciduous trees.

From the Puigcerdá, take the C1313 and drive SW for about 20 km towards La Seu d'Ugell. The entrance to the site is at Km158.7, just after the turning for Prulláns.
All year.

7HEC ◆ H P lau R A245 V245 245 245

PUERTO DE LA SELVA

Girona (☎972)

Port de la Selva ☎387287

Level, grassland site with young poplar trees.

1.5 km from the village, in a valley off the Puerto de la Selva to Cadaques road.
Jun–Sep.

3HEC ◆ H P Ⓟ lau s

PUERTO DE SANTA MARÍA

Cádiz (☎956)

Gaudalete ☎861749

Undulating in parts, very sandy terrain, 0.9 km to the sea.

Access from Km65.8 off the NIV–25 Sevilla–Cádiz road. Signposted.
All year.

5.5HEC ◆ H P lau A245 V200 245 175–245

PUERTO REAL

Cádiz (☎956)

Pinar ☎830897

Extends from edge of sparse pine woodland to a tree covered hill, 2 km to nearest good beach.

1 km SE of the village and approx 200 m inland E of the above the NIV (Sevilla–Cádiz) at Km666.
All year.

1.4HEC ◆ H lau

PUNTA UMBRIA
Huelva (955)

Pinos del Mar 310812

Undulating sandy terrain with pine woodland, sub-divided. 800 m from the sea.

SW from Huelva via bridge over the River Odiel past Camping Club Las Vegas.
15 Jun–15 Sep.

4HEC lau

REINANTE
Lugo (982)

Reinante 124509

Longish site beyond a range of dunes on lovely sandy beach.

On N634 at Km391.7.
Jun–15 Sep.
1.3HEC H lau

RIBERA DE CABANES
Castellón (964)

Torre la Sol 310212

Turn seawards at Km90.6 on N340 (Tarragona–Valencia) and continue for 1 km on a stoney road.
All year.

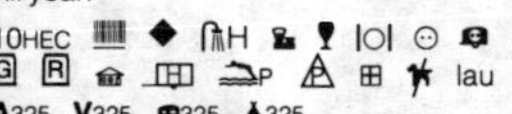

10HEC H lau A325 V325 325 325

RIBERA DE CARDÓS
Lleida (973)

Cardós 633012

Long stretch of meadowland divided by four rows of poplars.

Near the electricity plant in Llavorsi turn NE onto the Ribera road and follow it for 9 km. Entrance near hostel Sol y Neu.
Jul–Sep.
2.2HEC H lau RP A245 V245 245 245

RODA DE BERÁ
Tarragona (977)

Arco 800902

About 200 m SW of the Arco de Berá (triumphant arch), on the seaward side of the N340 at Km269.9.
All year.
3HEC H lau S A300 V300 300 300

Playa Bará 802701

Extensive site well kept and laid out in terraces. Separated from the beautifully situated beach by railway line with an underpass.

For access turn off the N340 near the Arco de Berá (triumphant arch) and drive towards the sea for about 1.5 km.
10 Mar–Sep.
13HEC H P lau L

Stel 802002

Spain

Via motorway (A7) exit 31.
Apr–Sep.
10HEC H P lau S A400 V400 400 400

ROMPIDO (EL)
Huelva (955)

Catapum 390165

Extensive site in clean sparse pine woodland above the beach and the coastal road.

Jun–Sep.
13HEC H R

ROSES
Girona (972)

Bahia de Roses 256669

Flat, grassy site. About 200 m from the sea.

On left of road as you enter the village from the W.
Etr–Sep.
3.5HEC H lau S A350 V350 350 350

Salatà 256086

On level terrain on the SW outskirts of Roses, surrounded by 2m-high walls.

Approaching from the W turn right just after entering the village and drive about 100 m to the Hotel Nautilius. Turn right again and continue for a further 150 m to the site.
15 May–Sep.
1HEC H S A310–350 V310–350 310–350 310–350

ROTAS (LAS)
Alicante (96)

Pinos 5782698

On two terraces in shade of pine woodland. Access to sea through bungalow estate via an alley of palms.

2 km SE of Denia turn left to Las Rotas after 1.5 km turn left at SPAR supermarket, site 300 m.
All year.
3HEC H lau S A210 V220 240 220

Tolosa 5782041

Two terraces with deciduous trees and sunshade roofing by the sea.

Turn left off the Jávea coast road about 2 km SE of Denia and head towards Las Rotas. After 1 km turn left and drive towards the sea for 150 m.
Apr–Sep.
0.8HEC H S A250 V250 280 250

SAGUNTO
Valencia (96)

Malvarrosa de Corinto

All year.
12HEC H S A225 V200 300 225

SALOU
Tarragona (977)

Cala Garbí 370847

Clean tidy site laid out in terraces and planted with pine trees. Slopes gently from the coast road down to the beach.

Take the road from Salou to Cabo, about 1 km before the turning towards Tarragona.
Apr–Sep.
3HEC H S lau

Playa Larga Salou 381800

Divided into two sections, which lie on both sides of the coast road. The section of the camp between the road and the sea is laid out in terraces and almost completely shaded. The other section is only partly shaded.

Apr–Oct.
4HEC H SP lau

Sangull 381641

In two parts on two levels separated from the sea by the road, a row of houses and a railway. Front section is landscaped with good facilities and a pool, rear part consists of sparse and stony grassland with poplars.

SW outskirts, 200 m inland from coast road to Cambrils.
All year.
14HEC H P lau S A195–385 V195–385 195–385 195–385

See advertisement page 372

Siesta 380852

Divided into pitches and planted with young deciduous and old olive trees. Sunshade roofs.

If approaching from Tarragona, turn right off the main road on outskirts of Salou and drive a further 150 m to the camp. The site is between the railway and road 0.4 km from the sea.
Mar–Nov.
5HEC H P lau S A330 V330 330 330

SAN MARTIN DEL PIMPOLLAR
Avila (918)

Choza de Gredos 348213

On gentle incline to river, amidst meadowland, with trees. Discotheque.

About 500 m E of El Barco de Avila (N110) on the C500.
Jun–Oct.
1.5HEC H P lau R A175 V175 200 175

camping sangulí

SALOU TARRAGONA

Tel. (003477)

CAMPING SANGULÍ Salou tel.381641

CAMPING CARAVANNING SANGULI is because of its situation, its climate and installations, one of the best sites in Spain and one of the most appreciated in Europe.

It is situated only 50 m from the beach and the town of SALOU, in the very heart of the COSTA DORADA, and one of the most beautiful tourism centres of the Mediterranean coast. Well known for its golden beaches, crystal-clear water and and extraordinary mild climate throughout the year.

On the site, 3000 trees — typical of the Mediterranean region, such as pine, palm, mulberry eucalyptus, olive, and carobean trees, as well as poplars, provide abundant shade.

In the shopping area you will find a supermarket, boutique, souvenirs, bar, restaurant, pub-discotheque, laundry service, nursery, children's playground, ice-cream shop, etc.

The sports and leisure complex gives you the opportunity to practise all kinds of sports, such as tennis, squash, mini-golf, frontón, boules, swimming, football, basketball, handball, and table-tennis. You will also find a games room, cinema, satellite TV, etc.

Four marvellous swimming pools, surrounded by grass, invite you to free swimming fun.

The site is fenced-in, guarded day and night and well illuminated. Daily doctor's visit. Large, modern and well kept ablution blocks provide free hot water 24 hours a day. Abundant water of excellent quality in all taps.

All this — and more — makes CAMPING SANGULI an ideal site to spend unforgettable holidays!

DISCOUNTS: 10% AA members. 25% from 1.4 till 15.6 and in September; 50% from 1.10 till 31.3.

SAN SEBASTIAN (DONOSTIA)
Guipúzcoa (☎943)

At **IGUELDO**

Garoa Camping Igueldo ☎214502

Terraced site on Monte Igueldo divided by hedges.

Follow signs Monte Igueldo from town, and beach road, about 4.5 km.
All year.

SAN SEBASTIAN DE LOS REYES
Madrid (☎91)

Aterpe Alai ☎6544640

Partly divided into pitches by tall hedges and planted with many poplar trees.

E of N1 at Km25.
All year.

1.8HEC H P lau A220 V220 220 180–220

SAN VINCENTE DE LA BARQUERA
Cantabria (☎942)

Rosal ☎710263

In tall pine woodlands beyond the dunes, with several sandy hollows.

On N634 before bridge turn right, after 800 m turn left.
Jun–Sep.

3HEC H s lau

SANTA CILIA DE JACA
Huesca (☎974)

Pirineos ☎377351

On meadowland in an oak wood and has a beautiful view of the Pyrénées.

N of C134 at Km34.5.
All year.

5HEC H RP lau

SANTA CRISTINA D'ARO
Girona (☎972)

Santa Cristina ☎835573

In a forest of pine and deciduous trees, on the slopes of a valley to the SE of the village.

To the right of the C250, Girona to Sant Feliu road, beyond Km30.
All year.

2.5HEC H sP lau A315 V315 315 315

SANTA EUGENIA DE RIVEIRA
La Coruña (☎981)

Coroso ☎838002

15 Jun–15 Sep.

3HEC H lau s A250 V250 275 250

SANTA FÉ
Granada (☎958)

Alamos

Level site in dense poplar woodland.

7 km W of Granada.
Mar–Oct.

0.4HEC H P

SANTA MARINA DE VALDEON
Léon (☎987)

El Cares

N off N621 from Portilla de la Reina.
Jun–Sep.

1.2HEC H R lau A195 V195 250 195–255

SANTA MARTA DE TORMES
Salamanca (☎923)

Regio ☎200250

Divided into several fields.

100 m from the N501 (Salamanca–Avila) behind Hotel Jardin-Regio.
All year.

3HEC H P lau A275 V275 275 225–275

SANTANDER
Cantabria (☎942)

Bella Vista ☎271016

Municipal site on edge of pine woodland. Many steps leading to beach.

About 10km N along coastal road to Cabo Maior. Turn left shortly before lighthouse.
All year.

4.4HEC H lau s A180 V170 210 125–210

SANT ANTONI DE CALONGE
Girona (☎972)

Costa Brava ☎650222

Level site with tall pine woodland partially subdivided under deciduous trees.

Access via the Calonge de les Gavarres turn off from the C253 S of Calonge and behind the hotel.
Jun–Sep.

2.4HEC H

Euro ☎650879

May–Sep.

7HEC H P lau s A295–360 V295–360 310–385 310–385

Internacional de Calonge ☎651233

Well-kept terraced site on slopes of hill in a pine forest.

At Km7.6 on Sant Feliú-Palamós road.
All year.

10HEC H sP lau

Treumal ☎651095

Entrance on Sant Feliú-Platja d'Aro-Palamós road.
May–Sep.

6HEC H P lau A480 V480 560 480

SANTA OLIVA
Tarragona (☎977)

Santa Oliva ☎661252

At Km3 on Calle Vendrell-Santa Oliva road.
All year.

1.8HEC H P lau A230 V230 230 230

SANTA POLA
Alicante (☎96)

Bahia de Santa Pola II Valverde Bajo 10 ☎5411012

On large terraces, scattered with old olive and carob trees. Straw mat roofs also provide shade.

It lies to the left of the C3317, from Elche at Km26, and just before the junction with the N332 and the big EL CRUCE petrol station. 1 km from the sea.
All year.

5HEC H P lau s A250 V250 280 250

SANTA SUSANA
Barcelona (☎93)

Bon Répos ☎7634075

In pine woodland between railway and the beach with some sunshade roofing.

Turn off the N11 at Km681 and approach via the underpass (height limit 2.5 m) just before reaching beach.
All year.

4HEC H P lau s

Oasis ☎7634003

Level site under deciduous trees and conifers, separated from the beach by the railway line (underpass).

Turn off N11 towards the sea.
All year.

3HEC H lau s

SANT CEBRIÁ DE VALLALTA
Barcelona (☎93)

Verneda ☎7630087

Inland and among tall trees.

Leave the N11 Girona-Barcelona road at the far end of Sant Pol de Mar, turn inland at Km670. Continue for 2 km to edge of the village and short of the bridge over the Riera Vallala turn right.
May–Sep.

1.6HEC H lau A225 V225 225 225

SANTIAGO DE COMPOSTELA
La Coruña (☎981) ➔

Spain

Santiago de Compostela ☎888002

Divided into 3 sections. Zone A along the road with almost no shade. Zones B and C in mixed woodland.

On the N550 (La Coruña–Santiago) at Km55.4, about 7 km N of the place of pilgrimage.
20 Jun–Sep.

2HEC ◆ H lau

SANTILLANA DEL MAR

Cantabria (☎942)

Santillana ☎818250

Slightly sloping meadow with bushes on a hillock within the area of a restaurant adjoining a swimming pool.

Access from Santander via C6316 turn off shortly after the Santillana sign and continue up the hill.
All year.

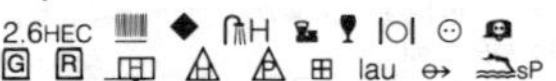

SANT PERE PESCADOR

Girona (☎972)

Aquarius ☎520003

Level meadowland. Partially in shade, quiet well organised site by the lovely sandy beach of Bahia de Rosas.

Travel in direction of L'Escala and turn towards the beach following signs.
25 May–Sep.

3.5HEC H s lau A390 V390 390 390

Ballena Alegre 2 ☎520302

Extensive site near wide sandy beach with dunes. Large shopping complex.

Access from L'Escala to San Martin de Ampurias, then onward to site in 2 km on unmetalled road.
15 May–15 Sep.

24HEC ◇ H P lau s

Dunas ☎520400

Level extensive grassland site with young poplars, some of medium height on the beach, totally subdivided.

It lies 5 km SE of village. If approaching from L'Escala follow an asphalt road to San Martin, then follow a dusty earth track for 2.5 km.
15 May–15 Sep.

18HEC H sP lau A225 pitch1000–1750

Palmeras ☎520506

On level grassland with, as yet, little shade.

Off the road from Sant Pere Pescador to the beach about 300 m from the sea.
All year.

2.1HEC ◆ H lau sR A360 V360 360 360

SANT POL DE MAR

Barcelona (☎93)

Spain

Kanguro ☎7600205

On the terraced slopes of a hill overlooking the sea. Large sandy beach is accessible via rather low pedestrian tunnels under the road and railway line.

Off the N11 at Km668.5.
Apr–15 Sep.

2HEC H lau sP A280 V280 280 280

SEGOVIA

Segovia (☎911)

Acueducto ☎425000

SE next to N601 at Km85.
Jun–Sep.

2.5HEC ◆ H P lau A275 V275 300 275

SEU D'URGELL (LA)

Lleida (☎973)

Valira av Valira 10 ☎351035

Meadowland site in three sections, rear part surrounded by deciduous trees with pleasant views.

W of C1313 towards Lleida at Km130.
All year.

3HEC ◇ H P lau

SEVILLA (SEVILLE)

Sevilla (☎954)

Sevilla ☎514379

Level site near airfield, road and railway.

About 2 km from airfield, 100 m from the NIV (Madrid–Sevilla) at Km533.8.
All year.

1.2HEC H P lau A250 V250 250 250

SIMANCAS

Valladolid (☎983)

Plantió ☎590082

In a poplar wood, on the river bank.

On outskirts turn off N620 at Km132.2 and continue 500 m on narrow asphalt road and a long single track stone bridge over the Rio Pisverga.
15 Jun–15 Sep.

1HEC ◆ H RP lau

SITGES

Barcelona (☎93)

Garrofer ☎8941780

Terraced site on mountain, partially under high sunshade roofing and pines. 0.4 km from the sea.

At Km24.7 on mountain side of C246. Turn inland at large bend in road.
Mar–Nov.

8.4HEC ◆ H lau s A275 pitch550

Roca ☎8940043

On three terraces with a view of Sitges. Shade is provided by pines and deciduous trees. Separate section for young people. 1 km from the sea.

Turn off the C246 (Barcelona–Tarragona) in the direction of Sant Pere de Ribes/San Pedro de Ribas. In 15 m turn right to site.
May–Sep.

2HEC ◆ H lau sP A300 V300 300 300

SORIA

Soria (☎975)

Fuente de la Teja ☎222967

On slightly rising terrain with poplars.

Follow the N11 to Km224.3 in direction of Madrid, about 2 km S of Soria. Then follow signs to Navalcaballo for 200 m and turn left.
Jun–Oct.

0.8HEC H P

SORT

Lleida (☎973)

Noguera Pallaresa ☎620820

On a meadow between a canal, the Rio Noguera Pallaresa and below the C147.

Turn off the road at Km110.9 on the N outskirts and below the turning signed 'Llesay 16' and drive towards the river.
Jun–Sep.

3HEC ◆ H R A200 V200 200 200

TALARN

Lleida (☎973)

Gaset ☎650737

Meadowland with trees providing shade below the main road and by the Embalse San Antonio reservoir.

Turn off at Km71 on C147 and continue for 400 m.
Apr–Oct.

3HEC ◆ H L lau A245 V245 245 245

TAMARIT

Tarragona (☎977)

Caledonia ☎650098

All year.

3.5HEC H P lau s

Trillas ☎650249

About 100 m from the sea. On several terraces planted with olive trees next to a farm.

For access, turn off the N340 at Km259.3, about 8 km N of Tarragona. Follow road and cross a narrow railway bridge. (Beware of oncoming traffic).
All year.

4.5HEC ◆ H lau A370 V370 370 A370

TARIFA
Cádiz (☎956)

Paloma ☎684203
All year.
2.5HEC ◆ H lau

Rió Jara ctra National ☎684279
Extensive site on meadowland with good tree coverage. Long sandy beach.
On the N340 Málaga–Cádiz road at Km79.7 turn towards the sea.
All year.
2HEC ◆ H sR lau

At **TORRE DE LA PEÑA** (7 km NW)

Torre de la Peña ☎684903
Terraced, on both sides of through road. Upper terraces are considerably more quiet. Roofing provides shade. View of the sea, Tarifa and on clear days N Africa (Tangier).
Entrance on the N340 Cádiz–Málaga, at Km76.5 turn inland by the old square tower.
All year.
3HEC ◆ H sP lau A235 V235 235 A235

TARRAGONA
Tarragona (☎977)

Gaya ☎653070
On level grassland with single poplars on the Rio Gaya.
Turn N inland at Km259.7 off the N340 (Barcelona–Tarragona). Continue on metalled road in 7.5 km via T202 and T203 to just before the Gaia river bridge at El Cattlar. To site via unmade road to right in 0.2 km.
15 May–Sep.
1.5HEC ◆ H lau A200–220 V200–220 200–220 A200–220

Palmeras ☎236722
Divided into three parts under trees between railway and sea.
From Barcelona on N430 before reaching town turn seawards at Km255.6 and continue 200 m via guarded level crossing.
Apr–early Oct.
10HEC ◆ H lau A280–390 V280–390 280–390 A275–350

Playa Larga ☎381800
Close to the sea.
At Km254.9 on N3409.
Jun–Sep.
4HEC ◆ H lau

Tamarit Playa Tamarit ☎650051
Well-kept site at the sea beneath the ruins of Tamarit Castle. One section lies under tall shady trees, and a new section lies in a meadow with some trees.

Spain

Turn off N340 and Km259.3 about 8 km N of Tarragona and drive 800 m seaward along a narrow track.
All year.
7HEC H lau

Torre de la Mora ☎650277
Beside the sea, overlooking a rocky bay and a sandy beach. Laid out in terraces on the slopes of a hill and is divided into pitches, which are mainly reserved for tents. Becomes very full early in the season.
Approaching from Barcelona turn off N340 about 5 km N of Tarragona and short of Km258. Follow asphalt road seaward and pass through railway underpass.
Apr–Oct.
7HEC ◆ H

TIERMAS
Zaragoza (☎948)

Mar del Pirineo ☎887009
On broad terraces sloping down to the banks of the Embalse de Yese. Roofing provides shade for tents and cars.
Situated on the N240 Huesca–Pamplona road at Km317.7.
May–Sep.
3.2HEC ◆ H P lau L A290 V260 290 A290

TOLEDO
Toledo (☎925)

Greco ☎220090
Few shady terraces on slope leading down to the Rio Tajo. On SW outskirts of town.
Approaching from the town centre take the C401, Carretera Comarcal and drive SW for about 2 km. Turn right at Km28 and drive 300 m towards Puebla de Montalban.
All year.
2.5HEC ◆ H P lau R A275 V275 300 A275

TORDESILLAS
Valladolid (☎983)

Astral ☎770953
Apr–Sep.
3HEC ◆ H P lau R A230 V220 220 A175–220

TORLA
Huesca (☎974)

Ordesa ☎486146
On three terraces between well-kept hedges.
2 km N of the village at Km96 and N of the C138.
Jun–Sep.

3.5HEC ◆ H P

TORREBLANCA
Castellón (☎964)

Mon Rossi ☎420296
Apr–Sep.
0.8HEC ◆ H lau A280 V280 280 A280

TORRE DEL MAR
Málaga (☎952)

Torre Del Mar ☎540224
All year.
2.4HEC ◆ H lau A350 V350 375 A350

TORRE DEL ORO
Huelva (☎955)

Doñana Playa ☎376281
All year.
2.6HEC ◆ H P lau A250 V250 250 A250

TORRE DE LA PEÑA See **TARIFA**

TORREDEMBARRA
Tarragona (☎977)

Norla ☎640453
The beach is reached over a level crossing.
Between the road and railway on the seaward side of the N340 Barcelona to Tarragona road near Km265.4
May–Sep.
3HEC ◆ H lau

Relax-Sol ☎640760
Situated near the sea, between the main N11 road and the railway line.
Access at Km265 of the N11.
All year.
2HEC ◆ H lau

Valle de Oro ☎640902
On level, rather barren meadow with some trees on the outskirts of village, between the road and the railway.
Turn seawards at Km264.7 of the N340.
All year.
2HEC ◆ H lau sP

TORROELLA DE MONTGRI
Girona (☎972)

Delfin Verde ☎758450
On undulating ground with some pine trees, and open meadow beside the long sandy beach.
Turn left off the road to Begur approx. 2 km S of Torroella de Montgri, and head towards Maspinell following a wide asphalt road 4.8 km towards the sea.
20 May–20 Sep. ➤

20HEC |O| ⊙ P ⊞ lau s A200 pitch1000–1650

Sirena ☎758542

Level site with some grass near the beach.

Approaching from Torroella de Montgri turn right about 400 m from 'Estartit' sign at Km1 and continue 300 m.
Apr–Oct.

2HEC H |O| ⊙ sP ⊞ lau

TOSSA DE MAR
Girona (☎972)

Cala Llevadó ☎340314

Magnificent terraced site with hairpin roads overlooking three bays, all suitable for bathing. Narrow, winding drives which are quite steep in parts. Separate section for caravans.

Take the coast road for about 4 km towards Lloret de Mar and turn towards the sea.
May–Sep.

13HEC ◆ H |O| ⊙ sP ⊞ lau **A**315–425 **V**315–425 360–480 315–425

Can Marti ☎340851

1 km from the sea.
Apr–Sep.

11.5HEC ◆ H ⊙ P ⊞ lau |O| s **A**290–350 **V**265–292 290–350 290–350

Pola de Luxe ☎341050

Partly on flat ground and partly on terraces, in a valley which opens out into a rocky bay with a sandy beach. Advance booking necessary for July and August. In height of the season cars are accommodated in separate car parks.

From Tossa take the winding coast road, GE684 and drive N for 5 km towards Sant Feliú. The camp lies between Km27 and Km28.
4 Apr–19 Oct.

◆ H |O| ⊙ s ⊞ lau

Tossa ☎340547

On a meadow in a quiet, isolated valley, in a deciduous forest. 3 km from the sea.

3 km SW near the GE681 (Tossa de Mar–Llagostera), in 600 m to site along an unmade road.
15 Apr–Sep.

5.6HEC H |O| ⊙ P Ⓟ ⊞ lau

Turismar ☎341105

Partly terraced on a slope. Shade is provided by plane, olive and poplar trees.

On both sides of the GE681 to Llagostera between Km14 and 15, 1.7 km NW of Tossa de Mar.
Apr–Sep.

8HEC ◆ H |O| ⊙ P ⊞ lau **A**380 **V**380 380 380

TOTANA
Murcia (☎968)

Totana ☎420609

All year.

1.5HEC ◆ H |O| ⊙ P ⊞ lau

VALDEMORILLO
Madrid (☎91)

Valdemorillo ☎8990002

On sandy meadowland under trees surrounded by hills.

1 km E at Km10.4 on the C600 road between Madrid and El Escorial.
All year.

3HEC H ⊙ P ⊞ lau |O| **A**200–300 **V**200–300 200–300 200–300

VALDOVIÑO
La Coruña (☎981)

Valdoviño ☎487076

Six gently sloping fields partially in shade. Located behind Cafeteria Andy and block of flats with several villas beyond.

Turn off the C646 towards Cedeira seawards and continue 700 m to site.
Jul–Sep.

1.8HEC ◆ H |O| ⊙ ⊞ lau **A**265 **V**265 275 265

VALENCIA
Valencia (☎96)

Saler ☎3670411

Amongst pines providing shade with its own entrance to sandy beach in 300 m.

Access from Valencia via coastal road towards Cullera as far as El Saler, then left at SE end of village and turn right.
All year.

9.2HEC H |O| ⊙ sP ⊞ lau **A**270 **V**320 320 160–270

VALENCIA DE DON JUAN
Léon (☎987)

Pico Verde ☎750525

Turn E off the N630 (Léon–Madrid) at Km32.2 and continue for 4 km.
15 Jun–15 Sep.

2.7HEC H |O| ⊙ P ⊞ lau **A**200 **V**200 200 200

VALL-LLOBREGA
Girona (☎72)

Castell Park ☎315263

Level and gently sloping meadow with poplars and pine woodland on a hill.

At Km40 about 100 m to the right of the C255 to Palamós and 3 km S of Montras.
Jun–Sep.

4.9HEC ◆ H |O| ⊙ ⊞ lau sP **A**225–280 **V**225–280 225–280 225–280

VALLROMANES
Barcelona (☎93)

Vedado ☎5681392

Beautiful site in a valley, with plenty of shade from poplar trees backing onto a forest.

Leave motorway at exit no. 3 and drive towards El Masnou. From El Masnou or from the N11 take the minor road towards Granollers and drive NW almost up to Km7.
All year.

4HEC ◆ H |O| ⊙ P ⊞

VEGA DE LIÉBANA
Santander (☎942)

Molino ☎730489

In an orchard by river about 300 m outside town.

Apr–Sep.

1HEC ◆ H |O| ⊙ RP ⊞ lau **A**180 **V**180 200 175

VENDRELL (EL)
Tarragona (☎977)

Franca's ☎680725

Slopes gently towards the sea, between the beach and the railway line which separates the two sections. These are connected by a pedestrian underpass.

Lies about 100 m away from the N340 on the seaward side at Km273.
Apr–Sep.

3.5HEC ◆ H |O| ⊙ s ⊞

San Salvador ☎680804

On two large grassy terraces and has some sunshade roofs. Near the sea and next to some tall buildings.

Easiest route is to turn off the N340 at Km275 and drive towards the sea and Comal-Ruga.
Etr–Sep.

2.9HEC ◆ H |O| ⊙ ⊞ lau s **A**340 **V**340 340 340

VERGEL
Alicante (☎96)

Llanos ☎5750273

In a field next to an orange grove and shaded by tall trees.

Turn off N332 between Km176.3 and Km176.4 and continue on gravel road for 200 m.
All year.

3HEC ◆ H ⊙ P ⊞ lau |O| s **A**300 **V**300 400 300

Patos ☎784325

15 Jun–15 Sep.

3.2HEC ◆ H |O| ⊙ s ⊞ lau **A**325 **V**325 325 325

VIGO
Pontevedra (☎986)

Samil ctra d'Samil 155 ☎232198

In a hollow surrounded by pine woodland separated from the sea by road and dunes.

SW of Vigo and E of the coast road towards Canido.

All year.

1HEC ◆ ⊙ lau

VILADECANS

Barcelona (☎93)

See also **CASTELLDEFÉLS**

Ballena Alegre 1 ☎6580504

May–20 Sep.

22HEC ◆ ⊙ lau

A375 V375 ⛟375 Å375

Filipinas ☎6582895

Large site on level ground in a pine forest and stretching down to the sea. Separate 'Quiet Section' where radios are not permitted.

Leave the C246 (Barcelona–Castelledeféls) at Km12 and follow a 0.5 km long, narrow dirt track. Well signposted.

All year.

30HEC ⊙ lau A330–360

V330–360 ⛟330–360 Å330–360

Toro Bravo ☎6581250

Level site in extensive pine woodland area by the sea. To the left of the access road on the banks of a stagnant canal about 1 km long is a leisure and sports complex with many facilities including evening entertainment in the season. ➤

Spain

Leave the C246 (Barcelona–Castelldeféls), at Km11 and continue towards the sea for 1 km.
All year.

30HEC ◆ H sP ⊞ lau **A**360 **V**360 360 360

VILLAJOYOSA
Alicante (96)

Garoa Camping la Cala 5851461
On level ground on the seaward side of the N332. Large pitches, asphalt interior roads. Different types of trees provide shade.

On N332 at Km17.2
All year.

4HEC H P ⊞ lau s

Hércules 5891343
Section near sea is well shaded. Asphalt interior road, separate section for caravans with numbered pitches.

Turn E off N332 near Km114.4 then turn S.
All year.

7HEC ◆ H P ⊞ lau s **A**250–275 **V**250–275 200–330 250–275

Sertorium Partida Torres 83 5891599
On level ground on the seaward side of the N332. Small stony beach, suitable for non-swimmers.

On N332 at Km117.2.
All year.

2HEC H sP ⊞ lau **A**250 **V**250 250 250

See advertisement page 377

VILANOVA DE LA BARCA
Lleida (973)

Racó d'en Pep 190047
On level terrain under poplars. Next to a restaurant and adjoining a swimming pool.

On the River Segre at Km8.3 off the C313 Lleida-Puigcerdá road. N of the bridge over the River Corp.
All year.

0.3HEC ◆ H RP ⊞ lau

VILANOVA I LA GELTRÚ
Barcelona (93)

Spain

Vilanova Park 8933402
All year.

40HEC ◆ H P ⊞ lau **A**415 **V**415 415 415

VINAROZ
Castellón (964)

Garoa-Sol de Riu 454917

5HEC ◆ H sP ⊞ lau **A**175 **V**175 175 175

See advertisement page 377

VIVERO
Lugo (982)

Vivero 560004
In tall woodland near beach road and sea.

Turn of the C642 Barreois-Ortgueire road at Km443.1 and follow signs.
Jun–Sep.

1.6HEC H s ⊞ lau

ZARAGOZA
Zaragoza (976)

Casablanca 330322
Totally enclosed on flat terraces, subdivided by paths.

Turn off N11 in Madrid direction between Km316 and 317, at traffic lights turn towards Valdifiero and follow signs.
All year.

7HEC H P ⊞

ZARAUZ (ZARAUTZ)
Guipuzcoa (943)

Talai Mendi 830042
In meadowland on hillside divided by interior roads without shade. 0.5 km from the sea.

On outskirts of town at FIRESTONE filling station at Km16.9 on N634 turn towards the sea and continue for 350 m along narrow asphalt road.
Jul.–15 Sep.

3HEC ◆ ◇ H ⊞ lau s **A**220 **V**220 220 220

Zarauz 831238
Site with terraces separated by hedges.

1.8 km from the N634 San Sebastian–Bilbao road. Asphalt access road from Km15.5.
All year.

2HEC H lau s

ZUBIA (LA)
Granada (958)

Reina Isabel 590041
In a park-like setting at the foot of the Sierra Nevada, S of Granada.

From Granada 4 km S on N323 and turn E.
All year.

0.5HEC ◆ H P ⊞ lau **A**250 **V**250 225 250

Andorra

Prices are in French Francs or Spanish Pesetas.

ENCAMP
Bons 31938
Jun–Sep.

1.75HEC ◆ H ⊞ lau P **A**170 **V**170 170 170

MASSANA (LA)
At **ERTS** (4 km NW)

Xixerella rte de Pals 36613
Jun–15 Sep.

6HEC H RP ⊞ lau **A**10 **V**10 10 10

SANT JULIÂ DE LÒRIA

Huguet 41019
On a level strip of meadowland with rows of fruit and deciduous trees.

Off La Seu d'Urgell road N1, S of village and drive W across river.
All year.

1.5HEC H P lau s **V**220 440 440

SWEDEN

The lovely Dalsland Canal takes travellers to the Norwegian border

Sweden is bordered by two countries, Norway in the west and Finland in the north-east. About half the country is forested and most of the many thousands of lakes are situated in the southern central area. Vänern, the largest, occupies 2,140 sq miles. Swedish Lapland to the north is mountainous and enters the Arctic circle.

In spite of its northerly position, Sweden has a mild climate although its great length does lead to variations. The summers can be very hot, but the further north you travel the shorter they become. The midnight sun can be seen during June and July above the Arctic Circle. The language is based on the ancient Norse and is closely allied to Norwegian and Danish. There are local variations and the Lapps have their own language.

HOW TO GET THERE

Sweden can be approached direct by ferry services operating from Harwich or Newcastle to Göteburg (Gothenburg). The crossing takes 23–26 hours. It is also possible to reach Sweden via Denmark, using the Newcastle or Harwich to Esbjerg car ferry services; sailing time is about 20 hours. Alternatively you can take one of the short Channel crossings to France or Belgium, then drive through the Netherlands, northern Germany, and Denmark to Sweden, using the ferry connections between Puttgarden–Rødbyhavn, and Helsingør–Helsingborg. Crossings from Harwich to Hamburg give a shorter overland journey via Germany or Denmark. The distance from Calais to Stockholm, the capital, is about 1,000 miles and would normally require three night stops.

See page 326 for location map

GENERAL INFORMATION

(see also *Things you need to know*, page 33–64)

British Embassy/Consulates

(see also page 57)

The British Embassy together with its Consular Section is located at *11527 Stockholm* Skarpögatan 6–8 ☎(08)670140. There are British Consulates with Honorary Consuls in Gävle, Göteborg and Malmö.

Camping

Sweden has around 600 campsites approved and classified by the National Organisations Camping Committee. These display a sign showing a white C on a black tent with a green background. Approach roads to sites are marked with blue and white signs. Sites are generally open from 1 June to 31 August, but some open 1 May and a few are open all year.

The Swedish Tourist Board, Hamngatan 27, 10392 Stockholm ☏(08)7892000 and the Svenska Turistforeningen (STF), (see *Motoring clubs*) can supply information on campsites. *International camping carnet* is compulsory on most sites. No reduction in campsite charges is given to the holders of a camping carnet. See page 37 for further information.
Off-site camping is permitted for 24 hours, except in military zones, which are restricted areas and can be visited only with a special permit issued by the defence district commander and on application to the police. Regulations covering a temporary stay are displayed at ferry berths, ports, railway stations and hotels within the neighbourhood. Overnight parking in parking areas is tolerated provided you do not exceed the permitted time allowed and you do not contravene local regulations.

Currency including banking hours

(see also page 57)
The unit of currency is the Swedish Krona (*SKr*) divided into 100 *Öre*. At the time of going to press £ = *SKr* 10.18. Denominations of bank notes are *SKr* 10, 50, 100, 1,000, 10,000; standard coins are *SKr* 1, 5, and *Öre* 10, 50. There are no restrictions on the amount of foreign or Swedish currency that a *bona fide* tourist may import into the country. No more than *SKr* 12,000 in local currency may be exported including bank notes with a value in excess of *SKr* 1,000. There are no restrictions on the export of foreign currency provided it was obtained outside Sweden.

In towns banks are generally open 09.30–15.00 hrs but some may be open until 18.00 hrs Monday to Thursday. In the country banks are usually open from 10.00 hrs to 14.00 hrs Monday to Friday.

Foodstuffs

(see page 60)
Travellers of at least 12 years of age may import free of duty, foodstuffs up to and not exceeding 15kg, of which a maximum of 5kg of edible fats (including 2.5kg of butter) and up to 5kg of fresh fruit and vegetables for their personal use, is permitted. As a rule, meat products (other than tinned meat) may not be imported without a permit from Lantbruksstyrelsen (Board of Agriculture).

Medical treatment

(see page 60)

Shopping hours

Shopping hours vary, especially in large cities, but most are open 09.00–18.00hrs from Monday to Friday, and 09.00–14.00 or 16.00hrs on Saturday.

Tourist information

(see also page 63)
Local tourist information is available from tourist offices throughout Sweden. Persons requiring information in the UK should contact the Swedish National Tourist Office, 3 Cork Street, London W1X 1HA ☏01-437 5816.

Visitors' registration

(see page 63)

MOTORING

(see also *Things you need to know*, pages 33–64)

Accidents

(see also page 46)
Fire, police and **ambulance** ☏90000. The emergency telephone number should only be used in the case of personal injury or illness.

Breakdowns

(see page 48)

Dimensions and weight restrictions

Private **cars** and towed **trailers** or **caravans** are restricted to the following dimensions – height: no restriction; width; 2.60 metres; length: 24 metres which is also the maximum permitted overall length of vehicle/trailer or caravan combination.

Trailers without brakes must not exceed twice the maximum weight of the towing vehicle.

Driving licence

(see also page 33)
A valid UK or Republic of Ireland licence is acceptable in Sweden. The minimum age at which a visitor may drive a temporarily imported car is 18 years and a temporarily imported motorcycle 17 years.

Lights

(see also page 50 and *Headlights* page 41)
Dipped headlights must be used by motorists and motorcyclists during the day throughout the year.

Motoring clubs

(see also page 61)
The *Motormannens Riksforbund* (M) has its headquarters at *10240 Stockholm* Sturegatan 32 ☎(08)7823800 and the *Svenska Turistforeningen* (STF) at *10120 Stockholm* Vasagatan 48 ☎(08)7903100. Both have branch offices and agents in main towns.

Passengers

(see also page 51)
It is recommended that children do not travel in a vehicle as front seat passengers unless seated in a special child restraint.

Petrol

(see page 61)

Roads

There is a comprehensive network of numbered, well-signposted highways, but minor roads are not numbered. There are several stretches of motorway, but these are mainly in the southern part of Sweden. Although many roads in the south are being improved, others – particularly in central and northern Sweden – are still surfaced with loose gravel.

In various parts, chiefly along the Baltic coast, there are *protected areas* where only certain roads are open to motorists, and in these areas visitors may stay only at certain places for a limited time. The two areas likely to concern visitors are around Boden and Kalix in the provinces of Norrbotten. Warning notices are displayed in English and other languages on the boundaries of these areas.

Road number changes Road numbers have been revised and changes to the classification and numbering of some roads throughout the country have taken place during 1986. 910 kilometres of national roads have been *downgraded* to county roads, and 1750 kilometres of county roads were *upgraded* to national roads.

Seat-belts

(see page 52)

Speed limits

Car
Built-up areas
50 kph (31 mph)
Other roads
70 kph (43 mph)*
Motorways
110 kph (68 mph)

Car/trailer/caravan fitted with braking system
Built-up areas
50 kph (31 mph)
Other roads
70 kph (43 mph)

Car/caravan not fitted with braking system
Built-up areas
40 kph (24 mph)
Other roads
40 kph (24 mph)
Motorways
40 kph (24 mph)
*The speed limit for cars may be raised to 90 kph (56 mph) where conditions permit.

Warning triangle

The use of a warning triangle is compulsory in the event of accident or breakdown. See also *Warning triangles/Hazard warning lights* page 54.

Prices are in Swedish Kroner.

ÅHUS
Skåne (☎044)
Idyllen ☎241188
On uneven grassy ground, fenced off with tall pine trees and divided into two sections by a road.
Road 118 to crossroads N, then road to beach.

ALMÖ
Bohuslän (☎0304)
Tjörnbron ☎61787
In a hollow surrounded by boulders, below the remarkable Tjörn bridge.
On the inside of the bend of road no. 160 which leads in a wide sweep downwards from the bridge.
15 May–15 Sep.
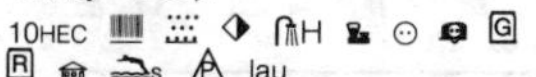

ÅLVSBYN
Norrbotten (☎0929)
Solholmens ☎7205
Level meadowland on two terraces above the right bank of the Pileälv. Pleasant common room with open fire and TV.
For access cross the bridge in direction of town and follow signs.
Jun–15 Aug.

AMBJÖRBY
Värmland (☎0564)
Backebo ☎42033
8 km N.
15 Jun–Aug.
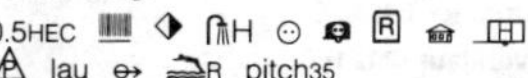

ANASET
Västergotland (☎0934)
Lufta ☎20488
On hillock amidst meadowland and sparse pine woodland.
Located about 1.5 km SW of town on the E4 Hoperarda road then turn left opposite MOBIL filling station for 200 m.
All year. ➤

7.5HEC lau pitch30–50

ANGELHOLM
Skäne (0431)
Räbocka-Baden 10543

In a forest 200 m from a sandy beach, protected from the wind by sand dunes. Can become very crowded during the peak season.

Turn off the E6 at the Ångelholm junction and follow signs to Hausbaden.

5HEC lau

ÅNN
Jämtland (0647)
Lilla Åreskutan 71006

1 km NE of railway station. 300 m N of E75.
All year.

3HEC lau pitch35

ARBOGA
Västergötland (0589)
Krakaborg 12670

N of E3.
May–15 Sep.

5HEC lau pitch40

ÅRJÄNG
Värmland (0573)
Sommatvik 12060

Above the E bank of the Bredviker, which is hardly visible. On grassland, sub-divided by numerous paths and slightly sloping.

Turn off E18 at BP garage, continue to MOBIL garage, left 2 km.
All year.

1.2HEC lau pitch38–58

ARNÅSVALL
Ångermanland (0660)
Bygdomsgården 61085

On gently sloping, undulating meadow between road in village and River Ovansjö.

Drive 20 km E of Ornsköldsvik, turn off the E4 onto the Taftea road for site in 3.5 km.
Jun–1 Sep.

3HEC pitch38

ARVIDSJAUR
Norrbotten (0960)
Arvidsjaur 12180

500 m S on road 95.
Jun–21 Aug.

1.5HEC lau 45 25

ARVIKA
Värmland (0570)
Ingestrand 14840

In hilly, natural woodland terrain without shade by the shore of Ingesund lake.

Follow road 175S for 5 km.

Sweden

15 May–Sep.

12HEC lau pitch45

ÅSA
Halland (0340)
Åsa 51774

Level grassland site in 3 sections beyond the dunes by the sea between two ranges of boulders. The greater part is fenced in. Separate section for caravans.

May–5 Sep.

3HEC lau

ASARUM
Blekinge (0454)
Långsjönäs Fritidsområde 20691

Between the Långsjön and the Store Kroksjön in a magnificent nature reserve, divided into many section by undulating ground, groups of trees and large rocks.

From town follow the road to Fritidsområde then after 3 km drive uphill following signs to the site.
May–14 Sep.

2HEC lau pitch45

BENGTSFORS
Dalsland (0531)
Grean 11797

On hilly terrain, partly adjoining woodland, near the road at Artingen lake.

2.5 km W of town, site entrance is immediately after Ford garage.
May–Aug.

3HEC lau pitch48

BERGKVARA
Småland (0486)
Dalskär 20587

On a peninsula of the Kalmar-Sund, adjoining a small harbour. Divided in two by a road.

3 km E of N15 on N outskirts of village.
15 May–15 Sep.

5HEC lau

BJÅSTA
Ångermanland (0660)
Kornsjøgårdens 38008

For access turn off the E4 at the camping and Kronsjö 3 km sign.
All year.

3HEC lau

BÖDAHAMN
Öland (0485)
Bödahamns 22457

On a meadow amidst woodland about 100 m from harbour with a flat sandy beach.

From the Öland Bridge follow road N136 to Böda. Turn off here onto the Bödahamn road, and continue for 500 m.
Jun–Aug.

8HEC lau

BORGHOLM
Öland (0485)
Ekerumsbadets 55190

On mainly level ground amidst sparse pinewoodland and open meadowland. Asphalt internal roads.

11 km S of Borgholm turn W off road 136, and continue for 1.5 km.
May–Aug.

lau

Kapelludden 10178

Among pine trees on a peninsula N of Borgholm.

Access via road 136, turn towards the centre at traffic lights then straight on; shortly before reaching the mole (breakwater) turn right and continue 300 m to site.
16 May–Aug.

1.5HEC lau pitch50–60

BORLÄNGE
Dalarna (0243)
Mellsta 38255

On hilly ground in sparse forest, overlooking the Dalälven 30 m below.

5 km N of the town.
3 Jun–12 Aug.

9HEC lau

BRÄKNE-HOBY
Blekinge (0454)
Jarnaviks 32166

Slightly undulating grassland with isolated groups of trees. Bay with 200 m beach. Partially fine sand, partially rocky.

Turn off E66 W towards the sea. Signposted.
May–15 Sep.

lau pitch48

BYSKE
Västerbotten (0912)
Byske 10850

Extensive level site with high pine trees, next to bathing beach.

Well signposted from E4.
Jun–Aug.

15HEC lau

BYXELKROK
Öland (0485)
Böda Sand 22195

In extensive woodland with asphalt interior

roads. Separate field for dog owners, caravans and tents.
Jun–Aug.
32HEC H |O| lau s

DALHEM
Gotland (0498)
Åminne 34011
In woodland on the Vitviken on E shore of the island.
3 km N of Gothem.
Jun–Aug.
1HEC H |O| lau s

DALS-LÅNGED
Dalsland (0531)
Laxjöns-Friluftsgård 40041
In a beautiful setting on a hill surrounded by forests, in the centre of a big recreation area.
From Billingfors 5 km S on N172, turn SE for 1 km then turn left on track over railway line and continue for 300 m.
All year.
23HEC H |O| lau LP pitch48
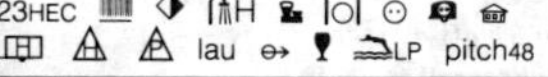

DEGERFORS
Värmland (0586)
Degernäs 42835
1.5 km N on road 205 to Karlskoga turn left at lake.
12 Jun–22 Aug.
1.2HEC H |O| lau L pitch35

DEGERHAMN
Öland (0485)
Sandvik 60080
On narrow stretch of pinewood approx 100 m from Kalmar-Sund.
300 m from Hammarley road.
16 May–23 Aug.
7HEC H |O| lau s pitch55

DOROTEA
Västerbotten (0942)
Björnens 10238
All year.
H lau |O|

ED
Dalsland (0534)
Gröne Backe 10862
Signposted from V166, 2 km from Ed.
All year.
6HEC H L lau |O| pitch47

ERIKSÖRE
Öland (0485)
Eriksöre 36187
Well-maintained, park-like family site on a quiet bay of the Kalmarsundes.

Sweden

Access from the Öland Bridge S in direction of Mörbylanga. In 7.5 km turn right and continue for 500 m.
May–1 Sep.
15HEC H L lau pitch50

ESKILSTUNA
Södermanland (016)
Vilsta 136227
Between roads 230 and 222.
May–Aug.
10HEC H lau s

FAGERSTA
Västmanland (0223)
Eskilns 13022
Grassy, slightly sloping site with adjoining large beach.
S of the town on the banks of the Asperlake, between road 65 and the railway.
15 May–15 Sep.
3HEC H lau |O| L

FALKENBERG
Halland (0346)
Olofsbo 92022
In meadowland between the beach road and a farm, about 500 m from the beach.
10 km NW of Falkenberg. Access from E6 to Skogsdorf and continue for 2 km. At crossroads turn right.
May–15 Sep.
1.1HEC H |O| lau L pitch55

FÅRJESTADEN
Öland (0485)
At **SAXNÄS** (5 km N)
Saxnäsbadet 35277
On several fields situated on both sides of the access road and within a public bathing beach.
Turn towards Saknäs beyond the Öland Bridge and continue for 1.5 km to the site on the Kalmar-Sund.
May–Aug.
10HEC H |O| s pitch45

FIDENÅS
Gotland (0498)
Fidenås 83910
On a narrow strip of land between the Burgsviken and the Baltic in the S of the island amidst woodland with a flat beach.
Access from Visby on road 140.9 km before Burgsvik.
15 May–Aug.

5.5HEC H lau s

FILIPSTAD
Värmland (0590)
Munkeberg 12616
Clean well-kept site beside the Lersjön.
800 m N of village off N246.
All year.
1.5HEC H L lau |O|

FJÄLLBACKA
Bohuslän (0525)
Fjällbacka 31490
A part level, part sloping site near the sea set between boulders. Section reserved for caravans.
Access from road 163 in seaward direction for about 1.5 km towards Säluik.
May–12 Sep.
2.5HEC H lau |O| s pitch56
Längsjo 12116
On somewhat uneven terrain between grassy hillocks.
4 km N of the village and 250 m off road 163.
May–15 Sep.
4.5HEC H lau s

FURUVIK
Gästrikland (026)
Furuviks 98028
On E4, 11 km E of Gale.
15 May–8 Sep.
5.2HEC lau |O| LPs

GÖTEBORG (GOTHENBURG)
Bohuslän (031)
Askim 286261
10 km S via road 158 to station.
15 May–24 Aug.
H s lau P
Kärralund Olbersgatan 252761
On grassy terrain with paths surrounded by woodland in the E part of town.
Approach from the S or N of E6 and the E3 is well signed.
All year.
4.25HEC H |O| lau L pitch50

GOTLAND (ISLAND OF) See **DALHEM, FIDENÅS, TOFTA, VISBY**

GRANEBERG
Uppland (18)
Graneberg 324133
8 km S on Lake Ekoln 200 m W of road.
May–Aug.
0.6HEC H lau |O| L

GRÄNNA
Småland (0390)

Grånnastranden ☎10706

On the edge of a lake, 100 m from the ferry port.

From the E4 follow signs Visingsö from the town centre and cross ferry to site.
May–Aug.

10HEC ◇ H ⊙ G R ⊞ lau L

GRAVOL
Värmland (☎0563)

Björkeho ☎85086

On slightly sloping natural grassland with two terraces. Beside the River Klarälven.

Access via road 62. Turn off about 7 km S of Stöllet and continue towards river in Gravol.
All year.

4HEC H ⊙ R lau pitch40

GREBBESTAD
Bohuslän (☎0525)

Edsvikbadets ☎10394

Level, mainly divided into plots by shrubs and high boulders, near a small fjord. Internal roads and low wooden fences divide the well cared for lawns.

From Grebbestad, drive 3 km NW in the direction of Haustensund.
May–15 Sep.

5HEC ◇ H ⊙ G lau S pitch53

Grebbestads ☎11211

A horse shoe-shaped site set around a granite boulder.

Access from S, approach well signed.
All year.

4.4HEC ◇ H ⊙ G R lau S

HALLSTAHAMMAR
Västmanland (☎0220)

Skantzôbadet ☎10378

On sloping, park-like ground in a beautiful location.

Turn off the E18 in the village and follow Badet signs.
15 May–30 Aug.

4HEC H ⊙ P ⊞ lau pitch38

HALMSTAD
Halland (☎035)

Hagöns ☎125363

A large site, divided by wide rose hedges and asphalt drives.

It is 6 km SW, near Östra Stranden.
May–Aug.

10.5HEC H ⊙ G R lau S pitch50–65

Karistorps ☎36316

A grassy site with tall trees, subdivided by sandy drives.

Signposted from Halmstad and from direction of Tylösand.
15 Jun–15 Aug.

H ⊙ G R lau S pitch40–50

Tylösand Kungsvägen 3 ☎30510

Well signposted from town.
May–Aug.

11.5HEC ◇ H ⊙ G lau L pitch50–135

HAMMAR
Västmanland (☎0583)

Hargebaden ☎70027

Level grassland terrain almost without shade divided by footpaths and rows of pines. Separated from the neighbouring holiday village by the access road.

Access is off road 50 about 1.5 km S of Hammar. Turn W onto the Harge road and follow it for 1.2 km.
May–15 Sep.

2.5HEC ◇ H lau

HÅSSLEHOLM
Skåne (☎0451)

Tykarpsgrottan ☎35087

An extensive site, close to the grottos after which it is named.

For access, from Kristianstad follow the road to Hässleholm for 4 km SW, then follow signs 'Ingaberget'.
All year.

2HEC H ⊙ G R lau pitch32

HELSINGBORG
Skåne (☎042)

Stenbrogården Rausvågen ☎290600

The site lies on meadowland and has asphalt pitches for caravans.

S along N106 to Råå, then E for 2 km and follow signs.
All year.

◇ H ⊙ R lau S

At **RÅÅ**

Råå Vallar ☎260685

Divided by hedges and fences with numbered pitches. There are hot showers in only one of the sanitary blocks and the washing facilities in one of these are in the open.

5 km S, near the port installations beyond the sea dyke. Access from the ferry, turn right onto the Malmö road as far as Råå, then follow signs.
15 May–25 Aug.

9HEC H ⊙ G ⊞ lau SP

HÖLICK
Halsingland (☎0650)

Hölicks ☎65032

Situated amidst pine woodland in a typical holiday area. Separate section on camp contains bungalows.

15 May–Aug.

◇ H ⊙ lau S pitch28–45

HOLJES
Värmland (☎0564)

Höljes ☎20260

3 km SE Norra Finsskoga.
6 Jun–24 Aug.

◆ H ⊙ G lau P

HORN
Östergötland (☎0494)

Hornåberg ☎30357

On level meadowland in a nature reserve, on the right bank of the River Stångån.

It lies about 300 m SW of the village from which it is signposted.
All year.

1.5HEC ◇ H ⊙ G R ⊞ lau pitch40

HOVMANTORP
Småland (☎0478)

Gôkaskratt ☎40807

A well-equipped site in parkland next to tennis courts by Rotten Lake.

For access, turn off opposite the church and cemetery and across the railway line for the site in 400 m.
All year.

3HEC H ⊙ L lau pitch40–50

HUNNEBOSTRAND
Bohuslän (☎0523)

Ramsvik Ramsvik 2 ☎50875

Situated by a fjord on the peninsula opposite Hunnebostrand, in typical nordic setting. Very busy in Jul and Aug.

From town drive S for 4 km, cross swing bridge and continue N for 3 km.
Jun–1 Sep.

3HEC ◇ H ⊙ R S Ⓟ ⊞ lau pitch75

HUSSJÖBY
Medelpad (☎060)

Bye Rast ☎45055

On meadowland subdivided by high bushes and situated between road and lake.

Situated on the E4 close to the café of the same name.
All year.

3HEC ◇ H ⊙ L lau pitch35

IGGESUND
Halsingland (☎0650)

Ankarmon ☎20505

Partly on sandy ground, partly on grass in a sparse forest of tall pine trees sloping down towards the Iggsjön with its clean, wide beach.

Off E4 at TEXACO station.

15 May–Aug.
5.4HEC H L lau pitch35

JÖNKÖPING
Småland (036)

Rosenlund 122863

On the E outskirts of the town, partly in birch and oak woods and partly on open meadowland in a depression about 15 m above the steep shores of Lake Vättern.

Turn off the E4 at the Rosenlund exit, pass below ESSO Motor Hotel and take third road to right uphill.
All year.
5HEC H lau

KALMAR
Småland (0480)

Stensö 83600

2 km S of town, next to a beach of the same name, which is very busy at weekends.

Access is from road 15, across Södra Vägen, then turn right via Stensö Vägen to the site.
Jun–Aug.

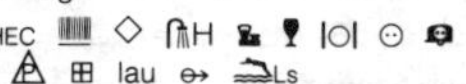

14HEC H lau Ls

KARLSBORG
Västergötland (0505)

Karlsborg 11916

In a forest of tall birch and pine trees between Lake Botten and Lake Vättern.

100 m off the busy N49/202 near the GULF service station, after the bridge over the Göta Canal.
31 May–1 Sep.
4HEC R L lau

KARLSKOGA
Värmland (0586)

Sandviksbadet 37860

Pleasant site on grassland and small wooded areas on northern shore of Lake Möckeln, next to a mill. Some air traffic during the day.

15 Jun–Sep.
5.5HEC H lau L pitch40

KARLSKRONA
Blekinge (0455)

Dragsöbadet 15354

Clean site on rocky hillock on island S of town.

Access from road 15 towards Dragsö.
May–Aug.
8HEC H G R lau s pitch48

Skönstavik 23700

A beautifully grassy site with trees and shrubs, near the busy road 15. The pitches near the road are noisy.

0.3 km W of the OK Motel.
May–Aug.

Sweden

10HEC H G R s lau pitch48

KARLSTAD
Värmland (054)

Skutbergets 35139

On a meadow divided into many sections of low fences and hedges. Separated from Lake Vänern and its beach by a 200 m-wide belt of forest.

7 km W of the town on the E18, turn left and drive for 1 km.
All year.
15HEC H G R lau L pitch40–55

KIL
Värmland (0554)

Frykenbaden 10974

On E shore of Lower Fryken Lake, partially hilly grassland without shade and a pleasant view of surrounding area.

For access, about 4 km from the road 61, 2 km W of Karlstad.
Jun–Aug.
4HEC H lau P

KIRUNA
Norrbotten (0980)

Kiruna 13100

Meadowland with dense bushes situated at the edge of a residential area between the ski-jump and the lake. Hardstandings for caravans.

Access is through the town, past the town hall. Well signposted.
Jun–Aug.
10HEC H lau P pitch35

KISA
Östergötland (0494)

Pinnarpsbaden 43088

On meadowland surrounded by a pine forest, beside the Ovre-Fölingen. One side of the camp is a holiday centre.

From the town centre take road no. 134 and drive W for 8 km, then follow signs towards Boxholm for a further 2 km.
All year.
3HEC H lau

KOLMÅRDEN
Östergötland (011)

Kolmårdens 92142

Situated amidst hilly woodland with boulders on the N shore of Bråviken.

Access from E4 at Kolmården exit then continue forward to Bråviken and left along shore to the site beyond a sports field.
4 May–Aug.

10HEC G R lau

KÖPINGSVIK
Öland (0485)

Grönhags 72116

Level grassy sections, sheltered from traffic noise by wooden chalets. Adjoins sandy beach.

Access near the church.
May–15 Sep.
3HEC H G R lau s

Klinta 72156

In a beautiful location on several levels above the bay. Divided into many sections by poplars and bushes, and is therefore well sheltered.

4 km E of Borgholm on N136. Well signposted.
May–Aug.
7.2HEC H G R lau s

Klintagårdens 72240

Level site situated on meadowland, divided by low groups of bushes and junipers.

Located 5 km E of Borgholm, in Kop.
Apr–Oct.
2.2HEC H G lau s pitch53

Lundegård 72341

On four large meadows that slope gently down to the beach. Each is divided by rows of bushes into individual pitches.

Situated 3 km N on road 136.
Jun–Aug.
12HEC H G R sP lau pitch70

KRAMFORS
Ångermanland (0612)

Flogstabadet 10005

Situated on meadowland with some terraces. There is no shade above swimming pool within the sports complex.

Turn off road 90 in Flogsta and continue uphill 1.5 km.
Jun–Aug.
5HEC H L lau pitch35

KRISTIANOPEL
Blekinge (0455)

Kristianopel 66130

On level meadowland, on a peninsula of the Kalmar Fjord, not far from a little harbour S of the village. Separated from the Vandrarhem (Hikers' Home) by a tall stone wall.

Turn off the N15 near the ESSO and GULF petrol stations and drive towards Kristianopel and the coast for 7 km. Well signposted.
May–Aug.
4HEC H s lau pitch48

KRISTIANSTAD
Skåne (044)

Charlottborgur ☎110767

On meadowland surrounding an old villa now serving as a youth hostel.

Between motorway and ring-road. Approach via road 21. Entrance to site in Längebrogaten.
All year.

2.8HEC lau A42 Vn/c 42 42

KRISTINEHAMN
Vårmland (☎0550)

Kvarndammen ☎14771

Set in a woodland area on the NE of the town, close to the Kvarn reservoir, in a hilly pine forest. Separate section for caravans.

Turn off the E18.2 km E of the town centre and drive for 100 m.
15 May–Aug.

KUNGSHAMN
Bohuslän (☎0523)

Ögårdens ☎37202

On a long stretch of grassland in a hollow, surrounded on two sides by shrubs and trees, between the hoad and high cliffs.

400 m from 'Kungshamn' sign in N outskirts on coastal road.
12 Jun–17 Aug.

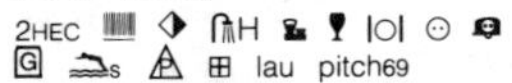

Solviks ☎31870

On level grassland between high boulders in a quiet, sheltered bay.

Turn off E6 in Hallinden towards Smögen. Then follow signs to site.
25 Apr–25 Sep.

2.5HEC H lau s pitch65

LANDSKRONA
Skåne (☎0418)

Borstahusen ☎10837

The site slopes down towards the Öresund, providing views of the Sound.

W of road 106. Access is from road 107, 3 km N of Landskrona turn towards the coast about 200 m N of large factory.
25 Apr–9 Sep.

10HEC H R lau s pitch45

LEKSAND
Dalarna (☎0247)

Orsandbaden ☎11224

On a slight incline, amidst sparse, tall trees and divided by internal roads.

Turn off road 70 in town centre then continue N on Tälberg for 2 km.
5 Jun–22 Aug.

6HEC H lau LP

Västanviksbadet ☎11201

In a pleasant setting on ground sloping down towards Lake Siljan off a busy main road.

Sweden

Towards Siljansnäs from town centre and turn towards Köstervit.
All year.

3.5HEC H L lau pitch50

LIDKÖPING
Västergötland (☎0510)

Filsbäcksbadet ☎46027

Partly on a meadow and partly in woodland on the E bank of Vänern Lake.

6 km E of town between the railway and road 44.

3HEC H lau Ls

Framnäs ☎46027

A rather long site in two stretches of dense woodland. Separate pitches for caravans.

NW, 150 m off road V44 in direction of Läcko, signposted.
15 May–Sep.

1.5HEC H lau LP

Läcko ☎10501

Above extensive grounds of a castle on slightly sloping meadowland on a peninsula reaching into Vänern Lake.

20 km N of Lidköping.
15 May–Aug.

1.5HEC H lau L

LINKÖPING
Östergötland (☎013)

Glyttinge ☎174928

Municipal site on pleasant grassland, divided into separate fields by rows of shrubs.

Access via Vikingstad exit on E4, past motel and waterworks.
15 May–15 Sep.

5.5HEC H P lau pitch30–60

LJUNGBY
Småland (☎0372)

Ljungby ☎10350

On meadowland around a pine covered hill and completely enclosed.

Turn off the E4 on the N outskirts of town, near the SHELL petrol station and the BETONE VERKEN, then continue for 300 m.
May–15 Sep.

4.5HEC H G R lau P pitch40

LJUNGBYHOLM
Småland (☎0480)

Aktiv Center ☎37200

In three slightly uneven fields within the grounds of a fairly large hotel.

Access from road 15 about 24 km S of Kalmar in direction of Löverslund.
Jun–Aug.

1HEC H sP

LJUNGSKILE
Bohuslän (☎0522)

Ljungskile ☎20807

Divided by trees and shrubs. 100 m from bathing facilities.

Signed from the E6 in town, about 0.3 km to site.
May–Sep.

9HEC H G lau s pitch55–60

LÖTTORP
Öland (☎0485)

Löttorps ☎23270

Situated on gently sloping meadowland divided into separate sections by bushes and access roads.

3 km N of Högby turn off road 136 Kesnäs road, to the site in 1.5 km.
Jun–Aug.

20HEC H G R lau sP

Sandby Sands ☎23212

Situated on extensive meadowland divided partly by hedges.

Turn off 2 km N of Högby onto a single track lane and continue for 0.7 km, site located E of road 136.
15 Jun–15 Sep.

10HEC H G s

LULEÅ
Norrbotten (☎0920)

Luleå Camp ☎50780

A grassland site between sports field and beach.

Turn left off the E4 N of the town close to Mercedes dealer.
All year.

5HEC H lau s V10 45–60 35

LYSEKIL
Bohuslän (☎0523)

Gullmarsbadens ☎11590

Extensive rocky site with some stretches of grassland extending down towards bay.

Well-signposted N of town.
15 May–Aug.

1HEC H Ls lau pitch50–60

Siviks ☎11528

Level grassland and sandy beach in the bay of Siviks.

Turn W towards sea off road 162, 2 km N of Lysekil. Continue for 1 km.
May–Aug.

8HEC H G R L lau

Trellebystrands ☎12183

Grassy site between rocky hills below a farm.

Turn off road 162 towards sea 5 km N of Lysekil.
May–Aug.
10HEC ◇ G R
lau pitch55

MALMKÖPING
Södermanland (☎0157)

Malmköping ☎21070

Grassland site surrounded by woodland, edging on one side onto the railway line which is not used at night. Next to the bathing lake of the same name.

Access from town via road 222 in direction of Eskilstuna. On northern outskirts of town turn right and continue for 0.5 km to site.
May–Sep.
3HEC |O|
lau |O|

MALMÖ
Skåne (☎040)

Sibbarp ☎155165

Subdivided by hedges, lying between Strandgatan and the Öresund near Limhamn.

5 km SW of Malmö. Access via E6 in direction of Limhamn, then follow signs.
All year.

⊞ lau s

MARIEFRED
Södermanland

Strandbadet ☎(0159)10230

In three meadows separated by trees, one adjoining the public pool. Lovely views of Gripsholm Castle from the pool.

Access from E8. At signpost 'Mariefred' turn off and continue for 3 km then onto bypass in direction of Hästaas to the site.
May–13 Sep.
◇ |O| L
lau pitch33

MARIESTAD
Västergötland (☎0501)

Strandbaden-Ekudden ☎10637

2 km NW of the village, on a peninsula of Lake Vänern, in a beautiful birch and pine forest.

May–15 Sep.
10HEC H |O| G
R ⊞ lau LP pitch55

MELLERUD
Dalsland (☎0530)

Vita Sannars ☎12260

All year.
15HEC ◇ |O|
G R ⊞ lau L

MÖNSTERÅS
Småland (☎0499)

Oknöbadens ☎11902

In a pine forest, on the Oknö peninsula by a splendid bay, 4.5 km SE of Mönsterås.

Sweden

Access is well signposted from the N15. Turn off between the GULF and TEXACO petrol stations.
Jun–Aug.
5HEC H |O| s
lau pitch60

MORA
Dalarna (☎0250)

Mora ☎26595

A large site, divided into many sections stretching over meadows and woodland.

Signposted from the village centre.
All year.
12HEC H G R
LRP lau |O| pitch45

MÖRBYLÅNGA
Öland (☎0485)

Haga Park ☎36030

A level site, situated on well tended grassland with junipers, low pines and birches. Separated from the sea by woodland.

Access from Öland Bridge, follow the Mörbylånga road along the coast for 14 km.
Apr–Sep.
10HEC ◇ H |O|
G R Ⓟ ⊞ lau
s pitch50

NORA
Västmanland (☎0587)

Trängbo ☎12361

800 m from town centre.
15 May–1 Sep.
3.2HEC ◇ H lau
|O| L pitch40

NORDINGRÅ
Ångermanland (☎0613)

Norrfällsviken ☎21382

Situated amidst sparse pine woodland near this pleasant holiday resort. Near to bathing beach, with extensive nature park. Harbour nearby.

From Gallsetter turn off E4 at BP filling station in direction of Nordingrå and continue for 29 km via Mjällom to Norrfällsviken.
18 Jun–Aug.
10HEC H |O| lau

NORRKÖPING
Östergötland (☎011)

Himmelstalunds ☎171190

On slightly sloping grassland beside a river.

300 m from E4.
15 May–Sep.
5.5HEC H |O|
G ⊞ lau P

NORSJÖ
Västerbotten (☎0918)

Rannuddens ☎20135

All year.
◇ |O|
⊞ lau s pitch30–45

NYBRO
Småland (☎0481)

Joelskogen ☎45112

S on road 31.
Jun–Aug.
2HEC H lau
|O|

NYKÖPING
Södermanland (☎0155)

Oppeby ☎11302

N at crossroads 58/222 and E4.
28 Apr–Sep.
1HEC H lau
|O| pitch29

ÖLAND (ISLAND OF) See **BÖDAHAMN, BORGHOLM, BYXELKROK, DEGERHAMN, ERIKSÖRE, FÄRJESTADEN, KÖPINGSVIK, LÖTTORP, MÖRBYLÅNGA**

ORSA
Dalarna (☎0250)

Orsa ☎52169

Beautifully situated partly on meadowland and partly amidst scattered pines on the N shore of the Orsasjon. After heavy rainfall the ground near the shore becomes waterlogged.

Signposted from the village.
All year.
30HEC ◇ H (Jun–Aug)
|O|(Jun–Aug) R LP lau
pitch45

OSBY
Skåne (☎0479)

Ebbarp ☎11135

Mainly sloping, grassy site on NW bank of the Osbysjan, about 800 m S of Osby.

Turn off road 23 onto road 14 in Osby and follow signs.
All year.
4HEC ◇ H ⊞ lau
|O| L

OSKARSHAMN
Småland (☎0491)

Gunnarsö ☎13298

Beautifully situated in pine woodland interspersed with huge boulders.

Access from road 15 in direction of harbour, past shipbuilders' yard 3 km SW. Signposted.
May–15 Sep.
|O| G s lau

Havslätts ☎15325

Grassy site surrounded by birch and pine trees. Near to beach.

Turn off road 15 in centre of Oskarshamn, ➤

towards harbour. Continue N following signs to reach site in 2.5 km.
15 May–15 Sep.
1.5HEC H lau s

ÖVERTORNEÅ
Norrbotten (0927)

Övertorneå 10141

Level grassy site between the river bank, museum and hostel.

Near Volkswagen workshop on northern outskirts.
Jun–15 Sep.
1.5HEC H R lau pitch35–55

PAJALA
Norrbotten (0978)

Pajala 10811

Municipal site in grassy terrain and woodland by Torne River.

Approach from Haparanda travelling N on road 400. The site is located about halfway to Karesuando.
15 May–15 Aug.
2.5HEC H lau R pitch30–40

PITEÅ
Norrbotten (0911)

Norrstrandbadet 15590

In northern outskirts totally divided into numbered pitches within the area of bathing beach.

Turn off E4 in town centre into Uddmansgaten and continue to site 0.8 km.
14 Jun–15 Aug.
5HEC H lau s

Pite Havsbad 32200

An extensive site amidst pine woodland near to a large parking area for beach.

Turn off E4, signed Munksund Pite Havsbad, and cross by ferry (no charge).
All year.
15HEC H G sP lau pitch60

Pitholmens Havsbad 32074

Municipal site situated on lovely sandy beach.

At Pitsund ferry 1 km E of E4.
Jun–Aug.
6.2HEC H lau s

RÅÅ See **HELSINGBORG**

RAMSELE
Ångermanland (0623)

Turistgården 10680

From roads 331/341, at the church and SHELL filling station drive towards Vandarhem. Continue down to river and cross bridge.
All year.
3.5HEC H lau R RP

Sweden

RÄTTVIK
Dalarna (0248)

Siljansbadet 11691

Between Siljan Lake and railway station.

Signposted from bridge and BP filling station.
May–4 Oct.
6HEC H L lau pitch40

RONNEBY
Blekinge (0457)

Järnaviks 32166

In a nature reserve, close to the Baltic.

May–15 Sep.
H G lau s pitch48

SÄFFLE
Värmland (0533)

Duse Udde 14305

Grassy terrain in extensive woodland area.

6 km S at Duse Lighthouse on Lake Vänern. Access from road 45 in Säffle.
Jun–15 Sep.
5HEC H sR lau L pitch50

SALA
Västmanland (0224)

Silvköparen 59003

6 km NW of the village.
22 May–23 Aug.
3HEC H L lau pitch40

SÄTER
Dalarna (0225)

Säters 50945

1 km S. Signposted from Säter.
All year.
1.5HEC H L lau pitch40

SAXNÄS See **FÄRJESTADEN**

SIMRISHAMN
Skåne (0414)

Tobisviks 11905

Municipal site with well cared for grassland which is divided into sections by hedging. Pine trees separate site from the beach.

Turn off the N10 about 2 km N of the harbour.
15 Apr–Sep.
2.2HEC H G lau sP

SJOBO
Skåne (0416)

Orebacken 10820

Mixed woodland with individual pitches in clearings.

SE of village off road 12.
All year.
3HEC H G lau P

SKANÖR-FALSTERBO
Skåne (040)

Ljungens 471132

Divided into plots with shrubs providing shelter from the wind.

Approach from Malmö on E6 then road 100. Immediately after the open heathland area and before the village, turn left and continue for 0.4 km.
1HEC H R lau P

SKARA
Västergötland (0511)

Skara 13510

Meadow divided by a ditch, behind Motel Tre Snäkor with a low wall protecting site from noise. Slightly undulating and separated from the sports area by high wire fence.

Access from the E3/49 at OK filling station.
May–Sep.
6HEC lau P

SKELLEFTEÅ
Västerbotten (0910)

Skellefteå 18855

In large grassy terrain with no shade. Separate section for caravans.

About 1 km N of the village, off the E4 near the SHELL petrol station.
All year.
5.5HEC H lau pitch50

SLAGNÅS
Norrbotten (0960)

Slagnasforsens 60039

On road 343.
15 Apr–Sep.
1HEC H G lau L pitch30–35

SÖDERTÄLJE
Södermanland (0755)

Farstanäs 50215

On two large meadows, partly level, partly sloping. Separate section for teenagers. Bathing area.

Turn off E4 at exit Järne 12 km S of Södertälje, passing ESSO-Taverna and continue towards Pershagen for 4.5 km.
28 Apr–18 Sep.
20HEC H s lau pitch35–45

SOLLERÖN
Dalarna (0250)

Sollerön 22434

A municipal site situated on a gently sloping meadow on an island in Lake Siljan with some pine trees.

From Gesunda turn right at the end of the dam.
All year.
10HEC H |O| lau L pitch35

SÖLVESBORG
Blekinge (0456)

Hällevik 52714

On the peninsula of the bay of Hanö, separated from the beach by a small wood.

Access from road 15 in direction of Hälleviks and continue for 6 km in the direction of Hälleviks Strand.
May–Aug.
2.4HEC H G lau |O| sP pitch46

Norje Boke 31026

Grassy site with shrubs and large boulders, stretching down to Purkaviks Bay.

From Sölvesborg turn right at Motel Norje and TEXACO filling station. Continue uphill past holiday village for 0.4 km.
May–Aug.
7HEC H |O| G R lau |O| s

Tredenborg 12116

In open ground on a peninsula and adjoins a car park.

Turn off road 15 towards town centre near the NYNÄS filling station and Volkswagen workshop and continue S for 4 km.
May–6 Sep.
12HEC H G s lau |O| pitch46

SÖRBERGE
Medelpad (060)

Bergeforsparken Timrå 599040

A level grassy site situated in Bergeforsparken, across the dam.

From northern exit follow signs Kraftverk.
All year.
3.5HEC H |O| P lau |O|

STOCKHOLM
Södermanland (08)

Bredängs 977071

Generously laid out with asphalt drives and separate sections for caravans and tents.

10 km SW towards Bredäng.
All year.
1.2HEC H |O| G lau L pitch65

STRÄNGNÄS
Södermanland (0152)

Löt 25237

Stretched over two terraces on pleasant meadowland, partly surrounded by a forest of coniferous and deciduous trees.

Turn off the main road 4 km E of the town, signed Reumatikersjukus and in 2 km drive past a concrete building. The camp is 3 km

Sweden

further on.
May–15 Sep.
2.5HEC H |O| lau L

STRÖMSTAD
Bohuslän (0526)

Daftö 26040

On several unconnected fields between boulders and woodland.

Access from E6 via southern approach to Strömstad, turning off at Vik, to Tjarno fork, then turn left to site and continue for 400 m.
Jun–Aug.
17HEC H |O| G R s lau pitch60

Fritidscentrum 12290

Quiet site in valley surrounded by woodland and rocks close to owner's pony farm. Separate pitches.

4.5 km NW of S outskirts of Seläter.
Jun–Aug.
5HEC H |O| G R lau |O| s pitch65

Ylseröds 30033

Grassy site, surrounded by woodland, sloping towards beach.

Well-signposted from E6 in vicinity of Strömstad.
All year.
5HEC G R s lau pitch60

STUREFORS
Östergötland (013)

Sätravallen 1240019

Access via road No. 34, turning W in Brobeind, in direction of Atvideberg. Signposted.
All year.
H |O| lau L pitch30–50

SUNDSVALL
Medelpad (060)

Bergafjärden 34598

An extensive holiday site in a sparse pine forest, beside a beach on the Baltic sea.

Turn off E4 in the village, drive towards Bjork, then continue for 5 km.
Jun–Aug.
5HEC H |O| lau s

Fläslan 554475

Terraced site on the Gulf of Bottnischen. It can be affected by fumes from nearby aluminium works if wind is in a certain direction.

6 km S on E4, then turn right.
Jun–Aug.
8HEC H |O| lau s

SVEG
Jämtland (0680)

Svegs 10881

Partly divided into pitches on meadowland between the banks of the Ljusnan and the busy N81.

Turn towards river by GULF and ESSO petrol stations.
15 Mar–Dec.
2HEC H lau |O| G P pitch40

SVINESUND
Bohuslän (0526)

Svinesunds 40175

In small grassy valley bordered by woodland.

3 km S of border and to the right of the E6. Near GULF filling station.
6 Jun–23 Aug.
2HEC |O| R lau pitch54

TINGSRYD
Småland (0477)

Tingsryd 10554

Grassy site on banks of lake surrounded by trees and shrubs.

1.5 km W of Tingsryd between road 120 and lake.
May–15 Oct.
5HEC H |O| L lau pitch30–45

TOFTA
Gotland (0498)

Tofta 65076

Amongst dunes set in woodland with part grassland.

5 km S between road 140 and the beach.
Jun–Aug.
38HEC H |O| s lau

TORSBY
Värmland (0560)

Bredviken 11095

On W bank of Övre Fryten on road 234 to Stöpafors.

Jun–Aug.
H |O| lau L

TRANÅS
Jönköping (0140)

Hättebaden 17482

3 km E.
May–Aug.
10HEC H |O| lau s pitch50

TRELLEBORG
Skåne (0410)

Dalabadet 14905

Well cared for grassland site with plenty of trees. ➔

E between sea and road.
May–Sep.
lau s

TROLLHÄTTAN
Västergötland (☎0520)

Hjulkvarnelund ☎30613

Slightly hilly site with some pine trees. 1 km N of town centre.

Access via road 42 and 45 across the Kungsgatan.
Jun–Aug.
3.5HEC H lau RP pitch45

URSHULT
Småland (☎0477)

Urshults Rävabacken ☎20243

15 May–Sep.
2.5HEC H lau L pitch50

VÄGSJÖFORS
Värmland (☎0560)

Nötöns ☎31038

In a beautiful setting beside the Övre Brockensjö.

Turn off the N234 N of the village, and proceed for 3 km along gravel road.
Jun–Aug.

4HEC H L lau pitch25–52

VARBERG
Halland (☎0340)

Apelviken ☎14178

Grassy seaside site surrounded by groups of trees and hedges.

Access via E6 to S bypass on outskirts of town.
May–15 Aug.
8.4HEC H lau

Getterons ☎16885

Grassy site on peninsula.

Sweden

Take road over railway and continue past aerodrome.
May–Sep.
7HEC H lau s pitch64

VÄSTERVIK
Småland (☎0490)

Lysingsbadet ☎11183 (Jun–Aug) 88700 (other times)

Extensive holiday and camping complex.

2 km S of town on a peninsula.
May–3 Jun & 14 Aug–Sep.
44HEC H s lau pitch70

VÄXJÖ
Småland (☎0470)

Evedal ☎63034

Site with own beach on Helgasjön close to marine and bathing facilities in extensive leisure complex.

Access from Växjö on road 23, follow signs.
All year.

3HEC H lau L pitch55

VEMDALEN
Härjedalen (☎0684)

Vemdals Campen ☎30122

In sparse woodland on either side of the N315.

1.5 km S of the village.
All year.
3.2HEC H lau pitch45

VILHELMINA-STRÖMÅKER
Lappland (☎0940)

Forsnäs-Strömåker ☎33012

7 km S turn off towards Forsnäs on road 351 SE of Vilhelmina.

25 May–15 Oct.
1.5HEC H R lau

VIMMERBY
Småland (☎0492)

Nossenbaden ☎11410

Grassy site sloping towards lake next to the bathing beach.

Turn off road 34 into road 33 towards Västervik and continue through Vimmerby 2 km E, then follow signs to the swimming facilities 'Nossenbaden'.
8 Jun–Aug.
L lau pitch45–55

VISBY
Gotland (☎0498)

Norderstrand ☎69659

Terraced site scattered with many trees and bushes, some aircraft noise. On road 149 in direction of airfield, beyond old town wall turn left towards northern bathing beach.

N of Visby not far from the Baltic Sea and between two roads, one of which runs between the camp and the beach.
Jun–Aug.
4.5HEC H lau L pitch20–55

VITTSJÖ
Skåne (☎0451)

Vittsjö ☎22131

Off E4, 1 km N.
All year.
1.5HEC H lau

YSTAD
Skåne (☎0411)

Sandskogen ☎77295

Between road 10 and railway in a pine wood 2 km E of Ystad.
25 Apr–24 Sep.
8HEC H lau s

SWITZERLAND & LIECHTENSTEIN

Oberhofen offers a pleasant cruise on mountain-fringed Lake Thun

Bordered by France in the west, the Federal Republic of Germany in the north, Austria in the east, and Italy in the south, Switzerland is one of the most beautiful countries in Europe. It has the highest mountains in Europe and some of the most awe-inspiring waterfalls and lakes, features that are offset by picturesque villages set amid green pastures and an abundance of Alpine flowers covering the valleys and lower mountain slopes during the spring. The highest peaks are Monte Rosa (15,217ft) on the Italian border, the Matterhorn (14,782ft), and the Jungfrau (13,669ft). Some of the most beautiful areas are the Via Mala Gorge, the Falls of the Rhine near Schaffhausen, the Rhône Glacier, and the lakes of Luzern and Thun.

The Alps cause many climatic variations through Switzerland, but generally the climate is said to be the healthiest in the world. In the higher Alpine regions temperatures tend to be low, whereas the lower land of the northern area has higher temperatures and hot summers. French is spoken in the western cantons, German in the central and northern cantons and Italian in Ticino. Romansch is spoken in Grisons and there are numerous regional dialects throughout the country of which the Swiss-German dialects are a notable example.

HOW TO GET THERE

From Great Britain, Switzerland is usually approached via France. The distance from the Channel ports to Bern, the capital, is approximately 470 miles, a distance which will normally require only one night stop.

GENERAL INFORMATION

(see also *Things you need to know*, pages 33–64)

British Embassy/Consulates

(see also page 57)

The British Embassy together with its Consular Section is located at *3000 Berne* 15 Thunstrasse 50 ☎(031)445021/6. There are British Consulates in Genève and Zürich, a British Consulate with Honorary Consul in Lugano and a British Vice-Consulate with Honorary Vice-Consul in Montreux.

Camping

Switzerland has over 450 campsites, about 90 of them are run by the Touring Club Suisse (TCS) who publish details of classified sites annually. Information can also be obtained from tourist offices, which are to be found in most provincial towns and resorts. The season extends from April or May to September or October, although some sites are open all year, particularly at winter sports resorts.

International camping carnet not compulsory but recommended. Some non-TCS campsites will allow a reduction in the advertised charge to the holders of a camping carnet. See page 37 for further information.

Off-site camping regulations differ from Canton to Canton. However, overnight parking may be

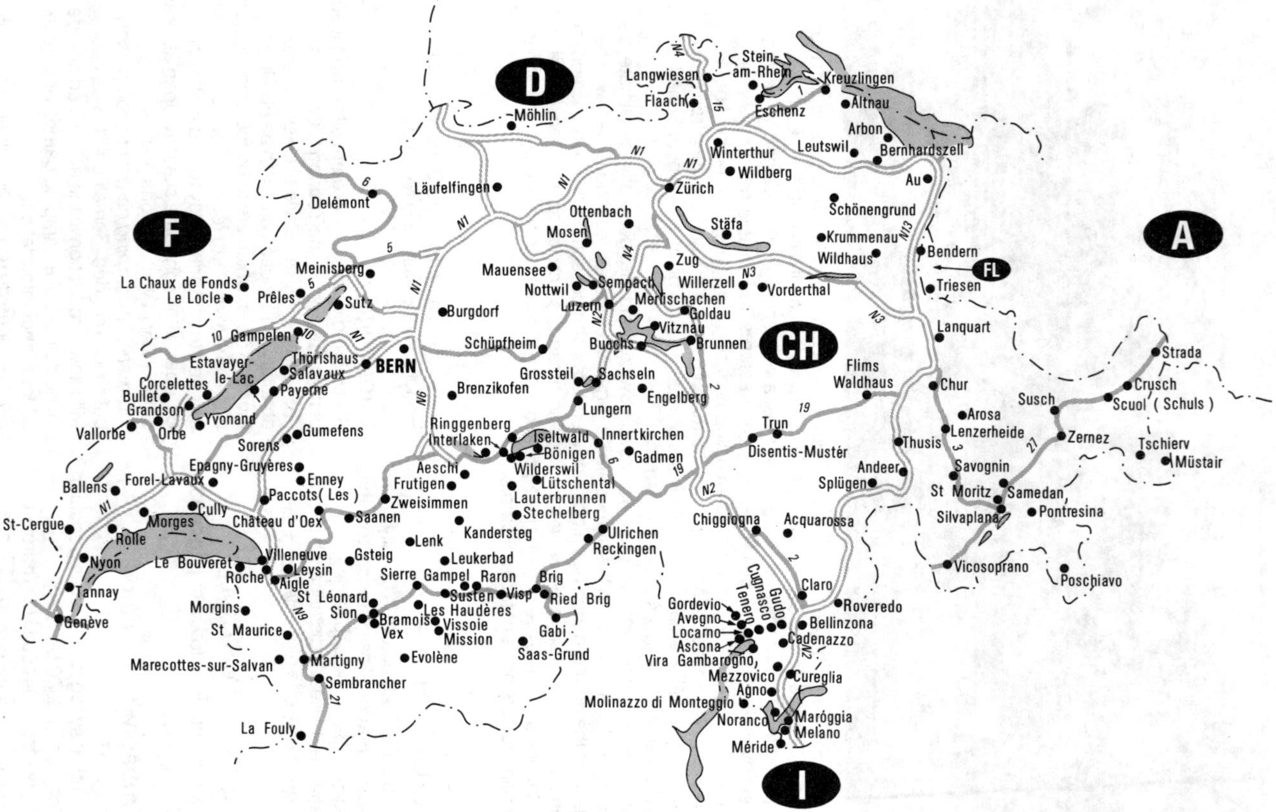

For key to country identification -see "About the gazetteer"

tolerated in rest areas of some motorways, but at all times the high standard of hygiene regulations must be observed. Make sure you do not contravene local laws. It is recommended that an official site should be used for this purpose.

Currency including banking hours

(see also page 57)
The unit of currency is the Swiss Franc (*SFr*) divided into 100 *Centimes* or *Rappen*. At the time of going to press £ = *SFr*2.40. Denominations of bank notes are *SFr* 10, 20, 50, 100, 1,000; standard coins are *SFr* 1, 2, 5 and *Centimes* or *Rappen* 5, 10, 20, 50. There are no restrictions on the import or export of foreign or Swiss currency.

Banks are open Monday to Friday and closed on Saturday. The opening hours in Basel are 08.15–17.00 (Wednesday or Friday 18.30); Bern 08.00–16.30 (Thursday 18.00); Genève 08.30–16.30/17.30; Lausanne 08.30–1200 and 13.30–16.30 (Friday 17.00); Lugano 09.00–12.00/12.30 and 13.00/13.30–16.00; Zürich 08.15/09.00–16.30/17.00 (Thursday 18.00).

There are exchange offices in nearly all TCS offices open during office hours. At railway stations in large towns and at airports, exchange offices are open 08.00–20.00 hrs although these hours may vary slightly from place to place.

Foodstuffs

(see also page 60)
Each traveller may import a total of 2.5 kg of provisions made up of 125 gm of butter, 500 gm of meat, 1 kg of meat products or 2.5 kg of one of the following: cooked poultry, poultry products, rabbit, game, fish and shell fish. The importation of pork or pork products from Africa, Brazil, Malta, Portugal, Sardinia or Spain and fresh or frozen poultry is strictly forbidden.

Medical treatment

(see page 60)

Shopping hours

Generally shops are open from 08.00/09.00–18.30/18.45 hrs Monday to Friday and 08.00/09.00–16.00/17.00 hrs on Saturday. In large towns some shops close on Monday morning; in suburban areas and smaller towns shops normally close on Wednesday or Thursday afternoons.

Tourist information

(see also page 63)
The Swiss government maintains an excellent information service in London at the Swiss National Tourist Office, 1 New Coventry Street, W1V 8EE ☏01-734 1921. In all the provincial towns and resorts throughout Switzerland there are tourist information offices who are pleased to help tourists with local information and advice.

Visitors' registration

(see page 63)

MOTORING

(see also *Things you need to know*, pages 33–64)

Accidents

(see also page 46)
Fire ☏118 **police** and **ambulance** ☏117. (144 for ambulance if the first two or three figures of the number on the telephone from which you are making the call are 01, 031, 042, 043, 052, 056, 057, 061, 062 and 064).

Breakdowns

(see page 48)

Dimensions and weight restrictions

Private cars and towed trailers or caravans are restricted to the following dimensions – **car** height: 4 metres; width: 2.30 metres; length: up to 3,500 kg 8 metres, over 3,500 kg 12 metres. **Trailer/caravan** height: 4 metres; width*: 2.10 metres; length*: 6 metres (including tow bar). The maximum permitted overall length of vehicle/trailer or caravan combination is 18 metres.

It is dangerous to use a vehicle towing a trailer or caravan on some mountain roads; motorists should ensure that roads on which they are about to travel are suitable for the conveyance of vehicle/trailer or caravan combinations.

The fully-laden weight of trailers which do not have an independent braking system should not exceed 50% of the unladen weight of the towing vehicle, but trailers which have an independent braking system can weigh up to 100% of the unladen weight of the towing vehicle.

*The Swiss Customs authorities can authorise slightly larger limits for foreign

caravans for direct journeys to their destination and back *ie* caravans up to 2.20 metres (7ft 2 in) in width and up to either 6.50 metres (21ft 4in) or 7 metres (23ft) in length depending on whether Alpine passes are used. A charge is made for these special authorisations.
Caravans up to 2.50 metres (8ft 2in) in width may also enter Switzerland if towed by a four-wheel-drive vehicle or one exceeding 3.5 tonnes, but no special authorisation is required.

Driving licence

(see page 33)
A valid UK or Republic of Ireland licence is acceptable in Switzerland. The minimum age at which a visitor may drive a temporarily imported car is 18 years and a temporarily imported motorcycle (exceeding 125cc) 20 years.

Lights

(see also page 50 and *Headlights* page 41)
Dipped headlights must be used at all times in tunnels, whether they are lit or not, and failure to observe this regulation can lead to a fine. Switzerland has a tunnel road sign (a red triangle showing a tunnel entrance in the centre) which serves to remind drivers to turn on their dipped headlights.

Motoring club

(see also page 61)
The *Touring Club Suisse* (TCS) has branch offices in all important towns and has its head office at *1211 Genève 3* rue Pierre Fatio 9 ☎(022)371212. TCS offices are usually open from 08.30–12.00 hrs and 13.30–17.00 hrs during the week and between 08.00–11.30 hrs on Saturday mornings (summer only). They are not open on Sunday.

Motorway tax

The Swiss authorities levy an annual motorway tax. A vehicle sticker, costing *SFr* 30 for vehicles up to 3.5 tonnes (unladen) and known locally as a *vignette*, must be displayed by vehicles using Swiss motorways including motorcycles, trailers and caravans. Motorists may purchase the stickers from AA Centres and AA Port Service Centres or at the Swiss frontier. Vehicles over 3.5 tonnes (unladen) are taxed on all roads in Switzerland; a licence for one day, 10 days, one month and one year periods can be obtained. There are no stickers and the tax must be paid at the Swiss frontier.

Passengers

(see also page 51)
Children under 12 are not permitted to travel in a vehicle as front seat passengers when rear seating is available.

Petrol

(see page 61)

Roads

The road surfaces are generally good, but some main roads are narrow. Traffic congestion may be severe at the beginning and end of the German school holidays.

On any stretch of mountain road, the driver of a private car may be asked by the driver of a postal bus, which is painted yellow, to reverse, or otherwise manoeuvre to allow the postal bus to pass. Postal bus drivers often sound a distinctive three note horn and no other vehicles may use this type of horn in Switzerland.

Seat-belts

(see page 52)

Speed limits

Car	***Car/caravan/trailer***
Built-up areas	*Built-up areas*
50kph (31mph)	50kph (31mph)
Other roads	*Other roads*
80kph (49mph)	80kph (49mph)*
Motorways	*Motorways*
120kph (74mph)	80kph (49mph)

*If the weight of the caravan or luggage trailer exceeds 1,000kg a speed limit of 60kph (37mph) applies on roads outside-built-up areas, but 80kph (49mph) is still permissible.

Warning triangle/Hazard warning lights

The use of a warning triangle is compulsory in the event of accident or breakdown. The triangle must be placed on the road at least 50 metres (55yds) behind the vehicle on ordinary roads and at least 150 metres (164yds) on motorways. Hazard warning lights may be used in conjunction with the triangle on ordinary roads, but on motorways and semi-motorways they must be switched off as soon as the warning triangle is erected. If this is not done the police may impose an *on-the-spot* fine (see page 51). See also *Warning traingles/Hazard warnings lights*, page 54

LIECHTENSTEIN

The principality of Liechtenstein lies between the upper reaches of the Rhine valley and the Austrian Alps. The scenery is typically Alpine and the country is noted for its great variety of wild flowers.

Traffic regulations, insurance laws, and the monetary unit are the same as for Switzerland and prices are adjusted to match those in the major country.

Prices are in Swiss Francs
Abbreviation:
str strasse
TCS Touring Club Suisse

ACQUAROSSA
Ticino (092)

Acquarossa 781603
Beautifully situated on large, unspoilt area of land.
1 km above Acquarossa and road to Lukmanier Pass.
All year.
3HEC H P lau A4 V2 4 4

AESCHI
Bern (033)

Panorama Rossern 544377
400 m SE of Camping Club Bern.
May–Sep.
1HEC H lau P

AGNO
Ticino (091)

Eurocampo 592114
Part of site is near its own sandy beach and is divided by groups of trees.
600 m E on road from Lugano to Ponte Tresa. Entrance opposite Aeroport sign and Alfa Romeo building.
Apr–Oct.
6HEC H G R L lau A5 V2 5 5

Golfo del Sole 594802
By lake. Separate play area for children.
Apr–Oct.
0.6HEC H G R L P lau A5 V2 6–9 5–7

Palma 592561
On level sandy lakeside beach.
1 km E on road from Lugano on Ponte Tresa.
Etr–Oct.
2.7HEC H G R L lau A4 V2 5–8 3–8

Piodella 547788
Enclosed on a beautiful, flat sandy beach, and partly level grassland with trees.
1 km E on shore of Lake Lugano.
Apr–Oct.
3.2HEC H G R LR P lau

Tropical 594317
Situated within the area of the bathing beach, between the road, railway and lake.
On S outskirts of Agno in direction of Ponte Tresa.
Etr–Oct.
1.2HEC H lau L A5 V2 8 3–8

AIGLE
Vaud (025)

Glariers (TCS) 262660
Near railway line and the avenue des Glariers.
800 m NE off the N9 near SHELL/MIGROL petrol station.
Apr–Sep
1HEC H G P A4–5 pitch5–9

ALTNAU
Thurgau (072)

Ruderbaum 651885
By Lake Bodensee between Constance and Romanshorn.
Apr–Oct.
6HEC H G L

ANDEER
Graubünden (081)

Andeer 611453
All year.
1.2HEC G R P lau A3–4 V5–8 5–8 2–3

Sut Baselgia (TCS) 611453
N towards Chur.
All year.
1.2HEC H G R lau P A4 pitch8

ARBON
Thurgau (071)

Arbon Strandbad 466545
By Lake Bodensee.
1 km W.
14 Apr–15 Oct.
1.2HEC H G P A4 pitch5

AROSA
Graubünden (081)

Arosa 311745
All year.
4.5HEC H G sP A5 V2 2 2

ASCONA
Ticino (093)

Segnale 352970
Level site, partly under tall trees, near large sandy lakeshore.
Cross bridge near VW service station, and drive in direction of aerodrome.
Etr–Oct.
3.3HEC H L lau A7 V2–3 8–12 6

AU
St-Gallen (071)

Ascot Kobelstr 1 711738
500 m W.
Apr–Oct.
0.15HEC H G R P lau A4 V2 3 2

AVEGNO
Ticino (093) ➔

Piccolo Paradiso ☎811581

In the Maggia Valley between the main road and River Maggia.

6 km NW from Locarno on the Maggia Valley road.
Mar–Oct.

2.7HEC H lau R

BAD Each name preceded by 'Bad' is listed under the name that follows it.

BALLENS
Vaud (☎021)

Bois Gentil ☎775120

200 m S of station.
Mar–15 Oct.

2.5HEC H P lau A4 V2 3 3

BELLINZONA
Ticino (☎092)

Molinazzo (TCS) ☎291118

2 km N of city.
23 May–13 Sep.

1HEC H lau A5 pitch2–16

BERN (BERNE)
Bern (☎031)

At **HINTERKAPPELEN** (6 km NW)

Kappelenbrücke (TCS) ☎361501

On grassy terrain.

S of the River Aare and E of Bern–Aarberg–Wohlen road.
All year.

1HEC H L

At **WABERN**

SC Eichholz ☎542602

In municipal parkland. Separate section for caravans.

Approach via Grossetstr and track beside lake.
May–Sep.

3.6HEC H R lau

BERNHARDSZELL
St-Gallen (☎071)

Leebrücke ☎384969

Beside River Sitter.

1 km W of Wittenbach.
May–15 Oct.

1.5HEC H lau P

Switzerland

BÖNIGEN
Bern (☎036)

Seeblick (TCS) ☎221143

Lakeside site divided into pitches.

400 m NW.
May–27 Sep.

1.5HEC H P lau

See Terrasse ☎222041

In a quiet beautiful setting near a lake.

All year.

0.4HEC H lau LP A5 V2 5 5

BOUVERET (LE)
Valais (☎021)

Rive Bleue ☎(025)812161

Beside lake.

Turn off the N37 to Monthey in the SW district of Bouveret and drive NE for about 0.8 km.
Apr–Sep.

2HEC H LP lau A6–7 V2 6–8 4–7

BRAMOIS
Valais (☎027)

Valcentre ☎311642

1 km NE of Bramois to the right of the road towards Grône.
15 Apr–15 Oct.

1HEC H lau L A4 pitch4

BRENZIKOFEN
Bern (☎031)

Wydell (TCS) ☎971141

8 km N of Thun.
11 Apr–27 Sep.

1HEC H P

BRIG (BRIGUE)
Valais (☎028)

Geschina (TCS) ☎232698

1 km S of town on the banks of the River Saltina.
May–27 Sep.

1.8HEC H lau

BRUNNEN
Schwyz (☎043)

Hopfreben ☎311873

On the right bank of the Muotta stream 100 m before it flows into the lake.

1 km W.
25 Apr–26 Sep.

1.5HEC H A4 V2 5–10 3–8

Urmiberg ☎313327

16 km N of Altdorf.
Apr–Oct.

1.5HEC H L A4 V2 2 1

BULLET
Vaud (☎024)

Cluds ☎611440

In beautiful mountain setting.

1.5 km NE.
All year.

1HEC H lau A4 V2 4 4

BUOCHS
Nidwalden (☎041)

Sportzentrum (TCS) ☎643474

Near local football field and tennis courts.

Signposted.
Apr–Sep.

2.2HEC H lau sP A5 pitch6–10

BURGDORF
Bern (☎034)

Waldegg (TCS) ☎227943

On Oberburg road, turn left at petrol station.
Etr–15 Oct.

0.8HEC H RP A4 V2 3 2

CADENAZZO
Ticino (☎092)

Cadenazzo (TCS) ☎622653

Divided into two parts by a stream, and by rows of trees and a gravel path.

Turn off at GULF filling station in direction of Mignos and continue 100 m.
27 May–Sep.

0.8HEC H lau P

CHÂTEAU-D'OEX
Vaud (☎029)

Berceau (TCS) ☎46234

On level strip of grass between the mountain and the river bank.

1 km SE at junction of roads 77 and 76.
27 May–27 Sep.
1HEC ◆ H ⊙ G P lau

CHÂTELET (LE) See **GSTEIG**

CHAUX-DE-FONDS (LA)
Neuchâtel (☎039)
Bois du Couvent ☎232555
Partly on uneven ground.
Take turning off Neuchâtel road near the Zappella and Moeschier factory and drive for 200 m.
May–15 Oct.
2.2HEC ◆ ◆ H ⊙ G R ⊞ lau RP A3 V3 5 4

CHIGGIOGNA
Ticino (☎094)
Gottardo ☎381562
Open meadowland on mountain slope partly on natural terraces.
1 km S of Faido, 20 m above N2.
All year.
0.8HEC ◆ H ⊙ G RP ⊞ lau A4–5 Vn/c 4–6 3–4

CHUR (COIRE)
Graubünden (☎081)
Camp Au (TCS) ☎242283
Take exit Chur-Süd from N13.2 km NW of town centre on bank of Rhein. Access is via outskirts of town.
All year.
3HEC ◆ H ⊙ G R ⊞ lau P A5 V3 6–10 3–10

CLARO
Ticino (☎092)
Censo ☎661753
Below a woodland slope.
Off the N2 (E9).
Apr–Sep.
2HEC ◆ H ⊙ G R P lau A5 pitch8–11

CORCELETTES
Vaud (☎024)
Belle Rive ☎243800
SW of Neuchâtel and 500 m SE of town.
Apr–Sep.
1.4HEC ◆ H ⊙ G L Ⓟ ⊞
Pins ☎244740
In a quiet lakeside setting interspersed with trees.
1 km E.
3 Apr–27 Sep.
2.5HEC ◆ H ⊙ G L ⊞ lau A4 V2 3 3

CRUSCH
Graubünden (☎084)
Piz Lischana ☎93544

Switzerland

Quiet site beautifully situated in a wooded area on right bank of the River Inn.
Left off N27. 150 m before Post Crusch drive down into valley and cross wooden bridge.
All year.
3HEC ◆ ◆ ◇ H ⊙ G R ⊞ lau A4 V2–5 3–5 3–5

CUGNASCO
Ticino (☎092)
Park-Camping Riarena ☎641688
Beautiful park-like site.
1.5 km NW. Turn off road 13 at BP filling station 9 km NE of Locarno and continue 0.5 km.
16 Apr-18 Oct.
3.8HEC ◆ H ⊙ G RP ⊞ lau

CULLY
Vaud (☎021)
Moratel ☎991914
On main Lausanne–Vevey road E of Cully.
Mar–Sep.
3HEC ◆ H ⊙ G ⊞ lau L A5 pitch6

CUREGLIA
Ticino (☎091)
Moretto (TCS) ☎567662
Open meadowland, wide strips which gently slope towards the Vedeggio Valley.
On outskirts, on road to Lugano.
11 Apr–25 Oct.
3HEC ◆ H ⊙ ⊞ lau

DELÉMONT
Bern (☎066)
Grand Écluse (TCS) ☎223080
In a meadow beside the River Sorne, surrounded by trees and bushes.
11 Apr–27 Sep.
1HEC ◆ H ⊙ G R lau

DISENTIS-MUSTER
Graubünden (☎086)
Fontanivas (TCS) ☎74422
Next to a swimming pool in a pine forest.
Take N61 for 1.5 km towards Lukmanier Pass then turn left and drive on for 100 m.
27 May–27 Sep.
2.5HEC ◆ H ⊙ G R ⊞ lau

ENGELBERG
Obwalden (☎041)
Eienwäldi ☎941949
1.5 km SW behind restaurant Eienwäldi.
All year.
4HEC ◆ H ⊙ G P ⊞ lau A5 V1 3 3

ENNEY
Fribourg (☎029)
Haute Gruyère (TCS) ☎62260
8 km S of Bulle on road 77.
All year.
1.5HEC ◆ H ⊙ G R ⊞ lau

EPAGNY-GRUYÈRES
Fribourg (☎029)
Sapins ☎29575
1 km N on the edge of a forest.
Apr–Sep.
2.5HEC ◆ ◆ H ⊙ G R ⊞ lau RP A4 V2 4 3–4

ESCHENZ
Thurgau (☎054)
Hüttenberg ☎412337
Terraced site lying above village.
1 km SW.
All year.
5HEC ◆ H ⊙ G R P ⊞ lau L A4 V2 4 2–3

ESTAVAYER-LE-LAC
Fribourg (☎037)
Nouvelle Plage (TCS) ☎631693
Situated beside the lake.
11 Apr–4 Oct.
1.5HEC ◆ H ⊙ ⊞ lau

EVOLÈNE
Valais (☎027)
Evolène ☎831144
200 m from town.
All year.
5HEC ◇ H ⊙ G ⊞ lau A4 V1 2 1–2

FLAACH
Zürich (☎052)
TCS ☎421413
In village turn off at Ziegelhaus Restaurant continue for 600 m.
16 Apr–11 Oct.
2HEC ◆ H ⊙ G R RP ⊞ lau A4 pitch2–9

FLIMS-WALDHAUS
Graubünden (☎081)
Prau ☎391575
500 m N of village, about 30 m below the Ilanz road.
All year.
1HEC ◆ H ⊙ R lau A4 V1

FOREL-LAVAUX
Vaud (☎021)
Forel-Lavaux ☎971464 ➤

12 km NE of Lausanne on Mondon Vevey road. 2 km N of Lac de Brêt.
All year.
3.6HEC H P lau A5 V1 4–6 2–4

FOULY (LA)
Valais (026)
Glaciers 42498
At end of village.
Jun–Sep.
5HEC H lau A4 V2 5 4

FRUTIGEN
Bern (033)
Grassi 711149
Scattered with fruit trees beside a farm on the right bank of the River Engstilgern.
From the Hauptstr, turn right at the Simplon Hotel.
All year.
1.5HEC H R lau P A4 pitch3–8

GABI (SIMPLON)
Valais (028)
Simplon (TCS) 291165
3.5 km from Simplon behind BP petrol station.
23 May–27 Sep.
0.2HEC H A2–3 pitch2–7

GADMEN
Bern (036)
Alpenrose 751155
About 150 m above the Alpenrose Hotel Restaurant.
May–Oct.
0.7HEC H P lau A3 V3 3–6 3–6

GAMPEL
Valais (028)
Rhône 422041
By the railway station towards the bridge over the Rhône. Reduction for International Camping Carnet holders.
29 Mar–20 Oct.
3.8HEC H P lau

GAMPELEN
Bern (032)

Switzerland

Fanel (TCS) 832333
On the shore of Lake Neuchâtel.
16 Apr–4 Oct.
11.3HEC H L lau

GENÈVE (GENEVA)
Genève (022)
At **VÉSENAZ** (6 km NE)
Ponte à la Bise (TCS) 521296
Small pool for children. On shores of lake.
NE between Vésenaz and Bellerive.
Apr–Sep.
3.2HEC H L lau

GOLDAU
Schwyz (041)
Bernerhöhe 821887
On the edge of a forest with a beautiful view of Lake Lauerz. Separate field for tents.
1.5 km SE and turn left.
All year.
2.5HEC H lau L A3 V1 1 1
Buosingen 823898
All year.
1.5HEC H A3 V2 2–3 2

GORDEVIO
Ticino (093)
Bellariva 871444
In quiet location between the road and the left bank of the River Maggia.
Apr–Oct.
15HEC H RP lau A5–6 Vn/c 10–12 9–10
Renato 871364
Gently sloping meadowland.
Site lies off main road running through the Maggia Valley.
Apr–Oct.
2.5HEC H P lau

GRANDSON
Vaud (024)
Pécos 244969

400 m SW of railway station between railway and lake.
All year.
2HEC H L lau A4 V2 4 3–4

GROSSTEIL
Obwalden (041)
Sarnersee 681298
On SW shore of Sarnersee. Reduction for International Camping Carnet holders.
Apr–15 Oct.
2HEC H L lau A4 pitch3–10

GSTEIG (LE CHÂTELET)
Bern (030)
Heiti (TCS) 51029
27 May–13 Sep.
0.4HEC H

GUDO
Ticino (092)
Gudo Hauptstr 641642
In deciduous woodland surrounded by meadows.
Off the main road (via Cantonale) running from Bellinzona to Locarno, about 0.6 km S of village.
27 Mar–12 Oct.
3HEC H P lau R A4 V3 4–5 4

GUMEFENS
Fribourg (029)
Basse-Gruyère 52162
On the borders of the lake.
15 May–15 Sep.
1.25HEC H L lau A5 V2 6–8 6

HAUDÈRES (LES)
Valais (027)
Molignon 831296
Terraced site beside the river in a beautiful setting.
All year.
1.2HEC H lau

HINTERKAPPELEN See **BERN**

HORW See **LUZERN (LUCERNE)**

INNERTKIRCHEN
Bern (036)
Grund 711379

Next to a farm on southern outskirts of village.

Turn S off main road in centre of village at BP petrol station. Drive for 0.3 km, turn right. All year.

0.5HEC lau A3 pitch3–5

Switzerland

Innertkirchen ☎711348
S bank of River Aare.

Mar–Oct.

0.5HEC A3 pitch3–5

INTERLAKEN
Bern (☎036)

Alpenblick Seestr 135 ☎227757 ➤

On the left bank of the River Lombach upstream from the bridge in a meadow bordering a forest opposite the Neuhaus Motel and the Strandbad Restaurant.

8 km N of Interlaken.
Mar–Nov.

2HEC H LR A4 V3 4–8 2–6

Hobby Lehnweg 16 229652

Accessible from the road running along the northern shore of the lake from Interlaken-West to Thun. Turn off at the Golf Motel, and drive on for 200 m.
Apr–Oct.

1.2HEC H lau RL A4 pitch3–12

Jungfrau Steindlerstr 60 227107

Has a beautiful view of the Eiger, the Mönch and the Jungfrau.

Turn right at Unterseen, drive through the Schullhaus and Steinler Str to site.
All year.

2HEC H P lau LR A5 pitch6–14

Jungfraublick Gsteigstr 80 224414

Take Autobahn N8 through tunnel, leave at Lauterbrunnen–Grindelwald exit, site on left, 300 m from N8 sliproad.
15 Dec–Sep.

Switzerland

1.3HEC H lau P

Lazy Rancho 228716

Motorway N8: exit Unterseen, turn toward Gunten. After 2 km turn right, then at Motel Golf turn left.
Apr–Oct.

1.6HEC H P lau LR A4 pitch5–12

Manor Farm 222264

From motorway N8 (Bern–Spiez–Interlaken–Brienz), exit Gunten/Beatenberg; follow signposts.
All year.

7HEC H LR lau A4–5 pitch4–21

Sackgut (TCS) 224434

Between a hill and the River Aare.

From Brienz turn left before Interlaken opposite the Ost railway station.
May–27 Sep.

1.2HEC H lau P A4 pitch2–8

ISELTWALD
Bern (036)

Lac 451148

Beside an inn of the same name.

Turn off the road along the lake shore E of village just before Gasthof.
May–Sep.

0.6HEC H lau L A4 pitch4–12

KANDERSTEG
Bern (033)

Rendez-Vous 751354

750 m E of town.
All year.

1HEC H P lau LP

KREUZLINGEN
Thurgau (072)

Fischerhaus 754903

Near Fischerhaus Restaurant, separated from lake by a road and car park.

From Romanshornstr turn into Bleicherstr and continue 1 km.
Apr–Oct.

2HEC H lau L A5 V2 3–4 2–4

KRUMMENAU
St-Gallen (074)

Adler 41030

On edge of village.
All year.
0.8HEC H G R P lau A2 V1–2 3 2

LA Each name preceded by 'La' is listed under the name that follows it.

LANDQUART
Graubünden (081)

Neue Ganda (TCS) 513955
Undulating grassy site in a wood, separated from the trunk road by a narrow stream lined with bushes.

Access from N28 towards Davos between Km2 and Km2.5 N of CHEVRON petrol station.
Dec–15 Oct.
4.5HEC H

LANGWIESEN
Zürich (053)

Rheinwiesen (TCS) 55700
In grounds of Langwiesen municipal beach.

From Constance turn sharp right at the large left-hand bend in Langwiesen.
May–15 Sep.
1.25HEC H G R R lau A3–4 Vn/c 6–9 6–9

LÄUFELFINGEN
Basel (062)

Läufelfingen 691189
On road from Basel to Olten.
Apr–Oct.
1.2HEC H S lau A3 V7 8 7

LAUTERBRUNNEN
Bern (036)

Switzerland

Jungfrau 552010
Widespread site in meadowland crossed by a stream. Partly divided into pitches.

100 m before the church turn right, drive a further 400 m.
All year.
5.5HEC H G R lau P A4 V2 5 2–5

Schützenbach (TCS) 551268
About 300 m from the lake.

S of village to the left of road leading to Stechelberg opposite B50. 0.8 km SE towards Stechelberg.
All year.
3HEC H G lau S A4–5 pitch4–8

LE Each name preceded by 'Le' is listed under the name that follows it.

LENK
Bern (030)

Seegarten 31616
Only winter camping. 700 m S.
10 Dec–Apr.
1HEC H G lau P A4 V4 4 3

LENZERHEIDE
Graubünden (081)

Gravas (TCS) 342335
Closed Nov.

1HEC H R P lau

LES Each name preceded by 'Les' is listed under the name that follows it.

LEUK See **SUSTEN**

LEUKERBAD
Valais (027)

Leukerbad 611138
On road N of Leuk.
May–Oct.
1.6HEC H G R lau P A4 V2 3 2

LEUTSWIL BEI BISCHOFFZELL
Thurgau (071)

Sitterbrücke 813831
Signposted from Bischoffzell on the Konstanz–St Gallen road.
Apr–Sep.
1HEC H G R A3 V1 1 1

LEYSIN
Vaud (025)

Semiramis 341148
After entering the village turn left at SHELL filling station and continue for 400 m.
All year.
1.7HEC H G R lau P A4–6 V3 3–6

LOCARNO
Ticino (093)

Delta via G–Respini 316081
A beautiful, well-equipped and well-organised site.

1.6 km S of Lake Maggiore. ➔

15 Mar–20 Oct.
4.5HEC ▥ ◈ ⋒H ▮ ▼ |O| ⊙ ◘ Ⓖ Ⓡ ⌂ ⊞ ≈LRP ⛺ ⊞ ✱ lau
pitch27–28 (incl 4 persons)

At **LOSONE** (4 km W)

Zandone ☎356563

A level site amidst deciduous forest behind an extensive military area.

Situated between the Losone–Golino road and the River Melezza.
Etr–Sep.
1.8HEC ▥ ◈ ▮ ◘ Ⓡ ⊞ ≈P ⛺

LOCLE (LE)
Neuchâtel (☎039)
Communal (TCS) ☎317493
Dec–Oct.
1.2HEC ▥ ◈ ⋒H ▮ |O| ⊙ ◘ Ⓖ ≈P ⛺ lau A4 pitch2–8

LOSONE See **LOCARNO**

LUCERNE See **LUZERN**

LUNGERN
Obwalden (☎041)
Obsee ☎691463
Beside lake.
1 km W.
All year.
1.5HEC ▥ ◈ ⋒H ▼ |O| ⊙ ◘ Ⓖ ≈L ⛺ ⊞ lau ⇸ ▮ A4 pitch6

LÜTSCHENTAL
Bern (☎036)
Dany's Camp ☎531824
Etr–15 Oct.
0.4HEC ▥ ◈ ⋒H ▮ ⊙ ◘ Ⓖ ⛺ ⊞ lau ⇸ ▼ |O| A4 V1 ◘6 ⛺6

LUZERN (LUCERNE)
Luzern (☎041)
Lido Lützelmattweg 4 ☎312146
Park-like site lying behind the beach. No admittance for vehicles or new arrivals 22.00–07.00 hrs.
Signposted.
15 Mar–Oct.
2.7HEC ▥ ◈ ⋒H ▮ ▼ |O| ⊙ ◘ Ⓖ Ⓡ ⊞ ⛺ ≈P ✱ lau ⇸ ≈L

Switzerland

At **HORW**
Steinibachried (TCS) ☎473558
In gently sloping meadow next to the football ground and the beach, separated from the lake by a wide belt of reeds.
3.2 km S of Luzern.
Etr–27 Sep.
2HEC ▮: ▥ ◈ ⋒H |O| ⊙ ◘ Ⓖ Ⓡ Ⓟ ⊞ lau ⇸ ▮ ▼ A4–5
pitch6–10

MARÉCOTTES-SUR-SALVAN
Valais (☎026)
Médettaz (TCS) ☎61830
10 km NW of Martigny.
All year.
0.6HEC ▥ ◇ ⋒H ▮ ▼ |O| ◘ Ⓖ ⛺ Ⓟ ⊞ ⇸ ≈P

MAROGGIA
Ticino (☎091)
Piazzale Mare (TCS) ☎687245
2 km S on lake.
May–11 Oct.
0.6HEC ▥ ◈ ⋒H ▮ ▼ |O| ⊙ ◘ Ⓖ ⛺ ⊞ ✱ lau ⇸ ≈L

MARTIGNY
Valais (☎026)
Neuvilles (TCS) ☎24544
All year.
1.5HEC ▥ ◈ ⋒H ▮ ▼ |O| ⊙ ◘ Ⓖ ⛺ ✱ lau

MAUENSEE
Luzern (☎045)
Sursee ☎211161
Next to Waldheim Country Estate.
0.8 km W of Sursee, 100 m of Sursee–Basel road.
Apr–Oct.
1.5HEC ▥ ◈ ⋒H ▮ ⊙ ◘ Ⓖ Ⓡ ⛺ lau A3 V2 ◘2 ⛺2

MEINISBERG
Bern (☎065)
Alte Aare ☎524540
3 km from Lengnau on main Biel-Solothurn road on banks of River Aare.
15 Apr–Oct.
0.5HEC ▥ ◈ ⋒H ⊙ ◘ Ⓖ ⊞ ⛺ ⊞ lau ⇸ ▮ ▼ |O| ≈R A4 V2 ◘2 ⛺2

MELANO
Ticino (☎091)
Paradiso ☎482863
Leave motorway N2/E9 at Bissone exit. Turn off road no. 2 on northern outskirts of village towards lake. After motorway underpass, continue 200 m to site.
May–Sep.
2HEC ▥ ◈ ⋒H ▮ ⊙ ≈L ⛺ A4 V2 ◘6–9 ⛺6–9

Pedemonte ☎688333
Between railway and lake with own private beach.
Turn off road no. 2 in S outskirts of Maroggia towards lake.
Apr–10 Oct.
2HEC ▥ ◈ ⋒H ▮ ▼ |O| ⊙ ◘ Ⓖ Ⓡ ≈LP ⛺ ⊞ lau A5 V2 ◘7–10 ⛺7–10

MÉRIDE
Ticino (☎091)
Parco al Sole (TCS) ☎464330
On gently sloping ground surrounded by a bushy wood, next to a small lake suitable for bathing.
Turn off motorway N2/E9 at Mendrisio and follow signs for Serpiano. Turn left past the railway station, then right via underpass, continuing through Rancate, Besázio, and Arzo to site.
5 Jun–13 Sep.
1.2HEC ▥ ◆ ◈ ⋒H ▮ ▼ |O| ◘ Ⓖ ⛺ A4 ◘2–8 ⛺2–8

MERLISCHACHEN
Schwyz (☎041)
Unterbergiswill am See ☎371804
Beside lake. Own beach.

Apr–Sep.
1.4HEC H G R L lau

MEZZOVICO
Ticino (091)
Palazzina 951467
On Bellinzona–Lugano road 100 m after restaurant.
Mar–Sep.
1.5HEC H G lau R A4 V3 5 A2

MISSION
Valais (027)
Pont de Mission 651391
In a meadow partly divided into pitches.
15 Jun–20 Aug.
0.7HEC H R P A3 V1 3 A2

MÖHLIN
Aargau (061)
Bachtalen (TCS) 882863
2 km N.
11 Apr–27 Sep.
1HEC H P

MOLINAZZO DI MONTÉGGIO
Ticino (091)
Tresiana 732342
Meadowland with trees on riverbank.
Turn right after bridge in Ponte Tresa, then 5 km to site.
May–20 Oct.
1,5HEC H G lau A5 V2 4–6 A4–6

MORGES
Vaud (021)
Petit Bois (TCS) 711270
Follow Geneva road from town. Site by lakeside.
Apr–2 Oct.
3.5HEC H G R lau LP A5 pitch8–14

MORGINS
Valais (025)
Morgins (TCS) 772361
Terraced site below pine forest.
Turn left at end of village towards Pas de Morgins near Swiss Customs.
All year.
1.3HEC H lau

MOSEN
Luzern (041)
Seeblick 851666
In two strips of land on edge of lake, divided by paths into several squares.
N on the N26.
Apr–Oct.

Switzerland

3HEC H G L lau A4 V2 2 A1–2

MÜNSTAIR
Graubünden (082)
Clenga 85410
Next to small river near the Italian frontier.
15 May–Oct.
2HEC H G A4 V2 2–4 A2

NORANCO
Ticino (091)
San Salvatore 541946
Meadowland with numerous plane trees, partially surrounded by hedging.
On N2 turn off at Lugano-Süd, site 300 m towards Figiro.
Etr–15 Oct.
10HEC H G R lau

NOTTWIL
Luzern (045)
St-Margrethen 541404
Natural meadowland under fruit trees, with own access to lakeside.
Turn off road to Sursee 400 m NW of Nottwil and drive towards lake for 100 m.
Apr–Oct.
0.7HEC H G L A4 V2 2 A1

NYON
Vaud (022)
Colline (TCS) 612630
Terraced site in a beautiful setting between the shore road and lakeside.
1.4 km S.
11Apr–4 Oct.
1HEC H G R L

ORBE
Vaud (024)
Signal (TCS) 413857
800 m from Orbe, off the road towards Yverdon.
11 Apr–27 Sep.
2.1HEC H lau P

OTTENBACH
Zürich (01)
Reussbrücke (TCS) 7612022
By river of same name.
Access from Zurich via road 126 in SW direction, via Affeltern to Ottenbach.
11 Apr–11 Oct.
1.5HEC H G R R A5 V2 7 A7

PACCOTS (LES)
Fribourg (021)
Bivouac 9487849
Turn E in Châtel-St Denis and continue for 2 km.
15 Dec–Etr & 15 May–15 Sep.
2HEC H G R P lau A5 V2 3 A3

PAYERNE
Vaud (037)
Piscine de Payerne 614322
Apr–Sep.
6HEC H G R P lau A4 V2 3–4 A2–3

PONTRESINA
Graubünden (082)
Plauns Morteratsch 66285
Beautiful situation at foot of Pit Palü.
Access from road towards Bernina pass about 4.5 km beyond Pontresina. Turn off main road 29 towards Hotel Morteratsch then 0.5 km to site.
5 Jun–11 Oct.
4HEC H G R R lau A5 pitch3–7

POSCHIAVO
Graubünden (082)
Boomerang 50713
In a quiet setting.
2 km SE.
All year.
1HEC H G lau A5–6 V2 4–6 A1–4

PRÊLES
Bern (032)
Prêles 951716
Turn off the main Biel-Neuchâtel road at Twann and follow signs for Prêles. Pass through village, site on left.
May–Sep.
5HEC H G R lau A4 V2 3 A3

RARON
Valais (028)
Simplonblick 441274
300 m W of Turtig.
All year.
4HEC H G R P A4 7

RECKINGEN
Valais (028)
Ellbogen (TCS) 731355
400 m S on bank of Rhône.
27 May–25 Oct.
1.3HEC H P lau

RIED-BRIG
Valais (028) ➔

Tropic ☎232537

To the left of Simplon road near entrance to village. 3 km above Brig.
Mar–Nov.

0.6HEC lau A4 V2 3–4 3–4

RINGGENBERG
Bern (☎036)

Lac ☎222616

Between the slopes of a slate quarry and the shore of Lake Brienz.

NW on lakeside.
All year.

0.8HEC lau A4 pitch4–10

RÖCHE
Vaud (☎025)

Close de la George (TCS) les Ecots ☎265828

4.5 km from Aigle.
All year.

2.6HEC A4–5 Vn/c 5–9 2–3

ROLLE
Vaud (☎021)

Vernes (TCS) ☎751239

Off the Chemin de la Plage and on the outskirts of the village towards Lausanne, between shore road and the lake.

1 km NE.
11 Apr–4 Oct.

1.5HEC lau

ROVEREDO
Ticino (☎092)

Vera ☎821857

10 km N of Bellinzona.
May–Oct.

1.5HEC lau A6 V3 8–9 6–7

SAANEN
Bern (☎030)

Beim Kappeli (TCS) ☎46191

In a long meadow between railway and River Saane.

1 km SE.
Dec–Oct.

0.8HEC A4 pitch2–8

SAAS-GRUND
Valais (☎028)

Am Kapellenweg ☎571954

Turn right over bridge towards Saas-Almagell.
All year.

0.7HEC lau A3 V2 2 2

Schönblick (TCS) ☎572267

Lies next to the Schönblick Restaurant.

Switzerland

2 km from village, off road towards Saas-Almagell.
All year.

0.5HEC lau

SACHSELN
Obwalden (☎041)

Ewil ☎664454

On Lake Sarnersee.
All year.

1.2HEC lau A4 V2 4 2

ST-CERGUE
Vaud (☎022)

Cheseaux ☎601267

1 km W.
All year.

6HEC lau A4 V3 3 2–3

ST-LEONARD
Valais (☎027)

Treiz Étoiles ☎312525

In an orchard between a road and mountain slopes.

500 m towards Brig.
Etr–Oct.

1.5HEC lau

ST-MAURICE
Valais (☎025)

Bois Noir (TCS) ☎(026)84176

From Martigny, turn right at Bois Noir Motel, then left and uphill. Take next turning on right after underpass and continue for 200 m.
Etr–Sep.

3HEC lau A4 pitch7

ST-MORITZ
Graubünden (☎082)

Olympiaschanze (TCS) ☎34090

Above the River En.

1 km E of Champfèr.
25 May–13 Sep.

1.5HEC lau

SALAVAUX
Vaud (☎037)

Chablais (TCS) ☎771476

Beautifully situated in a deciduous wood.

800 m SE near Lake.
4 Apr–11 Oct.

6HEC lau

SAMEDAN
Graubünden (☎082)

Punt Muragl (TCS) ☎34497

Near Bernina railway halt, to the right of the fork of the two roads Samedan and Celerina/Schlarigna to Pontresina.
25 Apr–25 Sep.

2HEC lau

SARNER SEE See **GROSSTEIL & SACHSELN**

SAVOGNIN
Graubünden (☎081)

Nandro AG ☎741309

Next to the Touristen hotel.

Turn right off road from Chur to the Julier Pass 150 m after entering village from the N.

0.3HEC lau

SCHÖNENGRUND
Appenzell (☎071)

Schönengrund ☎571166

All year.

0.8HEC A4 V2 2 2

SCHULS See **SCUOL**

SCHÜPFHEIM
Luzern (☎041)

Bad ☎761163

Between railway and road, close by an inn of same name.

Turn off N10 Luzern–Bern about 2 km S in the direction of Sorenberg.
All year.

0.6HEC lau A4 V2 2 1

SCUOL (SCHULS)
Graubünden (☎084)

Gurlaina (TCS) ☎91501

Turn SE off N27 at OPEL garage in village and cross narrow bridge leading to the site.
17 May–5 Oct.

2HEC lau

SEMBRANCHER
Valais (☎026)

Moulin d'Allèves ☎88254

12 km from Martigny at first Alpine road tunnel on road to Grand-St-Bernard.
All year.

1HEC lau A3 V3 3 3

Prairie (TCS) ☎88206

12 km from Martigny and 500 m from town.
All year.

5HEC lau A3 V3 5 3

SEMPACH
Luzern (☎041) ➤

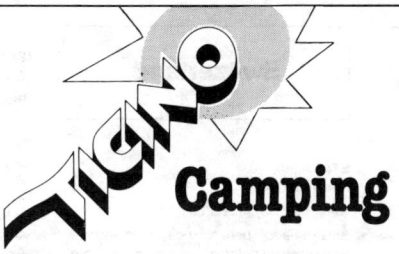

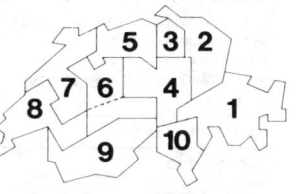

Seeland (TCS) ☎991466

Rectangular, level site on SW shore of lake.

700 m S on Luzern road by lake.
16 Apr–4 Oct.

5.2HEC lau A4–5 pitch2–11

SIERRA (SIDERS)

Valais (☎027)

Bois de Finges (TCS) ☎550284

Very beautiful site.

Access difficult for caravans.
Etr–Oct.

2HEC P lau A4–5 pitch6

SILVAPLANA

Graubünden (☎082)

Silvaplana ☎48492

Lies S of village, to left of the road leading to Maloja mountain pass.

May–15 Oct.

3HEC L lau A6 V3 3 2

SION (SITTEN)

Valais (☎027)

Iles (TCS) ☎36437

Site with leisure centre. Reduction for International Camping Carnet holders.

4 km SW of Sion on the road to Aproz.
All year.

5HEC L lau A4 Vn/c 6–10 2–4

Sedunum ☎364268

On right of road just before bridge over the River Rhône. Turn S off Simplon road W of Pont de la Morgue and follow signposts to Aproz.
Jun–Aug.

3HEC P lau A4 V1 3 3

SITTEN See **SION**

SORENS

Fribourg (☎029)

Forêt ☎51882

Turn right off the N12 in Gumefens and drive on to the village.
All year.

4HEC P lau A4 V2 7 7

SPLÜGEN

Graubünden (☎081)

Sand ☎621332

On left bank of River Hinterrhein.

Turn off the main trunk road in the village and follow signposts.
All year.

0.8HEC lau A4 V2 4 3

STÄFA

Zürich (☎01)

Kehlhof (TCS) ☎9263052

Small meadow between noisy road and lake with separate patch of grass near the shore.

Site lies opposite GULF petrol station, on edge of village towards Rapperswill.
May–27 Sep.

0.6HEC L lau

STALDBACH See **VISP**

STECHELBERG

Bern (☎036)

Breithorn ☎551225

3 km S of Lauterbrunnen.
All year.

1HEC lau A3 pitch3–7

STEIN AM RHEIN

Schaffhausen (☎054)

Grenzstein ☎4123

1.8 km E.
All year.

1.5HEC P lau A5 V2 5 4

STRADA IM ENGADIN

Graubünden (☎084)

Arina ☎93212

At the foot of a mountain, SW of village.
15 May–Sep.

0.6HEC RP lau A3 V1 1 1

SUSCH

Graubünden (☎082)

Muglinas ☎81244

200 m W.

1HEC A3–4 V1 2 2

SUSTEN

Valais (☎027)

Bella Tola ☎631491

In quiet position. Easy access for caravans.

2 km from village.
20 May–9 Oct.

4HEC P lau A6 pitch8–9

At **LEUK**

Monument ☎631827

Large site divided into small individual pitched. Set in forest, protected from traffic noise.

15 May–15 Sep.

5.5HEC P A4 V2 4 3

SUTZ

Berne (☎032)

Sutz ☎571345

7 km SW of Biel.
Apr–Oct.

4HEC L

TANNAY

Vaud (☎022)

Plage de Tannay ☎552465

Situated 12 km of Genève on W shore of the lake.

Access from autoroute N1 exit Divonne-Coppet. Drive SE on Coppet road for about 3 km to Commugny then on to Mies and Tannay.
Mar–Oct.

1HEC L A3 V2 6–7 3–7

TENERO

Ticino (☎093)

Campofelice ☎671417

Beautifully situated and extensive site completely divided into pitches, and crossed by asphalt drives.

1.9 km S. Signposted.
Apr–Oct.

15HEC LR lau pitch19–27

Giorgio ☎672220

Beside lake with large, well kept beach.

Follow signs from station.
Apr–Sep.

1.2HEC L lau A6 V2–3 6–30 6–30

Lago Maggiore ☎671848

Extensive site by the lake, well laid out and completely sub-divided.

Signposted.
11 Apr–17 Oct.

3.2HEC lau

Lido Mappo ☎671437

Beautifully situated, well appointed site on lakeside. Teenagers not accepted on their own. Minimum stay, 1 week in Jul–Aug.

700 m SW. Signposted.
23 Mar–20 Oct.

6.5HEC L lau A5–6 V2–3 10–12 6–10

Miralago ☎671255

Situated in pleasant position by the lake. Caravans only.

Access 1 km S from via St Gottardo to via Mappo and via Ronaccio.
All year.

1.5HEC lau LP A5–9 pitch22–38

Rivabella 672213

Beautiful lakeside site.

1 km S of village. Signposted.
All year.

1.3HEC lau A4–5 V2 2–19 2–19

Tamaro 672161

Partly on sandy shore.

Signposted.
Apr–20 Aug.

6HEC L A5–6 V2–3 14–22 14–22

Verbano 671020

Site in two sections, of which one is on the lakeside. The larger section has access to the lake about 150 m distance.

Signposted.
Apr–Oct.

2.7HEC lau A5 pitch4–14

THÖRISHAUS
Bern (031)

Friezelzentrum 880296

Clean site with well-kept grass.

9 km SW of Bern, Motorway 12; exit Flamatt, 1 km N, on River Sense.
15 Mar–15 Oct.

5.5HEC R lau A5 V2 5–10 4

THUSIS
Graubünden (081)

Viamala A.G. (TCS) 812472

May–Sep.

4.5HEC lau P A4 Vn/c 3–8 2–5

TRUN
Graubünden (086)

Trun (TCS) 81666

0.5 km from village centre. Take road 7166.
May–27 Sep.

3.5HEC

Switzerland

lau pitch4–10

TSCHIERV
Graubünden (082)

Sternen (TCS) Müstair 85551

In village behind the Sternen Hotel.

Between Ofen Pass and Santa Maria.
All year.

2HEC P lau A4 pitch3–8

ULRICHEN
Valais (028)

Nufenen 731437

1 km SE to right of road to Nufenen Pass.
15 Jun–Aug.

8HEC lau A3 V1 2 1

VALLORBE
Vaud (021)

Pré sous Ville (TCS) 832309

On left bank of River Orbe.
May–Oct.

0.7HEC lau RP A4 pitch4–5

VÉSENAZ See **GENÈVE**

VEX
Valais (027)

Val d'Hérens 221984

Near main road, about 500 m from village.
All year.

1HEC lau A4 V1 1–3 1–3

VICOSOPRANO
Graubünden

Albigna (082)41316

May–15 Oct.

1.5HEC A2 V2 3 1–3

VILLENEUVE
Vaud (021)

Horizons Bleus 601547

Near the noisy shore road and 800 m from the Lake.

From Montreux SW on road 9.
Apr–Sep.

0.6HEC L A4 V3 3–4 2–3

VIRA GAMBAROGNO
Ticino (093)

Vira-Bellavista (TCS) 611477

2 km W on lake.
23 May–27 Sep.

0.2HEC L A5 pitch4–15

VISP
Valais (028)

At **STALDBACH**

Staldbach 462856

1.5 km from Visp off road to Stalden.
All year.

1.9HEC P lau

VISSOIE
Valais (027)

Anniviers 651409

9 km S of Sion road to Ayer.
All year.

0.5HEC lau P A5 Vn/c 6 6

VITZNAU
Luzern (041)

Vitznau 831280

Well tended terraced site about the resort in lovely countryside with fine view of lake.

Approaching from N, turn towards mountain at church and follow signs.
Apr–15 Oct.

2HEC lau LP A5 pitch8

VORDERTHAL
Schwyz (055)

Wägital 691259 ➤

In a beautiful circular valley high up in mountains.

12 km SW of Lachen.
All year.
0.8HEC H lau A4 V2 2 A2

WABERN See **BERN (BERNE)**

WILDBERG
Zürich (052)

Weld 451198

In a terraced meadow surrounded by woods and is very peaceful.

In Winterthur, follow Tösstal signs, then turn right after spinning-mill in Turbenthal.
All year.
5HEC H lau

WILDHAUS
St-Gallen (074)

Dusl 52202

All year.
1HEC H lau L

WILLERZELL
Schwyz (055)

Grüene Aff 534131

Quiet, terraced site, separated from lake by the road.

Switzerland

1 km N of village beside lake.
All year.
3HEC H lau L A5–6 V2 6 A5

WILDERSWIL
Bern (036)

Oberei 221335

15Mar–15 Oct.
0.5HEC H lau P A4 pitch6–8

WINTERTHUR
Zürich (052)

Schützenhaus Rosenberg Schaffhauserstr 201 225260

To the left of the Schaffhausen road, near the Schützenhaus restaurant.
All year.
1HEC H lau

YVONAND
Vaud (024)

Pointe d'Yvonand 311655

6 km NE of Yverdon bordering Lake Neuchâtel with private beach 1 km away, boat moorings, private jetty and boat hire.

3 km W of Yvonand. Signposted.
Mar–Sep.
5HEC H L lau A4 V2 4–5 A3–4

ZERNEZ
Graubünden (082)

Cul 81462

Off road 27 W of Zernez.
15 May–Sep.
3.6HEC H P A4–5 V3 3 A1–2

ZUG
Zug (042)

Innere Lorzenallmend (TCS) 218442

Pleasantly situated with beautiful view of Lake Zug and surrounding mountains. Much traffic on railway which passes the site.

1 km NW by lake.
May–4 Oct.
1.1HEC H lau

ZÜRICH
Zürich (01)

Seebucht Seestr 557 4821612

Beautiful park-like site between the shore road and the lake.

1 km S.
May–Sep.
2.2HEC ▥ ◑ ⋒H ⛟ 🍷 |O| ⊙ ☎ Ⓖ ⌂ ⩳L Ⓟ ⊞ lau A4 Vn/c ☎6 Å2–6

ZWEISIMMEN
Bern (☎030)

Camping-Vermeille ☎21940
Well laid-out site along the River Simme.
1 km N towards Lake Thun.
All year.
0.9HEC ⛟ ◑ ⋒H ⛟ 🍷 |O| ⊙ ☎ Ⓖ Ⓡ Ⓐ lau ⊖ ⩳P

Switzerland

Liechtenstein

Prices are in Swiss Francs

BENDERN
(☎075)

Bendern Oberbendernstr 176 ☎31465
On partly terraced meadow beside the Rhine.
Signposted.
All year.
0.43HEC ▥ ◑ ⋒H |O| ☎ Ⓖ ⊞ Ⓐ ⊞ lau ⊖ ⛟ ⩳P

TRIESEN
(☎075)

Meierhof (TCS) ☎21836
Above the road to Malbun, near the Hotel Meierhof.
2 km S of Vaduz.
All year.
1.5HEC ▥ ◑ ⋒H ⛟ 🍷 |O| ⊙ ☎ Ⓖ ⩳P Ⓐ ⊞ lau

Europe's highest cablecar goes to the Klein Matterhorn

Yugoslavia

Pleasure craft replace the fishing boats of yore at picturesque Piran

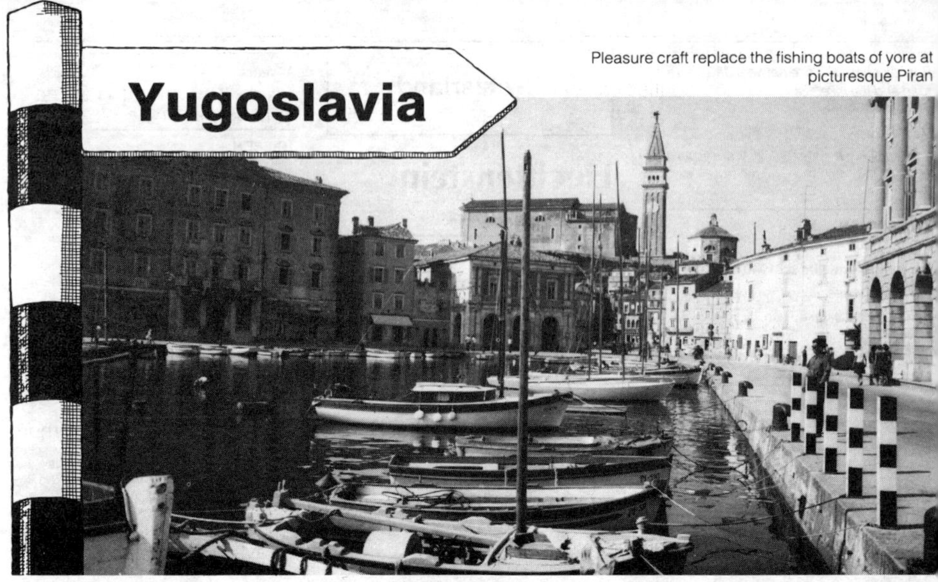

Yugoslavia, set on the Balkan peninsula and still largely uncommercialised, is bordered by Italy, Austria, and Hungary in the north, Romania and Bulgaria in the east, Albania and Greece in the south, and the Adriatic in the west. The mountains in the north follow the Alpine pattern, with wooded slopes, lakes, waterfalls, and gorges, whilst the southern ranges are bare and desolate. The Carpathian Mountains, on the Romanian border, are especially rich in woods and pastures. The rocky Adriatic coast stretches for some 390 miles, with many attractive islands lying off the shore.

The Adriatic coastal strip has a Mediterranean climate with warm summers, but the higher mountainous regions have an Alpine climate with short, cool summers. The remainder of the country has a Central European climate with hot summers. The three major languages of Yugoslavia are Serbo-Croatian, Slovene and Macedonian. Both the Latin and Cyrillic alphabets are used. The most common second languages are English, French, German and Russian which are taught in all schools.

HOW TO GET THERE

Yugoslavia is usually approached via Belgium, Federal Republic of Germany, Köln and München (Cologne and Munich) and Austria (Salzburg), or alternatively via France, Switzerland and Italy (Milan and Trieste). The distance from Calais via Germany to Beograd (Belgrade), the capital, is just over 1,200 miles, a distance which will normally require three or four overnight stops.

GENERAL INFORMATION

(see also *Things you need to know*, page 33–64)

Boats

(see page 33)

British Embassy/Consulates

(see also page 57)

The British Embassy together with its Consular Section is located at *11000 Beograd* Generala Zdanova 46 ☏(011)645034/43/55. There are British Consulates with Honorary Consuls in Split and Zagreb.

Camping

Yugoslavia has over 200 official campsites along the Adriatic, on the islands, and inland by rivers, lakes and woods. The sites along the Adriatic tend to become very crowded at the height of the season. Sites are generally open from May until September or October. Camping information is available from local tourist agencies in all main towns.

International camping carnet not compulsory but recommended. Some campsites will allow a reduction in the advertised charge to the holders of a camping carnet. See page 37 for further information.

Off-site camping is not permitted, unless

permission from local authorities has been obtained.

Currency including banking hours

(see also page 57)
The unit of currency is the Yugoslav Dinar (*Din*) divided into 100 *Para*. At the time of going to press £ = *Din*1,045. Denominations of bank notes are *Din* 10, 20, 50, 100, 500, 1,000, 5,000; standard coins are *Din* 1, 2, 5, 10, 20, 50, 100. A maximum of *Din*10,000 per person in Yugoslav currency may be imported or exported on a first journey during the course of a calendar year; for each subsequent journey during that year a maximum of *Din*5,000 is allowed. However, it is forbidden to import bank notes of a denomination larger than *Din*1,000. There are no restrictions on the import or export of foreign currency.

Visitors may exchange foreign currency at exchange offices, banks, hotels, tourist offices and some offices of the Yugoslav motoring organisation into dinar bank notes or dinar-denominated cheques. The dinar cheques may be used to pay for certain goods and services entitling the holder to a discount. They are easily re-converted into foreign currency unlike dinar bank notes and coins. Generally banks are open Monday to Friday from 07.30–12.00hrs, but in tourist areas they remain open until 18.00hrs. All exchange receipts should be retained until you leave the country.

Foodstuffs

(see page 60)

Medical treatment

(see page 60)

Shopping hours

Generally shops are open from 08.00–12.00hrs and 16.00–20.00hrs Monday–Friday and 08.00–15.00hrs on Saturday. Some *food shops* also open on Sundays 06.00–10.00hrs.

Tourist information

(see also page 63)
The Yugoslav National Tourist Office has an office at 143 Regent Street, London W1R 8AE ☎01-734 5243 and 01-439 0399 who will be pleased to help tourists before their departure to Yugoslavia. Additionally many resorts in Yugoslavia have their own tourist bureau where local information may be obtained.

Visitors' registration

(see page 63)

MOTORING

(see also *Things you need to know*, pages 33–64)

Accidents

(see also page 46)
Fire ☎93, **police** ☎92 and **Ambulance** ☎94 in main towns, but elsewhere the number will be found in the front of the local telephone directory.

Breakdowns

(see page 48)

Dimensions

Private **cars** and towed **trailers** or **caravans** are restricted to the following dimensions – height: 4 metres; width: 2.50 metres; length*: 6 metres. The maximum permitted overall length of vehicle/trailer or caravan combination is 15 metres.

*Trailers with two axles 10 metres (including towbar).

Driving licence

(see also page 33)
A valid UK or Republic of Ireland licence is acceptable in Yugoslavia. The minimum age at which a visitor may drive a temporarily imported car or motorcycle (exceeding 125cc) is 18 years.

First-aid kit

(see also page 50)
It is *compulsory* for visiting motorists to carry a first-aid kit in their vehicle.

Lights

(see also page 50 and *Headlights* page 41)
Dipped headlights must be used by motorcyclists during the day throughout the year when travelling outside built-up areas.

Motoring club

(see also page 61)
The *Auto-Motor Savez Jugoslavije* (AMSJ) has its headquarters at *11000 Beograd* Ruzveltova 18 ☎(011)401-699 and is represented in most towns either direct or through regional and associated clubs.

Passengers

(see also page 51)
Children under 12 and persons visibly under the influence of alcohol are not permitted to travel in a vehicle as front seat passengers.

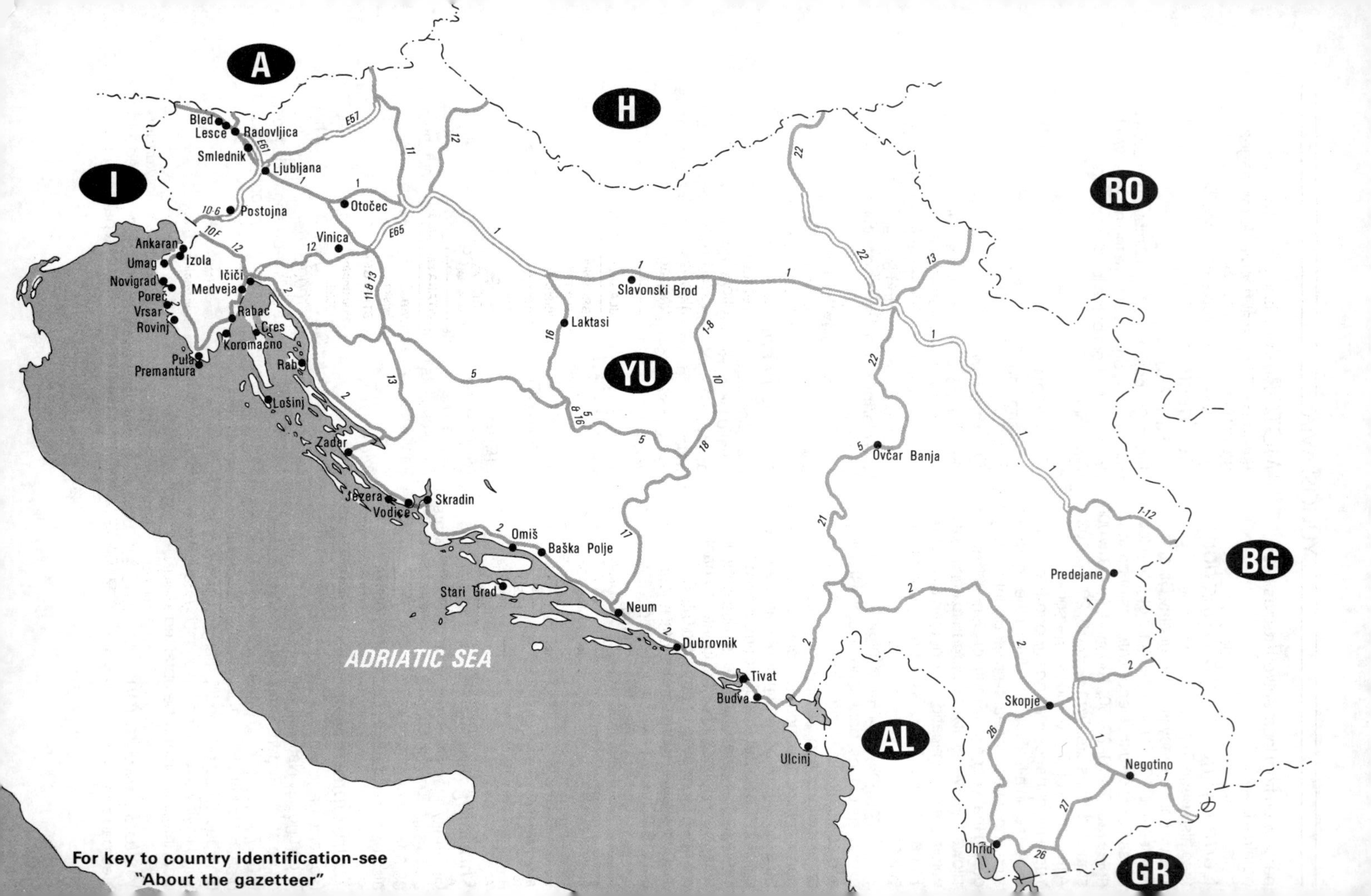
A
I
H
RO
YU
BG
AL
GR
Bled
Lesce
Radovljica
Smlednik
Ljubljana
Postojna
Otočec
Vinica
Ankaran
Izola
Umag
Novigrad
Poreč
Vrsar
Rovinj
Pula
Premantura
Ičiči
Medveja
Rabac
Koromacno
Cres
Rab
Lošinj
Zadar
Jezera
Vodice
Skradin
Omiš
Baška Polje
Stari Grad
Neum
Dubrovnik
Tivat
Budva
Ulcinj
Slavonski Brod
Laktasi
Ovčar Banja
Predejane
Skopje
Negotino
Ohrid
ADRIATIC SEA
For key to country identification-see
"About the gazetteer"

Petrol including petrol coupons

(see also page 61)
Tourist petrol coupons provide a discount on pump prices and may be purchased at road border crossings, but only with a freely convertible currency. They cannot be purchased in Yugoslavia. The border crossings at Škofije, Kozina, Fernetiči, Nova Gorica, Rateče, Korensko sedlo, Ljubelj, Vič, Sentilj and Gornja Radgona provide tourist services on a 24-hr basis. However visitors arriving by motorail cannot purchase tourist petrol coupons at Jesenice, the border crossing for rail traffic, but may obtain them in Ljubljana from the Kompas agency in the airport bank. Petrol in cans may be imported in an amount equal to the capacity of the factory-made tank of the vehicle, up to a total value of *Din* 80,000, provided customs duty is paid.

Roads

Roads have improved considerably in the last few years and many have been rebuilt. All the international transit routes are mainly in good condition, and so is the coast road from Rijeka to Dubrovnik and beyond. It is wise, when making a tour off the beaten track, to enquire at the local tourist agencies for the latest information on the next stage of the journey.

Make sure your car is in good order before you go, as telephones and service stations are far apart. A leaflet entitled '*Road Conditions in Yugoslavia*' is available to AA members.

Seat-belts

(see page 52)

Speed limits

Car
Built-up areas
60kph (38mph)
Other roads
80kph (49mph)*
Motorways
120kph (74mph)
*Unless varied by signs to 100kph (62mph).

Vehicle/trailer combinations not exceeding 750kg in weight are restricted to 80kph (49mph) on all roads outside built-up areas.

Warning triangles

The use of a warning triangle is compulsory in the event of accident or breakdown. The triangle must be placed on the road 50 metres (55yds) behind the vehicle to warn following traffic of any obstruction. Two triangles (placed side by side) are required for vehicle/trailer combinations. See also *Warning triangles/ Hazard warning lights* page 54.

In view of the fluctuation in rates of exchange, prices are shown in the currency quoted to us by the campsite ie. US dollars ($), Deutschmarks (Dm), or £ sterling. At the time of going to press the dollar stands at 1.73 = £1. See page 207 for Deutschmark conversion.

ANKARAN
Slovenija (☎066)
Adria Jadranska 25 ☎51387
On grassland near hotel of same name, partially under tall trees. Hard standings for caravans. Close to bathing facilities.
Turn towards the sea opposite Post Office on eastern outskirts to site in 250 m.
Map–Sep.
12HEC ◆ H lau s ADm12

Studentski Tabor ☎51826
Jun–Aug.
1.4HEC H s

BASKO POLJE
Hrvatska (☎058)
Autocamp Basko Polje ☎620066
On stony ground amongst pine trees. Terrain sloping down to sea.
Turn off road 2 (Split–Dubrovnik) at Km647.5 and drive downhill for about 500 m.
May–Oct.
10HEC ◆ H lau s

BLED
Slovenija (☎064)
Zaka Kidričeva 10 ☎77325
1.5 km from Bled on lake-shore.
May–Sep
6HEC H L lau ADm12

BUDVA
Crna Gora (☎082)
Avala ☎41205
In narrow sloping valley, partially in olive grove providing shade.
Entrance from the coastal road on outskirts in direction of Bar.
May–Sep.
1HEC H

CRES
Hrvatska (☎051)
Kovačine ☎871161
Apr–Oct.
27HEC ◇ H

DAJLA see **NOVIGRAD**

DUBROVNIK
Hrvatska (☎050)
Solitudo Babin Kuk ☎20247
On SW outskirts. Signposted.
All year.
5.5HEC H lau sP ADm6–9 VDm4–5 Dm5–6 ADm4–6

FUNTANA see **VRSAR**

HVAR
Hrvatska
At **STARI GRAD** (10.3 km NE)
Autocamping Jurlevac Stari Grad ☎75822
In woodland and partially in open meadow.
100 m from beach near harbour.
Jun–Sep.
2.5HEC H s

IČIĆI
Hrvatska (☎051)
Autocamping Opatija ☎711387
On sloping terrain, with a beautiful view, partly laid out on terraces. Private road leading to the narrow strip of rocky coastline and a small harbour. ➔

Leave the coast road no. 2 from Rijeka to Pula at Km 194 then continue for 600 m uphill on an asphalted road.
Apr–Oct.
6HEC

IZOLA
Slovenija (066)
Autocamp Jadranka Polje 8 61202
On extended strip of grassland with trees, between the road and sea.
Jun–Sep.
2HEC ADm8

JEZERA
Hrvatska (059)
Lovišća 78020
May–15 Oct.
12HEC ADm7 VDm7 Dm7 ADm5

KOROMACNO
Hrvatska
Tunarica (053)82219
15 May–Sep.
5HEC

LAKTAŠI
Bosna I Hercegovina (078)
Laktaši 830025
22 km N of Banja Luka.
15 May–Sep.
12HEC A$2 V$2 $3 A$2

LESCE
Slovenija (064)
Šobec 77500
Amongst pine trees on undulating ground and on two terraces stretching down to River Sava. Surrounded by grassland and wooded hills on the shore of an artificial bathing lake.
Between Bled (3 km) and Kranj.
May–Sep.
15HEC lau ADm1 pitchDm16

LJUBLJANA
Slovenija (061)
Ježica Titova 206A 371382
Ideally situated for overnight stops. Level grassland with some trees; bordering the river.
Entrance at N end of Ježica, right off the Maribor road, 6/E93, next to the swimming pool. 4.5 km N of Ljubljana.
May–Sep.
3HEC lau ADm7

LOŠINJ
Hrvatska (051)
At **MALI LOŠINJ**

Yugoslavia

Čikat 862125
Terraced site with many shaded walls on a rise (Punta Čikat) in tall pine woodland.
2 km from Mali Lošinj. Well signposted.
15 Apr–15 Oct.
15HEC lau

Poljana 861728
Terraced site in pine woodland on Privlaka peninsula with private beach. Very pleasant, well maintained site.
3 km from Mali Lošinj.
May–Oct.
16HEC ADm11

MALI LOŠINJ see **LOŠINJ**

MEDVEJA
Hrvatska (051)
Medveja M-Tita 1 731191
On level grassland with tall trees in a valley open to the sea.
Entrance to the right off coastal road no. 2 (Rijeka–Pula).
Apr–15 Oct.
9.2HEC lau ADm6 VDm4 Dm6 ADm4

NEGOTINO
Makedonija (093)
Antigona 72544
Small transit site with hard standings for cars and caravans.
On Autoput, 95 km S of Skopje about halfway to Greek border.
Apr–Oct.
2HEC A$2 V$2 $2 A$2

NEUM
Bosna I Hercegovina (088)
Autocamp Neum 870041
Below the Split–Dubrovnik road, extending over three wide terraces, each accessible by an asphalt drive. Beautiful view of the fjord-like bay of Neum.
Between Km 742 & 743 near JUGO petrol station.
2.5HEC

NOVIGRAD
Hrvatska
At **DAJLA** (4 km N)
Autocamp Mareda (053)31452
Extensive site on stony ground in sparse oak woodland with a strip of grassland without shade by the sea.
Signposted.
May–Sep.

30HEC ADm3 pitchDm5–6
Sirena (053)59050
In a pine forest on slightly sloping ground near the sea. Hotel Laguna facilities available to campers.
May–Sep.
10HEC ADm5 VDm3 Dm4 ADm3

OHRID
Makedonija (096)
Autocamp Gradište 22578
Terraced site in wide bay reaching down to the lake, partially subdivided.
13 km in direction SV. Naum then turn right to site.
May–Sep.
14HEC A$2 V$1 $3 A$3

OMIŠ
Hrvatska (058)
Autocamp Ribnjak 86046
Level site almost without shade between the coastal road and the sea. There are a few pitches in the shade between the tall shrubs on the flat sandy beach.
Approaching from Split, the site lies off the town road.
Jun–Sep.
13HEC ADm3–4 VDm2–3 Dm3–4 ADm3

OTOČEC
Slovenija (068)
Otočec 21830
Leave 1/E94 from Ljubljana–Zagreb at exit Otočec then 700 m to site over two island bridges, past castle then left.
15 Jun–15 Sep.
2HEC lau ADm5 VDm3 Dm4 ADm3

OVČAR BANJA
Srbija (032)
Ovčar Banja 816710
May–Sep.
2.5HEC lau ADm2 VDm2 Dm2 ADm2

POREČ
Hrvatska (053)
Lanterna 32488
Turn seawards off coastal road 10 km N of Poreč at INA petrol station, then 3 km to site.
15 Apr–Oct.
80HEC lau

Zelena Laguna (053)31844
On an uneven meadow next to a hotel complex.
2 km S. Turn off Vrsar road and continue for 3 km.

May–Sep.
9HEC H sP ADm5
VDm3 Dm5 ADm3

POSTOJNA
Slovenija (067)

Pivka Jama 21382
May–Sep.
2.5HEC H
lau ADm11

PREDEJANE
Srbija (016)

Predejane 86620
Two well tended grassland terraces next to a motel complex. Numbered pitches and concrete internal roads.
Turn right off the Autoput no. 1 Niš-Skopje and continue to site via underpass in 0.3 km.
May–15 Oct.
1.3HEC H lau
R

PREMANTURA
Hrvatska

Runke (052)75022
Jun–15 Sep.
8HEC H
s ADm5 VDm3 Dm4 ADm3

Stupice (052)75111
May–Sep.
30HEC H

Tašalera
Jul–Aug.
15HEC
s ADm3 VDm3 Dm4 ADm3

PULA
Hrvatska (052)

Indie 73066
May–Sep.
19HEC H
s ADm6 VDm3 Dm4 ADm3

Pomer 73128
Jul–10 Sep.
15HEC
s ADm5 VDm3 Dm4 ADm3

Yugoslavia

Autocamp Ribarska Koliba 22966
In long stretch of pine woodland sloping towards a narrow bay. The narrow approach road (single lane) is also the entrance to the Hotel-Restaurant Ribarska Koliba.
SE 3.5 km in direction of Verudela.
May–15 Sep.
3HEC H
s ADm5 VDm3 Dm4 ADm3

Auto Stoja 24144
On an island with a narrow causeway. Surface is not level. Tall pines, a small open meadow and many shrubs. Sanitary blocks subject to overcrowding. Bathing facilities for children on one side of the island only.
Access in direction of Stoja, signposted.
15 Apr–15 Oct.
19.6HEC H
G R s ADm6 VDm3
Dm4 ADm3

Valovine 23260
May–15 Sep.
3HEC H
s ADm5 VDm4 Dm7 ADm4

RAB
Hrvatska (051)

Rajska Plaža 771048
Hourly ferry services from Rijeka. 14 m from town of Rijeka.
May–Oct.
9HEC H
G R s lau

RABAC
Hrvatska (052)

Autocamp Oliva 872258
Slightly uneven ground in sparse olive grove in front of hotels, by the sea with a public beach. In the bay are drain pipes into the sea. Used by groups who are accommodated in hired tents and caravans.
Turn off Opatija-Pula road in Labin and continue 5 km towards the sea.

7 May–25 Sep.
14HEC H
G R s ADm5 VDm3
Dm4 ADm4

RADOVLJICA
Slovenija (064)

Kopališče 75770
A small site with a few trees.
Turn off main road to Kranj near airfield and follow road to Radovljica.
Jun–15 Sep.
0.8HEC H
RP

ROVINJ
Hrvatska (052)

Autocamp Poton Blondi 813557
On somewhat steep hillside in pine woodland, on terraces of various sizes. Separated from the sea by a busy coastal road. Nearest good bathing facilities in 800 m.
1 km in direction of Valaltao.
May–10 Oct.
11HEC H
s ADm5 VDm3 Dm4
ADm3

Polari 813441
3 km S.
10 Apr–10 Oct.
50HEC H
s ADm5 VDm3 Dm4
ADm4

Turističko Naselje Beograd 811244
On the peninsula, surrounded by pinewoods.
3.5 km from town.
Jun–Sep.
3HEC H
G P lau s

Veštar 811431
Sloping towards the sea with some terraces.
Turn off coast road 4 km S of town.
15 Apr–10 Oct.
15HEC H
lau ADm5 VDm3 Dm4
ADm4

Yugoslavia

SKOPJE
Makedonija (☎091)

Autocamp Park Gradski Stadion ☎228246

Small site on long stretch of grassland under tall, old deciduous trees.

Signposted from the Vardar bridge. Within the municipal swimming pool complex behind the football stadium near the restaurant by the River Varda.
Apr–15 Oct.
2.4HEC ◆ H P ADm4 VDm3 Dm4 ADm4

Bellevue Belimbegovo ☎223122

Beautifully laid out park-like grassland site. Hard standing for caravans. Some shade provided by poplars and willows. Next to hotel of same name.

Approaching from Niš, site is located about 10 km from town centre on the Autoput, near the turn off for Athens.
May–Sep.
0.3HEC ◆ H P A$2 V$1 $2 A$2

SKRADIN
Hrvatska (☎059)

Autocamp Slapovi Krke Skradinski Buk ☎22367

Set amongst shady trees, on the rushy banks of River Krka, not far from well known waterfalls.

Over bridge N of Lake Prokljan, site 4 km on narrow road.
Jun–Sep.
1.5HEC H R

SLAVONSKI-BROD
Hrvatska/Slovenija (☎055)

Vinogorje ☎231118
1HEC H

SMLEDNIK
Slovenija (☎061)

Smlednik Dragočajna-Moše Dragočajna Moše ☎627002

On a meadow bordering a forest, above the River Sava and next to a farm.

Turn left off road no. 1 Ljubljana–Kranj, just before bridge over the Sava. Drive for about 10 km following signposts.
May–15 Oct.
1.4HEC H L lau ADm6

STARI GRAD See **HVAR**

TIVAT
Crna Gora (☎082)

Autocamp Ciparis ☎61359

On slightly sloping meadow in an orange grove.

On coastal road in northern outskirts.
15 Jun–15 Sep.
2HEC H s

ULCINJ
Crna Gora (☎085)

Autocamp Neptun Velika Plaža ☎81888

Situated near the sea.

4 km from town. 1 km from 'Great Beach' hotel.
Apr–Oct.
9HEC ◆ H G s ADm6 VDm1

UMAG
Hrvatska (☎053)

Arena ☎51474
May–Sep.
1HEC ◆ H s ADm10

Autocamp Finida Lovrečica ☎51844

Undulating terrain slightly sloping towards the sea in deciduous woodland. Bare soil, some interior gravel roads.

Access from Umag 4 km in direction of Novigrad.
May–Sep.
4HEC ◆ H s ADm5 VDm2 Dm3 ADm2

Kanegra 71104

May–Sep.

0.2HEC H ADm5 VDm2 Dm3 ADm2

Ladin Gaj 52028

May–Sep.

H s ADm5 VDm2 Dm3 ADm2

Pineta 74518

May–Sep.

H sP

Stella Maris 51424

May–Sep.

15HEC H s ADm6 VDm3 Dm4 ADm3

VINICA

Slovenija (068)

Kolpa 55318

On meadowland with a few trees set below a castle and beside the River Kopla. 3 km off Zagreb–Rijeka road.

Take road 9 from Karlovac and drive W to Bocanci, then turn right towards Vinica.
May–Sep.

Yugoslavia

1HEC H R lau ADm8

VODICE

Hrvatska (059)

Imperijal 83200

On northern outskirts of Vodice hotel complex sloping towards a bay with many boulders. Campers may use the pool at the Hotel Imperial.

Turn off the road 2 to Split and continue in the direction of the sea at the INA filling station. Then bear left for 600 m.
May–Sep.

3HEC H G R s

VRSAR

Hrvatska

Turist (053)41330

In pine forest on N outskirts of town.

15 Apr–15 Oct.

30HEC H s

At **FUNTANA**

Puntica 31570

May–Sep.

40HEC H G R s ADm4 VDm3 Dm4 ADm3

Valkanella 32400

Apr–15 Oct.

120HEC H

ZADAR

Jadranska Obla (057)

Autocamp Punta Bajlo Omladinska 1 22336

On small peninsula. Largely pine woodland providing shade. Near Zadar harbour.

Turn off the road N2 (by-pass) towards the town. At end of dual carriageway to town turn left and continue along a very narrow one way street through an old part of town. 1.5 km to site.
May–Sep.

2.5HEC H s lau

The famous Postojna cave is an underground wonderland

MEASUREMENT CONVERSIONS

LENGTH

metres	yds or metres	yards
0.914	1	1.094
1.829	2	2.187
2.743	3	3.281
3.658	4	4.374
4.572	5	5.468
5.486	6	6.562
6.401	7	7.655
7.315	8	8.749
8.230	9	9.843
9.144	10	10.94
18.29	20	21.87
27.43	30	32.81
36.58	40	43.74
45.72	50	54.68
54.86	60	65.62
64.01	70	76.55
73.15	80	87.49
82.30	90	98.42
91.44	100	109.36
228.60	250	273.40
457.20	500	546.80

LENGTH

km	miles or km	miles
1.609	1	0.621
3.219	2	1.243
4.828	3	1.864
6.437	4	2.485
8.047	5	3.107
9.656	6	3.728
11.27	7	4.350
12.87	8	4.971
14.48	9	5.592
16.09	10	6.214
32.19	20	12.43
48.28	30	18.64
64.37	40	24.85
80.47	50	31.07
96.56	60	37.28
112.65	70	43.50
128.75	80	49.71
144.84	90	55.92
160.93	100	62.14
402.34	250	155.34
804.67	500	310.68

CAPACITY

litres	gallons or litres	gallons
4.546	1	0.22
9.092	2	0.44
13.64	3	0.66
18.18	4	0.88
22.73	5	1.10
27.28	6	1.32
31.82	7	1.54
36.37	8	1.76
40.91	9	1.98
45.46	10	2.2

PRESSURE

lb per sq in	kg per sq cm
18	1.266
20	1.406
22	1.547
24	1.687
26	1.828
28	1.969
30	2.109
32	2.250
34	2.390
36	2.531

WEIGHT

kg	lb or kg	lb
0.454	1	2.205
0.907	2	4.409
1.361	3	6.614
1.814	4	8.818
2.268	5	11.02
2.722	6	13.23
3.175	7	15.43
3.629	8	17.64
4.082	9	19.84
4.536	10	22.05

CONFIDENTIAL CAMP SITE REPORT FORM

You are invited to assist the AA by commenting on camp sites you have visited, whether listed in this guide or not, and by sending your remarks to:

The Automobile Association, Hotel & Information Services, Fanum House, Basingstoke, Hants RG21 2EA.

Block capitals please

Name

Address

Membership number

For office use: acknowledged recorded

Name of site

Town Country

Location

Description of site

Standard of cleanliness

Facilities

General remarks

Date of stay

Name of site

Town Country

Location

Description of site

Standard of cleanliness

Facilities

General remarks

Date of stay

Block capitals please

Name of site

Town | Country

Location

Description of site

Standard of cleanliness

Facilities

General remarks

Date of stay

Name of site

Town | Country

Location

Description of site

Standard of cleanliness

Facilities

General remarks

Date of stay

Name of site

Town | Country

Location

Description of site

Standard of cleanliness

Facilities

General remarks

Date of stay

We welcome comments on any sites you may have visited. If there is insufficient room on this report form please continue on a separate sheet, using this form as a guide.

USING THE TELEPHONE ABROAD

LOCAL AND INTERNATIONAL CALLS

It is no more difficult to use the telephone abroad than it is at home. It only appears to be so because of unfamiliarity with the language and equipment. The following chart may be helpful with elementary principles when making local calls from public callboxes but try to get assistance in case you encounter language difficulties.

Ringing tone: In most Continental countries, consists of a single tone of about 1–1½ seconds repeated at intervals of between 3 and 10 seconds (depending upon country). Engaged tone: Similar to UK or faster.

International Direct Dial (IDD) calls can be made from many public callboxes abroad thus avoiding the addition of surcharges imposed by most hotels. Types of callboxes from which IDD calls can be made are identified in the chart. You will need to dial the international code, international country code (for the UK it is 44), the telephone dialling code (omitting the initial 'O'), followed by the number. For example to call Bristol 12345(0272) from Greece dial 00 44272 12345. Use higher denomination coins for IDD calls to ensure reasonably lengthy periods of conversation before coin expiry warning. The equivalent of £1 should allow a reasonable period of uninterrupted conversation.

Note In *Denmark* coins used in a callbox are not returned even if the number is engaged, but repeat attempts may be made until time runs out. In *Greece* the coins used in a callbox must be dated 1976 or later. In *Italy* gettoni (tokens) are available from bars, tobacconists and slot machines. In *Yugoslavia* higher value coins are necessary in the new style callboxes when making national and international calls.➤

ACKNOWLEDGEMENTS

We thank the following tourist boards for permission to reproduce the black and white photographs in this book: Austrian National Tourist Office, Belgian National Tourist Office, Danish Tourist Board, French Government Tourist Office, German National Tourist Office, National Tourist Organisation of Greece, Irish Tourist Board, Italian State Tourist Board, Luxembourg National Tourist and Trade Office, Netherlands National Tourist Office (NBT), Norwegian Tourist Board, Portuguese National Tourist Office, Spanish National Tourist Office, Swedish National Tourist Office, Swiss National Tourist Office, Yugoslav National Tourist Office.

We also thank the following for permission to reproduce the colour photographs in the special feature: Belgian National Tourist Office, Danish Tourist Board, Netherlands National Tourist Office (NBT), Norwegian Tourist Board, Swedish National Tourist Office, Swiss National Tourist Office.

Country	Insert coin before or after lifting receiver	Dialling tone	Coins needed to operate callbox (local calls)	Highest value coin accepted	International callbox identification	What to dial for the UK	What to dial for the Irish Republic
Austria	After (instructions in English in many callboxes		1 Schilling piece	10 or 20 Schilling piece	Boxes with 3/4 coin slots	00 44	00 353
Belgium	After	Same as UK	5 franc piece	5 franc, 10 franc and 20 franc piece	Identified with European flags	00 *44	00 *353
Denmark	After	Continuous tone	2 ore (min of two) or 1 krone piece	1 krone 5 krone in some boxes	All callboxes	000 44	009 353
France	After	Continuous tone	Always dial 8 digit number except for calls to and from Paris area: – from province, add prefix '16.1' – in province, add prefix '16'	5 franc piece	Metallic grey	19 *44	19 * 353
Germany (W)	After	Continuous tone	3 × 10pf pieces (or 2 × 10pf)	1 DM (or 5 DM) piece	Green sign	00 44	00 353
Greece	After	As UK ringing	10 drachma piece Blue/grey callbox	20 drachma piece	Orange sign around top	00 44	00 353
Ireland, Republic of	After	Same as UK	5p and 10p	50p	Payphone or Telefon	03†	
Italy	Before	Short & long tones	200 lire *gettoni* (tokens) or coins in new payphones	(tokens) or 200 lire in new payphones	Yellow sign showing telephone dial	00 44	00 353
Luxembourg	After	Same as UK	5F (Lux. or Belg.)	5F or 20F	Roadside callboxes	00 44	00 353
Nether-lands	After (instructions in English in many callboxes)		25c	2½ guilder piece	All callboxes	09 *44	09 *353
Norway	After (instructions in English in many callboxes)		2 one kroner coins	5 krone coin	Most callboxes	095 44	095 353
Spain	Before		5, 25 and 50 peseta coins (min 2 × 5 peseta coins)	50 peseta coin	Light green sign	07 *44	07 *353
Sweden	After (instructions in English in most callboxes)		1 krone	1 krone piece (or 5Kr)	Callboxes with 1 or 3 slots	009 *44	009 *353
Switzer-land	After	Continuous tone	40 cents	1 franc (or 5 franc) piece	All callboxes	00 44	00 353
Yugoslavia	After	Long & short tones	5 Din	100 Din (10 Din in some	Certain boxes with	99 44	99 353

INDEX

SYMBOLS AND ABBREVIATIONS

For a more detailed explanation refer to About the Gazetteer (see contents page).

Pour plus amples informations venillez vous référer â About the Gazetteer (voir la table de matières).

Für weitere Angaben beziehen Sie sich auf About the Gazetteer (siehe inhaltsverzeichnis).

ENGLISH

A adult
V car
pp per person
caravan or motor caravan
charge per night (see **Example of a Gazetteer Entry**)
tent
telephone
HEC 1 hectare (equals approx 2 acres)
grass
sand
stone
◇ little shade
partly shaded
◆ mainly shaded
shower (cold only)
H shower (hot and cold)
shop
cafe/restaurant
bar
no dogs
electric points for razors
electric points for caravans
G Camping Gaz International
R gas other than Camping Gaz
bungalows for hire
caravans for hire
tents for hire
swimming:
L Lake
P Pool
R River
s sea
parking by tents permitted
Ⓟ compulsory separate car park
facilities not on site, but within 2km
⊞ first-aid facilities
site belongs to *'Castle & Camping'* chain (France only)
CM *camping municipal, parque municipal de campismo, or parque de la cămara municipal* (local authority site)
GC *Gemeinde Campingp* (local authority site)
KC *Kommunens Campingplads* (local authority site)
lau laundry
n/c no charge
pitch pitch charge per night for car with tent or caravan (there is usually a charge per adult in addition to this)
SC *Stadt Camping* (local authority site)
➤ Entry continued overleaf

Entries in italics indicate that particulars have not been confirmed by management.

FRANÇAIS

A Adulte
V Voiture
pp par personne
Caravane ou camping car
tarif pour une nuit (voir **Example of a Gazetteer Entry**)
Tente
Téléphone
HEC 1 hectare (correspond à environ 2 acres (mesures impériales))
Gazon
Sable
Pierres
◇ Peu ombragé
En partie ombragé
◆ Surtout ombragé
Douches (froides seulement)
H Douches (chaudes et froides)
Magasin
Café/restaurant
Bar
Chiens non admis
Prises de courant pour rasoirs électriques
Branchements électriques pour caravanes
G Camping Gaz International
R Gaz autre que Camping Gaz
Bungalows à louer
Caravanes à louer
Tentes à louer
Natation:
L Lac
P Piscine
R Rivère
s Mer
Stationnement voiture près des tentes autorisé
Ⓟ Utilisation des parkings voitures obligatoire
Aménitiès par sur le terrain, mais au plus, à 2km
⊞ Poste de premiers-secours
Terrain fait partie de la chaîne 'Castle & Camping' (en France seulement)
CM Camping municipal
GC Gemeinde Camping (camping municipal)
KC Kommunens Campingplads (camping municipal)
lau Blanchisserie
n/c Gratis
pitch Tarif d'un emplacement pour une nuit pour voiture avec tente ou caravane (en général s'ajoute un tarif par adulte)
SC Stadt Camping (camping municipal)
➤ Suite au verso

Une insertion imprimée en italiques indique que la direction de l'établissement n'a pas confirmé les précisions.

DEUTSCH

A Erwachsene (r)
V Auto
pp Pro Person
Caravan bzw. Campingbus
Preis pro Nacht (seihe **Example of a Gazetteer Entry**)
Zeit
Telefon
HEC 1 Hektar (ca 2 acres)
Grasboden
Sandgelände
Steiniges Gelände
◇ Wenig Schatten
Teilsschattig
◆ Grösstenteilsschattig
Dusche (nur Kaltwasser)
H Dusche (Warm- und Kaltwasser)
Laden
Imbiss/Restaurant
Bar
Hundeverbot
Stromanschlüsse für Rasierapparate
Stromanschlüsse für Caravans
G Camping Gaz International
R Gas ausser Camping Gaz International
Mietbungalows
Mietcaravans
Mietzelte
Schwimmen
L See
P Schwimmbad
R Fluss
s Meer
Abstellen des PKWs neben dem Zeit gestattet
Ⓟ Separates Abstellen des PKWs obligatorisch
Einrichtungen nicht an Ort und Stelle aber nicht weiter als 2 Kilometer entfernt
⊞ Unfallstation
Platz gehört der Schloss und Camping Gruppe (nur Frankreich)
CM camping municipal, parque municipal de campismo oder parque de la camara municipal (stadtischer Campingplatz)
GC Gemeinde Camping (städtischer Campingplatz)
KC Kommunens Campingplads (städtischer Campingplatz)
lau Wäscherei
n/c Gebührenfrei
pitch Stellplatzpreis pro Nacht für Auto mit Zelt bzw. Caravan (normalerweise eine zusätzliche Berechnung pro Erwachsener)
SC Stadt Camping (städtscher Campingplatz) Fortsetzung
➤ siehe umseitig

Eine kursiv gedruckte Eintragung zeigt an, dass die entsprechenden Angaben nicht von der Direktion bestätigt worden sind.